KU-461-199

SALES MANAGEMENT

Concepts and Cases

Seventh Edition

SALES MANAGEMENT

Concepts and Cases

Seventh Edition

Douglas J. Dalrymple
Indiana University

William L. Cron
Southern Methodist University

Thomas E. DeCarlo
Iowa State University

JOHN WILEY & SONS, Inc.

ACQUISITIONS EDITOR   Jeff Marshall
MARKETING MANAGER   Jessica Garcia
PRODUCTION EDITOR   Patricia McFadden
SENIOR DESIGNER   Kevin Murphy
ILLUSTRATION EDITOR   Anna Melhorn
PRODUCTION MANAGEMENT   Hermitage Publishing Services

This book was set in Times Roman by Hermitage Publishing Services and printed and bound by
R. R. Donnelley & Sons. The cover was printed by Lehigh Press.

This book is printed on acid-free paper. ∞

Copyright 2001 © John Wiley & Sons, Inc. All rights reserved.

No part of this publication may be reproduced, stored in a retrieval system or transmitted in any form or by any
means, electronic, mechanical, photocopying, recording, scanning or otherwise, except as permitted under Sections
107 or 108 of the 1976 United States Copyright Act, without either the prior written permission of the Publisher,
or authorization through payment of the appropriate per-copy fee to the Copyright Clearance Center, 222
Rosewood Drive, Danvers, MA 01923, (978) 750-8400, fax (978) 750-4470. Requests to the Publisher for
permission should be addressed to the Permissions Department, John Wiley & Sons, Inc., 111 River Street,
Hoboken, NJ 07030, (201) 748-6011, fax (201) 748-6008, E-Mail: PERMREQ@WILEY.COM To order books
please call 1(800)-225-5945.

ISBN 0-471-38880-7

Printed in the United States of America

10 9 8 7 6 5 4

LEEDS METROPOLITAN
UNIVERSITY
LEARNING CENTRE
1703676122
BT-BV
BP- 36732
11.2.03
658.81 DAC

PREFACE

This book is designed to help students learn sales management concepts and how to apply them to solve business problems. Most marketing students start their careers as salespeople and they need to understand the role of the sales manager to function effectively in their jobs and prepare themselves for promotion. Effective management of salespeople is critical to business success because many goods and services demand personal contacts to close the sale. However, selling costs are growing rapidly and managers must know how to handle this resource effectively. Customer contact is a key weapon in the marketing game, and managers need experience in this area if they expect to move up the executive career ladder.

Approach and Objectives

Sales Management focuses on the activities of first-line field sales managers. To function effectively as managers, students must know how salespeople perform their jobs. With this in mind, we have positioned chapters on personal selling, account relationships, territory management, and sales ethics near the front of the book to emphasize how salespeople interact with customers and prospects. This information is particularly useful for students who have not taken—and for schools that do not offer—courses in personal selling.

Our approach to sales management is comprehensive, up-to-date, and practical. We use many real-world examples and present them in an easy-to-read style. Stories in boxes highlight recent developments and issues associated with specific sales management competencies. We conclude each chapter with competency based problems, two short in-class exercises, and several detailed cases so that students can apply what they have learned by resolving realistic business dilemmas.

Changes in this Edition

With the new seventh edition we have made some significant changes to the pedagogy of the text while keeping the same 15 chapter structure of the last edition. Six new cases have been added to this edition for a total of thirty-one cases. The most significant change is the focus on sales management competencies. Competencies are defined as the skills necessary to be an outstanding sales manager in any company and industry setting. Based on our review of the sales management literature, we have identified six competencies critical to be an effective or even a great sales manager: strategic action, coaching, team building, self-management, global perspective, and technology competency. We have restructured the discussion in each chapter and the activities associated with each chapter to reflect a focus on these competencies. Specifically, the following changes have been incorporated into the seventh edition:

- Boxed inserts in the text are identified as focusing on one of the six sales management competencies. At least four competency inserts are included in each chapter. The boxed inserts usually present company examples of each competency within the subject area of the chapter. Wherever possible the web site of the company has been included in the boxed insert.
- A section titled, "Building Your Competencies", has been included at the end of each chapter. This section consists of six problem questions, one question for each competency. The nature of these questions is to focus on situations requiring students to think more deeply about the competency. In many cases these are "live problems" that companies are currently addressing. These are **not** memorization type questions.
- A "Problems" section has been added to the end of 7 chapters (2, 5, 7, 8, 9, 14 and 15). These are all Excel based problems for which the data is available on pre-edited Excel worksheets. This change was prompted by the competencies focus, specifically the technology competency. Increasingly, employees are expected to have a functional understanding of Excel to address basic data manipulation issues. Most of the problems require only a basic understanding of Excel.
- An "In-Class Exercises" section has been added to the end of each chapter. Every chapter now includes at least two exercises. Each exercise is approximately a page in length and can be assigned as written case exercises, videotaped role-plays, or as the basis for in-class discussion. These exercises also deal with problems that companies are currently addressing that require concept application rather than just memorization. The common thread throughout each of the exercises is the focus on people issues related to each chapter's topical area.

With the many changes that have been made to the text, some changes to the format of the chapters were made. Specifically, the TQM principles are now incorporated into the body of the text which is consistent with the integration of these principles by companies into their regular practices. Likewise, the discussion of ethical issues has been incorporated into the Self-Awareness Competency discussion. Finally, the "Review Questions" section has been taken out of the text itself and included as a student resource that can been found at the book's web site (*www.wiley.com/college/dalrymple*). These questions are a straightforward review of the topics discussed in the text and are useful when reviewing for exams.

Learning Aids

- **Chapter Objectives.** Each chapter begins with a set of objectives to show students what they will learn.
- **Boxed Inserts.** Each chapter has at least four boxed inserts that highlight issues related to the competencies necessary for success in sales management.
- **Summaries.** All chapters end with a summary for each of the chapter objectives listed at the beginning of the chapter.
- **Key Terms.** Key terms are highlighted in the text and listed at the end of each chapter.
- **Developing Your Competencies.** Each chapter includes six problems related to each of the sales management competencies.

- **Problems.** Excel based numerical problems have been added to the end of seven chapters where appropriate for helping students develop their technical competency in Excel and to work with numerical data.
- **In-Class Exercises.** All chapters include two in-class exercises calling for managerial decisions with respect to personnel issues.
- **Case Studies.** Thirty-one cases for class discussion and written assignments are grouped at the end of each chapter. These meaty cases challenge students to apply sales management principles to realistic situations.
- **Appendices.** Discussions on "In-Class Exercises" and "Getting a Job in Sales" at the end of the book help students learn how to use in-class exercises effectively, as well as how to write application letters and creative resumes.
- **Indexes.** Cases, Author, Company, and Subject indexes help students find information and examples.

Supplements

Successful sales management courses require a well-written text and an effective set of supplementary teaching materials. We have assembled an outstanding package of these aids to support *Sales Management.*

- *Instructor's Resource Guide.* Includes suggested course syllabi, chapter outlines, lecture notes, lecture enhancement examples, case notes, Developing Your Competencies tests, Excel problems, and In-Class Exercise instructor notes. It also includes a test bank with a wide assortment of multiple-choice and true/false questions that have been completely revised for this edition. The test bank is also available on computer disks; it allows you to compose exams on a personal computer.
- *Personal Selling Videotapes.* A set of 17 short (three- to five-minute) selling tapes prepared by Wilson Learning Corporation. These tapes provide models of good sales skills, mistakes to avoid, and coaching suggestions for sales managers. Integrated with text discussion.
- *Sales Management Simulation.* Encourages students to practice their sales management skills in a game environment by making decisions on hiring, deployment, retraining, termination, compensation, forecasting, and the design of sales contests for a field sales force. This new edition updates game parameters and features the sales of computer network servers. Student manual sold separately or as a set packaged with this text. Instructors manual available.
- *TTG Territory Mapping Program.* Helps students design new sales territories for Case 9-2 on a personal computer.
- *Sales Call Planning Software.* Helps students use a computer to allocate sales calls to customers in the Zygar supplementary case.
- *Excel Worksheets.* Edited worksheets are available for student use when working on the problems at the end of selected chapters or when performing data analysis on the cases. These can be downloaded from the book's website at *www.wiley.com/college/dalrymple.*
- *Powerpoint Transparencies* for lecture planning and note taking are available to both professors and students and may be downloaded from the book's Website at *www.wiley.com/college/dalrymple.*

ACKNOWLEDGMENTS

This book could not have been published without the spirited comments and suggestions from a host of colleagues and reviewers. A special note of appreciation is due to Eli Jones,

University of Houston, and Raymond Rody, Loyola Marymount University, for their contributions in developing the In-Class Exercises and to Avery Abernethy, Auburn University, for his contributions in developing the chapter problems. Although we don't have room to mention everyone, we would like to express our appreciation to the following professors, who provided valuable tips for the seventh edition,

Tim A. Becker, Point Loma Nazarene University
Ned J. Cooney, University of Colorado at Boulder
Kevin Coulson, Northeastern Illinois University
Robert S. Owen, SUNY Oswego
James A. Stephens, Emporia State University
John H. Summery, Southern Illinois University at Carbondale

as well as numerous reviewers on previous editions, whose comments and suggestions live on:

Zafar Ahmed	Jon Hawes	Jose Rosa
Ramon A. Avila	Karen E. James	Bob Smiley
Robert Collins	Madhav Kacker	Fred Smith
Jill W. Croft *National Sales Manager* *Disc Manufacturing, Inc.*	Thomas Leigh Richard Leventhal	Winston Stahlecker William Strahle
Daniel Gardiner	Elaine Notorantino	Harish Sujan and his class of 25 MBA students *Pennsylvania State University*
James Gray	Keith Paulson	
Bill Greenwood	Robert Roe	Shelley Tapp

A special acknowledgment is due to the sales and marketing executives and consultants who served as chapter consultants to this book. They both reviewed the chapters and offered important insights into the chapter's subject matter. The result of their efforts is a text that is both practical and cutting-edge with respect to current sales and sales management practices. We are deeply indebted to the contributions of the following people:

Bob Braasch
Manager Sales Planning
SABRE

Carol Caprio
Software Business Unit Executive
IBM

Randy Cimorelli
President/COO
Massey-Fair Industrial, Inc.

Joseph P. Clayton
President & CEO
Global Crossing
North America

Robert Conti
Vice President
The Alexander Group, Inc.

Neil Cronin
Director of Training and
Specialist Manager
John Wiley & Sons

Liz Crute
Vice President
Pitney Bowes Credit Corporation

J. Kevin Cummings
National Sales Manager
ABTco, Inc.

Russel Donnelly
Sales Manager–Central Region
Ericsson Inc.

Robert P. Eschino
Executive Vice President
Gold

William I. Evans
Principal
The Evans Group

Elizabeth Forbes
Director, International Results &
Analysis
GTE International

Keith Hall
Area Manager
Anderson Chemical Co.

David Henry
General Sales Manager
CBS Radio: KVIL

Don James
Principal
Human Dimensions, Inc.

Christopher Jander
National Account Manager
GTE

Michael Mahan
Account Manager
IBM

George Michaud
Director of Environment/Health
Safety & Ethics Northern
Telecom

Greg Miller
Senior Vice President, Strategic
Planning and Human Resources,
Sunburst Hospitality Corporation

George Petagrew
Sales Training Manager
Johnson & Johnson Medical

David Pinals
President
TTG, Incorporated

B. J. Polk
Associate Director—Marketing
Procter & Gamble Distributing Co.

J. Tim Prevost
Director—Sales & Marketing
Stuart C. Irby Co.

John Schreitmueller
Partner
Ray & Berndtson

Scott Smith
Vice President – Sales &
Marketing
SABRE Group, Inc.

Howard Stevens
President
Chally Group

Paulette Turner
Sales Operations Business Unit
Executive
IBM Corporation

Ken Whelan
Director, Business Development
Qwest Communications

Jerry Willet
National Sales Manager
Software Spectrum

We also want to thank all the people at John Wiley & Sons who helped develop this book. Jeff Marshall our editor, worked tirelessly to upgrade and improve the seventh edition. Our production editor, Patricia McFadden, has been a great help in guiding the book through the many steps of the production process.

Finally, we want to thank our wives, Nancy, Deborah, and Tiffany for their help and encouragement.

BRIEF CONTENTS

CONTENTS

PART II   DEVELOPING THE SELLING FUNCTION

PART III   SALES GOALS AND STRUCTURE

PART IV BUILDING A SALES PROGRAM

INTRODUCTION TO SELLING AND SALES MANAGEMENT

> If you sincerely believe that "the customer is king," the second most important person in this kingdom must be the one who has a direct interaction on a daily basis with the king.
>
> MICHAEL BON
> CHAIRMAN & CEO, FRANCE TELECOM

Chapter Consultant:
Paulette Turner, Sales Operations Business Unit Executive, IBM Corporation

LEARNING OBJECTIVES

After studying this chapter, you should be able to:

→ Define sales management and its relation to other marketing activities.

→ Describe the changes in personal sales and the reasons for these changes.

→ Describe the sales management process.

→ Discuss the competencies of successful sales managers.

SELLING AT DELL COMPUTER

Marty Sedlacek is an account executive at Dell Computer. Dell's roots are in the mail-order business, which did not include outside salespeople like Marty. It relied instead on PR, advertising, and direct mail; targets individuals and small companies; and is all about getting the phone to ring. Today, however, 90 percent of Dell's sales are to corporate and government customers, most of whom have a complex continuing relationship with Dell that probably began with a visit from someone like Marty.

Marty is married, has a 9-month-old son, and lives in a new four-bedroom house in Round Rock, Texas. Although he lives within 7 minutes of the office, Marty spends more time in airplanes than he does in his car. In a normal week, he leaves Austin on the 7:07 A.M. flight to O'Hare, rents a car at the airport, dives into a four-day schedule of sales calls, and flies home Friday night. "I don't want to be doing this job forever," Marty says, but he is not complaining. In fact, just the opposite. He's 32 years old. He has topped his quota 22 months straight. Last winter he and his wife unwound for a week in the Canadian Rockies, all expenses paid. This spring he's shooting for the trip to Costa Rica, and he likes his chances.

Marty's base salary is $44,500. If he makes 100 percent of his quota, he doubles that. Beyond 100 percent, the incentives quadruple. In addition, Marty has enjoyed five years at Dell accumulating one of the hottest stocks of the 1990s. He participates in his company's 401 (k) plan in which the company matches 100 percent of his contributions in Dell stock. In addition, he spends 15 percent of his after-tax pay on discounted shares available through the employee stock-purchase plan.

A recent call on Ace Hardware's headquarters is typical for Marty. Ace is a new account for Dell. Marty broke the ice with Ace in February with an order for $250,000 of Dell desktops. Marty is calling on Ace to gather competitive intelligence on who Dell is competing with for Ace's notebook and server business. He is also equipped with a testimonial from a client who praises Dell notebooks and a consultant's report that does the same for Dell servers. Mostly, though, Marty asks questions during the call. He takes careful notes in his planner with a multipoint pen: red ink for action items, black ink for intelligence tidbits, and a carbon for chores he can hand off to others. By the end of the meeting, Marty knows which companies Dell is competing against (Toshiba, IBM, and NEC on notebooks; HP on servers), who at Ace will decide the order, what matters most to them, and when they'll make up their minds.

One subject that never comes up is price. Marty doesn't talk terms. He doesn't take orders. He's what's known in Dell's internal lexicon as a hunter, one of 20 in the preferred-accounts division. A hunter's job is to establish a new account, get the order flow started, and then give way to an inside salesperson.[1]

These are very exciting times to be in sales and sales management. Many organizations, are finding that sales force changes are needed to match the needs of more demanding customers in an increasingly competitive world. Giant retailers such as Wal-Mart and Kmart are leveraging electronic data technology and are requiring manufacturer sales forces to assume responsibility for "just-in-time" inventory control, ordering, billing, sales, and promotion. Hewlett-Packard will now rent an office in a key customer's headquarters building and station an account manager there.

These innovations in the way suppliers and customers interact have necessitated changes in the way sales forces are organized, compensated, developed, and measured. Our goal with this textbook is to explain how the sales team operates in this new environment and how they may be supervised for maximum efficiency and effectiveness. We begin by defining personal selling and describing its role within a firm's promotion mix. We then turn to some of the changes taking place that have had an important impact on the sales function. Next, we direct our attention to the sales management function by describing the activities they perform, a process of sales management, and the competencies needed to successfully perform these activities and the sales management process. The final section of the chapter profiles the types of career paths that you can expect to find in your first sales job and the challenges in becoming a sales manager.

PERSONAL SELLING

According to the U.S. Department of Labor's Bureau of Labor Statistics, people working in sales number close to 15 million or about 14 percent of the total workforce in the United States. Personal selling is critical to the sale of many goods and services, especially major commercial and industrial products and consumer durables, and can be defined as:

> Direct communications between paid representatives and prospects that lead to purchase orders, customer satisfaction, and account development.

The relationships between selling and other elements of the marketing mix are highlighted in Figure 1-1.

Marketing programs are designed around four elements of the marketing mix: products to be sold, pricing, promotion, and distribution channels. The promotion component includes advertising, public relations, personal selling, and sales promotion (point-of-purchase displays, coupons, and sweepstakes). Note that advertising and sales promotions are nonpersonal communications, whereas salespeople talk directly to customers. Thus, where advertising and sales promotion "pull" merchandise through the channel, personal selling provides the "push" needed to get orders signed. With public relations, the message is perceived as coming from the media rather than directly from the organization. Personal selling involves two-way communication with prospects that allows the sales message to be adapted to the special needs of the customer.

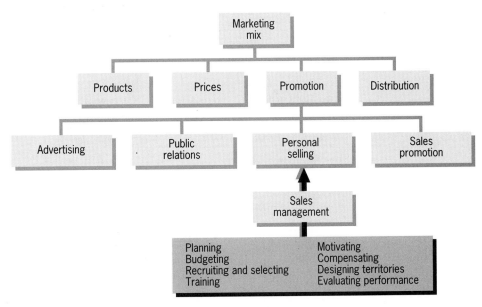

FIGURE 1-1   Positions of Personal Selling and Sales Management in the Marketing Mix

When customers have questions or concerns, the salesperson is there to provide appropriate explanations. Advertising can only respond to objections that the copywriter thinks are important to customers. Furthermore, personal selling can be directed to qualified prospects, whereas a great deal of advertising and sales promotions are wasted because many people in the audience have no use for the product. Perhaps the most important advantage of personal selling is that it is considerably more effective than advertising, public relations, and sales promotion in identifying opportunities to create value for the customer and gaining customer commitment.

The person responsible for management of the field sales operation is the sales manager. He or she may be a first-line manager, directly responsible for the day-to-day management of salespeople, or the manager may be positioned at a higher level in the management hierarchy, responsible for directing the activities of other managers. In either case, sales management focuses on the administration of the personal selling function in the marketing mix. This role includes the planning, management, and control of sales programs, as well as the recruiting, training, compensating, motivating, and evaluating of field sales personnel. Sales management can thus be defined as:

> The planning, organizing, leading, and controlling of personal contact programs designed to achieve the sales and profit objectives of the firm.

Regardless of whether the sales manager directs salespeople or other sales managers, all managers have two types of responsibilities: achieving or exceeding the goals established for performance in the current period and developing the people reporting to them. Each of these responsibilities includes a number of more specific functions and activities that will be discussed throughout this book. Now it is important that you understand the context in which sales managers execute these two responsibilities. In the next section we discuss the consequential changes taking place in the marketplace and in selling operations.

A CHANGING MARKETPLACE

It is certainly a time of change. Powerful forces are at work that are irrevocably changing the way that salespeople and sales managers understand, prepare for, and accomplish their jobs. Few sales forces will be immune. Some of the more important competitive and customer-related forces of change are illustrated in Figure 1-2. In this section we briefly examine these forces and the consequent changes in selling processes.[2]

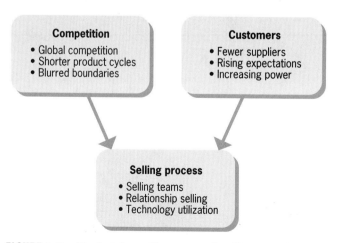

FIGURE 1-2   Marketplace Changes and Selling Consequences

Competition

The 1970s and 1980s were generally a seller's market. In the past 15 years the number of competitors in most markets has literally exploded. In this section, we explore three key reasons for this development—globalization of markets, shorter product cycles, and a blurring of market boundaries.

Globalization   Even companies that compete only in the United States or even in a region of the United States are feeling the effects of globalized competition. It is not unusual to compete with companies from other countries, to use suppliers located in other parts of the world, or to sell to customers that are selling in other countries. Any of these situations may result in intensified competition and requires that the sales force adjust from a local to a global focus.

The most obvious need for a global perspective is for those companies competing in other countries. World trade accounts for more than 20 percent of U.S. gross national product. This is because almost 95 percent of the world's population and 75 percent of its purchasing power are outside of the United States. The majority of sales by such well-known companies as Coca-Cola, Colgate-Palmolive, and Avon Products are made outside the United States. Sales managers know that their companies' growth is likely to depend on how well they manage customer relationships in global markets. This means more travel, hiring the right people, defining new roles and duties, and developing a global perspective and world-class skills at addressing an increasingly eclectic sales force.

Shorter Product Cycles   The rate of technology transfer is increasing. Processes and products that were once proprietary are quickly becoming widely available to competitors. As a result of the porousness of technology and increasing number of competitors, product cycles are shorter, imitation is more rapid, and as a consequence, the window of product differentiation has narrowed considerably. Sales and customer relationship skills are most important when a product is new and again when it is late in its life cycle. New products need careful presentation because a buyer's risk is highest owing to lack of experience with the product. The sales force's task is to help customers understand that the benefits of the new product outweigh the risks and costs associated with the requisite business changes. In the late stages of the life cycle, the salesperson again becomes very important. With very few important differences in competing products, the personal relationship and intimate customer knowledge of the sales force becomes the primary point of differentiation and leverage. Shorter life cycles and more new products mean that sales forces spend less time on the relatively easy, moderately new, moderately differentiated products.

Blurred Boundaries   Contributing importantly to increased competition is the phenomenon of boundary blurring: formerly indirect competitors entering each other's businesses. Steel, aluminum, plastic, paper, and glass, for instance, compete for the same applications. Banks, insurance companies, mutual funds, new Internet companies, and credit-card companies all compete for the same consumer savings and investment dollars. Developments in information and communication technology are often at the heart of boundary blurring. Besides technology, boundary blurring has increased owing to the rise in independents, for example, personal financial consultants and systems integrators, professionals who offer purchasing advice and bundle products from a variety of sources. As a consequence, sellers are having to call on new decision influencers interested in a new value proposition. These developments have made it more difficult and complex to sell effectively against a broader set of competitors.

Customers

The increase in competition clearly calls for new selling and sales management approaches. However, identifying the correct selling and sales management approach is further complicated by customer developments such as rising expectations, purchasing from fewer suppliers, and increasing power. We explore these issues here.

Fewer Suppliers   The traditional practice of buyers rotating purchases across multiple supplier sources is increasingly being questioned in many industries. Not too long ago, Xerox Corporation had 18,000 suppliers; now they have fewer than 500. Ford has taken its supplier base from 75,000 down to 5,000. These companies are finding that the costs of maintaining relationships with a large number of suppliers far exceed any possible price savings. Consider the results of a Department of Defense study which found that it costs hospitals $1.50 in administrative costs associated with a dollar's worth of medical supplies. These administrative costs include purchasing and sales call time, receiving, inventory, space, handling, paperwork, processing, leakage, and so forth. Addressing these internal costs associated with procurement and customer inventory holding costs requires a closer supplier-customer relationship than is usually possible when purchasing from a large number of suppliers.

At first glance, customers purchasing from fewer suppliers would appear to benefit suppliers. But what if a large customer asks you to address the total cost issues associated with a purchase, such as those listed above, and your company has not developed the capacity to do so? You are likely to lose this important customer. What if you are not chosen as one of the "In Suppliers"? Among wholesalers of periodicals and magazines, for instance, the shift by large retailers to single-sourcing has resulted in intense consolidation. Contract-winning wholesalers rapidly acquired former competitors in an effort to cover larger territories and service larger accounts. As a result, the number of wholesalers dropped from nearly 182 firms in 1990 to 56 today.[3] In other words, the revenue stream from individual customers had become so important that survival had become dependent on maintaining the supplier-customer relationship.

Rising Expectations   Despite a focus on quality and service, customer satisfaction remains low, according to research by J.D. Power and Associates. Customer satisfaction is difficult to manage because as customers receive good treatment, they demand even better treatment. In other words, the bar is being constantly raised. Customer expectations are raised not just by how well a business performs versus competitors, but also by the higher standards set in other industries. People are aware of the standard in the consistency of service at McDonald's, the cleanliness at Disney, and the product quality at Sony. Although you may not think you are competing directly with these companies, your customers are aware of the product and service quality they receive from these companies and are holding everyone else to a higher standard.

Higher customer expectations also extend to expectations of cost savings. As efforts intensified to make companies more competitive, purchasers' attention shifted from price, "first cost," to that of "lifetime" cost. This shift in focus from first cost to total cost is both a blessing and a curse for sellers. On the blessing side, this allows sellers to move beyond the confrontational game of negotiating price and may provide greater opportunities for differentiating their offerings. The curse is that many companies are not used to selling from this perspective; it really is a different type of sale. The more sophisticated and informed that buyers become, the less likely they are to be impressed with unsupported assertions, slick presentations, and a focus on product alone as the solution to their needs.

Enron is an energy company that started out selling and transporting natural gas. Now its sales force is just as likely to be offering sophisticated financial instruments such as options, swaps, caps, collars, floors, or firm forwards. During an Enron sales discussion, the salesperson is likely to sound more like a high-level financial specialist than someone from a company that sells gas and electricity. The customer is not really interested in natural gas, but in how they can improve their financial condition and their product offering. While having the right product is necessary, it may not be sufficient to meet the expectations of these customers.

Increasing Power   Fewer than 10 percent of all retail stores, for instance, account for more than half of U.S. retail sales. Wal-Mart, Kmart, Sears, Toys 'R Us, and many other dominant retailers have grown bigger and more powerful than the manufacturers that supply them, and are now dictating the supplier-customer relationship. Consider the situation of Merck & Company and Pfizer, Inc., two very large pharmaceutical manufacturers that failed to offer sufficient price discounts to Group Health Cooperative of Puget Sound. Salespeople from both companies were barred from calling doctors at the cooperative. In other cases, salespeople who once sold to doctors by offering samples and freebies, now face astute financial managers and buyers who want data on cost-effectiveness. Because of Group Health Cooperative's size, it is not only able to require more from its suppliers, but it will get it.

Selling Process

The changes discussed so far are rapidly dooming the traditional sales attitude of "I can sell anything to any account." The financial stakes are too high and the problems too complex for a single salesperson to handle, and the resources needed to address customer needs are embedded deeper in the supplier's organization than the traditional sales force. In this section we briefly discuss three important changes that are taking place in many companies' selling efforts: relationship selling, sales teams, and productivity.

Relationship Selling   The traditional selling model emphasizes selling products in the short-term. The value added by the sales force is in communicating the benefits of the product or service to the customer, helping customers make a purchase decision, and making the whole process convenient and easy for the buyer. In many situations, especially when the product or service is not of strategic significance to the buyer, this type of relationship is appropriate. However, many buyers and sellers are finding that this selling model does not work for all customers, particularly those that are most important. This has led to the development of an alternative selling model referred to as relationship selling. Relationship selling involves creating customer value by addressing important customer problems and opportunities through a supplier-customer relationship that is much more intimate than that of traditional transactional selling. Figure 1-3 contrasts some of the differences between the traditional transactional model of selling and the new relationship selling mode.

Perhaps the best way to understand what is meant by relationship selling is to see an example of it. Until the late 1980s, Procter & Gamble's (P&G) sales focus was very transactional. Multiple P&G divisions serviced the same retail account. As a result, buyers and P&G salespeople operated at an arm's-length buying-selling environment. Sellers took orders and aggressively pursued shelf space, while buyers negotiated fiercely for lowest prices and sought the highest shelving allowances in the form of fees for premium shelf facings. In contrast, relationship selling involves a collaborative effort to create added value from this synergy. P&G has reorganized into Customer Business Development Teams composed of a variety of functional areas and organizational levels focusing on individual customer needs. For example, P&G is able to manage the stock inventory for the retailer or wholesaler in certain high-volume categories through its continuous inventory replenishment system. This system has increased customer product turnover by 20 to 30 percent, and the retailer often sells the inventory before paying for it.[4] Of course for this program to be suc-

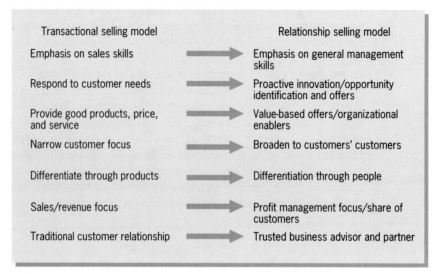

FIGURE 1-3   Contrasting Transactional and Relationship Selling Models

cessful, customers must allow P&G to have critical data on inventory levels and trust that the system will operate in the customer's best interest.

As the preceding example illustrates, relationship selling requires a greater level of trust and commitment by both parties. Note also that the focus is not on the individual transaction, and a long-term focus is necessary to realize its benefits. Notice also that P&G had to reorganize its sales force in order to implement a relationship selling model. In fact, virtually every aspect of their sales program had to be adjusted to foster a relationship selling orientation. It is not surprising that some buyers and sellers are not prepared to make adjustments of this magnitude. The key to successful sales management rests in the ability to strike a strategic balance between relational and transactional opportunities. We will discuss this issue further in Chapter 2 when investigating strategic sales management issues.

Sales Teams   As the P&G experience suggests, the importance of the "lone-wolf" salesperson winning and losing on strength of his or her own efforts and skills is likely to diminish in the future. In the case of relationship selling, no one person possesses the necessary knowledge and resources to address the bigger opportunities to create value that goes beyond selling the product. Figure 1-4 illustrates the changes made by P&G. Under the traditional buyer-seller interface model, all of P&G's capabilities and communications with the retailer were funneled through one salesperson whose customer contact was a purchasing

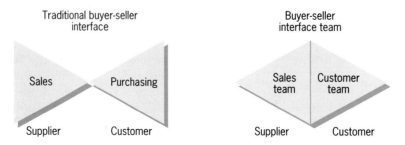

FIGURE 1-4   Traditional Buyer-Seller Interface versus a Team Interface

agent. With selling teams, the model is reversed, with multiple contacts being established between P&G and retailers. This allows for a broader transfer of capabilities and communications. Notice also that both the seller and buyer must change, so the degree and extent of interaction expand dramatically. Obviously, not all buyers and sellers are prepared to make these adjustments.

The switch to selling teams incorporating a relational sales orientation produces a number of critical consequences in a firm's sales program and management processes. Certainly teams will require changes in the organization, selection, training, compensation, supervision, and evaluation of the sales force. Even with strong top management commitment and support, it took P&G five years to transition to relationship selling and selling teams, and there is still a commitment to constantly revisit progress and make further adoptions. In recognition of its importance, we will discuss team building later in this chapter as an important competency for sales managers.

Productivity Focus   Historically, sales performance metrics were simple—increase revenue over the previous year. Sales managers typically rewarded and compensated salespeople by evaluating sales volume over a certain period of time. Although sales volume is important, companies are discovering that not all sales are equally profitable. The profitability of the sale may depend on the following issues:

- The amount of time necessary to complete the sale.
- The gross margins associated with the sale.
- The level of price discounting.
- The amount of promotional support.
- The amount of post-sale support.
- The impact of future product sales.

The sales force has an important influence on all the preceding issues listed through their account selection, account penetration, account retention, pricing, and servicing decisions. For example, packaged goods sales forces for large food manufacturers selling through grocery stores are responsible for trade promotion spending decisions. Trade promotions refer to the money manufacturers give to grocery stores for certain merchandising activities such as coupon promotions, advertising, using display racks, and price promotions. A recent McKinsey report indicated that trade promotion spending consumes approximately 50 percent of the marketing budgets of these companies and represents about 12 percent of sales.[5] Effectively spending this money is critical to these firms' profitability. As a result, salespeople are being evaluated on a wider array of performance metrics which places greater emphasis on gathering more and better performance data. We discuss these performance metrics further in Chapter 15.

The shift to productivity and profitability also has an important impact on the sales manager's job. Today's managers are faced with many complex tradeoff decisions. Illustrative of the decisions that must be made include the following:

- Should we increase the size of the sales organization or should we focus on our indirect sales channels?
- What is the appropriate mix of sales and field engineering support personnel?
- What is the optimum mix between sales resources and customer service resources, and how does this balance differ by types of customers?
- Should we grow our geographic sales group or our telesales group?
- Should we allocate more resources on our "strategic accounts" or should we focus on our midsize accounts?

As indicated at the beginning of this chapter, it is an exciting time to be in sales and sales management. The breadth of skills and knowledge required to excel in sales has increased dramatically. As a consequence, sales is becoming an important proving ground for top marketing and operating officers in many companies. In the next section we discuss a process approach to sales management.

THE SALES MANAGEMENT FUNCTION

As stated earlier, the two primary responsibilities of sales managers are to achieve their firm's goals for the current planning period and to develop the people reporting to them. To better understand how sales managers execute these responsibilities we describe in this section a fundamental process for sales management, the activities in which sales managers are engaged, and the competencies needed to be a successful sales manager.

The Sales Management Process

When managers fail to follow a defined sales management process, chaos reigns and field reps merely react to customer requests rather than help them solve problems. When Filemon Lopez looked at the selling process at Comcast Cable, he found there were no systems to help a salesperson convert leads into a sale.[6] There were no territories, salespeople sold advertising space on price rather than value, and lead generation was haphazard. Lopez instituted training classes showing reps how to prospect, analyze needs, solve problems, and make value-driven sales. He also established sales territories so reps were not competing with one other, and he hired telemarketers to get leads for field reps. Now that Comcast Cable has a defined sales process, reps know what steps to follow and sales revenue is up 20 percent.

The sequence of activities that guides managers in the creation and administration of sales programs for a firm is known as the sales management process. First, the firm must determine the role of the sales force in developing and executing its overall strategy. Then sales management must clearly understand and define the activities and responsibilities of the sales force and construct the formal organization of the sales operation. Then a competent sales force must be developed by recruiting, selection, and training. The last phase of the process focuses on managing the sales force, including leading, motivating, compensating, and evaluating performance. Each step in the sales management process is briefly described here.

Strategic Sales Planning   Sales management is concerned with strategic decision making, as well as with implementing marketing plans. For example, sales executives often become involved in the design and development of marketing programs, and contribute to changes in the product line, the pricing of products and services, and the selection of advertising campaigns. Sales managers are involved in developing strategies for accessing different markets and building account relationships. Sales managers and the salespeople they supervise are in an excellent position to obtain information about customer needs, product applications, and market conditions. This knowledge of the market allows sales managers to contribute to corporate decision making.

In addition to its role in developing and executing marketing plans, sales management is also responsible for developing budgets for implementing the company's marketing plans. This involves determining both a target sales level and the amount that will be spent on the sales function. A key determinant of how much to spend on the sales force is deciding how many salespeople will be needed to meet the company's sales target for the year. The issues involved in this process are discussed in Chapter 2, whereas sales forecasting methods are discussed in Chapter 7.

Understanding the Selling Function   Because sales management is responsible for developing and achieving results through salespeople, it is important to understand the role and responsibilities of the sales force. Therefore Chapter 3 describes the steps salespeople go through to convert prospects into repeat buyers. Chapter 4 stresses the importance of understanding how salespeople manage individual accounts and develop long-term customer relationships. Chapter 5 explains how salespeople manage a territory and their portfolio of sales opportunities. Because salespeople are continually confronted with ethical dilemmas, Chapter 6 provides some background on these problems so that informed decisions can be made.

Sales Goals and Structure Sales planning is easier when managers have good data on where potential customers are located and how much they can be expected to buy. Sales managers need to be able to project sales for existing accounts. A variety of techniques that can be used to estimate potentials and forecast sales are presented in Chapter 7.

Another dimension of sales planning is concerned with designing organizational structures (see Chapter 8). An example of a typical consumer goods sales organization competing nationally is shown in Figure 1-5. The diagram shows 96 salespeople reporting to 8 zone managers, organized into 6 regions. It is important to note that companies vary considerably from this typical sales organization structure. One study found that those with few geographic units and wide spans of control may be asking too much of their managers, whereas those with numerous units and narrow spans may be overstaffed.[7]

The next step in the sales management process is to assign salespeople to individual territories to minimize travel and contact costs, as discussed in Chapter 9. The proper design of sales territories helps the sales department provide optimum customer service and satisfaction at a reasonable cost.

Building Sales Competencies Sales managers are responsible for hiring salespeople with the appropriate skills and backgrounds to implement the sales strategy. Research has revealed that failure is more likely among candidates who lack initiative, organization, enthusiasm, customer orientation, and personal goals.[8] This means that good sources must be found for new hires, and those who are weak in these areas must be carefully screened out. These and other recruiting issues are covered in Chapter 10.

After salespeople have been hired, they should be trained before they are sent into the field. Sales managers are responsible for making sure that training is completed, and they

LEEDS METROPOLITAN UNIVERSITY LEARNING CENTRE

	Number
Vice president of marketing	1
National sales manager	1
Regional sales manager	6
Zone manager	8
Field sales representative	96

FIGURE 1-5 Sales Organization in a Typical Consumer Packaged Goods Company

often conduct some of the classes. Most initial training programs are designed to familiarize salespeople with the company's products, services, and operating procedures, with some time devoted to development of selling skills. Because sales training is expensive, the sales manager is responsible for selecting the most cost-effective methods, location, and materials. A detailed discussion of training is given in Chapter 11.

Leading the Sales Force   Effective sales managers know how to supervise and lead their salespeople. Sales managers provide leadership by inspiring people to grow and develop professionally, while achieving the revenue goals of the firm (Chapter 12). Good leaders provide models of behavior for employees to emulate, often developing strong mutual trust and rapport with subordinates. Leadership styles vary, but effective leaders are adept at initiating structure—that is, organizing and motivating employees, setting goals, enforcing rules, and defining expectations.

Sales managers use a variety of tools in their efforts to motivate salespeople to work more efficiently and effectively. Chapter 13 describes a proven process for achieving goal-directed effort. The chapter also discusses other techniques that have proved to be effective motivators, including sales meetings, quotas, sales contests, and recognition awards.

The most powerful motivator for salespeople is often a well-designed compensation package. Money is an important consideration for attracting and motivating people to work hard (Chapter 14). A key task for sales managers is to devise an effective mix of salary, bonuses, commissions, expenses, and benefits without putting the firm's profitability in jeopardy.

The final step in the sales management process is to evaluate the performance of the sales force. This involves analyzing sales data by account, territory, and product line breakdowns (Chapter 15). It also means reviewing selling costs and measuring the impact of sales force activities on profits.

Sales Management Activities

One field sales manager described the job as follows:

> People development is my main mission in life: 50 percent people development, 30 percent sales and product leadership, 10 percent administration, and 10 percent compliance—you go to jail if you are not the policeman on the block.[9]

Although the activities of each sales management position will vary somewhat according to the industry and company involved, this is probably a fair description of most field sales management positions. To provide a better understanding of the field sales management position, we turn our attention to how sales managers spend their time.

An excellent way to learn about sales management is to ask a representative group of sales managers how they spend their time. The results of just such an exercise are shown in Table 1-1. Most people are surprised to learn that the largest proportion of a sales manager's time (29 percent) is spent selling. Sales managers typically spend 17 percent of their time in

TABLE 1-1   Sales Managers' and Salespersons' Time Allocations

Job Responsibility	Manager's Time Allocation (in percent)
Selling	29%
Face-to-face	(17)
Telephone selling	(12)
Administration	25%
Account service/coordination	17%
Travel/waiting	15%
Internal meetings	14%

face-to-face conferences with customers and another 12 percent talking with them on the phone. These findings dispel the common misconception that sales managers sit behind desks issuing orders. For example, when Dan LeFever took over as sales manager for Bard Access's Northeast district, he began to travel three days a week with his reps to meet with customers and help tailor presentations to buyers' needs. He found that the buying center for his medical equipment had shifted from doctors to administrators who based decisions on cost. LeFever counseled his eight salespeople to broaden their prospect list to include chief financial officers, materials directors, and others involved in equipment decisions.[10] Two salespeople were unable to make this change and had to be replaced. By working closely in the field to train and motivate his salespeople, LeFever was able to move his district from last to first and earned a promotion to Director of Sales of the Davol Division of Bard, Inc.

Research shows that sales managers spend a significant amount of time selling to their own accounts. This activity can take time away from important administrative responsibilities; however, in some cases this activity can be justified. Occasionally sales managers will handle one or more large accounts because they merit and need their attention. In smaller firms, there may be no need for a full-time sales manager, in which case the sales manager is likely to handle personal accounts along with administrative responsibilities.

Administration   Administrative duties take one-quarter of the available time of sales managers. For managers, these activities include management of field sales offices, training, preparation of budgets, expense control, and administration of compensation programs. Sales managers must continually deal with people both to help new hires get adjusted and to improve the selling skills of more experienced members of the sales team. For example, Jan Howard of MONY insurance boosted the revenue of her top producer group $2.3 million a year and won a Best Sales Force award from *Sales & Marketing Management* magazine by helping them become more efficient.[11] Jan had the reps keep track of their activities and pointed out where they were wasting time on meetings and paperwork. By delegating some of this work and making better use of technology, face-to-face time with customers increased from 8 hours a week to 13 hours, and sales boomed.

Managers also spend time consulting with salespeople who are performing below standard. Encouragement, personal counseling, retraining, or assignment to a new territory can improve the performance of many of these people. Because poor sales records are occasionally the result of serious personal problems, sales managers must know how to recognize and deal with difficult situations and when to refer people to professional help. Poor performance may also be a function of factors beyond the control of the salesperson, such as unusual competitive activity, loss of a key customer, or weak company support. In other cases, problem salespeople are not always the result of poor hiring decisions.

Account Service/Coordination   Students sometimes wonder why sales managers spend 17 percent of their time servicing accounts. The reason is that customers need an advocate within the firm to make sure their interests are protected. Sales managers share responsibility with salespeople for ensuring that customers' orders are processed and delivered on time. This means that sales managers help coordinate customers' needs with the production department to make sure that quality and service standards are maintained. They also work to gain credit approval, and they check with customers to make sure that post-sales adjustments and service are satisfactory.

Travel   Typical sales managers spend about 15 percent of their time traveling (Table 1-1). This is less than the 18 percent spent by field salespeople who are on the road four or five days a week. Sales managers have larger territories than salespeople but travel less often. The most common reasons for sales managers to travel are to keep in touch with conditions in the field, to help close important sales, and to observe and train field sales reps.

Meetings   Sales meetings are important training and motivational tools for field reps, so it is not surprising that sales managers spend 14 percent of their time on this activity. When Steve Bannigan, the new sales manager of McBride Electric, had his first meeting with his sales team he found that only two thought of themselves as salespeople.[12] The rest saw themselves as "estimators" who just priced electrical work and took orders. To give his team more of a sales focus, Bannigan held a series of meetings to develop basic selling skills so they could solicit business and close orders. As a result McBride Electric has been growing between 10 and 25 percent per year.

Sales Management Competencies

We've talked about what sales managers do, but you may still be wondering what it takes to be an effective or even an outstanding sales manager. So, let's look more closely at the competencies that managers need in order to succeed.

Sales management competencies are defined as sets of knowledge, skills, behaviors, and attitudes that a person needs to be effective in a wide range of industries and various types of organizations.[13] People use many types of competencies in their everyday lives. Here we focus on six competencies (Figure 1-6) that you will need for today's sales management responsibilities. In practice, it is difficult to know where one competency begins and another ends. Drawing sharp distinctions between them is valuable only for purposes of identification and description. Keeping these six sales management competencies in mind, however, will help you remember how the material you are studying can improve your performance on the job. To help you in this process, we have included inserts into each of the following chapters describing these competencies in the context of the chapter's subject matter. Often these are examples from actual companies. In addition, exercises are included at the end of each chapter focusing on each of the six competencies. Let's examine the dimensions of each of these competencies more closely.

Strategic Action Competency   Understanding the overall strategy and goals of the company and ensuring that your actions and those of the people you manage are consistent with these goals involve strategic action competency. Strategic action competency includes:

- Understanding the industry
- Understanding the organization
- Taking strategic actions

Today's sales managers are being challenged to think strategically in order to improve their job performance. One dimension of strategic thinking is to anticipate strategic trends in

FIGURE 1-6   A Model of Sales Management Competencies

STRATEGIC ACTION COMPETENCY
Dimensions

Understanding the Industry:

- Understands the history and general trends in the industry and their implications for the future
- Stays informed of and anticipates the actions of competitors and strategic partners
- Identifies attractive market segments and their buying needs

Understanding the Organization:

- Understands the vision, overall strategy, and goals of the organization
- Appreciates the distinctive competencies of the organization with respect to market opportunities and limitations
- Understands how to marshal organizational resources to meet the needs of the customers

Taking Strategic Actions:

- Assigns priorities and making decisions that are consistent with the firm's mission and strategic goals
- Implements specific account selection, retention, and dominance strategies
- Develops an appropriate portfolio of account relationships
- Considers the long-term implications of actions in order to sustain and further develop the organization
- Establishes tactical and operational goals that facilitate the firm's strategy implementation

the industry and to make the appropriate adjustments to take advantage of these changes. A failure to do so may be very costly.

The plight of Encyclopedia Britannica Corp. is a good example of the possible penalty for ignoring important industry trends. First published 225 years ago in Edinburgh, Scotland, sales of *Encyclopedia Britannica* peaked in 1990 at $650 million with profits of $40 million. As CD-ROM technology gained acceptance, however, Britannica's management failed to respond and continued to market through a direct sales force of 2,300 people. Part of the reason Britannica found it hard to change is that a typical sale pays the salesperson a commission of $300. With CD-ROM encyclopedia packages priced from $99 to $395, a significant drop in commissions would have been required. It also would have required marketing through competing channels of distribution such as retail outlets, direct mail, and telemarketing, a change the powerful direct sales force would have resisted. Sales have drastically declined, the company is in financial trouble, and the sales force is now less than half its former size.[14]

This competency also involves understanding the organization—not just the sales unit in which the manager works. One sales manager in noting the importance of networking within an organization said, "Goals and standards will cascade from above. Unless you are well connected and can influence them, your point of view goes unheard at the top."[15]

A sales manager with a well-developed strategic action competency can diagnose and assess different situations and think in terms of relative priorities rather than ironclad goals and rules. In sales, executing a company's strategy involves making the right decisions with respect to customer account selection, account penetration and retention, product line emphasis, and managing selling and service costs. All managers—especially top managers—need strategic action competency. For more details about strategic action competency, refer to the Strategic Action Competency box.

Coaching Competency   Comparisons are often made between the competitive worlds of sports and business sales. Athletes compete against opposing players to win the game, whereas salespeople compete with other companies' salespeople to win accounts. Like the athletic coach, the sales manager plays an important role in this competition by helping to develop the skills of the sales team.[16] The president of a large distribution company developed the habit of calling a district sales manager into his office and bringing up an account on his computer. He then asked the manager to comment on what he or she had done to support the salesperson's relationship-building efforts in that account. He didn't tell the district managers how to help salespeople build better account relationships, but he did want to reinforce the importance of this management responsibility. At first, managers were unprepared, but as soon as the message was delivered, helping salespeople build better customer relationships became a priority among the district managers. Soon other senior officers began copying the president's actions.

Coaching is defined as a sequence of conversations and activities that provides ongoing feedback and encouragement to a salesperson or sales team member with the goal of improving that person's performance. Performance improvement is achieved by

- Providing verbal feedback
- Role modeling
- Building trust

Coaching helps salespeople develop through one-on-one feedback and encouragement. The best coaches don't tell salespeople what to do, they collaborate with them to achieve

---

COACHING COMPETENCY
Dimensions

Providing Verbal Feedback:

- Provides specific and continuous performance and selling skills feedback
- Builds a feeling of appreciation and recognition by taking the time to acknowledge a job well done, an effort beyond the call of duty, or an important victory
- Reinforces successes and positive attempts to support desirable behaviors

Role Modeling:

- Leads by example, rather than decree
- Provides role models, either themselves or others, and shares best practices
- Models professional attitudes and behaviors

Trust Building:

- Maintains good rapport with the sales team and fosters open communications, collaboration, creativity, initiative, and appropriate risk taking
- Adds value through communicating relevant selling experiences
- Helps salespeople to "look good" through two-way communications

mutually agreed-upon goals. In this role, a sales manager works with each person to create and implement a developmental plan to improve performance. This process often includes providing ongoing training and coaching in selling skills, sales strategy, and product and market knowledge.

Sales coaching, however, involves more than just providing verbal feedback on what a salesperson has done. Successful sales coaches also provide a role model of positive example through their own behavior or that of others. According to a successful sales manager at Xerox, "I believe in the power of personal example. You can rant and rave and threaten, but the most effective way to get results is to show someone what you want done."[17] Many sales managers believe that being a good role model is the most effective way to gain the respect of their salespeople.

Still, a salesperson must be open to coaching, taking feedback constructively and following the sales manager's example, for the sales manager's efforts to be effective. This requires a level of trust between a salesperson and a sales manager.[18] A climate of trust is created when a manager is honest, reliable, and shows a genuine concern about the needs of the salespeople. This is achieved by listening and maintaining an open, two-way channel of communications. As the saying goes: "They won't care what you know, until they know you care." For more details on dimensions of coaching competency, refer to the Coaching Competency box.

Team-Building Competency   Accomplishing tasks through small groups of people who are collectively responsible and whose work is interdependent requires a team-building competency. Sales managers in companies that utilize sales teams can become more effective by

TEAM-BUILDING COMPETENCY
Dimensions

Designing Teams:

- Implements an organizational architecture that will support teams
- Creates a reward system that is fair within the context of a team effort
- Coordinates team goals with the overall goals of the organization
- Coordinates team activities with the requirements of functional areas within the organization

Creating A Supportive Environment:

- Hires people who will be successful in a team environment
- Trains with programs that encourage teamwork
- Integrates the individual members of the sales team together to form a functioning and supportive team

Managing Team Dynamics:

- Understands the strengths and weaknesses of team members and uses their strengths to accomplish tasks as a team
- Facilitates cooperative behavior and keeps the team moving toward its goals

- Designing teams properly
- Creating a supportive environment
- Managing team dynamics appropriately

In a recent study of 243 employers, the Hay Group found that two of every three companies plan to increase their level of employee participation in teams. The primary reasons for the change are to improve customer service and productivity.[19] Increasingly companies are realizing that they are not selling a product; to remain competitive, they must provide system-oriented solutions to a customer's business problems. Allegiance Healthcare recognizes that the foremost mission of its hospital customers is the care of patients. Allegiance enables its customers to focus more closely on their mission by providing the support of a wide range of functional experts. Financial experts monitor regional economics, whereas information service specialists help customers with their information systems needs. Marketing Liaisons analyze product-specific data such as usage trends and pricing options. With an in-depth understanding of its customers' internal operations, the Logistical Support Group can offer improvements that will streamline customers' logistical processes. Designing an organizational structure so that teams effectively and profitably work together to bring added value to the customer can be very challenging, as the Allegiance example suggests. Team design involves formulating goals to be achieved, defining tasks to be done, and identifying the staffing needed to accomplish those tasks.

A well-designed team is capable of high performance, but it needs a supportive environment to achieve its full potential. In a supportive environment, team members are empowered to take actions based on their best judgment. This means that it is very important to hire people who can get along with others and who work well within a team environment. This is quite different from the traditional salesperson who survived by relying on his or her own abilities. In fact, some companies conduct interviews with team members as a crucial part of their hiring process. Successful team development undoubtedly will require team training, which is necessary to allow team members to assume each other's roles and to work interdependently.

Conflicts and disagreements among team members are natural, which means that managing team dynamics is necessary for effective team building. Essentially this means maintaining cooperative relationships while pursuing a common goal. If managed well, conflict can be productive; if poorly managed, however, it can destroy the team. For more details about the team-building competency, refer to the Team-Building Competency box.

Self-Management Competency   Taking responsibility for your actions at work and elsewhere involves self-management competency. When problems arise, people often blame their difficulties on the situation or on others. Effective managers don't fall into this trap. Self-management competency includes

- Integrity and ethical conduct
- Managing personal drive
- Self-awareness and development

Sales managers are in a particularly sensitive position with respect to integrity and ethical conduct. To achieve success the sales force must trust and respect a sales manager. How is it possible to respect people you feel have no integrity and do not conduct themselves ethically? As a person who influences or controls the rewards salespeople receive, a manager's ethics and integrity are constantly under review. As the leader of the sales team, salespeople take their cues from the sales manager with respect to the ethical treatment of customers. If salespeople are aware of instances in which a sales manager has bent the rules to make a sale to one customer, they are more likely to model this behavior. At the same time, there is increasing emphasis on ethical professional behavior and important penalties associated with unethical behavior. Consider the following recent examples:

SELF-MANAGEMENT COMPETENCY
Dimensions

Fostering Integrity and Ethical Conduct:

- Has clear personal standards that serve as a foundation for a sense of integrity and ethical conduct by the sales team
- Projects self-assurance and doesn't just tell people what they want to hear
- Willing to admit mistakes and accepts responsibility for own actions

Managing and Balancing Personal Drive:

- Seeks responsibility, works hard, and is willing to take risks
- Shows perseverance in the face of obstacles and bounces back from failure
- Ambitious and motivated to achieve objectives, but doesn't put personal ambition ahead of the organization's goals
- Understands that goals are achieved through the success and development of the salespeople

Developing Self-Awareness and Management Skills:

- Has clear personal and career goals and knows own values, feelings, and areas of strengths and weaknesses
- Analyzes and learns from work and life experiences
- Willing to continually unlearn and relearn as changed situations call for new skills and perspectives

---

- In 1994 Prudential Securities Inc., formerly Prudential-Bache Securities, reached an agreement with federal and state securities regulators on settling a securities fraud case that hinged on misleading sales documents distributed to brokers and passed on to customers. The settlement would ultimately cost Prudential in excess of $1.4 billion.
- Columbia/HCA Healthcare Corporation, the largest for-profit hospital company in the United States, has been accused of improperly inflating costs in reports to the government, and pocketing more Medicare reimbursement than deserved. Industry sources predict that Columbia will pay a $1 billion fine.
- Sears, Roebuck & Company recently admitted to having used flawed judgment after it collected debts from some of its credit-card holders who had sought bankruptcy. The retailer took a $475 million pretax write-off to cover the costs of the settlement.

Perhaps because of the size of these judgments, developing corporate cultures that encourage ethical behavior is becoming a prominent concern of management. Companies are developing and enforcing codes of ethics, instituting formal ethics training programs, hiring ethical consultants, and maintaining standing ethics committees. Despite all these efforts, ethical conduct by managers is critical to developing an ethical corporate culture.

Sales managers are involved in a constant balancing act. On a typical day, they will work on many problems simultaneously from the insignificant to the important. In the words of one new sales manager:

> You have eight or nine people looking for your time ... coming into and out of your office all day long. Who is going to come in with the real hot one today and how do I escalate myself to listen to that one today because I can't listen to all eight or nine?

A sales manager's job is more than just balancing the many issues that arise each day. Most important is achieving a balance between one's personal goals and those of the organization and of the people they manage. After being promoted to sales management a year earlier, one manager responded as follows to the question of what satisfied him:

> What satisfies me about the job? Well, you do get feedback. Every month you can see how much your team has generated and you can see which people have developed and maybe even been promoted. You know you are doing something that is important to the company, something that needs to be done—both making money and helping people grow and move—both aspects bring their own satisfactions.

Perhaps the biggest adjustment that new sales managers must make is understanding the difference between selling customers and leading salespeople. At first glance there appears to be quite a bit of overlap in what you do as a salesperson and a manager. For instance, both the salesperson and the manager must be good listeners and know how to take decisive action. To understand the difference between the two situations, consider the comments of one sales manager:

> With clients you have to decide quickly, in one or two meetings of twenty minutes or so, what you think of them. You make quick, almost snap, judgments. You're constantly reading people. You can't judge so quickly when trying to read your own people. You need to really get to know what they're like, because you'll have to trust them. It can't be superficial.[20]

Self-awareness is a critical element of being a good sales manager. This begins with the reason for wanting to be a sales manager in the first place. People are attracted to management for a variety of reasons including being tired of their present job, the opportunity to assume more authority and make more money, and the opportunity to exercise power and influence. New managers quickly discover that these reasons don't help them much in the day-to-day life of a sales manager, which often leads to self-doubts and a focus on the question of "Will I be good at it?" Following are comments from three new sales managers regarding what they discovered about themselves through their salespeople:

- I saw my style as very aggressive, demanding, interested, and involved. They saw me as a dictator, a tyrant on their backs.
- I was just being myself. But after three weeks on the job it was coming back to me that people thought I was harsh, harsh. I needed to soften.
- What an eye-opener. People were trying to tell me I was too indecisive. I made them nervous because I seemed timid. No one had ever called me timid before.[21]

To help you in your own self-awareness, a number of self-assessment exercises have been included in the following chapters. The best way to develop self-awareness, however, is to do something; take some action. A number of experiential exercises are suggested at the end of the chapters along with in-class exercises in which the feedback from other students and your instructor will be helpful in developing self-awareness. The Self-Management Competency box provides more details about this competency.

Global Perspective Competency Drawing on human, financial, information, and material resources from multiple countries and serving customers who span multiple cultures requires a global perspective competency. Not all companies compete in global markets or service customers who sell throughout the world, but during the course of your career, it's likely that you will work for an organization which has a global sales component. To be prepared for such an opportunity, you should begin to develop your global perspective competency, which in sales is reflected in

- Cultural knowledge and sensitivity
- Adapting a global selling program

GLOBAL PERSPECTIVE COMPETENCY
Dimensions

Cultural Knowledge and Sensitivity:

- Stays informed of political, social, and economic trends and events around the world
- Recognizes the impact of global events on the market and the organization
- Sensitivity to cultural cues and ability to adapt quickly in novel situations
- Travels regularly and has a basic business vocabulary in languages relevant to the position

Adapting Global Selling Program:

- Adopts an appropriate sales force architecture for global accounts
- Appropriately adjusts sales force measurement, competency creation, and motivation systems to the local culture
- Appropriately adjusts own behavior when interacting and managing people from various national, ethnic, and cultural backgrounds

---

By the time you become a sales manager in your home country, your own culture has become second nature to you. However, unless you have traveled extensively, or studied other cultures as part of your education, you probably have much less general knowledge and understanding of other countries, even those that share a border with your own country. Yet because business is becoming global, many managers are now expected to develop a knowledge and understanding of at least a few other cultures, such as where the company is marketing its products or where customers are selling their products. For example, Wyeth-Ayerst International sells pharmaceuticals in 100 countries and employs 50 international sales trainers. The skills component of their training programs emphasizes that listening, asking the right questions, and probing for needs are the same throughout the world. Nevertheless, the company adapts training to local conditions in response to cultural differences. Salespeople are taught when to drink tea, when to schedule appointments, and when to close.[22]

Selling globally or to global accounts impacts almost everything a sales manager does. Selection, for instance, becomes more difficult. One study reported that sales executives rated up to 50 percent of expatriates as ineffective or marginally effective.[23] Coordination also becomes problematic as issues arise between sales efforts at global headquarters and in individual regions and locations are exacerbated. In recognition of this complication, global issues are discussed in each of the following chapters. The Global Perspective Competency box provides more information on the dimensions of this competency.

Technology Competency Understanding the potential for technology to improve sales force efficiency and effectiveness and knowing how to implement the integration of technology into the sales force is referred to as possessing technology competency. Technology competency includes:

- Understanding new technology
- Implementing sales force automation

TECHNOLOGY COMPETENCY
Dimensions

Understanding of New Technology:

- Awareness of the potential for technology to increase sales force efficiency and effectiveness
- Experience in using new technology
- Attitude toward adopting new technology

Implementing Sales Force Automation:

- Knows what is to be accomplished and the possible benefits
- Adapts personal management style and procedures
- Fosters sales force acceptance and use of selling technology

Imagine Willy Loman, the central figure in Arthur Miller's classic *Death of a Salesman,* several times a day punching in his activities—his contacts, sales calls, results, and so forth—on a small PalmPilot and then each night uploading the information to his personal computer and, ultimately, to his boss. Impossible, you say? Maybe, maybe not. Many experts consider the integration of communications technology, more commonly known as sales force automation (SFA), as not only a source of competitive advantage, but increasingly a necessity to stay competitive. According to a recent survey of top sales executives, 83 percent of respondents' companies plan to upgrade existing sales and marketing service and customer relationship management systems. The average budget companies have slated for these initiatives is $1.5 million.[24]

When implemented correctly, sales force automation can streamline a company's entire selling process. Although most companies can't afford not to automate, an estimated 55 percent of SFA projects fail to deliver the expected benefits. According to SFA experts, company efforts to automate are jeopardized by one of three reasons, each of which causes the sales force to resist SFA. One reason for resistance is that the sales force does not understand how SFA will help them in their efforts to sell. In other words, management has not clearly identified and communicated what they want to accomplish. Second, sales management may expect SFA to allow better control of remote and mobile salespeople. Experience shows that when the balance shifts to management control and data collection from increasing sales-rep productivity, SFA will be resisted by the sales force. (Isn't this what is really going on in the Willy Loman scenario described earlier?) Third, resistance is likely when top management is not committed to automation by adapting technology themselves. Unfortunately, it is still almost a badge of honor among top corporate officers to not know how to use their own personal computer. Because the opportunities for sales force automation are so widespread and important and because management plays such an important role in the successful implementation of SFA, we consider technology competence a sales management competency. In addition to the box inserts and end-of-chapter questions focusing on technology, problems have been included in the appropriate chapters accompanied by Excel spreadsheets. The companies we have talked with and the sales managers who have been chapter consultants for this text have indicated that they expect their new hires to have a basic proficiency in the use of spreadsheets, which is why we have included the problems along with Excel files for your analysis. For more on technology competency, see the Technology Competency box.

CAREER PATHS

We believe it is important for students to understand how someone moves into the position of sales manager and what the opportunities are for further advancement. Sales managers almost always begin their career paths as salespeople. According to a survey of first-line sales managers, the median age of newly appointed field sales managers is about 35 with about 6 $\frac{1}{2}$ years of prior sales experience.[25] Research has shown that there is a significant positive correlation between the appointment of new sales managers and subsequent performance.[26] Because of their enthusiasm and fresh ideas, new sales managers are often able to boost the sales of the salespeople they supervise. The bottom line is that you can make a difference with a career in sales management. Following is one person's story.

Rob Prazmark

When Rob Prazmark graduated from college, his first job was selling Xerox copy machines in Buffalo, New York. After learning the basics, he moved on to sell ad space at an independent television station. Then he got a job selling ABC network news time. He was so creative at squeezing extra cash from each sale that he was offered a sales vice-president's position at ISL Marketing at the young age of 31. In this job he had to find 11 sponsors for the Olympic Games and raise $300 million. The key sale was a $20 million pitch to Visa; from then on, Prazmark made each successive campaign even more successful. Prazmark's skyrocketing career shows that a basic foundation in selling often leads to a progression of increasingly rewarding sales positions.[27]

Sales trainees with undergraduate degrees are promoted into sales management positions after a few years of field-selling experience. The amount of time required to make this step depends on the ability of the individual, the size of the firm, and the types of products sold. In some organizations that sell directly to consumers, it is possible to become a sales manager after six months. On the other hand, a person may spend 5 to 10 years in several positions before being promoted to sales manager in a firm marketing industrial products. An example of sales career paths for Hallmark Cards is now presented.

Hallmark Cards

Sales careers with consumer product firms begin in the field, where trainees gain valuable experience that becomes the springboard for promotions into other marketing areas. At Hallmark Cards, salespeople who lack field sales experience start as retail installation coordinators (Figure 1-7). This allows new hires to familiarize themselves with customers and their needs before they move up to a sales representative position. Each sales representative is assigned a geographic territory that consists of several counties and about 30 retail accounts. Sales representatives work with their retail accounts to improve space productivity, visual appeal, personal selling skills, inventory control, and local advertising programs.

Successful reps move up to the position of sales executive with more responsibility and larger accounts. From this position, some people move to jobs as multiple account coordinators, district sales trainers, or district sales managers. The position of multiple account coordinator is designed for career salespeople who are not interested in staff or sales management positions. Hallmark thus offers three promotion opportunities for those who want to stay in sales rather than move on to management.

District sales trainer is an important job at Hallmark Cards, because it can lead to a regional sales trainer job, district sales development specialist, new-business specialist, or staff positions outside the sales organization. Promotion to district sales manager at Hallmark usually takes 7 to 10 years and can lead to a position as one of four regional sales vice presidents. A key advantage of a Hallmark sales career is the wide variety of positions available that provide experience needed to climb the ladder of success.

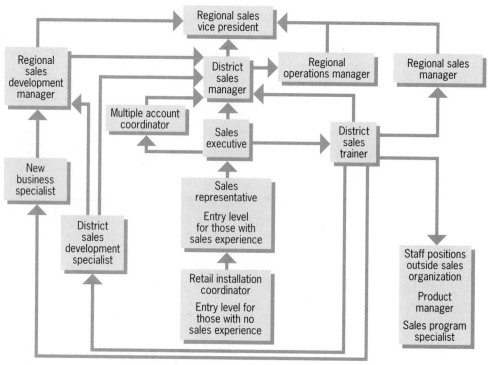

FIGURE 1-7   Sales Paths at Hallmark Cards

SUMMARY

This chapter has introduced the topics of personal selling and sales management. Where personal selling focuses on direct contacts with prospects, sales management is concerned with the planning, organizing, leading, and controlling of personal contact programs to satisfy customers and achieve the objectives of the firm. You should now be able to do the following:

1. **Describe the major changes taking place in selling and the forces causing these changes.** The competitive marketplace is becoming more globalized, product life cycles are shortening, and competitive boundaries are blurring. At the same time, customers are buying from fewer suppliers, their service and performance expectations are increasing, and their power is increasing so that they can not only demand, but obtain higher service and offerings from suppliers. As a result of these forces, the selling process is becoming more focused on relationship selling, selling teams are often necessary to fully address customer needs, and sales force success is increasingly measured in terms of productivity and profits as opposed to top-line revenues.
2. **Define sales management.** Sales management is defined as the planning, organizing, leading, and controlling of personal contact programs designed to achieve the sales and profit objectives of the firm.
3. **Describe the sales management process.** For pedagogical purposes and by way of organizing the variety of activities involved in sales management, the sales management process is grouped as follows: strategic sales planning, developing the selling function, setting sales goals and structures, building sales competencies, and leading the sales force. Though these steps are not usually performed in sequence, this organization of

sales management activities provides a good overview of the decisions in which sales managers at all levels in the organization are involved.

4. **Discuss the competencies required to be a successful sales manager.** To be an effective sales manager in a dynamic environment requires six competencies: strategic action, coaching, team building, self-management, a global perspective, and a technology competency. You can develop these competencies through study, training, and experience. By doing so, you can prepare yourself for a variety of sales and sales management positions in various industries and countries. You can continue practicing your managerial competencies by completing the exercises at the end of this and subsequent chapters.

KEY TERMS

Advertising	Personal selling	Sales manager
Advertising pull	Personal selling push	Sales organization
Business products	Public relations	Sales promotion
Career paths	Relationship selling model	Sales representative
Consumer products	Sales force automation (SFA)	Sales teams
Globalization	Sales management	Span of control
Leadership	Sales management competencies	Transactional selling model

DEVELOPING YOUR COMPETENCIES

1. **Technology Competency.** When JVC Company of America, an audio and visual equipment manufacturer, decided to explore sales force automation (SFA) with its 200-plus reps, mostly working from their homes, it asked them two questions: "What would you like to have on your desk at home?" and "What questions do you get asked?" JVC reps wanted to be able to provide answers to their customers' queries about purchase orders and inventory. JVC implemented a software program that lets reps download that information from a mainframe every day, providing them with instant information and saving them considerable time in having to call headquarters and customers the next day. What did JVC do right in this SFA effort and what other things could they have done to ensure a successful SFA implementation? For more on JVC Company, visit the company's home page at *www.JVC.com.*

2. **Team-Building Competency.** GoldMine Software Corporation is a leading developer of software solutions for sales and marketing teams. Firms like GoldMine that sell complex analytical software are relying more on sales teams to work with customers, partly because a single salesperson can never know everything about the product. Nonetheless, companies have found it difficult to transition to a sales team selling effort from a more traditional model. What are some of the problems that GoldMine is likely to encounter with a team sales operation? For more information on GoldMine Software Corporation, visit the company's home page at *www.goldminesw.com.*

3. **Coaching Competency.** Sales consultants are advising businesses that female sales representatives should move away from dresses and slacks and adopt a more professional look. Is it part of your job as sales manager to tell your reps what to wear? If so, how should this be done?

4. **Strategic Action Competency.** Carter Diamond Tool has been a leader in manufacturing and designing high-quality synthetic and natural diamond cutting tools and dressers since 1920. Until recently, they employed 10 salespeople to call on accounts. Dissatisfied with the results, Carter Diamond discharged all 10 in favor of 8 independent manufacturer's

representatives. (Manufacturer's reps are not employed by the company; usually they sell for a number of companies.) The reps in this case sold other industrial products along with the Precision line to the same customers. Immediately, sales began to increase, old business was retrieved, and new accounts were acquired. What possible reasons might explain this? What are the advantages and disadvantages of manufacturer's reps compared to an in-house sales force? For more on Carter Diamond Tool, visit its home page at *www.carterdiamond.com*.

5. **Self-management.** A good way to learn about sales management is to spend a day with an actual sales manager. Contact a sales manager and arrange to observe his or her activities during a typical day. Ask him or her what it was like becoming a sales manager. Why did this person want to be a manager? What did they think it would be like? What was it like during the first six months? How did they come to their present perspective? If possible, keep a log of how the sales manager's time is spent and compare it with the data in Table 1-1. If you have difficulty finding a cooperative sales manager, contact the local chapter of the Sales and Marketing Executives Club or the American Marketing Association, or ask your instructor for help. A good way to get started is to visit the American Marketing Association home page at *www.ama.org*.

6. **Global Awareness.** Where in the world, literally, would you like to work? Choose a country where you would like to work sometime but that is unfamiliar to you. Begin to learn about it by compiling some basic facts, such as: What language is spoken? What is the system of government? What is the dominant religion? Which industries are most important? Which large companies are headquartered there? Which domestic companies have significant sales in this country? Use whatever sources of information you can to complete this activity, including speaking with people who have lived in or visited the country, visiting a professor who teaches about this country, and exploring the Internet.

IN-CLASS EXERCISES

1-1: Promotion to Manager

Skymation, Inc. has been experiencing fantastic growth during the past year. The introduction of its new product, StarDuster, has had salespeople working double-time. In fact, the company's overall sales have jumped an average of 60 percent per month, because of the added exposure StarDuster has given to all of the company's products.

Lester Mews is the vice president of sales. Lately, he spends most of his time interviewing and hiring new sales reps. After adding 10 people to the sales roster, and shuffling territories, Mews realized he needed to promote one of his senior reps to an area sales manager. Two candidates fit the position. Melinda Curtis is one of Skymation's best closers. She has been a President's Club member every year since she was hired five years ago. Her dynamic personality is an inspiration to other reps, and she has had great success with the two rookie reps she has mentored. Her "take-charge" personality has been a boon to Mews, who often asks Curtis to help him plan sales meetings. The other choice is Scott Lanier, who is a six-year veteran of Skymation. Lanier is a solid producer who is looked up to by many of the younger reps. He is great at building customer relationships, and always has supportive words and suggestions for his peers on how to improve their sales techniques. He is surprisingly detail oriented for a salesperson; his sales reports are always filled in perfectly and turned in on time.

Mews wants to choose the person who will keep sales growth high and keep the reps motivated, but who also can oversee the territory and keep records and budgets as if it were his/her own business. He doesn't want to lose one rep by promoting the other.

Questions:

1. Whom should Mews choose for area sales manager and why?
   - Consider the leadership issues discussed in the chapter. In particular, think about the duties of a sales manager. What skills do sales managers need to perform effectively?
   - Consider Melinda Curtis: she is obviously the best salesperson. As such, she can coach others. She also has some experience with planning sales meetings. Would Curtis make the best area sales manager? Why or why not?
   - Consider Scott Lanier: he is a veteran who also offers suggestions for others on how to improve their sales techniques. He is an effective administrator. Would Lanier make the best area sales manager? Why or why not?
2. What will happen to the other person she/he is not selected for the area sales manager's position?
3. Is there a win-win-win solution in this situation?

1-2: Ex-Employee

Jackson LeBlanc, a sales rep for TriCo Industries, met this morning with his best customer, Sue Daly. After working together for 10 years, LeBlanc and Daly are as much friends as business associates. That's why Daly felt comfortable telling LeBlanc that during a meeting with one of his competitors the day before, the salesperson criticized TriCo, its products, and Terry McCabe, the sales manager.

The rep, a former TriCo employee who was fired for underperforming, told Daly that TriCo's product quality has diminished significantly in recent years, and as a result the reps are having a hard time selling to prospects and are relying on past reputation to sell to current customers. He added that TriCo's make-quota-or-leave mentality is forcing reps to push products that customers don't really need, such as updates of new parts before old parts are worn out.

Daly was unmoved by the rep's accusations, but she thought his approach was in bad taste. She also was insulted by the suggestion that she's one of the customers being duped by TriCo, which implies that she isn't doing her job properly. She told LeBlanc that she now plans to buy solely from TriCo, but that other customers might be swayed by the rep's complaints.

When LeBlanc returned to the office, he met with McCabe immediately to discuss the situation. McCabe thanked LeBlanc for his quick action, and then shut the door to contemplate his next move.

Questions:

1. What should Terry McCabe, the sales manager, do now?
   - Consider the leadership issues discussed in the chapter. In particular, think about the sales manager's responsibility to keep track of what his/her reps are doing and inspire sales reps to develop professionally.
   - Consider Sue Daly's position: she now plans to buy solely from TriCo, because she was insulted by the accusations of the former TriCo rep. Will other customers and/or prospects think this way? Is there a different strategy for customers versus prospects?
   - What about other customers who may not tell TriCo reps about their encounter with the former employee?
2. If you were the sales manager, what would you do about the following:
   - The former TriCo rep's accusation concerning the company's product quality?
   - The former TriCo rep's accusation concerning the make-quota-or-leave mentality?
3. As a sales manager, how would you handle the next meeting with your sales reps?
   - What would you say to your sales reps to guide their actions with customers?
   - What are the possible reactions of the sales reps during the meeting?
4. What are the possible reactions of other customers?
5. Are there any ethical issues involved?

CASE *1-1*   THE CASE METHOD

The objective of the case method is to introduce a measure of realism into business education. A case approach forces you to deal with problems as they actually occur in a for profit or a not-for-profit organization. Each case is simply a written description of the facts surrounding a particular business situation. With the case approach, it is your responsibility to develop solutions to the problem. Instructors, for example, may set the stage for the case discussion by providing background material or by helping you gain insight into the problem. They may also act as devil's advocates and as critics to test arguments and proposals that you put forth. Finally, they evaluate your performance, assign grades, and make suggestions for improvement.

BENEFITS AND LIMITATIONS

The case method becomes an effective teaching device when students are encouraged to analyze the data presented and to formulate their own sets of recommendations. Because each case is different, the solution that is developed for one case cannot be randomly applied to another. This raises the question of what you actually learn by working with business cases. One obvious benefit is that preparation and discussion of case studies helps you improve your skills in oral and written expression. In addition, the case method provides an easy way to learn about current business practices. Perhaps the most important advantage of the case method is the experience it provides in thinking logically about different sets of data. The development of your analytical ability and judgment is the most valuable and lasting benefit derived from working with business cases.

Most cases, including those in this book, are drawn from the experiences of real firms. The names and locations may be disguised to protect the interests of the companies involved. In addition, final decisions are usually omitted to enhance the problem-solving orientation of the cases, thus permitting you to reach your own conclusions without being forced to criticize the actions taken by others. The case method departs from the typical business situation in that the business executive usually does not have the

facts presented as clearly and as neatly as they are in casebooks. Problem solving in business usually involves extensive data collection, something that has been essentially completed for you.

A FRAMEWORK FOR ANALYSIS

You can approach the analysis of business cases in many different ways. Each instructor has his or her own ideas on the number and nature of the steps involved. We believe the following six-step procedure is a logical and practical way to begin.

1. Define the problem.
2. Formulate the alternatives.
3. Analyze the alternatives.
4. Recommend a solution.
5. Specify a plan of action.
6. Prepare contingency plans.

Defining the Problem

Once you are familiar with the facts of the case, you should isolate the central problem. Until this is done, it is usually impossible to proceed with an effective analysis. Sometimes instructors provide questions to help you start your analysis. You should look at questions as guides for action rather than as specific issues to be resolved. All cases should be considered as problems in the management of the marketing mix, not as specific issues concerned only with some narrow phase of management.

We use the term *problem* loosely and employ it to indicate a state of nature that may involve either a negative situation possibly requiring corrective action or simply a situation needing opportunity assessment. You must distinguish between problems and symptoms of problems. Declining sales, market share, or the size of the sales force are symptoms of more fundamental underlying problems that are their cause. Any business situation may pose multiple problems. The key to solving unstructured problems is to identify the one that must be solved first, the one whose solution will either eliminate other problems or permit their solution. We are usually interested in solving the most immediate critical problem. For example, we may have problems maintaining the size of our field sales force, problems that have been created by a poor recruiting and selection process. Our immediate concern, however, is with finding ways to get new salespeople quickly into unfilled sales territories. We may well recommend an evaluation of the firm's recruitment process, but we will leave that for future study. Note that the central problem is a state of nature. A statement of it should not contain any action verbs (i.e., *to do* is part of the plan of action). Nor should it contain the words *or* and *and,* which are, respectively, part of the statement of alternatives, and an indication of compound problems and lack of identification of *the* central problem.

Selecting the Alternatives

The second step is to define possible alternatives available to resolve the problem. Some of these alternatives may be obvious from the material supplied in the case and from the statement of the main issue. Others may have to be supplied from your own review of the situation. You should be careful to limit your analysis to a reasonable number of alternatives. Three or four alternatives are usually sufficient for a typical case. One alternative that should always be considered is the maintenance of the status quo. Sometimes doing what you have been doing is the best course of action.

Analyzing the Alternatives

The heart of the case method is the analysis of alternatives. To analyze is to separate into parts so as to find out the nature, proportion, function, and underlying relationships among a set of variables. Thus, to analyze is to dig into, and work with, the facts to uncover associations that may be used to evaluate possible courses of action. Your analysis should begin with a careful evaluation of the facts presented in the case. You should be sensitive to the problem of sorting relevant material from that which is peripheral or irrelevant. In reviewing a case, you must be careful to distinguish between fact and opinion. You must also make sure that the facts are consistent and reliable. Some cases may contain errors, and the instructor may prefer to remain silent.

You are expected to base your analysis on the evidence presented in the case, but this does not mean that other information cannot be used. You should utilize facts that are available to the trade and information that is general or public knowledge. You should incorporate relevant concepts from other disciplines, such as accounting, statistics, economics, psychology, and sociology. The criterion in using outside material is that it must be appropriate to the particular situation. For example, do not use census data for 2000 to make decisions in a case dated 1995. For this book we have attempted to select cases that provide you with enough information to complete the analysis. In some situations, however, you may wish to collect additional materials from the library.

Sometimes the most important facts in the case are buried in some chance remark or seemingly minor statistical exhibit. Be careful to sift through the data to uncover all the relationships that apply to the alternatives being considered. This means that the quantitative information must be examined using a variety of ratios, graphs, tables, or other forms of analysis. Rarely are the data supplied in the case in the form most appropriate to finding a solution, and instructors expect students to work out the numbers.

Marketing analyses are usually based on incomplete information. Assumptions must be made.[1] However, they should be made only when necessary and must be clearly labeled as such. Moreover, a rationale should be given for any assumption made. For example, a retail chain stops carrying one of your product lines but continues carrying another. You are interested in what your sales of the dropped product line would have been. You might note that over the past few years the ratio of the sales of the two product lines had been relatively constant. You could assume that the ratio would have remained the same for the current year as well, and multiply this ratio by the current year's sales of the continuing product line to estimate sales of the discontinued line in that chain. Or perhaps you would calculate the lowest and highest ratios over recent history to calculate conservative and optimistic estimates of lost sales. In any case, at the end of any decision-making exercise, you always want to review your assumptions to see how dependent your conclusions are on the assumptions made. (At one extreme, you could assume away the problem!) You should make contingency plans in the event that major assumptions do not hold.

You should realize that a complete analysis is not one-sided. A review of a business situation is not sound unless both sides of important issues are exam-

---

[1] In most large companies, a corporate planning group provides certain forecasts, assumptions, and planning premises so that everyone in the company is using the same numbers, for instance, on future inflation rates. These tend to be long documents and are not included in casebooks.

ined. This does not necessarily mean that every point must be mentioned, but major opposing arguments should be addressed where possible. You will find it helpful to explicitly list the pros and cons or advantages and disadvantages of each alternative.

Making Recommendations

After you have carefully analyzed the data and alternatives, you are in a position to make recommendations. Sometimes more than one course of action will look attractive. This is not an unusual situation, as most cases do not have a single right answer. Still, you must come up with a concrete proposal. To arrive at a solution, you should judge the relative risks and opportunities offered by the various alternatives. The optimum choice is the one that provides the best balance between profit opportunities and the risks and costs of failure. Make a clear-cut decision, and avoid qualifications and other obvious hedges. Instructors are much more concerned with how a particular decision was reached than with what alternative was selected.

Students sometimes review the facts and decide that they do not have enough information to reach a decision. They recommend that the decision be postponed pending the results of further research. Usually, "get more information" is not an acceptable solution to a business case. Decisions cannot wait the length of time necessary to conduct good research. In addition, it is unlikely that you will ever have all the information you think you need. Because of the cost of research and the penalties of delay, business decisions are almost always made under conditions of uncertainty.

Specifying a Plan of Action

Having made your decision, how are you going to implement it? You should suggest, in as much detail as the case allows, what actions you would take, when they would be taken, and how much they would cost. You may want to provide pro forma income statements, and other relevant supporting material. Once you have proposed your actions, you would do well to reflect on the potential market reactions to them, especially competitive reactions. These possible reactions might lead you to modify your actions.

If you judge that collecting additional information is the only feasible means of solving a case, you must provide support for this decision. First, you should state exactly what the research will show and how this information will be used. In addition, you should indicate the research methodology to be followed and the anticipated cost of the study. After you have completed these tasks, you will be in a better position to decide

whether additional research is needed. Remember, managers should have a predisposition to act and then adapt, rather than to procrastinate.

Preparing Contingency Plans

When you make a decision, it is based on the facts at hand, as well as on your expectations about the future that you hold at that point in time. Since the future does not always unfold as we expect or wish, we must be prepared for any significant alternative future scenario. You must ask yourself what you will do if the market does not respond to your marketing actions as you anticipate, if competitors take actions that deviate from their usual behavior, if the economy is different than economists have forecasted, and so on.

WRITING THE REPORT

We believe that students who prepare written reports do a better job of analyzing business problems. Writing a good report takes a certain skill, and we would like to suggest a few ideas that may be of help.

When instructors read reports, they check to see whether students fully understand the situation and whether student interpretations of the facts are reasonable. They also like to see papers that are objective, balanced, consistent, and decisive. Perhaps the most common error made by students in writing case reports is to repeat the facts that have been provided. Instead of analyzing the data in light of alternatives, students frequently repeat statements that appear in the cases, with no clear objective in mind. Nothing upsets an instructor more than reading a paper that devotes several pages to explaining what he or she already knows about the case.

Another deficiency often observed in writing reports is lack of organization. Students who make this error begin with the first thought that enters their minds and continue, in almost random fashion, until they run out of ideas. The end result is a paper that has no beginning and no end, and often consists of one long paragraph. To avoid this problem, some instructors require that reports be presented in outline form. However, the condensed nature of such reports sometimes makes them hard to follow. Therefore, we prefer the more readable narrative approach.

There is no optimal length for a written case analysis. It depends on the amount of data provided, the preferences of the instructor, and the number of case reports the student turns in during the course. The report should be long enough to cover the subject adequately. It is fairly obvious that written reports must be neat, legible, and free of grammatical and spelling errors. Business professors are not hired to teach English composition, but they do expect certain minimal standards of performance in written expression. Their standards for written work reflect what the business community expects from college graduates.

SUMMARY

Case analysis is designed to give you an opportunity to develop a productive and meaningful way of thinking about business problems. The case method helps train you to use logic to solve realistic business issues. Remember, however, that solutions are worthless unless they can be sold to those who are in a position to act on the recommendations. The case approach provides you with practical experience in convincing others of the soundness of your reasoning.

CASE *1-2*   MOREGUARD INSURANCE

I was having another good year in sales. I've been one of the top four reps at MoreGuard Insurance, averaging $150,000 per year for the past 4 years and it looked like I would do it again this year. I've always taken pride in getting great results while doing things my way and not necessarily by the book. I really liked the competition and the excitement of sales, but lately I'd been thinking about moving to the next level. After all, many of my college buddies were making it in management. If they could do it, why couldn't I? Plus, I liked the thought of DOUG BLOOM—MANAGER emblazoned on my door. As far I as I could tell, a good sales manager would only work a little harder at the same things I'm doing now, but with more power, control and autonomy. Just work with the worst reps awhile, show them how it should be done and bring them up to speed, and everyone would be happy. The more I thought about it, the more I wanted it.

OPPORTUNITY KNOCKS

I was prepared to leave MoreGuard within 6 months if I received a management offer from another insurance brokerage firm. I didn't want to leave; MoreGuard had been very good to me. As luck would have it, the very next week a branch sales manager opening was posted in the company newsletter for the Midwest region. I wasn't excited about leaving Atlanta to go to Des Moines, Iowa, but the timing was perfect. Lady luck was shining on me again. I was finally going to get in the management game and I was ready for the move.

I had a good shot at landing the job, since MoreGuard had an unwritten policy to try and hire from within and I was probably the top producer who was applying for the job. I did some checking into the job and according to the company statement, the previous manager left because "a change was needed to take the branch office into a new direction." But, I heard through the grapevine that the manager was fired because sales were off the previous years. That might have explained the minimal competition from other eager sales reps who were ready to spread their management wings. Maybe they knew something I didn't. It was too late though; mentally I already had my bags packed.

SALES MANAGER TRAINING

After signing my new contract on February 1, the company flew me and 6 other manager wannabes to MoreGuard's headquarters in New York City for 5 days of management orientation. The training schedule was chaotic to say the least. I think they relished the idea that more information was better. The manuals alone reached close to three feet high when I stacked them up in my hotel room. I could have read the materials non-stop all week and still only be half finished. They gave us manuals on strategic analysis, competitor analysis, external environment analysis, product posi-

This case was prepared by Thomas E. DeCarlo of Iowa State University and William L. Cron of Southern Methodist University. Copyright @ by Thomas E. DeCarlo and William L. Cron.

tioning, pricing, promotion, personnel problems, coaching, feedback, performance evaluation techniques, and hiring and firing tips. Other than the consultants who wrote these books, I doubt anyone in the company has read them cover-to-cover. It didn't matter; they would look impressive on my office shelf.

The majority of the new manager training amounted to MoreGuard's rollout and promotion of the new First-Plus account program. Basically, it was a renewed effort by MoreGuard to increase revenues by encouraging sales reps to focus on larger accounts. All-Safe, our major competitor in the full service market, had already implemented their version of First-Plus and now MoreGuard was repositioning itself as well. The VP of Marketing expected us to redirect our staff's selling efforts on this new product line as soon as we started our jobs. I thought to myself, how in the world am I going to get all 25 salespeople interested in selling this new program? I remember that I felt intimidated by the larger, more sophisticated accounts back when I first started. In those days the smaller accounts were my bread and butter. I knew this was going to be a big change for some people.

On the last day George Treadgold, MoreGuard's CEO, showed up to make a few remarks and shake our hands to wish us luck. As he was shaking my hand he smiled and offered his life-in-the-trenches line, "bring in the numbers every month and everything else takes care of itself." He also mentioned using the company policy manual to avoid any personnel problems. I thought to myself what an odd combination of send-off messages. The VP of Human Resources, Ray Cody, gave me his card, slapped me on the back, and told me to call anytime if I had any problems. I had met him during my interview process five years ago; he said the same thing then. He didn't remember me.

MOVING TO DES MOINES

When I returned to Atlanta, I spent the next few days finalizing the details of my move to Des Moines. It was a hectic time. I had to bring the Atlanta office up to speed with my accounts, break my lease on my apartment, notify everyone of my new address, close bank accounts, shut off utilities and find a new apartment in Des Moines. At first, moving sounded like a good idea, but after all the small hassles, you understand why people stay where they are. Plus, I was really going to miss Atlanta, I had some good friends there.

When I arrived in Des Moines near the end of February, I felt like I had moved to the North Pole. It was 10 degrees below zero. My first stop was to the nearest

mall to buy the warmest coat I could find, then to the office to scope it out. MoreGuard's branch office was on the 27th floor of a new high-rise office tower that overlooked the Des Moines River. I had a corner office with a huge picture window overlooking the city. I thought, this is it. The big time. My hoop dream was becoming reality and I couldn't wait to get started. As I was unpacking and organizing my office, Liz Shute, my District Director, walked in. We exchanged chit-chat for a few minutes and then she invited me to lunch to get acquainted.

During lunch I tried to impress her with my understanding of sales management. I made sure that she understood that I was going to be an action-oriented manager and that the majority of my job is sales and sales leadership. The next biggest part of the job is fire fighting and solving salespeople's problems. Maybe five percent is human relations and counseling and another five percent is other administration duties such as recruiting. She smiled and nodded. I didn't understand why she wasn't getting as excited as I was. I got the sense she had heard this all before from previous managers. As I was finishing the last bite of my chocolate tort, she summed everything up by stating, "Doug, I like everything that I'm hearing, just remember though, you are accountable for the production of this office. I'll give you whatever support you need. You just get the reps to come up with the numbers and everything else should take care itself." I thought, first the CEO, now the District Manager; is that the company slogan, or what?

MY FIRST SALES MEETING

After lunch, I spent the rest of the afternoon organizing a presentation to the sales staff about the new First-Plus account program. I built in some humor, stories from my background and a model on how to operationalize the new strategy. I was thinking, what's not to like? This was going to be the perfect introduction—a new manager and a new direction. Liz was planning to introduce me, then I would take over and not look back. I was starting to get the feeling that management just might be my calling.

Liz gave me a great introduction. As I walked up to the podium, I could feel all eyes in the room were sizing me up. I wondered if everyone could see how nervous I felt. I launched into the new strategy and provided color graphs, charts, and percentages on how the new program works and how sales reps, if they followed just the minimum of my performance model, would be compensated. Some people were actually taking notes, some were staring blankly. I thought, good time to get them involved. "Any questions?" I asked. Big mistake. Tiffany Williams, the top performer for the past 8 years, raised her hand and said, "Doug, I make more than 10 times the income level you just described and I have a lot of smaller to medium-sized accounts that have taken me years to cultivate. They throw off a ton more commissions to me than my larger accounts. Why would I want to follow that model?" The room was silent. I cleared my throat. "This isn't my idea, the directive came from corporate." Tiffany responded, "I can't see why corporate would want us to completely abandon the smaller accounts." I pointed out that MoreGuard doesn't want us to neglect the smaller accounts, but the company was moving in a new direction. Someone in the back snickered. More questions followed, some of which only Liz could answer. Overall, not what I had planned. I knew I had to do something to stop the flood of questions. I recommended that people hold their remaining questions for the individual meetings planned for Thursday and Friday so we could finish on time. One-by-one the hands went down.

MEETING THE REPS

The rest of the week I spent preparing for the meetings. I pored over each rep's account history and revenue numbers for the past year to find ways to sell them on the new program. I knew that if I could find ways to get most to buy into the plan, then everyone else would eventually get on board. I scheduled the lower performers for my first meetings on Thursday morning. I figured they would help me warm up and gain confidence for the bigger hitters to follow. I was pretty sure I could get the lower performers to refocus their efforts on my model, but the higher performers might take more persuasion. Based on what I've seen, however, everyone would benefit by implementing aspects of the First-Plus program into their sales strategy. I just had to show them how.

Around 8:00 A.M. Thursday morning I was thinking how excited and nervous I was to be having my first official one-on one meeting as a sales manager. Bill Johnson, my lowest performer, was first. I had plans for this guy and I couldn't wait to see him begin implementing this new strategy. But before I could talk about my ideas, Bill starts telling me how the First-Plus program won't work. He said he was on the verge of a breakthrough and that changing course now would destroy all of his hard work. I couldn't believe what I was hearing. If the worst performer was telling me

this, I could be in for a long two days. After he finished, I gave him my pitch for the future and how he could become a player by changing strategy with his larger accounts. He said he would give it a shot and left. As he was walking out, I thought, he wasn't going to change a thing. I made a note to myself that I was going to have to spend more time with him to show him how the program would work.

Much to my surprise, most of the remaining meetings went smoother. A few were excited about the change, some just wanted to know how I pulled off the promotion, others wanted specifics about my expectations. One thing struck me though: I was not at all prepared for the individuality of my reps. No two were alike. Each one had different motivations and talents, and I spent most of each meeting figuring out each rep's hot buttons. I felt like I was dealing with 25 customers. When the final sales rep left on Friday afternoon, I was worn out. Some meetings went better than others, but all-in-all, not too bad.

TRYING TO KEEP UP

The first few weeks flew by and I was putting in a lot of overtime. I routinely stayed after 5:00 P.M. Monday through Friday and worked most of the day on Saturday. I always felt it was the manager's duty to set the example and, as a sales rep, I lost respect for managers who would leave at 5:00 P.M. while others were still working. Plus, the workload was much more than I expected, so it wasn't merely an act. In-between the 25 reps constantly vying for my time, I had to deal with system crashes, approve salesperson expense reports, review budgets, and prepare a 3-year strategic plan due to the home office at the end of the next month. I could have worked 24 hours a day and still not be caught up. I felt like I was speeding along a curvy highway at the top of a mountain at night with no signs such as slow, curve, narrow bridge, and stop. If I drove off a cliff, the entire branch office would follow me right over too.

The results for my first month were not good—revenues slipped 15%. I felt like my wheels were slipping off the road. Based on the numbers, though, the sales force was not implementing the new program. I knew the reps would not like the First-Plus program to be forced down their throats, but I didn't want a repeat performance next month, so I had to take action. It was time I showed them who was running the office. I fired off a memo to all sales personnel requiring them to complete a weekly sales planning report, including their First-Plus activities for the week. Although I didn't need additional work, I was sure they would read between the lines and start focusing on the First-Plus program. The next morning Tiffany Williams called me from her car phone. "Doug," she said, "I got your memo yesterday." "Good, looking forward to seeing your plan," I said. She said, "Look, Doug, I can't control when my clients want to meet with me and I'm just a little bit too busy to be filling out reports about how I'm going to spend my time." Based on the sarcasm in her tone, I could tell she wasn't happy about the memo. I explained that some reps (including Tiffany) reached their overall quota, but everyone was behind on their First-Plus targets last month and that people need to take some steps to work toward those goals. She responded by informing me that she single-handedly produced 20 percent of the office's revenue last year, so she was exempting herself. I said, "I don't think so, Tiffany, have it on my desk first thing in the morning." As I hung up, I stared at the phone thinking, why did I say that? I shouldn't have demanded she fill it out, but too late.

HELPING REPS RESCHEDULE THEIR TIME

The following Monday everyone, except Tiffany, turned in their weekly reports. I worked through lunch making comments and re-prioritizing the reps' week. I couldn't believe the inefficiencies in their schedules. Some were spending too much time with smaller accounts. Others had large chunks of time devoted to "administrative." No wonder we didn't make quota last month. It felt like this was my first real management breakthrough. Later that afternoon Bill Johnson appeared in my office, obviously upset. I had completely reorganized his schedule. He said, "Doug, what are you trying to do?" I told him I was just trying to help. His voice rose. "Maybe I'm not the best rep in the office, but I'm not incompetent. I'm close to getting things turned around." I told him I wasn't suggesting that, I was just showing him how to implement the First-Plus account management principles. He clenched his jaw and said, "Let me know when you want to take over my accounts too." He threw the reorganized schedule on my desk and stormed out of the room. I sat in my chair in disbelief for a few seconds; I could feel myself tightening up. I dashed after him and motioned him back into my office. I lost it. I started hollering, "You're lucky I'm even helping at all." He looked completely surprised. I continued: "Corporate wants you fired. But, I've been covering for your ass." The rest was a blur. It felt like I was on the outside looking in while this lunatic occupied my body. It wasn't me.

I figured a salesperson has to always be as cool as a cucumber while dealing with problem clients, but it's nothing compared to management. One of the fundamental lessons in management training was that the manager, more than anybody else in the branch, stands for professionalism. Finding and maintaining composure under every situation is all you've got. But, it was too late and I couldn't have a "do over." I wished the entire Human Resources Department was working down the hall.

BILL JOHNSON RESIGNS

The next Monday I got a call from Liz to let me know that she'd had complaints from corporate. I wasn't getting my expense forms in on time. I told her I've been swamped. Not only was I busy working with the reps so we could make our quarterly quota, but that I was also trying to be meticulous before I sent them over to corporate. She shot back, "You're job is to make quota *and* have the reports in on time." As soon as I hung up the receiver, my secretary brought in Johnson's letter of resignation. What a relief. It was just a matter of time before I had to let him go. I immediately called the top rep at AllSafe, our biggest competitor, and tried to lure him away with the promise of his own corner office and an excellent compensation package. I had met him at a conference a few years ago and I knew I could work with him. He accepted immediately. I think he liked the idea that if he continued to perform as he did at Allsafe, he would be the highest paid rep in our office. The very next day, Tuesday, rumors were flying around the office that I hired my buddy and threw lots of guaranteed cash at him. Needless to say, most of the reps were not happy about it—Williams in particular, though she didn't say anything.

The rest of the quarter was a constant struggle to get something completed. Someone always needed a "minute" to resolve a crisis—which usually meant sorting out head-on collisions reps had with clients. But, there were malfunctioning computers, squabbles over accounts and commissions and basic jealousies I had to constantly deal with. I thought that a sales manager had the primary responsibility for taking care of the customer, but I wasn't prepared for the sheer volume of fires to be put out every day. I could count on about 15 totally different conversations within any 2-hour time span. The only place where I could get some peace was the men's room. Not only was I falling even farther behind on paperwork, but I needed to update the reps on some new policies and come up with a new sales idea for our Friday afternoon sales meeting. At times I felt like a babysitter who was also running his own $30 million business.

The day after my first quarterly numbers came in, Liz called me. "Bloom, she said, "you're under quota. What are your plans for turning it around next quarter?" A fair question, I thought, but I didn't like the tone of her voice. I told her I'd looked over the numbers and a few of the reps are close to landing some big accounts. If I have to, I'll close those accounts myself. I also said that my reps don't like having the First-Plus program pushed on them. She said, "Look, Bloom, this is our new direction. It's your job to sell it to the reps and get the branch back on track with First-Plus account volume. If you need anything from my end, just call." "Will do," I said.

CLOSING THE TOP 10 FIRST-PLUS ACCOUNTS

My first plan of action was to identify the top 10 unclosed First-Plus accounts with the most revenue potential. I couldn't afford to lose those accounts. As a sales rep, I was the big account guru, so why not handle those accounts personally? Plus, the customer would love it if the sales manager was their primary contact person. If I was going to get fired, it wasn't because my office couldn't sell the large accounts. I knew some reps weren't going to be happy, but at this point I didn't care whose toes I stepped on. They would just have to understand. The following Monday morning I circulated a memo explaining the new policy for the 10 accounts. Later that same morning, just as I had started working on some salesperson expense reports that were already a month overdue, Williams and another rep named Bill Barone walked into my office. They had the memo in their hands and were obviously upset about it since two of the biggest accounts came from them. Williams started out, "Doug, what's going on here?" I said, "For two months now I have been trying to get people to close more First-Plus accounts, but it's not happening. Corporate wants me to take responsibility, so I am." Bill responded, "Everybody in the office is pissed about the lost commissions on the account." I said, "As of right now, nobody is getting any commissions on those accounts because no one seems able to close them. Once they're on board, everyone will get them back." I thought, didn't they even bother to read the memo? Williams said as she was walking out the door, "Doug, this isn't a threat, but I can guarantee you that if you keep pulling this stuff, you'll find yourself taking over more accounts than you can handle." This is getting ridiculous; as a rep I would have accepted it and moved on. These ungrateful reps were resenting the fact that they were going to get a big account handed to them on a silver platter after someone else closed it.

DOUG BLOOM PLANS FOR THE FUTURE

I was glad when the month ended. Not because I made quota for the first time, but because I had a chance to rethink this whole management thing. I didn't want to quit, but I'd rather quit than get fired and I saw nothing but a downward trend. I was working 80-hour weeks, but I constantly felt like I was treading water. Plus, Williams was probably going to leave soon and it would take time to replace her volume. I also got word that some of my other reps had been looking around. If I stay, I've got to do something about Williams and the other reps who might leave. I had to get a handle on my time and most of all, put the fun back into my job. Was it possible?

CASE 1-3 ARAPAHOE PHARMACEUTICAL COMPANY

As he reread the annual report that he had prepared for Phil Jackson, his regional sales manager, John Ziegler, shook his head and kept repeating to himself, "What a year!"

He could not forget the surge of pride he felt when his district sales manager asked him to call Phil Jackson to let him know whether or not he wanted to accept a promotion to district sales manager for the Dallas area. As he remembered, he couldn't get to the telephone quickly enough, and it was only after Phil had asked him how his wife had taken the news, that he realized that he had forgotten to ask her. He immediately telephoned Lynn and found that she was thrilled both with his promotion and the move to Dallas even though neither one of them had been there before. Lynn was particularly pleased that her company had a sales opening in Dallas and she felt that she could obtain a transfer to that city. John once again expressed his appreciation to his sales manager, Betsy Warner, for all of the help that she had given him so that he could qualify for the promotion.

John had joined Arapahoe Pharmaceutical as a sales rep immediately after graduating from San Francisco State University. While he had been interested in science in high school, and he had taken one course in chemistry and another course in biology at San Francisco State, he was more interested in marketing communications. When Arapahoe Pharmaceuticals recruited at the college in his junior year and again in the spring of his senior year, John decided that he might combine the interests in science and marketing communications as a sales representative. He was interviewed, hired, and assigned to a territory near Omaha in Betsy Warner's district. John's willingness, personality, and communications skills, plus Betsy's encouragement and guidance, helped him in quickly achieving above average productivity and allowed him to win a transfer to a territory in the greater metropolitan Denver area. The new territory offered him additional experience in working with food and drug chain headquarters, large hospitals, and drug wholesalers. John reviewed these experiences with considerable pleasure as he recalled the events of the past year.

Betsy worked regularly with him, and delegated to him some of the training of new sales reps, which he found both challenging and rewarding, especially when the new sales trainee did well. His selling skills flourished as did his income and the recognition of his achievements by Betsy and the regional sales manager. A year later he was selected to attend his company's leadership training program, which was a milestone in his career.

Even before his first trip to Dallas, John was asked by Tom Boyle, the general sales manager, to spend a couple of days at the corporate headquarters in Philadelphia with him and various department heads in marketing, legal and human resources. They were all very complimentary about his past performance and how much he deserved his promotion. However, each of them in a different way seemed to repeat the same message: "Managing people is different from selling products." How well the events of the past year were to bear that out. The thrust of Boyle's message was a bit different. He wanted John to realize that he had full confidence in his ability, that John had earned his promotion, and that although John was a sales rep one day, and a district sales manager the next, the company recognized the change wouldn't take place overnight and it would provide him with further training. In the meantime, Boyle advised John that the Dallas district was productive, operating efficiently, and staffed with well-trained sales reps, and that he was not expecting John to "Sweep the district clean" and make radical changes. He also emphasized that (1) John should give the sales reps in Dallas time to get to know him and he them; (2) he would be surprised and disappointed to discover that all the reps didn't operate with the same level of efficiency that he did nor use the same methods he used when he was a rep; (3) he shouldn't try to correct too many deficiencies at one time; (4) telling someone to do something doesn't necessarily get it done; (5) everyone doesn't remember hearing something the same way; and (6) it's better to have three sales reps working with you than ten working for you.

One year later, John realized that at the time he and Boyle talked, he didn't understand or appreciate the

---

This case was prepared by Professor Richard C. Leventhal of Regis University in Denver, Colorado. Reproduced by permission.

full meaning of that advice. The legal department wanted him to be aware of his increased responsibilities as a manager in speaking or acting for the company. The various departments in sales, marketing and human resources emphasized the importance of his new role and his support in administering the company's promotional programs and gaining the compliance of his sales reps. Increasingly, he realized the duality of his role as a member of management and of the field sales force. The sales management training programs he attended during the succeeding months reinforced these points and helped prepare him for the types of problems he was to encounter.

His introduction to the ten sales reps in the Dallas district went quite well. His predecessor, Chuck Morgan, who was retiring after 30 years with Arapahoe, fully reviewed all of the sales statistics for the district and the human resource records of the sales reps. He also gave him the benefit of his thoughts for the future and what John's immediate concerns should be. John had inherited a district that was operating on target both for sales and expenses, and appeared to have no major personnel problems other than one territory that had been open for four weeks. Chuck even had two resumes on promising candidates who needed processing.

John telephoned both applicants and scheduled interviews for the following week, along with trips of two days each with two of his sales reps. The interviews seemed to go well, but they took almost a full day. On his first day at his office the following week, John called the references and previous employers of both applicants, scheduled a second interview several days later with Larry Palmer, the most promising applicant, and, in accordance with the company's interviewing procedure, set up an information session with Larry and his wife for the following evening. Since this was John's first session of this type, he was pleased that it went well. Jean Palmer, Larry's wife, had numerous questions about transferring, the amount of travel, and how much extra time that her husband would have to spend responding to e-mail and other computer-type reports. John was glad that he was able to address her concerns. The telephone conversations with the other applicant's references and previous employers had been an interesting experience and tended to confirm what the applicant had said, except in two instances. A previous employer and one reference were guardedly enthusiastic about the applicant. When John pressed the issue, the reference refused to say more, while the previous employer provided specifics which confirmed an earlier impression John had noted at the initial interview. Comments about Larry Palmer all emphasized the great personality he had and what a terrific job they thought he would do in sales. Following the second interview with Larry Palmer and the spouse information session, John completed the company's applicant appraisal reports on both applicants and decided that Larry was the better of the two. He telephoned his regional sales manager, Phil Jackson, to set up a final interview for Larry. Then he faxed Phil his applicant appraisal reports and wrote the other applicant a polite turndown letter.

The day following Larry's interview, Phil Jackson called to say that while he had some misgivings, he had hired Larry to begin training in a class at the regional office the first of the month. John's reaction was a sigh of relief because of all of the time he had put into the screening and the hope that he wouldn't have to do that too often. The reports that he completed on his first field trips with his reps took longer to prepare than he anticipated. Coupled with the correspondence and appraisal reports on the applicants, John realized that communications were going to be a bigger part of the job than he had realized. He would have to learn how to use the computerized information system in a more effective and efficient manner if he were to have the necessary time for his other responsibilities.

John's relationship with his sales reps seemed to go well during the first few months on the job, with the exception of Dick McClure, an above average producer, aged 50, with 12 years experience, and the senior man in the district. Dick had been described by Chuck Morgan as a friendly, outgoing individual with a good sense of humor and a highly individualistic style of selling. As John worked with Dick, he was able to confirm in Dick's interaction with his customers, the general description Chuck had given him. However, Dick was curt with John, relatively subdued, and at other times almost hostile. For the next several working trips, John tried to ignore Dick's conduct and concentrated on the calls that they were making and the objectives that they were trying to achieve. At a recent sales meeting, Dick seemed to take delight in being argumentative and disruptive until John jokingly asked him if he would like to take over the sales meeting. After that, Dick settled down but made almost no contribution to the discussions for the rest of the meeting.

The situation came to a head immediately following a physician call, during which Dick introduced John without indicating who he was or his purpose for being there. The physician's reaction was: "Oh a new rep, eh?" and to Dick, "Are you being promoted?" This forced Dick, somewhat embarrassed, to indicate that John was his new district sales manager. As they left the office, it was clear that Dick was furious, as he muttered in a sarcastic manner, "Are you being promoted?" John decided that it was time to take action, whereupon he said emphatically, "Dick, I don't know what is eating you, but I think that it's time that we get it out in the open. You've been complaining from the day that I arrived. You're sarcastic, uncooperative, and just as cool as ice. If you and I are going to continue to work together, things had better change. I don't know what I have done that has upset you, but whatever it is or whatever I've said, it certainly wasn't intentional and I'm sorry. You're too good a person to go around perpetually angry. What the heck is bothering you?"

Dick's reaction was an angry, somewhat subdued and embarrassed, "I just guess it's not really your fault or anything that you did. I've been here 12 years and I'm the best rep in this district. Chuck even told me so. And bam—you get promoted and I'm left hung out to dry. Man, that's gratitude for you!"

Now that the problem was out in the open, John realized how long Dick had been carrying his anger locked up inside himself, and felt sorry for him. With that, he said, "Dick, I've sure been blind. Let's knock off and sit down somewhere to talk this thing out." Three hours later they shook hands and parted on a much better understanding. Their relationship improved steadily, and now as John reflected on the district's productivity for the past year, he realized that Dick's support had been of paramount importance in terms of the district's overall success.

Thinking about the successful year reminded him of Peggy Doyle, the sales trainee who was doing such a terrific job. She was the one who had taken Larry Palmer's place. When he thought of Larry Palmer, he winced thinking about the mistake that he had made. Larry was the first sales rep that he had recruited. He had completed the basic sales training class, but just barely. The report from the sales training manager was anything but encouraging. Larry had difficulty acquiring the necessary product knowledge and his scientific communication skills were marginal at best. The qualities that saved him from being dropped from the sales training class were his desire, his willingness to work, and the fact that he was such a great guy—everybody loved him! Notwithstanding Larry's shortcomings, John was convinced he could turn Larry around. He worked with him every opportunity he had, quizzed him, coached him, and drilled him in an effort to improve his knowledge and skills so that

Larry could be able to capitalize on his sincerity and personality.

As the months wore on, John became increasingly aware that while Larry's customers liked him, he couldn't sell and his sales showed it. It was a tough decision John had to make to let Larry go, and an even tougher decision to implement, but John realized it really was in everyone's best interests. As he looked back on all the time and effort he had put into Larry's ultimate failure, John realized that it was at the expense of the time and effort he should have spent with his more productive sales reps. He also realized that in spite of the overwhelming evidence, he had carried Larry much longer than he probably should have, and was thankful that Phil Jackson did not remind him of it. Sometimes, however, events have a bright side. As much as John regretted the amount of time that it took to recruit Larry's replacement, he felt that he had lucked out with Peggy Doyle. She seemed to do everything right. In the four months since she'd been in the territory, sales had taken a noticeable increase and her enthusiasm was infecting the other sales reps in the district. John hoped her progress and productivity would continue on in this manner for a long time to come. Some performance data for Peggy and the other reps are shown in Exhibits 1 and 2.

Peggy's performance, however, did not eliminate the logjam that recruiting her had created in John's other activities. Her interviews, reference checking, early sales orientation and training, plus the extra time he had spent over the last few months helping Larry try to succeed, extended the intervals since he last worked in the field with his above average sales reps, to the extent that several were beginning to make humorously sarcastic comments about being "orphans." John tried to explain that they were practically self-sufficient, while others needed his help more urgently. While they were willing to listen, John could see that they weren't buying into his excuse.

To further compound the problem, he received an e-mail that his semiannual appraisal interviews were to begin within 30 days. This would be the second time he would be holding these performance reviews, but it would be the first time alone since Phil Jackson had helped him. As John began to review the trip reports and correspondence in each sales rep's file, along with sales performance data generated from the company's computerized database (Exhibits 1 and 2), he realized the files of the above average producers were relatively thin. If it hadn't been for performance data, John would have been at a serious loss to justify his appraisal of their productivity.

EXHIBIT 1   Performance Data for Sales Reps in the Dallas/Ft. Worth District

Sales Rep	Last Year's Sales	This Year's Sales	Sales Quota Current Year
Larry Palmer[a]	$180,000	$181,000	$275,000
Dick McClure	450,000	583,000	535,000
Peggy Doyle[b]	–	120,000	150,000
Tom Jones	445,000	555,000	550,000
Bill Morrison	465,000	560,000	550,000
Sam Hanna	435,000	535,000	525,000
Jared Murphy	365,000	370,000	420,000
Marty Nakai	475,000	625,000	575,000
TOTALS	$2,815,000	$3,529,000	$3,580,000

[a] Sales and quota figures are for eight months.

[b] Peggy Doyle has been in her territory for only four months, there is no sales figure for the previous year. This year's sales and quota are for four months.

Preparing for and conducting the performance reviews took a lot of time and this was when he really earned his salary. When the reps and John had different evaluations, the differences were resolved and then it became a matter of jointly agreeing on a plan of action to close the gap between actual and desired performance. As difficult as it was to achieve the agreement at times, and harder still to implement the agreed-upon plan, John felt that it was at this point that he was making a significant contribution to the success of the company and the growth and development of the individual sales reps in the district.

The second appraisal and counseling session of the year had its peaks and valleys. It had been a pleasure to provide several with the recognition their performances merited, and to help them to further define the goals they would achieve for the forthcoming year. The case of Jared Murphy was another matter. Jared had been in the training class at the time John was hired. He had done reasonably well, but hadn't really lived up to his potential. Lately, Jared seemed to have lost interest. When John challenged Jared's own evalu-ation of his performance Jared sheepishly commented that he "wondered whether you'd let it pass." When John pressed him for an explanation of his performance in view of the potential in his territory, Jared quickly replied: "I didn't know you cared that much."

John also stated he felt that Jared had sufficient experience and intelligence to exert the necessary self-discipline to do what was required without a lot of personal attention from him. At this point, John said: "Jared, I think that it's time to decide whether or not you really have a future with Arapahoe. You definitely have the capabilities to be an above average performer. If you really want to do a better job, I'll make every effort to help you to do a better job, but you will have to help me and really want to work at it. So what I want you to do is to go home, think about what I said, talk it over with your wife, and we will get together next Wednesday and make a plan for your future."

The problem John faced with Marty Nakai was almost the opposite. Marty was a young, single sales rep who had three years' experience in a territory that required quite a bit of travel in the Texas panhandle.

EXHIBIT 2   Input Factors Affecting Territory Coverage in the Dallas/Ft. Worth District

Sales Rep	Number of Sales Calls	Annual Expenses ($)	Physicians in Territory
Larry Palmer[a]	800	$6,300	1,600
Dick McClure	1,500	9,300	2,100
Peggy Boyle[b]	400	2,500	1,650
Tom Jones	1,300	8,000	1,850
Bill Morrison	1,350	8,300	1,800
Sam Hanna	1,350	8,500	1,900
Jared Murphy	1,050	7,800	2,000
Marty Nakai	1,550	9,800	2,200
TOTALS	9,300	$60,500	15,100

[a] Number of sales calls and expenses are for an eight-month period.

[b] Number of sales calls and expenses are for a four-month period.

He had about every good quality anyone could want in a salesperson, except maturity and self-control. He was smart, eager, highly motivated, and extremely ambitious. His favorite question of John was: "What else do I have to do to get promoted?" and he posed that question on every field trip and frequently at sales meetings. In addition, John could count on Marty calling him at home on weekends. In a way, John wished he had more sales reps who were as productive and as eagerly cooperative, but he also wished that Marty would develop more patience and self-discipline. While John certainly didn't want to do anything to dampen Marty's enthusiasm, he was running out of ways to help Marty grow up.

As he thought about the challenges he had with his reps and the logjam he had created as a result of his recruiting activities, he realized that he had to formalize a set of objectives and specific plans for the coming year to discuss with Phil Jackson during his own coming appraisal session. Although the year had been a successful one, their performance on a couple of major products could have been at a higher level and he would have to figure out some kind of action plan to correct that situation. And then there were the territory revisions to be done to take advantage of the growth potential in the Ft. Worth area. Not the least important or urgent matter he needed to address was to evaluate his own performance during the past year and to set some personal objectives.

In addition, John had to prepare some written comments on the performance of each of his reps for the past year to put in their personal files. He thought he should calculate some ratios from the data in Exhibits 1 and 2 such as sales growth, sales to quota, sales per call, sales per physician, expenses per call, and selling expenses as a percent of sales to include in his report on each rep. Also he had to decide what to do about Jared and Marty. Overall, John saw his problems were really people problems and people opportunities, and their interaction and interdependence were what made his job both challenging and fun.

CHAPTER 2

STRATEGIC PLANNING AND BUDGETING

"Sharing a Vision"
Two men were struggling to get a large crate through the door. They struggled and struggled, but the crate would not budge. Finally, one man said to the other, "We'll never get this crate in." Replied his partner, "I thought we were trying to get it out."

Chapter Consultants:
Scott Smith, Vice President – Sales & Marketing, SABRE Group, Inc.
Joseph P. Clayton, Vice Chairman of the Americas, Global Crossing

LEARNING OBJECTIVES

After studying this chapter, you should be able to:

- ► Know what is meant by strategic management planning.
- ► Distinguish the major steps involved in strategic marketing planning.
- ► Identify the two strategic sales force decisions and their implications for selling and sales management.
- ► Discuss the purpose and scope of a sales force budget.
- ► Describe three approaches to setting a sales force budget.

"WHEN YOU BUY THE IRON, YOU GET THE COMPANY"

This is the philosophy of Caterpillar Inc. (Peoria, Ill.), which sells machinery and engines worldwide. Despite sales of $10.2 billion, the company faces the twin challenges of global competition and a sputtering global economy. Part of Caterpillar's strategy for winning in such a tough environment is to strengthen its network of 2,400 independent dealers. Says Pat Dalton, business operations manager for Caterpillar's North American commercial division, "We want the entire distribution network to focus on the customer first." Dealer owners, for example, attend classes taught by top Caterpillar managers.

Caterpillar's 2,400 salespeople are instrumental in implementing its strategy. In 1992, Caterpillar introduced "customer sensitivity training" for all of its salespeople. Among other things, the sales force learns how to train customers to operate the machinery. "Our salespeople must demonstrate the benefits of our products," says Dalton, "to show why buying our products will help the customer make more money. We want our salespeople to roll up their sleeves and work closely with customers to be business partners with them."

Sales force compensation has also been adjusted to reward the sales force for being good dealer partners. Salespeople don't receive bonuses just for meeting quotas; they can accumulate bonus points for scoring high on product knowledge tests, customer-satisfaction surveys, and evaluations from their managers.[1]

This example shows how one company is attempting to meet its objectives in a highly competitive environment. They are trying to be successful based on the competitive advantage of their strong dealer network. As the primary company contact with the dealers, the sales force is critical to the success of the strategy. As this case illustrates, strategic decisions will usually have implications for the sales force in terms of how the market is accessed and the type of relationship established with the customer. These decisions make up the sales force strategy, which, in turn, has implications for the budget plan and how the sales force is organized and managed. In this case, training, compensation, and individual salesperson evaluation were adjusted to reflect the "partnering" focus of Caterpillar's strategy.

The purpose of this chapter is to show the implications of business and marketing strategy for sales management. We do not attempt to explain organization or marketing strategy; this is better accomplished elsewhere. Instead, we offer an overview of marketing strategy, while focusing mostly on sales force strategy and budgeting and the connection between marketing and sales strategy.

Strategic management planning	• Mission • Goals • Strategies
Strategic marketing planning	• Situation analysis • Segmentation & target marketing • Marketing mix program
Sales force strategy	• Market access strategy • Account relationship strategy
Operating budgets	• Promotion • Selling expenses

The sequence of topics to be covered is depicted in the diagram on page 42. Key sales force decisions are made within the limits set by the organization. *Strategic management planning* consists of the steps taken by the organization to ensure the long-term survival and growth of the business. In contrast, *strategic marketing planning* involves the allocation of resources to programs designed to achieve specific marketing objectives derived from the organization's overall objectives.[2] The *sales force strategy* is derived from the marketing strategy and includes decisions about how to access the target market and the type of relationships the company will have with its customers. Finally, the strategic plan must be converted into an operating budget. Budgets are working documents that help sales managers keep track of expenses. Actual results can be compared with budgeted figures, and any changes in the objectives and strategies planned for the subsequent period can be recommended.

STRATEGIC MANAGEMENT PLANNING

Strategic planning is employed to make better use of company resources and to create and sustain an advantage over the competition. At a basic level, competitive advantage arises from a firm's choice of markets to serve, its distinct competencies, and the deployment of resources that gives it an edge over its competition in chosen markets. The factors influencing the strategic management planning process are depicted in Figure 2-1. Both marketing and sales personell should be intimately involved in an organization's strategic planning process because they understand the customers' requirements and how they value the fulfillment of needs.

Business Mission

A well-defined business mission provides a sense of direction to employees and helps guide them toward the fulfillment of the firm's potential. The basic character of an organization's business is defined by the *three Cs*—customers, competitors, and the company itself. Top managers should ask "What is our business?" and "What should it be?" The goal is to determine an overarching mission from a consideration of the firm's history, resources, distinct competencies, and environmental constraints. The *business mission* is a

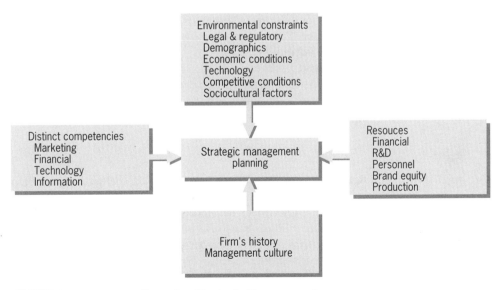

FIGURE 2-1 Factors Influencing Strategic Management

statement about (1) the types of customers it wishes to serve, (2) the specific needs to be fulfilled, and (3) the activities and technologies by which it will fulfill these needs. Thus organizations will not only know the focus of their business, they will also be able to identify strategic opportunities.

As the competitive environment changes, companies may need to alter their mission. Figure 2-1 describes how marketplace changes affect field sales activities. Merck and Company, the $4 billion pharmaceutical firm, has adjusted to meet the needs of the evolving customer base in the health care industry. In the past, Merck's 3,000 salespeople called primarily on individual physicians. Now reps must also call on business administrators of hospitals, health maintenance organizations (HMOs), and preferred provider organizations (PPOs), which have vastly different information needs than those of physicians. These new customers are more interested in issues such as order processing, distribution, and after-sales servicing. One change has been to reorganize the sales force so that more people are calling on the managed-care customers. Merck has also had to adjust their training by adding team building and negotiating and developing more expertise on the managed-care environment in general.[3]

Establishing Goals

Once the mission for an organization has been decided, the next step is to translate the mission into the *organization's goals*—specific objectives by which performance can be measured. These objectives are usually stated in terms of profits, sales revenue, unit sales, market share, survival, and social responsibility. Firms will typically pursue multiple objectives. Procter & Gamble, for example, seeks a 10 percent after-tax profit and a doubling of sales revenue every five years.

When priorities change, the sales force is often affected. Faced with major competitors such as Procter & Gamble, demanding retailers, and mature markets, Scott Paper Company switched its mission from gaining volume at any cost to profitability. This called for massive changes in how Scott's 500 salespeople related to the retail trade. "It's no longer a volume or promotional approach to customers," states one Scott marketer, "it's a lot more than that. It's understanding brands and how the consumer's response to various actions on our part is timed so that we can eliminate waste and improve profit." To support this changed relationship, sales training has been altered to include market knowledge and understanding marketing data in order to achieve the most profitable product mix for both the company and the customer. Some salespeople were unable to adapt to the discipline required in this new business approach. To reinforce this new approach, Scott shifted its compensation plan from volume to profitability.

The Scott Paper example illustrates another important characteristic of organizational goals: the hierarchical nature of the goals. Measurable organizational goals must be communicated down the organizational structure. Figure 2-2 illustrates this point by showing how an organizational sales goal is translated into a major account goal.

Strategies

Once business objectives have been identified, the next step is to translate them into strategies. A *strategy* is the means an organization uses to achieve its objectives. Several classification schemes have been developed to delineate the overall thrust of a strategy. One of the most popular is Porter's *generic business strategies*.[4] According to Porter, all successful businesses focus on one of three generic strategies—*low cost, differentiation, or niche*. Each of these strategies is described in Figure 2-3. Each strategy is based on offering a customer value distinct from its competitors. The success of the strategy in the marketplace generally requires that the sales force execute the strategy properly. A good example of how strategy

FIGURE 2-2   Hierarchy of Sales Objectives

influences the job of the sales force is described in the Strategic Action Competency box, "We Aren't Selling Lightbulbs."

One of the most widely recognized analytical tools for developing strategies is *business portfolio analysis,* developed by the Boston Consulting Group (BCG). This approach helps large firms allocate resources by grouping their organization into individual profit centers called *strategic business units (SBUs).* Ideally, an SBU is a product line or group of products (1) for which plans can be developed independently, (2) that has its own competitors and unique set of customer needs that it fulfills, and (3) that has one manager with profit responsibility. Depending on relative market share and market growth rate, one of four growth strategies is recommended—*build, hold, harvest,* or *divest.* These strategies are described in Figure 2-4, together with the primary sales tasks associated with each strategy.

STRATEGIC MARKETING PLANNING

Strategic marketing planning is a process whereby an organization allocates marketing mix resources to reach its target markets. This planning process is similar to the overall strategic management planning process in that it begins with a situation analysis. This information is then used to segment the market and choose target markets on which to concentrate the

STRATEGIC ACTION COMPETENCY
"We Aren't Selling Lightbulbs"

Philips Lighting Company, the North American division of the Dutch company Philips Electronics, recently decided to take a different approach to the lighting business by selling lightbulbs on the basis of customer value. Traditionally, the industry focused on the customer's purchasing managers who bought on the basis of how much the lightbulbs cost and how long they lasted. Everyone competed on price and length of life, which resulted in constant margin and profit pressure.

After a closer study of the customer, Philips came to understand that the price and life of bulbs did not account for the full cost of lighting to the customer. Because lamps contained environmentally toxic mercury, companies faced high disposal costs at the end of a lamp's life. So in 1995, Philips introduced the Alto, an environmentally friendly bulb.

What was the impact on the sales force? Huge. The purchasing agents whom they had traditionally called on were not held accountable for the costs of lamp disposal, but the CFOs were held accountable for disposal costs. So instead of calling on the purchasing agents, Philips' salespeople called on the key influencers, including CFOs and public relations people. The Alto reduced customers' overall costs and garnered customers positive press for promoting environmental concerns. The new market Alto created has superior margins and is growing rapidly in stores, schools, and office buildings throughout the United States.

For more on Philips Lighting Company visit *www.lighting.philips.com.*

firm's marketing resources. The third step is to develop the complete marketing mix. Each of these steps has important selling and sales management implications.

Situation Analysis

Suppose that you are the head of marketing for Glaxo Holdings PLC, a large pharmaceutical company. You have been very successful to date spending 20 percent of your revenues on

Low-Cost Strategy: Vigorous pursuit of cost reductions from experience and tight cost control.	**Sales Force Role:** Service large current customers, pursue large prospects, minimize costs, sell on the basis of price, often with significant order-taking responsibilities.
Differentiation Strategy: Creating an offering perceived as being unique leading to high brand loyalty and low price sensitivity.	**Sales Force Role:** Sell non-price benefits, educate the customer, provide consulting, order-generating, servicing and be responsive to needs of customers. High-quality sales force usually required.
Niche Strategy: Servicing a target market effectively, focusing all decisions with the target market needs in mind, dominating sales with the segment.	**Sales Force Role:** Experts in the operations and opportunities associated with a target market. High margins needed, focus on non-price benefits, and allocate selling time to the target market.

FIGURE 2-3   Generic Business Strategies and the Role of the Sales Force

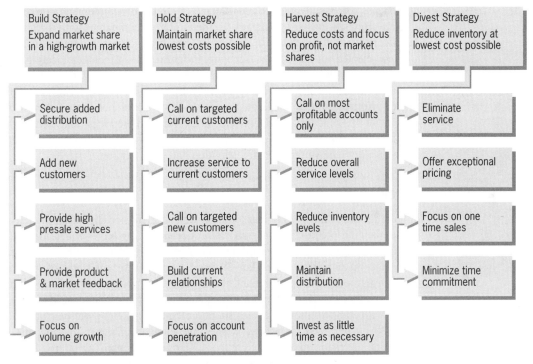

FIGURE 2-4   Business Portfolio Analysis and Sales Force Strategy

marketing and sales. Most of the money goes to the army of sample-toting representatives who call on individual doctors to get your drugs prescribed. More and more doctors, however, are joining managed-care organizations. One of the largest managed health care networks is Kaiser, which plans to buy more than $700 million worth of pharmaceuticals this year. In order to reduce costs, however, Kaiser has cracked down on having representatives in their facilities. All representatives, called detailers in the industry, must abide by 32 rules, including not being able to visit a facility without an appointment.[5] Why is the growth of managed care and Kaiser's actions significant factors for Glaxo to consider when developing its marketing strategy? Will Glaxo place less reliance on its sales force to promote its products? At what point should Glaxo change its marketing strategy? These are only a few of the questions raised by Glaxo's situation analysis.

This is the essence of *situation analysis*—taking stock of where the firm or product line has been, where it is now, and where it is likely to end up in the future. This analysis must often consider legal, economic, competitive, customer, and technological factors. As the primary contact with customers, the sales force is often critically involved in gathering information for a situation analysis. In the Glaxo situation, a special 45-person sales team was formed to help determine how to deal with managed-care networks.

Segmentation and Target Marketing

Because marketing programs require a customer focus to be effective, companies segment the market and select target markets on which they will concentrate their marketing efforts. *Market segmentation* involves aggregating customers into groups that (1) have common needs and (2) will respond similarly to a marketing program. *Target marketing* refers to the selection and prioritizing of segments to which the company will market.

These marketing decisions have obvious implications for how management would want salespeople to set priorities and allocate their time among different customers. Sometimes the sales force must even be reorganized to effectively implement a targeted marketing program. Hewlett-Packard Company decided to target companies with three characteristics: significant worldwide presence, large size, and high growth potential. In all, 1,000 accounts were selected for the Global Accounts Program, which includes locating technical and selling teams at the headquarters of each account. Revenue growth in these accounts is more than 10 times the growth rate in the $350 billion information technology industry. As a further effort to target specific customers, H-P has developed separate sales organizations for discrete manufacturing, process industries, financial services, and telecommunications customers.[6] In this reorganization, H-P is attempting to ensure that markets targeted in its marketing plan receive the intended attention and sales support.

Marketing Mix Program

Having settled on specific marketing goals and identified the target market, the third step in the planning process is to design the proper *marketing mix*—price, product, promotion, and channels. Once again, an important change in any of these elements usually necessitates changes in the sales force plan. It was found, in a recent study of organizational actions when introducing a new product, that a significant proportion of responding firms modified nearly every element of the sales management program. The most likely change was in quotas, with compensation and sales support elements also likely to be changed.[7]

The sales force, however, is only one element of the promotion mix. Other elements include television advertising, company literature, coupons, print ads, direct mail, radio ads, catalogs, trade shows, and public relations. With so many communication tools, companies must decide how and when to use each of these tools and how to coordinate their messages to produce the greatest impact. *Integrated marketing communications* is a popular term used to describe how firms attempt to coordinate their communication tools to deliver a consistent and high-impact message. To get an idea of how complicated this process can become, consider Hewlett-Packard's integrated marketing communications efforts in the recent introduction of a new printer. First, Hewlett-Packard sent sales kits to customers and dealers, followed by a mailing program and telemarketing. Next, they sent sales reps to the dealerships to make follow-up calls and give management briefings. Afterward, a committee of dealers met to evaluate the success of the program. This marketing program included a coordinated effort among advertising, sales promotion, channels of distribution, and the sales force.[8] As this example illustrates, a company's marketing program has an important influence on sales and sales strategy, which we will consider next.

STRATEGIC SALES FORCE DECISIONS

Throughout the remainder of this text, many important issues are discussed with respect to organizing, building, leading, and controlling an organization's selling effort. Two management decisions in particular have an important and pervasive impact on these sales force issues and an organization's sales management program: (1) how the company will access its customers, and (2) the type of relationships the company wishes to have with its various customers. We address these decisions in this section.[9]

Market Access

Most large companies access their markets in more than one way—through a direct sales force, for instance, or through distributors. To defend their customer base, expand market coverage, and control costs, companies today are adopting multiple methods for reaching different target markets. IBM, for example, once sold computers through the company's

5,000-person sales force. When low-cost computers hit the market, IBM reacted by expanding into new channels. Now they sell through dealers, value-added resellers (VARS), catalog operations, direct mail, and telemarketing. In total, IBM added 18 new channels in addition to their own sales force to communicate with customers.[10]

To better understand why companies are seeking alternatives to the traditional direct sales force, it may be helpful to identify the customers to whom a company markets. The typical customer base of many organizations consists of a few very important customers in terms of sales and profits. In other words, a classic 80/20 rule exists in which 80 percent of revenues are generated from 20 percent of the customers. This is depicted in Figure 2-5 as a triangle with the horizontal dimension representing the number of customers and the vertical dimension the size of the accounts. There are typically a few major accounts at the top and many "minor" accounts at the bottom. All too often, the traditional sales force has had difficulty in meeting the needs of the top accounts and found it too expensive to call on the large number of small accounts. At IBM, for instance, 20,000 distributors and resellers, referred to as "business partners," have become the primary sales force for small and medium-sized accounts.[11] Technology has also created alternatives to face-to-face selling for accessing and servicing customers. (See the Technology Competency box, "The Net Effect.") In the remainder of this section, we will briefly describe some of the more common alternatives to the traditional face-to-face sales force. Two of these alternatives, telemarketing and independent reps, will be discussed further in Chapter 8 when we examine organizing of the sales force.

Distributors   *Distributors* are channel members who take title to the offerings that they sell to end-users. They perform many functions within the channel, including warehousing, breaking bulk, extending credit, and providing information, but one of their primary functions is to market their suppliers' offerings to their own customers. It is in this capacity that they function as a possible substitute to a supplier's sales force by calling directly on the end-user. Distributors have many, even hundreds, of salespeople calling on thousands of customers, in effect multiplying the efforts of the supplier's salesperson.

This does not mean that a salesperson has no role with this channel alternative. Consider the case the Gates Rubber Company. Gates establishes strong partner relationships with its distributors in order to compete with price competition from offshore manufacturers. The role of the sales force in Gates's marketing strategy is critical. Among other responsibilities, they must determine the distributor's objectives and needs, provide product knowledge, share information regarding industry trends, and communicate Gates's expectations of the distributor.[12] As a consequence, all aspects of the sales organization and man-

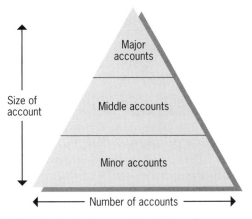

FIGURE 2-5   Customer Base Triangle

TECHNOLOGY COMPETENCY
"The Net Effect"

More and more marketers are turning to the Internet in search of new, improved ways to link with customers and suppliers. One company, Industry.Net, is going one step further in bringing together companies that have something to sell with companies that have something to buy. Through Industry.Net, more than 200,000 companies are reaching the more than 150,000 buyers that are attracted to the site each day. Large companies like FedEx, Holiday Inn, and Air Products & Chemicals, Inc. are finding success on the Internet:

- FedEx has set up their Web site so that instead of calling a customer service center, Web surfers just type their package ID number to get an update on the location of their package.
- Holiday Inn allows guests to check availability and price, and book rooms at any of its 2,100 hotels.
- Air Products & Chemicals Inc. has its complete product catalog online in an interactive format that will allow customers to conduct searches for Air Products offerings by typing in what they're looking for.

agement are affected, including the type of person who will be successful in this situation, that is, one who has to work through the distributor and the distributor's sales force to make their revenue objectives. In addition to calling on the distributor, the Gates salesperson will also call on some end-users, usually the larger ones, either independently or concurrently with the distributor's salesperson.

Telemarketing   *Telemarketing* refers to customer contacts utilizing telecommunications technology for personal selling without direct, face-to-face contact. Business-to-business telemarketing is growing at a rate of 30 to 40 percent a year and generates sales in excess of $100 billion yearly.[13] More than two million people are employed in consumer and business-to-business telemarketing operations. The effectiveness of telemarketing is indicated by the $1,000 value of the average business-to-business telemarketing sale. Corporations such as IBM, Procter & Gamble, Chase Manhattan Bank, and Union Pacific Railroad have all developed telemarketing systems.[14]

Companies are using telemarketing in a variety of ways. In some cases, it is utilized as a substitute for the sales force. This is particularly likely when selling to the many small customers at the bottom of the triangle shown in Figure 2-5. This is because the cost of telemarketing per customer contact is far less than that of a field salesperson. Alternatively, many companies utilize telemarketing at certain points in the selling process to enhance the effectiveness and efficiency of the regular sales force. This is the case with Wright Line, Inc., a leading supplier of accessories used to store, protect, and provide access to computer tapes, diskettes, and other media, which focuses the sales force where it can be most effective. For many years, it sold only through a direct sales force responsible for all steps in the selling cycle—lead generation, qualifying, pre-selling, closing, post-sales service, and account management. Now direct mail and telemarketing perform the complete selling cycle for small and medium-sized customers. Telemarketing is also responsible for generating and qualifying leads among big customers, and a special technical support group handles post-sales servicing for large customers. These changes have resulted in adjustments to sales force deployment, training, and compensation.[15]

Integrators   In a number of industries a new channel member has arisen which we call integrators. An *integrator* is a service supplier unaffiliated with specific products, whose advice the end customer has sought to help them with a complex choice. We have already discussed one of these integrators, value added resellers (VARS) in the computer industry. They may advise a client to buy an IBM one day and advise another client to purchase a Dell computer the next day. Other examples of integrators are Personal Financial Advisers, Building Contractors, and Systems Integrators. Because they typically do not take possession of the supplier's offering, as do distributors, and are not under contractual agreement with a supplier, integrators represent a new and complex situation. Since the end-user seeks out the integrator's advice, a supplier must sell to the integrator as well as to the end customer. On the other hand, the integrator is also a new competitor to the extent that they may advise clients to purchase a competing offering. At a minimum, they have changed the role of the supplier's salesperson in that they represent a new and powerful buying influence.

Independent Sales Agents   An important alternative to the direct sales force is to hire independent sales agents (sometimes referred to as manufacturer's reps, reps, or brokers) to perform the selling function. *Independent sales agents* are not employees, but independent businesses given exclusive contracts to perform the selling function within specified geographic areas. In this way, they are different from integrators. Unlike distributors, they take neither ownership nor physical possession of the products they sell and are always compensated by commission. Agents are often used to develop new markets through a combination of persuasive selling skills and technical competence. This technical competence exists in part because agents usually handle five to eight noncompeting but related product lines that they know fairly well and sell to similar types of buyers. In certain situations, independent sales agents represent a cost-effective alternative to a direct sales force, provide greater flexibility and a quicker response to competitive threats and opportunities. These issues are explored more extensively in Chapter 8 when we discuss how to organize a sales force.

Internet   The extensive use of the Internet to gather information and to make purchases is the key business channel development of the 1990s. As household penetration of computers increases and the speed of the information access over the Internet increases, the importance of this channel of distribution will also increase. A recent study by Forrester Research indicated that the greatest impact of the Internet will be on direct company sales either over the telephone or by the sales force. Although there is considerable concern that the Internet will take sales away from other channels of distribution, it is also likely that the Internet will allow companies to better access additional market segments.

Consider the case of Herman Miller Inc. of Zeeland, Michigan. Its hmstore.com was the first online sales channel in the office furniture industry. Herman Miller has traditionally sold its premium cubicle systems (its $1,150 Aeron chair has become an office status symbol) to major corporations through its network of more than 250 contract dealers. These big contracts may be for five years to purchase, configure, deliver, and install millions of workstation components to thousands of a single customer's employees. With a contract of this size, the dealers will obviously go to extraordinary lengths to serve those customers. But while contract dealers were able to deliver a vast array of components and services to their large clients, they practically ground to a halt if they had to provide one chair or one desk to one person. That is the market served by the Internet, although Herman Miller went to considerable lengths to assuage the concerns of its 250 contract dealers that they would not be hurt by the Internet.

Many companies are finding that the Internet should not be viewed as a substitute for the traditional sales force, but as an enabler to help the sales force and other channel partners become more effective and efficient.[16] Hewlett-Packard, for example, has aggressively pursued electronic channels with HP Shopping Village (for consumers), HP Commerce Center (for businesses buying from authorized resellers), and Electronic Solutions (for contract customers). Thanks to a tight integration between HP's intranet and resellers' home pages, however, HP will take the customer's order and, at the last moment, kick the order over to the reseller's home page. The reseller completes the order, ships the product, and gets the commission. In this way, HP helps to alleviate the conflict that often arises when selling through multiple channels.

Alliances   An increasingly popular alternative for accessing markets is to establish an *alliance* with another organization in a joint venture to sell products to specific markets. This strategy has often been used to expand globally. AT&T, for example, negotiated a variety of computer sales partnerships with companies in France, Germany, Italy, Belgium, and the Netherlands.[17] The Chrysler Corporation contracted with Hyundai Motor Company to sell certain Chrysler products in South Korea.[18] General Mills and Nestlé SA have set up a joint venture to form a separate company for marketing breakfast cereal throughout Europe.[19]

The use of alliances is not exclusively a global selling strategy. The formation of alliances to sell new drugs is fairly common. A new drug may have enormous profit potential, but there is a limited time period in which to capture the profits. When a drug goes off patent and generics become available, the bulk of the profit opportunity is gone. So there is enormous pressure to fully penetrate the market as soon as possible. Even if it were feasible to hire-up to introduce a new drug, it is unlikely that newly hired people would be capable of gaining the physicians' support.

The number of new channel arrangements continues to mushroom. The net effect has been, first, that many large firms have reduced the size of their field sales forces by focusing them on medium- and large-size accounts. Second, firms have had to struggle with the problems of coordinating the alternative means by which they access their markets. IBM, for example, attempts to limit the direct competition between its value-added resellers and its direct sales force by crediting 85 percent of the volume generated by resellers in the salesperson's territory against the salesperson's annual sales quota.[20]

Third, many companies find that *where* to sell and distribute is equally or more important than *what* to sell. In the commercial airline industry, for example, one of the biggest challenges is allocation of inventory to Internet sellers, travel agencies, and bulk buyers, such as corporate customers. Airlines are finding that their "distressed" inventory is a valuable commodity to resellers because of the market draw potential. Depending on one's view, this may be a marketing decision, but channel allocation certainly has huge ramifications to the sales organization as well.

Account Relationship Strategy

A firm's *account relationship strategy* refers to the type of relationship a firm intends to develop with its customers. Some firms, for instance, take a transactional approach to customers because customers can quite easily switch their business from one supplier to another, depending on which offers the lowest price. Other firms may establish contractual relationships with their key customers. To further complicate the situation, a firm may decide to establish a different type of relationship with different customer groups. Selection of the right customers for the right type of relationship becomes strategic for both the customer and the supplier.

The management of account relationships has grown more varied and strategic in today's business-to-business environment, in some cases actually defining how a company competes in the marketplace.[21] Impetus for this development are the issues discussed in Chapter 1, including industry mergers and acquisitions, global competition, information technology, maturing markets, and more sophisticated customers.

Account relationships may take a variety of forms, each having major implications for the sales force with respect to recruiting and selection, compensation, necessary competencies, and behaviors. Figure 2-6 illustrates several generic alternative relationships along the dimensions of customer and supplier investment in the relationship. Notice that both the supplier and the customer must choose the type of relationship in which they will engage; it is not just a seller's decision.[22] Notice also that the three relationships in Figure 2-6 are depicted on the diagonal. This suggests that an appropriate convergence of selling and purchasing approaches is needed for a particular relationship to be successful. To get a better idea of the investments involved, the nature of the relationships, and the role of the sales force, we will discuss each of the three types of relationships described in Figure 2-6.[23]

Transactional Relationship   Most business-to-business transactions take place as part of an ongoing relationship between supplier and customer. A *transactional relationship* is one in which the relationship is based on the need for a product of acceptable quality, competitively priced, and a process and relationship convenient for the buyer. Often a good transactional relationship involves a personal relationship between the buyer and the seller. The relationship is based on the nurturing elements described in Chapter 4, including a history of trust, bargaining, value, and meeting or exceeding customers' expectations, but the relationship is usually a personal one between individuals. At a recent meeting of a group of European sales and marketing executives, a Scandinavian vice-president of sales remarked, "You know, I personally have never bought anything from someone I didn't like." This is at the heart of a transactional relationship—personal relationships.

The efforts of Jim Roberts, a salesperson with Holston Building Supply, to sell oak balusters and other staircase parts to a small chain of lumberyards in eastern Tennessee, illustrates the advantages and limitations of this type of account relationship. While the customer had long purchased other Holston products, they informed Jim that they were quite satisfied with their present supplier of staircase parts and had excellent profit margins on these items. Jim persisted, however, saying, "Just give me a chance to prove that you could sell even more and make better margins with our products." When the buyer did give them a trial run, they sold so well that he soon switched completely to Holston's stair parts. "I would not have had the slightest chance of getting him to try our line," says Roberts, "no matter how good my arguments might have been, if I had not already established a solid,

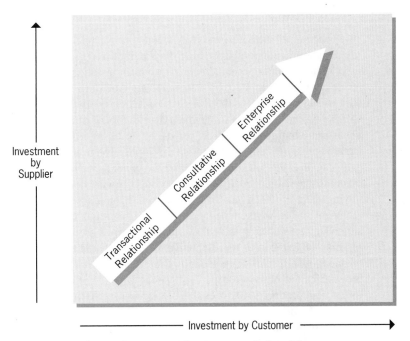

FIGURE 2-6   Alternative Types of Account Relationships

trusting relationship with him."[24] Notice that the personal relationship between Jim and the account was critical to obtaining the sale, and that trust was a key element in the relationship. On the other hand, another supplier of staircases offering a higher profit margin and able to generate equal demand is likely to take business from Jim in the future. Also notice that the customer's investment in the relationship is mostly at a personal level—that is, between the Jim and the customer's purchasing manager, not between the customer and Jim's company.

While repeat transaction relationships may sound as if they are the traditional buyer-seller relationships, this is not necessarily the case.[25] Michael Dell was one of the first to recognize the enormous opportunity to provide sophisticated buyers with the kind of relationship they were seeking. By offering a direct sales channel for computer equipment, Dell was providing buyers who knew what they wanted with a low-cost and convenient way to purchase a personal computer. The Dell selling approach through telemarketing and self-customization of the equipment was roughly 15 percent lower than selling through computer retailers. The only sales function that had to be performed by Dell was efficient order taking, which could be accomplished at a fraction of the traditional full-service model of selling through retail outlets.

Consultative Relationship   Quite common in industrial markets, a *consultative relationship* is based on the customer's demand and willingness to pay for a sales effort that creates new value and provides additional benefits outside of the product itself. While suppliers may want to establish a consultative relationship with their customers, the success of consultative relationships rests on the ability of the salesperson to become very close to the customer and to intimately grasp the customer's business issues. In these relationships, the sales force attempts to create value for the customer in three ways:

- Helping customers understand their problems and opportunities in a new or different way
- Helping customers develop better solutions to their problems than they would have discovered on their own
- Acting as the customer's advocate inside the supplier's organization, ensuring the timely allocation of resources to deliver customized or unique solutions to meet the customer's special needs

The role of the salesperson in a consultative relationship is quite different from their role in a transactional relationship. Much more time is spent learning the special needs of the individual customer and marshaling resources inside the supplier's company to meet those needs. A good example of a company implementing successful consultative relationships with its key customers is the Boise Cascade Office Products Corporation (BCOP), one of the world's premier business-to-business distributors of office products. BCOP has repositioned its award-winning sales force personnel as business consultants. The Boise sales force strives to differentiate itself through the application of value-added techniques. Through pre-call planning, the sales representative develops a comprehensive understanding of the specific customer. Using Data Base Marketing software, the salesperson examines a customer's buying pattern, which can lead to a formal business review with the customer. The BCOP salespeople seek areas in the customers' organizations where process improvements are possible. This effort can involve flow charting various processes with the customer. Sales usage reports enable the sales representative to advise customers on buying trends in the categories of paper, furniture, computers, and office supplies. Sales representatives also use a software program called Activity Based Cost Management (ABCM) to measure costs by activity, customer, and product. ABCM enables Boise to directly assign more than 90 percent of actual costs to specific customer-related activities. As a consequence, opportunities such as cost savings possibilities can be explored and presented to customers. The usual end result is improved financial results for both the buyer and Boise.

Boise Cascade's efforts at establishing consultative relationships with its customers illustrate several important characteristics of this type of customer relationship and how it differs from transactional relationships. Notice that the additional customer value resides in nonproduct resources that the salesperson brings to the relationship. This type of relationship also puts a premium on gathering and analyzing information about customers and their business issues. As a result, the selling process is usually longer, so the value of the customer to the supplier must be great enough to cover the higher selling costs. This usually requires that the relationship be long-term in nature. Notice also that the salesperson must have a great deal of skill in gathering customer information, business acumen, and technical competency. Finally, the support, software programs, and training Boise provides to its sales force is critical to their success, but is also a significant up-front cost to Boise.

Figure 2-6 indicates that both the seller and the buyer's investment in the relationship are greater in consultative relationships than in transactional ones. The Boise Cascade example clearly shows that the seller's investment increases, but what about the buyer's investment? Gathering information to understand the customer's problems and opportunities requires by its very nature an investment of time and a sharing of information by the customer. A vice president of distribution for a large utility firm put it this way: "It's a big investment of time bringing a new vendor aboard. You need to know that the time you spend with them is worth it. You can't just give a free education to everyone who comes knocking at your door."[26]

It is critical to choose the right situations in which to invest in consultative relationships. Experience indicates that a consultative relationship is most appropriate when one or more of the following conditions are present:

- The product or service can be differentiated from competitive alternatives.
- The product or service can be adapted or customized to the needs of the customer.
- The customer is not completely clear about how the product or service provides solutions or adds value.
- The delivery, installation, or use of the product or service requires coordinated support from the selling organization.
- The benefits of the product or service justify the relatively high cost of consultative relationships.

When more of these conditions are present, it usually means that there is an opportunity for the sales force to create customer value through consultative selling.

Enterprise Relationship   In recent years, customers have been downsizing their supplier base, and replacing their myriad vendors with a very small number of possibly long-term relationships offered only to a select few suppliers. A widely quoted figure is that customers are working today with one-third fewer suppliers than they did 10 years ago. Combined with merger mania and market consolidation, the trend toward purchasing from fewer suppliers has resulted in companies capable of leveraging the volume of their purchases for enhanced services and cost-cutting opportunities. Many sellers' response to the emergence of very large and powerful customers has been to develop a system of enterprise relationships to better meet the needs of their major customers. According to one study, the number of enterprise relationship programs within the Fortune 1000 companies has tripled over the last five years.[27]

An *enterprise relationship* is one in which the primary function is to leverage any and all corporate assets of the supplier in order to contribute to the customer's strategic success. In such a situation, both the product and the sales force are secondary and the customer must be of strategic importance to the selling organization. Adjectives to describe this category of relationships abound, and include Major, Strategic, National, Global, Corporate, and Key Account Programs. Accounts that qualify for an enterprise-level relationship are

GLOBAL AWARENESS COMPETENCY
"An International or a Global Company?"

In 1993, IBM was an international company, but not necessarily a global one. For instance, McDonald's, a major IBM account, was operating in more than 90 countries, as was IBM. McDonald's needed standard solutions that could be delivered to any location globally, but IBM was not equipped to deliver the consistent solutions that the world headquarters of McDonald's was seeking. Each of IBM's local operations had evolved its own processes. As a result, McDonald's needs in Indonesia were handled very differently by IBM Indonesia, than the way in which, say, IBM UK dealt with McDonald's requirements in London. In some geographies the traditional silos had been eliminated and cross-functional teams were creating real success stories, but in other areas old functional thinking persisted. As a consequence, it was difficult to deliver the full potential value of IBM to its customers.

Starting in 1994, IBM began to rethink its approach to the global market. The company designed what it calls a "customer relationship management process." The process redesign put the issue of creating customer value firmly at the center of the new strategy, while beginning with the best local practices and adapting them for worldwide use. As the general manager of IBM North America explains, "Our intention was to create value for our customers worldwide, and that meant centering everything on customer wants and needs. We could no longer afford the old functional ways of thinking."

In McDonald's case, IBM created a cross-functional global team to work with McDonald's worldwide headquarters. The team is designed to mirror McDonald's own worldwide management structure. It includes a senior IBM executive sponsor and specialist food service representative for each of McDonald's major markets in Asia Pacific, Europe, and Latin America. Together with global pricing and improved responsiveness to McDonald's needs, the process approach has been successful in creating customer value at the corporate level. As IBM's client executive for the McDonald's team says, "Our ability to communicate efficiently and effectively a common message around the world is a tremendous competitive advantage." See *www.ibm.com* and *www.mcdonalds.com*.

characterized by their relative level of complexity and by a number of common traits: a centralized, coordinated purchasing organization with multi-locations; multiple purchasing influences; a complex, diffuse buying process; very large purchases; and a need for special services. To achieve successful enterprise relationships, the supplier must deliver exceptional customer value, while also extracting sufficient value from the relationship. This is always challenging, especially when the customer has worldwide needs. To better understand this point, see the Global Awareness Competency box, "An International or a Global Company?"

Many of America's premier industrial firms such as GE, IBM, DuPont, Monsanto, and Honeywell have established strategic partner relationships with customers such as American Airlines, Ford, Milliken, Procter & Gamble, and the federal government. The customer often initiates this radically different type of relationship. In 1989, for instance, Chrysler was on the ropes. One of its responses was to change the way it did business with its suppliers. Figure 2-7 lists some of the ways in which Chrysler changed its supplier relationships. Instead of forcing suppliers to win its business anew every two years and focusing on lowest list price, it decided to give suppliers business for the life of a model and beyond. Excruciatingly detailed contracts gave way to oral agreements. Instead of relying solely on its own engineers to create the concept for a new car and design all the car's components, DaimlerChrysler now involves suppliers. Instead of DaimlerChrysler

Traditional Relationships	Enterprise Relationships
Little recognition or credit for past performance	Recognition of past performance and track record
No responsibility for supplier's profit margins	Recognition of suppliers' need to make a fair profit
Little support for feedback from suppliers	Feedback from suppliers encouraged
No guarantee of business relationship beyond the contract	Expectations of business relationships beyond the contract
No performance expectations beyond the contract	Considerable performance expectations beyond the contract
Adversarial, zero-sum game	Cooperative and trusting, positive-sum game

FIGURE 2-7   Changes in Customer Expectations of Suppliers

dictating price, the two sides now work together to lower the costs of making cars and to share the savings. Today DaimlerChrysler has improved its market share and profitability significantly by speeding up product development, lowering development costs, and reducing procurement costs.[28]

The Chrysler example illustrates some ways in which enterprise relationships differ from traditional supplier relationships. Following are some of the ways in which other companies have made strategic partner relationships work:

- Suppliers are involved in the early stages of need identification, specification, and new-product development. Texas Instruments targets key emerging accounts in which they participate in these firms' product design process as early as possible and, in doing so, suggest improvements that enable these firms to design products that fully capitalize on the strengths and capabilities of TI system products.

- In conventional relationships, the primary players were the salesperson, the customer service representative, and perhaps a design engineer. With enterprise relationships the supplier fields a team that interfaces with the customer on a regular basis, and includes a variety of functional areas and management levels. John Deere workers, for instance, solve production problems with their counterparts at suppliers such as McLoughlin Body Co.[29] See the Team-Building Competency box, "An Advisory Board" for another example of the selling teams in an enterprise relationship situation.

- In enterprise relationships there is an unusually high degree of intimacy resulting in immediate responsiveness from suppliers, sharing of information, and radical empowerment of suppliers. For instance, a small group of nine suppliers, called "in-plants," work on-site, full time at Boise. This insider status gives them unparalleled opportunities to grow with the customer and to influence requirements for their products. Based on their access and knowledge, the suppliers decide what, when, and how much of a particular product or service is needed, and write orders to themselves to make it happen.[30]

The role of the sales force, the structure of the sales program, compensation, and even the sales philosophy differ for each type of relationship.[31] For instance, as the buyer-seller relationship becomes more sophisticated and complex, the sales force's role as the primary point of contact between customer and supplier often diminishes. The focus also shifts from sales volume generation to management and maintenance of the relationship and the conflicts that are likely to arise over time.[32] Growing with the customer, as opposed to expanding the customer base itself, is the seller's strategy for increasing sales and profits. The skills needed, compensation, incentive programs, and evaluation criteria all need to be adjusted from those of a general field sales force to be appropriate for these relationships.

TEAM-BUILDING COMPETENCY
"An Advisory Board"

To add value to the customer's business, General Electric Industrial Control Systems (GE ICS) has reorganized into Local Customer Teams that work within their specialties to fully research and understand a customer's business and to solve complex customer problems, including productivity issues. GE ICS provides a complete line of ac and dc electric motors for commercial and industrial applications, including steel and paper mills, cranes, automotive, appliances, and farm equipment, among others. GE ICS provides customer value beyond its products through sharing its process and application engineering knowledge, providing complete industrial systems, as well as the services to improve, maintain, or monitor the system.

To bring GE ICS' capabilities to bear on their customers' issues, 20 Local Customer Teams (LCT) composed of 30 to 70 people have been established throughout the Americas. An advisory board of seven individuals runs each LCT. An LCT could have an account manager from sales, a representative from distribution, and a representative from OEM sales on its advisory board. There are only two management level functions on the board: a business development leader and an engineering manager. The LCT teams also select two individuals from the technical ranks (field engineers and application engineers), and one who holds an "at large" position that does not fit into any of the other categories. Within the team framework, the advisory board is responsible for establishing the sales strategies and tactical plans, allocating and positioning its resources to best meet the customers' challenges. See *www.ge.com/indstrialsystems/index.*

Summary   One of the key ideas expressed up to this point is that a sales force strategy should be derived from the business and marketing plans of the organization. Numerous company examples have been presented to illustrate this idea. The other important idea is that a sales force strategy should include two key decisions: (1) the organization's strategy for accessing the target markets defined within the marketing plan, and (2) the type of account relationships that will be pursued—transactional, consultative, and enterprise. It is important to keep in mind, however, that in today's business world these strategic decisions can be quite complex. To appreciate this, it is not at all unusual for a buyer to want to "cross-leverage" the supplier. At IBM, for example, American Airlines is viewed as both a customer and a supplier; that is, American sells airline seats to IBM, but IBM is also a primary supplier of computer equipment and software to American. This type of relationship requires that the supplier's account manager navigate within his or her own procurement area, as well as that of the customer.

Another difficulty that may arise in executing a marketing strategy is that the sales force may not understand and thus not execute the product strategy. The sales manager's ability to understand marketing strategies and apply them in the field has been examined in some recent research.[33] Table 2-1 shows how marketing executives and sales managers classified products into four basic strategies. If the views of the two groups matched perfectly, then all the numbers would be on the diagonal. Instead, sales managers tended to be more aggressive in pushing products that marketing wanted either to divest or harvest. Not only does there appear to be widespread misallocation of selling time and effort, but continued emphasis on building product sales volume when inappropriate may also cause the company's relationship with its customers to suffer. (What is the firm's strategy when marketing says they are doing one thing but sales says another?)

TABLE 2-1   Sales Manager's and Marketing Executive's Product Classifications by Strategy

		Sales Manager Classification				
		Build Strategy	*Hold Strategy*	*Harvest Strategy*	*Divest Strategy*	*Total*
Marketing executive classification	Build strategy	71[a]	22	2	0	95
	Hold strategy	29	57	3	1	88
	Harvest strategy	10	49	23	6	88
	Divest strategy	21	21	27	25	94
	Total	129	149	55	32	365

[a] A total of 71 sales managers classified their products as build strategies out of 95 so classified by marketing executives.

Another mistake is to assume that more investment in the customer relationship will automatically create a better relationship with improved results. The experience of a packaged materials manufacturer provides a typical example of this mistake. Because the manufacturer's costs were slightly higher than competitors', they were losing business. This manufacturer decided that the best way to halt this decline was to upgrade its sales force. Their "packaging consultants" were charged with adding value to their products through providing customers with help and advice. The investment in upgrading the sales force, including retraining and recruiting, together with the development of a new marketing strategy, was in excess of $10 million. The average cost of each sales call increased to $890 and the average sales cost to acquire a new account was $112,000. It turned out, however, that the customer just didn't want advice or help, they needed packaging material, pure and simple, and that's all they were prepared to pay for. The company was soon taken over at a fire-sale price. The moral of the story is that a successful relationship must create value for the customer.

A final point to keep in mind is that moving up the diagonal to more intimate and complex customer relationships also entails greater risks. More money is at stake because these customers represent significant revenues, and the costs to implement are significant. The challenge suppliers experience with major and strategic account relationships is suggested by the results of a survey asking companies with major or strategic account programs to rate the effectiveness of these relationships. As indicated in Table 2-2, more than half of these programs were rated as failing miserably with a self-rating of "Poor." While the challenges of these programs are significant, the risks of revenue and profit loss associated with losing these accounts to competitors are often of even greater significance.

Strategic planning implies that choices will have to be made. One of these choices is the allocation of resources. Indeed the marketing and sales force strategy is often motivated by cost and revenue considerations. One of the goals of the strategic planning process should be to set an operating budget for controlling the implementation of the strategy. The next section concentrates on how sales force budgets can be set and administered.

TABLE 2-2   Partnering Effectiveness Index

THE SALES BUDGET

Budgets are a key element used by sales managers in planning programs to reach their objectives. A *sales budget* is essentially a set of planned expenses that is prepared on an annual basis. The sales budgeting process is described in Figure 2-8. Sales budgeting begins when senior management designs a marketing plan and sets spending levels for advertising and sales promotion. Once these demand creation factors are determined, sales forecasts can be made (forecasting is discussed in Chapter 7). The sales forecast, in turn, provides a guide for estimating how many salespeople will be needed. Sales managers must also project travel and other expenses for the sales force. Next, the actual expenditures for a period are compared with the budget. When expenditures exceed planned levels, the sales manager has to revise the categories or ask for more funds. The main concerns in preparing budgets are to decide how much to spend on personal selling and how to allocate the money in various selling activities.

Sales Budget Planning

For budgeting purposes, it is usually necessary to further refine and identify the strategic avenues for achieving an overall sales volume target. For instance, the overall sales target may be broken down by geographic area, region or district, and by product line. For example, if one region represents a greater growth opportunity than others, then management may wish to add more salespeople and spend more on marketing programs in this region. When combined with market share and market growth figures for individual product lines, product-focused avenues for achieving sales targets can be identified and costs can be budgeted to support product sales targets.

Many companies have found the *Customer-Product Matrix* shown in Figure 2-9 to be very useful for analyzing the basic revenue generating avenues of the firm. This matrix identifies four strategic sources of sales revenue based on a combination of new and/or current customers and products. Companies have found this to be a useful analysis tool because the sales job and resulting expenses are quite different for each quadrant in the matrix. New Business Development revenues (new customers and new products) will require much higher training and promotion expenses and may require additional salespeople, for instance, than Account Management revenues (current customers and products). Conversely, Account Management revenue development may call for additional sales support such as telemarketers and service people. Even the sales force compensation plan can be quite different

FIGURE 2-8   The Sales Budgeting Process

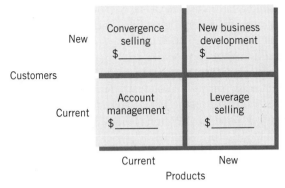

FIGURE 2-9   The Customer-Product Matrix

depending on the quadrant representing the source of company revenues. When New Business Development is a significant growth opportunity, sales force compensation should include significant incentive opportunities for generating new customers. This and other compensation issues are discussed further in Chapter 14. The point being made here is that a sales figure for each of these four sources of revenue illustrated in the customer-product matrix should be budgeted so that the total of the four quadrants equals the company's total sales volume target. This analysis will help considerably in determining expense budgets and in designing an overall sales program.

How Much to Spend?

At some point in the budgeting process, management must settle on a specific dollar amount that will be spent on the sales force. Three methods for arriving at this number are described in this section: the percentage of sales approach, the workload approach, and the incremental sales approach.

Percentage of Sales   Perhaps the most popular method for determining a sales budget is the percentage of sales method. This technique bases a sales budget on what managers think is a reasonable percentage of planned revenues. The percentage is usually derived from historical spending patterns and industry standards for a particular line of trade. Table 2-3, for example, provides the average sales force expenses for 19 major industries. A typical firm selling industrial services spent 11.7 percent of sales on sales force expenses.

Let's say that the management of a paper products company is trying to determine how much to spend on the sales force next year. They have forecasted sales for $20 million and have noted that manufacturing companies spend 6.8 percent of their revenue on the sales force. Let's also say that traditionally 15 percent of the sales force budget was spent on sales management. In this case, the sales force budget and the number of salespeople the budget supports could be derived as follows:

$20,000,000 Expected sales
$\underline{\times\ .068}$ Field sales expense ratio (wages, commissions, and travel expenses)
$ 1,360,000 Sales budget
$\underline{\times\ .85}$ Percent for sales force (i.e., 15% for supervisor)
$ 1,156,000 Available for salespeople

$$\frac{\text{Dollars available}}{\text{Wages and expenses per person}} = \frac{\$1,156,000}{\$57,600} = 20 \text{ (number that can be hired)}$$

The preceding example indicates that of the $1,360,000 expected sales budget, $1,156,000 would be available to hire salespeople after supervisory expenses had been deducted. If salespeople cost an average of $57,600 per year for wages and expenses, then the company could afford to hire a total of 20 people.

Despite its widespread use, there are several notable drawbacks to the percentage of sales approach for setting sales force budgets. There is no guarantee, for instance, that the use of industry percentages in setting sales budgets will lead to optimal results for individual firms. Note in Table 2-3 that smaller firms tend to spend a larger percentage of sales on the sales force than do larger firms. Another drawback to this approach is that budget allocation for selling expenses changes in the same direction as sales. The percentage base, however, may not provide the appropriate amounts of funds when market conditions change. If a firm is losing market share, for instance, an intensified selling effort may require greater funding than would be appropriated under the percentage of sales method.

Despite its drawbacks, the percentage of sales method is practical and provides useful standards for comparison. A company might adjust the industry average according to its own needs and plans, using sales budgets that are higher or lower than average to see if they lead to greater effectiveness. This latter approach is similar to the workload approach described next.

Workload Approach   The workload approach to determining a sales force budget derives the budget figure from what the workload will be to meet a revenue target. An example may best illustrate this approach. Loctite North America sells adhesives and sealants to heavy industry. To improve short-term profitability, Loctite allowed its field sales force to decline through attrition. Because of the resulting greater size of the sales territories, however, Loctite's reps were unable to provide adequate service to existing customers. Industrial adhesives are a special applications business that requires a lot of technical support. Loctite decided to hire 30 additional salespeople during a one-year period. The added expense depressed profitability for six months, but soon afterward, sales began to grow. Loctite's decision to add salespeople incorporated the idea behind the workload method of calculating sales force size, which is to focus on the work to be done in determining the number of salespeople needed to do the work, which would also drive the budget decision.

TABLE 2-3   Sales Force Selling Expenses as a Percentage of Sales

	Sales Force Total Cost as a Percentage of Sales		Sales Force Total Cost as a Percentage of Sales
COMPANY SIZE		**INDUSTRY**	
Under $5 Million (MM)	12.7%	Business services	10.5
$5–$25 MM	14.0	Chemicals	3.4
$25–$100 MM	9.3	Communications	9.9
$100–$250 MM	7.4	Educational services	12.7
Over $250 MM	10.1	Electronics	12.6
		Fabricated metals	7.2
PRODUCT OR SERVICE		Health services	13.4
Industrial products	10.4	Hotels and other lodgings	11.4
Industrial services	11.7	Instruments	14.8
Office products	10.8	Machinery	11.3
Office services	11.1	Manufacturing	6.8
Consumer products	11.3	Office equipment	2.4
Consumer services	11.6	Paper and allied products	8.2
		Printing and publishing	22.2
		Retail	15.3
		Trucking and warehousing	12.2
		Wholesale (consumer goods)	11.2
		Average	**10.0%**

One commonly used way to implement a *workload approach* is to determine the size of the sales force based on decisions concerning the frequency and length of calls needed to sell to existing and potential customers. An estimate of the total number of salespeople required using this approach can be made using the following formula:

$$\text{Number of salespeople} = \frac{\left\{\begin{array}{c}\text{Number of} \\ \text{existing} \\ \text{customers}\end{array} + \begin{array}{c}\text{Number of} \\ \text{potential} \\ \text{customers}\end{array}\right\} \times \begin{array}{c}\text{Ideal} \\ \text{frequency} \\ \text{of calls}\end{array} \times \begin{array}{c}\text{Length} \\ \text{of} \\ \text{call}\end{array}}{\text{Selling time available from one salesperson}}$$

For example, if a computer software development firm had 3,000 existing customers and 2,250 potential clients to be called on five times per year for two hours (including travel time), and if available selling time per salesperson is 1,500 hours per year, the size of the sales force would be:

$$\text{Number of salespeople} = \frac{(3,000 + 2,250) \times 5 \times 2}{1,500} = 35$$

This estimate of 35 salespeople is based on the assumption that the desired frequency and length of calls are the same for all customers. If it is decided that these should vary according to the size and type of customer, then the formula can be modified accordingly. The sales force budget is then calculated based on the cost of hiring, training, supervising, and supporting the desired number of salespeople.

Perhaps the biggest disadvantage of the workload strategy is its failure to consider the costs and profits associated with different levels of customer service. Because the ideal call frequencies used in the model are based on judgment, the firm never really knows whether it has set the number of calls to maximize sales and profits. Thus, the workload approach finds the number of salespeople needed to cover the market, but it does not lead to an optimum solution. For existing firms, the incremental approach can be used to determine the number of salespeople needed and resulting sales force budget.

Incremental Approach Experience has shown that as firms add salespeople within an existing trading area, the increase in new business is usually smaller with each new employee. Sales grow because customers receive better service, but the total number of potential accounts does not change. That is, eventually all prospective customers are adequately covered, and sales do not increase as selling expenses grow. This situation suggests that salespeople should be added until the gross profit on new business is equal to the costs of deploying another person, which is the philosophy on which the *incremental approach* to determining sales force size and budget is based. Because the new business associated with additional sales staffing varies over time and among salespeople, firms must continue to monitor sales activities closely and determine whether they are approaching the point where costs exceed potential benefits.

Each of the methods for determining sales force size focuses on a particular aspect of the problem—revenue, workload, and cost. Since the decision involves consideration of each of these factors, the best approach may be to triangulate the problem by using all three methods to determine the boundaries of the budgeting problem. With the results of this analysis as decision aids, management judgment is needed to determine the final choice of sales force size.

Where to Spend It?

Sales managers set target figures for the various selling expense categories for each planning period. The goal is to keep actual expenditures at, or under, the budgeted figures to ensure that overall financial objectives are achieved. Some of the more common *expense classifications* are:

- Sales force salaries, commissions, and bonuses
- Social Security
- Retirement plans
- Hospitalization and life insurance
- Automobile
- Travel, meals, lodging, and entertainment
- Sales manager salaries, commissions, and bonuses
- Office supplies and postage
- Office rent and utilities
- Clerical and secretarial services
- Recruiting and training
- Samples and other sales aids

The amounts budgeted for the different expense categories tend to vary widely by product and type of customer. Often managers make their initial allocations using the previous year's budget, and adjust for inflation and program changes.

Budget Administration

One of the prime benefits of sales budgets is that they force managers to think about how marketing funds should be spent. Decisions must be made about whether sales representatives should receive more training, whether more money should be spent to purchase complementary hockey tickets, whether to provide more sample books, or to increase bonuses, and so on. Budgets, therefore, aid sales managers in designing the optimal combination of the marketing variables under their control.

Another advantage of a budget is that it facilitates the control of sales operations. If sales objectives are not being reached, for instance, the manager can see from the budget how much money has been spent in each expense category and where adjustments are needed. In this case the sales manager might be able to use funds from the training budget to buy prizes for a sales contest.

Budget administration has been greatly simplified in the past few years with the development of the *electronic spreadsheet*. Computer programs such as Lotus 1-2-3 and Excel, and the widespread availability of personal computers, have made it easier to keep track of sales force expenditures.

SUMMARY

The sales force strategy and management structure should be planned and designed within the context of an organization's overall business strategy and its marketing strategy. This chapter has given numerous examples of how sales force decisions are subject to the overall strategy of the company and its marketing strategy. You should now be able to do the following:

1. **Describe the major elements of strategic management planning.** The strategic management process includes defining a business mission, setting specific measurable goals for the organization, and deciding on a strategy for meeting these objectives. A well-defined business mission should provide a sense of direction for the organization, defined in terms of customers, competitors, and the company itself. Goals should be measurable and should guide goal setting throughout the organization. Strategies should be based on developing a sustainable competitive advantage.

2. **State the basic elements of strategic marketing planning.** Strategic marketing planning is a process whereby an organization allocates marketing mix resources to reach its target markets. This process starts with a situation analysis that consists of taking stock of where you have been, where you are now, and where you are likely to go in the future. The next step is to define market segments and to choose target markets. Once you have made these decisions, an appropriate marketing mix program should be designed, including integration of the various promotion tools. The sales force strategy should follow from and be consistent with the earlier business and marketing strategy decisions.

3. **Explain what is meant by strategic sales force decisions and several alternative approaches.** Strategic sales force decisions refer to the key sales force decisions that when once made will influence how the sales force will be organized, built, led, and controlled. Two decisions are particularly important with respect to the sales force: (1) how the company will access the market segments that it has targeted, and (2) the types of relationships in which the company chooses to engage and the choice of customers within for each type of relationship. The chapter discusses six channel alternatives in addition to a direct sales force and three types of customer relationships, including transactional, consultative, and enterprise.

4. **Describe what is meant by a sales budget.** Sales budgets follow from the long-term strategic plans of the organization. Sales budgets are essentially a set of planned revenues and expenses that are prepared on an annual basis. How much is spent on personal selling and sales force expenses will vary from industry to industry and among competitors within an industry.

5. **Describe three approaches to setting a sales force budget.** The affordability approach to budgeting starts with how much money a company can allocate to the sales force and then considers the cost of hiring, training, maintaining, and managing a certain size sales force in arriving at a final determination on the size of the sales force. The workload approach is based on decisions regarding the frequency and length of calls needed to meet a certain sales and customer service level. The incremental approach to budgeting suggests that salespeople should be added until the gross profit on new business is equal to the costs of deploying another person.

KEY TERMS

Account relationship strategy
Alliances
Analyzers
Benchmarking
Build strategy
Business mission
Business portfolio analysis
Consultative relationship
Customer product matrix
Defenders
Distributors
Divest strategy

Electronic spreadsheet
Enterprise relationships
Expense classifications
Generic business strategies
Harvest strategy
Hold strategy
Independent sales agents
Integrators
Low cost
Market segmentation
Marketing mix
Niche

Organizational goals
Prospectors
Sales budget
Situation analysis
Strategy
Strategic business units (SBUs)
Strategic management planning
Strategic marketing planning
Target marketing
Telemarketing
Transactional relationships

DEVELOPING YOUR COMPETENCIES

1. **Strategic Action.** Merrill Lynch & Company has finally decided to enter the low-cost business of on-line trading. On-line brokerage firms such as E*Trade Group Inc. have been growing rapidly and taking business from full-service brokerage houses owing primarily to the low price per transaction and the record bull market since 1994. With the Internet now accounting for 30 to 35 percent of all stock trades by individuals, Merrill executives finally decided they could no longer afford not to embrace such trading. Not only is this a major change in strategy for Merrill, but the move to the Internet could spark rebellion within its army of 14,800 well-paid brokers. An internal Merrill Lynch study, for example, suggests that brokers who are paid chiefly in commissions might see their incomes decline by 18 percent initially. How big a problem does Merrill face? What would you suggest they do about their brokers? For more on Merrill Lynch visit their Web site at *www.ml.com.*

2. **Technology.** Claudia da Costa knows how tough implementing sales force automation (SFA) can be: When she was hired as a marketing manager at Access Radiology Corporation in Lexington, Massachusetts, in January, da Costa's job was to clean up after a previous, unsuccessful attempt at automation and try again. "It failed—and it failed miserably," because of an installation error on the vendor's part and a lack of training on the part of Access, she says of the first SFA project. What advice would you give Claudia to ensure that this second foray into SFA will have a better chance of success than the first one?

3. **Coaching.** Perhaps one of the best role models for today's sales and marketing managers is Lou Gerstner, who became the chairman of IBM. There were major problems at IBM and it was probably tempting for Lou to turn all his energy inward to resolve these difficulties. Instead, he decided to become actively involved in the company's sales efforts. IBM's relationship with Monsanto, the St. Louis-based agricultural and pharmaceutical giant, is a good case in point. Gerstner hosted a number of one-day strategy seminars for small groups of chief executives from significant companies in a variety of industries. The chairman of Monsanto, Robert Shapiro, who was an attendee at one of these events, asked whether any of IBM's research or cutting-edge technology might have an application for Monsanto, which was involved in genetic research. IBM found some interesting material on gene mapping in both animal and plant cells that they thought might be useful to Monsanto. A few weeks later an IBM executive team arrived at Monsanto headquarters, and discussions began. As discussions progressed, it became apparent that IBM had other more important strategic-level contributions to make. Within a year, Monsanto and IBM signed a contract, reputedly worth several hundred million dollars, that had IBM running the total Monsanto mainframe and PC network of more than 20,000 personal computers. What did Lou Gerstner do right? Which type of customer relationship do IBM and Monsanto have and what makes it work? IBM: *www.ibm.com.* Monsanto: *www.monsanto.com.*

4. **Team Building.** The need for coordination and teamwork has been emphasized throughout the discussion of relationship management in this chapter. WESCO Distribution, Inc., a $3 billion electrical equipment and supplies (EES) distributor, presents an interesting case study on the issues involved in coordinating the implementation of a national account contract with large customers.

   WESCO regularly carries and sells more than 210,000 products from over 6,000 suppliers to satisfy the electrical equipment needs of any customer anywhere in the world. What they are really selling, however, is the capability of a single source of supplies, customized delivery, technical support, application development, and customer product training. In other words, they offer the latest in integrated supply chain systems including inventory management options, inventory reduction initiatives, and related efficiency improvements to customers such as industrial manufacturers, original equipment manufacturers (OEMs), municipal power authorities, and other utilities.

Recently WESCO established a national account program for its 300 largest industrial customers who collectively accounted for almost 70 percent of WESCO's total revenues. The national account contract offered customers a 2 to 3 percent price discount on products purchased from WESCO in exchange for consolidating all their purchases of these product lines with WESCO. WESCO's account penetration with these customers ranged from 60 to 90 percent for the product lines covered by the contract, so the lower prices in the contract could be offset by greater volume through 100 percent penetration. Contracts were signed at the customer's corporate headquarters, but most of the purchasing was left to purchasing agents at the local plants. This is where the coordination problems began. Despite corporate enthusiasm, some plants were reluctant to abandon local distributors with whom they had long-established and close relationships. In addition, the local availability of supplies was often highly valued in case of emergency. Problems in coordinating between corporate and local interests also existed inside WESCO. A customer may purchase a lot of supplies in total, but the volume generated at the local plant level may be fairly small in comparison with larger single plant customers serviced by the WESCO branch salesperson. The branch salespeople report to the branch manager and are paid a base salary plus commission on sales volume, so they are reluctant to call on a relatively low-volume plant, especially one with a long commute, even if they are on a national account contract. What would you recommend the national account manager do to encourage teamwork and local support for a national account in such a situation? What actions would you recommend for the vice president of marketing and sales?

For more on WESCO Distribution, Inc., the products and services it offers, and its customer base, see *www.wescodist.com.*

5. **Self-Management.** Every baseball player must throw, catch, and hit the ball. Yet what it takes to be a winning pitcher or a great hitter are quite different. The same is true of sales—all salespeople must talk to customers and take orders; however, what it takes to excel at transactional relationships is quite different from that required for enterprise relationships.

The H. R. Chally Group has built a large database of salespeople information from which they have identified four different sales roles and skills. Each sales job requires a certain amount of each skill to be a top performer. Rate yourself from 1–10 in terms of how much each of the following four skills describes yourself.

- **Closing:** Can aggressively initiate personal contacts. Does not have a high fear of personal rejection. Can quickly establish another person's emotional desire and personal concerns. High self-confidence.
- **Consultive:** Possess a combination of patience, good interpersonal skills, and aggressiveness. Have good persistence. Are very career oriented. Somewhat academically inclined. Are willing to take risks, but only after careful thought and calculation. Pay a high level of attention to detail. Can handle personal rejection and the fear of failure extremely well. Team oriented.
- **Relationship.** Like independence and the freedom of sales (i.e., the feeling that you are your own boss). Exercise discipline and take responsibility for their actions. Once again, low fear of failure. Have a strong work ethic.
- **Display.** Easily bored, need to have something to do. Enjoy people. High physical energy level. Impulsive. Work tends to revolve around home and other goals.

What is your profile on these four dimensions? Name two types of sales positions (e.g., stockbroker, telephone sales, corporate jet sales, computer software sales, etc.) for a person rating high on each of the four dimensions. What would be the composite profile on each of the four skills (rate from 1 to 10) of a person who would be successful at each of the three customer relationships discussed in this chapter: transactional, consultative, and enterprise relationships. For more on H. R. Chally, see *www.chally.com.*

PROBLEMS*

1. Your company has 2,500 regular customers on which your sales force calls on once every other month. In addition, you would like to obtain 500 new customers to meet your company's growth target. The average number of calls to convert and service a new account for the year is expected to be six calls. Your salespeople are in the field calling on accounts 40 weeks a year. They spend 60 percent of their time calling on customers and prospects, with the average sales call taking 30 minutes. If the average number of hours your salespeople work each week is 50 hours, how many salespeople would you need in your sales force to maintain this level of customer service and also generate 500 new customers?

2. SOMA Inc. has been in business for a little under two years. SOMA is a Web-based information technology training company currently employing one salesperson and a sales manager. They have been successful in two rounds of financing and have a $5 million cash balance. Their target for 2000 is to have revenues of $4 million. Revenues in 1999 are anticipated to be $1.3 million. The issue they are struggling with is to determine a sales force budget for 2000 that will be sufficient to meet their sales projections. Sales force expenses in the training industry average 22 percent of sales, but they can be quite a bit higher; in fact, a recent start-up company in the training field had spent more than 50 percent of their revenues on the sales force. An executive recruiting firm had supplied SOMA with the following data on typical sales compensation ranges in the computer-based training industry.

	Salesperson	*Sales Manager*
Typical Quota	• $800,000–$1,200,000	• Sometimes carry personal quota
Cash Compensation		
• Base salary range	• $45,000–$85,000	• $60,000–$110,000
• Commission rate	• Varies by company	• Varies by company
• Total cash compensation	• $65,000–$135,000	• $110,000–$160,000
• Top earnings	• $250,000	• $250,000

IN-CLASS EXERCISES

2.1: "How's This Budget?"

Last year had been a very good year for Bubble Wrap, a manufacturer and distributor of cellophane sheets of air-filled bubbles used to protect merchandise during shipping. Sales had increased by 10 percent to $134 million, mostly due to increased shipments by existing customers. Tom Thornton, president and chief operating officer of Bubble Wrap, was even more excited about the coming year because of an exciting new product development and plans for a geographic expansion beyond Bubble Wrap's Southeast Atlantic Coast trading area. He was just meeting with Bill Singler, vice president of sales and marketing, to discuss next year's budget.

---

*Excel spreadsheets for working on these problems are available at www.wiley.com/college/dalrymple. Go to "Student Resources."

"Bill," greeted Tom, "I'd like to thank you for such a great year in pushing our sales over $130 million. As you know, I've been working on our budget for next year and feel that we have an opportunity to become one of the real players in this industry. With our earnings from last year, I feel that we are finally in a position to expand beyond our present eight-state geographic territory by adding on New York, Pennsylvania, and West Virginia in the north and Louisiana and Arkansas in the south. On top of that," he continued, "I feel that at least 10 percent of our sales next year will be in the new Instatight packaging technology."

"Instatight sounds like a great product," Bill commented, "but what I really like about it is that it is best suited for the high end of the market, expensive products that are easily broken if not handled correctly. We've needed a product of this kind for some time and it shouldn't cannibalize our existing technology which is really best for the middle of the market."

"Bill, I'm as excited as you are about our opportunities. Now we just have to aggressively execute our plan," added Tom. "I've forecasted sales next year for $174 million which is right at a 30 percent increase over this year's projected sales. We have got to maintain our bottom line to help finance our growth plans, so I'm setting a sales and marketing budget of $19 million which is the same as this year's projected 10.9 percent of revenue. This is nearly a $5 million increase in your budget, which should be enough to reach our target of $174 million."

Questions:

1. As vice president of sales and marketing, what would be your reaction to Tom's budget?
2. How would you begin to analyze this budget?
3. What are the possible budget implications of the expanded geographic trading area?
4. What are the possible budget implications of the new product introduction?

2-2: "Are You Prepared to Work with Us?"

An insurance company is starting to see some fundamental changes in the attitudes of its independent brokers. The salespeople for this insurance company called on independent brokers (i.e., insurance agents who are not employees and sell policies from a number of companies) who in turn sold to individual companies and households. In the past, brokers were primarily interested in getting the lowest price or "quotes" from the insurance company for a plan having features the broker's customer requested. The lower the price, the easier it was for the broker to sell the plan and to show the customer the savings that resulted. Brokers were also interested in how quickly the company responded to a request for a quote. The role of the insurance company's sales force was to ensure that brokers were aware of any new plans the company developed and to handle any possible service problems.

Increasingly the insurance company's salespeople were hearing a different story from the large brokers who had grown by merger and consolidation in the industry. Typical of the comments heard is the following from one of their largest brokers: "We need a lot of help. Every one of our offices does things its own way. We don't have a common set of procedures, and we haven't got a common information system. We'll write a lot of business with you if your people are prepared to work with each office individually and help them get their act together." The insurance company was not sure how to respond to this request, but knew that it could not afford to lose this customer's business and that of other large brokers making similar requests.

Questions:

1. How fundamentally different is the role of the sales force in addressing these new customer needs from that addressing the needs of more traditional brokers?
2. How will the selling effort change when addressing these new broker needs?
3. How will the changes affect sales management?
4. What are the threats and possible downside of addressing these emerging broker needs?

CASE 2-1   AT&T (A)

*D*ick Falcone, head of Sales Operations at AT&T, America's largest telecommunications company, had been saying for years that small business would be critical to AT&T's continued pre-eminence in the marketplace. By mid-1989, after sub-stantial marketshare drop and a recent spate of ads by competitors such as MCI (Microwave Communica-tions, Inc.), his point began to hit home. Typical ads zeroed in on AT&T's weak spots, e.g.:

"How can Goliath ever understand David?"

"Who can better understand the needs of a small business ... than a small business?"

"When was the last time you saw your AT&T rep?"

The obvious answer—"never"—underscored a fact that had long worried Falcone: while AT&T had made certain that its large, national customers were served by a face-to-face salesforce, the small business accounts were being handled by its telemarketing department.

Ten or even five years earlier, Falcone agreed, that kind of sales approach may have been adequate. But now, with the irreversible changes happening in the competitive landscape, AT&T had no option but to change with it. As he saw it, these changes were being driven by two related factors: (1) the emergence of small business as the source of growth, productivity and wealth; and (2) fueling this growth, the informa-tion and communications services offered by AT&T as well as—to an ever growing extent—by competitors entering the newly opened market nearly every week.

Since the United States district court consent decree in 1984 to dismantle AT&T's legal monopoly of most telecommunications services in the U.S., over 300 competitors had entered a market which, for almost 100 years, had been overwhelmingly AT&T's. But, of all these new players, one in particular had become synonomous with "competition": MCI. Many found this fact to be ironic: MCI was a small company which had started out during the '60s in microwave technology applications. Unlike Sprint—another key competitor that was strategically and financially aligned to the telephone manufacturer GTE—MCI had no major partnerships or financial backing. Yet, in less than five years, the company had inched its way into AT&T's market to such an extent that it had achieved double digit share.[1]

For Falcone, the reasons for MCI's impact in the market were obvious: it had targeted an end of the market where AT&T had traditionally been little involved, and was therefore also unaware of the strength and potential of this small business sector. By the same token, MCI had formed and trained a sales-force specifically for the small end of the market—a sector whose needs from a services' salesforce were, Falcone was convinced, profoundly different from those of the large customers with whom AT&T had historically cultivated relationships.

By the end of 1989, what Dick Falcone had long been advocating finally happened, and he was appointed to create, staff and lead a brand new unit in AT&T's Business Network Sales division: the Com-mercial Market Group. By covering the small business market across the United States, he was expected to deliver multi-billion dollar revenue to AT&T annually.

When he began this new journey in January 1990, Falcone was reminded of the old Chinese proverb: "Be careful what you ask for in life: you just might get it."

DE-MONOPOLIZING THE MONOPOLY

Since its inception in 1885, AT&T—the driving force behind the Bell System—functioned as a regulated monopoly providing the bulk of telephone service throughout the U.S. The Bell System had been a verti-cally integrated monopoly with over one million employees who had assumed they had secure employ-ment. The company's activities included: communica-tions technology research; production and distribution

---

[1] According to Federal Communications Commission News Report, March 20, 1990.

This case was prepared by Professor Sandra Vandermerwe and Dr. Marika Taishoff as a basis for class discussion rather than to illustrate either effective or ineffective handling of a business situation. Copyright (c) 1993 by IMD-International Institute for Management Development, Lau-sanne, Switzerland. All rights reserved. Not to be used or reproduced without written permission directly from IMD, Lausanne, Switzerland.

of equipment; installation and maintenance of facilities, as well as provision of the necessary services; and handling accounts and revenues for the entire system. In 1974, antitrust proceedings against AT&T were launched; ten years later, AT&T agreed to divest itself of its Bell Operating Companies that provided local exchange service. And from that agreement, AT&T was dismantled and the Bell System existed no more.

AT&T was allowed to retain $34 billion of the $149.5 billion in assets it had on December 31, 1983. Of its over 1 million employees, only 373,000 remained; even the well-known Bell name and logo had to be discontinued. But, in recompense, the company was permitted to pursue more fully the technology being developed at Bell Laboratories.

The newly-created AT&T was still the largest telecommunications company in the United States and one of the worldwide leaders in information technology. It had been allowed to retain several activities from the former Bell System, most notably: long-distance services; equipment manufacture and supply; and research and development, including integrated communications and computer solutions. All told, by 1989 the AT&T network handled 135–140 million calls a day.

A constantly changing number of Strategic Business Units (SBUs), each headed by a President and all of them under the direction of AT&T's President of Business Communications Services, could either choose to use AT&T's sales channels or to engage third parties like independent retailers to sell their products and services to the market. The principal SBUs were Inbound Services, Outbound Services and International Services. *(Refer to Exhibit 1 for a simplified organization chart.)*

As accelerating leaps in technology allowed ever wider use and different applications of existing lines and cables, services became the key source of innovation at AT&T and at other communication companies.

Small business customers were sold to by a variety of salespeople:

- *Product Sales:* AT&T's General Business Systems (GBS) sold telecommunication equipment and systems to the small business market.
- *Business Network Service Sales:* Telemarketers sold telecommunication network services to the small business market. They were organized into four geographic regions. In contrast, large business customers were handled by a direct, face-to-face—otherwise known as premises—salesforce.

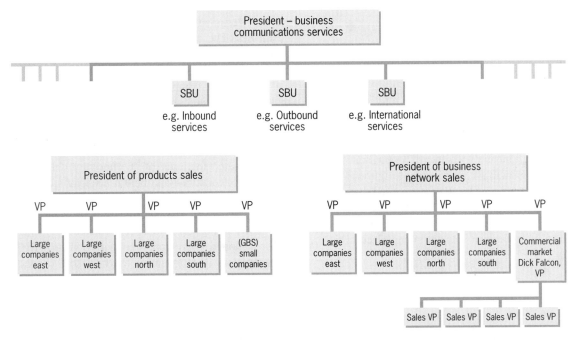

EXHIBIT 1   Organizational Chart (Simplified)

FROM A LARGE CAPTIVE MARKET TO A SMALL COMPETITIVE ONE

Beginning in the mid-'80s, the demand for telecommunications line capacity increased dramatically. Fueling this demand was the exponential growth in new communications technologies—particularly fax machines, computers, video conferencing and tele-conferencing—which in turn created a need for new kinds of services. The acceleration in business conducted across boundaries also spurred the need for more international telephone services. Total revenues in the industry grew, on average, by 5% a year beginning in 1984. This was combined with an equally dramatic decrease in communication service prices.

Competitors sprang up in many facets of the telecommunications industry. They targeted various areas and, to varying extents, were successful or unsuccessful. By 1989, Sprint had acquired about 7% of the market in pre-subscribed long-distance lines— i.e., lines which customers had deliberately specified as their choice for long-distance services, and MCI had about 15%. In five years, AT&T's percentage of the 134 million pre-subscribed lines had fallen from 100% to 75%.[2] MCI's inroads were typically ascribed to its almost exclusive focus on small businesses and its ability to undercut AT&T's prices by 1–2 cents. Because MCI was small, as its ads claimed, it did not have to support an infrastructure the size of AT&T's. A number of smaller competitors—about 300 dispersed throughout the country—were primarily regional or niche providers.

Market share in the industry was measured by the number of minutes a line was used. AT&T's share steadily diminished from 98.7% of premium interstate minutes to 65% by the end of 1989.[3]

Throughout the decade of the '80s, the small business market had been growing steadily and, in a stark reversal of previous trends, had overtaken large business as the key source of economic growth. By the end of the '80s, small business was worth $10 billion, with 100% of the growth in employment figures from 1980–1989 due to this sector. Falcone figured that even if AT&T were to recapture 100% of the large business market, the company would not be able to grow, simply because future growth was not taking place in that market.

---

[2] According to Federal Communications Commission *News Report,* March 20, 1990

[3] According to Federal Communications Commission *News Report,* March 20, 1990

A survey commissioned by the National Foundation of Women Business Owners had in fact indicated that, if trends continued, by 1992 more people would be employed by female business owners than by all the Fortune 500 companies combined. In Falcone's view, AT&T had lost huge chunks of market share simply because it did not fully appreciate the power and importance of small business. Historically, AT&T had cultivated relationships with a relatively small number of large companies, with whom it had conducted a huge, and therefore, cost-efficient volume of business. Substantial volume was especially important in this market, since large users tended to demand tariff revisions, thus lowering prices. The primary focus of the AT&T salesforce was to sell new products and services to this market as soon as they became technologically feasible and commercially viable.

THE COMMERCIAL MARKET GROUP: TO DEVELOP THE SMALL BUSINESS SECTOR

In late 1989, AT&T determined that the company's future success lay in two areas: expanding business internationally, and regaining and growing the ever-more important small business market share domestically. To achieve this goal, top priority would be given first to winning back those customers who had moved over to the competition.

It was clear to the SBUs that the time had come to meet the just created demand in the marketplace for services designed and delivered specifically for small businesses. The creation of a national sales organization for this market—together with a new set of disciplines to guide it—was, they had decided, the one critical way for the company to remain competitive. The most important step, though, was finding the right person to make it work. It did not take long.

Dick Falcone had been working at AT&T since graduation. He worked for a short period of time at the Massachusetts Institute of Technology's Industrial Guidance Laboratory—and held a bachelor's degree in Engineering. He had had a variety of positions at the company across all key disciplines, with considerable time in marketing. Up until 1989, he had been in charge of the national sales support organization at AT&T's GBS division—the organization which sold telephone equipment to small business customers—where he had been responsible for ensuring appropriate training, compensation plans, quotas and the like for a multithousand person salesforce. Just prior to being assigned to the new position, he had designed and established one of the largest information and database systems; it gave all AT&T salespeople anywhere in the U.S. instant access to any and all unrestricted customer files.

When the President of Business Communications Services told him that he had been selected as head of the soon-to-be-created Commercial Market Group—responsible for the eight million small business customers nationwide—and, as such, the fifth Vice President in AT&T's Business Network Sales Department, Falcone was ready. Designing and establishing a world-class salesforce, he admitted, interested him far more than implementing technology—even though he was an engineer. The cardinal objective given by the SBUs to the Commercial Market Group was to create and achieve a "win-back" strategy: to recapture the market base which had left AT&T.

Falcone, his direct boss (the President of Business Network Sales), and his internal constituents—the SBUs, which he called his "client customers," all concurred that the only way to accomplish this goal was to "get as many feet on the street and into customers' premises as possible." But, where should they start? Falcone recalled at that time:

> I was given a title, assigned major responsibilities, and presented with an entirely new department to run. There were a few startup problems, though: expectations in the small business market were changing on a daily basis, and we hadn't been keeping up with those new requirements; we had to create a salesforce and train them to sell to those customers and meet their expectations: and to top it all off, we had to do all of this from scratch.

At first, the telemarketing salespeople who had been working in one of the four major regional divisions were realigned into the national Commercial Market Group. Falcone knew that telemarketing was an integral component to meeting the needs of small businesses across the U.S. The objective was not to dismantle what already existed but to complement it with a direct, face-to-face salesforce.

THE FORMING OF A NEW SALESFORCE: THE FIRST WAVE

Of the eight million customers who fell into the small business category, about 4 million were very small businesses that were satisfied with telemarketing. The other half typically had more employees and more specialized needs. It was for these customers that a face-to-face salesforce would have to be created. From his own research and from market data from consultants, Falcone knew that he would need at least a multi-thousand strong force to satisfy these customers.

But, while the Commercial Market Group was a priority for AT&T, the company was also instituting an across-the-board cost-cutting exercise. Hiring an employee base of this magnitude would be difficult. Therefore, rather than look outside, it was decided that the majority of the salesforce should be hired from within.

Falcone put together a marketing program—including brochures, presentations, etc.—throughout AT&T nationwide, offering an option to AT&T employees whose positions were being eliminated and who wanted to recycle their professional competence, as well as to those who basically wanted to do something else with their lives. He asked his sales managers to become personally involved. A salesforce was being created, he announced, which would focus on the growth sector of the American economy and would give each individual the opportunity to grow with it. Surplus headquarters employees, 5,000 in all, from every level of the company—accountants, nurses, middle managers—applied. They were all given a test designed specifically to assess their sales talent and potential. The several thousand who passed then attended a basic, one-month sales training program before being sent to one of the 27 branches across the U.S., from where they would play their role in the "win-back process."

Falcone was fully aware that he was taking a gamble by building the foundations of his salesforce on a group of people who had never sold before. But, he had confidence in AT&T people, their intelligence, their work-ethic and most importantly their cultural propensity to serve customers well. "After all, isn't that what quality selling is?" he thought. One of the nurses was an example: she claimed that, despite all her qualifications and her successful career, she felt that she had been doing the wrong thing all her life; she had always wanted to sell, but had never had the chance to do so. She was not going to let this opportunity slip away. Other candidates were less interested in sales *per se* than in changing their careers entirely. One of the accountants bluntly explained that he was tired of dealing with numbers and wanted to work with people instead.

The drive of these people to do something different with their lives encouraged Falcone. Still, he decided not to expect too much too soon. His main objective was to create a physical presence in the marketplace and convince small business customers that AT&T, in creating a salesforce to handle their needs in a uniquely personal way, did indeed care about them. Changing the perception that small businesses had formed of AT&T would, Falcone knew, be sufficient challenge for his people. But, if that goal were successful, it would be the first step toward rebuilding market share.

SETTING THE DRUMBEAT...

Throughout 1990, Falcone concentrated on creating the framework in which these new salespeople could most effectively work and be evaluated. Four managers who had previously overseen the telemarketers in their respective geographic territories reported to Falcone on a dotted line basis; they reported to his four peers—VPs for each of those regions—on a solid line basis. As he put it:

> I believed in the idea, and I had responsibility for the group, but I didn't have any authority to make decisions: I had to get the agreement from the other four VPs. But that never really stopped me: if I thought it was the right thing to do, I did it. Sometimes that meant counting on the fact that forgiveness is a lot easier to get than permission.

Convinced that only something which is measured gets done, Falcone began thinking about what he should be expecting of his newly-created, multi-thousand salesforce. His years at Product Sales' small business division, GBS, had exposed him to this kind of market, yet he did not want to rely on that experience to create a strategy for the Commercial Market Group. He knew that selling services was completely different from selling products and that fighting this year's wars with last year's strategies was a sure route to defeat. So, he decided to start with a clean slate.

Falcone soon began to sense how many customers needed to be contacted and/or visited in a day, as well as how many deals should be signed daily. Still, more needed to be done in order to achieve all his goals. It was not enough for his people to be "as good" as the competitors—they had to be better. Having a competitive salesforce selling network communication services to small businesses would not satisfy him; he wanted a world-class salesforce as good as that of the best company—regardless of industry—when it came to serving the needs of the small business sector. To meet such a goal, Falcone did several things:

- Using consultants' data, he set best-in-industry performance levels for his people, based on benchmarking against his direct competitors.
- Best-in-class performance standards were also set by identifying, studying and establishing the benchmark for firms which were not in the industry but serviced the small business sector. He traveled and met with Vice Presidents of Sales from other industries who were selling into the small business market to learn

what metrics of performance they used. He was able to do this through the many good relationships AT&T had with other firms. He concluded:

> You have to visit a certain number of potential customers a day and close at least a given amount of deals every day if we are to get the sales we expect. And if we don't, the cash registers won't be ringing, and we as a group—and as a company—will have to bear the consequences.

- More and better training programs would also be needed. His salesforce was a patchwork quilt of people and experience, and simply setting targets would not suffice for getting consistently high performance. The salespeople would have to be fashioned to meet those targets.

The sales training programs initiated over the past year had undergone a quantum leap, with two or three generational improvements. Now, more than ever, the intent of these courses was not just to demonstrate effective selling techniques but to instill a real sense of team spirit which would differentiate the Commercial Market Group—in mentality, outlook and results—from the traditional AT&T salesforce. These training courses were entirely paid for by the SBUs.

- A remuneration package was designed to help Falcone achieve his objectives. The salesforce was paid on a 60% salary and 40% commission basis. Falcone decided early on that there would be no limit on how much the high achievers could earn: the more money they brought in, the more they could earn for themselves. Even in that first year of operation, a few salespeople began to stand out as real stars, earning four to five times above average; others were nearer to the 80% mark. Any salesperson who underperformed for a specific period of time was eligible to be reassigned or terminated.
- He also laid out his expectations for branch managers. First and foremost, their responsibility was to motivate and drive the Commercial Market Group salesforce. And although the branch managers were directly responsible for running the branches, Falcone himself also set some key guidelines for them to follow. For instance, to meet the profitability target he expected of them, they had to be able to constantly challenge their employees to do better. As Falcone explained:

> In our lives, the one thing that gives us real satisfaction is stressing our capabilities against some challenge. We are not here to control the salesforce, but to get their commitment by constantly challenging them to do better. Management's *raison d'etre* is to let people be "ever in a state

of becoming more," and this can only be done by constantly setting challenging and rewarding hurdles.

Branch managers had been given the mandate to train their people, direct them and offer appropriate career advice. Salesforce satisfaction, Falcone recognized, would be directly related to how well branch managers succeeded in these tasks. Managers would be judged by the overall financial results of their branches.

INTEGRATING THE SECOND WAVE

By the end of 1990, market share was still eroding, but at a slower pace than over the past five years. The SBUs insisted that more coverage was needed on the small business front. The sales support requirements in the high end of the market, because of advances in technology, had been lessened. Therefore, they boosted Falcone's salesforce by taking about 15–20% of the sales support away from the four major regional groups and reassigning them to the Commercial Market Group. This second wave that joined the Group was a combination of salespeople—already trained and accustomed to selling at the high end of the market—as well as technical people who were not strictly "sales" people; rather, they were technical support specialists.

The SBUs told the four VPs responsible for large national customers which accounts they thought needed fewer people, based on achieved results and changes in technology. These employees were then sent to the Commercial Market Group to form the "second salesforce wave." More than a thousand people joined Falcone in this way, and now there was a salesforce which Falcone felt was sufficient in number to beat the competitors and satisfy the customer. The training course, by this stage perfected still more, was mandatory for the second wave. Falcone recalled their reaction to being allocated to the Commercial Market Group, and to being obliged to attend the initial briefings and training sessions:

> It was a real eye opener: here I was, telling them how great this journey was going to be, and they were hating every minute of it. I remember one of my sales managers coming into my office the first day they joined us, and saying he had never seen such an "ugly"—and he didn't mean in physical appearance—group of people in his life. What they were basically saying was that AT&T owed them something: that they were entitled to the job that they wanted, and no one had the right to tell them that they had to work here or there.

Falcone rearranged his entire schedule over the next few months so that he could visit and personally participate in every training group. At each session, he discussed his objectives, requirements and aims for the group, and then gave the salespeople three options.

One: they could decide to stay, consciously seize the opportunity and make the best of it. He emphasized that they would learn something new, perfect their skills and grow, and that he in turn would do everything he could to help them succeed. Falcone reiterated that his expectations were high and that nothing would interfere with achieving the results he wanted for the group as a whole. He told them that he was counting on them and would invest in them so that they could invest in themselves. He conveyed his philosophy that what was in it for them was one opportunity to become more than they were, to become even stronger professionals and that, in the final analysis, the value of their improved professionalism would be something that they uniquely owned. They could apply their strength in the future to AT&T or anywhere they chose.

Two: they could decide that they just could not work in this kind of market. Perhaps they had done well dealing with large accounts—but the small business market, he emphasized, had its own pace and beat which was rather different. As he put it to them:

> You've got to wake up in the morning, get out there and pound the pavement, and meet as many customers as possible. And you've got to sign a deal—quickly. It's a totally different ball game and I'm not going to hide anything from you. Some may not want to. And if you decide you don't want to do this, we'll help you find something else at AT&T.

Three: they could decide not to make a choice: just sit in on the training classes, pass the time away, and then try to get some business. But, Falcone told them, this option would be a mistake. He encouraged them to "either stay, or go, but make a decision. After all, it's your life."

About 50% of the second wave decided not to join the Commercial Market Group. Falcone and his management team successfully placed the majority of them in other functions at AT&T; the remainder left the company.

THE UNLEARNING PROCESS: MOVING FROM SELLING LINES TO SELLING APPLICATIONS

The typical contacts for the Commercial Market salesforce were the small business firms' presidents who, although they wanted solutions, usually had very little time to give and no in-house technical expertise on hand. As Falcone explained:

> It's not only *what* they need that is different, it's also how and when they need it. And, they don't always even know what they need; their requirements are different, and so is their buying process. The salesperson has to be able to understand, meet and satisfy the ongoing needs of these customers—in as short a time as possible.

For Falcone, the only way to sell services to this kind of market was by somehow showing the customer the benefits of those services upfront. In his opinion, perfecting this approach would be pivotal for AT&T's overall profitability. As he saw it, AT&T and its competitors all had the same hardware—cables and wires. But, those assets only made a return when customers used them, which—given the nature of the phone business—they inevitably had to do, but only up to a point. Since that limit was money, competitors tended to cut prices to get customers to use the phone more often. Falcone did not want to compete that way, but rather demonstrate results. He wanted to show customers that, even if AT&T was a price leader for some services, it could help them make more money by reaching more people and thus having more customers come to them.

Persuading small business customers successfully, though, meant having a much keener insight into their operations than most salespeople were accustomed to. It also meant not just selling the attributes of a service, but emphasizing the results that customers would get from that service. Falcone called this "application selling," and insisted that even a butcher—who had probably never thought of his phone as a tool to extend his market and improve his results—could be a suitable candidate for such services. AT&T, for instance, could design an advertising campaign whereby existing or potential meat purchasers could call for information, prices and deliveries on a reversed charge, toll-free "800" line. By encouraging customers to use this line free of charge to place orders, the butcher would be getting results he otherwise would never have achieved. Such services, designed on the premise that toll-free "800" numbers could be just as beneficial to small businesses as they had always been to large companies, were a typical example of an application sale.

A completely different example was the "900" service numbers. Here, because of the specific and unique value of the service provided over the line, individual end users paid much more for the call than the use of the line alone. A pharmacy, for instance, installed a 900 number as a service to its customers: at any time of the day or night, if they had any questions about counter-indications from prescribed drugs, or their side effects, they could dial the service.

Some salespeople were apprehensive about being able to determine, in the short time period between the expected number of daily customer visits, the specific needs that these customers might have to get the results they were after. Falcone was determined, however, that this skill be learned and applied. Service was more than just efficiency, as had been assumed in the past. It was improving customers' bottom line performance.

TURNING THE CORNER

By the end of the third quarter of 1991, the results of the Commercial Market Group impressed everyone at AT&T. The SBUs, the direct clients of the Group, were especially satisfied with the results, which had exceeded financial expectations. The Group had helped the company turn the corner and had broken the back of market share erosion. The Group had also restored the AT&T name amongst the major contenders in the small business market, which continued to be the key growth sector in the economy. Customer satisfaction surveys continued to place AT&T above competitors.[4]

The SBUs now decided on a new strategy for the Commercial Market Group. Its salespeople were no longer to focus primarily on win-backs, but would also exploit untapped opportunities in the market, and protect and satisfy the customer base. Falcone was even more challenged than he had been on the first win-back round. He was certain that he now had the kind of employees who could meet the needs of both customer groups—the small businesses across the country, and the SBUs.

Yet Falcone, who had always regarded himself as a people person, despite his attention to results, began to question if he had truly achieved success. Was it enough to satisfy these two customer sets? Would their satisfaction alone yield sustainable success in the marketplace? What about the employees who created this success: did they need to be more motivated and inspired than others?

AT&T had always considered employees its most important asset, and so for decades the company had monitored employee satisfaction through surveys. Falcone was convinced that unless employee satisfaction results grew together with those of customer satisfaction, the success of the Commercial Market Group could not be sustained. He therefore decided to

---

[4] Statement about customer satisfaction from Data Communications "Data Comm User Survey," August 1992.

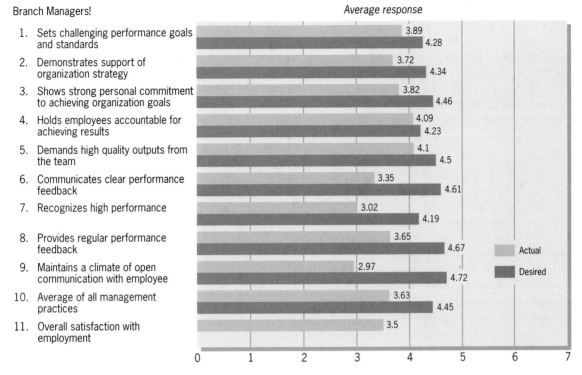

EXHIBIT 2   Eleven Point Employee Satisfaction Survey

conduct an employee satisfaction survey. Eleven key factors, related to how salespeople evaluated their branch managers, were tested on a scale of 0–7: employees were asked to indicate the kind of working relationship they *desired,* and their *actual* experience, Exhibit 2. Falcone was surprised at the results of the

Employee Satisfaction Survey. Although Falcone's team had done a good job fulfilling its sales goals for the SBUs, he had forgotten that the sales force were customers as well. Falcone realized some changes were needed if his sales force was to remain competitive in the future.

CASE 2-2   SHANANDOAH INDUSTRIES (A)

L ate in the evening of August 8, 1986, Charlton Bates, president of Shanandoah Industries, called Dr. Thomas Berry, a marketing professor at a private university in the Northeast and a consultant to the company. The conversation went as follows:

BATES: Hello, Tom. This is Chuck Bates. I'm sorry for calling you this late, but I wanted to get your thoughts on the tentative 1987 advertising program proposed by Mike Hervey of Hervey and Berham, our ad agency.

BERRY: No problem, Chuck. What did they propose?

BATES: The crux of their proposal is that we should increase our advertising expenditures by $400,000. They indicated that we put the entire amount into our consumer advertising program for ads in several shelter magazines.

BERRY: That increase appears to be slightly above your policy of budgeting 5 percent of expected sales for total promotion expenditures, doesn't it? Hasn't John Bott [vice president of sales]

This case was prepared by Professor Roger A. Kerin of Southern Methodist University. Reproduced by permission.

emphasized the need for more sales representatives?

BATES: Yes. John has requested additional funds. You're right about the 5 percent figure too, and I'm not sure if our sales forecast isn't too optimistic. Your research has shown that our sales historically follow the Industry almost perfectly, and trade economists are predicting about a 13 percent increase. Yet, I'm not too sure.

BERRY: Well, Chuck, you can't expect forecasts to always be on the button. The money is one thing, but what else can you tell me about Hervey's rationale for putting more dollars into consumer advertising?

BATES: He contends that we can increase our exposure and tell our story to the buying public—increase brand awareness, enhance our image, that sort of thing. He also cited data from *Home Furnishings* magazine which showed that the newly affluent baby boomers [consumers between the ages of 25 and 40] are almost three times more likely to buy dining room furniture and twice as likely to buy living room furniture than their elders in the next year. All I know is that my contribution margin will fall to 25 percent next year due to increased labor and material cost.

BERRY: I appreciate your concern. Give me a few days to think about the proposal. I'll get back to you soon.

After the parting remarks, Dr. Berry began to think through Charlton Bates's summary of the proposal, Shanandoah's present position, and the furniture industry in general. He knew that Bates expected a well-thought-out recommendation on such issues and a step-by-step description of the logic he used to arrive at his recommendation.

THE COMPANY

Shanandoah Industries is a manufacturer of medium-to high-priced living room and dining room wood furniture. The company was formed at the turn of the century by Bates's grandfather. Charlton Bates assumed the presidency of the company upon his father's retirement in 1982. Forecasted year-end gross sales in 1986 were $50 million; before-tax profit was $2.5 million.

Shanandoah sells its furniture through 1000 high-quality department stores and furniture specialty stores nationwide, but not all stores carry the company's entire line. The company is very selective in choosing retail outlets. According to Bates, "Our distribution

policy, hence our retailers, should mirror the high quality of our products."

The company employs 10 full-time salespeople and 2 regional sales managers. Sales personnel receive a base salary and a small commission on sales. A company sales force is atypical in the furniture industry since most furniture manufacturers use sales agents or representatives who carry a wide assortment of noncompeting furniture lines and receive a commission on sales. "Having our own sales group is a policy my father established 25 years ago," noted Bates, "and we've been quite successful having people who are committed to our company. Our people don't just take furniture orders; they are expected to motivate retail salespeople to sell our line, assist in setting up displays in stores, and give advice on a variety of matters to our retailers and their salespeople."

In 1985 Shanandoah allocated $2.45 million for total promotional expenditures for the 1986 operating year, excluding the salary of the vice president of sales. Promotion expenditures were categorized into four groups: (1) sales expense and administration; (2) cooperative advertising programs with retailers; (3) trade promotion; and (4) consumer advertising. The cooperative advertising budget is usually spent on newspaper advertising in a retailer's city. Cooperative advertising allowances are matched by funds provided by retailers on a dollar-for-dollar basis. Trade promotion is directed toward retailers and takes the form of catalogs, trade magazine advertisements, booklets for consumers, and point-of-view materials, such as displays, for use in retail stores. Also included in this category is the expense of trade showings. Shanandoah is represented at two showings per year. Consumer advertising is directed at potential consumers through shelter magazines. The typical format used in consumer advertising is to highlight new furniture and different living room and dining room arrangements. The dollar allocation for each of these programs in 1986 is shown in Exhibit 1.

THE INDUSTRY

The household wood furniture industry is composed of over 1400 firms. Industry sales at manufacturers' prices were $6.3 billion in 1985 and were forecasted to reach $7.1 billion in 1986. California, North Carolina, Virginia, New York, Tennessee, Pennsylvania, Illinois, and Indiana are the major furniture-producing areas in the United States. Major furniture manufacturers include Ethan Allen, Bassett, Henredon, and Kroehler.

EXHIBIT 1   Allocation of Promotion Dollars, 1986

Sales expense and administration	$ 612,500
Cooperative advertising allowance	1,102,500
Trade advertising	306,250
Consumer advertising	428,750
Total	$2,450,000

Source: Company records.

No one firm captured over 3 percent of the total household wood furniture market.

The buying and selling of furniture to retail outlets takes place at manufacturers' expositions at selected times and places around the country. At these *marts,* as they are called in the furniture industry, retail buyers view manufacturers' lines and often make buying commitments for their stores. However, Shanandoah's experience has shown that sales efforts in the retail store by company representatives account for as much as one-half of the company's sales in any given year. The major manufacturer expositions occur in High Point, North Carolina, in October and April. Regional expositions are also scheduled during the June–August period in locations such as Dallas, Los Angeles, New York, and Boston.

FURNITURE-BUYING BEHAVIOR

Results of a consumer survey conducted by the company provide information on furniture-buying behavior. Selected findings from the consumers survey are reproduced in Exhibit 2. Other findings from this research are as follows:

- Ninety-four percent of the respondents enjoy buying furniture somewhat or very much.
- Eighty-four percent of respondents believe that "the higher the price, the higher the quality" when buying home furnishings.
- Seventy-two percent of respondents browse or window-shop furniture stores even if they don't need furniture.
- Eight-five percent read furniture ads before they actually need furniture.
- Retail outlets used by respondents:
  Furniture specialty stores (32 percent)
  Furniture gallery stores (28 percent)
  Department stores (14 percent)
  Sears, Ward's, and Penney's (8 percent)
  Discount furniture outlets (7 percent)
- Ninety-nine percent of respondents agree with the statement "When shopping for furniture and home furnishings, I like the salesperson to show me what alternatives are available, answer my questions, and let me alone so I can think about it and maybe browse around."
- Ninety-five percent of respondents say that they get redecorating ideas or guidance from magazines.
- Forty-one percent of respondents have written for a manufacturer's booklet.
- Sixty-three percent of respondents say that they need decorating advice for "putting it all together."

THE BUDGET MEETING

At the August 8 meeting attended by Hervey and Bernham executives and Shanandoah executives, Michael Hervey proposed that Shanandoah's 1987 expenditure for consumer advertising be increased by $400,000. Cooperative advertising and trade advertising allowances would remain at 1986 levels. Hervey further indicated that shelter magazines would account for the bulk of the incremental expenditure for consumer advertising.

John Bott, Shanandoah's sales vice president, disagreed with the budget allocation and noted that sales expenses and administration costs were expected to rise $50,000 in 1987. Bott believed an additional sales representative was needed to service Shanandoah's accounts since 50 new accounts were being added. He estimated that the cost of the additional representative, including salary and expenses, would be at least $50,000 in 1987. "That's about $100,000 for sales expenses that have to be added into our promotional budget for 1987," Bott noted. He continued:

> We expect sales of about $50 million in 1986 if our sales experience continues throughout the remainder of the year. Assuming a 13 percent increase in sales in 1987, that means that our total budget would be about $2,825,000, if my figures are right, or a $375,000 increase over our previous budget. And I need $100,000 of that. In other words, $275,000 is available for other kinds of promotion.

Hervey's reply to Bott noted that the company planned to introduce several new styles of living room and dining room furniture in 1987 and that these new items would require advertising to be launched successfully. He agreed with Bott that increased funding of the sales effort might be necessary and thought that Shanandoah might draw funds from the cooperative advertising allowance and trade promotion.

EXHIBIT 2　　Selected Findings from the Consumer Survey[a]

Question: If you were going to buy furniture in the near future, how important would the following factors be in selecting the store to buy furniture? (Base 449)

Factor	Very Important	Somewhat Important	Not Too Important	Not at All Important	No Answer
Sells high-quality furnishings	62.6%	31.0%	3.8%	1.1%	1.5%
Has a wide range of different furniture styles	58.8	29.2	8.2	2.9	.9
Gives you personal service	60.1	29.9	7.8	.9	1.3
Is a highly dependable store	85.1	12.7	1.1	—	1.1
Offers decorating help from experienced home planners	26.5	35.9	25.4	10.9	1.3
Lets you "browse" all you want	77.1	17.8	3.3	.7	1.1
Sells merchandise that's a good value for the money	82.0	15.6	.9	.2	1.3
Displays furniture in individual room settings	36.3	41.2	18.7	2.4	1.3
Has a relaxed, no-pressure atmosphere	80.0	17.1	1.6	—	1.3
Has well-informed salespeople	77.5	19.8	1.6	—	1.1
Has a very friendly atmosphere	68.2	28.1	2.4	—	1.3
Carries the style of furniture you like	88.0	10.0	.9	—	1.1

Question: Please rank the following factors as to their importance to you when you purchase or shop for case-goods furniture, such as a dining room or living room suite, 1 being the most important factor, 2 being second most important, and so on, until all factors have been ranked. (Base 449)

	1	2	3	4	5	6	7	8	9	10	NA
Construction of item	24.1%	16.0%	18.5%	13.1%	10.5%	6.9%	4.9%	1.6%	.2%	1.1%	3.1%
Comfort	13.6	14.7	12.9	12.3	12.7	10.9	8.2	4.5	4.0	2.4	3.8
Styling and design	33.6	19.8	11.1	9.6	4.7	7.3	4.5	1.6	2.9	1.6	3.3
Durability of fabric	2.2	7.6	9.8	14.5	15.1	14.7	12.9	5.6	5.8	7.8	4.0
Type and quality of wood	10.9	17.8	16.3	15.8	14.7	5.8	5.3	3.1	4.9	2.0	3.4
Guarantee or warranty	1.6	3.8	1.6	5.3	8.7	10.0	13.8	25.2	14.5	11.1	4.4
Price	9.4	6.2	8.7	8.5	10.0	12.5	14.2	11.8	6.9	8.0	3.8
Reputation of the manufacturer or brand name	6.2	3.6	4.7	5.6	6.2	6.2	12.7	17.1	22.7	11.6	3.4
Reputation of retailer	1.6	1.8	1.6	2.4	4.0	7.3	7.4	13.6	22.0	34.5	3.8
Finish, color of wood	4.7	7.6	10.2	8.0	8.9	13.4	10.7	10.0	10.2	12.7	3.6

Question: Below is a list of 15 criteria that may influence what furniture you buy. They are ranked from 1 as most important to 5 as least important. (Base 449)

	1	2	3	4	5	No Answer
Guarantee or warranty	11.4%	11.1%	26.3%	16.9%	5.3%	29.0%
Brand name	9.1	6.5	14.3	25.6	11.6	32.9
Comfort	34.7	27.8	14.5	8.5	4.7	9.8
Decorator suggestion	4.0	2.4	2.7	8.2	44.8	37.9
Material used	14.9	24.1	14.9	13.4	6.2	26.5
Delivery time	.7	.5	1.3	2.9	55.2	39.4
Size	7.6	10.7	13.6	30.9	4.0	33.2
Styling and design	33.4	17.8	21.8	13.6	2.2	11.2
Construction	34.3	23.6	13.1	11.4	2.9	14.7
Fabric	4.0	25.6	24.9	14.0	4.5	27.0
Durability	37.0	19.4	13.6	6.9	4.9	18.2
Finish on wooden parts	5.8	14.7	16.7	10.7	16.7	35.4
Price	19.4	21.8	16.0	10.9	15.4	16.5
Manufacturer's reputation	4.2	9.1	15.4	22.9	14.3	34.1
Retailer's reputation	2.2	4.7	10.5	21.2	26.5	34.9

EXHIBIT 2 (Continued)

Question: Listed below are some statements others have made about their homes and the furniture pieces they particularly like. Please indicate, for each statement, how much you agree or disagree with each one. (Base 449)

Statement	Agree Completely	Agree Somewhat	Neither Agree nor Disagree	Disagree Somewhat	Disagree Completely	NA
I wish there was some way to be really sure of getting good-quality in furniture	61.9%	24.7%	4.7%	4.2%	3.6%	.9%
I really enjoy shopping for furniture	49.2	28.3	7.6	9.8	4.2	.9
I would never buy any furniture without my husband's/wife's approval	47.0	23.0	10.9	9.8	7.1	2.2
I like all the pieces in the master bedroom to be exactly the same style	35.9	30.7	12.7	11.1	7.6	2.0
Once I find something I like in furniture, I wish it would last forever so I'd never have to buy again	36.8	24.3	10.0	18.9	9.1	.9
I wish I had more confidence in my ability to decorate my home attractively	23.1	32.3	12.5	11.6	18.7	1.8
I wish I knew more about furniture styles and what looks good	20.0	31.0	17.1	13.4	16.7	1.8
My husband/wife doesn't take much interest in the furniture we buy	6.5	18.0	12.3	17.8	41.4	4.0
I like to collect a number of different styles in the dining room	3.3	10.5	15.2	29.8	38.3	2.9
Shopping for furniture is very distressing to me	2.4	11.6	14.3	18.0	51.9	1.8

Question: Listed below are some factors that may influence your choice of furnishings, 1 being most important, 2 being second most important, and so on until all factors have been ranked. (Base 449)

	1	2	3	4	5	No Answer
Friends and/or neighbors	1.3%	16.9%	15.8%	22.1%	41.7%	2.2%
Family or spouse	62.8	9.4	14.3	9.8	2.0	1.7
Magazine advertising	16.3	30.3	29.6	17.6	4.2	2.0
Television advertising	1.1	6.7	14.7	32.5	42.3	2.7
Store displays	18.9	37.2	22.1	14.0	5.6	2.2

Question: When you go shopping for a *major* piece of furniture or other smaller pieces of furniture, who, if anyone, do you usually go with? (Base 449—multiple response)

	Major Pieces	Other Pieces
Husband	82.4%	59.5%
Mother or mother-in-law	6.2	9.1
Friend	12.0	18.9
Decorator	4.2	1.6
Other relative	15.6	15.4
Other person	2.9	3.3
No one else	5.1	22.3
No answer	.9	3.1

Question: When the time comes to purchase a *major* item of furniture or other smaller pieces of furniture, who, if anyone, helps you make the final decision about which piece to buy? (Base 449—multiple response)

	Major Pieces	Other Pieces
Husband	86.0%	63.5%
Mother or mother-in-law	2.4	4.5
Friend	3.6	8.0
Decorator	3.1	2.7
Other relative	10.1	12.9
Other person	1.6	1.8
No one else	7.1	24.3
No answer	.9	2.2

[a] Survey interviews were conducted using shopping center intercepts at five cities throughout the United States. A total of 449 responses were obtained in the survey.

Bates interrupted the dialogue between Bott and Hervey to mention that the $400,000 increase in promotion exceeded the 5 percent percentage-of-sales policy by $25,000. He pointed out that materials cost plus a recent wage increase were forecast to squeeze Shanandoah's gross profit margin and threaten the company's objective of achieving a 5 percent net profit margin before taxes. "Perhaps some juggling of the figures is necessary," he concluded. "Both of you have good points. Let me think about what's been said and then let's schedule a meeting for a week from today."

As Bates reviewed his notes from the meeting, he realized that the funds allocated to promotion were only part of the question. How the funds would be allocated within the budget was also crucial. Perhaps a call to Tom Berry would be helpful in this regard, he thought.

CASE 2-3   SALES MANAGEMENT SIMULATION

The Sales Management Simulation (5th ed.) is a computer game in which you operate a sales force in competition with other firms in a search for fame and fortune. SMS allows you to select salespeople, set prices, and make other decisions during each round of game play. Your decisions are processed on a computer, and you will receive regular printouts showing the impact of your choices on sales, profits, and customer satisfaction.

THE SELLING ENVIRONMENT

The sales force is the primary focus in this simulation game. Thus, performance in the simulated environment depends on your skill in selecting high-quality salespersons and deploying them effectively over the various regions of the country. Although the products and advertising are the same for all teams, you may adjust your prices, sales force compensation levels, sales contests, and market research requests each period of play.

THE INDUSTRY

Your team will act as the managers of the sales force of one of three to five companies making up the industry. All companies are independent divisions of large firms in the mushrooming office machine industry. The firms manufacture and sell two models of computer servers that are designed for a variety of industrial and consumer markets.

THE PRODUCT

Many offices are buying network servers to improve communications efficiency. These machines are special computers that allow networks of personal computers to communicate with each other. The basic model will handle networks with 50 machines and the advanced model will work with up to 100 machines.

Each of the companies in this simulation has announced an initial price of $3,500 for its basic machine and $5,500 for its advanced model. There will be no quantity or cash discounts. The purchase price from manufacturing divisions is initially $3,000 for the basic unit and $4,000 for the premium model. This transfer price is based on full overhead and administrative expenses and a contribution by manufacturing to the corporate overhead and profit. The gross margins retained by the Sales Department must cover all compensation and expenses of the sales force, transportation costs, and inventory or expediting costs and generate a contribution from sales operations to corporate overhead and profit.

This simulation was developed by Professor Douglas J. Dalrymple of Indiana University, Professor Harish Sujan of Penn State University, and the late Professor Emeritus Ralph Day of Indiana University.

THE MARKET

The market for your product is divided into 10 clearly defined geographic regions. Your plant and national headquarters are located in the Midwest. All shipments are made directly to the customer from the factory by motor freight to eliminate the need for regional warehouses. Industry practice calls for the seller to pay the freight, and in your company the Sales Department pays for shipping.

The servers you will sell are potentially useful in a variety of offices that are widely, but far from uniformly, dispersed throughout the country. You can expect that many firms will first experiment with one or two units before considering wider uses of the machines for their offices. Also, customers can choose from among a half-dozen server suppliers with similar products and prices. Therefore, server salespersons must have a good grasp of their product's features, have an understanding of office problems, be skilled in selling, and have the drive and persistence to handle the "tough-close" situations they are likely to encounter.

THE SALES FORCE

To get into the market quickly, an initial sales force of ten salespersons will be hired and trained on an emergency basis. Highly qualified salespersons will be sought and given a brief but intensive training program prior to the beginning of the first quarter of sales operations. They will be provided unusually close support from the field sales managers and technical people from the factory during the first quarter. All salespeople beyond the initial ten will be required to complete a three-month training program consisting of two months of training in the headquarters and factory and one month in the field. Training programs will start at the beginning of a quarter so that graduates can be assigned to a territory at the beginning of the following quarter.

Up to five salespersons can be either hired for training or retrained in each quarter. This means up to five trainees may be hired at the same time as the initial ten salespersons. The student manual for the game contains 55 application forms from those applicants who passed an initial screening by the corporate personnel manager. A number of applicants who lacked the basic communications skills required for selling and/or lacked the background education needed to acquire the skills used in selling servers were rejected by the personnel manager. The personnel manager's evaluation after each interview is provided for each application. Applicants in the first group of 20 who are passed over are generally *not* available for the following quarter. Instead, a new group of five applicants (for up to five positions) will be made available each quarter.

GAME PERFORMANCE

Students enjoy playing the Sales Management Simulation because of its competitive interactions and its realism. How well you do depends on the quality of your decisions as well as those of your competitors. Performance of individual companies is usually measured by sales revenue, profits, and market share. Instructors compare performance across firms to determine the grades to be assigned to each simulation team.

Sales performance depends on your team's skill in selecting and assigning salespersons, your choices in setting prices, and the amounts spent on sales contests. Performance as reflected by cumulative net profit will depend on the team's ability to control costs as well as its ability to obtain sales. The most common error teams make is to cut prices sharply to increase volume without considering the impact on profits. Additional information on the operating rules of the game is available in the student manual.

Copies of the Sales Management Simulation Participant's Manual (5th ed.) and the SMS Instructor's Manual with the game diskette can be obtained from:

John Wiley & Sons
605 Third Avenue
New York, NY 10158

Telephone inquiries concerning the SMS should be made to:

Cynthia Snyder, Editorial Assistant
John Wiley & Sons
605 Third Avenue
New York, NY 10158
(212) 850-6515

PERSONAL SELLING

> People are more apt to buy when they're talking than when you're talking!
>
> ROBERT FROST

Chapter Consultants:
S. Keith Hall, Area Manager, Anderson Chemical Company, Inc.
Neil Cronin, Regional Sales Manager, John Wiley & Sons, Inc.
William Evans, President, Evans & Associates

LEARNING OBJECTIVES

After studying this chapter, you should be able to:

→ Describe the basic types of selling approaches.

→ Describe the skills utilized in the preinteraction phase of the selling process.

→ List the skills involved in the interaction phase of the selling process.

→ Explain the skills involved in the postinteraction phase of the selling process.

AN ELECTRONIC SOS

Exxon Chemical Co. wanted a software-development tool that would help it blend off-the-shelf software packages with the oil giant's custom business applications. Project manager Ed Baugh, head of the sales team for CAP Gemini Sogeti, a French computer-services giant, was aware that his customer had for five months combed the market without finding a solution to their problem. Baugh's sales team had also determined that building the tool from scratch would take at least 18 months, too long for Exxon's needs.

Hoping CAP Gemini's 17,000 software engineers and technicians might have a lead, Baugh sent out an electronic SOS across the company intranet. Forty-eight hours later, an engineer with CAP Gemini's British unit responded that he knew of a software tool that might be tailored to meet Exxon's needs. Within three weeks, Baugh presented a solution to Exxon and clinched a hefty development contract.[1]

The CAP Gemini sale described above is indicative of how sales is changing today. A sales team is frequently involved rather than a single salesperson. Sales force automation is often key to success. Addressing a critical customer solution often requires marshaling diverse resources within the selling company. It is for these reasons that some people feel that selling will never be the same.

Before we talk further about sales management, it is vital that you have a general understanding of personal selling. Sales managers are usually promoted from field sales and, as we noted in the first chapter, are often expected to spend part of their time (29 percent on average) selling. In addition, sales managers need selling skills in order to train, coach, and evaluate field sales personnel, and earn their respect.

This chapter is designed to provide you with a basic understanding of the selling process. One thing you should recognize is that a business-to-business sale rarely occurs in one sales call between a supplier and a customer, but is likely to result from multiple interactions between the two parties. Accordingly, we have adopted an appropriate terminology. For discussion purposes, we have divided the selling process into three phases:

- **Preinteraction.** Actions that are initiated prior to interaction with key decision makers requiring skills in precall planning.
- **Interaction.** Actions initiated while interacting with decision makers, calling on skills in relating, discovery, advocating, handling objections, and closing.
- **Postinteraction.** Activities following a transaction involving supporting skills.

This chapter takes a skills-based approach to selling. The three phases of selling and the skills associated with each phase are specified in Figure 3-1.

It is important to note that these steps are ordered in a logical sequence for discussion purposes. The actual process may backtrack to earlier phases many times before concluding in a sale. These phases are highly interrelated, and it may be difficult to specify the exact

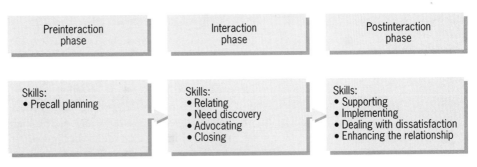

FIGURE 3-1   Phases and Steps of the Selling Process

step at a specific point in a sale. Finally, it should be recognized that the process is not necessarily completed in a single sales call.

As we discuss each skill, we will point out its purpose, as well as strategies for achieving these objectives. In many cases, common mistakes to be avoided are also highlighted. Throughout the discussion, company practices and viewpoints of sales executives have been included to facilitate your learning. After you have achieved a basic understanding of the selling process, sales force automation is discussed. First, different basic types of selling approaches are discussed.

BASIC TYPES OF SELLING APPROACHES

Sales consultants have devised numerous titles or labels for the selling approaches they teach, but most are based on one of the following basic selling process models: standardized, need-satisfaction, and problem-solution. Each approach is appropriate in certain situations and for different types of account relationships. Accompanying a description of these sales approaches is an analysis of situations and relationships in which each is most efficient and effective.

Standardized Approach

With a *standardized presentation,* a series of statements are constructed about an offering, so as to stimulate a positive response by the customer. This is often referred to as *benefitizing* an offering. Benefitizing means translating features of a product into benefits believed to be of value to the customer. A benefit of a new software package, for example, may be the ease with which it can be learned by employees. At an extreme, specific statements are developed using phrases that tend to elicit a positive response. These may include words such as *user-friendly, satisfaction guaranteed, productivity improvement,* and *no money down.* The ease-of-learning benefit may be stated as "Clear, easy-to-follow, step-by-step instructions containing no confusing buzzwords." This is referred to as a *canned presentation* because the same basic presentation is given to each customer.

The standardized approach is most appropriate in situations where a product is standardized or when the benefits are generally the same for all customers. In such a situation, the sales pitch can be studied and refined to such a degree that even voice tone can be studied for its impact on sales.[2] Recalling our discussion in Chapter 2 of different types of account relationships, this type of selling approach would be most appropriate for transactional relationships in which the customer is concerned about lowest cost and convenience.

Because standardized sales presentations are easiest to learn, they are also used in cases where the sales force is relatively inexperienced and employee turnover is high. Such is the case with many direct marketing organizations such as Mary Kay Cosmetics, Cutco, and Avon Products. This also helps to ensure uniform, high-quality presentations. This selling approach is particularly dangerous, however, when listening to customers is necessary to enhance the relationship.

Need-Satisfaction

A *need-satisfaction presentation* is oriented to discovering and meeting customers' needs. Needs discovery is achieved by skillfully asking questions that will elicit a customer's buying needs. This type of selling requires more selling skill because if it is not tactfully handled, customers may become irritated by the questions or find them intrusive. Needs discovery takes place early in the selling cycle, often during the first call, and replaces the presentation as the most important step in the selling process.

A needs-satisfaction selling model is most appropriate when two conditions exist: when *the dollar value of the sale is significant enough* to cover the added time required by the selling process, and when *different benefits need to be emphasized* for different customers. An office manager of a law firm, for example, is likely to look for different reproduction qualities in a laser-jet printer than would an administrator of a school district. In both cases, a salesperson would need to investigate the nature of the documents to be produced, along with the capabilities of their present printers. The sales force must be trained to ask the right questions to uncover customer needs that will lead to a purchase decision. The general line sales forces of most consumer goods and office products companies are trained to use this selling model. The key is to develop good listening skills, as opposed to concentrating on how to respond to what the customer is saying. Overall, the need-satisfaction type of selling approach is most appropriate for consultative-type customer relationships. Both the customer and the supplier are investing more time and resources in the relationship than is typical of transactional relationships.

Problem-Solution

A *problem-solution presentation* is similar to the need-satisfaction method in that both involve an analysis of each customer's circumstances. The primary difference is that a problem-solution selling process is based on more formal studies of the customer's operations. Instead of identifying the customer's needs on the first sales call, the early selling objective is to get the customer's permission to conduct a formal study. The sales rep or sales team will conduct the study and typically submit a written proposal based on the study. A formal presentation, perhaps by a team including a salesperson, management, and technical personnel, often accompanies the proposal.

This selling model usually involves very significant dollar expenditures, and the selling cycle may be quite long. The types of products being sold by this selling approach include computer systems, advertising campaigns, telecommunications systems, and information systems. The problem analysis study may be so involved that the customer may be asked to pay to have it performed. EDS's customers for instance, may be asked to pay several hundred thousand dollars for a study of their computer systems to determine if EDS can help them. It is not unusual for clients to pay several advertising agencies to research and prepare a proposed ad campaign before deciding which agency will be awarded the account. As is probably obvious from this description and the EDS example, a problem-solution selling approach is most appropriate for the enterprise type of relationships where there is a very high investment in the relationship by both the seller and the buyer.

Which is the best selling approach? There is no unequivocal answer to this question. The most appropriate approach will depend, among other factors, on the offering, the professionalism of the sales force, the dollar value of the transaction, and the type of customer relationship involved. With small chains or individual grocery stores, for example, Procter & Gamble may use a needs-satisfaction selling style, but with major accounts such as Wal-Mart, a problem-solution approach may be most appropriate.

In the next section of this chapter, the skills associated with each phase of the selling process are presented. These skills are considered to be fundamental to all types of selling approaches and account relationships, but the level of skill development becomes greater as one moves toward problem-solving selling and enterprise relationships. Much of the discussion that follows is based on the Counselor selling method developed by Wilson Learning.

PREINTERACTION PHASE: PRECALL PLANNING SKILLS

As the term *precall planning* implies, this stage occurs when you collect your thoughts and organize your sales strategy prior to meeting the buyer face to face. A recommended approach to precall planning is to ask yourself a series of questions.

FIGURE 3-2   Some Important Pretransactional Information

What Do I Want to Accomplish?

Many selling experts have stated simply that salespeople should not make a call unless they can specify an *action* that they want the client or prospect to take. Don't set a vague objective such as "to collect information" or "to build a good relationship." Here are some examples of good objectives:

- The client agrees to supply information on historical inventory levels.
- The client tells you who will be involved in the purchase decision.
- The client arranges for a meeting with the chief design engineer.
- The client agrees to a trial run on the system.

Note that each of these examples calls for the customer to take a specific action. Objectives should be stated in terms of actions so that the salesperson will know whether the objectives have been met. Also, note that the first two objectives involve gathering information.

In more complex selling situations involving multiple calls over a period of time, a customer action objective may be more subtle. For example, it may take a number of calls to understand a customer's needs, identify the key decision-influencers, and fully educate a buyer on the benefits of the product. Alternatively, you may be calling to ensure that the customer is satisfied after the sale or to handle a specific customer complaint.

What Do I Know About the Customer?

Precall planning is also a good opportunity to review information about buyers and their company relevant to achieving your sales objective. Basic information that may be useful to know about an individual includes exact spelling and pronunciation of their name, title, age, residence, education, buying authority, clubs and memberships, hobbies, and idiosyncrasies. The experience of a medical equipment salesperson illustrates the value of this information. The salesperson was finding it very difficult to persuade doctors at the hospital to allow him to make a presentation. The doctors were usually pressured for time while at the hospital and were concerned about their immediate patients. He found out that many of the doctors belonged to a health club near the hospital, and that in this environment they were more relaxed and willing to listen to his sales pitch. He eventually became the top salesperson in his district—and an accomplished racquetball player.

Not only is personal information important, but you should also review what you know or do not know about the buyer's organization. Figure 3-2 lists of some of the questions that a salesperson should be able to answer about a customer. This information is often critical when planning a presentation and when demonstrating competency, trust, and commitment to the buyer.

Where Can I Find the Information?

When you know what information you need to make a successful sales call, you can usually identify a number of sources for obtaining the data. These sources include company records, salespeople, customer employees, published information, and observation. Observation of the prospect's business operations provides a wealth of information to the experienced salesperson. By observing a prospect's retail operations, for instance, a veteran consumer goods salesperson can tell a lot about a buyer's pricing strategy, merchandising strategy, vendor preferences, and deal proneness.

The Internet is a powerful source of information, ranging from customer information to competitive information to industry information. For instance, you can obtain information about industry trade associations and a list of companies in different industries at *www.mfginfo.com.* Several other locations on the Web are excellent for identifying and locating prospects (e.g., *www.switchboard.com*).[3]

Customer Relationship Management Software (CRM)   The purpose of customer relationship management software is to ensure that every person from a supplier's organization (most important, the salesperson) who comes into contact with a customer has access to all the latest information on a customer and that the information is relevant, accurate, and up-to-date. In other words, the purpose of this software is to eliminate the "islands of information" that have developed in most companies, allowing people to share information easily. For example, CRM software can provide salespeople with accurate and timely leads from telemarketing, as well as with information about specific needs that a prospective customer might have expressed. Or it can give an account manager access to a customer's entire sales and service history—including the flurry of phone calls that took place just a few days ago—so that he or she isn't caught off-guard when making the big pitch to the customer's CEO. Because enhancing the customer's experience of doing business is so important, CRM software sales are expected to grow by a compounded annual rate of 44 percent over the next three years.[4]

So what information is stored on these programs? Almost all CRM programs start with a customer's sales and service history. In addition, they may track every conversation, every letter, and every contact that occurs between the supplier and a customer. They also provide a source of information about the customer's operations, including equipment used, type of manufacturing processes, all the customer information that may be relevant to making a customer needs assessment and sale. Not all the information is about the customer's business, however. Some CRM programs also include information on people who are key decision makers and influencers in the account. For instance, the Brooklyn Union Gas CRM system will track information on architects, landlords, and real estate agents. Although generating customer information is important, having timely access to the information is also critical.

What Am I Going to Say?

All salespeople should have at least some idea of how they will initially start the sales presentation, what questions they will ask, and what benefits they plan to present. Salespeople should anticipate concerns a customer is likely to raise and prepare strategies for addressing these concerns.

When preparing to call on clients, it is helpful to put yourself in their position. What would you want to know about your company and its products if you were the buyer? If you are prepared to address such questions, you are probably ready for the call and have a much better chance of success. Figure 3-3 shows some of the questions a client may have about you and your company when there is no prior experience on which to rely. Note that although these questions may be in the client's mind, they are often not asked because they expect a good salesperson to address these questions without requiring them to be asked by the customer. Therefore not addressing these questions may prevent a sale if they are left unanswered.

One other suggestion that has proven useful in a variety of situations is to visualize a successful sales encounter. This technique simply means creating a mental picture of the sequence of events that will lead to accomplishing your call objective. With practice, this exercise should help you to reduce your anxieties and increase your confidence.

THE INTERACTION PHASE

The *interaction phase* generally refers to what takes place during a face-to-face encounter with a customer. Our discussion of this phase of the selling process focuses on three skills that are important in all business and social interactions: relating, discovering, and advocating. In addition, there are two skills that are critical to successful selling in certain situations: gaining access and closing. Gaining access to key personnel is very important when calling on prospects (i.e., businesses that have never purchased from your company). Closing the sale is a necessary step in all selling situations, but is most problematic during transactional selling and in stimulus-response type of selling. We start with a discussion of gaining access.

FIGURE 3-3   A Buyer's Questions

Gaining Access

Usually, it is fairly easy to get appointments with established customers, but it can be much more difficult when prospecting, especially with the senior officers of a company. Following are three commonly used alternatives for gaining access to decision makers.

Direct Personal Contact   The most difficult approach occurs when the sales call is the first meeting and no prior attempts have been made to communicate with the prospect. In making a personal visit, the salesperson has the opportunity to check out the facilities of the prospect and to become better prepared to talk with the buyer. However, problems are likely to arise. For example, the person may be busy, so the salesperson must wait. The key is not to waste the time. Use this opportunity to learn more about the prospect from others in the organization, prepare for other scheduled calls, or complete necessary reports. A more difficult problem is the buyer's negative reaction to being called on without an appointment. Many purchasing agents do not like to meet with a salesperson who walks in without an appointment. Indeed, many clients simply will not see you without an appointment.

Phoning Ahead   Using the telephone to approach prospects has a number of advantages. Appointments make better use of the salesperson's time and reduce the hours spent in waiting rooms. Even prospects who are too busy to see anyone often will answer the phone and give salespeople a chance to introduce themselves and set up a future meeting. The major problem with a phone approach is that it is too easy for prospects or their secretaries to turn someone down over the telephone. Salespeople, therefore, must develop tactics to secure the cooperation of switchboard operators and receptionists. Referring to buyers by their first name, for example, implies familiarity with the buyer.

Phone contacts are quite common with current clients. Recall the discussion in Chapter 1 about the time sales managers spend selling and that almost half of the selling time occurs over the phone. A special problem that arises both with new and existing customers is leaving voice messages. In today's business world the most likely outcome of a phone call is getting someone's voice message center. Veteran salespeople will tell you that there are several rules to keep in mind when leaving voice messages. First, keep the message as short as

---

SELF-MANAGEMENT COMPETENCY
"You're Not Prepared! You Don't Listen! You Promised!"

One of the better methods for self-learning is learning from the mistakes of others. In this case a panel of purchasing executives was asked to comment on some of the typical gaffes they had seen salespeople commit. Following are some excerpts from their responses: "The first rule of selling is to know how your product or service impacts or adds value to your client," stated Jeri Sessler of A.T. Kearney in Illinois. "If you don't know anything about your client and have no conception of how your offering can be employed by him or her, you have no right to be there." "There are times when salespeople just won't let their clients talk," noted Gary Slavin, president of Multimedia Marketing, Inc. "The salesperson thinks it's more important for him or her to be heard. They don't realize how important listening is in determining the needs of their customer. Consequently, they wind up talking themselves out of a sale." "I've seen many salespeople who over-promise the delivery of their product and simply don't follow up enough," said Maria DiNuzzo of John H. Harland Company. "To avoid this, I suggest they develop a contact sheet of all their accounts in order to make sure they call each one periodically and see them as often as possible." See *www.atkearney.com, www.amtexpo.com* and *www.harland.net.*

possible. State your name at the beginning and again near the end of the message, and always repeat your phone number. Also, state your phone number slowly, slower indeed than you think is necessary.

Personal Letters   The first approach to a prospect may be made by means of a personal letter. Letters are more difficult than phone calls for the secretary to screen. In addition, letters allow the person to include brochures that describe the product assortment and benefits, enabling prospects to learn more about a potential supplier than they can over the phone. Approach letters should close by suggesting dates for a meeting. This may also be accomplished by a follow-up phone call. In doing so, the salesperson focuses the prospect's attention on the issue of *when* to meet rather than *whether* to meet.

E-mail Messages   An increasingly common method of communications, whether with new or existing clients, is to leave an e-mail message. E-mail messages have at least two advantages over voice messages. First, it is possible to send the message at very little cost in time or money to a large number of people to whom the same message is applicable. Second, graphics and detailed promotional material may be included with the message as an attachment to the main message. Many of the same rules of thumb that were mentioned with respect to leaving voice messages also apply to e-mail messages. In particular, the body of the message should be kept as short as possible. It is not unusual for busy executives to receive 50 to 100 e-mail messages a day, and deleting an e-mail message is easier and faster than erasing a voice message. There is also the problem of communicating effectively via e-mail. Grammatical and spelling errors are quite common in e-mail messages. Also a lot of information is communicated by how you say something in addition to the actual words you may use. This communication is lost when using e-mail. A new service from Onebox.com addresses this issue by allowing you to record an audio message to send in an e-mail. You can describe your new services or products to your customers by recording one message and e-mailing it to all of them. All anyone needs to listen to the message is computer speakers. To record messages, you need a microphone. Onebox.com is a free service, so try it.

Relating Skills

In most social situations, there is a degree of tension or defensiveness when people meet for the first time. This defensiveness, referred to as *relationship anxiety,* is especially likely to occur when meeting a salesperson.[5] This anxiety arises because people don't like to be sold, they like to buy. In one sense, the role of the salesperson is to help the customer buy wisely. This calls for well-developed *relating skills,* which refers to the ability to put the other person at ease in a potentially tense situation. The first few moments of the selling encounter are important because people formulate initial impressions at this time. Buyers formulate impressions about salespeople's competence, trustworthiness, and likability based largely on nonverbal visual cues. To help establish rapport, salespeople should be forthcoming about the purpose of the sales call. Many experts, for example, admonish salespeople to avoid asking "How are you?" because this question is meaningless and contrary to what the salesperson should be, which is genuinely helpful and direct.[6] A good idea is to hand the prospect a business card and introduce yourself. As a result, the prospect then can both see and hear the salesperson's name. A sample introduction might go as follows: "Hello, Mr. Smith, I am Mary Johnson of the Hamilton Company, and I am here today to see if we can help you save money on your duplicating budget." Ms. Johnson tells who she is, the purpose of the visit, and that she plans to focus on a possible customer benefit (lower costs). Many salespeople prefer to use this type of opening. It is simple, direct, and informative.

Propriety	Show buyer respect; dress appropriately
Competence	Know your product/service; third-party references
Commonality	Common interests, views, acquaintances
Intent	Reveal purpose of call, process, and payoff to the buyer

FIGURE 3-4 Means of Reducing Relationship Anxiety

Although nonbusiness topics are often discussed initially in the selling process, this is not always the case. The buyer may be more concerned with getting down to business if they are interested in what a salesperson has to say, because they feel that the salesperson could help them in their business. They may also respect the salesperson's time demands. Discussing nonbusiness issues may be seen as a waste of time and the person judged as being someone who cannot provide solutions to the buyer's business problems. The message is clear: Don't overdo the nonbusiness pleasantries before getting down to business. If the customer gives signals that he or she is pressed for time, then get on with the call. The key is to be flexible and focus on the other person.

Much more is involved in demonstrating relating skills than simply getting a dialogue started between you and the buyer. Figure 3-4 discusses four strategies by which salespeople can reduce relationship tension. It is critical that salespeople utilize each of these means to reduce tension when meeting with a prospect. With established customers a relationship already exists; thus many of the rules of the relationship are already set. However, salespeople should constantly strive to reinforce these impressions.[7]

NEEDS DISCOVERY SKILLS

After establishing initial rapport with the prospect, the salesperson should begin a customer *needs discovery*. Many experts claim that what makes a great salesperson is the ability to forget about the product and try to understand what's in the prospective buyer's mind. This seems counterintuitive, but it's true. Remember, customers do not buy products or services, they buy solutions that address problems or enhance opportunities. Contractors do not want a bulldozer; they want dirt moved quickly and at low cost. Plant managers do not buy computer-controlled milling machines; they are interested in reduced setup time, closer tolerances, and fewer defects. Thus the salesperson's job is to discover the true needs and then inform the prospect about the characteristics, capabilities, and availability of goods and services that can address these needs.[8]

Research has shown that there is a direct relationship between the number of needs a salesperson uncovers and selling success. A study by Xerox of more than 500 sales calls revealed that successful sales calls contained three times more identified needs than failed calls.

What you perceive as being a good relationship and a distinct set of customer needs is not enough to make the sale. The buyer must also perceive the same needs.[9] Recommending a solution that the buyer does not perceive or does not rank high in importance will fall on deaf ears. In fact, this recommendation will probably hinder further progress toward a sale because buyers may conclude that you do not really understand their situation. Therefore, needs discovery is much more than just matching your products or services to your perception of the buyer's needs. Needs discovery is about understanding the buyer's perceptions of his or her needs. In the new model of personal selling in today's business environment, *80 percent of the selling process focuses on discovering and matching customer needs.*[10] Indeed, this is one of the goals of enterprise relationships; that is, to become so intimate and

---

STRATEGIC ACTION COMPETENCY
Enron Energy Services

Enron Corporation's latest energy start-up is Enron Energy Services (EES). In 1996 EES sold next to nothing, but within three years the 170 person sales team's sales topped $8 billion. Enron Corporation is known for providing natural gas and electricity, but also for starting new energy businesses that turn out to be enormous. EES is simply the latest in a long line of successful ventures.

Enron's sales team sells long-term outsource energy solutions. Essentially, they ask businesses to turn all their energy management needs over to Enron. That includes letting Enron supply both the commodity (the power that keeps the lights on), and the funding and maintenance of all the interior workings: the boilers, chillers, heating, ventilation, and air conditioning equipment—basically, any piece of equipment you might see James Bond crawling around in.

All this began when Enron discovered that companies actually spend far more on what they refer to as the private utility, all that energy equipment inside their facilities (and the employees who maintain it), than they do paying for the gas and electricity. So the market for Enron's services is even bigger than executives anticipated. The business-to-business commodity market is estimated to be worth $120 billion and the market for energy-related services to the private utility to be worth an additional $120 billion.

Central to Enron's service offering is the financing of the deals. The company will actually invest money up front in a customer's energy equipment, or they can write a check for a lump sum worth what customers will save through the duration of the outsourcing contract. Customers can then reinvest that capital in their core businesses. One Enron salesperson describes the company as a combination investment bank, consulting firm, and energy business. For more on Enron see *www.enron.com*.

---

knowledgeable about the customer's business that the intimacy becomes a barrier to entry for your competitors. Enron Corporation took intimate customer knowledge one step further when it discovered that customers spend more on the energy equipment inside their facilities than they do paying for the gas and electricity. Enron's response was to start up a new company called Enron Energy Services. See the Strategic Action Competency box for more information.

Identifying Motives

In selling to other businesses, the situation is complicated because both task and personal motives influence the purchasing decision. *Task motives* can be defined as the logical, practical, or functional reasons for buying. They usually involve either money or productivity. Typical financial motives may include cost savings or profit increases. Productivity motives may involve increasing output, increasing quality, or reducing effort. Organizations tend to emphasize different task issues in their culture, so it is important for salespeople to understand these tendencies.[11]

At the same time, people will have personal motives for purchasing a product or service. Personal motives are the individual preferences that spur a person to buy. They are generally psychological in nature and involve relationships with other people. *Personal motives* include the need for respect, approval, power, and recognition. The *respect*-oriented buyer wants to demonstrate and prove his or her expertise. These buyers are interested in research that not only supports your product or service, but also reinforces the work they have already done. Buyers focusing on *approval* want to be sure that those affected by the decision to buy will be pleased. They are responsive to products or services that reduce conflict and provide minimum risk. Buyers interested in *power* are seeking ways to gain greater control over some real, practical aspect of their situation. Products or services that will enable them to make quicker decisions, choose from among more options, or get desired results in a better way will be most appealing. For some buyers, the desire for *recognition* is the dominant personal motive. They are interested in products or services that give them greater visibility and provide opportunities to demonstrate their leadership ability. These people are often unique or innovative in their approach to problem solving. Although respect and approval motives are somewhat timid and defensive, power and recognition are fairly aggressive in nature.

It is important for a salesperson to identify these personal motives for each person involved in the buying process. Discovery of personal motives is challenging because the buyer rarely states them. In many cases, buyers may be reluctant to share their personal agendas because of their political sensitivity in the organization and because people are often reluctant to share these personal insights. Nevertheless, you must infer these motives from the actions and statements of the buyer.

Many companies have problems in getting close enough to the customer to make the necessary inferences. Anderson Chemical Company, a manufacturer of specialty chemicals and related equipment, has experienced success in what it refers to as its Back-up Vendor program. To write a proposal or price quote on prospect's business, Anderson needs to know the technical data about the plant. The facility engineers, however, must have confidence in Anderson or have other motives for supplying the data. This is where the Back-up Vendor program has worked well. Most prospects see no harm in allowing Anderson to come into their plant site and perform surveys, tests, and such, and provide information to them free of charge. In effect, Anderson offers a second opinion about their operation. This is done very professionally and without "throwing rocks" at the current vendor. The prospect becomes more familiar with and confident in the Anderson representative over the 6- to 18-month period the program is in effect. This is a large investment on Anderson's part, but Anderson estimates that its success rate in converting prospects improves from approximately 10 to 60 percent when using the Back-up Vendor program.

Questioning

Discovering a customer's perceived needs naturally involves asking *questions* and actively *listening* to the customer's responses. Asking questions is not as easy as it may first appear. Not only do you want to know perceived needs, but you want to obtain the information in a way that does not irritate or alienate buyers and helps them to better understand their own needs.

Questions may be classified as closed-ended or open-ended. *Closed-ended questions* can be answered with a simple "yes" or "no" or by selecting from a list of responses. "Would you like delivery Friday, or is Monday of next week all right?" These questions are easy to answer, and are used to gain buyer feedback and commitment. *Open-ended questions* cannot be answered with a simple "yes" or "no" and are used to identify a topic. "How are the new tax laws affecting your decision regarding the purchase of fleet cars for your salespeople?"

Sales experts have identified several types of questions that may be used in the discovery process.

- **Permission.** This closed-ended questioning technique involves asking the buyer's permission to ask questions or to probe further into a subject. It is designed to put the buyer at ease and observe social courtesies. "May I ask you a few questions about your current shipping process?"

- **Fact finding.** These are questions that focus on factual information about the business, the person, and the current situation. Factual information might include a question such as: "Who is your current supplier of sutures?" A follow-up question about the buyer's current situation might be: "Do you have a JIT arrangement with Ethicon in supplying sutures?"
- **Feeling finding.** These are open-ended questions that try to uncover the buyer's feelings about a situation and the potential consequences of the situation. These inquiries help to determine the buyer's perceptions and the importance of the need. "How do you feel about your current inventory levels in sutures?" "What effect does this level of inventory have on your operating costs?"
- **Checking.** At this point, the seller is checking to see if he or she understands exactly what the buyer has said and to get the buyer's agreement concerning the statement. "If I understand you correctly, you have said that you are happy with the quality of your current supplier but feel that you may be able to get the same quality of service at a lower price from another supplier. Is that accurate?" This type of question may result in an open or closed type of answer.

Discovering a customer's needs usually requires a series of questions. This process usually begins with a *permission question* and *open-ended questions,* followed *by fact-finding* and *feeling-finding questions* and *checking questions.*

Effective salespeople are also good listeners. This means that they are actively involved in listening to the buyer (e.g., by nodding in agreement, smiling, taking notes). However, active listening means more than engaging in these nonverbal cues. For instance, salespeople should not focus solely on their own response to the buyer's statement, but rather on hearing all that the buyer said or did not say. Indeed, research suggests that the odds of success increase if the customer states a problem, as opposed to the seller stating the problem. This requires a series of questions based on the buyer's responses and the implications of the responses.[12]

Companies that uncover customers' real needs are in a better position to fill them. Consider again the Exxon sale discussed at the beginning of the chapter. The CAP Gemini Sogeti sales team not only needed to know that Exxon was actively seeking a software integration solution, but that an immediate solution was needed.

Team Selling

With today's more complex problems and solutions, the execution of the discovery process is also changing. Now a team of people may be involved in the process of discovering and providing solutions to customer needs. At Allegiance, Inc. a person called a sales generalist may be responsible for discovering customer problems and needs. Owing to the breadth and technical complexity of Allegiance's product lines, the sales generalist can call on people known as a surgical generalist, an I.V. systems generalist, a distribution generalist, and a variety of product specialists to uncover and address customer needs. In other words, Allegiance is organized to discover and meet different levels of customer needs.

Advocating

Following the discovery of customer needs, the skill that takes on critical significance is advocating. *Advocating skills* refer to the ability to clearly and fully present a solution that customers can see helps to address their needs. In this section, two aspects of advocating are considered: (1) presenting a specific solution to a problem, and (2) addressing customer concerns regarding the solution being proposed.

Solution Presentation   The objective of a solution presentation is to convince the customer that the goods and services which are offered match the customer's requirements and satisfy his or her needs. It is very important to remember, however, that the purpose of the sales presentation isn't just for your prospects to understand what you are selling. The sales presentation should make them visualize the end-result benefits—how your product or service will satisfy their task and personal needs.[13]

A sales presentation is primarily a discussion of a series of product features connected with benefits that the buyer has indicated are important during the previous needs discovery stage, and is followed by evidence that the benefits will in fact be delivered. *Features* are tangible or intangible characteristics of the product or service. For example, a feature of a long-distance telephone service may be that billings are based on one-tenth of a minute rather than the usual full-minute increments. This feature may be emphasized because the task motive of this buyer is judged to be cost savings. A benefit is a statement about how a product or service can help a customer satisfy an explicit or stated need. Therefore, the salesperson may state the benefit of the previous billing feature in the following terms: "What this means is that on a call of 2 minutes and 6 seconds, you will be billed for only 2.1 minutes. Other companies would bill you for 3 minutes. This will provide you with a significant cost savings on those high monthly telephone bills that are contributing to your operating budget overruns."

Notice that the feature (one-tenth-of-a-minute billings) is connected directly with a stated *benefit* (billed for 2.1 versus 3 minutes). Also, notice that although the feature is product or service centered, the benefit focuses on the buyer and is related to a task motive (cost savings). The benefit is being sold, not the feature. There is also research to suggest that benefit statements are most powerful when connected to an explicit need expressed by the customer.

Finally, some *evidence* should be offered to support the claim that one-tenth-of-a-minute billing is a significant savings. Evidence may include presenting the product or a model of the product, showing test results, testimonials from satisfied customers, or trial periods. In the long-distance telephone service example, the salesperson may use testimonials from satisfied customers, as well as actual savings from other installations or test results to show savings. With any presentation, salespeople must be careful what they say about competitive products. In the case of a chemical salesperson's statements about a competitive product, for instance, the courts found the statement "The stuff is no good" permissible as an exaggerated statement. On the other hand, the salesperson's statement that the competitive product was "only about 40 percent as effective" as the salesperson's product was found to be an "assertion of fact" and therefore actionable.[14]

Perhaps the most widely used means of providing evidence to prove problem-solving claims is the use of *demonstrations*. Demonstrations encourage participation and often allow the buyer to experience the product benefits firsthand. Communication is improved by involving more of the buyer's senses than just hearing. A good demonstration should impress—even startle—a buyer so that interaction is stimulated. *The objective is to get the prospect to ask questions and to become more involved in the selling process.* Demonstrations shift the focus from selling to showing how the buyer's needs will be fulfilled.

Demonstrations become more difficult when selling heavy equipment. Heavy-machinery salespeople may encourage prospects to observe the equipment in action at a construction site, factory, or office. As a less expensive alternative, demonstrations are often made in the prospect's office through the use of visual aids. Audiovisual equipment is used primarily because it improves retention and recall of sales messages. Because people receive more than 80 percent of their knowledge visually, salespeople who use visual aids are better able to communicate a product's benefits to prospects.

Type of Customer Relationship   Presentation skills, like the other skills discussed in this chapter, are related to success regardless of the type of customer relationship being developed. Utilizing these skills, however, is quite different in a transactional relationship than in a consultative or enterprise relationship. To better understand this point, consider the following research findings:

- In most successful transactional-type relationships, the seller can make a solution presentation immediately after uncovering a customer problem. Presenting solutions too early is one of the most common mistakes, however, in high investment relationships, such as consultative or enterprise relationships.
- Listing features and advantages often leads to success in transactional relationships. In high investment relationships, however, these types of presentations often lead to more buyer objections and raise barriers to buyer commitment.[15]

These are just a few ways in which the type of customer relationship can influence successful use of selling skills. Nonetheless, these selling skills are necessary in all selling environments.

Written Sales Proposals   In today's competitive world, most prospects want to "see it in writing." There is simply too much at stake to make an uninformed decision. This is especially true of *complex sales.*

Although proposals may be organized in various ways, a proposal should convey the following five quality dimensions:

- **Reliability:** identifies solutions and strategies to achieve the prospect's needs and wants.
- **Assurance:** builds trust and confidence in your ability to deliver, implement, and produce benefits.
- **Tangibles:** enhances and supports your message and invites readership.
- **Empathy:** confirms your understanding of the prospect's business and needs.
- **Responsiveness:** develops proposal in a timely manner.[16]

Formal sales proposals are advantageous because everything is in writing, which means there is less chance of misunderstanding. Written proposals also improve communication when purchase decisions are made at buying or executive committee meetings that are off-limits to salespeople. Sales proposals have a durability that allows them to be read and evaluated over a period of time. However, written sales proposals take time and money to prepare, and they may not be cost-effective for many selling situations. In addition, formal sales proposals must be constructed carefully because they are binding contracts (see the Technology Competency box, "Five Weeks or a Few Minutes?").

Addressing Customer Concerns   Customer concerns or questions about a proposed solution to a problem are likely to arise in any sales presentation. In traditional sales training, these concerns were often referred to as objections. David Mercer, in his book *High Level Selling,* expresses well our reasons for preferring the term *concerns* rather than *objections* when he says:

> Even using the term "objections," I believe, puts a sales professional in the wrong frame of mind. It immediately relegates the whole sales call to an adversarial game of verbal tennis, instead of concentrating on helping the prospect. I believe that he should be on the same side of the net as the prospect; this automatically makes verbal tennis impossible.[17]

Ideally, a customer's most fundamental concerns should have been uncovered in the discovery phase before recommending a solution. Because customers are not likely to be aware of all their concerns until faced with making a decision, customer concerns are probably best considered a natural part of any sales presentation and should be viewed by the salesperson as an opportunity rather than an obstacle. Research on presentations by Xerox salespeople found that successful calls have 50 percent more objections than failed calls. When prospects raise concerns, they are actually showing interest and are asking for more

---

TECHNOLOGY COMPETENCY
"Five Weeks or a Few Minutes?"

Sales force automation can help improve performance, sometimes dramatically. Consider Ascom TimePlex, a company that monitors and manages complex wide area netwarks for its customers. TimePlex equipped its account executives with Apple Computer's PowerBooks in an effort to improve its business-order cycle time.

One of the important processes in TimePlex's selling cycle is developing customer proposals for the sale of large communication networks. One account executive with TimePlex described the process prior to the introduction of automation: "After huddling with my sales engineer, I'd prepare a quote or proposal and hand it over to an administrator, who had it typed. When I got it back, I reviewed it to make sure it was correct; then I'd worry about having someone fax or mail it to the client. The customer invariably made changes, and I'd have to insert them by hand, calculate the new costs, and double-check, again, the quote and the drawings that always accompanied it."

With TimePlex's new computers, account executives are able to prepare quotes and proposals at the customer's site, as well as handle client-induced changes and calculate the resulting costs during the sales call. An account executive describes how he won a major telecommunications carrier account from two competitors: "A customer using an RFP (request for proposal) called me in with the two other vendors. During our meeting, he made twelve changes to the proposed network that affected my preliminary quote, drawings, and paperwork. I took out my PowerBook, edited the quote, and, using the customer's printer, gave him a revised quote, cover letter, terms and conditions, and network drawings, all within a few minutes. One competitor took four weeks to provide the same documentation; the second competitor, over five weeks."

As a result of the proposal-generating ability and other capacities of their automation system, TimePlex has realized significant benefits, including the following:

- Order cycle time slashed by 50 percent
- Order accuracy improved by 25 percent
- Order administration costs cut by 20 percent

See *www.timeplex.com* for more on TimePlex.

---

information. They may be trying to make a clearer connection between their needs and your offering. Instead of being passive buyers, they are actively involved in the buying process. The most difficult prospect is one who does not say anything during the presentation, refuses to buy, and gives no reason for the decision. Xerox has also found that failed calls contain significantly more customer statements of indifference than successful calls. Concerns should be welcomed as a chance to get the prospect involved and to expand the discussion into areas of concern to the buyer. Most concerns are nothing more than innocent questions and should be viewed as an opportunity for deeper insight into customer needs.

Once *rapport* is *established,* most buyers have no reason to want to score points at the salesperson's expense. It is important that salespeople distinguish between real and pseudoconcerns. Each type is described below, along with ideas about how to approach these concerns.

Real concerns arise in most sales presentations. Concerns are likely to involve your company, product, timing, or price. In a well-developed selling situation, a need concern should not arise, because it should have been established earlier, when qualifying the prospect and during the needs discovery phase of the selling cycle. Many successful sales professionals view these concerns as pleas for more information.

The question remains as to how to handle real concerns raised by buyers. Wilson Learning Corporation suggests a method for handling objections that it refers to by the acronym LSCPA. The process involves the following steps:

- *Listen* to the buyer's feelings.
- *Share* the concerns without judgment.
- *Clarify* the real issue with questions.
- *Problem-solve* by presenting options and solutions.
- *Ask for action* to determine the commitment.

These steps are recommended because buyers are in no mood to listen to a logical clarification or solution when they are feeling tense. A customer concern is a signal that the buyer is feeling discomfort with the buying process. It is a natural part of the process. The listening and sharing steps can reduce tension by helping the buyer get objections out in the open and showing that you, the salesperson, care enough to acknowledge and try to understand them. Listen actively and encourage the buyer to talk. Don't think about how you will respond while listening to the buyer. In the sharing stage, you are trying to demonstrate understanding of the buyer's feelings. Listening and sharing take maturity, energy, and patience. Remember that the buyer is not attacking you personally, so concentrate on not being defensive.[18]

The clarifying step often takes the form of a question, such as "It seems to me you are saying…" This step will often uncover misinterpretations. When this happens, you need to go back to the beginning of the process in order to listen to and share new understandings with the buyer to demonstrate your acceptance and to help the buyer relieve tension.

How the problem-solving stage is handled will depend on the concern and the situation. One strategy is to present a list of the pros and cons for the action requested. Another approach is to admit that the concern is valid but to point out advantages that compensate for the concern. Alternatively, a case history could be presented describing how another prospect purchased the offering and benefited.[19]

Salespeople must learn to distinguish between real concerns and *pseudo-concerns,* or excuses. Pseudo-concerns are designed to hide the fact that the prospect just doesn't want to show his or her hand or is not ready to make a decision. People often fear change and may not trust their own decisions. For example, the following concerns may be valid in some situations, but they usually are employed to get rid of salespeople:

- "I'll get back to you."
- "I'm too busy right now."
- "Our budget is tight this year."

The astute salesperson recognizes such excuses, sometimes choosing to ignore them, and continues with the presentation. If the concern is legitimate, the customer will bring it up again and the salesperson can handle it then. As with real concerns, one of the best ways to uncover the real reason for the excuse is to ask questions that call for action by the buyer. A suggestion for responding to the preceding excuses is the following:

- "If you are too busy now, may I see you for half an hour this afternoon at three, or would tomorrow morning be better?"

Closing Skills

Closing occurs when a salesperson asks for a commitment from the customer. In a simple selling situation, such as in inventory replenishment, the commitment is for an order. Only 10 percent of sales calls in most major business-to-business relationships result in an order. In the other sales calls the customer is asked to commit to advancing the buying process.

Many salespeople find this the most difficult step of the selling process and are very reluctant to close. As one sales manager said when asked about the common mistakes salespeople make, "I think one of the big mistakes salespeople tend to make is not asking for the order."[20] The major reason salespeople are so hesitant to close seems to be fear of rejection. If salespeople do not ask for the order, they cannot be turned down and thereby they avoid embarrassment or disappointment. All professional purchasing agents, however, expect a sales representative to attempt to close. It is the job of the salesperson to make the first move. Research shows that it is important to keep a positive attitude for a sales presentation to be effective.[21] If you have successfully performed the earlier steps in the selling process, the close will follow naturally. In this case, closing is simply asking for a decision when you're fairly certain a person is going to say yes.

When to Close   An often-heard suggestion is to "close early and close often." This advice is not consistent with efforts to build trusting relationships with customers and is inherently adversarial in nature. The buyer is likely to regard asking for the order before being ready to buy as pushy. "You can be too pushy because if you want the sale too badly and become overly aggressive, your client is going to close up and start pushing to end the meeting," notes Tim McCarthy, director of sales and marketing for The Gregory Group.[22]

Does this mean that successful salespeople expect to close only once? No. Often there are undisclosed needs that still need to be addressed. One of your customer's needs may be to have other people listen to them. Salespeople must be prepared to use multiple closes. It is often said that most acceptances are made on the fifth closing attempt.

If undiscovered needs are likely to exist and multiple closes are often required, how does a salesperson avoid being pushy while uncovering hidden needs and making the sale? We suggest the use of *trial closes*. Although closes call for decisions, trial closes are questions that ask for opinions which will serve as indicators of how close the buyer is to making a purchase decision. You may, for example, ask:

- How does this look to you?
- How important is this to you?
- Is this what you had in mind?
- Will this equipment be consistent with what you have now?

If a prospect makes a positive response to one of these questions, the salesperson can assume that the customer is leaning toward buying and can move directly to the final close. The salesperson should be prepared to continue the sales presentation, however, if the prospect does not appear ready to make a decision. He or she may then proceed, boldly but discreetly, to ask the simple question "Is there anything I presented that is unclear or doesn't meet your particular needs?" This question will help the salesperson uncover the real needs of the buyer.[23]

Successful salespeople learn to time their closing remarks on the basis of *buying signals* given by the customer. These cues can take the form of gestures (the customer nods in agreement, picks up the product and examines it closely, or leans back in his or her chair) or they can be verbal comments. When prospects make comments such as:

- "Shipments must be completed in five months?"
- "We like the speed-control feature."
- "Would we be able to install the custom model within three weeks?"

The salesperson should recognize them as signs of interest and shift to a specific closing routine. Notice that each of these signals suggests an action by the buyer, not just a problem.

Closing Techniques   There are many different closing techniques and salespeople have personal preferences, depending on the circumstances. This suggests that salespeople need to be familiar with a number of closing techniques so that they can choose methods that are appropriate for each selling situation. Two popular closing techniques are the alternative choice close and the summary close.

Alternative Choice   When the prospect is faced with a variety of colors and models, the alternative choice close may be effective. With this technique, the salesperson poses a series of questions designed to narrow the choice and help the prospect make a final selection. For example: "These couplings can be packed in units of 24 or cases of 72. Which is more convenient for you?"

Summary Close   One of the best closes provides a summary of the benefits accepted during the call, combined with an action plan requiring the customer's commitment.

SALESPERSON: George, you have said that our word processor has more memory, better graphics, and is easier to use than other machines you have seen. Is that correct?
PROSPECT: Yes.
SALESPERSON: Well, I recommended that you lease one of our machines for three months, and the lease payments will apply to the purchase price if you decide to keep it.

In a Xerox-sponsored study of 500 sales calls, the *summary close* gave a 75 percent success rate; in only 7 percent of the calls was the summary method a failure.[24]

There are myriad other closing techniques that have been suggested and can be found in any selling textbook. There are popular business books entirely devoted to presenting different closing techniques.[25] Although some of the techniques are very creative, in practice, most veteran salespeople prefer one of the more straightforward closes discussed in this section. It is our belief that if the previous steps have been performed correctly, the close may be kept simple. This is also supported by research on the influence of different closing techniques on the customer's trust of the salesperson.[26] "If the salesperson has a clear vision of what benefits his or her product or service has to offer and he or she has made those benefits tangible for the prospect," says Arnold Wechsler, president of Wechsler Partners, Inc., "there's no reason for the salesperson not to be blunt in asking for the sale."[27] Perhaps part of the problem is terminology. "I've never been a believer in *closing,*" a sales consultant once said, "because my objective is to open a relationship."

POSTINTERACTION PHASE

A sale only begins the relationship between buyer and supplier. Once a salesperson has helped a buyer make a purchase, attention shifts to the follow-up activities. *Follow-up* refers to all the efforts involved in servicing the sale and building a lasting and growing relationship. Customers expect after-sale service, and it is frequently the sales representative's job to make sure that these activities are carried out.

The Wilson Learning Corporation has identified four pillars of sales support involved in after-sales follow-up. These are shown in Figure 3-5. *Supporting the buying decision* means reducing any anxiety that may arise with the purchasing decision. This may be accomplished through a follow-up sales call or by sending a card or letter thanking the buyer for the order. *Managing the implementation* includes offering support services, assisting with any personnel training, and reporting implementation and utilization progress. *Dealing with dissatisfaction* may include responding in an empathetic manner to any problems that arise. Salespeople should always try to *enhance the relationship* by being available, ensuring that the quality of the offering is maintained, and being a source of information, help, and ideas. It is very important to perform these activities successfully because the bulk of most salespeople's volume is in repeat business.

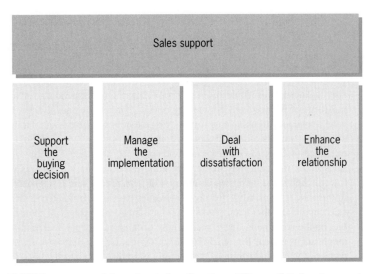

FIGURE 3-5   Servicing the Sale: The Four Pillars of Sales Support

Delivering after-sale service is more difficult than it sounds because salespeople have to depend on the actions of others. Other people drive the trucks to get the product to the customer. Other people service the product to keep it operating. Someone else sends out the manuals and bills to the customer. If something goes wrong, however, the salesperson is the one the customer turns to for help. Therefore, salespeople must learn to follow up on *everything* that they ask others to do for the customer.

An example of the power of follow-up occurred at a paper products company. The company handled many complex orders and prided itself on not missing one delivery date in four years. To highlight its achievements, the firm attached a new sheet to the monthly invoice that showed requested delivery dates and actual delivery times. A final column listed the number of days behind or ahead of schedule that the firm delivered the orders. This helped emphasize the company's excellent record, and it has led to considerable new business.

Follow-up also refers to callbacks to check the status of prospects who don't buy on the initial call. Some salespeople who get put off on a first call fail to return when the prospect may just need a little extra time or help to make a purchase decision. As a general rule, when an order is not obtained on the initial call, the salesperson should express appreciation for the time made available and suggest a later visit. In this way, the salesperson shows continued interest in helping the prospect and in getting the order. When leaving, the salesperson should inquire if there are any brochures, samples, or other information that the prospect needs before their next meeting.

Whenever salespeople leave without an order, they should immediately write down what they have learned about the prospect—for example, the prospect's chief concerns, who makes the final decision, and the prospect's primary needs. If the salesperson made any critical mistakes during the presentation, they should be noted so that they will not be repeated on the next visit.

Salespeople who do not follow up on sales are unlikely to establish long-term relationships with customers or secure repeat business. Purchasing agents expect post-sale service, and it is the salesperson's responsibility to see that they remain satisfied. The importance of salesperson follow-up in Japan is described in the Global Perspective Competency box, "What Would You Say If You Were Called an 'Okyaku-Sama'?"

GLOBAL PERSPECTIVE COMPETENCY
"What Would You Say If You Were Called an 'Okyaku-Sama'?"

Are Japanese salespeople different from American salespeople? According to George Leslie, president of Meitec Inc., the answer is yes. "Today's Japanese sales reps," says Leslie, "still have a tendency to behave as if they're at the bottom of the social ladder, respecting and trying to satisfy their customers. In fact, customers are often referred to as okyaku-sama, sama used in reference to God, the emperor, and others deserving honor." While the lower social status of salespeople in Japan may hinder recruiting efforts, there are benefits to the Japanese attitudes toward clients and their own company. For instance, Japanese salespeople are trained to assume immediate responsibility for any difficulties that are associated with their product. Japanese salespeople are also team players, who are fanatically proud of their company. U.S. salespeople, on the other hand, have traditionally been more independent and often taught the merits of independent action. Being rewarded with commissions may also reinforce the image of independence and responsibility. Interestingly as industries mature and selling becomes much more complex, traditional salesperson orientations are changing in the United States and in some important ways adopting the perspective of Japanese salespeople with respect to service and teamwork.

SUMMARY

Sales managers are first-line supervisors of field salespeople and need to understand the personal selling process in order to properly execute the strategic sales force plan. In addition, salespeople respect a sales manger who can help them achieve greater personal success in sales. A sales manager does not need to be the best salesperson in the unit, but he or she must at least have an understanding of the process involved and the skills needed to execute the firm's sales program.

1. **State the different types of selling approaches.** We have discussed three basic selling process models—standardized, need-satisfaction, and problem solution. Each approach is appropriate in certain circumstances. A standardized presentation is designed to stimulate a positive customer response. The presentation is well rehearsed and places minimal emphasis on problem discovery. A need-satisfaction type of presentation is oriented toward discovering and meeting customer needs. It relies on well-developed questioning skills to elicit customer buying needs. A problem-solution selling approach also involves an analysis of the customer's circumstances, but the analysis is more extensive and based on formal studies of the customer's operations.

2. **Describe the skills involved in the preinteraction phase of the selling process.** The preinteraction phase takes place prior to meeting with the customer. The planning skills involved in this phase focus on setting a good objective for the sales call, obtaining relevant information about the customer, and deciding how to open the conversation with the customer.

3. **List the skills involved in the interaction phase of the selling process.** The interaction phase includes all face-to-face interactions with the customer prior to arriving at the sale. Our discussion of this phase of the selling process focused on three skills important to all business situations: relating skills, discovery skills, and advocating skills. In addition we described two skills more critical to success in transactional type selling situations: gaining access and closing skills.

4. **Explain the skills involved in the postinteraction phase of the selling process.** The postinteraction phase takes place following the purchase and involves the servicing of the sale and building a lasting and growing customer relationship. Four skills were described in this phase: supporting the buying decision, managing the implementation, dealing with dissatisfaction, and enhancing the relationship.

KEY TERMS

Alternative choice closer benefits	Fact-finding questions	Precall planning
Benefitizing	Features	Problem-solution presentation
Buying signals	Feeling-finding questions	Pseudo-concerns
Checking questions	Follow-up	Real customer concerns
Closed-ended questions	Needs discovery	Relating skills
Closing	Need-satisfaction presentation	Relationship anxiety
Customer Response Management (CRM)	Open-ended questions	Stimulus-response presentation
	Open systems	Summary close
Demonstrations	Permission questions	Task motives
Establishing rapport	Personal motives	Trial close

DEVELOPING YOUR COMPETENCIES

1. **Coaching.** Talking to the person with responsibility and authority for purchasing is considered critical for success. According to Dave Douglas, a salesperson with Western Electric, this is not always enough. Western Electric, headquartered in Kansas City, sells high-fidelity audio amplifier vacuum tubes. Prices range from $250 to $1,500 each. According to Dave, "if a purchasing agent shows any reluctance to my product, I go right to engineering and ask the department to specify my line." Are there any potential problems with this approach? What would you tell Dave if you were his manager? Do you think Douglas's sales approach is the same for engineering and purchasing? For more on Western Electric, see www.westernelectric.com.

2. **Self-Management.** A better understanding of the role of personal selling can be obtained by traveling with a field salesperson for a day. Contact a salesperson and arrange to observe his or her activities for a day. Keep a log of how much of the salesperson's time is spent on meetings, travel, and waiting, and how much is spent talking to customers. Write a report describing your experience and the salesperson's activities. The Yellow Pages and your college placement office can be used to identify firms with salespeople in your area. Local chapters of Sales and Marketing Executives clubs and the American Marketing Association are also good sources of salespeople for this assignment.

3. **Strategic Action.** A strategic decision in sales is the level in the customer's organization on which the sales force focuses its selling efforts. Selling to a CEO is quite different from selling to a purchasing manager. The selling focus must be a well-thought-out decision to be successfully executed. Recall, for instance, Enron Energy Services (EES), the start-up by Enron discussed in the Strategic Action Competency box in this chapter. EES sells long-term, outsource energy solutions. In essence, they convince businesses to turn all of their energy management needs over to EES. Naturally, customers don't take the decision to outsource lightly. Those decisions are usually made at the "chief" level—by a CEO, CFO, or COO. This means that the sales force has to be able to sell to the highest-ranking people in an organization. Negotiating the first deals in a given industry can take

from 9 to 15 months. What are the implications for Enron's salespeople; that is, how do you think selling to a CEO is different from selling to mid-level managers? What are the implications for Enron's sales program, for example, prospecting, organization, motivation programs, competency development, and evaluation program? Does this decision impact the role of top management at EES? For more on Enron, see *www.enron.com.*

4. **Global Awareness.** Expanding into foreign markets often involves a healthy dose of research and development. Experts recommend that companies set a specific goal to be achieved in a 12-month time period and to make sure that a significant portion of business is coming from these new markets instead of just seeing it as a way to dump product in a new place. A good example of a company that needs to thoroughly research and understand its goals when entering a new market is Speech Works International Inc., which sells conversational speech recognition technology and other products used for telesales. Before opening a new overseas office, the company relies on experts at local universities who understand the nuances of a local language. The technology needs to translate such expressions as "I want to fly from Singapore to Hong Kong next Tuesday afternoon," into a language the computer will understand. Besides getting the language translated correctly, what additional information would you gather if you worked for Speech Works and what additional actions would you take to ensure a successful expansion into a city such as Mexico City or Singapore? *www.speechworks.com*

5. **Technology.** Sales Force Automation (SFA), according to recent reports, represents the fastest growing segment in the computer software business. Unfortunately, many of these efforts face the prospect of failure. To date, more than 60 percent of all SFA projects have been unsuccessful according to industry reports. Given this prospect, the results of a recent study by Mark Rivers and Jack Dart on the factors that are related to success in SFA are particularly interesting. First, recall that SFA involves converting manual sales activities to electronic processes through the use of various combinations of hardware and software applications. This means that an SFA project may be as simple as substituting electronic equivalents for paper daytimers, or as complex as developing advanced systems relying on computer-telephony integration to allow salespeople to enter orders electronically, create their own presentations, correspond via e-mail, and do their own pricing. Which of the following factors do you think were found to be related to achieving SFA success among the 210 manufacturing firms participating in the study?

   - The extent to which top management was involved in the purchase decision.
   - The extent to which sales force management is involved in the purchase decision.
   - Sales management's predisposition toward the SFA concept.
   - The management's difficulty in assessing sales force performance.
   - The resistance of the sales force to the adoption of SFA.

6. **Team Building.** It is estimated that half of all U.S. companies use manufacturers' representatives or agents. Manufacturer reps are independent firms who sell for a number of companies. They are almost always paid on commission and generally work alone. A recent study, however, observed that a little over 75 percent of the more than 350 manufacturer rep organizations surveyed were periodically using team selling in which more than one person from the rep organization would call on a customer. However, team selling was likely to be used only in certain buying and selling situations. In which type of selling and buying situations do you think manufacturers' rep organizations were most likely to have more than one person calling on the purchasing organization?

IN-CLASS EXERCISES

3-1: "Unkept Promise"

WHOT, a Latin music radio station in Miami, after considerable market research, decided to update its format from Latin standards to new, hip Latin music in an attempt to reach young, upscale Hispanic residents. As part of the changeover station manager Jorge Moreno hired salesperson Rita Vasquez, a 30-year-old, Cuban-American woman with a master's degree in business, whom he felt embodied the station's new target audience. Besides, Vasquez had a proven track record in advertising sales from her six-year stint with a radio station in Tampa.

Most customers were pleased with the new format and planned to continue advertising on the station. However, one media buyer at an agency that represented three of WHOT's largest accounts, was unhappy and planned to cancel his current contract.

Moreno decided to send his new rep to call on the disgruntled media buyer. Having already succeeded in bringing in several new accounts, Vasquez happily accepted the challenge. After an unsuccessful attempt to sway the buyer, Vasquez offered a guarantee that the buyer's clients would get "editorial mentions"—casual comments from the deejay about the clients' products and/or services—on the station's popular morning show if the agency agreed to maintain its current media plans. With that, the buyer was sold.

A month later the buyer called Moreno to complain that his clients were never mentioned on the morning show as promised by Vasquez; he planned to pull additional advertising if the station didn't meet its promise beginning the following morning. Vasquez put Moreno in a difficult position. He wants to keep the customer, but editorial mentions are strictly against station policy. Worse, Vasquez knew this when she made the promise to the buyer. It was 4:00 P.M. when the customer called. Moreno needed to think quickly.

Questions:

1. Consider the postinteraction phase discussed in the chapter. In particular, think about the Four Pillars of Sales Support. Which stage is the buyer in? How, then, should the buyer be handled?
2. If you were the station manager, what would you do about the following:
   - Rita Vasquez's blatant disregard for station policy?
   - The fact that Vasquez has a lot of experience and can add so much value to the station?
   - The customer's dissatisfaction with the broken promise?
3. As a sales manager, how would you handle the meeting with Rita Vasquez?
   - What would you say to her about her actions with the customer?
   - What are her possible reactions during the meeting?
4. As a sales manager, how would you handle the meeting/phone call with the customer?
   - What would you say to him about Vasquez's actions?
   - What are his possible reactions during the meeting? Is the relationship salvageable?
   - What can Moreno do to regain the client's trust?

3-2: "Selling Software"

William Banks, vice president of sales and marketing for U.S. Industries, loves technology. Six months ago he signed a deal with a vendor, Primary Software, which would provide a comprehensive, custom software package for his sales force. Among the package's features are a database, a contact and schedule manager, and a price and specification estimator. Banks wants to tie his sales force to every other department in the company, allowing everyone real-time access to customer activities, product availability, and other necessary information.

When he called Primary today, he learned that the project had fallen behind schedule and the beta version wouldn't be ready for at least three months (it had been promised to him in one month). The vendor apologized, saying, "It's the best we can do." Banks was aghast. He had already purchased laptops for his 500-person sales force, expecting the software to be running internally by the time the shipment of laptops arrived. He had also based year-end sales projections on the increased productivity and sales he expected as a result of automating the company's sales process.

Coincidentally, a salesperson from another vendor, AllBright Software, called Banks to discuss some industry information he thought Banks would find useful. After a few minutes, the conversation turned to Banks's automation problem. The vendor offered his company's services, promising to complete the project within three months, and offering extensive training and support that surpassed what the current vendor was offering. The price would be about the same, but Banks had already paid $100,000 in unrecoverable dollars to Primary. Banks said he needed time to consider the offer.

Questions

1. Should Banks be patient and wait for Primary to complete the job, or should he risk going with AllBright?
2. What other options does Banks have?
3. Are there ethical issues involved?

CANTERBURY BANK AND TRUST COMPANY

At 5:15 P.M. on a moist March afternoon, John Bryan, vice-president and corporate lending officer for the Canterbury Bank and Trust Co., Inc., of Houston, Texas, was sitting in his cool, wood-paneled office reviewing the calls he had made that day. John believed that the day had been a success, but he wondered if there was anything that he could have done to improve his performance.

THE BANK

Canterbury Bank and Trust Company was the largest bank within Canterbury Bancorp., a holding company with assets in excess of $30 billion, and as such, one of the largest financial institutions in the country. Canterbury was preparing aggressively for regulatory changes that would allow interstate banking in the United States. With retail banking offices in 11 western states, Canterbury expected to be a major force in the financial future of that region.

The bank was engaged in virtually every form of bank business allowed by law, including commercial lending. The group within Canterbury primarily responsible for commercial lending was known as the World Banking Group.

Commercial lending was essentially an asset-management function. The Group's officers' primary responsibility was to lend funds, or core deposits,

This case was prepared by Chris A. Christopher, Jr., and Robert B. Parks under the supervision of Derek A. Newton. This case was written as a basis for class discussion rather than to illustrate effective or ineffective handling of an administrative situation. Copyright (c) 1982 by the University of Virginia Darden School Foundation, Charlottesville, VA. All rights reserved. To order copies, send an e-mail to dardencases@virginia.edu. No part of this publication may be reproduced, stored in a retrieval system, used in a spreadsheet, or transmitted in any form or by any means—electronic, mechanical, photocopying, recording, or otherwise—without permission of the Darden School Foundation.

raised by the bank's retail and corporate sectors in a manner that would maximize the bank's earnings. The bank's clients were diverse and included a good number of the largest companies in the world.

The commercial loan business was highly competitive. Unlike the lucrative energy lending business, where loans were often made at substantially above the prime rate, loans to corporate customers typically were made at or very near the prime rate. Despite the fact that loans to corporations did not have the highest yields of all commercial loans, the large dollar volume of these loans made corporate lending to established customers only moderately risky and very profitable on an incremental basis. The bank's average annual growth rate of the commercial loan portfolio was well over 20 percent.

In addition to its lending services, the bank also offered a full range of other "financial products" to its corporate clients. These products included cash management, corporate finance, investment management, employee benefit trust services, equipment leasing, inventory financing, zero-balance checking, and lock-box capabilities.[1]

THE BANKING LOAN OFFICER

John was representative of his fellow loan officers at his level within the bank. After graduating from the University of Texas, he joined the bank in its Houston office and had been with the bank for 15 years. He was a rather tall, neatly groomed man with dark hair that was graying at the temples. He favored charcoal-gray suits and starched white shirts. He and his family lived in the River Oaks area of Houston.

John was a vice-president and district manager within the Metropolitan-South section of the U.S. Banking Division. This division was part of the larger World Banking Group. A vice-president at his level had two primary responsibilities: supervision and account representation/lending. John supervised six other loan officers, each of whom normally had a loan portfolio of between $150 and $200 million. In addition, John was the account representative of up to 15 relationships, and he called directly on as many as 100

more companies. John's annual salary was $50,000. He and the other vice-presidents at his level were also eligible for bonuses, which were based on the profitability of the bank. There was no financial compensation (e.g., commission) for performing any particular aspect of a bank officer's duties.

Canterbury used a peer-group evaluation system. Periodically, people with the same performance categories within the divisions were evaluated as a group. A loan officer's ranking within the group was determined in part by performance and in part by his or her supervisor's ability to market the loan officer's achievements. Essentially, this system emphasized relative as opposed to absolute performance evaluation. The evaluation system was formalized, in the sense that performance categories and goals existed. The former were set by upper management, while the latter were the result of mutual agreement between loan officers and their supervisors. The peer-group evaluation system, coupled with the compensation scheme, encouraged the development of an informal model of a good banking loan officer in the managers' minds. On the whole, John believed this system contained more good than bad.

John considered himself successful in his job, which he viewed as selling clients *all* the services his bank had to offer, even though he was primarily concerned with lending. In his view, to be "tied in" with the client in as many ways as possible was to the bank's advantage. Consequently, he made it his business to be familiar with all of the bank's financial products.

The bank stressed the development of long-term relationships with its clients. Lending officers attempted to become financial consultants to their clients, to build good personal relationships with them, and to know the clients' businesses so that they could anticipate clients' needs. Lending officers were generalists, responsible for a number of different types of businesses.

The Metropolitan section's accounts ranged from Fortune 1000 companies to small companies with sales in the $50–$150 million range. John believed that the smaller companies presented a greater challenge for the lending officer. He also believed that lending to these accounts was much more fun. With the small companies, the lending officer had to structure the loan as well as sell it within the bank. This internal sales task was a major part of the lending officer's job. Large loans had to pass through as many as six levels of approval. For a typical $100 million company, the bank structured the whole transaction, which could

[1] In a lock-box system, payments to a corporation by its customers are directed to a post office box that the bank is authorized to empty daily. The bank opens the mail, endorses and deposits the checks in the corporation's account, and sends a record of the deposits to the corporation for bookkeeping purposes. The lock-box is intended to speed the flow of money into the corporation's account and to transfer most of the paper handling to the bank.

include loans, cash-management services, and lock-boxes as well as normal checking and deposit accounts. Much of the bank's business from smaller companies was the result of solicitation by the lending officers.

With any of the larger corporations, however, the lending officer was still in a more traditional role of order taker. If a large corporation needed another $5 million, it would simply phone the bank. The relationship between Canterbury and its large corporate clients was at the organizational, not the individual, level. A corporation looked to the bank as a whole. John believed that, with large clients, a sale was more a question of whether the bank could provide a service the company was looking for.

Normally with a large corporation, banks competed on the basis of "tierings." A bank's tiering was determined by the percentage of the corporation's bank debt that bank held, compared with other banks. The bank with the largest percentage was in the top tier. The largest corporate accounts were served usually by a vice-president, assisted by an assistant vice-president who, in turn, took care of the day-to-day dealings with the account.

John believed that banking was not a high-mentality business. Rather, he saw common sense and experience as the keys to success. The best bankers were the ones who possessed intuition bred through experience. With large corporations, he believed that customers were less impressed with a bank officer's MBA than with his or her years of experience in a particular area or with a particular problem. Finally, to be a good lending officer, John believed that it was essential to know how to close a deal.

THE CALLS

Lonestar Bag Company

At 9:00 A.M., John pulled his ice-blue Mercedes into the parking lot of the Lonestar Bag Company. He entered Lonestar's small, wood-paneled reception area and greeted the receptionist with a warm smile. He gave her his name and told her that he had an appointment with Michael Ramsey, the Vice-President—Finance. Lonestar was a moderately sized, well-run company specializing in the manufacture of grocery store shopping bags. It had never entered a business relationship with Canterbury before, and John was unsure what to expect from the call. Within a minute, Mike Ramsey appeared at the entrance to the offices.

Mike: Good morning, I'm Mike Ramsey.
John: Good morning, I'm John Bryan from the Canterbury Bank.

The two shook hands, and Mike hung John's top-coat in a hall closet and escorted him into his corner office. Mike was a tallish man in his late 40s. He had rather curly, silver hair, wore wire-rimmed eyeglasses, and was dressed in a camel-hair sport coat, brown slacks, and a tie. His office reflected its occupant. It was warm, contemporary, and well organized. The walls and carpeting were in shades of brown, and the furniture was varnished natural wood. Several large plants filled different corners of the room. Mike directed John to a pair of sofas in one corner of the room where they could talk. John noticed that Mike's secretary had followed them into the room.

Mike: Would you like a cup of coffee?
John: Yes, I like mine light and sweet, please.

The secretary disappeared and returned momentarily with two cups.

John: So, how's the paper bag business?
Mike: Well, it's pretty good these days, although there have been times when it was better. As you may know, our business is primarily the manufacture of shopping bags for grocery stores. Consequently, our customers' demands vary somewhat with the health of the economy and the buying power of the purchaser in the grocery store.
John: I see.
Mike: However, we have very strict controls over our manufacturing process. The production of paper bags is a very clean operation. We have the latest in manufacturing technology in all of our three plants. This allows us to be very responsive to our customers' demands in a short time. A happy result of this is that we are rarely stuck with a lot of finished inventory. I'd like to take you on a tour of the plant when we're finished here if you're interested.
John: Oh yes, I'd be very interested in seeing it.
Mike: Since our operation is so clean, our borrowing needs are fairly straightforward. Right now we have a $3.75 million revolving-credit term loan with two large New York banks. We are currently negotiating a new agreement with them. The company is owned by two principals. They have been with the company for years and are respon-

sible for the growth of the company to its present size. We have manufacturing facilities in Texas, North Carolina, and New York, and our market is basically the eastern half of the United States.

John: Which banks do you deal with in New York?

Mike: Right now we have part of our credit arrangement with the Universal Bank and the rest with Central National. We also have a lock-box arrangement with Central National. These relationships were begun before I got here, however. I joined the company several years ago. Before that, I was a partner in Couch, Rose and Co.

John: Oh, so you're familiar with Canterbury?

Mike: Oh, yes. As you know, Canterbury and Couch, Rose have a long relationship.

John: Have you been satisfied with these banking relationships?

Mike: Generally, yes. Central National has a particularly good lock-box system.

John: I had heard that they and the Bank of Gotham are rather good with that service. You know, Canterbury does quite a bit of that as well.

Mike: Yes, I had looked into it.

John: Have your credit arrangements with these banks been satisfactory?

Mike: Well, as I mentioned, we're presently negotiating a new agreement with the banks. At present, they lend to us at about 1 percent above prime.

John: Uh-huh.

Mile: They also have balance requirements of about 10 and 10.[2] Our principal concern with the agreement is that the covenants are rather tight. Specifically, the agreement is restrictive on the use of funds for the company buy-back of corporate stock. We'd like to be able to arrange things so that the company or an entity controlled by the company could purchase the shares from the principal over time after his retirement. We also feel that those balance requirements are a bit high as well.

John had begun taking notes.

John: Humm-m-m. That sounds reasonable. Does your agreement with these banks contain the usual covenants?

Mike: Oh, yes, concerning the use of funds, balances, and so forth. We have no problem with the types of covenants. We just feel that several of them are too tightly drawn.

John: I see. OK. How is your financial condition?

Mike rose, went to his desk, and pulled out a folder, which he handed to John.

Mike: These are our financial statements for the last several years, including the latest one. I'll get my secretary to make copies for you. As you can see, we're in pretty good shape. Our sales have grown steadily over the last several years, and our debt-to-equity ratio has remained about the same.

John: Are these inventory figures here high or rather normal?

Mike: They are pretty much the norm. We buy our paper in huge bulk rolls. The majority of our inventory is this bulk kraft paper. Paper in this form is basically a commodity. If we have too much, it can be resold with no problem. We rarely have this trouble, however, as we're pretty good at anticipating our demand. We have the capacity to handle 150,000 tons of paper per year. Presently, we handle about 100,000.

John: How do you trace your receivables?

Mike: Our receivable records, like all our others, are fully automated. We do our record keeping on one of the latest systems. We also have one person working for us whose job it is to stay on top of our customers by phone. She knows nearly all of our customers, and she does an excellent job in a very nice manner. The result, as you can see, is that we collect rather quickly and have few outstanding overdue receivables. In addition, we've found that the few receivables we have had to write off usually end up being paid at some point anyway. It's very satisfying.

John: How do you sell to your customers?

Mike: We use a professional sales force, which we feel is one of our strengths. This group is a mix of in-house salesmen, manufacturers' representatives, and regionally selected paper wholesalers. They are able to cover most of the eastern United States, which is where we concentrate our sales.

---

[2] Meaning: 10 percent of line of credit and 10 percent of amount of loan in use.

John: Who are your competitors in this area?

Mike: We compete mainly with Weyerhauser, International Paper, and some other smaller producers like ourselves. We've been able to maintain our strong position, however, because we constantly upgrade our production and delivery systems. I feel that we are one of the most efficient producers. Our machines are fairly simple, and we own them all. We also have our own machine shop to repair them. We own all of our buildings, and we have our own fleet of trailers for delivery. Many of our customers also come to us for delivery. Would you like to see our plant now?

John: Yes, I'd love to. I've never seen a paper bag plant before.

Mike escorted John through the manufacturing area, explaining the workings of the various machines as they walked along. They also walked past huge stacks of paper rolls and pallets of finished paper bags waiting to be loaded for shipment. Mike knew every employee that he passed by name. Mike also took John to the computer area and arranged for a short demonstration of the computer's record-tracing and record-keeping capacity. Soon they returned to the office.

Mike: I hope you enjoyed your tour.

John: That was very interesting. Tell me, if we can get a set of covenants drawn to our mutual satisfaction, how much business would you do with Canterbury?

Mike: Well, we never like to take all of our credit from one bank. However, I should think we'd be willing to do at least one-third of our business with Canterbury.

John: I'll begin working something up, and I'll be back in touch with you in about a week.

Mike: If I have any questions, do I contact you at the bank?

John: Yes, please. Here is my card.

The two men exchanged business cards, and Mike retrieved John's coat from the closet.

Mike: Well, I'll look forward to hearing from you next week.

John: Thank you very much. It has been a pleasure to meet you.

The two men shook hands.

Mike: Thank you, have a good day, good-bye.

John: Good-bye.

John believed that Mike knew the other banks were giving him a bad deal. He felt that Canterbury could get at least half of Lonestar's business. He smiled as he walked to his car to travel back to the bank for his next meeting.

YORK CORPORATION

At 11:45 A.M., John was sitting at his desk at the Canterbury Bank reviewing a few notes before his luncheon meeting with Troy Thermapolos from the treasurer's department of the York Corporation. He was looking forward to this meeting, because York was a good customer of the bank and Troy was a good friend of his.

At noon, John's secretary escorted Troy into John's office. They greeted each other warmly, and John put Troy's umbrella in a nearby closet. Troy was a tall, dark, curly-headed man of about 35. He was single. John had known Troy for about two years. They walked across the bank's modern lobby, where a commercial was being filmed, toward the elevator to the bank's private dining room.

Troy: Hey, what's going on in here?

John: Oh, they're filming a new commercial for the bank to be used on TV.

Troy: Oh, really? Hey, we showed up at just the right time. I've always wanted to be on TV.

John: Are you kidding? The bank needs responsible-looking people in its commercials.

Troy: Hey, aren't I surrounded by that air of confidence?

Both men laughed as they got onto the elevator and were still chuckling as they entered the dining room. The bank's dining room was quiet and elegant. The floors were covered with thick red carpet, the tables were made of rich wood, and the windows were framed by heavy draperies. Gleaming silver and crystal greeted each diner.

John: So, what's this I hear about you getting a new car?

Troy: Yeah. I'm going to get a Porsche 944. It's a new model they're coming out with. I thought about getting the old Audi fixed up, but someone swiped my stereo out of it, so I'm just going to sell it. I'm tired of it anyway.

The two men ordered lunch.

Troy: You know, I'm also thinking about buying a house down in Galveston, on the shore. It's really beautiful down there, but the prices are pretty steep. Even that wouldn't be so bad, but the mortgage rates are awful. Do you know of any place where a guy can get a reasonable mortgage?

John: Well, I've been thinking about buying a condo at Galveston myself. I know Canterbury's interest rates are high now, so I'm going to do some calling around. If I find anything, I'll let you know.

Troy: That's great. I've had real estate on the brain lately. My family holds some land over in Greece that some guy has been trying to hoodwink from us. I told the family not to do anything until we got a lawyer. Ah, get a lawyer—the American way!

The food began to arrive.

John: So, what's the story on York borrowing?

Troy: Well, we recently issued about $20 million in commercial paper to finance some textile deliveries. The problem is that this puts us pretty close to our limit on issuing commercial paper. As a result, we're going to need bank financing to pay for a cotton delivery next week. The loan would be about $3 million.

John: What's your commercial-paper limit?

Troy: It's about $37 million, but we don't want to hit the limit, because it would significantly reduce our flexibility. With economic conditions being what they are, we'd rather not do that. As you know, we've tried to establish our name in the commercial-paper market to assure ourselves of availability. We are comfortable at the $37 million level, which leaves bank financing to satisfy less predictable needs.

John: You know that we hold a money market facility available to York which you've used from time to time. It's still available. We'll begin calling you with rates so that you can get a feel for the market.

Troy: Great! Here we are in the era of Reaganomics, and I feel like a Democrat. I mean, where I am in the company, we're really moving the money around. We're growing so fast, everyone needs cash. Did you know we are reorganizing my department?

John: You said something about that the last time we met. Where does it stand now?

Troy: Well, you know that York began as a textile company. In recent years, the company bought into a number of different businesses. For all practical purposes, York is now a conglomerate. But we had a problem in that the textile people were still making most of the financial decisions. This reorganization will take most of the financial decisions out of the textile people's hands and give them to a corporate treasury staff. This will be very good for the company. One result, though, has been a lot of movement among the office staff.

John: How come?

Troy: Well, they're combining several different offices into one at the staff level. I've had several new people come to work for me. Two of them are women.

John: How is that working out?

Troy: Well, I'm not sure. I'm all for women in the work place, you understand, but they're so sensitive. I mean, if I'm in my office and one of the guys there passes by on his way to the coffee pot and I ask him to grab me a cup, he'll say "What do you want in it?" and get it, and that's that. But if I ask one of the women, boy, do they get upset. And it happens about a lot of other things, too. You ever have that happen to you?

John: Well, not really. Maybe it's because female calling officers have been at the bank for a while, and we've all come up through the ranks together. I never have problems with my secretary either in that regard.

Troy: Boy, I wouldn't have problems with her either. She's a knockout. I tell you, you set me up with her and we'll do a lot more borrowing with the bank.

John: Yeah, OK. You can talk to her big Swedish boyfriend.

Troy: Hey, the boyfriend wasn't part of the deal. Say, there's a woman that looks rather like her at the Sports Club. That's not a bad place to meet people. Hey, do you want to play racquetball sometime soon?

John: Sure, that sounds great. Let's set it up when we've got our calendars handy.

Troy: OK.

They ordered dessert and coffee.

Troy: You know, they've put me in charge of directing the reorganization of the treasury staff. It's a real mess right now, but we should have it straightened out pretty soon. We're going to take over all of the payroll functions and assign borrowing and investment functions to a single individual. I think you've met Don Coggin. He will be responsible for our borrowing and investing.

John: Yes, I have met him before. Would you suggest that I meet with him to discuss York's borrowing plans?

Troy: I think that would be best. While he's not on his own, he will coordinate our borrowing on a day-to-day basis.

John: I'll give him a call this week to arrange a meeting.

Troy: OK. Boy, this job is a zoo. I'm actually waiting for my 60-year-old boss to retire. He's the assistant treasurer. If I don't get his job after this, I'll quit the company. There's no excuse. I've really worked hard there.

John: Yes, I know what you mean.

Troy: I'll tell you what else. I'm glad I'm single right now. It gives you a real advantage. They can't put pressure on you as well, and you're always free to leave. There are no other ties to hold you back. That flexibility sure makes it easier in the political fight for executive positions.

John: That's interesting. Do you really think he'll retire soon?

Troy: I'm not sure, but he's considering it.

The two men finished dessert and walked out to the elevator.

Troy: You know, it's too bad that your dining room doesn't serve liquor. Hey, you know, I wouldn't mind discussing a few executive positions with your secretary. You sure you don't want to set me up?

John: Remember the boyfriend.

Troy: OK. Hey, maybe if I changed my name so that it sounds more WASPish, I'd get promoted faster. What do you think?

John: (laughing) What are you going to do with a name like yours?

Troy: Beats me. Maybe I'll shorten it to Therman. I don't know.

John: Well, you let me know if you do.

The two men walked back across the banking floor to John's office where John retrieved Troy's umbrella.

John: OK, Troy. Tell Don that I'll be calling him in a day or so to arrange an appointment.

Troy: Great, John. Don't forget the racquetball game.

John: You bet. I'll be in touch.

Troy: OK, John. Take care.

The two shook hands. Troy waved to John's secretary on his way out. John swallowed a laugh.

LAMBETH INDUSTRIES

John drove from lunch out to his last call of the day at Lambeth Industries. He parked the Mercedes in a parking garage across the street from Lambeth's impressive corporate headquarters in Houston's fashionable Galleria area. The sprawling building was formerly the headquarters of a major fashion company. The Greek columns, white exterior, and gravel walkway winding through flowers and fountains gave the building the look of a Hollywood set.

John had invited Sandra Ming, a 30-year-old Asian woman and a Columbia University graduate with a Masters in Chinese Culture, to make this call with him. Sandra was with the bank's international division. During the ride to the Galleria area, Sandra and John had discussed Lambeth's financial position and an article Sandra would give to Lambeth's people about technology transfer from the United States to China. She and John were taking this opportunity to explain to two of Lambeth's assistant treasurers, R. F. "Bob" Runcie and Rebecca West, some of the services that Canterbury could offer Lambeth in financing its activities with the People's Republic of China. John did not expect any business to be consummated during this call.

Upon entering the building, John asked a woman at the front desk for Bob and Rebecca. After standing for a few moments in the hardwood-paneled reception area with its ornate furniture and an oriental rug covering a marble floor, they were greeted by a secretary who appeared from one of the elevators. She smiled as John introduced Sandra. After a brief elevator ride to the second floor, John and Sandra were shown to a small conference room in the interior of the building. A few moments later, Bob, a man of medium height with a beaming smile, and his attractive, blond-haired co-worker Rebecca entered the room.

Bob: Good afternoon, John.

John: Good afternoon, Bob, Rebecca. Let me introduce Sandra Ming. She's with our international division.

Sandra shook hands with Bob and Rebecca, and everyone took their seats around a small round table. The modern furniture was made of aluminum and hard plastic. Earth tones predominated in the color scheme, giving the small conference room a sense of cool efficiency. Bob, Rebecca, and John were friends, and everyone was smiling as the conversation resumed.

John: We're here to talk to you about China.

Bob: Good. Lambeth wants to be at the forefront in China. In the treasurer's office, we want to be ready when one of our divisions is ready to begin business in China.

Sandra: As you know, the head of the Bank of China is planning a trip to New York. Before returning to China, he will stop in Houston where Canterbury will host a dinner in his honor. Is your president planning to come to our dinner?

Bob: We don't have a president right now, but I believe our chairman will be at the dinner. He intends to appoint a president soon; the chairman doesn't want to do both jobs.

Sandra: It should be a productive dinner.

John: Yes, it's a very casual affair. We expect many of our corporate customers will be there.

Sandra: Yes, that's right.

After a few more pleasantries about the dinner, the conversation returned to business.

Rebecca: Is China buying or selling?

Sandra: China is definitely in the market for fertilizer.

Rebecca: Do they pay cash?

Sandra: The Chinese do pay cash for some of their purchases.

Bob: Really? It seems much more natural for them to use some sort of barter transaction.

Sandra: Canterbury is trying to establish an office in Shanghai. It is very hard to get space in Peking. For example, Chase Manhattan took a hotel room six years ago and has never given it up. One thing all the workers said is your R&R [rest and recreation] has to be very good, living in the Peking Hotel. And Hong Kong—I wouldn't want to live there. Family conditions are too difficult. Have you been to China?

Bob: No, I haven't.

Sandra: Well, it's very unusual. For example, by 5 o'clock every evening, they dim the lights.

But now there is much more cultural activity. They have a night club. It's mostly patronized by Chinese students. The club is kind of tacky. I don't like to go to tacky clubs.

John: What's tacky about it? It doesn't sound tacky to me.

Sandra: They're still playing music from the beatnik era—they're not even up to the Beatles yet.

John: Are there actually any private banks in Peking?

Sandra: Yes, there are some branches of overseas banks there. There are British banks from pre-1949. The ex-pats [expatriates] left, but the office stayed.

Bob: I'm surprised the banks could keep their offices. They must not have done much business.

Sandra: No, they didn't do a lot.

John: Does China only have one bank?

Sandra: No, there are two, the Bank of China and the People's Republic Bank.

Bob: But no private banks?

Sandra: No, there are no Chinese private banks.

Rebecca: Is there a Canterbury Branch yet?

Sandra: No, we have a space problem. But a lot of our business is done over the phone.

John: Do they [the Chinese] require letters of credit like they do in Hong Kong?

Sandra: Basically yes, but if they know you very well, some transactions are done without a letter of credit.

John: Will they actually ship goods without a letter of credit?

Sandra: Yes—mostly only the Chinese you know very well. We have built up a rapport with the Bank of China. The business is very competitive. One of our biggest competitors can process business in 20 days. We can do it in 10 days. Again, this is because of our relationship with the Bank of China. The reason we are so competitive is that we send documents directly to Hong Kong—then our people there act as liaison with the Chinese. We use a daily courier service to Hong Kong. China always insists on payment in China. They are not a party to the international equivalent of the Uniform Commercial Code. But if you're a good customer and your documents are in order, payments can be expedited. If you want, I can send you the proper addresses.

Bob: You have a branch in Hong Kong. Will you move a representative from Hong Kong or Los Angeles to China?

Sandra: Yes, we will.

Bob: Will you [Sandra] go to China?

Sandra: I'd like to, but I don't know yet. I've only been with the bank for a few months. I moved to Houston after I got mugged in New York City.

A brief discussion followed of the relative safety and quality of life in New York and Houston. The consensus was that one had a better chance for long-term survival in Houston.

Sandra: I am going to China this spring with the National Council on United States and China Trade. I will travel with another officer from the bank. We will be doing work for clients.

Bob: We'd like to talk to you when you get back. I imagine a few of our people will be in China as part of the project.

Rebecca: Our customers are arranging for space. Do you know of any brochures with information? For example, I know that people and companies who are working in Korea are listed. You can also get a list of banks doing business there.

Sandra: I'll try and send you a list of who is in China. [Sandra jotted down a few notes.]

At this point Sandra handed Bob and Rebecca a copy of an article concerning technology transfer from the United States to China.

Sandra: Do you know about the National Council on United States and China Trade? They have 5,000 members. They gather information about trade and exchange. There are a lot of contacts presently between the United States and China. Members are very generous with the information.

Bob: I imagine that there has to be enough business to go around at this point.

John: Can you get a list of banks for them, Sandra?

Sandra: Yes.

Bob: Korea and China potentially are big areas for Lambeth. Our chairman made a trip to South Korea and talked to their president about licensing. Perhaps we might make some of our defense and navigation equipment there. Essentially, we make a little black box. China and Korea are both busi-

ness possibilities. It's an area we would like to be in.

John: Is the equipment sold to OEMs [original equipment manufacturers] or end users?

Bob: The equipment is very flexible. You can take it in and out. Often a plane will have three [of these black boxes]. If one breaks down, you simply take it out and fix it while you slap another one in in the interim. It really depends upon the buyer.

Sandra: Do you know our country manager? He is a China expert. He had done business in five areas.

A brief discussion of who knew whom in China followed.

Bob: We will recognize the businesses much better after we see the list of who is in China. Is movement within China by its people free or limited?

Sandra: It is much freer than it used to be. For instance, you don't need a guide anymore. Today, the ideal thing is to bring your own interpreter. Without an interpreter, it is very difficult to travel in China. All the signs are in Chinese, and not many people speak English. Fortunately, I went to graduate school and studied Chinese culture. There is a small clique which runs the international business community. If you would like, our China expert, Ed, can help you set up any meetings you might need.

Bob: Doesn't First Chicago have a presence in China?

Sandra: Yes, First Chicago was the first major U.S. bank in China. They stopped doing business in Taiwan. First Chicago didn't have much exposure in Taiwan. However, it's not good business to concede a market. The Chinese really shouldn't force banks to do this.

Bob: Uh-huh.

John: Well, we appreciate your listening to our story.

Bob: Well, thanks. [Everyone smiled.] We're interested and we will be glad to follow up.

Rebecca: Yes, it certainly isn't like doing business in St. Louis.

Sandra: Do you have any other questions I can answer? For instance, we can easily do a funds transfer.

Rebecca: Really? We've just started with an investigation into how to transfer funds, and we have all kinds of questions on letters of credit. So far, we only have letters of understanding. No actual funds have been transferred.

Bob: The business people went over and got a big contract, but they didn't figure how to get the money out.

Rebecca: Are there any currency problems?

Sandra: We can do any exchange transactions also. Right now the exchange rate is about 56 yuan to the dollar. It's pretty stable. It's not like Indonesian currency. There is no need to shop around for the best rate.

Bob: Is the Chinese currency a tradeable currency?

Sandra: No, not like pounds or marks.

Bob: Oh.

John: Can you do business in United States dollars?

Sandra: Yes.

Bob: China has U.S. dollars it's willing to pay out?

Sandra: Yes, but this year they are projecting a big deficit, or at least that's what Chase Manhatten predicted. The official Chinese projections don't show this deficit. The Chinese are importing wheat and cotton. They want to export coal and oil. According to the recent World Bank report, there are nine areas in which the West will help China. The first is education.

Bob: You mentioned oil. Isn't Japan a big trade partner?

Sandra: Yes, Japan is a big partner. But China still has some trade problems. For instance, with oil, China has what is known as dirty oil, "waxy." Oil is representative of China's basic trade problem. They have the resources, but not the ability to turn the resources into marketable products. Coal, on the other hand, is different. China has very rich coal deposits in the Batung area. They are exporting a lot of coal—even to a place like Korea where the political relations are very poor. To get around legal restrictions, they use what is known as "switch trading." There are ways around restrictions if you really want to do business.

There truly is a large Cultural Revolution aftermath. China wants to catch up. I was quite shocked when I first visited China and people asked me, "What's a refrigerator?" Instead, they preserved food in plastic bags. It would be great if you could go. We could meet again and compare impressions.

Bob: Well, that's very interesting.

Sandra: One last problem you should be aware of is the difficulty in getting any equity out of the country. I'll hunt for the new laws for you. China has recently published them. I'll get them in April and send you copies. It's mostly procedural stuff concerning small letters-of-credit transactions. Right now we have $400 million of business in China and hope to double that this year.

Bob: Well, thanks a lot, John. It's been very helpful. It's been a pleasure to meet you as well, Sandra. I hope your trip to China goes well.

At this point, the meeting broke up. The four people left the room and parted on the second floor. John and Sandra were left to find their way back out to the street. Once outside, they broke out in smiles, obviously pleased with their last hour's work.

CONCLUSION

After John dropped off Sandra at the bank, he returned to his office. Even though he felt that the day had gone very well, on particularly busy days like this one, John liked to take some time to review his performance and reflect on what, if anything, he might do to improve it. As the daily thunderstorm began to rumble through Houston, John sat back in his chair and thought about his day.

CASE 3-2   THE AKILI SYSTEMS GROUP

*I*n August of 1999, Andrew Thorby, president of Akili Systems Group, was considering a sales opportunity at Taylor Corporation, a retail chain in North America and Canada. A meeting was scheduled with Taylor's chief financial officer in one week to present Akili's proposal for the project. In two weeks, Akili would make a presentation to Taylors' entire project team outlining Akili's approach to the project and to address any concerns the project team might have. The problem is that Thorby had not yet made up his mind whether this was the right opportunity for Akili at this time. Akili had grown to $20 million in sales last year and had set an objective of $30 million in revenues for 1999. Synectics, a competitor of Akili, had already estimated the project at $9 million. Thorby was very concerned whether Akili could successfully deliver on a project of this size without straining the organization and taking away potential revenue from other accounts. On the other hand, the project was in an area, the Internet, which Akili had targeted for future growth and in which they needed to build a reputation.

The Taylor opportunity had come to the attention of Mike Chaffin, one of Akili's sales representatives, several months after Synectics, a large systems integration firm with over $1 billion in revenue, had already established its presence at Taylor. Taylor wanted to design and build an Internet infrastructure to connect all of its remote stores and prospective customers in order to provide online access to catalogs, inventory, and employee certifications. The objective of this project was to allow Taylor to meet some of its strategic repositioning objectives, along with reducing costs and improving customer service.

Despite the attractive size of the project and its fit with several of Akili's strengths, Thorby kept coming back to the comment made by Alan Boyer, a project manager with Akili:

> With our existing customers' demands for more of our people, we need to focus on supporting their needs. Furthermore, the retail environment has not been the most pleasant working environment for our consultants. It will be difficult to motivate our consultants to move out of their existing projects to do this one. In this employment market, we can't force them to go.

INDUSTRY OVERVIEW

The term "systems integrator" was a broad characterization for companies that provide information technology related services. A systems integrator could be industry-focused such as with information technologies used in the oil and gas exploration industry; information technology-focused such as with Internet application development, year 2000 conversion development, data warehouse, etc.; or, a mix of both.

Competitors in the systems integration business are divided into two groups of firms depending on their size. On the one hand, there are a limited number of very large systems integration firms consisting of companies such as IBM, Andersen Consulting, and Synectics. Each firm has a worldwide presence with several thousand consultants. With the Year 2000 causing information systems departments to scramble for resources, systems integrators' prices and fees are skyrocketing.

There are also a large number of smaller systems integration firms. The Houston, Texas, market alone is home to over 2,200 technology consulting firms. There are at least two reasons for the large number of small systems integration firms. First, there is very little barrier to entry into this business, as the initial capital requirements are minimal. Second, most large systems integration organizations will not look at projects that are less than seven to eight million dollars in size. These smaller firms fill the void created by large firms not taking on the smaller projects.

The large and small systems integration firms also differ in their operating models. The large firms follow a leveraged model where they provide one senior consultant and several junior consultants. This process helps to ensure high quality and consistency, while achieving scale economies. This approach is also attractive to people early in their careers or those who just received their MBAs, they are usually more risk adverse and still learning the ropes. Despite its advantages, customers' experiences with this approach are somewhat mixed.

> A number of our customers have told us that they have to provide parking for the school bus when the large systems

This case was prepared by Michael Chaffin of Akili Systems Group, James Boles of the University of South Florida, William L. Cron of Southern Methodist University. Copyright © by Michael Chaffin, James Boles, and William Cron.

integration firms show up. Even though this frustrated many of our customers, they had several projects that required an enormous amount of people. The large systems integration firms could provide these resources on a moment's notice, whereas the small boutique systems integrators could not.—Chaffin

The smaller firms, on the other hand, tend to attract top-level, experienced talent because these individuals are confident in their ability to find other work quickly should the company go out of business. In return, they have the opportunity to make a big return should the company successfully go public. This may make smaller firms more attractive to customers because of the quality of the human resources put on each project.

The average number of consultants who are not assigned to projects for the large systems integration firms is typically around 15%–25% of their workforce, whereas the unassigned in the smaller firm is usually around 5% or less. The large systems integration firms are the more expensive alternative, but from the customer's perspective are potentially the least risky in regard to their own job stability. Management rarely gets fired should a project fail when they utilize a large systems integration firm.

> It seems that our customers have a much more pleasurable experience working with us. They have a lot of involvement with our projects and they get to work with senior people. The large systems integration firms can be frustrating to their clients at times when they send 20 people to do a project and don't involve the customer.—Boyer

Small systems integration firms have to be more creative with their approach to marketing. Small firms might utilize independent contractors or engage in joint ventures in order to gain client referrals and muster the resources necessary to compete with the larger firms.

> Cambridge Technology Partners (CTP) could not compete against McKinsey in the strategy business. CTP could have hired experienced management consultants but it would have taken a significant amount of time to build up the experience to compete effectively. When CTP acquired the management consulting firm Peter Chadwick, they instantly could compete. That acquisition primarily bought CTP a strategy consulting track record.—Thorby

Like most consulting and service industries, the key resource in this industry is the expertise and experience of the firm's human capital. Salary requirements for individuals with similar experience, for instance, vary widely. The large demand for consultants has increased their demands for pay, benefits, and stock.

> In 1990, compensation for a technical consultant ranged from $35,000 to $50,000. By 1997, the range grew from $60,000 to over $100,000. One of our customers has an information systems staff of over 700 people. Three hundred of those people are consultants on assignments from numerous systems integration firms.—Chaffin

A TYPICAL PROJECT

A typical project in the systems integration industry has three distinct phases (see Exhibit 1). The first phase is to define the technical and organizational change requirements of the project. The first phase, often referred to as the design phase, of each project requires generalists in five categories: business analysis, technical architecture, application architecture, data architecture, and change management (Exhibit 2). At the end of phase 1, there would be a minimal switching cost to change systems integrators should there not be a fit between the organizations. Phase 1 averaged about 10% of each project's total effort.

The second and third phases are systems development and implementation (Exhibit 1). Typically the bulk of the consultants during these phases are specialists in each of the previously mentioned categories. While the first phase utilized a smaller number of resources (3 to 5 people on average), the latter phases for large projects required in excess of 20 consultants.

Prior to receiving approval for the project, a systems design firm would usually spend some time with the potential client to develop accurate numbers to present to the client's management team so that they could determine a project's return on investment (ROI). Systems integrators would usually spend a week or more, depending on the size of the project, performing a high level analysis (usually at no cost) to determine the overall size of the project (all three phases). In addition to giving the client an understanding of the general size of the project, it also gave the systems integrator a chance to sell itself and give the prospective clients a comfort level with the systems integrator before moving ahead with the project.

THE INTERNET

The Internet has had an important impact on the systems integration industry. Historically, information systems departments had developed applications such as order entry and accounts payable that their business units had to use. The end users of the application were

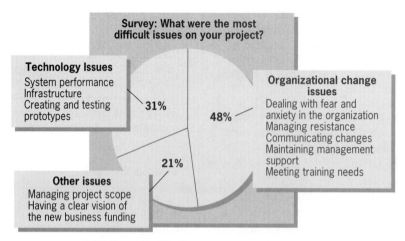

Survey: What were the most difficult issues on your project?

Technology Issues
System performance
Infrastructure
Creating and testing
prototypes
31%

48%

Organizational change issues
Dealing with fear and
anxiety in the organization
Managing resistance
Communicating changes
Maintaining management
support
Meeting training needs

21%

Other issues
Managing project scope
Having a clear vision of
the new business funding

FIGURE 1   Problems with Systems Integration

well defined and their needs fairly easy to see. The Internet, on the other hand, did not have well defined users, nor were the users required to use the system. This created much more pressure for organizations to focus on the user side of the process. Who would be using the system? What would they need from the system? What are their personal preferences? Figure 1 shows that the human factors and how they connect the Internet to an organization's existing infrastructure are the most complex pieces of the project.

> The Internet spawned the introduction of many new small Internet development companies that are very good at the technical requirements needed to develop an Internet site. Most of these firms had the creative talent and developers, but lacked the experience to connect the Internet with their customers' existing systems, or to understand the human factor needs for projects of this nature. As the Internet moves from more of a passive medium to an interactive one, the smaller firms will need to partner with firms like ours to compete.—Boyer

THE AKILI SYSTEMS GROUP

In late November 1992, Kaushik Shah and Andrew Thorby, two independent consultants, sat around the dinner table discussing the current systems integration industry's business model.

> Our customers always complained about the way the large systems integration firms worked. They felt that they were paying a lot of money for inexperienced people to build their large scale mission critical systems. We saw an opportunity to build an organization with seasoned consultants. Unfortunately we did not recognize that, as

much as our customers despised the large systems integration firms, they viewed them as job security.—Thorby

With this in mind, Akili was born. Akili built its practice rapidly; by 1998 it had grown to approximately $20 million in sales with over 125 employees. With more and more organizations looking for industry specific expertise, Akili had narrowed its focus to three: energy, telecommunications, and financial services. Akili also narrowed its product offerings to management consulting and custom application development. Within management consulting, Akili focused on business process reengineering and change management. Within the custom application development, Akili wanted to shift its focus toward the Internet due to strong growth potential. Forrester Research had estimated that over $3.2 trillion would be transacted over the Internet by the year 2002.

> The Internet appears to be the fastest growing segment in the market. Akili as a company has little experience in this area. We need to get some experience quickly in order to stay even with or slightly ahead of our competition. Currently we would lose in a direct qualifications battle with our competitors for an Internet project.—Thorby

> Our management consulting practice is extremely competitive with the large systems integration firms. The projects we typically go for are considered small in the eyes of the larger systems integrators. When we compete against them, they often send in the "B Team" while we send in our "A Team." They frequently use a direct strategy to sell against us, by showing the customer how many references they have. For the first phase of any project, however, we can compete against anyone.—Boyer

Akili's objective was to do an initial public offering (IPO) within the next 18 months. It was critical for Akili to maintain revenue growth and high profitability in order to have a successful IPO. However, well-publicized project failures could have an adverse effect. Since everyone at Akili had stock options, opportunities were scrutinized to avoid any high-risk projects. A large part of Akili's past success derived from its ability to attract and retain experienced consultants. Akili's plan to do an IPO was a large part of its attraction to prospective employees. Offering the opportunity to work on interesting and leading edge projects is considered important to future recruiting.

THE TAYLOR CORPORATION

The Taylor Corporation traced its history back to 1919 as a wholesaler of woolen products. The company survived the Great Depression and following World War II opened its first two retail stores specializing in wool products. This was the beginning of a successful retail and mail order chain store business that eventually grew to $6 million in sales. In 1950, the company was taken public. In 1963, Taylor acquired a small, virtually bankrupt company that was an electronics retailer. The company had nine retail stores and a mail order business that sold primarily to ham operators and electronic buffs. Since 1963, Taylor has grown to more than 7,000 locations throughout the U.S. and over $5.6 billion in annual sales. In addition to its flagship retail stores, Taylor also launched a separate computer superstore concept, a chain of electronic product repair shops, telephone specialty stores, and a computer servicing business.

Taylor Corporation has undergone a lot of changes in the past five years, spinning off several unsuccessful business ventures and consolidating and refurbishing their retail outlets. They also experienced a large information systems project failure in the previous year, causing the business units to be less than confident in the ability of their internal information systems department.

> Our organization was not prepared to take on a project of that nature. People were comfortable supporting our older systems. They were not ready for change. Unfortunately, management did not recognize this soon enough. The project was 100% over time and budget before anyone even thought to look at the problem. The technology was ultimately blamed for what I think was clearly a people issue.—Former information systems employee

Senior management had brought in a whole new team to revamp the information systems department. The new chief information officer (CIO), Teri Sullivan was determined to tear down any walls that had been built between her new department and the business units. The proposed project had to be successful in order to regain the confidence of the business units.

> Being a retail organization, the company is fairly price-sensitive and willing to accept a bit more risk in order to save a dime. This is why we had a high failure rate.—Former information systems employee

This was Taylor's first attempt at building an interactive Internet site, so the technology portion of the project was viewed as very complex. Taylor felt that it was important that the systems integration firm involved in this project should have experience with large-scale Internet projects. Taylor's current company-information only Internet site was relatively inexpensive to create and could only be accessed within Taylor by certain employees. This experience established expectations with Taylor's senior management that the costs for this Internet project would be relatively low.

> Taylor's senior management expected hardware costs to be the most expensive item on this project. Early estimates from our hardware vendor were approximately $750,000 for the necessary hardware.—Boyer

> Teri was previously the vice president of human resources so she had an appreciation for the human factors involved in the project. The project team for Taylor was made up of information system technical and project management resources. Teri gave the project team significant input into the decision process. The project team's decision criteria were the following: Can the vendor deliver? And can we team with them to enhance our skills? While the project team wanted to insure a successful implementation, they appeared concerned that by bringing in Synectics, their roles in the project would be substantially reduced, therefore limiting their professional growth with the Internet.—Chaffin

A project of this nature is a significant undertaking for Taylor. The technologies are new, and this is the first time its information systems department would be building a system for customer use. While technical issues associated with developing the screens that the individuals saw will present some challenges, Thorby felt that this was not the main challenge of the project. Understanding how end users (customers and employees) would want to interact with the system and organizational issues associated with building and supporting the new systems he considered to be most critical to the success of the project. This played into several of Akili's strengths, particularly its experience in change management.

THE TAYLOR OPPORTUNITY

After spending a week interviewing all the senior management at Taylor, Synectics had put together some rough estimates for the entire project. The estimate was $9 million for full implementation of the project. Taylor was certainly shocked by Synectics' initial cost estimate. Taylor's management was considering this proposal when Akili was introduced to the CIO through a current customer of Akili.

While Akili did not have experience with large-scale Internet projects, this could be a great opportunity for Akili to gain the references it needed in the Internet practice. This may also be an opportunity for Taylor to reduce its cost. Akili had a much lower overhead than the larger systems integration firms and a low price offer might be considered the cost of entry for Akili into this growing business.

The Akili team had spent some time reviewing notes from the original interviews but did not have enough information to propose costs for the entire project. There were also concerns as to whether Synectics had captured all of the requirements or estimated the project cost at a realistic number. Two meetings had been scheduled for Akili to walk through its approach with Taylor. The first meeting, scheduled for next week, will be a thirty-minute session with Taylor's CIO. In this meeting Akili would be expected to present its overall approach to the project and its cost estimates. The CIO's confidence in Akili's ability to deliver and the recommendation of Taylor's project team will be critical for Akili to have an opportunity to win. The second meeting, two hours with the entire project team (12) from Taylor, was to discuss Akili's approach and allay any concerns the project team might have with Akili. This meeting is scheduled for two weeks from today.

This is a very tight schedule for Akili and not at all typical of how the selling cycle of most projects develops. Commenting on this opportunity, Mike Chaffin explained:

> When we first entered the sales process, it appeared that we had such a remote chance of winning that delivery didn't pay much attention to what happens should we win. Because of the size and strategic nature of this project, most people at Akili thought we were wasting our time because we had no Internet client references. My

company felt that we were being used by Taylor to get a better price from Synectics. I think Akili is now beginning to worry that we might actually win this project. We're still the underdog, and we have to develop a "win theme" to present to the executive sponsor and project team.

It was also clear that Akili's sales approach would have to be well thought-out to have any chance of succeeding. This would not be a straightforward features-benefits comparison type of presentation. Neither Mike nor his boss Rudy George, sales director at Akili, felt that they could slug it out with Synectics standing toe-to-toe and win the sale. In summarizing the situation, Mr. George commented:

> Synectics has positioned itself with Taylor as an Internet specialist. They have been in the account longer than we have, they have a lot more experience as a company with the Internet than we have, and they have the resources on board now to do the entire project. Synectics will attack us directly on our lack of Internet technology experience and our size. Based on our competition successfully positioning this project as strictly Internet-only with Taylor, the customer has to view Synectics as the least risky alternative because of its number of Internet references compared to Akili. We need to find a way to position this opportunity to allow us to compete.

Not only did Mike and Rudy need to develop a sales strategy for Taylor, but they also realized that they would need to sell the merits of the project internally to Akili.

> This is considered a large project for Akili and a mid-to-small size project for Synectics. Unfortunately we have one large and several medium-to-small size projects that we are currently working on. All of our consultants are currently involved in these projects. The latter phases of the project for Taylor would eventually require a bunch of people over the next two years. Staffing it with all new people would raise our risk of delivery. But they pay me based on a percentage of revenue from new customers, not to be risk-averse. A project of this size would take care of half my quota for next year.—Mike Chaffin

WHAT SHOULD AKILI DO?

Thorby realized that he had to make a decision with respect to Taylor before things developed too far and events made the decision for him. Due to the size of the project and its Internet focus, Thorby recognized that this sale had to be considered strategic in nature:

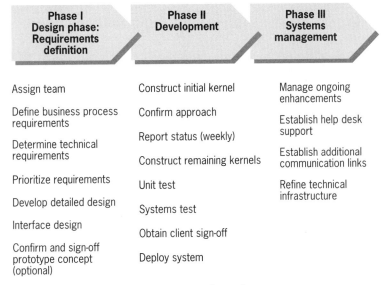

Phase I Design phase: Requirements definition	Phase II Development	Phase III Systems management
Assign team	Construct initial kernel	Manage ongoing enhancements
Define business process requirements	Confirm approach	Establish help desk support
Determine technical requirements	Report status (weekly)	Establish additional communication links
Prioritize requirements	Construct remaining kernels	Refine technical infrastructure
Develop detailed design	Unit test	
Interface design	Systems test	
Confirm and sign-off prototype concept (optional)	Obtain client sign-off	
	Deploy system	

EXHIBIT 1 Project Phases

We will be only a $20 million company this year and could be putting $9 million of next year's projected revenue of $30 million on one customer. Can we deliver a project of this size successfully without straining the organization or taking away potential revenue from a strategic account? This opportunity is not in an industry that we typically pursue. Although this service offering is an area that we want to get into, we currently don't have the experience Taylor desires. They have clearly stated that relevant Internet experience is required. Should we expend the resources chasing something that we are not well positioned to win or successfully take on? We would have to substantially increase the size of our company to take on the latter phases of this project not counting the growth that will be required to service our existing customers.

It is clear that Akili is coming into the game late, and Thorby was wondering if it was too late. It was even questionable whether Akili had enough information to accurately estimate the price for the entire project. Thorby's concern was that any numbers given to Taylor could be invalid and could potentially set their expectations too high.

When talking to sales, Thorby got the impression that it was very important to win this opportunity. This is a multi-year project involving a service offering in which Akili had no current experience. On the other hand, Akili has several people who have the requisite experience from previous jobs. Should Akili win this

EXHIBIT 2 Design Phase Team

Business Analysis—determines the business requirements for the project
Technical Architect—determines the computer hardware platform to support the business requirements. This position is a generalist who understands a wide range of computer hardware platforms.
Application Architect—determines the development architecture and toolsets. This position is also a generalist who understands a wide range of development toolsets (i.e., PowerBuilder, Visual Basic, etc.).
Data Architect—models the data requirements for the project and makes recommendations on the type of database required for the project (i.e., Oracle, DB2, etc.).
Change Management—determines the people factors that might impede the success of the project and how to correct them.

project, the customer has a recognizable name, which can be used as leverage with other prospective clients.

But Thorby also recognized that he had to consider the big picture. Was this opportunity right for Akili, and how could they minimize their risks? "We have revenue goals for sales," he thought, "low turnover goals for human resources, and delivery goals for our consultants. Is this business aligned with those goals?"

CHAPTER 4

ACCOUNT RELATIONSHIP MANAGEMENT

> The sale, then, merely consummates the courtship, at which point the marriage begins. How good the marriage is depends on how well the seller manages the relationship.
>
> THEODORE LEVITT

Chapter Consultants:
Ken Whelan, Director, Business Development, Qwest Communications
Chris Jander, National Accounts Manager, Marconi Communications

LEARNING OBJECTIVES

After studying this chapter, you should be able to:

→ List the steps in the professional purchasing process.

→ Identify the different buying influences in the buying center.

→ Explain how relationships are likely to evolve.

→ Describe factors critical to gaining commitment to a relationship.

GROWING THE RELATIONSHIP

Owens-Brockway's relationship with a major beverage producer began to change with a business lunch in the client's executive dining room. Owens, the Glass Container Division of Owens-Illinois (Toledo, Ohio), had been selling glass containers to the beverage producer for a number of years. "As I recall, the company's worldwide sourcing director and I were talking about cost-reduction opportunities," notes account executive Henry A. Casazza, Jr. "The director had attended the Owens-Brockway Glass School and was familiar with the blow-mold concept. That was the gestation of a partnership agreement that was termed the Multi-Serve Juice Rationalization Program," he reports.

The beverage company was expanding its product line by offering its product in many new sizes and shapes. This offered the marketing advantage of differentiation but was also very costly. Teams from each side were reviewing crucial issues, such as how to standardize the bottling line and how much time it would take to change over to new molds. Owens-Brockway's program was chosen over that of another supplier and resulted in a multiyear agreement.

In commenting on the relationship, Casazza stresses, "Partnering has emotional costs. You must develop a very trusting relationship. And you and the customer need mutual reasons to lock into each other for a period of time." Casazza emphasizes that partnerships "require relationships with all departments. You'll work with plant, marketing, logistics, operations, and traffic personnel—and in virtually every aspect of the business."

"The account manager usually makes the initial contact and steers the agreement through," he notes. "However, that individual requires the support of all the others—on both sides—all of whom become part of the partnering team."[1]

This chapter focuses on building lasting and profitable relationships with customers, referred to as *accounts*. In Chapter 2 we discussed the strategic sales force decisions companies should make. One of these decisions is the type of relationship the company wished to have with its target customers. In this chapter we will examine four key aspects of business-to-business relationships shown in Figure 4-1. The concepts discussed in this chapter are important regardless of the type of customer relationship desired by the supplier, though there are differences in their relative importance and execution depending on the type of relationship. Trust and productive relationships are important regardless of whether there is a transactional, consultative, or enterprise relationship between the customer and supplier.[2]

The discussion of the selling process in Chapter 3 focused primarily on an individual sales call. In professional selling to other businesses, multiple calls are typically required to close a sale, and transactions usually take place within the context of an ongoing relationship. The Owens-Brockway example illustrates some of the most important developments in business-to-business marketing—selling teams, buying centers, close cooperation between buyers and sellers, strategic project involvement, long-term relationships, and a high level of trust. This chapter examines each of these issues and provides practical examples of their significance.

One additional point that should not go unnoticed in the Owens example is that companies are increasingly looking for significant growth opportunities within current accounts. In a recent Gallup survey, more than 60 percent of responding salespeople indicated that it took one or two calls to consummate a sale with existing customers, but only 18 percent indicated

FIGURE 4-1   Account Relationship Management Concepts

a sale could be made to new customers with only this number of calls.[3] Results of a recent study by Weeks and Kahle further underscores the importance of existing customers in meeting sales objectives. This study investigated whether the amount of time spent calling on established accounts versus potential new accounts affected sales force performance. The results show that neither the total amount of time spent face-to-face with customers nor the amount of time prospecting is related to performance; only the time spent with established accounts has a positive impact on performance.[4]

Our discussion of relationship management begins by presenting the typical stages in the business-to-business purchasing process. Examples of different types of account relationships will be discussed within the context of each stage. The concept of a buying center is introduced, along with the development of selling teams. Following this, our focus changes to understanding how relationships develop and what steps sellers can take to ensure profitable account relationships.

ACCOUNT PURCHASING PROCESS

One of our basic premises is that in order to be successful the sales force must create value for the customer. To better understand how the sales force can create customer value, let's look at the different points in the purchasing process where a sales force can potentially add value. The typical sequence of steps that purchasers go through in business-to-business acquisitions can be viewed as a process consisting of four steps (Figure 4-2).[5] It is not at all unusual for this process to last a year, especially with large projects that overhaul some aspect of a customer's organizational infrastructure, such as its communications or information systems. It is also important to keep in mind that it is not just the customer's purchasing department that is involved in this process. In fact, the purchasing department may have minimal or no involvement in a customer's strategic purchases.

Recognition of Needs

The first stage occurs when the account *recognizes that a need exists*. In some cases the need is immediate and focuses on resolving a problem, such as when a manager observes a bottleneck in a production process or when existing machinery breaks down. Not only is it the sales force's responsibility to address known customer problems, but often the sales force must uncover opportunities that the customer didn't even know existed. Transcend Services, Inc. of Atlanta, Georgia, for example, will conduct an operational assessment of the medical records department in a hospital, evaluating how the department processes work, proce-

FIGURE 4-2   The Typical Purchasing Process

dures, adherence to performance standards, and interface with the rest of the hospital. Transcend will submit a proposal to the hospital to take over total management of the hospital's record department, including having the hospital's employees become Transcend's employees, if the audit indicates that cost savings are feasible within predetermined performance standards. According to Transcend's president, Larry Gerdes, an audit may take two to three days to perform; the report takes an additional week to complete. The whole purchasing process typically takes about six months. The key for Transcend is getting customers to understand and quantify the magnitude of the problem.

One of the first things a salesperson needs to understand when identifying business-to-business buying needs is the concept of *derived demand.* Professional buyers do not purchase for themselves, but rather help to produce goods and services for resale. This suggests that suppliers can gain a competitive advantage by knowing and understanding the needs of the customers' customers.[6] This also means that the demand for industrial goods is derived from demand for the client's final product.

Derived demand is an important concept because it determines whom the sales force calls on, what customer benefits are emphasized, and how much of a product or service is ultimately sold. To convince GTE to carry its line of ethernet connections, for example, RELTEC demonstrated to apartment owners the advantages of ethernet connections for the computer needs of their customers. Since this feature could reduce the apartment's client turnover, the apartment owners convinced GTE to include RELTEC's ethernet connection with its product lines.

Evaluation of Options

Businesses may spend considerable time and money in searching and evaluating alternative suppliers, depending on the strategic significance of the purchase.[7] Purchased materials represent from 30 to 80 percent and average 50 percent of an original equipment manufacturer's (OEM) total product cost.[8] The cost of misunderstandings among the parties involved and post-sales problems can be enormous. Often the biggest cost is the opportunity cost associated with not selecting the right supplier. On the other hand, the search for and evaluation of suppliers can be quite expensive. Consider the chapter-opening case of Owens-Brockway relationship and their efforts at cooperative problem solving. Most purchasers would not have the resources to establish this type of working relationship with all of their suppliers. It is very important the supplier understand the customer's situation with respect to both costs and opportunities at this phase of the purchasing process.

Specifications   One of the key activities taking place during this phase is the development of a precise statement of the requirements and tolerances, referred to as a product's *specifications.* The exact specifications are usually dictated by the anticipated demand for the organization's products and by the technological requirements of its operations. This stage is often critical for potential suppliers because final specifications can favor one product over another. Therefore, selling the benefits of a technology is often critical at this point in the purchasing process. Because each supplier may emphasize different product features, getting specifications established that are best met by your offering may be important to landing the sale.

Traditionally, customers developed their own product specifications very early in the evaluation stage of the purchasing process. In some of the more advanced and successful partnering relationships however, customers work with suppliers to meet product specifications. Take the case of Johnson Controls, Inc., chosen to supply seats for Neon, Chrysler's new compact car. Johnson was able to meet Chrysler's cost target but fell far short on safety, weight, and comfort. Ten Chrysler engineers met with 10 Johnson counterparts, led by the sales director. After five 11-hour days, they agreed on weight, cost, and performance targets and subsequently helped Johnson meet these targets.[9] This example also illustrates that in more advanced buyer-seller relationships, the supplier is actually chosen prior to completion of detailed technical specifications that are jointly developed by the supplier and customer.

Proposals A *sales proposal* is a written offer by a seller to provide a product or service to a purchasing organization. The proposal may represent the culmination of sales activities spanning several months involving extensive client analysis. On the other hand, a proposal may result from receiving a *Request for Proposal* (RFP) from a buyer. An RFP is a notice that a customer sends out to qualified suppliers asking them to bid on a project with a certain set of specifications. Regardless of how the process was initiated, it is important that the proposal development process is integrated into the selling process. In purchasing materials and equipment, for example, building contractors may consider service, quality of product, supplier support, low price, and/or reputation for fair dealing among their most important purchasing criteria when choosing suppliers. The relative importance of these criteria, however, may vary from one contractor to the next. One contractor may place more importance on low price, whereas another may be more concerned about the willingness of the supplier to stand behind the product. To win a contract, it is important that a supplier's proposal is geared toward meeting the customer's priorities. In this case, the proposal is actually the outcome of the first two phases of the purchasing process: identification of needs and evaluation of options.[10]

Purchase Decision

It is common to describe a purchase decision using one of the three labels: a *straight rebuy, a modified rebuy,* and *new buy.* The reason for using these labels is because the nature of the purchasing process is quite different among the three and thus the selling approach is also different. In a straight rebuy, the product has been previously purchased and the current purchase does not involve any changes in the product or the offering. In a modified rebuy some changes in the offering are present and in the new buy situation the customer has not previously purchased the offering. The modified rebuy and new buy purchase situations are discussed in the next section when describing the complex selling situation and buying center concept.

In straight rebuy cases, the purchase usually involves replenishing inventories in products that have been purchased many times with no modification in specifications. An individual may make the purchase decision and the decision itself is limited to one of quantity and delivery timetable, as opposed to specification of the product's requirements. In such a situation, the seller can add value to the customer by helping to make the purchase easy, convenient, and as hassle-free as possible. When customers have been dealing with one company and salesperson for a long time, salespeople may even write the purchase order themselves thereby saving the customer time.

The use of *Extranets* to facilitate inventory replenishment-type orders is becoming quite common in business-to-business transactions. Extranets link trading partners' internal, Internet computer networks to provide a secure private electronic environment for real-time communication. By connecting with the customer's computer system and accessing a customer's inventory information, a supplier is able to automatically ship product for purposes of inventory replenishment. More companies are in fact requiring their suppliers to support just-in-time inventory practices, improve supply chain management, and furnish instant order-status information via Extranets. Marshall Industries, a leading distributor of steel products, has developed an Extranet that allows customers to track order status, expedite shipping by linking to freight forwarders, participate in live engineering seminars with video and audio, and get live online support.

In cases where the product is significantly altered or where the customer considers the purchase strategic, a *buying committee* may make the final purchase decision. A buying committee may be made up of personnel from a variety of functional areas affected by the decision, often including management from finance, operations, purchasing, manufacturing, and marketing.

Price is usually a crucial factor in business-to-business marketing, especially for commodity-type items, for which there are many comparable alternatives from which to choose. The role of price in many buyer-seller relationships is changing in today's competitive environment. Instead of looking for the lowest price, some buyers are realizing that by working together with sellers, they can operate more efficiently and effectively in satisfying the needs of the ultimate consumer and may do so at a lower overall cost. Grief Brothers Corporation, which manufactures fiber and plastic drums, routinely conducts what it calls *cost-in-use* studies to document the incremental cost savings that a customer gains by using Grief's more expensive products and services, rather than a less expensive alternative. One of Grief's technical service managers works with customer managers to estimate the customer's current total costs and to identify system solutions for the customer. Solutions might include just-in-time deliveries, a new delivery system, and drum recycling. In giving the customer a variety of service alternatives together with estimates of cost savings, Grief helps the customer make a more informed purchase decision based on the total worth of the system solution to the customer.[11]

An important development in the purchasing process is purchasing on the Internet. According to Forrester Research, the value of business-to-business purchases on the Internet was $32 billion in 1998. This figure far exceeds the $7.8 billion in retail sales over the net in the same year. More important, experts expect business-to-business purchases to grow to $331 billion by the year 2002. The message to suppliers is clear: Develop Internet purchasing capabilities or lose business.

Implementation and Evaluation

As was pointed out at the beginning of this chapter, the sale is only the beginning of the relationship in most business-to-business selling situations. The seller's obligation during this phase in the purchasing process is to ensure that all promises are fulfilled and customer expectations met or exceeded. This will include making sure that the product has no defects, arrives on time as promised and at the right place, warranties are honored, repairs or exchanges handled quickly and smoothly, needed information is provided, and adequate training is provided.

In any relationship, conflicts are likely to arise. Some have argued that conflict management is the key competency that salespeople must develop to succeed in the partnering relationships that characterize many modern supplier-customer relationships.[12] When effectively managed, conflict can have a positive effect on relationships and sales. Some of the potential benefits include (1) stimulating interest in exploring new approaches, (2) providing an opportunity to air problems and explore solutions, and (3) mobilizing the resources of the parties in a relationship.[13]

Many organizations will evaluate their suppliers by a formal value analysis and/or a vendor analysis. *Value analysis,* developed by General Electric as a basis for cost reduction, is a detailed analysis of vendor offerings focusing on the relative cost of providing a necessary function or service at the desired time and place with the necessary quality. Value analysis focuses on total cost, not just invoice cost. For repetitively purchased items, *possession costs* (i.e., costs related to holding inventory) and *acquisition costs* (e.g., costs associated with originating requisitions, interviewing salespeople, expediting deliveries, receiving and editing invoices, follow-up on inaccurate and late deliveries) usually far exceed the price on the invoice that the customer pays for the product.[14]

Vendor analysis is similar to value analysis but focuses on the vendor by looking at such things as delivery reliability, product quality, price, service, and technical competence. Vendor analysis focuses on eliminating marginal suppliers in order to reduce contact costs and improve efficiency. General Motors, for example, used vendor analysis to help concentrate its steel purchases among a smaller number of suppliers. GM felt it could get better service and prices by favoring a few vendors with most of its steel business.

In some high-tech industries there is a movement away from extensive vendor analysis. Instead, suppliers are offering a warranty that says in effect the supplier will share the cost of any changes in specifications that are needed during a period of time. The supplier is essentially sharing in the customer's risk while reducing the selling and purchasing cycle.

Summary

This section discussed the distinct phases of organizational purchasing to illustrate the typical process and to demonstrate how suppliers can win or lose the sale at any point in this process. In Chapter 2 we stressed that one of the strategic sales force decisions companies make is the type of customer relationship desired. Figure 4-3 illustrates the implications of the type of relationship on how the sales force creates customer value during each phase of the purchasing process. In transactional relationships the opportunities for creating customer value are highest during the final two phases of the purchase process. Making purchasing easy and hassle-free and preventing post-sale headaches are important opportunities for creating customer value in transactional relationships. Consultative customer relationships create customer value by creatively helping customers solve problems and identify growth opportunities during the first two phases of the purchasing process. The intent of enterprise relationships is to create exceptional customer value during all four phases of the purchasing process.

Selling in each type of customer relationship requires a high degree of customer intimacy—knowing the customer's problems, their priorities, expectations, needs, and culture.[15] Similarly, it is important that salespeople know who within the customer's organization is involved in the purchasing decision and understand this person's role in the process. This is particularly important in complex sales situations. *Complex sales* situations are ones in which several people in the customer's organization must give their approval before the sale can take place. Complex sales situations are defined by the structure of the purchase decision, not by the product or price. Consider selling basketballs for example. The salesperson who sells a dozen basketballs to Mr. Jones, owner of the local sporting goods store, is mak-

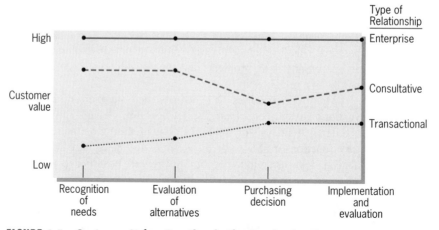

FIGURE 4-3   Customer Value Creation in the Purchasing Process

ing a simple sale. But the salesperson selling a hundred gross of basketballs to Wal-Mart is probably involved in a complex sale, because making the sale will require not just one approval, but several, especially if this is a new line of basketballs. The added complexity of selling to more than one person in an organization and a framework for doing so is discussed in the next section.

BUYING CENTER

The term *buying center* is used to refer to all of the people formally or informally involved in the purchasing decision. That is, all the people who must say yes for a sale to occur or influence the people who will ultimately say yes or no to the purchase. The buying center changes over time and is not a formal department in the organization. The number of people included in the buying center may vary from 1 to 15 or more, depending on a number of factors, including how many departments use the item, the dollar value of the purchase, and the product's degree of technical sophistication. Four people, for instance, are typically involved in the purchasing of new office equipment—a purchasing agent, an office manager, a controller, and a supervisor of the department using the equipment. Each of these people is likely to have a unique perspective and purchasing concern when selecting an office equipment supplier.

A *purchasing role* refers to the set issues or concerns that a member of the buying center will consider when deciding whether to approve or recommend either a purchase or a specific supplier. For purposes of clarification and simplification, these concerns may be grouped into one of three purchasing roles: economic buyers, user buyers, and technical buyers. An individual buying center member may occupy multiple purchasing roles, but each purchasing role is expected to be held by at least one individual in any major purchasing situation.[16] A fourth person must also be present for the sale to be successfully concluded. This person is referred to as an advocate. Each of these four roles is described in this section.

Economic Buyer

An *economic buyer* is the person or committee who has the power to give final approval to buy your product or service. These people have the money to make a purchase and are able to release the cash to buy should they choose to do so. The focus of the economic buyer is not exclusively on price or technology, but also on performance; that is, what will the organization get in return for spending this money?

Obviously this buyer must be identified in each sale. Although these people are rarely very far down in the organization, their exact organizational position will depend on a number of factors. The economic buyer is likely to be farther up the organizational ladder in the following situations:

- The more expensive the product
- The more depressed the organization's business condition
- The less experience the customer has with you, your firm, and the product
- The greater the potential impact a wrong purchase decision will have on the organization

The person who assumes the role of economic buyer may change if the role the product or service performs for the customer changes. The regional Bell operating companies (RBOCs) of a downsized AT&T, for example, are experiencing this in the telecommunications industry. The role played by telecommunications has changed as a result of the movement toward distributed data processing and networked computer systems.[17] Many companies now view telecommunications as a strategic asset rather than just "utilities." This has far-reaching implications for sales and marketing in the industry. "In the last three years," says a vice president of operations at AT&T, "we have changed from selling to purchasing agents and dealing with only the communications managers. We have expanded our horizons to where we must gain acceptance with people in the customer organization who are policy makers." This change in focus has necessitated many changes in AT&T's sales practices; for instance, the RBOCs' sales force training has been beefed up to place more emphasis on strategic business decision making in addition to the usual technical training of salespeople.

User Buyer

The role of *user buyers* is to determine the impact of the purchase on the job that they or their people perform. Their focus is much narrower than that of the economic buyer because they are primarily concerned with their own operating areas or departments. As users, they represent a very powerful buying influence and one that is important for the seller to identify. This point is made quite well in the now-famous story of 3M's Post-It notes. Initial efforts to sell the stick-on notes to office managers met with little success. It wasn't until 3M gave secretaries and office workers free samples that the notes took off.

Identifying user buying influences may be more complex than often anticipated. In selling axles for trucks, for example, at least three sets of users are involved. First, there are the manufacturing engineers who design manufacturing processes. Second, there are the people on the manufacturing line at the assembly plant who fit the axle onto the truck. Third, the ultimate end-user is the customer who buys the truck. In recognition of this, some leading-edge axle supply companies are questioning their customers' customers directly about the performance of their axles.[18]

Technical Buying Influence

The role of *technical buyers* is to act as gatekeepers by screening out products and suppliers that do not meet the needs of the buying organization. Their function is to narrow down the choices to those alternatives that are most likely to fulfill particular organizational objectives. These people can have a powerful influence on the final decision, but by themselves they can't say yes, only no.

These buyers are called technical buyers because they focus on the quantifiable aspects of the product or service as they relate to the product's specifications. A number of people may perform this function, including engineers, legal counsel, and purchasing agents. In our earlier truck axle example, product engineers and designers would probably assume this role. A company that has enjoyed success by cultivating relationships with technical buyers is discussed in the Coaching Competency box, the "High Test Safety Shoes Company".

One problem salespeople have experienced with some technical buyers is that they take on the appearance of the economic buyer, that is, the person who makes the final decision. This may occur because of the person's screening function and also from self-deception or an attempt to elevate their perceived importance within the organization. At any rate, salespeople may be misled, and as a result, a purchase decision may be a surprise to them because the competition has dealt with the real economic buyer.

Advocate

In a complex selling situation involving multiple buying influences, it has been suggested that salespeople need to develop a special relationship with a buying influence referred to as an *advocate*. The role of the advocate is to help guide you in the sale by providing critical information about the organization and the people involved in the purchase decision. These

COACHING COMPETENCY
High Test Safety Shoes Company

The High Test Safety Shoes Company manufactures and sells a variety of shoes designed to protect workers from job-related injuries. They sell a non-slipping shoe to the airlines, which workers wear when performing repairs and maintenance on airplanes. One key user-buying influence High Test must sell is the personnel and benefits department of the airlines, because once every six days an airline worker will fall off the wing of a plane. These accidents may result in higher insurance rates, workman's compensation, and other medical-related expenses, not to mention the cost of possibly replacing the injured employee. If High Test can show that their shoes can reduce accidents and lower the costs associated with accidents, it is addressing the concerns of the personnel and benefits office of the airline, an important buying influence in this case.

people may be internal or external to the buying organization. They do not necessarily make the sale or make referrals, but are willing to provide key information about those who do influence the sale. They are often able to sell for you when you cannot be there, for example, during purchasing committee meetings. Their motivation for providing this information is that they are convinced that your product is best for the organization, and therefore they have a personal interest in seeing that you get the sale. This person is obviously critical, and must be selected and developed with care. Others in the buying center must feel that the person is trustworthy and competent. Ideally, the advocate will be recognized by others in the buying center as a group leader and major influence. One way to identify a good advocate, in fact, is to listen for the name of a person whom others in the buying center mention frequently. A strong advocate may be important to the seller's long-term success, because people are less likely to change after having established a publicly stated position.[19]

Summary

The buying center concept has several important implications for salespeople in business-to-business selling. First, salespeople must be quite diverse in their knowledge and flexible in their behavior. Salespeople may find themselves, for example, selling to purchasing agents, engineers, production managers, and controllers in order to close a sale.

Second, a supplier may need to sell to different people with different concerns depending on the stage of the purchasing. Purchasing agents, for example, have been found to have the greatest influence during the later stages of the purchasing process. They are experts at negotiation and tend to know a lot about the suppliers' and competitors' product offerings and terms of sale. Production, on the other hand, is usually most influential during the need identification stage, while engineering is most involved in establishing specifications.

Finally, always be sure that you know who the real decision makers are, because people tend to exaggerate their role in any decision. In addition, most people enjoy the special treatment—golf or dinner—a supplier may extend to the decision makers in a big potential sale.

EVOLUTION OF RELATIONSHIPS

Most marketers would like to establish a long-term relationship with their customers to ensure a stream of purchases and an upgrading of the equipment a client purchases over

Relationship Stage	Description	Key Selling Objectives
Awareness	Recognition that a supplier may be able to satisy an important need.	1. Gain customer's attention. 2. Demonstrate how the product/service can satisfy a need.
Exploration	A tentative, initial trial with limited commitments by both parties. This trial period may go on for an extended period of time.	1. Gain initial acceptance. 2. Build a successful relationship.
Expansion	Expanding the rewards for each party in the relationship.	1. Get to know customers and their business better. 2. Expand ways to help the customer.
Commitment	The commitment by both the buyer and seller to an exclusive relationship.	1. Interaction at levels between the buyer's and seller's organizations. 2. Early supplier involvement in development processes. 3. Long-term focus to the relationship.
Dissolution	Total disengagement from the relationship. This may occur at any point in the relationship.	1. Look for warning signals. 2. Attempt to reinitiate the relationship.

FIGURE 4-4   Stages in a Buyer-Seller Relationship

time. Many companies are emphasizing to their salespeople the importance of understanding how to build and enhance professional relationships at all levels in the organization.[20] It is helpful in this regard to understand how relationships are likely to evolve over time. According to research in social psychology, growing relationships evolve through five general stages: (1) awareness, (2) exploration, (3) expansion, (4) commitment, and (5) dissolution.[21] Although it may be difficult to determine exactly when a relationship progresses to each stage, each represents a major shift in the nature of the relationship; consequently, salespeople should be aware of these changes and proceed accordingly. These five stages of *relationship evolution* and the objectives associated with each stage are summarized in Figure 4-4.

Awareness

This stage refers to recognition by the client that a seller may be a viable source for a particular product or service. Commitments at this stage are nonexistent or very limited. Buyers' and sellers' actions are largely unilateral; that is, they are each looking out solely for their own objectives.

Although this stage may seem obvious in beginning a relationship, it makes a subtle but important point. Relationships are based on a number of sales calls, and customers want to know who you and your company are before they agree to spend much time with you and certainly before making any commitments. The Ball Corporation recognizes this explicitly in its selling strategy, which they refer to as the *planned selling approach.* Ball Corporation is a packaging company with a high-technology base. Its products consist of glass, metal cans, barrier plastic packaging, and industrial product lines and items used in space technology. The purpose of the first sales call is to give a more detailed explanation of the Ball Corporation. On subsequent calls, salespeople tell buyers about each of the four product groups.

The importance of this stage and the validity of Ball Corporation's selling approach are backed by research comparing the sales approaches of average and higher-performing salespeople. This research found that higher-performing salespeople believed that assessing the prospect's knowledge of the seller's company and discussing the prospect's background were more important activities in the initial sales call than did lower-performing salespeople.

Conversely, lower-performing salespeople felt that making a complete presentation and explaining each product benefit were more important than did the higher-performing salespeople.[22]

Exploration

When both parties develop a heightened sense that the possibility for mutual benefit exists, this signals the beginning of the exploration stage of the relationship. The buyer is willing at this point to make a greater effort to explore the seller's offering and capabilities. The Ball Corporation, for example, invites prospects and their fellow decision makers to visit its research labs, a manufacturing plant, and corporate headquarters in Muncie, Indiana. A certain level of interest must have been developed up to this point for a buyer to commit time to this type of visit.

From the seller's perspective, the selling process shifts to understanding the unique needs and viewpoints of the account in order to better understand whether and how a product can be of benefit. At this point, buyers are more willing to share their needs and feelings with a seller. This suggests that salespeople should be aware that many buyers will be unwilling to share their true concerns with a salesperson on the first visit. The relationship has not yet progressed to this point of heightened trust and interest. This phase is critically important to the selling of services to business because the services are often customized to fit the particular needs and values of the customer. When selling communications services, for instance, communication features, technical aspects, information reporting, and price all are adjusted to fit the preferences of individual customers. Indeed, the larger the customer, usually the greater the customization of the offering.

The exploration stage focuses on a *trial relationship*. If feasible, trial purchases (small quantities or tests) may take place in an effort to better understand the benefits, consequences, and costs or problems associated with a product. For example, it is common in the furniture industry for large furniture chains to purchase a sofa from a manufacturer in order to examine its durability, workmanship, and general appearance. Recall from the opening vignette on Owens-Brockway that teams from Owens-Brockway and the beverage producer met to review crucial issues with respect to the cost of glass containers for its beverage line. There must be a certain level of trust and expectation of success to commit to this type of relationship. At this point, however, the relationship is very fragile, allowing for relatively easy termination.

Expansion

During this phase, the parties have experienced some of the benefits and problems associated with the relationship and attempt to expand the benefits. Returning again to the Owens-Brockway example, Owens was awarded a five-year contract as a result of its work with the beverage producer. At the end of this period, it will need to renegotiate. How strong Owens-Brockway's position will be at that time will depend partially on how well it has lived up to its agreement.

Expansion doesn't simply refer to increased sales, although this will usually occur in a good relationship. Expansion also occurs in the joint activities in which a seller and customer may engage. These activities include tool development and product design, value analysis and cost targeting, design of quality control and delivery systems, and long-term planning.[23] This also suggests that one of the distinguishing characteristics of this stage is increased dependency between supplier and buyer. Both parties will have made unique investments in the form of personnel, time, and information sharing.

In some cases, increased business will take place naturally because a customer's business grows over time. However, salespeople should not expect sales to increase as a natural phenomenon; they must be earned. As suggested earlier, calling on existing customers is often the most productive use of a salesperson's time. One practical suggestion for increasing business with an existing account is to survey (either formally or informally) as many parts of the customer's business as possible and examine in some detail all aspects of the operation. For each department visited, a comprehensive report of its requirements should be produced. In the context of what the salesperson is selling, the following elements should be established:

1. **Existing uses.** What limits current operations? What makes current operations more difficult than they need be? Which of these difficulties are most important? What do managers consider their worst problems?
2. **Possible needs.** What do managers need to improve their operations? What do they need to make their lives easier and more pleasant?
3. **Possible solutions.** What does the client think might be the best solutions?
4. **Possible new uses.** What new operations does the client believe might be possible? Which ones are favored?
5. **Decision criteria.** In supporting any solution, what would the business and personal criteria be?

Often a single salesperson will not be sufficient to identify all the opportunities for a supplier and customer to work together. As a result, cross-functional teams are being assigned to large customers identified as key business growth opportunities. See the Teamwork Competency box for a discussion of how Marconi Communications decides that a selling team is needed.

TEAMWORK COMPETENCY
Marconi Communications

Marconi Communications, a subsidiary of UK-based The General Electric Company, provides integrated systems and components for data, voice, and video communications. Marconi's customers include telephone, cable TV, and wireless providers. Its parent is not related to the U.S. electronics firm General Electric.

Selling teams are expensive to organize and maintain. Therefore, the significant opportunities must exist to justify investment in selling teams. Marconi Communications has found that forming sales teams to meet with cross-functional customer teams is particularly effective when one or a combination of the following situations exists:

- **Rapidly changing technology.** New products are being added and old ones improving at such a pace that individual salespeople cannot stay current.
- **Customer consolidation.** Individual customer operations are becoming so geographically diverse and important to the supplier that a team approach is needed and financially justified.
- **Demanding customers.** Customers are demanding solutions to problems that individual salespeople are not equipped to handle.
- **Competitive advantage.** Teams bring more of an organization's competencies to bear on the customer's problems so as to gain an advantage over the competition.

Many of the current business developments discussed in this and previous chapters suggest that selling teams will become more prominent in the future, so companies are well advised to figure out how to form, manage, and direct selling teams.[24] These issues are addressed throughout the remaining chapters of this text.

For more on Marconi Communications, see *www.marconicomms.com*.

One of the important benefits of this type of survey is that it will provide the salesperson with the knowledge necessary to demonstrate expertise in the customer's business. The United Parcel Service (UPS), for example, will set up private branch exchange, and telecommunications services, as well as perform time-and-motion studies for its clients. What does this have to do with the delivery of packages? These value-added services make UPS more valuable to the customer, often resulting in access to decision makers higher up in the organization.

Commitment

This stage consists of a high degree of commitment by the buyer and seller to their relationship. The commitment is more than just between individuals, it is also between organizations. In fact, a buyer may commit to purchase from only one supplier, while a supplier sells exclusively to one buyer within a specified trading area.

As was mentioned earlier, customers are consolidating their supplier base for a very obvious reason. Cheap technology, easily available information, and the explosion of global markets have commoditized their businesses and driven down their prices. In response, customers are looking to suppliers as a resource where there is potential to find new productivity and competitiveness. As a result, choosing the best suppliers and developing close working relationships are becoming critical to the success of many businesses.[25]

Customer evaluation and selection is becoming critically important to suppliers, especially in an enterprise type of customer relationship. Enterprise-type customer relationships, while generally few in number, are likely to represent a disproportionately large percent of the supplier's total sales base. As a result, the supplier is more dependent on the customer's success for his or her own success. The supplier must select a winner with which to establish a committed relationship. This is true for both large and small suppliers. For instance, IBM recently signed a $16 billion agreement to sell parts to Dell Computer and a $3 billion contract to supply disk drives to storage leader EMC. This leaves IBM in the curious position of betting on the success of both Dell and EMC, which are in some respects rivals in the PC market.

Some important considerations when choosing a customer with which to partner include the following:

- **Potential for impact.** Is there some real value for both parties that can come out of partnering that could not be achieved from a traditional supplier relationship?
- **Common values.** Is there sufficient commonality of values—what the parties consider to be important? In particular, it is important that both companies be ethical and look at quality and the quality process similarly.
- **Good environment for partnering.** How does each party look upon the partnership—long-term relationship versus profit on the sale, future oriented or present? Are there frequent interaction and transactions between the two companies?[26]
- **Consistency with supplier's goals.** Is a partnering relationship with this customer consistent with our own product and market strategy, and with our overall direction as a company?

Enterprise relationships represent the extreme in interorganizational commitment. Even in more transactionally oriented buyer-seller relationships there may develop a deep level of personal and professional commitment between the parties. Indeed, research indicates that buyers often have greater loyalty to salespeople than they have to the firms employing the salespeople.[27] This is likely to be the time when the customer is most profitable for the supplier.

Dissolution

The possibility of disengaging from a relationship is not a direct consequence of commitment, but it is implicit at each stage. If the criteria discussed for each stage in the relationship are not met, then the parties may choose either to limit the relationship to one of the earlier developmental stages or to disengage from the relationship entirely.

The world of business is dynamic, and the forces of change require that the seller stay alert to the possibility of dissolution even when a relationship with a client is in a strong commitment stage. Specific issues that sellers should continually monitor include (1) increasing costs of transactions; (2) financial health of the client; (3) changing barriers to switching suppliers; (4) changes in key personnel; and (5) changing organizational needs, resulting in less relative value for the benefits of the seller's products and services.

Salespeople must be alert to signs that a relationship is changing. Following are five warning signals that a relationship may possibly change:[28]

1. **Missing information.** You are unable to specify the purchasing role (e.g., economic, user, or technical buyer) of each person involved in the buying decision or you do not know the person involved in a particular purchasing role.
2. **Uncertainty about information.** You are unsure about what a piece of information means to the sale. For example, you may not know how a change in the size of new retail stores affects your client's merchandising strategies.
3. **Uncontacted buying influence.** Each buying influence should be contacted, either by the salesperson or by someone else from the selling organization. For example, Saga, Coca-Cola, and Hewlett-Packard employ a strategy of like-rank selling to cover all the bases of a sale. This means that salespeople contact people at a comparable level in the client's organization.
4. **Customer personnel new to the job.** This occurs when a new person is employed by the customer's organization or is transferred from another part of the organization. This person must be convinced of the benefits of an existing relationship.
5. **Reorganization.** Like the new buying influence, when people assume a new role, they must be sold. That is, the relationship changes when people change, even though the name of the account stays the same. Reorganizations can be particularly difficult because a person's role may change, even though the person occupies the same office and has the same title.

On the other hand, dissolution of a customer relationship should not always be considered a failure. Consider the experience of a respected South American metropolitan newspaper, where the advertising sales force has developed a deeply ingrained never-lose-a-client culture. The salespeople regularly offer significant discounts from their standard ad rates just to keep advertisers from walking away. The average discount rate is 45 percent. As long as the ad revenue exceeds the marginal cost, they argue, the paper is coming out ahead. What is not being considered though, is how their discounting behavior has led advertisers to expect ever-greater discounts. The advertisers, knowing the paper will do anything to keep them, have all the leverage. Each heavily discounted ad may indeed be marginally profitable, but in combination they dramatically reduce the paper's overall revenue and profits.

RELATIONSHIP BINDERS

It should be obvious from the previous discussion that there are certain factors that drive parties, whether individuals or organizations, to progress to a fully committed relationship. Salespeople should be aware of these factors. This section reviews four important underlying factors necessary for a fully developed relationship, which every salesperson and marketer should know and understand—value, expectations, negotiating, and trust.[29]

Value

Value refers to the perception that the rewards exceed the costs associated with establishing and/or expanding a relationship. Highly committed relationships provide the seller with the opportunity to leverage his or her skills and resources, develop long-term customers, and build strong competitive positions. Investment in building relationships may be considerable, so the financial returns must also be significant to justify their cost.

Value to a buyer is not always the lowest list price; it may also save time, labor, or result in higher sales of the customer's products. Value must ultimately reach the customer's customers in the form of better quality or less expensive products, wider choices, and/or quicker access to those choices. At the same time, customers will also consider the costs in terms of time and resources in establishing and building a relationship when determining the value of a relationship.

Consider Motorola, Inc.'s approach to selling customized pagers. Motorola's pager sales force will use the customer's own specifications to design a pager system perfectly suited to the customer's needs. The specs, put together on a laptop computer by the Motorola sales rep, are sent via modem to the company's factory. This individualized product development, however, requires an investment of time and effort on the part of the buyer. Motorola executives believe that it is partially this initial investment by the customer that makes them so resistant to competition.[30]

Expectations

In any relationship, the involved parties develop *expectations,* sometimes referred to as rules or norms, with respect to acceptable conduct and performance. Acceptable behavior varies by individual preferences, company policies, and national cultures. See the Global Perspective Competency box for a discussion of the cultural tendencies of different countries.

In some strategic relationships, buyers and sellers derive a mutually agreed-upon set of team values. These are sometimes put in writing in order to remind all members that these are the accepted standards of conduct of the relationship to which every individual must subscribe. Each may agree, for instance, to be the advocate for the other partner within their own company. It is especially important to ensure that new members to the team are aware of and comply with these values.

Salespeople must be careful not to encourage unfavorable buyer expectations as a result of present behaviors. If a salesperson agrees to a special price discount at the buyer's request, for example, the buyer may think this is standard practice, and expect some sort of discounting in the future. Because of this behavior, many companies (e.g., IBM and Procter & Gamble) do not give their salespeople the flexibility to discount prices in order to avoid the development of a discounting rule.

Expectations also develop with respect to performance. Customer performance expectations include the performance of the product, as well as a number of service activities such as frequency of sales calls, notification of price changes, lead time in delivery, order fill rate, emergency orders, and installation. A recent study comparing the performance perceptions of salespeople and buyers in a wide variety of industries shows that there is considerable inaccuracy in salespeople's perceptions of buyers' performance expectations.[31] Furthermore, accuracy in identifying the buyer's performance rules is related to high sales performance. Interestingly, the more experienced salespeople in this study were less accurate in their buyer performance expectations.

To encourage accuracy in customer assessment, some companies require their salespeople to provide a yearly written assessment of their key customers. This assessment process involves answering a series of questions. Writing the answers helps to identify key assumptions, inconsistencies, and missing information. This assessment could be done every time a competitor wins a key piece of business.

GLOBAL PERSPECTIVE COMPETENCY
National Culture and Selling in France

Because people from the same country are conditioned by similar background, educational, and life experiences, they are likely to have similar cultures or dispositions to see things a certain way. Researchers have classified national cultures along four dimensions:

- **Uncertainty avoidance:** how people accept and handle uncertainty and tolerate opinions and behaviors different from their own
- **Individualism:** the extent to which people enjoy individual freedom and are expected to take care of their nuclear family alone
- **Power distance:** the extent to which inequalities in power and wealth are condoned and supported
- **Masculinity:** whether traditional masculine traits such as assertiveness, respect for super-achievers, and acquisition of money and material possessions are valued versus feminine traits such as nurturing, concern for the environment, and championing the underdog

Relative to other countries, for example, France displays a strong tendency to avoid uncertainty and a willingness to condone and encourage inequalities in power and wealth. When selling in France, emphasis should be placed on such factors as established name brand, superior warranty, and money-back guarantees as uncertainty reducers. An appeal to the status value of the offering is also likely to be favorably received in France. Individuals will develop their own styles, but it is very helpful to be aware of national cultures in international sales.

Negotiating

Negotiating refers to the willingness to consider each party's obligations, benefits, and burdens. Two aspects of negotiating are of particular interest in a buyer-seller context. First, buyers must perceive a seller's willingness to negotiate on significant factors in the relationship. A firm may be unwilling to negotiate on price, it should demonstrate considerable flexibility in other important areas such as delivery service, maintenance agreements, installation, and so on. Second, sellers should engage in negotiating early in the relationship in order to avoid misconceptions regarding future obligations and norms of conduct. There may be some reservations among salespeople, especially new ones, about engaging in such bargaining out of fear of losing the sale. Veteran salespeople are probably more aware of the hazards of failing to bargain early in the relationship. They have probably learned that the costs of terminating a relationship are higher when a customer is alienated later in the relationship.

Trust

Trust refers to the opinion that an individual's word or promise can be believed and that the long-term interests of the customer will be served. Trust in salespeople and their companies is essential to buyers' evaluation of the quality of a relationship and to establishing working partnerships.[32] How does a salesperson earn the buyer's trust? Studies of buyers and sellers have shown that the five most important trust-earning attributes of salespeople are the following:

- **Dependability.** Salespeople who follow through on their promises.
- **Competence.** Salespeople who know what they are talking about.

STRATEGIC ACTION COMPETENCY
Eastman Kodak and IBM

As partnerships, alliances, and long-term customer relationships become more important in business, it is becoming increasingly important to distinguish between the deal and the relationship. Salespeople fear that if they push too hard to get the best deal possible today, they may jeopardize their company's ability to do business with the other party in the future. According to Danny Ertel, an expert in negotiations, the problem lies in the notion that the relationship and the deal function like a seesaw—to improve one, you have to be willing to sacrifice the other. A recent deal negotiated between Eastman Kodak and IBM is illustrative of the problem, and of how two companies successfully addressed the issue.

When Eastman Kodak transferred its data center operations to IBM, a lot of money was at stake, and both sides wanted the terms of the deal to be in their best interest. Kodak wanted to reduce its costs; IBM wanted to increase its revenues. But the companies also knew that the ultimate success of the outsourcing arrangement would hinge on the health and openness of their long-term relationship.

Rather than treat the deal and the relationship as intertwined, the companies separated the two explicitly. Key managers from each side sat down and first laid out what particular benefits they hoped to achieve through the terms of the immediate agreement. They then articulated as precisely as possible what would constitute a successful relationship over the long haul. They developed two discrete lists of issues, one related to the deal and the other to the relationship, and agreed to keep the two sets of issues separate at all times. Following are excerpts from the two lists.

Deal Issues	Relationship Issues
Retirement and replacement of hardware	Reliability
Use of third-party software	Giving each other the benefit of the
Service levels	doubt
Ease of communications	Absence of coercion
Record storage, maintenance, and security	Understanding each other's objectives
Termination and return of data center	Timeliness of consultations
operations to Kodak or transfer to another party	Mutual respect

www.kodak.com and *www.ibm.com*

- **Customer orientation.** Salespeople who put buyers' interests ahead of their own.
- **Honesty.** Salespeople who tell the truth.
- **Likability.** Salespeople whom the buyer enjoys knowing.[33]

There is also evidence that people place greater trust in those whom they feel have good listening skills.[34] Components of good listening skills include focusing on the speaker, not interrupting, paraphrasing questions, answering at the appropriate time, and using complete sentences instead of saying simply yes or no.

SUMMARY

Increasingly a company's profitability and growth depends on establishing good relationships with the right customers and managing each relationship so as to deliver value to the customer. Skills and concepts important to the successful management of account relationships were discussed in this chapter.

1. **Describe the steps in the professional purchasing process.** We have described four basic steps in the typical purchasing process: recognition of needs, evaluation of options, the purchase decision, and implementation and evaluation of performance. The sales force has the opportunity to create customer value during each of these steps; however, the level of customer value created is likely to depend on the type of buyer-supplier relationship—transactional, consultative, or enterprise.

2. **Identify the influences in the buying center.** A number of people are likely to be involved in most organizational purchasing decisions. These people are collectively referred to as the buying center. It is important that salespeople identify all those involved in the process, as well as the nature of their involvement. Regardless of functional area or level in the organization, people in the buying center will assume one of three roles: economic buyer, technical buyer, or user buyer. In addition, salespeople should selectively choose and cultivate an advocate in the buying center.

3. **Explain how relationships are likely to evolve.** Growing relationships evolve through five general stages: (1) awareness, (2) exploration, (3) expansion, (4) commitment, and (5) dissolution. Because each stage represents a major shift in the nature of the relationship, salespeople should be aware of these changes and proceed accordingly.

4. **Describe factors critical to gaining commitment to a relationship.** Certain factors are important to gaining increasing levels of commitment in relationships. We have reviewed four important factors necessary for a fully developed and productive relationship: value, expectations, negotiating, and trust. Each factor has been described within a professional account relationship situation and the means by which to identify and enhance these factors have been described.

KEY TERMS

Account purchasing process
Acquisition costs
Advocate
Buying center
Buying committee
Complex sale
Derived demand
Dissolution
Economic buyer
Enterprise relationships
Expectations

Modified rebuy
Need recognition
Negotiating
Possession costs
Proposals
Purchasing concerns
Rebuy
Relationship evolution
Request for proposal (RFP)
Specifications
Straight rebuy

Switching costs
Systems selling
Technical buyer
Trial relationship
Trust
User buyer
Value
Value analysis
Vendor analysis

DEVELOPING YOUR COMPETENCIES

1. **Technology.** The popular press has focused on the Internet's business and marketing applications with respect to consumer goods sold directly to households. In contrast, there have been very few investigations of business-to-business implications of the technology, which is surprising since forecasts predict greater growth of Internet use in this area, rather than in household use.

A recent study in the U.S. plastics industry, however, sheds some light on the use of the Internet between suppliers and processors of resin suppliers. Overall, 20 percent of firms were communicating with their suppliers and customers via the Internet. It was also found that contrary to much of the advertising on business Internet use, larger firms are more likely to use the technology than small firms.

One particularly insightful part of this study was on the content of Internet communications between buying firms and suppliers. Buyers were asked how frequently they personally engaged in communication with resin suppliers via the Internet on each of the following 10 factors:

1. Placing an order
2. Checking on order/shipping status
3. Checking on inventory status
4. Requesting price quotations
5. Submitting bid requests
6. Resolving problems/conflicts
7. Seeing catalog of products
8. Gaining general information
9. Receiving technical advice
10. Sending product specifications

Responses were in the form of a 5-point scale, with the extremes being never = 1 and very frequently = 5. How frequently do you think the Internet is being used for each of these 10 communication reasons? Why do you think the Internet would be especially valuable for the uses you have specified?

2. **Strategic Action.** Services Shipping, Inc., provides trucking services to large customers. It has an excellent reputation for reliable scheduling and careful handling. With decreasing regulation, Services' management decided that they needed more of a marketing orientation. They wanted to build and maintain long-lasting, profitable relationships with their customers. Services invested time and effort to study customers' shipping needs and were especially effective at helping customers plan for their needs. After two years, Services' managers were very disappointed with the results. Customers were pleased with the new marketing approach and frequently complimented Services, but sales were down. Low-cost competitors were particularly bothersome. What went wrong? Why didn't customers want to commit to long-term relationships?

3. **Self-Management.** American business firms and the purchasing managers continue to stress the importance of ethics in purchasing activities. Although such "perks" as the business lunch are common business practice, there is increasing concern about the ethics of such things as free tickets to sporting events and shows. In contrast to the United States, the purchasing function in Mexico is at a relatively early stage in its development as a profession. No professional organization of purchasing agents exists, and the agents are often viewed as necessary evils within their own organizations. Given this discrepancy in their professional development, American and Mexican purchasing agents are likely to disagree on the ethics of particular practices. From the following list of five ethical dilemmas, on which do you think purchasing agents from Mexico and America are likely to differ? How would they differ and why?

1. Accepting free trips from salespeople is okay.
2. Accepting free entertainment from salespeople is okay.
3. It is acceptable to make exaggerated statements to a supplier in order to gain a concession.
4. Giving preferential treatment to suppliers who happen to be good customers is sound business practice.
5. It is acceptable to obtain information about competitors by asking suppliers for that information.

4. **Coaching.** Building successful, long-term customer relationships is a specialty of WESCO International, Inc. WESCO is the number 2 distributor of electrical equipment in the United States. It warehouses and supplies more than a million different products including fuses, connectors, tools, tape, circuit breakers, transformers, lightbulbs, and data communications products. Customers include manufacturers, contractors, utility companies, and government agencies. WESCO's sales strategy is to profitably expand its relationship with key customers. To get an idea of how they accomplish this, consider the following description of how they established a partnership with an industrial customer in the paper business.

"Even though we had done relatively little business with this customer before, their headquarters people asked us to compete for their business in November of 1997. We distributed questionnaires to develop details of programs to reduce the customer's inventory and energy costs. We determined that we could serve all but three of their plants. We secured the account in June 1998 after making presentations to their selection committee.

"As soon as the agreement was signed, we formed an account team and held a national rollout meeting to begin implementation. During the next few months, we moved toward compliance at each customer plant, agreeing to hold monthly meetings to address customer concerns at the customer's various mill sites. As planned, we acquired two distributor branches and opened one new branch. We conducted a complete energy audit and recommended more energy efficient systems for all their plants. We also reduced inventory and implemented an EDI (Electronic Data Interchange) ordering system.

"By June 1999, the intensive implementation phase was over. Sales had increased tenfold from the year before, reaching $1 million per month. Between transaction cost reductions, energy savings, and inventory reduction, WESCO was able to document over 20 percent cost savings to the customer. This was far more than the customer had expected."

From this description of a successful business expansion effort, what do you think are the keys to successful business expansion, what are the pitfalls? For more on WESCO, see *www.wescodist.com*.

5. **Team Building.** Opportunities to expand sales to customers often result from signing agreements at a customer's headquarters to cover all their product and service needs, similar to the WESCO agreement discussed in the Coaching Competency question above. Implementation of these headquarter-initiated agreements depends on local service and compliance. This is where real teamwork is needed. In the agreement discussed above, one of the customer plants, which generated only $50,000 per year in sales, was located two hours away from the WESCO branch and demanded semimonthly sales calls. The salesperson responsible for calling on this plant is paid a combination of fixed salary and commissions on sales volume. He offered a blunt opinion on the situation:

"They may be a good customer for WESCO, but from where I stand, they demand a lot of service that is not commensurate with their sales volume—either current or potential. Unless I am ordered to do it, I wouldn't call on this customer, even without the long drive they require. The opportunity costs of serving these customers are way too high. I would rather spend my time selling to other local customers who value my services and from whom I make greater commissions."

If you were this salesperson's branch manager, what would you say to him? If you were the the national account manager for this customer, how would you get this salesperson on board the team? If you were the national sales manager for WESCO, what would be your reaction?

6. **Global Perspective.** In business after business, the physical product is no longer enough to create a sustainable competitive advantage. Increasingly, advantage relies on superior after-sale customer service. It has been generally agreed that customer expectations form the basis upon which service satisfaction is determined. Expectations are formed from previous experiences, promises made or implied, and are cultural in nature. This presents special problems and requires careful attention from companies competing globally.

   To better understand this point, consider the experience of a large Swedish company with nearly 50 years' experience selling engineered industrial products to more than 50 countries. After-sales services such as installation, training, routine maintenance, emergency repair, parts supply, and software services are responsible for about 25 percent of this firm's total revenues and are growing more rapidly than overall product sales. In describing their customers' service expectations across the globe, marketing managers at the Swedish company made the following statements:

   - "They want instant service and they want it for free."
   - "They are very willing to pay in advance for after-sale services in the form of service contracts."
   - "After-sales service was accepted as part of the cost of doing business, but not so well accepted that prepayment on a contract basis could be expected."

   Match the service expectation statement with what you think is the appropriate world location: the Far East, Europe, and U.S./North America. Be prepared to give the reasons for your choices.

EXPERIENTIAL EXERCISE

1. Make an appointment to interview an industrial purchasing agent. Ask the buyer to explain how parts, raw materials, or equipment are bought at his or her company. Prepare flow diagrams showing all the steps in the purchase process. Write a report comparing your diagrams with the model found in this chapter. Explain how a salesperson could make use of your charts.

IN-CLASS EXERCISES

4-1:"Late-Paying Large Account"*

Major Contracting has always been one of Phil Dario's biggest accounts—until last year. A downturn in the local economy has slowed both construction and renovation projects. Moreover, Major reorganized its management team, including hiring a new CFO—The result? The company has been slow paying its bills for the past six months.

   Construction Suppliers Corporation's accounting department, as is customary, hired a collection agency to obtain payment. The agency is now threatening to create credit-rating problems for Major if it doesn't pay within in a week. Dario, a senior account executive with CSC, received a call from Troy Hamilton, his contact at Major (not to mention his friend of 15 years), asking him to intercede on his behalf. Hamilton pleaded with Dario to get him a month, promising to be back on track with bill payment, saying that Major has bid on a few big projects that should get it back on track financially.

---

*Contributed by Eli Jones, University of Houston.

Dario is now in an awkward position. Not all of the projects are firm, so Major may be unable to settle its debt in a month. He wants to help Hamilton, but he also feels he has a responsibility to the company, and to himself—his compensation is based in part on the profitability of his territory. On the other hand, Dario doesn't want to risk losing the account and the sales that would come from those expected projects.

Does he try to get Major the month it needs to pay its bills? Does he claim it's out of his hands? Is there a better solution?

Questions:

1. As discussed in the chapter, the final stage in the buyer-seller relationship is dissolution. Is the relationship between Major and CSC a candidate for dissolution? Why or why not?
2. Consider Major's history. What if Major's bad luck turns around? What are some of the short- and long-term implications of Major getting back on track financially, as they relate to CSC?
3. Obviously, Hamilton is asking Dario to serve as an advocate. Given the awkwardness of the situation, what should Dario do next? What are some of the main factors that Dario should consider?
4. Are there any ethical issues involved?

4-2: "Someone Who Is More Professional"*

All Allen Freeman could think was, "Why me?" Freeman, sales director for Pace Manufacturing, had just received the kind of phone call no manager wants: one that pits his salesperson against a customer.

The call was from Stella Burnar, the new purchasing manager for Stateline International, Pace's fifth-largest national account. Burnar explained that although she is happy with Pace's products and pricing, she is uncomfortable with Cathie Simon, the national account manager for Stateline. She finds Simon to be too informal, too concerned about when they can meet for lunch; a glad-hander who talks far too much and wastes time. Burnar asked Freeman to transfer the Stateline account to a salesperson who has a more "professional" demeanor, who strictly discusses business problems and solutions. And she wants to meet with that new person in a week, at which time she'll be ordering for the next quarter.

Freeman thinks that in a situation like this, he has to comply with a key customer's wishes. At least he knows which salesperson to give the account to: Ray Harley, who fits Burnar's request perfectly and is ready for a promotion from regional rep to national account manager. The problem is, how does he tell Simon that he has to take her off her largest account?

Questions:

1. Should Freeman acquiesce to a customer's request to change salespeople?
2. What are the potential problems with moving Simon from this account?
3. Assuming you decided to move Simon from the account, how would you present the move to Simon?
4. What alternatives besides moving Simon from the account should be considered?

---

*Contributed by Eli Jones, University of Houston.

 **TORONTO-DOMINION BANK: MONEY MONITOR**

*I*n February 1990, Gary Shore was transferred from Toronto to be the branch manager of the Richmond and King Street branch of the Toronto-Dominion Bank in London. Among other issues, he was considering options for the marketing of Money Monitor, a computer-based product which allowed commercial clients to access their financial data. Although the product had been introduced as a corporate product in 1981 and redeveloped for commercial use in 1986, sales had been below target and were sporadic. The bank executives in Toronto considered this product to be of long term strategic importance. As the largest and most profitable unit in the Ontario Southwest Division, Gary Shore's branch was considered the flagship, and he therefore felt an obligation to increase sales.

THE TORONTO-DOMINION BANK

The face of the Canadian financial industry had changed significantly in the previous decade and was set to experience further adjustment. Deregulation had increased competition both among the "big five" banks and from foreign institutions. Since there was little differentiation among financial products, the institutions were looking for new ways of adding value to their services. The Toronto-Dominion (TD) bank was focusing on computerization as a means of providing added value to its customers.

The TD bank was Canada's fifth largest chartered bank with assets of nearly $60 billion. Although much smaller than the country's largest bank ($130 billion in assets), the TD bank had consistently outperformed the other "big five" banks in return on equity and return on assets.

The TD bank had over 1,000 branches across Canada, but was strongest in Ontario. There were two types of branches—those which performed retail bank-

ing only (providing mortgages, loans and deposit services to individuals) and those which also provided commercial services (lending funds to businesses). Gary Shore's branch was the commercial banking center for the London region, with customers as far as 50 kilometers away. Other large commercial branches in the Ontario Southwest Division were located in Windsor, Kitchener, and St. Catherines. Smaller commercial branches were located in Cambridge, Chatham, Sarnia and Guelph.

The TD bank's strategy was to be conservative in lending policies, innovative in products and information technology, and competitive on providing customer service. The bank was not overly aggressive on pricing commercial loans, and considered relationship building as key to their success.

Branch Management

The typical commercial banking center was divided into three sections: retail banking (personal lending and deposits), commercial banking, and administration. Exhibit 1 provides an organization chart for the Richmond and King Street branch. This branch was the largest in the Ontario Southwest Division and had a history of low loan losses, excellent customer service and, as a result, good profits.

The branch's commercial client base was diversified among many industries including real estate developers, manufacturers, and service businesses such as moving companies and advertising firms. There was also a substantial group of professional firms—doctors, lawyers and accountants. The scope of the businesses also varied, with small proprietorships on the one hand, and large retail chains and multi-plant manufacturers on the other. Some clients borrowed regularly and some infrequently. There were approximately 500 non-borrowing customers who only utilized deposit, investment and cash management services.

This case was prepared by Alicia Cestra and Royal Mathews under the supervision of Professor Donald W. Barclay for the sole purpose of providing material for class discussion. Certain names and other identifying information may have been disguised to protect confidentiality. It is not intended to illustrate either effective or ineffective handling of a managerial situation. Ivey Management Services prohibits any form of reproduction, storage, or transmittal without its written permission. This material is not covered under authorization from CanCopy or any reproduction rights organization. To order copies or request permission to reproduce materials contact Ivey Publishing, Ivey Management Services c/o Richard Ivey School of Business, The University of Western Ontario, London, Ontario, Canada, N6A 3K7; phone (519) 661-3882; fax (519) 661-3882; e-mail cases@ivey.uwo.ca. Copyright © 1992 The University of Western Ontario. One time permission to reproduce granted by Ivey Management Services on November 3, 1999.

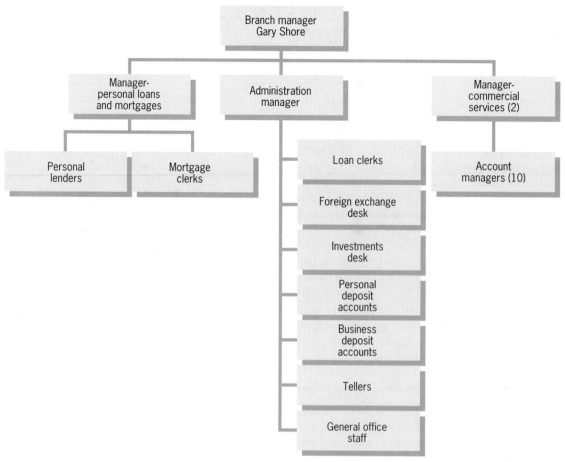

EXHIBIT 1   Organization Chart—Richmond and King Street Branch, London, Ontario

Each branch was operated as a profit center. As such, the branch manager was responsible for marketing (with some regional advertising and promotion support), cost control, loan losses and human resource deployment. General staff hiring was the branch manager's responsibility, but he/she could not hire management personnel, create a new position, or fire any personnel without division approval.

The Account Manager

An account manager was responsible for a portfolio of business customers to which he/she lent funds. He/she was responsible for the bank's profitability on the account, the risk level of the portfolio, and the servicing of each account.

Since the account managers had little control over the timing or complexity of loan requests or client problems, they had to be well organized and efficient, yet flexible. As indicated in Exhibit 2, the account managers had a considerable range of responsibilities

and answered to the needs of numerous stake-holders both inside and outside the bank. Bottom line responsibility, however, rested on the avoidance of loan losses, which necessitated open, effective communication with clients.

A commercial banking center utilized three levels of account managers, as follows:

Independent Business Account Managers: These individuals managed a portfolio of 140 to 160 small accounts borrowing between $10,000 and $200,000 each. They were given full responsibility for their portfolios and tended to operate independently. The smaller customers had less sophisticated needs and usually required constant, but not detailed, attention. These portfolios were expected to generate higher margins to compensate for the required administration. The Richmond and King Street branch had four independent business account managers.

EXHIBIT 2   An Account Manager's Responsibilities[a]

1. Direct Loan Products: operating loans, commercial installment loans, small business loans, commercial mortgages, leases.

2. Direct Non-Loan Products: credit insurance, corporate Visa cards, export receivable insurance, business credit service, Money Monitor, interest bearing business accounts.

3. Referral Products: payroll services, foreign exchange, lock box services, pension fund management, personal mortgages, personal loans, RRSP's, Visa cards, personal accounts.

4. Administration:
   - For each account in a given portfolio, one credit review (usually ten pages) outlining a full analysis of the company's borrowing arrangements, financial performance and future requirements, was completed yearly. For higher risk or more active accounts, reports would be required on a semi-annual, quarterly or even monthly basis. Annual reviews required a visit to the client's premises.
   - Daily administration—required 30 minutes to one hour for checking and initialing reports on overdrafts, loan activity, loan expiries.
   - Credit reviews for new loan requests (volume varies with business/economic cycle).
   - Security documentation was also the responsibility of the account manager. Considerable time was spent following up on security changes and corrections.

5. Marketing:
   - All account managers were expected to grow their portfolios. It was expected that they spend at least one half day per week visiting clients or prospective clients.
   - Account managers were also expected to attend social functions, such as receptions, golf tournaments, chamber of commerce dinners, etc.
   - Much time was spent talking to clients on the telephone. Such communications were of three types: relationship building, client monitoring, and negotiating.

     (A) Relationship building
     Often telephone calls occurred in both directions on a "how are things going" basis. A client might call to ask about the bank's perspective on the economy or to bounce ideas off the manager. An account manager might call to get information on the client's industry sector and to see how the client was doing relative to the competition.

     (B) Monitoring
     Clients usually provided monthly financial information and often had to be reminded to submit the data. A client was called if the company was in an overdraft position and upon the expiry of a credit facility.

     (C) Negotiating
     Whenever the client requested changes to the credit package or the company's performance warranted a change, negotiations were required. Negotiations could include rate changes, security changes, loan limit revisions, loan extensions, company restructuring, and changes in the fee structure.

The breakdown of an account manager's time among the above activities depended on the economic environment. However, every contact with the client would likely involve at least two of the above types of communications and each represented an opportunity to cross sell products.

[a] Based on discussions with two account managers and the branch manager.

Account Managers: These account managers were responsible for approximately 100 clients borrowing from $200,000 to $1,000,000 each. Since this position was an entry level posting for commercial lenders, they were generally assigned less complex accounts. The account managers were expected to cross-sell to existing accounts. (Identify and capitalize on opportunities for selling new products to existing clients rather than attempting to find new clients.) There were three account managers at the Richmond and King Street branch.

Senior Account Managers: These individuals handled 30 to 60 clients, each of whom generally borrowed in excess of $1 million. Some smaller but complex accounts might also be assigned to these managers. The accounts were much more complicated and therefore the manager of Commercial Services and in some cases the branch manager, were more often involved. Extensive financial analysis and a greater understanding of the clients' business were required. These clients interacted with the bank on a number of levels since they were more likely to require payroll, foreign exchange and other services. Cross-selling was also done with these clients. There were three senior account managers at this branch.

The account managers were paid a salary ranging in the mid five figures. Each account manager's performance was reviewed on an annual basis by his/her immediate supervisor. Account managers were rated on a four-point scale. The rating reflected the supervisor's view of the account manager's performance in a number of defined areas including loan volumes, account control, product knowledge, cross-selling, professionalism, and administration capability. The account manager's evaluation was based on specific targets negotiated at the beginning of the year. Account managers received an annual percentage increase in salary which was computed by the Divisional Human Resource department based on the performance rating, education level and mobility. Promotions, which also resulted in higher salaries, were similarly based on the above criteria.

MONEY MONITOR

Money Monitor was a personal computer software package which allowed clients to access the bank's mainframe via a modem and telephone line. Once the initial link parameters had been established, clients could easily obtain information on their loan balances, account balances, account statements, check clearing, plus foreign exchange rates and money market rates. Clients could also transfer funds between their own accounts. Exhibit 3 outlines the initial features of Money Monitor.

EXHIBIT 3   Money Monitor Features

1. Consolidated statement of account and loan balances, providing net cash position.
2. Downloading of account statements—95 days of account information available at any time.
3. Foreign exchange rates.
4. Money market rates.
5. Searches for specific checks by number or dollar amount.
6. Previous days' account activities, and on-line real-time reporting.
7. Autodial: Daily access to items 1–6 can be pre-programmed into the Money Monitor software. The user enters the password each day and the system then retrieves and prints the specified data. Average user PC time for this procedure is under one minute, as the user does not have to attend to the computer during this process.
8. Customer initiated transfers.
9. Full security system with passwords and system utilization report.

Strategic Fit

The TD bank's executive believed that cash management services would be an important source of future profits. Money Monitor was viewed as a key element of the bank's cash management services. Additional PC based products were being developed which would allow clients to format documentary letters of credit, disburse and collect preauthorized payments, execute wire transactions, process financial Electronic Data Interchange, issue commercial paper and manage investment portfolios. These additional products, along with Money Monitor, would be marketed under a single menu-driven communication software gateway known as "Business Window." Money Monitor was viewed as a tool to further cement the bank's relationship with the client. In essence, Money Monitor was considered the commercial equivalent of the automatic teller machines used in retail banking.

It was anticipated that significant savings in the bank's personnel costs would eventually result as the number of Money Monitor accounts grew. Nevertheless, there was no exact data on the extent of the savings, if any.

The TD bank's Head Office estimated that 50% of all commercial clients used IBM compatible personal computers, and that 50% of these clients would have use for Money Monitor. In other words, all commercial clients, regardless of size or type of business, were targeted. Individual branch goals were established by division offices and, to date, these goals had not been met. Furthermore, utilization rates were below expectation as some clients were connected to the system but were not accessing data. Exhibit 4 shows the divisional targets, branch performance, and utilization rates between 1988 and 1990.

Pricing

The system operated on any IBM compatible personal computer. The client was required to purchase a modem (usually costing $200), but was provided with the software free of charge. The client paid for the information provided by Money Monitor at a flat rate of $40 per month for the first three accounts interfaced and an additional $14 per account thereafter. These fees were highly competitive, with fees charged by other banks ranging from $80 to $1,000 per month for similar services. Clients typically interfaced their operating loans, general accounts and payroll accounts. Some clients also connected to U.S., trust, and interest bearing accounts.

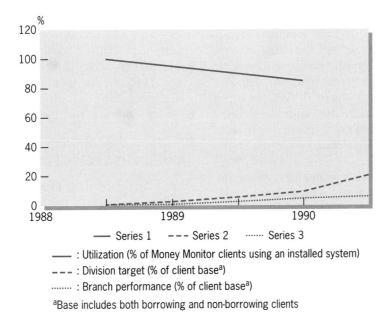

EXHIBIT 4 **Targets, Performance, and Utilization of Money Monitor**

Distribution and Selling

The OSW Division had decided to place the marketing of Money Monitor in the hands of the account managers. This was done to accomplish a number of objectives, including:

- utilizing the account managers as a "ready and inexpensive distribution channel";
- promoting a selling orientation among account managers;
- encouraging computer literacy among account managers; and
- ensuring the account manager's understanding of Money Monitor's capabilities.

This distribution method was in contrast to that used for the bank's other cash management products. For example, specialists operating out of Toronto sold payroll systems based on referrals from account managers. A specialist would visit the potential payroll client with the account manager but, once the introduction had been made, would handle the demonstration, price negotiation, installation, user training, and follow up. The payroll specialist responsible for London was professional, enthusiastic, and well-liked by the account managers.

To sell Money Monitor, account managers were expected to identify potential clients, demonstrate the system, sell the product, install the computer link which involved using DOS, and complete the registration paperwork. A 1-800 telephone number was pro-

vided to the customer and the account manager in case of technical difficulties.

The selling approach varied according to the size of the account. Price was an issue with the smaller accounts who had less need for Money Monitor services due to the lower complexity of their businesses. They often had only one business account, an operating loan and one or two term loans. The owners of the businesses often kept their own books and were therefore the Money Monitor users.

On the other hand, price was not an issue with larger accounts, although they sometimes felt they were being "nickeled and dimed." The larger clients had the greatest need for Money Monitor due to the high complexity of their operations. These clients more often utilized payroll services, foreign exchange services and multiple accounts. The larger clients often expected and received good service from bank personnel. The decision to buy Money Monitor was usually made by senior company personnel rather than by the clerk who would use the system.

The buying behavior of the medium-sized clients was a hybrid of the small and large clients.

Reactions of the Account Managers

When the product was introduced to the account managers, they were immediately enthusiastic about its capabilities. They hoped that the Money Monitor system would reduce their work load, especially with respect to account and loan information. For example, account managers would have to call accounts which were unknowingly in an overdraft position. Money Monitor clients often detected and corrected the overdraft position without account manager involvement. In addition, customers often complained that late arrival of bank statements slowed the completion of their monthly financial statements. Since some clients were required to provide monthly financial statements to the bank, prompt completion would assist the account managers.

While impressed with the above advantages, the account managers were largely unsuccessful in their efforts to sell Money Monitor. Account managers frequently did not have previous selling experience. In addition, they had difficulty setting aside the two to four hours required to install the system and train users. Since some account managers were not computer literate, they were uncomfortable performing the installations. Exhibit 5 provides an account manager's description of a typical installation.

EXHIBIT 5   An Account Manager's Description of a Typical Installation[a]

"An installation was often time-consuming and cumbersome because the necessary equipment was not always available. I can remember a number of situations where the telephone line was too far from the personal computer and we had to move things around, or they wouldn't be using DOS and we would have to find the DOS disk and boot the computer. More often, we could not set the parameters up correctly or were not able to link up with TD and had to call Toronto who would call us back with an answer. As a result, the customer wasted time and, in one case, the decision maker had to leave the room before the demonstration was completed.

"Money Monitor is user friendly, but there are still enough screens to require at least an hour's training. Even then, it was inevitable that the client would call you later with questions. If the client was convinced that the system was useful, he/she would make an effort to use it, if not, he/she would forget what screen did what and their utilization would drop. Since the security system required a password change every 28 days, clients who used the system less frequently would be irritated when they could not get on the system without making password changes. These customers would inevitably be the ones who didn't have a clear grasp of Money Monitor's full capabilities.

"At one business, we found that two separate people in the same office were obtaining bank information. One used Money Monitor while the other just called the bank. When we found such situations we would have to go back and provide training. Money Monitor is a great product and the concept is easy to sell but the actual implementation is tricky."

[a] From a discussion with an account manager.

Finally, the TD bank's strategy of providing good service proved to be a tough competitor. Many clients knew bank staff by name and were used to getting information quickly over the telephone. Some staff would even prepare information in anticipation of certain customers' calls. It was more difficult to sell Money Monitor to such clients.

GARY SHORE'S PERSPECTIVE

The issues concerning Money Monitor interconnected with other changes in the banking environment. It was clear that the Canadian economy was heading into a recessionary period and this had implications for branch staff. Client difficulties increased account managers' workloads, while division managers emphasized closer account monitoring and control. Considerable internal changes were occurring as the TD bank introduced new products, systems, and concepts. As a result, the true effectiveness of Money Monitor in personnel savings and improved customer service was nebulous.

As Gary Shore further considered Money Monitor, he questioned the most effective means of motivating the account managers and, indeed, whether the account managers should sell the product at all.

A possible option was to use an outside vendor to install the system once the account manager had sold the concept. Some other commercial branches had designated one account manager as the Money Monitor specialist with a reduced portfolio. Their effectiveness had been debatable. It was evident that an in-branch specialist would be an expensive addition to the branch and Gary Shore would have to influence the division office to have the position created.

Although tangible incentives were typically not used by the bank to encourage the account managers to sell a given product, the possibility of increasing their enthusiasm via incentives was worth considering. Nevertheless, commissions were discouraged by the bank's executive to avoid setting a precedent, as a commission might indicate that selling Money Monitor was in addition to their other responsibilities.

How could customers be convinced that Money Monitor was the future of banking? This challenge was especially difficult given the past success of the Richmond and King Street branch in providing excellent client service.

CASE 4-2 · THE CENTRUST CORPORATION

While at the Chicago airport, I was awaiting a flight to Los Angeles. I checked voice mail and there was another message from Bill Short, who is Vice President of Strategic Planning. He was concerned over the apparent loss of Joysco Technological Surgeries (JTS). The message was: "Please call me tomorrow at 7:00 A.M. to discuss the loss of JTS. I am extremely disturbed at losing this account. I have reviewed your records on this account through the last quarter. The records do not have third-quarter profiles." He continued, "Be prepared to discuss how you approached this strategic account and why we lost the business. As the most senior sales representative for Centrust, I am discouraged that you have not called before now to discuss this matter."

Each quarter, the field sales force downloads all account profiles and sales activities from their laptops to home office computers. Current-quarter records are due next week, containing information that Bill Short has not yet examined. I decided it would be a good idea to look over all of the information on this account which had been logged on my laptop for the last eight months. If I could discover why this account was lost, obviously I could make some changes in my selling strategy.

It was only a week ago that I had caught a flight to Cincinnati on a sales call to JTS, only to be frustrated by this account. I was certain that prior to my arrival, everything was in order to close this sale. I was shocked that JTS had purchased what I believed to be a substantially inferior surgical system for performing cataract surgery from Bayson Laboratories. Bayson Labs is a relative newcomer in the medical supplies field, and JTS always had dealt with vendors who have an established reputation. I was given no indication that any other vendor was being seriously considered for this purchase.

As I reflected on the situation, I wondered how much the loss of the JTS sale would impact my division in the upcoming budget for the year. I also wondered how the loss would impact my own position.

THE CATARACT SURGERY MARKET

The cataract surgery market has grown tremendously over the last decade. Much of this growth occurred as a result of Medicaid and Medicare reimbursement for the procedure. In 1993, there were 6,000,000 cataract surgeries performed in the United States, of which almost 65 percent were covered by government Medicare and Medicaid programs. Cataracts typically occur in patients after forty-five years of age. When patients develop cataracts, the lens of their eye forms an opaque mass and light rays are unable to pass to the back of the eye. With the diminishing ability of the lens to pass light, patients will eventually go totally blind. Estimates indicate that 35 percent of the population will develop cataracts. Approximately 40 percent of all Medicare and Medicaid patients can be certified as needing cataract surgery.[1]

There are 12,000 board-certified eye surgeons in the United States. The number of board-certified eye surgeons is the only specialty that has not grown in total members in the last 10 years. Only under the rarest conditions would any doctor other than an eye surgeon perform cataract surgery. The average reimbursement for an office visit by Medicare, Medicaid, and most private insurance payers in 1993 was $72.00. Most patients will see a surgeon five times, including pre- and postsurgery visits. The average gross income after three years of practice for eye surgeons in 1993 was $2,000,000 for either a sole practitioner or one in a group practice. Net income for an eye surgeon in the United States during this year was $494,543 (less costs for opening the practice and paying off student loans).

Cataract surgery is a procedure requiring superb skills, yet it is not time-consuming; the surgery can be performed in less than one hour. Patients feel little, if any, discomfort, and the surgery is usually performed

---

[1] Information on the profiles of cataract surgeons and the number of procedures supplied by the U.S. Office of Medical Statistics, Washington, D.C.

This case was prepared by John Cheneler and Professor William Cron of Southern Methodist University. Neither names nor financial data are intended to reference anyone or a particular business. All cataract surgery information is accurate; however, competitive and product information has been modified for reasons of company security.

on an outpatient basis. In 1993, the total cost for the procedure was $8,200, with the surgeon receiving $3,000. As recently as three years ago, the total cost for the procedure was $17,000, with a $5,000 surgeon's fee. Today, surgeons typically operate two days a week, averaging 10 surgeries weekly.

Most eye surgeons practice for 50 weeks each year. Surgeons also offer ancillary services such as offering eyeglasses and contact lenses, thus offering a complete package to their patients. Frequently, a surgeon will lease space to an optometrist, receiving a percentage of the profits, typically 10 percent.

Eighty percent of eye surgeons prefer to be sole practitioners. A sole practitioner will usually need two nurses and a receptionist to manage four examination rooms. The remaining eye surgeons belong to large group practices. The average group practice has four surgeons with 12 examination rooms. In 1993, the cost to open a practice with equipment for examinations and office supplies was $720,000.[2] On average, a first-year surgeon will owe $195,000 for schooling and resident training.

With increased competition and better equipment, many hospitals are fighting to maintain market share by having the latest equipment available. In the early stages of the cataract surgery market, all surgery was performed at hospitals. Soon off-site surgery centers began to compete actively with hospitals for the patients of large surgical group practices.[3] Now some large group practices are even soliciting other surgeons to use the group's facilities for performing cataract surgeries, rather than going to either hospitals or off-site surgery centers.

Suppliers and Equipment

The main competitors in this market are the established medical vendors that have broad lines of medical products. Two of the major competitors are Alcon Laboratories and Storz Medical, Inc. Centrust's loss of patent protection on its new product line allowed competitors to obtain previously protected digital/laser technology by copying Centrust's new products. Competitors' R & D departments were able to alter their surgical product

lines with Centrust's technology and market to Centrust's accounts. The competition was also very aggressive at targeting other surgical specialties with these modified products. The purchaser was often unaware that this technology originally belonged to Centrust.

Most of the full-line vendors in the cataract surgery market carried a complete line of products. Niche manufacturers were typically able to hold market share for only two or three years. Vendors have offered lines of diagnostic units, surgical units, and disposable instruments. Centrust, along with Storz and Alcon, offered office products, but margins on these products are very thin.

Diagnostic Units. Diagnostic units are used to determine the relative focal ability of an eye. Even though a physician can determine that a patient suffers from eye degeneration with a routine examination, there is still a need to quantify eyesight to justify the need for cataract surgery.

While a patient places his or her chin on a leather strap, a laser beam is projected into the eye. The patient reads a series of randomly generated letters or numbers. The diagnostic unit predicts how much eye sight will be regained by the patient after surgery. When cataract surgery is completed, patients will see as well as they did using the diagnostic unit. An examination can be performed in less than five minutes.

Centrust introduced the first diagnostic unit in 1990 and offers the highest-priced diagnostic unit on the market at $60,000. Competitors have attempted either to continue to sell the Snellen Chart method, using dilation, or to use a variation of the Centrust diagnostic unit, though with limited success.[4] Competitors' products range in price from $4,500 to $27,000. Surgeons considered Centrust's diagnostic unit as the only one currently on the market in which they could have 100 percent confidence in diagnosis. The U.S. government had ruled only the Centrust unit as acceptable in confirming the need for cataract surgery for Medicaid and Medicare patients without a second medical opinion. No other competitor is currently able to offer a product that can duplicate this process with as much reliability. Centrust was quite successful in selling this unit by emphasizing that it lasts for the life of a medical practice and, further, that no dilatation drops are needed.

---

[2] Financial data on the costs of maintaining an ophthalmological practice found yearly in *News in Ophthalmology,* a private trade publication.

[3] Off-site surgery centers are conveniently located centers for performing a variety of surgeries in which the patient needs to stay for less than a day. Surgeries that can be performed at these centers include removal of gallbladders, cosmetic surgery, liposuction, and cataract surgery.

---

[4] The Snellen Chart consists of rows of letters or numbers that decrease in size with each row. One major concern of a physician is that patients will often memorize the letters after repeated examinations.

Centrust was the only vendor offering lifetime warranties on diagnostic products for eye care.

Surgical Units. The price for a surgical unit used in cataract surgery varied between $200,000 and $600,000. This price differential was due solely to the name recognition of the vendor and the number of modifications needed to adapt the unit to other equipment in the operating room as opposed to distinguishable product difference. Modifications can be as simple as adapting electrical outlets or as complex as writing computer programs to link the unit to other surgical units.[5]

The surgical unit is a large console, usually four feet long by two feet wide by five feet tall. It consists of a computer that sends an electric impulse to hand-held cutting tools, tubing for flowing fluid into the surgery area and suctioning the fluid back, and several exasperating tubes to remove the lens of the eye after incision. The minuscule pieces of material around the lens must be removed without damaging the surrounding area. The surgery site is smaller than the size of a period on a piece of paper. Most units offered by manufacturers appear to have similar capabilities; therefore, surgeons and hospitals often shopped vendors on price. Seldom would surgeons be aware of the difference in a vendor's products. In the past, surgeons always purchased the highest-priced unit, believing that quality and price were absolutely related. As their surgical techniques improved, surgeons were less willing to pay higher prices unless they observed a distinct difference in product quality. Hospital surgery management viewed a surgical unit, however, as much more critical for their success in attracting doctors and patients than a diagnostic unit.

Disposable Instruments. Disposable cutting instruments used in cataract surgery typically cost $170. Every surgical procedure requires a new set of disposable surgical hand pieces each time an incision is made. Disposable hand pieces are plugged into surgical units which supply electrical current, along with proper irrigation and as apiration.[6] After completion

of the surgery, disposable cutting tools and gauze patches must be discarded. Little difference exists among the disposable products of various vendors; therefore, most disposable instruments were purchased primarily based on the lowest price available through distributors. Pictures of a diagnostic unit, a surgical unit, and a disposable instruments pack are shown in Exhibit 1.

Centrust Corporation

Centrust has been a pioneer in the development of digital/laser technology in the medical field. They started almost exclusively as a fledgling medical manufacturer in New York City, with a limited product line. However, in the last few years with the introduction of new diagnostic products, Centrust had grown to a leadership position in medical diagnostics and surgical products for cataract eye surgery. See Exhibit 2 for financial information on Centrust. Few medical companies enjoy Centrust's reputation for quality.

Although the technology for the diagnostic unit is protected by patents, the cataract surgery units and disposable instruments are not. With its superior manufacturing processes, however, R & D was able to modify slightly its line of surgical units to fit the needs of off-site surgery centers and other medical specialties. The delicate aspirating capabilities of the surgical unit, for instance, have been modified for use by vascular surgeons in nerve and vascular reattachment. The success of product extensions depends on both the identification of viable extension opportunities and the manufacturer's reputation. Most successful vendors develop a strong association with a particular specialty and use this relationship for product line extensions. Due to Centrust's success in the cataract area and resulting selling time demands, the sales force has not been aggressive in promoting Centrust's products to other specialties.

Centrust's marketing strategy had been to establish their reputation through aggressive promotion of their high-quality products. The margins on cataract equipment had been high, but with increased competition and product maturity, they had declined. After 1992, numerous competitors for Centrust's digital/laser products appeared. This was not unusual, as typically a breakthrough product could hold market share for only three years or less.

With its reputation and high margins, Centrust was able to attract extraordinarily skilled and established sales representatives plus similarly qualified sales

---

[5] Centrust was not aggressive in requiring the purchaser to share the costs of modifying surgical units, in which extensive modifications could add up to 50 percent to the cost of the unit. In 1990 Centrust made major modifications to 11 percent of their units; in 1993 the percent of units requiring adjustments soared to 38 percent.

[6] The hand-held piece makes a quite thin incision along the lens of the eye, and the surgeon removes the lens and extraneous materials with suction tubes supplied via the unit. The cleaner the incision, the quicker the recovery of the patient.

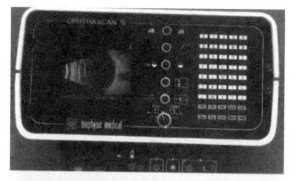

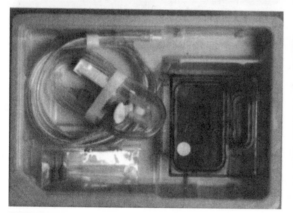

EXHIBIT 1

managers. The sales force consisted of six sales representatives, three sales managers, and one national sales director. There had been no turnover in the sales force in the last two years. The average sales representative had over 10 years' industry experience and covered a large territory.

Centrust had watched their market share dwindle from 70 percent in 1990 to 42 percent in 1993. The total U.S. sales for equipment in cataract surgery in 1992 was $1.075 billion, up from $579 million in 1990, not including disposable instruments. In reaction to this, the strategic planning unit developed a New

EXHIBIT 2   Centrust, Inc.: Income Statement and Statement of Retained Earnings for the Year Ending December 31, 1993 (in Millions)

	1990	1991	1992	1993
Sales revenues	$436.6	$515.5	$558.5	$456.1
Cost of sales	330.6	372.7	385.4	345.8
Gross margin	106.0	142.8	173.1	110.3
Expenses				
Depreciation	$24.0	$24.1	$24.4	$24.6
Sales expenses	28.1	30.3	32.5	34.1
Other expenses	10.9	10.7	10.3	10.2
Income taxes	18.9	35.0	48.7	19.1
Total expenses	81.9	100.1	$115.9	88.0
Net income	$24.1	$42.7	$57.2	$22.4
Less: Cash dividends	7.2	12.8	17.2	6.7
Net retained earnings	$16.9	$29.9	$40.0	$15.7

Account Planning Program (NAPP), which Centrust hoped would return the company to its previous high level of performance. NAPP is described in Exhibit 3.

Although other companies relied on distributors when selling disposable instruments, Centrust sells all of its medical products directly to the health care provider, relying on distributors to promote only office supplies. Centrust does not want to lose control of their medical products to distributors. The competition has been extremely active in using a distribution network over the last two years. Distributors provide a local inventory of products, logistical services, filling customers' reordering needs, and supplying manufacturers with market information. Armed with market information from their distributors, for instance, competitors have been quite successful in imitating Centrust's dis-

posable cutting tools and promoting these to other specialties.

Market Purchasing Behavior

To complete the selling cycle for a surgical system, sales representatives need to work through several layers of approval. Sales representatives typically meet with several individuals to identify their needs and to demonstrate the product's advantages. This process becomes quite confusing if the sales representative tries to sidestep anyone influential in the decision-making process. The commitment to buy medical products is seldom impulsive; therefore, sales representatives who try to complete the sale without total buyer commitment to the product will become frustrated. A suc-

---

EXHIBIT 3   National Account Planning Program (NAPP)

NAPP is an effort by Centrust to change the selling behavior of the sales force to a more consultative approach, emphasizing account relationship building, value-added selling, identification of product line extension opportunities, an account tracking system, and coordination with management. Following is a brief description of this program.

1. **Relationship Building:** With all important members of the buying center, build a relationship based on trust, rapport, and meeting each member's concerns and expectations. Backgrounds on people who may be involved in the purchase include the following:

Marketing Manager:	Promotes the hospital and is often involved in its strategic planning.
Hospital Administrator:	Acts as CEO of the hospital. Concerned with financial matters and the strategic direction of the hospital. Usually does not have a technical background in medicine.
Purchasing:	Establishes and maintains vendor relationships and ensures continuous supply at the lowest price. Usually a business or liberal arts education.
Reimbursement Officer:	Determines and tracks billing of patients and third parties (e.g., insurance and government) to meet government guidelines. Usually has some medical background.
Head of Nursing:	Primary user of many medical supplies; acts as a budget director for surgery and is highly influential in deciding which products will be used in surgery.
Safety Director:	Concerned with government safety regulations compliance and exposure to lawsuits. Frequently a highly technical individual; often an engineer.
Head of Surgery:	Usually a senior, well-respected surgeon who is highly influential in the hospital. Would have worked solely with one hospital in the past; this is not necessarily the case today.

2. **Value-Added Selling:** With hospitals' recent emphasis on low price, emphasis should focus on nonprice benefits, such as demonstrating technical superiority of equipment and instruments, fewer complications following surgery, lower cost per surgery due to greater speed, value in hospital's marketing to doctors, and exceeding government-mandated safety specifications.

3. **Product Line Extension Opportunities:** In an effort to expand sales opportunities for current cataract equipment, salespeople should be on constant alert for opportunities to apply cataract technology to other medical specialties.

4. **Opportunity Tracking System:** In order to better track the current selling situation, salespeople are to classify all sales opportunities into one of the following classifications:

"Unqualified"	When salesperson thinks there may be an opportunity but has not identified all buying influences.
"Qualified"	When a need has been verified, there is a confirmed intention to buy, and funding is available within a defined time frame.
"Best"	All influencers have been identified and concerns addressed, and there is a 90 percent probability of a sale.

5. **Management Coordination:** Salespeople are to update management quarterly on the status of all opportunities. In addition, management is to be personally involved in all "Best Opportunities" valued at more than $500,000, must approve all equipment discounts, and should be notified of all line extension opportunities by completing Form LEO-2000.

cessful sales representative must be prepared to allot several months to gain the endorsement and commitment of everyone involved in the process.

To keep the selling process flowing, effective sales representatives must find a champion, either inside or outside the hospital, to help promote their products and to identify potential roadblocks hindering completion of the sale. The purchasing agent, for instance, may not be the most influential individual in the decision process. The head nurse, rather than the surgeon, most often purchases disposable surgical products and determines the budget. Hospital management may desire a particular surgical unit based on low price, but surgeons in many specialties may influence the decision in another direction by demonstrating that the slightly higher-priced unit has more applications. Each purchase decision is unique, though multiple people are always involved.

The medical community has come under greater scrutiny in the last few years concerning the purchase and costs of medical care. With the impending government legislation, purchasing agents have been instructed to acquire products at the lowest possible price. Often, the value of products and services is not readily apparent. Very seldom are vendors able to sell a purchasing agent on any point other than price without first establishing strong relationships with everyone influential in the decision process.

Laptop Records of Account Activities.   The following notes appear in their original grammatical form as copied from laptop notes. The sales representative is required to input daily activities on all accounts.

Business Practices at JTS

JTS is a rather large surgical hospital that has a solid business reputation. They performed the most surgical procedures in a three county region that served seven million residents. In an effort to retain the most skilled surgeons, JTS had one of the highest compensation programs in the industry and their turnover rate was low throughout the hospital. JTS had published several brochures recently that indicated they were establishing Total Quality Management (TQM) programs this year. I thought it might be advantageous to link this to Centrust.

January 6

JTS had been targeted as being an account that had tremendous profit potential by our Strategic Analysis Department. During a scheduled appointment with B. J. Avery, JTS Director of Purchasing, we examined the new product lines that Centrust is offering. I assessed the

potential purchases of this account as 4 diagnostic units, 16 surgical units, and around 4,000 disposable surgical instruments for the first year. The total potential is $10.5 million.

Spent the day doing informational interviews at the JTS facility. Developed a list of people who I think will be influential in the purchasing decision. The buyers assured me that Centrust had maintained a positive relationship in the past with delivery, service and quality. Spent two hours looking around to obtain information about their business. I noticed that there was a business services unit that actually marketed medical services and products.[7] Made an appointment to see Avery's boss, the Vice President of Purchasing, for the morning of January 22 and the Head of Surgery for the afternoon of January 22.

January 22

Met with Sandy Adams, who has been the Vice President of Purchasing for three years. In the past I had been able to sell at JTS without needing to meet Sandy Adams. I was informed that all bids must be at the lowest market price. I must find users of the products to champion the full price. Dropped off the proper brochures to show Sandy Adams the features of our products that fit perfectly into their existing surgical protocols. I have classified JTS as a "Qualified Opportunity."

I met with Dr. Stenz (a leading surgeon who works with JTS) to discuss the technical aspects of Centrust products. He appeared more comfortable with Centrust after understanding the surgical benefits of our products over our competitors' products. He seemed to be impressed by our products.

I asked if any other competitor had established solid relationships with JTS and I was guaranteed that we were in the "driver's seat." It was even suggested that I stop by the office of Dr. Stenz and speak with his four associates. We also discussed the delivery process and training. The order for $10.5 million from JTS should be coming soon and we are in a position to hold full price. Stenz does not feel that we will need to discount very much to JTS. He also indicated that he would be purchasing for his office seven diagnostic units; an unusually large order for an established practice. I wonder?

January 24

Stopped by to see the associates of Dr. Stenz. I was surprised that no one was aware that I was coming. Stenz had seemed so enthusiastic and promised that he would arrange my visit with his associates and pass along the brochures I gave him. Even though I was disappointed

---

[7] Even though hospitals are traditionally thought of as nonprofit, they will often have marketing and promotion departments that are extremely aggressive.

that they were unprepared for my visit I used this as an opportunity to speak with the office manager, whom I found was influential in the office's buying process.

One interesting development is that I found out during the meeting with the office manager that there were two other competitors that had spoken with the hospital and other surgeons during the last month. Dr. Stenz had assured me that there was no real competition. I am not worried too much since I know from the December Vendors Trade Show in New Orleans that there is no threat for upcoming products from any other vendor.

February 3

Called on JTS to check on the Purchasing Department's progress concerning the order. Took the Purchasing Vice President's Assistant to lunch to find new information. The discussion centered around the politics of the organization. Learned that they felt we are being too aggressive and need to slow down. I took this as an opportunity to discuss our company and try to establish a rapport rather than focus on true selling product. After lunch I stopped by surgery to see if any competitors' products were being used. It seemed like a smorgasbord of products with no one vendor in dominance.

Made an appointment to see the Nursing Head of Surgery on the 14th. It's interesting. When I mentioned this to the Purchasing Assistant, he said, "Go ahead and do that, but remember we are the ones who sign all the purchasing orders."

February 14

It's Valentines Day so I stopped by with candy and flowers for the Surgical Nursing Department. This has always paid off well. The atmosphere was light and everyone was very receptive to listening to benefits of our products. They seemed to be pleased with what I told them. Looks as though the "ducks are being lined up." Look for the order soon!

March 16

Called Stenz to schedule an appointment since I will be in the area in April. He said that I needed to talk to H. M. Jones over at JTS. Found out that Jones was the Head of Safety at JTS. Made an appointment for April 23 and sent a follow-up letter and brochures on every product that we could possibly offer. I am not sure who this individual is but I am sure his role will be explained at our meeting.

April 23

I arrived at JTS and initiated a discussion with H. M. Jones concerning purchases on the original "bid." I was surprised to find that Jones was rather unsophisticated and appeared confused by both the literature and our conversation. Centrust had hired the finest ad agency in the city

to prepare these brochures for a high school level education. Jones may actually understand the material and is simply testing me. I'm sure I passed the test. The last question I asked was, "If this is all clear, do you have any other questions?" The reply I got was "nope"—another duck lined up!!!! I have moved JTS' classification up to a "Best Few Opportunity."

May 15

Received a phone message from Stenz stating that our prices on the diagnostic units for his office are too high, and I need to come down on price immediately. I called and was unable to reach him, but I did speak with an associate who told me that they were actually looking for an order that might be twice as large as my original estimate but the problem is that we are too high on price. I asked him if they were basing this opinion on a price relative to someone else or if our price was too high in general. They assured me that their business could not support our prices. I set an appointment on May 18 to speak in person with everyone in their office.

May 18

I had prepared new proposals in accordance with the practices of Centrust. There had been an offer by our Vice President of Sales to attend the meeting, but I felt comfortable that I would finalize this sale in ninety days so I rejected the suggestion. I proposed to the Strategic Analysis Department that we offer a new pricing structure for Dr. Stenz and his associates if they are able to help us get the JTS contract. After some arm twisting I was given the authority to discount Stenz's order by 25% on the condition that they help us obtain the JTS order. All I need now is the JTS account. The shipment of diagnostic units to Stenz' office is scheduled for July 1, with some modification of mounting devices to fit on their examination equipment. Stenz wants this order rushed, but modifications always require a minimum of thirty days from R & D. I am sure he will negotiate on our behalf to JTS. Stenz said he would set an appointment with B. J. Avery at JTS for June 16.

June 16

I was shocked to find that Stenz was not present for the meeting at JTS. When I called Stenz' office, they said they were nervous about meetings with JTS. For the first time, I found out that they now compete with JTS over some surgical business.[8] Avery was very pleasant, but informed us that our prices appeared to be quite high. I

---

[8] It is becoming very competitive for the cataract business, with the ability of cataract surgeons to perform surgery in their offices. The U.S. Food and Drug Administration has been quite liberal on the restrictions of in-office surgery for this field.

explained that this was due to the "state of the art technology" and that the price is actually reasonable. He asked if I might supply him with technology specifications to verify this statement. While this may not be standard protocol, I agreed to share the information I had with him. I also stated that we would share anything else that they needed after the order was delivered. I again mentioned to Avery that in an earlier meeting everyone had agreed that pricing would not be an issue. He asked me to return on July 7 and meet with the purchasing board. I asked why it was necessary to meet with this board. He said that it was a formality that was rarely used; however, with the size of this order he wanted another opinion. I asked if there was anything else we needed to cover and he said, "No, I am comfortable for now. I am also looking forward to finalizing this transaction."

July 7 morning

Tried to see Dr. Stenz before heading to JTS. The delivery of the 7 diagnostic units had occurred and training was complete. The staff was not using the system and I am concerned about this. I'll bring this up with Dr. Stenz at the meeting with JTS this afternoon. With the discount I had given them they must be happy. Normally this discount is reserved for long-term accounts. All in all everything appeared to be in control.

July 7 afternoon

My meeting with the purchasing board took only three minutes. They were totally unaware of what we were to discuss. Since Avery had been so concerned about my meeting them, I was frustrated that they were not prepared for the meeting. Once again, Avery assured me that everything was OK and that we will meet on August 1st to finalize the sale.

August 1

When I arrived for my scheduled meeting with Sandy Adams and B. J. Avery, there was a note left for me at the front desk from Sandy Adams. It read:

> Sorry to miss you this time around. We are busy with R & D helping with the installation of new

diagnostic and surgical equipment. Again, sorry you lost this business. Better luck next time.
> Sandy Adams

I stopped by Adams' office and found a helpful secretary who informed me that Bayson Laboratories had won the business. They had apparently had a price similar to Centrust's.

Next, I proceeded to Avery's office and had the following conversation:

B. J. AVERY: Oh Hi! I was unaware that you were stopping by today. Did we have an appointment?

(I didn't let on that I had read the note and acted as though all was still in order. I wanted to see if I could gain some information as to what had happened)

ME: No, I was in the area and wanted to see if you were close to arriving at your decision. Is there anything more that I can supply you with?

B. J.:   No, I received the new brochures that you sent and passed them along to everyone that you indicated in your letter. I believe that everyone was quite impressed with them. The videos that you sent were very professional too. All in all, I would say that you have done an excellent job of presenting your company and your products.

ME: I am happy that you feel that way, and I hope that we will soon be engaging in a long-term relationship. As I indicated to you in one of our last meetings, we will also be able to offer substantial discounts with multiple units installed.

B. J.:   This was a hard decision, but we have decided to purchase all of our surgical products from Bayson Laboratories. There was no real reason other than that was the decision by all parties. We do want to thank you for your trouble. I have a meeting in five minutes, so I hope you will forgive me. Here is a note I was about to send you.

There was nothing different in this note from the one left by Sandy Adams. It appeared that they both wrote these together.

TERRITORY MANAGEMENT

> It almost goes against the nature of salespeople to think about time; they just want to hit the road and sell.
>
> MARTY WILEY (Vice President of Marketing and Sales, Loctite Corporation)

Chapter Consultants:
Greg Miller, Senior Vice President, Strategic Planning and Human Resources,
  Sunburst Hospitality Corporation
Jerry Willett, National Sales Manager, Software Spectrum

LEARNING OBJECTIVES

After studying this chapter, you should be able to:

⟶ Describe effective steps for generating new accounts.

⟶ Explain how to determine the minimum account opportunity a salesperson should pursue.

⟶ Describe four methods for setting account priorities and indicate when each method should be used.

⟶ Tell how salespeople can spend more time selling.

ALLOCATING TIME AT IBM

After 20 years with IBM in a variety of sales, sales management, and sales training positions, David Mercer was recalling one of his earliest experiences: "I well remember when I was an IBM trainee and had been given my first territory to develop. I spent an inordinate amount of time on a small food wholesaler which had been foolish enough to admit that it wanted to improve its financial systems. Over seven or eight extended calls I eventually developed a 50-page proposal, which just about managed to justify the $50,000 or so I was asking them to invest in the smallest mainframe computer. I ultimately lost the order. They actually bought a new electric typewriter and a new desktop electronic calculator at a total cost of less than $1,000."

Identifying your opportunities and using your time wisely is important with current customers as well as new prospects. According to Mercer: "In IBM I rarely worked on more than 10 or so accounts that I knew would deliver better than 90 percent of my business in the next year. I didn't totally ignore the next 20 or 30 accounts, which would give me almost all the remaining 10 percent, but they received significantly less attention. I didn't totally ignore the 100+ accounts which might provide, at best, 1 or 2 percent; like many sales professionals, I am too greedy for my own good. But I covered these marginal accounts by mass marketing activities—only getting personally involved when they actually asked to place an order. Even then, the size of the order usually made the business unproductive."[1]

As David Mercer's experiences indicate, the difference between rookie salespeople and experienced sales professionals often starts with their attitude toward their territory. Salespeople must carefully analyze their resources, opportunities, and constraints. All accounts and sales opportunities are not equally important. Similarly, time available for face-to-face communications with customers is an important constraint on performance.

Up to this point, we have concentrated on selling effectiveness: how to make a good sales presentation and how to cultivate a profitable long-term relationship. For many companies sales force efficiency has been an important issue because selling costs have been rising much faster than sales volume. With the average cost of a sales call for manufacturers above $200, the crisis in sales force productivity has grabbed top management's attention.[2] While most of this chapter's discussion focuses on the salesperson, you will see that there are numerous issues and implications for sales management and top level management. This is particularly true for the later parts of the chapter and in the competencies development at the end of the chapter.

There are essentially two paths by which to grow sales: obtain new customers and grow the business with existing customers. This chapter is organized accordingly. The first part of our discussion focuses on strategies for growing sales. We begin by discussing the importance of growing by acquiring new customer prospects and present various methods for generating qualified prospects. We shift our focus to existing customers by discussing specific

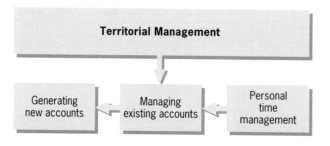

tools for allocating effort across a set of customers. First, we show how to determine the minimum size account a salesperson should try to sell, followed by a discussion of how to allocate time among selling opportunities. We conclude the chapter with a discussion of time management in sales. It is particularly important in this regard to increase the amount of time available for selling through efficient travel schedules and handling of nonselling time.

One way to increase sales force productivity is to focus sales force time on those prospects that have a high probability of becoming important customers. The next section discusses the importance of building your customer base by acquiring new customers and company efforts to increase sales force efficiency in this area.

GENERATING NEW ACCOUNTS

In the business press a lot of emphasis is placed on growing by getting closer to your present customers. Although this is certainly an important opportunity for businesses, many companies focus on finding new customers to achieve their growth objectives. A recent survey conducted by consulting company Towers Perrin indicated that 33 percent of sales executives cited acquiring new customers as their biggest opportunity for growth (see Figure 5-1). No matter how strong your products, how great your customer service, how aggressive your sales force, businesses lose customers every year when companies are bought and sold, management changes, industries consolidate, and global economies fluctuate. Few companies can afford to neglect new business development. For these and other reasons, many salespeople spend a good proportion of their time looking for new customers. The key to building sales in a territory through prospecting is to spend time with prospects who are likely to become good customers. Therefore an important first step in acquiring new customers is for salespeople to build a good prospect profile.

Building a Prospect Profile

Not all businesses will want or need your product or services. Some prospects will clearly be a waste of your time, while others will not buy enough to make it worth your time. You must first decide what factors determine who is a good prospect. This means building a *prospect profile,* which is simply a profile of what the best prospect looks like.

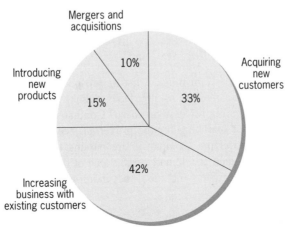

FIGURE 5-1   What's the Best Way to Grow?

A starting place for building this profile is a review of the target markets for your products, as specified in your marketing plan. Allnet Communications Services, a small long-distance phone company in Michigan, defines its target niche as small- to medium-sized business that bill between several hundred dollars and several tens of thousands of dollars per month. This target was identified to avoid head-to-head competition with AT&T, WorldCom, and Sprint. If a target market has not been clearly identified, a new salesperson may need to rely on the past experience of other salespeople in the company by asking them what types of business provide their most valuable customers. Veteran salespeople are probably best advised to examine their own past successes.

If you are selling blood processing machines, for example, then your best prospects may be hematologists (hospital consultants specializing in analyzing and treating blood disorders). Upon closer examination, the hottest prospects may be young (under 30) and trained at a handful of teaching hospitals.

The blood processing example points out a few important aspects of building a profile. First, the profile is defined in terms of demographics, the physical characteristics that define the individual buying environment. In the blood processing example, demographics included the customer's business, age, and educational background. Other examples of demographics frequently used to build a prospect profile include the following:

- Size of the business
- Age of the equipment to be replaced
- Geographic distance from shipping points
- Product line specialty

This information often can be obtained before meeting with the prospect. At Southwest Networks in Austin, Texas, salespeople keep a written profile of 12 characteristics on all leads, such as current vendor, percent savings, equipment specs, payback period, and such. After the first call on a prospect, the salesperson answers all 12 characteristic questions. The purpose of the profile is to tell salespeople how good a prospect a lead is and when to walk away from the lead.[3]

The Internet can also play an integral role in building a prospect profile. Once on-line, you can access databases containing government statistics, journals, books, and up-to-date newswires. There are also about 7,000 newsgroups, and any number of bulletin boards, forums, and roundtables that cover almost every subject imaginable. Web sites useful for target marketing and identifying new customers include *www.census.gov:80/stat-abstract* or *www.city.net*. A good site for identifying the top business in a geographic market area is *www.toplist.com*. If you are in the information technology business, for instance, you can receive by e-mail a report on any company within 15 minutes from *www.reports.infowizard.com*.

Building a Prospect List

With an ideal profile clearly in mind, a list of prospects should be developed. Here's the question that many companies are asking: Does it make sense for salespeople to spend four days out of five prospecting for new business? Companies are increasingly answering no,[4] and are concluding that searching for the proverbial needle in a haystack is not worth the investment in time and effort. Companies are passing the job of identifying prospects to lower-cost alternatives such as telemarketers. Some of the more widely used methods being used to identify good prospects include direct inquiries, trade shows, directories, referrals, and cold canvassing.

Direct Mail   All companies receive direct inquiries about products or services from potential customers. People making direct inquiries are often good prospects because they are, in effect, requesting that a salesperson call. Although some inquiries are unsolicited, the most common ways to generate leads are by advertising, direct mail, and trade shows. Advertising is not always used to sell the product or service, but it is an excellent vehicle for locating prospective customers. The fact that the potential customer initiates the contact allows salespeople to concentrate their efforts on those prospects most likely to purchase. The use of e-mail inquiries has made it possible to dramatically increase the speed with which companies can respond to a direct mail inquiry, which helps to increase the rate at which inquiries are converted to sales.

The quality of leads generated by advertising may vary, depending on the quality of the mailing list and the promotional copy in the advertising. Someone responding to an ad stating that a salesperson will call on them is a more qualified lead than one responding to a prize offered as a reward for completing the inquiry. The former indicates a greater commitment to further buying action.[5] At Tribute Inc., a software company in Cleveland, a business development coordinator will analyze the responses from mailings to discern the prospect's critical business issues, including their buying time frame and budget constraints. Using this approach, Tribute's high-priced salespeople are focusing their efforts only on high-quality prospects.[6]

Trade Shows   Trade shows are also an excellent vehicle for generating good prospects. It is estimated that more than 145,000 firms participate in over 8,000 trade shows at a cost of $10 billion annually. The National Restaurant Show held annually in Chicago draws more than 100,000 food buyers and business owners. One of the reasons for the growing popularity of trade shows is the relatively low cost per customer contact, approximately $89 per qualified contact. (A qualified contact is a customer contact whose interest in purchasing has been verified.) Another reason for this popularity is that organizations can project a coherent and consistent message to all prospects through exhibit structure, graphic and product displays, product demonstrations, and other support material. While some sales are consummated at trade shows, it is more likely that the lead is passed on to the appropriate salesperson; in fact, some trade shows do not permit the writing of orders.[7] Historically one of the problems arising from leads generated from trade shows or direct mailings has been passing along the leads in a timely manner and to the correct salesperson. E-mail and company internets are helpful in this regard because lead information can be passed along to the appropriate salesperson even before the trade show is over.

Directories   Special *direct inquiry directories* and open-to-bid announcements are important sources of leads for many firms. For example, the *Thomas Register of American Manufacturers* provides names, addresses, and other information compiled by types of products and by state. Furthermore, the firms in the *Register* are scored according to their assets, which enables the salesperson to judge the size of each potential customer. Industry trade associations often publish directories of their members by targeted segment or organization function.

Internet   The Internet has revolutionized the process of building a prospect list. Not only can potential customers inquire about your offerings over the Internet, but a wealth of information is available over the Internet. Most of the search engines available today are quite good at locating company Web sites. In addition, published information on companies is readily available at Web sites, such as at *Business Week* and the *Wall Street Journal.*

In addition to these public sources of company information the Internet is being used as a vehicle for supplying information specializing in particular industries. U.S. LifeLine, Inc., for example, will supply a wealth of information about health care providers such as hospitals, physician offices, and long-term care facilities to manufacturers and distributors selling to these organizations. They provide financial information, data on capital expenditures and procedural costs by area, as well as executive level profiles and photos. All this information can be downloaded from the Internet and used as graphical information in a PowerPoint presentation, which makes it more feasible to develop excellent sales presentations on the road.

Referrals   With *referrals,* a satisfied customer is asked to provide the names of others who might be interested in a product. In some cases, the person may also supply an introduction of the salesperson to the prospects. The advantage of referrals is that the person can say things about the salesperson and the product line that might not be as credible coming directly from the salesperson.[8]

One residential protection agency uses an interesting referral technique. The company holds a "walkthrough party" after completing an alarm system installation. The customer is encouraged to invite as many as four neighbors or friends to observe the well-organized indoctrination in the use of the system. The conversion rate on subsequent presentations to people who were present at the walkthrough party is more than 90 percent.[9]

Cold Canvassing   *Cold canvassing* involves contacting prospective customers without appointments; that is, salespeople call on firms or knock on doors until they find good prospects. Direct sales organizations such as Avon Products have had success with this approach. It is also used with some regularity by salespeople selling office supplies, air conditioning, cash registers, paper supplies, and insurance. Cold canvassing is used in these situations because the target markets for these products are fairly broad. The use of cold calls allows salespeople to concentrate their efforts in the best geographic areas and to fill gaps in their schedules. For example, if a stationary salesperson has an appointment canceled in the middle of the day, the time until the next scheduled call can be spent making cold calls on other potential customers in the same building or in the immediate area. The drawback to this approach is that it does not encourage calling on high-quality prospects, so a salesperson could waste time soliciting low-quality prospects. Canvassing may also be accomplished by telephone.

As the preceding discussion suggests, a variety of methods are available for identifying high-quality prospects. Salespeople are only limited by their own imagination and initiative.

Qualifying Prospects

Once salespeople have a list of leads, they must identify or *qualify a prospect,* that is, determine if the prospect is likely to be converted to a buying customer. Companies often initially qualify leads by telephone because of the lower cost of doing so. For example, Dow Corning, a specialty chemical affiliate of Dow Chemical and Corning Glass Works, uses an inside sales staff to qualify by telephone some of the 80,000 leads it generates annually.

To effectively qualify a prospect, the salesperson needs information about customer needs, buying authority, and ability to pay. Each of these is discussed below.

Needs   The most qualified leads are those that have a use for the seller's goods or services and are planning to buy in the near future. A prospect who is satisfied with the present supplier and has no desire to change is going to be very difficult to convert into a customer. You will sell such a prospect only if you can discover a desire or need that is not being fulfilled adequately by the present supplier and get the buyer to focus on these needs. This is not an easy task. Even if the prospect has an immediate need that you can meet and a desire to buy, you must still determine if the size and profitability of potential orders are sufficient to warrant further attention.

Buying Authority   Beyond the question of customer needs is the issue of buying authority. The plant manager may want a milling machine, but if he or she does not have the authority to buy, then a sales call may help create a favorable impression but will not necessarily pro-

<table>
<tr><td>

GLOBAL PERSPECTIVE COMPETENCY
Would You Sell to Crooks?

There is perhaps no more dramatic change in a business environment than that occurring in eastern Europe, which in the 1990s has attempted to transition from communism to capitalism. No one has to tell Rank Xerox how difficult it can be to sell in this environment.

Rank Xerox, a joint venture between Xerox and the Rank Organization of Britain, has been selling photocopiers in eastern Europe since 1964. The company believes the sales potential in eastern Europe and the former Soviet Union is fantastic. The former Soviet Union, which has about 50,000 copiers, is estimated to need 2.5 to 5 million. Eastern Europe has about 100,000 copiers and is estimated to need at least 1 million.

To realize this potential, significant obstacles must be overcome. To get around the shortage of convertible currencies in the area, a company must be adept at counter trade—arranging the sale of eastern European and Soviet goods to earn the hard currency to pay for photocopiers. Perhaps Rank Xerox's most important problem is deciding who are the best customers for Xerox photocopiers.

The problem is that the only people with the necessary capital to be independent copier dealers are those who were corrupt Communist officials or those involved in money changing or other black-market activities. "Nobody but the big crooks have the money," according to Rank Xerox's area director of Hungary and the Czech Republic, "and the question is whether you, as a respectable company, want to do business with the crooks." Rank Xerox is continuing to look for the honest entrepreneurs who are slowly emerging in eastern Europe. His primary prospect profile is people with expertise who might have worked for state-owned companies and are eager to go out on their own. See *www.rankxerox.com.*

</td></tr>
</table>

duce a signed order. Business-to-business salespeople often have problems identifying who has the authority to buy within an organization because of the number of people involved in making a purchasing decision. Methods for identifying the buying authority were presented in Chapter 4.

Ability to Pay   Finding prospects who want a product and also have the authority to buy will not be productive if they lack the financial resources to pay for it. Selling products that must be repossessed later for nonpayment of bills is not the way for salespeople to get ahead. Hence, salespeople should make an initial screening of prospects on their ability to buy. The objective is to eliminate prospects who represent too high a credit risk. Credit ratings are readily available from banks and credit services such as Dun and Bradstreet.

One study on how salespeople qualify prospects found that successful salespeople differed from less successful salespeople in the way they thought about prospects. While both groups of salespeople generally used the same cues to qualify a prospect (e.g., income, need, etc.), successful salespeople utilized higher qualifying standards and were more likely to cut their losses early. For example, they required a higher credit rating or a greater need for the product or service to consider a lead to be a hot prospect.[10] This is another example of how wasted time can hurt productivity and that time management is critical to sales success.

MANAGING EXISTING ACCOUNTS

Generating new customers is important, but many sales and marketing managers feel that the companies that will prosper will be ones that maintain strong customer loyalty. Referring to the results of the Towers Perrin survey shown in Figure 5-1, 42 percent of the sales executives surveyed felt that the greatest opportunities for growth lie in keeping and growing existing customer relationships; in short, winning a greater share of the customer's overall business.

From an efficiency perspective, we would want our salespeople to spend their time with their best opportunities. This means that we need to be able to identify our best sales opportunities and to know where we should spend less time. In other words, we want to avoid David Mercer's mistake in focusing on low-priority opportunities. A good starting point in deciding how to allocate your time across existing accounts is to determine the minimum size account that represents a good opportunity. A process for answering this question is discussed in the next section.

Minimum Account Size

In all likelihood, you will be given a list of existing customer accounts that will be the source of most of your sales volume. An important starting point in managing your territory is to determine the minimum size customer on whom you should be calling. The individual salesperson should be able to determine the long-term value of a customer. For example, salespeople should know customers' short-term growth potential, as well as their territory's competitive and demand situations. Salespeople who are supplied with proper direct selling expense information are in an excellent position to perform a minimum account size analysis. This analysis involves two steps: calculating a personal cost per sales call and a break-even sales volume. We turn our attention to these analyses in the following sections.

Cost per Call   The first step in addressing the minimum customer size issue is to calculate the costs of making a sales call. *Cost per call* will be a function of the number of calls you make per day, the number of days available to call on customers, and your *direct selling expenses.* Direct selling expenses include compensation, travel, lodging, entertainment, and communications. These expenses are referred to as direct selling expenses because they can be attributed to an individual salesperson. In other words, the company would not have incurred these costs had a salesperson not been present in the territory.

The procedure for computing the average cost per call is illustrated in Table 5-1 for an industrial sales representative with an average-size territory. In this example, compensation includes salary, commissions, and bonuses, as well as fringe benefits such as insurance and social security. These total $84,220, which is about average for an industrial salesperson.[11] Other direct selling expenses equal $21,250, for a total direct selling expense of $105,470.

For this salesperson, 205 days a year are available for selling. If the average number of calls per day is 3, then under normal circumstances the total number of calls for the entire year is 615 (3×205). Using these estimates, the representative can now compute the cost of an average call as $171.50 ($105,470/615).

How does the cost per call of $171.50 compare with that of other salespeople? According to one survey, the median cost per call for industrial goods is $202.19 and $242.24 for services.[12]

Break-Even Sales Volume   *Break-even sales volume,* the sales volume necessary to cover direct selling expenses, will help determine the minimum size customer that should be pursued. In addition to the cost per call, calculating the break-even volume requires that we also know the number of calls necessary to close a sale and what direct selling expenses should be as a percentage of total sales. It is necessary to know the number of calls needed to close a sale in order to calculate the total cost of generating the sale. A commonly referenced figure is that it usually takes five sales calls to close a sale, although this figure will vary considerably according to the industry and company involved. For calculating the break-even

TABLE 5-1   Computing the Cost per Call for an Industrial Products Salesperson

Compensation		
Salary, commisions, and bonus	$73,235	
Fringe benefits (hospital, life insurance, social security)	10,985	$84,220
Direct Selling Expenses		
Automobile	7000	
Lodging and meals	5250	
Entertainment	2250	
Communications	3500	
Samples, promotional material	1750	
Miscellaneous	<u>1500</u>	<u>21,250</u>
Total Direct Expenses		$105,470
Calls per Year		
Total available days		260 days
Less:		
Vacation	10 days	
Holidays	10 days	
Sickness	5 days	
Meetings	18 days	
Training	<u>12 days</u>	<u>55 days</u>
Net Selling Days		205 days
Average calls per day		3 calls
Total Calls per Year (205 × 3)		615 calls
Average Cost per Call ($105, 470/615)		**$171.50**

sales volume, a sales call refers to a personal face-to-face contact with the customer. Not considered sales calls in this case include telephone calls, e-mail, notes that are dropped off, chance meetings at neutral sites, and contact by nonsales personnel such as delivery people. Calls to close may be based on your own experience or that of other salespeople in the company. It is also necessary to know the company's target for direct selling expenses as a percent of sales because this figure indicates how large sales need to be for a given dollar amount of direct selling expenses. If direct selling expenses are higher than this target, then profits will be lower if there are no offsetting cost or gross margin adjustments. The target for direct selling expenses should be provided by management.

Both the number of sales calls needed to close a sale and direct selling costs as a percentage of sales will vary considerably among industries and even between companies in the same industry. Table 5-2 shows these numbers for 10 industries. The number of calls needed to close a sale varies from 2.8 in the construction industry to 5.3 in the instruments industry. Sales costs as a percentage of sales are 22.2 percent in printing/publishing but only 2.4 percent in office equipment.

Armed with this information, break-even sales volume for an individual sale can be calculated as follows:

$$\text{Break-even sales volume} = \frac{\text{Cost per call} \times \text{Number of calls to close}}{\text{Sales costs as a percentage of sales}}$$

If the sales representative is in the chemicals industry, where 2.8 calls are needed to close a sale and sales expenses are 3.4 percent of sales, then the break-even sales volume would be $13,654 ([$165.80 × 2.8]/.034). As a point of comparison, break-even sales volume for an average salesperson in the instruments industry is $8,093 ([$226.00 × 5.3]/.148). Notice that the higher cost per call and greater number of calls needed to close an order in the instrument industry are more than offset by the fact that direct selling costs are normally 14.8 percent of sales in this industry, compared to 3.4 percent in the chemicals industry.

TABLE 5-2 Selected Statistics on Cost per Call and Number of Calls Needed to Close a Sale

Industry	Cost per Call	Number of Calls Needed to Close a Sale	Sales Costs as a Percentage of Total Sales
Business services	$ 46.00	4.6	10.3%
Chemicals	165.80	2.8	3.4
Construction	111.20	2.8	7.1
Electronics	133.30	3.9	12.6
Food products	131.60	4.8	2.7
Instruments	226.00	5.3	14.8
Machinery	68.50	3.0	11.3
Office equipment	25.00	3.7	2.4
Printing/publishing	70.10	4.5	22.2
Rubber/plastic	248.20	4.7	3.6

So far, our discussion has focused on sales in which multiple calls are needed to close a sale. This is most typically the situation when calling on new customers or when selling high-ticket equipment or services to business. In many industries, a salesperson's primary function is a combination of selling new products and services and taking orders to replenish

STRATEGIC ACTION COMPETENCY
Dell Online

In late July 1996, Dell began conducting business through its Internet site. Almost immediately Dell began selling $1 million of computers per week through the Web. Within six months, more than 150,000 customers were visiting the Web site each week, generating sales of approximately $1 million per day. According to people inside Dell, everyone sensed that the Internet would be a big win because of its compatibility with Dell's overall strategy of selling computers direct to the end-user rather than through retailers, but few envisioned that it would be so big so soon. In fact, three months later Dell was selling $2 million a day over the Web and before 1997 sales had grown to $3 million in revenue per day. According to one source, Dell now moves $14 million per day in direct computer sales over the Internet. Dell's customer surveys indicate that about 25 percent of the volume was incremental business that Dell would not have obtained without the Web site. Perhaps the most important development, however, was the cost savings that were achieved through increased selling efficiency and productivity.

In the traditional Dell Direct model, dropping 100,000 catalogs would result in 10,000 customer calls to Dell's sales reps. On average, Dell was able to close 20 percent of these 10,000 incoming customer calls, resulting in 2,000 orders. These relations changed with Dell Online. Once customers logged onto the site and configured the system that best suited their needs, they had the option of purchasing the system using a credit card. If the order was incomplete, the sales rep called the customer for the missing information. Approximately 20 percent of the orders that Dell received from its online retail store were complete. About one-third of incomplete orders were due to customer concern over security and were lacking credit card information. As a result of this type of customer self-selection, the close rate for Dell sales reps increased to 35 percent and 500 orders out of every 100,000 Web site visits were complete and did not require a sales rep callback. As a result of the higher close rate of sales on the phone which originated from a Web site visit, individual sales reps have been able to increase their sales figures by 50 percent, resulting in increased income to the sales rep and significant cost savings to Dell. For more on Dell, visit *www.dell.com* or visit their online store at *www.dell.com/store/index.htm*.

inventory levels. This is typical of the job responsibility of most consumer and industrial goods wholesale salespeople, for instance. The process for calculating break-even in this case is quite similar to what we have done so far. Instead of examining the number of calls needed to close the sale, however, the number of calls made on an account each month may be substituted in the break-even sales volume equation to arrive at a break-even volume per month. For example, if the cost per call is $146.75, the number of calls made on a customer is four times a month, and selling costs are 9 percent of sales, then a customer should place, on average, $6,522 worth of business with a salesperson each month ([$146.75 × 4]/.09).

Territory Management Implications   Having performed a break-even analysis, how can a salesperson use this information? Should a salesperson not call on customers or prospects whose sales volume does not exceed the minimum sales volume?

The real world of selling is rarely simple or straightforward. Other factors must be considered before dropping a customer or reducing the selling effort. For example, sales to a customer may be growing, which may be due to one of two causes. The customer's business is growing rapidly, so their need for supplies is also increasing. Alternatively, your sales to this account may be growing because you are getting a larger share of the customer's business. If this is the case, then it is important to know how much your customer share is and how much more is available. What if a customer is located next door to a major account, so a call takes little time and no real travel time is involved? Should you walk away from this opportunity, even though it does not take as much time as your average sales call? Another important consideration is that a customer may purchase a mix of high-profit products, so that this customer's gross margins are 25 percent higher than the

---

TEAM-BUILDING COMPETENCY
How Cisco Is Partnering to Reach New Customers

In today's economy eight people gain Internet access every second and electronic mail messages outnumber regular mail by more than 10 to 1. If you have accessed the Internet or sent e-mail to a friend, it is likely that Cisco products transferred your data. Needless to say, demand for Cisco products has been robust. The growth and evolution of the Internet has caused Cisco to embrace a new set of customers which it had been unable to reach in the past—small- and medium-sized business. The obstacle was Cisco's traditional sales force system. Visiting each customer in person may be the preferred strategy, but with smaller accounts the costs aren't justified. According to Cisco management, "We can't put enough feet on the street," even though Cisco already employs several thousand field salespeople.

The new model Cisco has adopted is to have account managers work with resellers to tap the opportunity in the small to medium businesses. The new model forced account executives to switch roles from salespeople who pitch technology to business partners who create solutions, often for start-up businesses. This involves a whole new set of issues. The account executive must team with the reseller by coordinating his or her own activities with those of the reseller. With the vast number of businesses interested in Internet solutions, there are some activities that resellers can perform more efficiently because they already have a relationship with the customer and others that the Cisco salesperson with technical expertise is better equipped to address. This type of teamwork has resulted in a better than 50 percent increase in business from these new customers. The coordination issues are significant, but the rewards are worth the effort. For more on Cisco systems Inc., see *www.cisco.com*. You can also visit its Web site for small- and medium-size businesses to get more information on how they are working with resellers.

average for the territory. As you can see, a number of factors must be considered when judging the value of an opportunity.

Top management may choose to address the smaller, less profitable accounts in ways other than reducing the number of sales calls made on these accounts. The Gillette Company's Safety Razor Division decided to hire part-time merchandisers to assist salespeople in calling on individual small retailers. The Commercial Systems Division of Hewlett-Packard hired inside sales and technical reps to work the phones. Alternatively, a plumbing fixtures manufacturer chose to raise prices to discourage the "worthless" small customer orders that were disrupting its production scheduling. These small orders subsequently became the company's most profitable. The new higher prices more than compensated for the costs; customers weren't changing suppliers because of high switching costs; and competitors had shied away from these small accounts because of the conventional wisdom in the industry regarding their profitability.

As you can see from these examples, the minimum size customer on which a salesperson should call depends on the direct selling costs involved, the number of sales calls made over a period of time, and the cost structure of the company, as well as other considerations. There is rarely a hard-and-fast dollar volume below which a customer's business should not be pursued. However, when supplied with the right information, sales professionals will know each account well enough to judge if it is likely to become a profitable one.

Setting Account Priorities: Account Analysis

Break-even account analysis provides a starting place from which to determine the minimum size account that should be called on. This analysis does not fully address the issue of how much time should be allocated to prospecting and how much to existing accounts in a territory. With customer loyalty declining, many successful companies are finding that they need to differentiate their service levels according to the importance of the customer. This issue and the more general concern of prioritizing sales opportunities is the reason for performing account analysis. *Account analysis* refers to estimating the present and future importance of accounts to your business and allocating time so as to maximize sales productivity.

Single-Factor Model   The easiest and probably the most widely used models for allocating salespeople's time are single-factor models. These models examine a single customer characteristic, such as current sales volume, to arrive at an initial allocation of sales calls. Thomas Cook Travel, a division of the Thomas Cook Group, an international travel and financial services company based in the United Kingdom, divides its clients into A's (those who spend $750 or more in annual revenues), B's (those spending $250–$749), and C's (those who spend less than $250). Differentiating its client services according to their classification has freed up travel agents to spend more time with A and B clients.

The basics of a *single-factor allocation model* based on total sales volume is presented in Table 5-3. This is referred to as ABC *account classification.* Customers are first arrayed according to their total sales volume. In this case, the top 15 percent of all accounts are classified as A accounts, the next 20 percent are classified as B's, and the remaining accounts are classified as C's. Column 4 is a calculation of each type of account's sales as a percentage of total territory sales. In this example, A's generate 65 percent of total territory sales, B's account for 20 percent, and C's represent only 15 percent. Based on surveys of sales executives, these results are fairly typical for a variety of businesses.

If sales force performance is based on total revenue, then effort should be allocated according to sales volume. All too often customers are treated equally, so that each customer is called on with the same frequency. Columns 5 and 6 in Table 5-3 illustrate the problem with making equal numbers of calls on all customers. Notice that if you treat all accounts as

TABLE 5-3   ABC Account Classification

Account Classification	No. of Accounts (1)	Total Accounts (2)	Sales (000) (3)	Total Sales (4)	Total Calls Per Classification (5)	Sales ($) Per Call (6)
A	21	15%	$910	65%	105	$8,667
B	28	20	280	20	140	2,000
C	91	65	210	15	455	462
Totals	140	100%	$1,400	100%	700	$2,000 (Avg)

equal, say by calling on each account weekly, you would be spending 65 percent of your time on your C accounts. A call on an A customer, however, is on average 20 times as productive as a call on a C customer. Spending too much time with C customers may allow the competition to steal an A customer through better service.

The main limitation of single-factor models such as the ABC account classification procedure is that they may not include all the factors that should be considered when evaluating an account. They do not consider customer growth potential, for example, or the opportunity to obtain greater account penetration (a greater share of the account's total purchases), vulnerability to competitive efforts, or account profitability. On the other hand, salespeople are likely to make better time allocation decisions with the ABC systematic approach than when relying totally on judgment and intuition without the necessary data on past purchase patterns.

Portfolio Models   Portfolio models attempt to overcome the limitations of single-factor models by considering multiple factors when determining the attractiveness of individual accounts within a territory. Selling effort is allocated so that the most attractive accounts receive the most selling effort.[13] For instance, one company classified its portfolio of accounts according to their average gross margin and the cost to service each account. The Surgical Division of Cardinal Health, Inc. instituted a customer classification system based on the type of hospital (e.g., teaching/research, regional medical center, government/federal, community), location (rural versus urban), and size. Sales effort and marketing programs were designed for each type of customer within the classification system. The criteria a company uses to classify its customers will depend on their competitive situation, its ability to capture and disseminate relevant customer information, and what the sales force is being asked to accomplish.

Figure 5-2 illustrates one well-known portfolio model. This model classifies accounts into one of four categories by determining account attractiveness based on two criteria: account opportunity and competitive position. *Account opportunity* refers to the magnitude of an account's present and future need for the salesperson's offering. Ratings of account opportunity may be based on the account's present and projected growth rate, its financial health, and its present and future strength in the marketplace. *Competitive position,* the second dimension on which accounts are classified, refers to the strength of the salesperson's present relationship with an account. Competitive position may be based on outcome measures such as an account's total gross profit dollars, share of the account's total purchases, type of contract, and compliance with the contract. Additional indicators of competitive position may focus on the account relationship and may include the account's attitude toward the company and familiarity with the decision makers in the account. Once all accounts have been rated on both dimensions, we can proceed to prioritize our accounts by splitting them at the median of both dimensions and forming a four-quadrant grid, as shown in Figure 5-2.

As an extension of single-factor customer classification models, portfolio models offer several benefits that single-factor models do not:

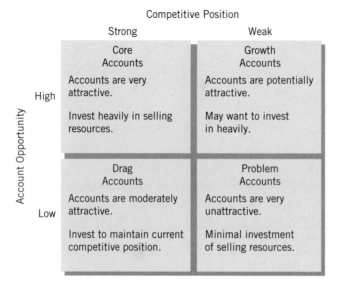

FIGURE 5-2   Portfolio Model

- They help the sales team to identify the important customer and relationship issues.
- They facilitate communication and sharing of judgments and assumptions between salespeople and sales managers.
- They help isolate information gaps and set priorities for customer data collection and analysis.
- They force the sales team to think about the future and consider ways of achieving a more desirable portfolio configuration.

Decision Models   Although portfolio models have the advantage of using multiple characteristics to classify accounts, several shortcomings remain. First, accounts must still be grouped into the four quadrants for the purpose of allocating sales calls. Differences between firms in the same quadrant are therefore not taken into consideration. Second, the process does not arrive at an optimal allocation of sales calls.

Decision models for allocating sales calls overcome these two shortcomings by focusing on the response of each account to the number of sales calls made over a period of time. Although mathematically elegant, these models consist of only two parts. The first part develops the relationship between the number of sales calls over a period of time and sales to a particular account. This is referred to as a *sales response function*. The response function may be derived either through regression analysis on historical data or judgmentally. With judgment-based decision models, salespeople are first given information about how many times they called on a particular account over a period of time and the sales generated. Salespeople are then asked to project sales in the next period of time if the same number of calls are made on the account, if the number of sales calls is decreased by 50 percent, if they make no sales calls, and if they make the maximum number of sales calls possible. These estimates are used to construct a sales response function like the one shown in Figure 5-3.[14]

Note that customers are assumed not to respond dramatically when only one or two calls are made per quarter, but sales are expected to increase dramatically when the number of calls increases from two to four. The response function flattens out after four calls, suggesting that there is little left for the salesperson to accomplish by calling on the account more than four times in a quarter. The software would construct such a response function for each customer on which the salesperson called, since the response curve is likely to differ between customers. For instance, some customers may be estimated to respond very quickly, in which case the response line would be very steep.

The second part of these models uses the individual response functions to allocate calls so as to maximize sales. Essentially, these models continue to allocate sales calls to an account until more sales can be generated by calling on another account. For example, a third and fourth call may be allocated to the account in Figure 5-3, but greater sales are likely to be generated by calling on another account rather than by allocating a fifth call to this account.

The allocation task in decision models is complex and involves a large number of calculations as the number of accounts in a territory increases. Therefore, computer models such as CALLPLAN have been developed. CALLPLAN is an interactive computerized program based on decision model logic. CALLPLAN is self-instructing, and salespeople can work with the model at remote computer terminals using simple conversational language. Research results on the use of decision models have consistently supported the use of these models, with reported sales improvements ranging from 8 to 30 percent.[15]

Sales Process Models Despite the advantages of sophisticated call allocation programs, they are not appropriate for all situations. See the Coaching Competency box for a discussion of Intel's sales force for an example of when a decision model would not be appropriate. Instead of calling on microprocessor customers, some people in Intel's sales force call on software vendors, information technology buyers, and retail outlets, selling the idea of PCs on every desk and in every household. In the case of these Intel salespeople, immediate and near-term sales volume is not a relevant measure of the opportunity these sales calls represent.

In other sales situations, the selling cycle can be quite long because of the dollar commitments associated with the sales. This is especially true in industrial goods and high-tech markets, as well as in major account selling where more effort is required and many people may be involved in the purchase decision. An 18-month selling cycle is typical, for example, in the Traffic Control Division of 3M. Similarly, new product introductions are more time-consuming in most industries. In such situations, the single-factor, portfolio, or decision models are not appropriate.

In complex selling situations or when significant time is spent prospecting for new accounts, a sales process model approach to effort allocation is probably most appropriate. Unlike the earlier models, which focus on the relative sales volume or profitability of oppor-

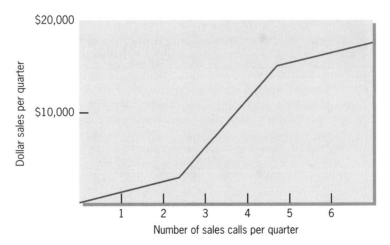

FIGURE 5-3 **Number of Sales Calls Response Function**

tunities, *sales process models* focus on where the opportunity is currently classified in the selling process. In these models, opportunities are assigned to different stages of the selling process according to the probability that they will ultimately result in a sale. This sort of opportunity categorization is most appropriate when the selling cycle is fairly long and multiple opportunities may exist within the same account.

One example of a selling process model is the *sales funnel*.[16] Initially developed for training salespeople at Hewlett-Packard, this system categorizes and prioritizes sales opportunities or objectives, not accounts.[17] This is necessary because a salesperson or sales team may have multiple selling objectives at one account at the same time. He or she may be attempting to get a pilot installation in one of the client's departments, for example, while wanting to upgrade to a more sophisticated piece of equipment in another department.

Each sales opportunity is categorized based on the level of uncertainty in meeting the opportunity:

1. **Unqualified opportunities.** In this case data suggest that a possible need exists, but this need has not been verified with key people in the account. For example, you have learned that a customer's existing contract with a competitor is about to expire. The selling job needed in this situation is to qualify the account by verifying that a need exists according to the criteria discussed earlier in this chapter.
2. **Qualified opportunities.** A qualified opportunity must meet four criteria:
   • The need has been verified with at least one of the buying influences (i.e., the technical, user, or economic buyers discussed in Chapter 4).
   • There is a confirmed intention to buy a new product or service, replace an existing one, or switch suppliers.
   • Funding for the purchase has been approved or already exists.
   • There is an identified time frame within which the purchase will be made.
3. **Best few opportunities.** All the buyers have been contacted and their needs identified, and in your judgment have been sufficient to make the sale. You have all but eliminated luck and uncertainty in the sale and are at least 50 percent along in the selling cycle. That is, it should take you half as long to close these sales as is normal in your territory.

The term *sales funnel* is derived from figuratively placing the sales opportunities in a funnel. Unqualified opportunities appear just outside the top of the funnel, qualified opportunities inside the funnel (depending on the probability of closure and the position in the selling cycle), and the few best opportunities at the bottom of the funnel.

COACHING COMPETENCY
Intel: Salespeople Who Don't Call on Customers

An important aspect of coaching is sharing best practices from other companies. Certainly Intel would qualify as a company whose marketing and sales practices are worthy of consideration. It would probably surprise many people to learn that a large number of Intel's salespeople don't call on customers. Instead they call on software vendors, information technology buyers, and retail outlets—companies that are traditional partners and customers of PC manufacturers. These salespeople don't sell the microprocessors made by Intel; instead they sell the idea of PCs on every desk and in every household. Salespeople are also responsible for knowing what is going on in those industries that impact Intel. For instance, Intel is represented on most software standards committees. That gives Intel a voice in what shape such things as the Internet will take. It's a voice Intel uses to foster consumer and corporate interest in PCs—rather than low-end devices that don't require Intel processors.

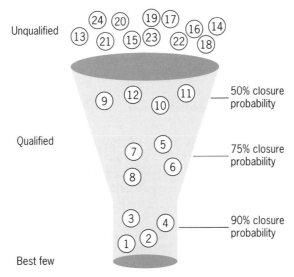

FIGURE 5-4   The Sales Funnel

In the sales funnel shown in Figure 5-4, each numbered bubble represents a unique selling opportunity. Notice that the qualified opportunities are divided into those with a 50 percent probability of closure and those with a 75 percent probability. This distinction is made to portray the current situation more clearly and to facilitate communication between salesperson and sales manager. The situation in Figure 5-4 appears to be healthy in that there are a number of opportunities likely to result in sales during the current period, but an even larger number of opportunities for future sales results. Some companies will alter the shape of the funnel to reflect the number of opportunities at each level, which quickly indicates the present and future health of the territory.

At first glance, it would seem advisable to work on your best few and qualified opportunities, while spending whatever time remains on unqualified opportunities. The problem with this approach is that when given low priority, prospecting rarely occurs. Having closed the best few and exhausted the qualified opportunities, there is nothing left to replace these opportunities. Therefore, experts suggest the sequence of (1) closing your best few sales opportunities first, (2) prospecting for unqualified opportunities next, and (3) working the qualified opportunities last to ensure a constant and predictable flow of sales over time.[18] It is always important to keep the funnel full through prospecting for new opportunities.

Because there are probably many sales opportunities during any review period, only the major deals and core or growth accounts should be included in the sales funnel. This will allow both the salesperson and manager to identify critical sales objectives accurately, monitor progress over time, and spend their time meeting key sales objectives.

Focusing on Profitability

There is a tendency in sales to evaluate opportunities in terms of dollar sales. Faced with tough buyers in mature markets, some companies are beginning to focus on the bottom line instead of the top line. A recent survey of 200 leading executives in North America, Europe, and Asia reported that 49 percent expected to track customer profitability based on return on investment.[19] Profit, of course, is the difference between net price and the actual cost to serve a customer. There can be dramatic differences between the price an account pays and the costs incurred in servicing an account.[20] Why is this true?

Customers may pay very different prices for similar products and services. Although there are some legal constraints, such as the Robinson-Patman Act, some customers are able to negotiate lower prices and higher discounts because of their size. In other words, large customers can demand and get lower prices because a seller cannot afford to lose their business. Other customers are simply able to get lower prices because of their negotiating skills. And still other customers exploit deals and promotions more than others and "forward buy," which means they buy a large amount of their annual needs at one time when the product is on discount.

The cost to serve is also likely to differ between customers. Some accounts are located far from the salesperson's normal route, so more travel time is involved. Some customers place their orders by phone or over the Internet, whereas others require endless face-to-face sales calls to close a deal or to place even a routine order. Some customers demand intensive presale services like applications engineering and custom design support, while others accept standard designs. Costs may also vary according to preferred transportation mode, number of receiving locations for an order, and opportunities to back-haul. (Back-hauling refers to transporting supplies back to an origination point after delivering supplies. As a result, a truck does not travel without a load which would waste time and money.) The list of customer service cost differences sometimes seems endless.

The main point we would like to make here is that companies and salespeople need to be aware of the price, cost, and profit differences between customers. It is not at all unusual for there to be between a 50 to 75 percent difference in the profitability of customers who purchase a similar quantity of product. This is what FedEx found out when it began studying the profitability of its customers. This issue is so important to FedEx that it now searches its database to compare the costs of doing business with particular customers and rates its customers according to profitability. FedEx also now matches transaction information with demographic data to pinpoint the characteristics to seek in prospects or existing customers that might offer more business.

Perhaps the most surprising discovery for firms that closely examine the profitability of their individual customers is that many of their largest customers are not their most profitable ones. Typical of the experience of many companies today is that of a major U.S.-based component manufacturer. They decided that it was time to examine the profitability of their 10 largest accounts. In 1987, these accounts had represented 72 percent of the company's overall profits. Ten years later, in 1997, their contribution had shrunk to less than 40 percent of profits. In fact, 2 of these 10 large accounts were producing a loss for the company and 2 others were barely breaking even. Many other organizations are finding that size is no longer a good proxy for profitability. As a result, businesses are investing heavily in information technology to help them identify their most profitable customers.[21]

The shift to managing territory profits requires that companies pinpoint their costs, measure account profitability, and provide this information to the sales force. Assuming that salespeople have the proper level of customer information made available to them, the sales force can manage the dispersion of customer profitability in at least three ways.

1. **Allocation of effort.** Salespeople can manage their time allocation according to the profit opportunity an account represents. Distributors of disposable medical supplies, for instance, look for small or single physician family practices because these practices use a lot of disposable supplies (such as exam table paper) and they tend to be less price sensitive, because most do not have a dedicated purchasing manager.

2. **Mix of products.** Because most salespeople sell a number of product lines with very different gross margins, they should allocate their efforts based on both volume opportunity and profitability of the product line. Management at Loctite Corporation, a manufacturer of industrial sealant and adhesives, compensates its sales force so as to emphasize the

sales of its larger, more profitable console adhesive applicators rather than the pencil applicators.

3. **Price concessions.** Salespeople should be very reluctant to offer price concessions in order to close a sale. Not only do they encourage the buyer to negotiate discounts in the future, but even a small concession can have a dramatic impact on profits. Studies indicate that companies giving salespeople wide latitude to negotiate price discounts are not only less profitable, but also grow less rapidly than those with tight control over sales force price discounting.[22] Some would argue that price discounting is often a result of competitive weaknesses and is therefore a symptom, rather than a cause, of poor overall performance. In either case, management should be cautious about giving salespeople wide latitude in discounting prices.

TIME MANAGEMENT

Time management was recently rated the third most popular subject in business training programs. Seventy-one percent of firms provide salespeople with training in time management.[23] Figure 5-5 shows how salespeople spend their time. The amount of time spent selling, either face-to-face or over the phone, has increased during the 1990s to 54 percent from only 50 percent in 1990. Most of this increase is due to a greater use of the phone when selling.

Improving the amount of time spent selling is an opportunity for producing significant productivity gains. A task force for one Fortune 100 company estimated that a 10 percent improvement in the time its sales force spent selling would generate more than a 5 percent increase in overall sales volume. This helps to explain why in a recent survey, 72 percent of sales executives listed a cellular phone as the technology most essential to their salespeople's job.[24]

Notebook computers and the Internet were also highly ranked by the sales executives as essential technologies. To understand the reason for this rating, consider how things have changed for the salespeople in Quaker Oats' chemical division. In the 1980s, tracing a shipment of solvent for a client meant numerous hours of phone calls and plenty of headaches. Today, Quaker Oats salespeople simply open their laptop, go into the company's internal Web site, click on a button that says "shipment information," and in just a few minutes they are able to tell the purchasing agent that the tank car is in Houston, 20 miles away. The

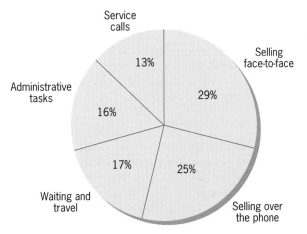

FIGURE 5-5 How Salespeople Spend Their Time

importance of this technology is indicated in Figure 5-5, which shows that salespeople spend 13 percent of their time on service calls.

Territory Coverage

On average, 17 percent of salespeople's time is spent traveling and waiting. Careful scheduling can produce substantial savings in travel time. The task of selecting sales routes is usually handled by the salesperson, but at some companies the sales manager or staff specialists develop it. The rapidly increasing costs of automobiles, gasoline, and automobile repairs, as well as the possible savings in time, have encouraged many firms to employ more sophisticated technologies to find the best travel routes.

Techniques used to schedule and route salespeople have received considerable attention from management scientists; the issue has become known as the *traveling salesperson problem*. The dilemma is usually stated as a search for a route through the territory that allows a salesperson to visit each customer and return to the starting point with a minimum expenditure of either time or money. A variety of techniques have been employed to search for the best routes, including linear, integer, nonlinear, and heuristic programming, and branch-and-bound methods. Discussion of these complex procedures is beyond the scope of this book.[25]

A simple way to find a good sales call route, and one that is often just as effective in minimizing travel time and costs, is to plan a travel route based on four basic rules:

1. The route should be circular.
2. The route should never cross itself.
3. The same route should not be used to travel to and from a customer.
4. Customers in neighboring areas should be visited in sequence.

Circular routes are reasonable because salespeople usually start at a home base and then return to it at the end of the sales trip. Similarly, if sales routes cross, a salesperson knows that a shorter route was overlooked. Sometimes a salesperson will be forced to use the same route to travel to and from a customer because of local road conditions or scheduled appointments, but this should be avoided when possible.

Additional Considerations　　In reality, other factors often interfere with plans that appear to be ideal on paper. In geographic routing problems, circumstances such as availability of good roads, traffic flows at different times of the day, traffic lights, and congestion often lead to a different route than that originally planned. This does not mean that operations research approaches are not of value; they are an excellent starting point for your analysis.

One additional factor to consider is the work schedule of the account. The best approach is to travel when clients are not available, to avoid wasting valuable selling time. If customers are not available early in the morning, then this may be a good time to get in the most travel miles. As a result, you may make your first call on the customer farthest from your home, rather than making a circular route. Better routing usually comes with experience and greater familiarity with the territory.

Overall Time Management

Despite all the emphasis companies are putting on increasing selling time, 16 percent of a salesperson's time is spent on administrative tasks. This figure has not changed much during the 1990s. While it is important for salespeople to provide customer and competitor information to their company, a key aspect of managing time effectively is to recognize and control things that tend to waste time. Following is a list of what many salespeople consider being some of the most common time wasters:[26]

1. Telephone interruptions
2. Drop-in visitors
3. Lack of self-discipline
4. Crises
5. Meetings
6. Lack of objectives, priorities, and deadlines
7. Indecision and procrastination
8. Attempting too much at once
9. Leaving tasks unfinished
10. Unclear communication

Note that the top two time wasters are telephone interruptions and drop-in visitors. The rest of the time wasters, such as lack of discipline, lack of objectives, and procrastination, indicate poor self-management by the salesperson. How different is this list from the one you would make for yourself? One aspect of time management that is particularly important in sales is to know when the customer is available. This is the key selling time during the day and salespeople should strictly adhere to customer contacts during these times. This time must be protected, while other duties and issues are handled at other times of the day.

A key step frequently recommended for improved time management is preparing a list of personal and professional goals and then pursuing them one step at a time. Planning does not have to be elaborate to be useful. Simply writing down a list of things you want to do tomorrow is a good place to start. The next step is to rank the tasks on the basis of their importance. Then when you start the day, begin task 1 and stay with it until it is completed. Recheck your priorities and begin task 2. Continue with tasks as long as they remain most important.

Once people get into the habit of daily planning, the next step is to plan a week or more ahead. Many salespeople, for example, are required to prepare weekly call plans. The idea is to encourage salespeople to plan a series of calls for each day, to call ahead for appointments, and to make better use of their time. A useful device that helps with planning is a small diary for the pocket or purse. Carrying a diary allows you to keep track of appointments and to reschedule them as needed.

Stephen Covey, a well-known consultant in personal and professional development, advises people to analyze their time management using a framework like the one shown in Figure 5-6.[27] *Importance* refers to activities that are of importance to you in meeting your objectives. *Urgency,* on the other hand, is the time pressure we feel to perform certain activities. Notice that we may feel this pressure for both important and relatively unimportant activities. According to Covey, activities in the Emergencies and Recreation quad-

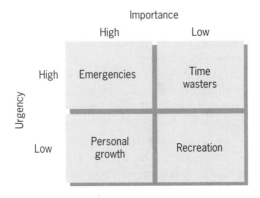

FIGURE 5-6 Time Management

rants will generally take care of themselves. People can gain control over their lives by spending less time on Time Wasters and more on Personal Growth activities. Time Wasters (high urgency but low importance) include phone calls, some meetings, and unnecessary administrative work—in other words, things that demand our immediate attention. Personal Growth activities (low urgency but high importance) are easily put off but are very important to our future growth and development. Activities in this category may include reading professional journals or books, enrolling in professional development or executive courses, learning how other functional areas operate, or prospecting for new customers. Notice that many people can indefinitely postpone these activities. Considering both urgency and importance may provide us with a useful perspective on how we can spend our time more productively.

SUMMARY

Over the past decade, sales force productivity has lagged behind the double-digit increase in selling costs. As a result, top executives are giving added emphasis to improving sales force productivity by increasing the amount of time salespeople spend face-to-face with customers. Salespeople are being armed with laptop computers, cellular phones, and the Internet to fight this battle.

1. **Describe effective steps for generating new accounts.** First, a prospect profile should be constructed which describes the best prospects for your company's offerings. The profile may be based on sophisticated database analysis of the purchasing patterns and profitability of your current customers. With an ideal prospect profile clearly in mind, a list of prospects should be developed using a variety of methods including direct mail, trade shows, directories, referrals, and cold canvassing. Finally, prospects need to be qualified based on their need for the seller's offerings and intention to buy in the near future, their authority to buy, and their ability to pay for the offering.

2. **Explain how to determine the minimum account opportunity a salesperson should pursue.** Two techniques for making this determination should be used. First the cost per sales call should be identified. This is calculated by identifying all direct selling costs for the period of time being evaluated and dividing this sum by the number of sales calls that are expected for the time period. The cost per call figure is then included in a break-even sales volume analysis, which consists of multiplying cost per call times the number of calls necessary to close the sale and dividing this product by the company's sales costs as a percent of sales target. This provides a base figure from which to determine whether a sales opportunity is of sufficient magnitude to warrant a face-to-face selling effort.

3. **List the available methods for setting account priorities.** The single factor model focuses on sales volume to classify account opportunities and allocate salespeople's time. Portfolio models expand the criteria for classifying account opportunities by considering both competitive position and account opportunity factors. Decisions models allocate effort according to a sales response function, which is based on the sales response to different numbers of sales calls during a period of time. The final models presented are sales process models, which allocate time to sales opportunities based on their stage in the selling process. The appropriate model will depend on the competitive and selling situation of the company.

4. **Tell how salespeople can spend more time selling.** A recent survey indicates that salespeople spend about 54 percent of their time selling either face-to-face or over the phone. Three avenues for increasing this percentage are incorporating technology into the selling and planning process, more efficient routing of sales calls within a territory, and reducing time wasters through personal time management techniques.

KEY TERMS

Account analysis
Account opportunity
Best few opportunity
Break-even sales volume
Cold canvassing
Competitive position
Cost per call
Decision models
Direct mail
Directories

Direct selling expenses
Minimum account size
Nonselling time
Portfolio models
Process models
Prospecting
Prospect profile
Qualified opportunities
Qualify a prospect
Referrals

Sales funnel
Sales response function
Sales routes
Selling cycles
Single-factor model
Time management
Trade shows
Traveling salesperson problem
Unqualified opportunity

DEVELOPING YOUR COMPETENCIES

1. **Self-Management.** One of the most important aspects of self-management is to develop a clear understanding of your personal and career goals. One highly successful method of arriving at a better understanding of your goals and of the steps that should be taken to achieve those goals is the time management analysis developed by Stephen Covey, which is discussed on pages 181-182 in this chapter. First, list your personal and professional goals in any order. Next list the actions that you will need to take to get yourself in position to achieve these goals. Third, draw the Time Management Matrix presented on page 181 labeling the axis as high versus low importance and high versus low urgency. List the activities on which you spent time over the past week or month. Now, compare these activities to the list that you developed for achieving your personal and professional goals. In which quadrant would these goal-directed activities fall? How could you adjust your time to put yourself in a good position to achieve your goals?

2. **Coaching.** You are spending the day with a new salesperson in your district who has been with your company, Consumer Research International (CRI), for less than a month. CRI is a marketing research company that competes with the likes of M/A/R/C Group, Market Facts, and Burke Marketing Research. Although CRI has a number of accounts with which it has worked for a number of years, each month between 20 and 30 callers will contact your company to investigate engaging it in a marketing research project. Each month, however, only about two or three of the calls warrant further attention. A new salesperson is having a problem determining in a reasonable amount of time, which of these callers is a real prospect and which is a waste of time. Time is precious, however, but you do not want your salespeople walking away from important growth opportunities. Because the salesperson is new on the job, you would like to give him a set of questions that he could ask to determine if this is a "hot" prospect or one that is "just looking." What would be your advice?

3. **Global Perspective.** Dendrite International is one of the world's leading suppliers of sales force automation software in the pharmaceutical industry. Pharmaceutical firms worldwide are arming their salespeople with laptop computers and looking for software to design call plans and collect call reports to increase sales force efficiency and effectiveness. More than 15,000 salespeople in 40 companies in 11 countries use Dendrite systems. One of the issues Dendrite faces is that software demands differ greatly from country to country. How would software requirements differ in each of the following countries? For more information on Dendrite, see *www.drte.com*.

- U.S. pharmaceutical sales forces are among the largest in the world, ranging from 500 to more than 3,000 reps per firm. Sales reps called on medical personnel every four to six weeks to leave product samples and literature, perform service tasks, and to build relationships with prescribing physicians.
- In western Europe, sales forces are generally 100 to 200 reps in size. Government funding of health care and large, managed-care organizations are common. In England, a rep sees a doctor once a year, always by appointment, and can only leave one sample.
- In Japan, sales forces are like those in the United States and, with fewer doctors, there is one pharmaceutical salesperson for every six physicians. Unlike in the United States, where physicians cannot sell drugs, Japanese physicians combine prescribing and dispensing of drugs. Sales reps negotiate prices with individual physicians, who also derive income from selling free drug samples to their patients. Most Japanese doctors work in clinics or hospitals that require sales reps to wait outside to see the doctor. As a result, "social selling" is very important in Japan. Reps develop face time with doctors by washing their cars, entertaining them, and running all sorts of errands.

4. **Technology.** Wisdom Ware Inc., a small software firm, has developed a slick tool that helps salespeople to be better informed and more efficient. It requires salespeople and their bosses to do things just a little differently. The issue Wisdom Ware attempts to address is keeping the sales force informed about products, the market, and the competition. Even more important, the software is designed to enable every piece of information to link with any other piece. That way, salespeople can assemble just the right combination of facts necessary for the immediate task without being inundated with information. In short, this software is the interactive equivalent of Cliff Notes. While planning a call, a sales rep makes a few menu choices to identify the customer, the product, and such. One click creates the most up-to-date qualifying questions, another reveals how the competition stacks up, another reports the most common objections, still another suggests an "elevator speech" for precisely those circumstances. Though only a few concise sentences pop on the screen, detailed reports are just a click away. Unfortunately, Wisdom Ware has been less than wildly successful so far. The problem isn't training, which takes less than an hour. Nor is it compatibility; Wisdom Ware works seamlessly with other front-office software. Neither has any customer winced at the price of $500 and up per user. What do you think could be the problem? For more on Wisdom Ware, see *www.sellmorenow.com.*

5. **Strategic Action.** IBM has proved it can market successfully to fellow corporate giants like General Motors and Citibank. But will the company be successful in selling to the millions of enterprises with 1,000 or fewer employees who make up the world's fastest-growing segment? It had better be because for IBM entrepreneurial companies are the future in information technology. In the United States, small businesses are responsible for 50 percent of the gross national product. That segment is growing at 11 percent annually, three percentage points higher than the growth of large companies. What's more, IBM estimates that last year 75 million small and medium-size companies worldwide spent $305 billion in information technology.

But IBM faces an enormous challenge simply trying to prove to smaller customers that it really cares about them. "My small customers don't feel comfortable with IBM," says Gunther Obhlschlager of TransCat, an IBM reseller in Karlsruhe, Germany. "Unless you spend millions of dollars with the company, you can't get someone on the phone," he says. Richard Laermer, a New York entrepreneur, adds, "I don't believe they're really going after small businesses." He adds, "Their attitude is, 'If you don't have a thousand employees, get out of my face'". Should IBM go after the whole market—large, medium, and small firms? Can they? If so, how?

6. **Team Building.** One of the most important jobs of the first line sales manager is to create an atmosphere in which individual salespeople feel that they are part of a team, and are also responsible for carrying their own weight. Perhaps one of the most controversial aspects of this balancing act is the degree to which the sales manager should get involved in territory and account planning.

The attitudes and advice of sales managers run the gambit from close supervision to a totally hands-off attitude. At Ziegler Tools, an Atlanta industrial distributor, for example, salespeople are required to fill out weekly detailed itineraries and call reports, which are compared with quarterly itineraries. Turner Warmack, vice president of sales and marketing at Ziegler Tools, states, "Generally speaking, salespeople are poor managers and can be thrown off course pretty easily. What we feel our system does is help them focus their efforts." At the other end of the spectrum are sales managers who do not require their salespeople to submit call reports and detailed reviews of customer status. Typical of this approach is Rick Horn, president of Stahl Company, a specialty truck body manufacturer, who states: "I didn't feel I had to tell them what to do. They were big boys and knew their territory. All I wanted to know is where they were in case I had to reach them." Which approach do you feel is best? Does it depend on the circumstances? If so, what circumstances should be considered?

PROBLEMS*

1. You are a rookie salesperson with Associated Medical Supplies, Inc., a wholesaler of disposable medical supplies. As a new salesperson, you are finding it difficult to convince accounts to switch from their current suppliers. The doctors with whom you are having the most success tend to be small, single practices located in rural areas. Competition for these accounts is not as intense, perhaps because their purchases are fairly small. They usually place about $900 worth of business with you every month. Nevertheless, they seem to be most appreciative of your weekly visit to take inventory of their supplies and write an order. Furthermore, it is better than no sales at all. Lately your boss has been hassling you because productivity has not increased as much as he had hoped when he placed you in the territory. In particular, direct selling costs, including compensation, are currently 15 percent of net sales, whereas the total company's target is for direct sales costs to be 10 percent of net sales. In light of this, you are wondering if spending time on small rural physicians is the best way to manage your territory. You have calculated that your cost per call is currently $34.50. Should you be calling on these small physician practices? What is the smallest size customer you should pursue in order to meet your company's selling cost objectives? What actions might you consider in managing your territory better?

2. As a salesperson for Strength Footwear, Inc., you have been very successful. Your commissions are well over $70,000 per year. Demand for your product line is strong, but so is the demand on your time. You work your territory 220 days a year and can make four calls a day. The maximum number of times you need to see any account is every other week, but you need to call on each account at least once a quarter. To help you allocate your time according to sales results, you have gathered the following information on customer sales:

Excel spreadsheets for working on these problems are available at www.wiley.com/college/dalrymple. Go to "Student Resources."

Accounts	Sales Last Year
Top 10 accounts	$150,000
Next 10 best accounts	37,500
Next 10 best accounts	37,000
Next 20 best accounts	56,250
Next 20 best accounts	55,500
Next 20 best accounts	18,750
Last 20 accounts	15,000
	$370,000

Develop and justify a call schedule for allocating time across the 110 customers in your territory.

3. You have just finished your annual account review of the telecom purchases of one of your largest customers. They had purchased $125,000 worth of telecom equipment from you last year, but are indicating that they want a 10 percent discount on next year's purchases or they will switch their business to one of your competitors. Technical, installation, and other account services that were provided to this customer last year totaled $11,000 and are expected to be about the same next year. You earn a commission of 10 percent on sales. Last year this account's gross margin was 40 percent, and they are expected to purchase a similar quantity of equipment next year. Assuming that the list price for the equipment would be the same as last year, but discounted by 10 percent, how would the discount affect the profit contributions this account is estimated to generate next year?

4. Continuing with the account analysis from problem 3, assume that the account purchases some of its telecom equipment from one of your competitors. How much would you need to increase your penetration of this account through increased sales in order to justify the 10 percent discount the account wants on next year's purchases?

5. Let's consider only the 40 accounts called on a regular basis last year (accounts called on when appointments are canceled or to fill in a schedule are omitted from the table); 600 calls are scheduled yearly. The top 40 accounts are scheduled for 450 calls, but due to appointments being canceled, 402 calls were made on top 40 accounts. Sixty calls are scheduled for prospects for which no sales have been made, and the remaining calls to smaller accounts.

   Average cost per call = $109 and 3 calls are made in an average day. Sales costs as a percentage of total sales are 6.3 percent. It took an average of 2.3 calls to close a sale across all three products. Your company sells three products P1, P2, and P3. P1 has a unit selling price of $25, P2 has a unit selling price of $50, and P3 has a unit selling price of $100. Unit contributions (excluding direct selling costs) are: $17 for P1, $29 for P2, and $53 for P3. How would you allocate your sales calls to the top 40 accounts given the information on page 187 about last year's revenues and sales calls per account?

Account	Sales Revenue			Units Sold			Calls Last Year
	Product 1	Product 2	Product 3	P1	P2	P3	
1	$0.00	$0.00	$5,000.00	0	0	50	9
2	$475.00	$1,700.00	$0.00	19	34	0	8
3	$0.00	$7,950.00	$0.00	0	159	0	12
4	$4,325.00	$0.00	$0.00	173	0	0	6
5	$0.00	$0.00	$8,900.00	0	0	89	13
6	$1,275.00	$0.00	$0.00	51	0	0	6
7	$2,750.00	$550.00	$0.00	110	11	0	8
8	$7,275.00	$0.00	$0.00	291	0	0	9
9	$0.00	$0.00	$2,500.00	0	0	25	9
10	$0.00	$0.00	$3,900.00	0	0	39	11
11	$5,275.00	$0.00	$0.00	211	0	0	7
12	$0.00	$1,950.00	$1,000.00	0	39	10	7
13	$5,825.00	$0.00	$0.00	233	0	0	9
14	$0.00	$0.00	$9,700.00	0	0	97	14
15	$3,325.00	$1,150.00	$0.00	133	23	0	8
16	$0.00	$3,750.00	$0.00	0	75	0	10
17	$6,875.00	$0.00	$0.00	275	0	0	7
18	$0.00	$4,900.00	$0.00	0	98	0	12
19	$1,250.00	$3,650.00	$0.00	50	73	0	11
20	$3,500.00	$0.00	$0.00	140	0	0	6
21	$0.00	$2,850.00	$0.00	0	57	0	13
22	$0.00	$0.00	$13,100.00	0	0	131	17
23	$1,275.00	$1,050.00	$0.00	51	21	0	6
24	$1,925.00	$500.00	$0.00	77	10	0	6
25(a)	$625.00	$250.00	$0.00	25	5	0	12
26(a)	$3,425.00	$0.00	$0.00	137	0	0	9
27(a)	$0.00	$0.00	$3,100.00	0	0	31	14
28(a)	$4,025.00	$0.00	$0.00	161	0	0	9
29(a)	$6,650.00	$0.00	$0.00	266	0	0	7
30(b)	$0.00	$500.00	$0.00	0	10	0	12
31(b)	$1,250.00	$0.00	$0.00	50	0	0	9
32(b)	$0.00	$450.00	$0.00	0	9	0	9
33(b)	$0.00	$0.00	$600.00	0	0	6	4
34(b)	$0.00	$0.00	$100.00	0	0	1	3
35#	$0.00	$0.00	$3,900.00	0	0	39	12
36#	$775.00	$350.00	$0.00	31	7	0	12
37#	$2,500.00	$0.00	$0.00	100	0	0	12
38*	$9,500.00	$0.00	$0.00	380	0	0	18
39*	$1,775.00	$0.00	$0.00	71	0	0	18
40*	$575.00	$0.00	$0.00	23	0	0	18
Totals	$76,450.00	$31,550.00	$51,800.00	3058	631	518	402

a = new accounts.

b = prospects just converted into accounts.

= accounts in a fringe area A. Requires a 1/2 day of travel to reach. Thus, one day is spent traveling for day selling.

* = accounts in a fringe area B. Requires a day of travel to reach. Thus, two days are spent traveling for one day selling.

IN-CLASS EXERCISES

5-1: Selling to Direct Competitors*

Andrew Newman has just accepted an offer he couldn't refuse. However, in the process he may have lost his biggest customer. Newman, sales manager of Rapid Logistics Company, took on the distribution business for Smith's Clothiers, a manufacturer of such specialty clothes as petites and big and tall men. The main reason Smith's chose Rapid Logistics was to gain the same improvements in just-in-time delivery, logistics, and warehousing, which are the areas that caused its main competitor, Stylers, to grow revenue and profits significantly over the past five years.

The company that improved Stylers' distribution is Rapid Logistics. In fact, Stylers is Rapid Logistics' largest customer, accounting for more than 30 percent of Rapid Logistics' revenues. When Stylers' president, Chris Turner, heard that Rapid Logistics had taken Smith's as a customer, he called Newman to set up a meeting, suggesting that he planned to find a new logistics vendor. He also told Newman he was shocked that Rapid Logistics would service its best customer's main competitor—and, that he was offended at having heard it through the grapevine. How should Newman handle the meeting?

Questions:

1. What are the main issues in this case?
2. If you were Newman, sales manager of Rapid Logistics Company, what would you do about the fact that Stylers is your largest customer and their president is upset with you?
3. What would you say to Turner about your actions?
4. Are there any ethical issues involved?

5-2: Lead Generation*

Standard Industries had its usual 40 × 40 booth at the annual industry trade show, but through a new marketing strategy used this year, qualified leads increased more than 60 percent. Standard's vice president of sales, Beth Mainard, was thrilled with the results. Back at headquarters after the show, Mainard and her assistant divided the 1,500 leads based on the reps' territories. Each of the 65 reps received 23 leads, all of whom had expressed interest in at least receiving information or a phone call from a Standard rep. Some leads were people ready to buy but who preferred to meet after the show.

A month later, at Standard's quarterly sales meeting, Mainard asked for a progress report on the status of the trade show leads. Only five of the reps had followed up on any of the leads. Of those five, there were 12 sales made and a few proposals in development. Mainard was now concerned. After all the hard work that went into generating these leads, she didn't want them to gather dust on her reps' desks. Moreover, she didn't want to lose easy sales from prospects who were ready to buy. She voiced her concern to the reps and said she would be creating a standard plan the reps would have to use when following up on the leads.

Questions:

1. Should Mainard have taken another approach as opposed to saying that she would initiate a plan?
2. If you were the sales manager, what would you do about the reps' obvious lack of motivation to follow up on the leads generated at the trade show?

---

*Contributed by Eli Jones, University of Houston.

3. What are the possible reactions from the leads not contacted by Standard?

4. What is an "ideal" course of action given all of the issues involved?

5. Write a brief step-by-step plan to handle this situation.

CASE 5-1 HANOVER-BATES CHEMICAL CORPORATION

James Sprague, newly appointed northeast district sales manager for Hanover-Bates Chemical Corporation, leaned back in his chair as the door to his office slammed shut. "Great beginning," he thought. "Three days in my new job and the district's most experienced sales representative is threatening to quit."

On the previous night, James Sprague, Hank Carver (the district's most experienced sales representative), and John Follett, another senior member of the district sales staff, had met for dinner at Jim's suggestion. During dinner, Jim had mentioned that one of his top priorities would be to conduct a sales and profit analysis of the district's business in order to identify opportunities to improve the district's performance. Jim had stated that he was confident that the analysis would indicate opportunities to reallocate district sales efforts in a manner that would increase profits. As Jim had indicated during the conversation, "My experience in analyzing district sales performance data for the national sales manager has convinced me that any district's allocation of sales effort to products and customer categories can be improved." Both Carver and Follett had nodded as Jim discussed his plans.

Hank Carver was waiting when Jim arrived at the district sales office the next morning. It soon became apparent that Carver was very upset by what he perceived as Jim's criticism of how he and the other district sales representatives were doing their jobs—and more particularly, how they were allocating their time in terms of customers and products. As he concluded his heated comments, Carver had said:

> This company has made it damed clear that 34 years of experience don't count for anything … and now some-

one with not much more than two years of selling experience and two years of pushing paper for the national sales manager at corporate headquarters tells me I'm not doing my job… Maybe it's time for me to look for a new job… and since Trumbull Chemical (Hanover-Bates's major competitor) is hiring, maybe that's where I should start looking … and I'm not the only one who feels this way.

As Jim reflected on the scene that had just occurred, he wondered what he should do. It had been made clear to him when he had been promoted to manager of the northeast sales district that one of his top priorities should be improvement of the district's performance. As the national sales manager had said, "The northeast sales district may rank third in dollar sales but it's our worst district in terms of profit performance."

Prior to assuming his new position, Jim had assembled the data presented in Exhibits 1 through 7 to assist him in his work. The data had been compiled from records maintained in the national sales manager's office. Although he believed that the data would provide a sound basis for a preliminary analysis of district performance. Jim had recognized that additional data would probably have to be collected when he arrived in the northeast district (District 3). To provide himself with a frame of reference, Jim had also requested data on the north-central sales district (District 7). This district was generally considered to be one of the best, if not the best, in the company. Furthermore, the north-central district sales manager, who was only three years older than Jim, was highly regarded by the national sales manager.

This case was prepared by Professor Robert W. Witt of The University of Texas, Austin. Reproduced by permission.

EXHIBIT 1   Summary Income Statements (thousands), 1995 to 1999

	1995	1996	1997	1998	1999
Sales	$39,780	$43,420	$38,120	$43,960	$47,780
Production expenses	23,868	26,994	24,396	27,224	29,126
Gross profit	15,912	16,426	13,724	16,736	18,654
Administrative expenses	5,212	5,774	5,584	5,850	6,212
Selling expenses	4,048	4,482	4,268	4,548	4,798
Pretax profit	6,652	6,170	3,872	6,338	7,644
Taxes	3,024	2,776	1,580	2,852	3,436
Net profit	$ 3,628	$ 3,394	$ 2,292	$ 3,486	$ 4,208

EXHIBIT 2   District Sales and Gross Profit Quota Performance (thousands), 1999

District	Number of Sales Reps	Sales Quota	Sales Actual	Gross Profit Quota[a]	Gross Profit Actual
1	7	$7,661	$7,812	$3,104	$3,178
2	6	7,500	7,480	3,000	3,058
3	6	7,300	6,812	2,920	2,478
4	6	6,740	6,636	2,696	2,590
5	5	6,600	6,420	2,620	2,372
6	5	6,240	6,410	2,504	2,358
7	5	5,440	6,210	2,176	2,260
		$47,600	$47,780	$19,040	$18,654

[a] District gross profit quotas were developed by the National Sales Manager in consultation with the district managers and took into account price competition in the respective districts.

EXHIBIT 3   District Selling Expenses, 1999

District	Sales Rep Salaries[a]	Sales Rep Commissions	Sales Rep Expenses	District Office	District Manager's Salary	District Manager's Expenses	Sales Support	Total Selling Expenses
1	$354,200	$38,852	$112,560	$42,300	$67,000	$22,920	$139,000	$776,832
2	286,440	37,400	101,520	42,624	68,000	24,068	142,640	702,692
3	314,760	34,060	108,872	44,246	70,000[b]	24,764	140,000	736,722
4	300,960	33,180	98,208	44,008	65,000	22,010	132,940	696,306
5	251,900	32,100	85,440	42,230	66,000	22,246	153,200	653,116
6	249,700	32,530	83,040	41,984	67,000	22,856	134,200	631,310
7	229,700	35,060	89,400	44,970	63,000	23,286	117,500	602,916
								$4,797,830

[a] Includes cost of fringe benefit program, which was 10 percent of base salary.
[b] Salary of Jim Sprague's predecessor.

EXHIBIT 4   District Contribution to Corporate Administrative Expense and Profit, 1999

District	Sales (thousands)	Gross Profit (thousands)	Selling Expenses	Contribution
1	$ 7,812	3,178	$ 776,832	$2,401,168
2	7,480	3,058	702,692	2,355,308
3	6,812	2,478	737,058	1,740,942
4	6,636	2,590	696,306	1,893,694
5	6,420	2,372	653,116	1,718,884
6	6,410	2,358	630,752	1,727,248
7	6,210	2,620	600,516	2,019,484
	$47,780	$18,654	4,797,272	$13,856,648

EXHIBIT 5 **District Sales and Gross Profit Performance by Account Category, 1999**

District	Sales by Account Category (thousands)			
	(A)	(B)	(C)	Total
Northeast	$1,830	$3,362	$1,620	$6,812
North-Central	1,502	3,404	1,304	6,210

District	Gross Profit by Account Category (thousands)			
	(A)	(B)	(C)	Total
Northeast	$712	$1,246	$520	$2,478
North-Central	660	1,450	510	2,620

EXHIBIT 6 **Potential Accounts, Active Accounts, and Account Call Coverage, 1999**

District	Potential Accounts			Active Accounts			Account Coverage (total calls)		
	(A)	(B)	(C)	(A)	(B)	(C)	(A)	(B)	(C)
Northeast	90	381	635	53	210	313	1297	3051	2118
North-Central	60	286	499	42	182	216	1030	2618	1299

EXHIBIT 7 **Product-Line Data**

Product	Container	List Price	Gross Margin	Sales (000)
SPX	400 lb drum	$160	$56	$7,128
ZBX	50 lb drum	152	68	8,244
CBX	50 lb drum	152	68	7,576
NBX	50 lb drum	160	70	9,060
CHX	100 lb drum	440	180	8,820
BUX	400 lb drum	240	88	6,952

THE COMPANY AND INDUSTRY

The Hanover-Bates Chemical Corporation was a leading producer of processing chemicals for the chemical plating industry. The company's production process was, in essence, a mixing operation. Chemicals purchased from a broad range of suppliers were mixed according to a variety of user-based formulas. Company sales in 1999 had reached a new high of $47,780,000, up from $43,780,000 in 1998. Net pretax profit in 1999 had been $7,644,000, up from $6,338,000 in 1998. Hanover-Bates had a strong balance sheet and the company enjoyed a favorable price-earnings ratio on its stock, which was traded on the over-the-counter market.

Although Hanover-Bates did not produce commodity-type chemicals (e.g., sulfuric acid and others),

industry customers tended to perceive minimal quality differences among the products produced by Hanover-Bates and its competitors. Given the lack of a variation in product quality and the industrywide practice of limited advertising expenditures, field sales efforts were of major importance in the marketing programs of all firms in the industry.

Hanover-Bates's market consisted of several thousand job-shop and captive (i.e., in-house) plating operations. Chemical platers process a wide variety of materials including industrial fasteners (e.g., screws, rivets, bolts, washers), industrial components (e.g., clamps, casings, couplings), and miscellaneous items (e.g., umbrella frames, eyelets, decorative items). The chemical plating process involves the electrolytic application of metallic coatings such as zinc, cadmium, nickel, and brass.

Regardless of the degree of plating precision involved, quality control is of critical concern to all chemical platers. Extensive variation in the condition of materials received for plating requires a high level of service from the firms supplying chemicals to platers. This service is normally provided by the sales representatives of the firm(s) which supply the plater with processing chemicals.

Hanover-Bates and the majority of the firms in its industry produced the same line of basic processing chemicals for the chemical plating industry. The line consisted of a trisodium phosphate cleaner (SPX), anesic aldehyde brightening agents for zinc plating (ZBX), cadmium plating (CBX), and nickel plating (NBX), a protective postplating chromate dip (CHX), and a protective burnishing compound (BUX). The company's product line is detailed in Exhibit 7.

COMPANY SALES ORGANIZATION

The sales organization consisted of 40 sales representatives operating in seven sales districts. Sales representatives' salaries ranged from $28,000 to $48,000 with fringe-benefit costs amounting to an additional 10 percent of salary. In addition to their salaries, Hanover-Bates's representatives received commissions of 0.5 percent of their dollar sales volume on all sales up to their sales quotas. The commission on sales in excess of quota was 1 percent.

In 1997, the national sales manager of Hanover-Bates had developed a sales program based on selling the full line of Hanover-Bates products. Anticipated benefits included the following: (1) sales volume per account would be greater and selling costs as a percentage of sales would decrease; (2) a Hanover-Bates sales representative could justify spending more time with such an account, thus becoming more knowledgeable about the account's business and better able to provide technical assistance and identify selling opportunities; (3) full-line sales would strengthen Hanover-Bates's competitive position by reducing the likelihood of account loss to other plating chemical suppliers (a problem that existed in multiple-supplier situations).

The national sales manager's 1997 sales program had also included the following account call frequency guidelines: A accounts (major accounts generating $24,000 or more in yearly sales)—two calls per month; B accounts (medium-size accounts generating $12,000 to $23,999 in yearly sales)—one call per month; C accounts (small accounts generating less than $12,000 yearly in sales)—one call every two months. The account call frequency guidelines were developed by the national sales manager after discussions with the district managers. The national sales manager had been concerned about the optimum allocation of sales efforts to accounts and felt that the guidelines would increase the efficiency of the company's sales force, although not all of the district sales managers agreed with this conclusion.

It was common knowledge in Hanover-Bates' corporate sales office that Jim Sprague's predecessor as northeast district sales manager had not been one of the company's better district sales managers. His attitude toward the sales plans and programs of the national sales manager had been one of reluctant compliance rather than acceptance and support. When the national sales manager succeeded in persuading Jim Sprague's predecessor to take early retirement, he had been faced with the lack of an available qualified replacement.

Hank Carver, who most of the sales representatives had assumed would get the district manager's job, had been passed over in part because he would be 65 in three years. The national sales manager had not wanted to face the same replacement problem again in three years and had wanted someone in the position who would be more likely to be responsive to the company's sales plans and policies. The appointment of Jim Sprague as district manager had caused considerable talk, not only in the district but also at corporate headquarters. In fact, the national sales manager had warned Jim that "a lot of people are expecting you to fall on your face. They don't think you have the experience to handle the job, in particular, and to manage and motivate a group of sales representatives most of whom are considerably older and more experienced than you." The national sales manager had concluded by saying, "I think you can handle the job, Jim. I think you can manage those sales reps and improve the district's profit performance, and I'm depending on you to do both."

CASE 5-2 PRACTICAL PARTIES

George Thompson is employed by the Howard Hills Holding Company, a conglomerate with its headquarters in the UK, but operating worldwide. He has a reputation as a trouble shooter, and has been given a number of assignments in the group where Thompson has successfully carried out turn-round operations on subsidiary companies. Some of these have been acquisitions purchased very cheaply as the companies have been in a state of near insolvency.

Arnold Newby, the group's managing director has invited you to his office to discuss a new assignment. "You are aware of our takeover of Practical Parties about two years ago. We are very unhappy with its performance and would like you to sort it out." This strikes Thompson as surprising, as he knew that the subsidiary concerned is profitable, but Newby goes on to explain further. "We paid a good price for Practical Parties on the basis of its prospects for growth, but to be frank, the growth has not happened. To make matters worse, the executive we put in charge has left suddenly after a major disagreement with us. We thought we had made a major coup in being able to recruit him

from another party plan company. All he seems to have done is upset some of our consultants by changing procedures to those of his previous company, and now he says that the growth we looked for is not possible. I would like you to take over from him, produce a plan for growth, and get it started before moving on to a new challenge. It will not be easy, but I know you won't let us down."

Newby explains that if a case can be made for it the group can make investment funds available. He does not expect you to agree to the assignment immediately, but would like your thoughts on how or whether sales and profits growth could be established in the next three years. This is expected in the form of an interim report to be delivered and discussed in only a week's time. To help, Thompson is given a folder prepared by Jane Fraser, a recent Business School Graduate who has worked for Practical Parties for the last year. The folder contains comments and material written by Jane, in addition to photocopies of material she thinks might be useful. On the basis of this material, which follows, Thompson is expected to complete his report.

EXHIBIT 1 Comments from Jane Fraser

1. Background

Practical Parties is a successful and profitable company. Its founder worked for another party plan company bringing with him some of the best staff. Unfortunately, sales have been nearly static for the last three years. In fact, after allowing for inflation, sales have declined somewhat.

Party Plan is a method of selling where a hostess (almost all party plan activities are female oriented) invites friends to her house, light refreshments are provided, and there is the opportunity to buy goods. In the case of Practical Parties, orders are taken and the goods delivered and billed later. This avoids problems of hostesses getting involved with the collection of money and storing goods. The hostess is rewarded with a relatively modest cash payment and a gift from the Practical Parties product range, which can broadly be described as giftware, but has a strong bias to glass and china goods. The hostesses are recruited by Practical Parties consultants, who are paid on commission, and classed as self employed.

Hostesses are seen as key factors in the success of the company's operations. If a hostess has a wide network of friends and acquaintances then a suitable mix of guests can be found which enables the party to be an enjoyable social and buying occasion. Prior to the arrival of the previous executive of Practical Parties, hostesses received incentives not only on sales made, but also on the number of guests attending and the number of further parties arranged. A dynamic and expanding network of hostesses, with parties held at regular and appropriate intervals, is the cornerstone of a consultant's success.

In all there are 2500 consultants, of whom about one in twenty are supervisors responsible for a group of consultants under them. These supervisors receive commission on the sales of the consultants under them. They are expected to recruit consultants, and they conduct usually fewer parties themselves than the average for the people under them. *(continued)*

This case was prepared by Mark Adams, Mike Easey, and Harry Robinson of the University of Northumbria at Newcastle England. Copyright © 1991 by the University of Northumbria at Newcastle. Reproduced by permission.

EXHIBIT 1   (Continued)

The consultants' role is to demonstrate the product, actively sell gift items, collect orders, and make deliveries. A minimum requirement is that at least one guest at the party agrees to host another party. The consultant is also responsible for recruiting all the hostesses and briefing them on such matters as invitations, refreshments, and the creation of a friendly atmosphere.

The quality of consultants varies considerably. Some consultants produce their own special invitation cards and follow-up brochures to encourage repeat orders independent of the parties. A number of consultants are also agents for other party plan companies and it is suspected that products for these other companies may be sold at functions organized in the name of Practical Parties. Training of consultants is the responsibility of the senior consultants who have themselves often been selected primarily for their sales performance. Training is not standardized, aside from the sales conferences.

Turnover of consultants has recently increased. Some of those with the most successful records have moved to recently started party plan companies undergoing rapid growth. Methods of recruiting more consultants are being considered. With more consultants, there will be more hostesses having more parties, thus giving more sales. Direct payments to consultants to recruit more consultants has been rejected for the time being, as that might be construed as pyramid selling (a form of selling that involves payment for recruiting people who would have to pay fees to join or for stock). This was considered illegal and unethical. Practical Parties was a member of the Direct Selling Association, and adhered to a code of practice which would make sure that it remained a respectable company which did not become involved in dubious practices.

In addition to commission, the company tried to motivate consultants through lavish sales conferences, competitions, and merit awards.

A full-time buyer scours the world for interesting giftware. If we are in the giftware business, perhaps we could consider opening a chain of gift shops using our economies of scale and sourcing knowledge as a distinctive competence. This could perhaps be turned into a franchising operation. On the orders of the recently departed managing director, slightly poorer quality products were being sold in order to at least increase margins if volume could not be increased. This had partly backfired, as it had led to experienced consultants moving on. In the past they had always been able to claim that the company sold reasonable products.

Administration is efficient, with deliveries being accurate and on time. This is made possible with a highly advanced computer operation. The computer manager boasted that the company had records of all the parties indicating who purchases what product, when the product was purchased, and where the purchaser lived. Not much use has been made of this data, but preliminary analysis reveals disappointment with performance in the South-East of England, where it was considered the most purchasing power lay.

Very little advertising is used, as it is deemed inappropriate for this type of operation.

2. The Market

It is very difficult to define the market for Practical Parties. If the market means any product that might be given as a gift, then it means almost any product. However, most of the products are in the china and glass category, and a fair amount of secondary data exist for that.

During the 1990's retail sales of tableware and kitchenware were valued at approximately £400m, and glassware at around £220m, giving a total of £620m. Both sectors have grown in real terms with tableware growing faster than glassware.

Growth has been attributed to increasing interest in the house, and home entertaining, as well as increases in income. The market was affected by cheap imports in the late 1980s, but made a recovery. Since 1990 there have been signs of a downturn due to lower rates of new house formation because of demographic factors, and a reduction in disposable income resulting from higher interest rates for mortgages. As a company we are not sure what the effects will be of the increasing trend to single person and single parent households.

China and porcelain are losing market share to stoneware and earthenware which are cheaper. The glassware market is divided into two categories, hand gathered glass and machine gathered glass.

Hand gathered glass can be either hand made crystal, with a high lead oxide content, or less elaborately cut glass with a lower lead content. Much of the better quality glassware is bought by tourists, especially Americans, and is therefore affected by fluctuations in the number of visitors caused by such things as the variations in exchange rates. Machine made glass is produced for the mass market and everyday use. It is hit at the cheaper end from time to time by petrol retailers using free glassware as promotions. Practical parties tends to sell either lower quality hand made products, or glassware at the higher end of the machine made market.

3. The Competition

If the competition is thought to be organizations selling similar goods, then department stores and gift shops would be considered the main competition. If the "product" is more of the party as a social occasion, then the competition would be other party plan operations, or perhaps other organizations engaged in direct selling.

Direct selling could include such things as direct mail selling and selling insurance door to door. For this reason, statistics from different sources never seem to tally on the total market for goods sold direct.   *(continued)*

EXHIBIT 1 **(Continued)**

Overall the direct selling sector is characterized by being very fragmented, with several hundred individual enterprises. The majority of these are very small, and the sector is dominated by a relatively small number of larger organizations. Most of the organizations which sell consumer goods direct, involving personal contact, use party plans. One notable exception is Avon Cosmetics, possibly the largest in personal selling terms, which uses individual to individual contact rather than the groups involved in parties.

The UK market for direct selling of consumer goods involving face to face contact was worth approximately £600m in 1990. The 1980s were characterized by slow growth rates, much of which came from new, smaller companies. Indeed, it appears that all the companies eventually become victims of the product life cycles of the goods they sell, with the company growth slowing as the product category growth slows. An alternative hypothesis is that as well as the advantage of the social occasion, parties need novelty to interest those attending, and once the novelty of a new organization wears off, then the attractiveness of the party also declines.

Brief profiles of some of the chief competitors in various forms of direct selling follows:

EXHIBIT 2   **Profiles of the Major Competitors**

Avon
Avon cosmetics is still the largest direct selling company in the UK. The company is a subsidiary of Avon Products Inc., the US conglomerate of New York. It is primarily involved in selling cosmetics and toiletries, and holds significant market share in many product sectors. Avon mainly sells by means of a small catalogue which is regularly changed and updated, although the customer can still sample the products if they wish. The catalog also features other products such as jewelry items and personal goods.

Rosgill
The Rosgill Group comprises a number of wholly owned subsidiaries which are listed below. It is the largest party plan company in the UK, with a current turnover somewhere in the region of £45m. The company has been quoted as holding 42,000 parties each year, by some 6000 demonstrators. Significantly they appear to be the only party plan company to encourage children to attend their parties, which may well be used as an added pressure to buy.

Rosgill Holdings (Pippa Dee Parties, Dee Minor Limited)   Merchandises clothing by direct sales
Pippa Dee International   Jewelry by direct sales
Wanderkurst   Clothing manufacture
Melrose Marketing   Consumer goods by direct sales
Matchmaker Parties Ltd.   Housewares by direct sales

Tupperware
Tupperware effectively established the party plan selling method in the UK, however recent years have shown a loss of presence and turnover has fallen slightly. This probably is because plastic housewares are now much more widely available through retail outlets and have lost some of the individual appeal they once had. In response to this, the company has widened its product range to merchandise plastic toys and general household goods.

The company started in the UK in 1960, although it originated in the USA in the 1950s. Internationally in 1996 Tupperware claimed a sales force of 800,000, worldwide net sales of US $1.4 billion, and 97 million attendances at parties worldwide.

The mode of operation remains predominantly Party Plan although it is now far less rigid and "kitchen consultants" are being used for house demonstrations. This is mainly a response to more women working and, as such, attempts have been made to sell the products at places of work. The Tupperware image which launched their initial success is now possibly proving more of a hindrance than a help, for although the company has a huge range of products, it is still strongly identified with its base products.

Amway
The company is a wholly owned subsidiary of the Amway Corporation and is most strongly identified with the sponsorship and multi-level approach to party plan. The Amway Corporation had worldwide sales of US $6.3 billion in 1995, which marked 11 years of consecutive growth for the organization.

They offer a wide range of merchandise, including household cleaning products, cosmetics, skincare, dietary aids, and jewelry.

EXHIBIT 3   **Practical Parties Consultants**

Average number of parties per week per consultant

0–1	1	2	3	4	5	6+
45%	26%	16%	9%	2%	1%	1%

Interpretation: The table should be read as percentage of consultants arranging a given number of parties, e.g. 45% of consultants arrange on average less than one party a week.

Performance of consultants by length of service

Length of Service	% of Consultants	% of Sales
0–12 weeks	4	1
13–18 weeks	8	6
19–24 weeks	12	7
25–30 weeks	12	10
31–52 weeks	15	16
1–2 years	18	25
2–3 years	16	20
3+ years	13	15

Twenty-five percent of consultants leave each year.

EXHIBIT 4   **Results of Survey of 948 Respondents on Party Plan Attendance**

Consumer reaction to Party Plans is difficult to express with any degree of accuracy, given the wide variability in quality of product offerings. Some secondary research, although dated, did indicate that roughly 80% of consumers thought the products were expensive at Party Plan schemes, but over 60% thought they were good value for money. Approximately 90% did feel under some pressure to buy something. The extent to which these findings apply to Practical Parties is unknown.

Percentage Yes response from the survey question "Have you ever been to a party or consultant where goods are sold?"

Base: 948 responses   % Yes response overall = 75%

Age Groups	%	Social Class %		% UK Adults
15–24	69	AB	64	22.3
25–34	75	C1	75	27.1
35–44	92	C2	82	22.5
45–54	81	DE	67	28.1
55–64	74			
65+	58			

Social Class Definitions

A Upper Middle Class: Higher Managerial, administrative or professional.
B Middle Class: Intermediate managerial, administrative or professional.
C1 Lower Middle Class: Supervisory or clerical, and professional, junior managerial or administrative.
C2 Skilled Working Class: Skilled Manual Workers.
D Working Class: Semi and Unskilled Manual Workers.
E Those at the lowest level of subsistence: State pensioners or widows unemployed, casual or lowest grade workers.
Television Regions.
The main Commercial Television Contracts in the UK are awarded on a regional basis.

TV Area	Contractor	% Attending Party Plan
London	Carlton/LWT	60
South & South East	Meridian	64
Wales & West	HTV	75
South West	West Country TV	73
Midlands	Central TV	78
East	Anglia	71
North West	Granada TV	75
North East	Channel 3	74
Yorkshire	Channel 3	78
Border	Border TV	72

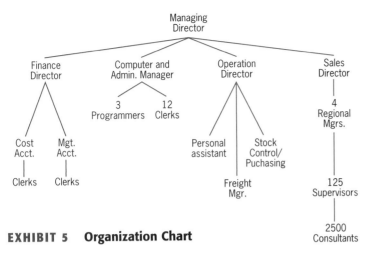

EXHIBIT 5 **Organization Chart**

EXHIBIT 6 **Summary Accounts for Practical Parties Ltd (Thousands of Pounds)**

	1999	1998	1997	1996
Sales	19379	19808	17629	15395
Commission	6775	6716	6522	6003
Net Sales	12604	13092	11107	9392
Interest paid	50	50	46	38
Sales Expenses	660	587	426	309
Manufacturing and Dist. Exp.	73	81	68	52
Other Expenses	197	183	126	102
Depreciation	420	381	261	222
Advertising	7	11	3	3
Variable Cost	8879	9133	7659	6545
Bad Debt	0	0	0	0
Admin. remuneration	1193	1040	999	943
Total Expenses	11479	11466	9588	8214
Non-trading income	58	50	48	35
Net profit before tax	1183	1676	1567	1213
Exports	0	0	0	0
Fixed assets	1974	2138	1836	1756
Stocks	1892	2004	2403	2399
Trade debtors	0	0	0	0
Other current assets	182	263	192	176
Total current assets	2074	2267	2595	2575
Total assets	4048	4405	4431	4331
Creditors	1653	1923	1836	1820
Short term loans	96	83	81	69
Other current liabilities	5	0	1	1
Total current liabilities	1754	2006	1918	1890
Net assets	2294	2399	2513	2441
Shareholders funds	1823	2017	2131	2109
Long term loans	471	382	382	378
Capital employed	2294	2399	2513	2487
Ratio Analysis				
Return on Net Assets	51.57	69.86	62.36	48.77
Return on Total Assets	29.22	38.05	35.36	28.01
Operating Margin	6.10	8.46	8.89	7.88
Asset turnover	4.79	4.50	3.98	3.55
Current ratio	1.18	1.13	1.35	1.36
Quick ratio	0.10	0.13	0.10	0.09
Interest cover	23.66	33.52	34.07	31.92
Debt/Equity	0.26	0.15	0.19	0.18
Stock turnover	10.24	9.88	7.44	6.42

CHAPTER 6

SALES ETHICS

> Make yourself a seller when you are buying and a buyer when you are selling, and then you will buy and sell justly.
>
> ST. FRANCIS DE SALES

Chapter Consultant:
Georges Michaud, Director of Environment/Health Safety & Ethics, Northern Telecom

LEARNING OBJECTIVES

After studying this chapter, you should be able to:

➤ Explain the moral bases for business ethics.

➤ Understand how to make decisions that involve ethical problems.

➤ Recognize the issues of common sales ethics.

➤ Discuss how to build a sales ethics program.

WHY ETHICS ARE IMPORTANT

Sales ethics provide a moral framework to guide salespeople in their daily contacts with customers. Ethical dilemmas are common in selling because salespeople often have to make decisions in the field in response to customers' demands and competitive offers. For example, Prudential Insurance Company of America had to take a $2.6 billion charge against earnings to pay policyholders damages after the company allowed its salespeople to use deceptive sales practices that encouraged customers to trade in old life insurance policies for new ones. Salespeople told clients that the new policies were no more expensive than ones they replaced when in fact, the new policies cost more and could not be paid for with future dividends.[1] In another case, salespeople for promotional material suppliers paid bribes in cash vacations, plane tickets, wine, luggage, football and theater tickets, golf clubs, golf trips, a table saw and a snow blower to purchasing managers at Hueblein, Warner-Lambert, and Philip Morris to secure orders at higher than normal prices. The companies are now suing 19 suppliers to recover millions of dollars in losses they suffered as a result of the bribery scheme.[2]

Other ethical problems occur with the issue of harassment. We know of one sales manager who asks his salespeople to credit his personal frequent-flier account whenever they take trips on company business. Salespeople who refuse fear they may be penalized on their next performance review. This occurs despite surveys that show 94 percent of firms allow their reps to keep frequent-flier miles for personal use.[3]

These examples suggest that the world of personal selling is full of ethical dilemmas. Sales managers must train reps in how to recognize these situations and how to respond when they occur. Remember that *business ethics* is a code of moral behavior that governs the conduct of a business community. This chapter focuses on the ethical problems faced by salespeople and sales managers and provides you with a set of guidelines to make better decisions.

MODELING ETHICAL BEHAVIOR

Procedures for making ethical decisions in business organizations are described in Figure 6-1. The process begins with the characteristics of individuals who are confronted with ethical choices (Part A). If people start out with high moral standards, the chances that ethical decisions will be made are enhanced. This suggests that hiring honest, principled salespeople is the first step in establishing high moral behavior in sales activities.

Part B of Figure 6-1 describes the sequence of activities a person goes through in making ethical decisions. First, you have to recognize the ethical issues, the affected parties, and the possible outcomes of your choices. This is not easy to do, since research has shown that marketing professionals identified fewer than half of the ethical issues when asked to review a case study and pick out issues to be discussed with a college-level marketing class.[4] Next you have to assign priorities to moral values and convert these intentions into actions. This decision process is moderated by the ethical standards of society, the organization, your peers, superiors, competitors, customers, and the law.

Part C of Figure 6-1 focuses on the outcomes of the ethical decision process. This can be measured in terms of job performance, customer satisfaction, and the achievement of organizational goals. For example, if salespeople who refuse to pay bribes to get business are supported by their managers, then the climate for ethical decision making is strengthened. On the other hand, if salespeople or sales managers who make ethical decisions are reprimanded and punished for their actions, then the organization is likely to get into trouble. For example, a former sales manager at Dean Witter who was fired for refusing to condone improper activities by the firm's brokers received a $2.4 million arbitration award for false statements that appeared on his termination notice.[5]

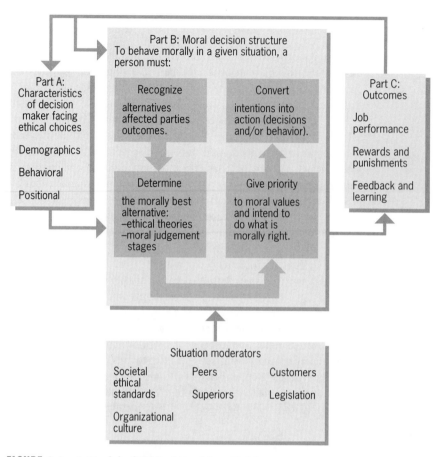

FIGURE 6-1   A Model of Ethical Decision Making

Our discussion of sales ethics is built around the ethical decision-making process described in Figure 6-1. We begin by focusing on the ethical rules and moderating factors that influence ethical choices in Part B of the diagram.

WHOSE ETHICS ARE RELEVANT?

Ethical problems are usually the result of poor decisions by individual salespeople, or company policies that encourage wrongdoing. For example, New York State investigators found that an information services director solicited bribes from computer suppliers for a $1.2 million computer installation. Salespeople were asked to contribute $8,000 to a scholarship fund for the buyer's late son. Salespeople from Data General contributed the largest $1,000 gift to the fund and got the order for the computer. When the scam was uncovered, Data General was asked to remove the computer, the salespeople were fired, and the buyer was demoted. Data General was also barred from making any sales to the state for six months.[6]

This example suggests that hiring the right people—people with principles—can save money in the long run. However, even the best salesperson can go wrong if forced to operate under policies that promote misdeeds. For instance, Sears lost millions of dollars in fines and sales as the result of a reward system that encouraged overselling of parts and services at its

SELF-MANAGEMENT COMPETENCY
Unethical Selling at Sears

In the early 1990s, Sears converted its service advisers in its automotive centers from hourly wages to a commission program that paid employees solely on the amount of repairs customer authorized. They also instituted a program of requiring service advisers to meet sales quotas on specific parts during their work shifts. However, in 1992 California officials found that in 90 percent of the cases it investigated, Sears service advisers recommended repairs that were not needed. Sears paid $15 million to settle customer claims of unneeded repairs at its auto service centers. Then in 1997, Sears paid $580,000 to customers in Florida for tire balancing services that were not performed. Again in 1999, Sears paid $980,000 to settle charges that its salespeople passed off used batteries as new. Sears' most expensive ethical lapse occurred in 1999 when it paid $475 million to settle charges that its lawyers improperly collected the credit card debts of bankrupt Sears' card holders. Finally Sears paid $36 million in cash and $118.5 million in merchandise coupons in 1999 to settle charges that the company improperly raised interest rates on Sears' credit cards. All of these activities have hurt the customer goodwill that Sears has carefully built up over the years. It appears that the incentives Sears provided to motivate its employees led some of them to employ unethical tactics in an effort to please superiors and raise their wages. If incentive strategies are to work as planned, they have to be monitored regularly and employees have to be carefully trained as to what activities are acceptable. Unrealistic sales and profit goals can lead to unethical selling and billing.

auto centers. A description of Sears' problems is given in the Self-Management Competency box. Remember, often there are no laws or court decisions to guide salespeople in specific situations, so actions must be taken in the "twilight zone" between the clearly right and the clearly wrong. This means you must understand the different moral rules that are available to guide business managers (Figure 6-1, Part B).

Role Morality

The moral philosophies held by sales managers are important to maintaining an ethical sales force because managers select field salespeople, provide ethical training, and enforce the moral codes of the firm. Two ways to describe individual moral philosophies are in terms of relativism and idealism. A relativistic manager tends to reject universal moral rules and make decisions on the basis of personal values and the ramifications of each situation. Idealists accept moral codes and believe that positive outcomes for all can be achieved by morally correct actions. In general, idealism leads to better ethical decisions than a reliance on the "it all depends" approach used by relativists. When 602 marketers were asked 20 questions to assess relativism and idealism, the scores of sales managers were not significantly higher on relativism or lower on idealism than other marketing personnel. This destroys the popular myth that salespeople have lower ethical standards than those in other business occupations. The study also showed that relativism declines with age and idealism scores increase with age. Also, female idealism scores were significantly higher than those for males. When sales managers were asked to evaluate unethical sales scenarios, idealistic managers were more sensitive to the moral problems exhibited.[7] These findings show that basic moral philosophies such as relativism and idealism held by individuals are important considerations in building and maintaining an ethical sales force.

Job Description

A good place to look for guidelines on ethical behavior in the workplace is the job description. A *job description* is a set of rules or practices that define the role an employee is expected to play at work. It resembles a legal contract because it specifies the number of hours of work, starting and stopping times, and the goals that are to be accomplished. If an employee fails to live up to the legal rules of a job description, there are grounds for dismissal.

When an accurate and complete job description is available, employees are in a better position to resolve ethical problems when they occur. If Data General had a written policy stating that salespeople could not donate to scholarship funds, hospital building funds, or special charities associated with customers, then it is unlikely that they would have gotten in such trouble with New York State officials. When job descriptions include questionable activities to be avoided, salespeople can respond that their job description does not allow them to make such payments.

Social Darwinism

The concept of *Social Darwinism,* based on the ideas of Charles Darwin and his theory of evolution, emerged in the latter half of the nineteenth century. Just as natural selection leads to stronger plant and animal species, free competition among business firms presumably leads to the survival of the fittest. That is to say, "natural laws" select the best and the most competent firms to enhance the good of society.

With Social Darwinism, there are no ethical standards. The law is the law of the jungle. Government does not interfere, cutthroat competition eliminates the weak, and only the strong survive. Social Darwinism was quickly embraced by the robber barons of the nineteenth century because it perfectly reflected the climate of their everyday business activities. However, this philosophy is generally considered too ruthless for today—an era in which the U.S. government protects the interests of small businesses and consumers. As a personal ethic, Social Darwinism is not publicly endorsed because of its inherent inhumanity.

Machiavellianism

Niccolò Machiavelli, Secretary of State in the Florentine Republic in the sixteenth century, is best known for his observations on human behavior and the workings of power. Many consider him to have been basically a realist—a person who focused on what is rather than on what ought to be. Machiavelli's political doctrine denied the relevancy of morality in public life and regarded expediency as the guiding principle. He was prepared to manipulate people and bend the laws of business to achieve his own goals. The opportunism that characterized Machiavelli's philosophy is reflected in the following quotation:

> Any person who decides in every situation to act as a good man is bound to be destroyed in the company of so many men who are not good. Wherefore, if a Prince desires to stay in power, he must learn how to be not good as the occasion requires.[8]

Dictionaries define *Machiavellianism* as the principles and methods of craftiness, duplicity, and deceit. Such practices are still employed by some sales executives to achieve personal or corporate goals. A survey of 98 salespeople revealed that those with Machiavellian tendencies were less ethical than other salespeople.[9] Sales managers should avoid hiring people with Machiavellian traits and should retrain their existing people to avoid this type of bad ethics.

"When in Rome"

Another ethical standard that can guide the actions of executives is known as *conventional morality* or *situation ethics*. This philosophy is reflected in the familiar phrase "When in Rome, do as the Romans do." The emphasis shifts from the *individual* to what *society* thinks about the ethical issue; that is, the standard of morality becomes what is acceptable to others at a particular time and place. Thus, social approval is the ultimate test of right and wrong. With conventional morality, relationships with others are more important than end results.

The *When in Rome* approach to morality has no absolute ethical standards to guide the actions of executives. Morality is based on social convention and group consensus. But the problem is that the majority can be wrong. Salespeople and sales managers sometimes justify cheating on expense accounts with the argument that "everybody does it" or "it's a way to reward salespeople with tax-free dollars." However, these are not acceptable reasons for violating organizational policy.

Another problem with conventional morality is that it is difficult for managers to adapt to changing contexts. Ten dollars given to a headwaiter is a tip, but $10 given to a customs official to get a perishable product moving is a bribe. While both transactions represent payment for extra services rendered, one is socially acceptable and the other is not—in the United States. Often, in fact, what is moral, ethical, or common in one country is unacceptable—or even illegal—in another. For example, hiring of relatives is called nepotism in the United States; in South America, it is viewed as an honorable family duty. Some ethical dilemmas encountered by firms selling in multinational markets are described in the Global Perspective Competency box.

GLOBAL PERSPECTIVE COMPETENCY
Overseas Ethical Dilemmas

The U.S. government has obtained information indicating that bribes were used to influence the outcome of 239 international contract competitions for $108 billion of new orders between 1994 and 1998. About 70 percent of the bribes were offered or paid to ministry or executive branch officials. The bribes were effective with companies paying bribes usually winning the contracts. Companies that were alleged to offer bribes included the European airplane consortium Airbus Industrie. U.S. government reports indicate that French and German firms were most frequently involved in paying bribes to influence contract competitions. In the United States, the 1977 Foreign Corrupt Practices Act prohibits American firms from using bribery across borders to get business. About 75 percent of the 239 international bribery cases involved companies from countries that belong to the Organization for Economic Cooperation and Development. Until recently, most OECD countries have had no laws against such bribery. However, in 1999, a major OECD bribery treaty took effect that committed member countries to pass antibribery laws. Although Germany and Japan have passed antibribery laws, others including France, Italy, Belgium, and the Netherlands have yet to ratify the OECD treaty. Interestingly, many businessmen and some politicians have made the point through the French media that the antibribery campaign is a ploy by the United States to gain competitive advantage. From the U.S. standpoint it appears that the French want to continue to use bribes to get orders, while at the same time take tax deductions on the bribes they pay.

Although U.S. firms are not allowed to use bribes to solicit overseas business, ethical dilemmas still arise. For example, Mobil Corp. paid consulting fees of $2.7 million to three Panama citizens after they obtained the right to operate a Panama Canal fueling terminal formerly used by the U.S. government. The Panama government did not consider these payments illegal, but others have suggested that they may violate the U.S. Foreign Corrupt Practices Act.

Different rules in different countries can create ethical problems.

MAKING DECISIONS ON ETHICAL PROBLEMS

Ethics are concerned with the effect of actions on the individual, the firm, the business community, and society as a whole. The relationships among the values and moral codes of conduct of these various entities were first described in Figure 6-1. A hierarchical diagram showing the order in which values evolve is given in Figure 6-2. Notice that the ethical values and standards of the business firm are derived from the general values and norms of society, and that business decisions represent a synthesis of the moral and ethical principles embraced by the various entities. Conflict is common because the values of the firm, as interpreted by its executives, may not match the values held by the individual. The difficult choice for managers is whether they should adhere to their own moral standards to solve problems or do what is expedient to maximize the short-run profits of the firm.

When faced with ethical problems, executives too frequently choose what is expedient rather than what is morally correct. When 400 executives were asked to play an "in basket" game, 47 percent of top executives directed underlings to avoid write-offs that would hurt profits and 14 percent inflated sales figures to meet expectations.[10] The presence of a company ethics policy did not change the results. This tendency to sell out personal ethical standards for a chance at corporate glory means organizations need to foster a business climate that reinforces ethical behavior, and establish ombudsmen who train and provide salespeople with guidance on ethical dilemmas.

Ethical Checklist

To help managers make difficult moral decisions, General Dynamics suggests the following checklist:

1. Recognize the dilemma.
2. Get the facts.
3. List your options.
   Are they legal?
   Are they right?
   Are they beneficial?
4. Make your decision.

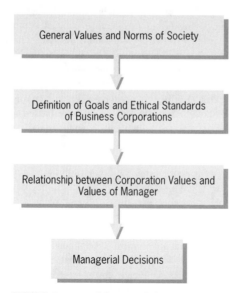

FIGURE 6-2   Making Decisions on Ethical Problems

Applying this checklist to an employee who is operating below expectations helps explain how it works.

The Case of the Drug Using Salesperson

Recognizing the Dilemma   Suppose sales manager Smith is concerned about Jones, who used to be the star member of the sales force. Jones's sales volume is slipping. At first, Smith ignores the problem. However, when customers start calling to complain about service, she can no longer put off deciding how to deal with the problem.

Assembling the Facts   The next step in the decision process is to assemble all the relevant facts. Smith could start by asking questions of the other members of the sales force and of customers who can be trusted to tell the truth. Suppose these inquiries reveal that Jones's family life is stable but that a possible drug problem is interfering with normal sales-call patterns.

The sales manager could summarize the problem in the following manner:

1. Jones had an excellent sales record in the past, and the firm is having trouble finding good replacements for salespeople who leave.
2. Jones's apparent drug use is preventing him, a potentially good salesperson, from performing up to standard.
3. Jones's apparent drug use is hurting company sales and profits, and the situation must be corrected.

Any solution should deal with all the facts. If some of the pertinent information is ignored, the sales manager is unlikely to find the best way to resolve the problem.

Making an Ethical Decision   Alternative plans that deal with all aspects of the problem include the following:

1. Smith could have a talk with Jones and indicate her concerns about sales in Jones's territory. The two could agree on an acceptable quota, and Jones could prepare a plan to achieve the new goals. Smith could explain that she does not believe in telling people how to lead their personal lives, but she does not allow personal problems to detract from job performance.
2. Smith could call Jones in and state that she is unhappy with Jones's poor sales and has heard rumors that Jones has a drug problem. Smith could give Jones an ultimatum that unless he submits to a drug test and resolves the problem if the test is positive, his employment will be terminated. Smith would agree to set a reasonable sales quota and express confidence in Jones's ability to meet the goal.
3. Smith could tell Jones that she is concerned with the dual problems of poor sales and possible drug use. Jones could be offered a three-month furlough at half pay to find a way to overcome his problem and be told that a reinstatement or termination decision would be made at the end of the furlough. Smith could suggest that Jones start seeing the company psychologist, explaining that the firm would like to keep Jones because of his impressive record of past successes. Temporary salespeople would be hired to cover Jones's territory during the furlough.
4. Smith could call Jones in and express her displeasure with Jones's poor sales and his possible drug problem. Jones could then be offered a choice of taking a drug test and going to a drug rehabilitation center for a month at company expense or of being terminated. Temporary salespeople would be hired to cover Jones's territory during his absence.

The first of these solutions is a step in the right direction, but it may not be sufficient. Smith alludes to the drug problem but stops short of offering any help. The second plan faces the sales and drug problems squarely. However, it is not clear that Jones would be able to handle the pressure of the "reform or get fired" threat made by the sales manager. The third plan takes some of the pressure off Jones and offers help for the drug problem. But Jones may be unable or unwilling to stop using drugs and this plan may simply postpone the inevitable decision to dismiss him.

The last solution to the possible drug problem is attractive because it offers advantages for all participants. The sales manager gains because Jones is removed from the territory and customers are handled by experienced reps. In addition, company sales volume in the territory should recover with the added attention. Furthermore, Jones is forced to confront his possible drug problem in a professional environment where chances for recovery are enhanced. The main risk with this approach is that Jones may refuse the treatment and his potential contributions to the firm will be lost forever.

COMMON SALES ETHICS ISSUES

Sales managers must make decisions in a wide variety of situations that have ethical dimensions. These include relations with superiors, salespeople, customers, competitors, dealers, and issues such as sexual harassment. There are no well-defined guidelines for moral conduct in each of the situations because what is right so often depends on the particular circumstances. Our objective is to raise some questions about business ethics and to point out potential problem areas.

Hiring and Firing

Various federal and state laws prohibit discrimination in hiring practices. Thus, firms that hire only white male Christians between the ages of 25 and 30 are breaking the law rather than operating unethically. An ethical problem, in contrast, usually requires considerable judgment as to the proper course of action—for example, in hiring candidates who are relatives of officers of the firm. Suppose a sales manager must choose between a man and a woman for a field representative position. Both candidates are well trained, but the man has somewhat more experience. Assume further that the woman is the daughter of a vice president of the company. If the decision is based strictly on qualifications, the man would get the position. However, the firm is under pressure from the federal government to hire women, so maybe she should get the position despite having somewhat lower qualifications. Although nothing has been said, the sales manager knows there could be personal advantages in hiring the vice president's daughter. Some would contend that hiring the woman instead of the man would be reverse discrimination and unethical. In this example, the sales manager must make a moral choice between what is best for the firm and what might enhance his or her own position in the firm.

Another sticky ethical question relates to hiring salespeople from competitors. The main advantages are that these people are trained and are likely to bring along some customers from their former employer. However, securing salespeople from competitors can increase selling costs and may lead to lawsuits if trade secrets are involved. Despite these risks, raiding competitors is common in the insurance, real estate, and stock brokerage fields. These firms operate on the premise that it is easier to hire successful agents than it is to train them. To prevent such practices, some firms have unwritten agreements that local competitors will not hire salespeople from each other. Although this arrangement helps to control selling costs, it often precludes salespeople from improving their positions by moving to another firm in the local area.

With so many firms concerned about reducing selling costs to boost profits, some companies are tempted to fire older salespeople who are paid high wages, and to replace them with younger people who earn less. This approach is clearly illegal if it is part of a general plan to discriminate against older employees. However, the courts have ruled that it is legal to fire older employees if the decision is based solely on the need to reduce costs.[11]

A study of 602 sales and marketing managers revealed that women had significantly higher idealism scores reflecting higher standards of ethical behavior than men.[12] This suggests that hiring more women might reduce ethical problems in sales organizations and improve compliance with government guidelines on hiring minorities.

House Accounts

A touchy problem for sales managers is how to handle large and important customers. These older accounts often require special attention that exceeds the time and skills available from the salesperson assigned to the territory. Should these accounts be left with the district salesperson or shifted to headquarters as *house accounts?* This is not an easy decision because the accounts often generate high commission income. The designation of a customer as a house account is usually defended on the grounds that it results in better service. However, the district salesperson who developed the account is likely to feel a proprietary interest because of the historical relationship with the client. Thus, a transfer to house account status is sure to be viewed as unfair by the salesperson losing the account. House accounts are clearly one area where firms need a specific and well-publicized policy in order to avoid misunderstandings and resentment.

Expense Accounts

Most ethical abuse in a sales organization takes place with expense accounts. Salespeople are expected to spend money contacting customers and are then reimbursed for their expenses. Those who abuse the reimbursement policy often claim higher expenditures than the amounts spent, keep the difference, and then don't report it to the Internal Revenue Service. A recent survey revealed that 25 percent of sales managers have caught a rep falsifying expenses within the past year.

Sales managers must decide how tight controls on expense accounts should be. For example, if all salespeople who pad their expense accounts were fired, there would be few people left in the sales organization. Tight control on expense accounts could result in salespeople not traveling to contact out-of-the-way customers. However, liberal repayment for expenses invites investigations by the IRS and results in selling expense ratios that are higher than they should be.

A good solution to this problem is to monitor the actual expenses of some reliable salespeople for a month each year and then use these figures to set reimbursement amounts for all field reps. This approach greatly reduces the costs of processing expense accounts and keeps expense payments in line with actual experiences.

Gifts for Buyers

American business has a tradition of giving small *gifts for buyers* to express appreciation for past and future business. These gifts include novelties and samples given out by salespeople, and gift-wrapped bottles of liquor at Christmas. The problem is that the gift giving may start out with a pair of hockey tickets and end up as a portable television set for the customer's den. How can a gift be distinguished from a bribe?

A survey of doctors by the Department of Health and Human Services revealed that 82 percent have received gift offers from drug salespeople to encourage them to prescribe their wares. Most physicians were offered small gifts such as pens and prescription pads, pocket calculators, and textbooks, but each was offered at least one more substantial gift or payment. The average gift offers for each doctor amounted to $727 per year, but three offers for research funding amounted to $20,000 or more.[13]

Today there seems to be more willingness among purchasing managers to accept gifts of clothing, pens, and calendars. However, management guidance on gifts has slipped, so it is increasingly difficult for salespeople to know what is right or wrong in a changing business environment. Some firms have set rules that prohibit buyers from accepting any gifts, meals, or favors that might compromise their integrity. Although rules appear to solve the problem, they are hard to enforce. Another guideline is the IRS ruling that only $25 can be deducted each year for company business gifts to any one person. In the absence of explicit policies, sales managers and salespeople must judge what is a reasonable gift and what others could interpret as a bribe.

Bribes

The use of *bribes* to obtain business is widespread, so you must know what to do when you feel it necessary to engage in this practice. Bribery is fairly easy to spot in its most blatant forms. If a customer says that an order will be placed if a $20,000 commission is paid to a third party, then the salesperson can be sure that someone is being paid off. Bribes of this size are not only unethical, they can be illegal.

The chief executive officer of Mid-American Waste System Inc. has been indicted on charges that he approved payment of bribes to members of the Gary, Indiana city council to influence voting on a lucrative landfill contract. Certain council members expected financial "help" for their upcoming elections and "all preferred cash." Mid-American attempted to limit the funding to the $2,000 allowed for political contributions, but it eventually agreed to pay one council member $10,000 disguised as the purchase of two vehicles. Other council members received $5,000 in cash and $2,000 checks from Mid-American's political action committee.[14] In another case, the vice president of sales for National Medical Care Inc. pleaded guilty to charges that he induced dialysis centers to order laboratory tests that were paid for by Medicare. In return, the centers received rebates on certain products, consultant fees, and study grants.[15]

Foreign payoffs are so common that the U.S. Congress passed the *Foreign Corrupt Practices Act* in 1977, making it a criminal offense to offer a payment to a foreign government official to obtain or retain foreign business. However, other industrialized nations have been slow to follow; France, Italy, Belgium, and the Netherlands have yet to pass laws prohibiting bribery and the deduction of bribes as a business expense for tax purposes. As a result, in the 1990s, the United States lost more than $100 billion of international competitions where bribery influenced the awarding of contracts.

Because of the difficulties caused by the Foreign Corrupt Practices Act in bidding on overseas contracts, the law has been amended so now U.S. companies break the law only if they knowingly make an illegal payment.[16] Also, "grease payments" are now permitted to facilitate a routine matter such as getting a visa or a permit. In addition, it is proper to make payments allowed under the written laws of a foreign country. Although these changes have helped, American firms can't engage in activities their local competitors carry out every day.

Unfortunately, much of the bribery and extortion in business dealings is disguised to make it even more difficult for the businessperson to choose right from wrong. For example, bribes have been disguised as gifts to hospital building funds, scholarships for relatives, memorial contributions, discounts on auto purchases, trips to professional meetings, golf outings, expensive dinners where speakers discuss state-of-the-art treatments of a given medical condition and the utility of the sponsor's drug, research grants, and illustrated reference manuals. The fine line between what is ethical and what is unethical in the marketing of infant formula is described in the Strategic Action Competency box.

STRATEGIC ACTION COMPETENCY
The Ethics of Selling Infant Formula

The three leading suppliers of infant formula in the United States are Abbot Laboratories with 51 percent of the market, followed by Bristol-Myers's 27 percent and American Home Products' 11 percent. These companies have built this dominant market position by having networks of sales representatives work closely with hospitals and doctors. The companies provide doctors with cash grants for research, school loans, payments for medical articles, and expenses for trips to conventions. They also make major contributions to hospitals for the privilege of giving away "discharge packs" of formula to mothers leaving hospitals. The market leaders have also agreed on an industry code to abstain from consumer advertising. This ban on advertising has been endorsed by the American Academy of Pediatrics. The Academy says its opposition is based on the fear that consumer advertising would reduce breast-feeding of babies. However, the objectivity of the Academy is suspect when you realize that the formula industry contributes $1 million a year toward its budget and paid $3 million of the $10 million cost of its headquarters in Illinois in 1983. Also the formula companies regularly pick up the tab for cocktail receptions at the American Academy of Pediatrics biannual meetings. The academy's opposition to advertising has made it very difficult for new entrants such as Nestlé and Gerber to break into the infant formula market.

The close cooperation among the three market leaders allowed them to increase the price of infant formula 207 percent since 1980, or six times the increase in the price of milk, its basic ingredient. Antitrust charges and bid-rigging allegations have recently caused the three market leaders to settle with the government for $230 million. The government fines appear to be primarily due to price-fixing charges rather than the payments to doctors and the American Academy of Pediatrics.

Are the actions of infant formula suppliers just an aggressive marketing strategy or are they being unethical?

Entertainment

Providing entertainment for potential customers is standard practice in American business, but it can lead to ethical problems. The issue is often "How much is too much?" Most would agree that taking a customer to lunch is fair, reasonable, and expected. Few would argue against occasionally taking a client and spouse to dinner and a nightclub. But what about the use of a company car or a weekend on the company yacht? On big orders, it is not unusual to fly personnel from the customer's plant to the supplier's headquarters in order to include plant tours and introductions to corporate executives as part of the sales presentation. Should the expenses of spouses taken on such trips be covered? Is it ethical to offer customers free use of the company hunting lodge in Canada? Sometimes out-of-town buyers are provided with call girls in addition to other forms of entertainment. What legitimately and ethically constitutes business "entertainment"?

An example of a difficult entertainment issue occurs when customers ask to be taken to topless bars. A survey revealed that 49 percent of male reps and 5 percent of female reps had taken customers to topless bars.[17] The survey also revealed that 72 percent of the visits were suggested by customers. Most women reps do not like topless bars, and believe that entertaining customers at these places gives men an unfair advantage over female salespeople. Although 40 percent of the surveyed firms do not allow reps to entertain at topless bars, many firms simply look the other way. This example suggests that it is hard to solicit business on the basis of product quality and service features when your competition is "buying" customers with exotic entertainment.

SEXUAL HARASSMENT

The Equal Employment Opportunity Commission defines sexual harassment as:

> Unwelcome sexual advances, requests for sexual favors, and other verbal or physical conduct of a sexual nature constitute sexual harassment when (1) submission to such conduct is made either explicitly or implicitly a term or condition of an individual's employment; (2) submission to, or rejection of, such conduct by an individual is used as the basis for employment decisions affecting such individual; or (3) such conduct has the purpose or effect of substantially interfering with an individual's work performance or creating an intimidating, hostile or offensive working environment.

Workplace sexual harassment is prohibited by Title VII of the 1964 Civil Rights Act. Although sexual harassment has been against the law for 36 years and higher penalties are being awarded, salespeople still may encounter it. For example, in 1996 *Business Week* described the sexual harassment endured by salespeople at the U.S. subsidiary of Astra AB, a major Swedish pharmaceutical firm.[18] This harassment was engaged in by managers at the highest level, and those who did not comply found life at the firm very difficult. When sexual harassment is this blatant, the courts may be called on to remedy the situation. However, salespeople often encounter sexual harassment in a more subtle and indirect fashion.

Salespeople are particularly vulnerable to what is known as third-party harassment, which is harassment by someone outside the boundaries of the firm, such as a customer, vendor, or service person. A typical situation could involve a male buyer at a key account asking a female salesperson for sexual favors in exchange for an order. In this case the salesperson may want the order to help make her quota and fear the contract will be given to a competitor if she refuses. She may also believe that if she complains to her boss, she will be seen as lacking the selling skills needed to resolve the harassment problem. Another worry is that efforts to reform the buyer could sour relations between the two firms.

Unfortunately, many employees are unaware that their own firm could be held liable for third-party harassment and that third-party harassment is prohibited behavior.[19] Each firm should develop formal policies on harassment within the organization and by those outside the organization, and provide a process for salespeople to remove themselves from a harassing situation perpetrated by an outsider without sanctions. Third-party harassers can be dealt with by writing them a letter, or asking them to stop. These actions attract attention because they imply that the victim may take further, more public action. Some firms take a more passive response and simply reassign accounts with harassing buyers to new salespeople. Although this approach does not stop harassment, it may help the seller retain the account.

WHISTLE-BLOWING

A whistle-blower is an employee who informs the public about an employer's or supervisor's immoral or illegal behavior. *Whistle-blowing* is a last-resort action that is justified when the employee has the appropriate moral motive. Before whistle-blowing takes place, the person who has observed the unethical behavior should have exhausted all the internal channels for dissent. This means talking to your supervisor or the company ombudsman if one is available. Another test of whistle-blowing is that the evidence should be strong enough to convince the average person that a violation is taking place. Furthermore, the observed moral violation should be serious enough to require immediate attention. Finally, the act of telling the public must have some chance for success. From a practical standpoint, it makes no sense to complain to the public unless something is going to be done about the problem. Why expose yourself to hardship if there is no moral gain?

Whistle-blowing is not taken lightly, because employees know they may suffer if they "go public" with a moral problem. A typical example of what happens to a whistle-blower occurred with a West Virginia bank manager who was fired for complaining about illegal overcharges for certain classes of his customers. The manager sued the bank and won an unfair firing judgment, but he received only $18,000 after paying his legal fees. Even worse, he was unable to find another bank job, even after applying to all of the other banks in the state. The former banker was eventually forced to take a lesser job as a state bank examiner.

Why are whistle-blowers treated so badly for simply following high personal moral standards? The problem seems to be that by speaking up, they violate the role morality that demands that employees be loyal and keep their mouths shut. Management can be embarrassed by whistle-blowing so they often try to get rid of people they feel can't be trusted. To help encourage whistle-blowers to come forward, federal laws have been modified to pay rewards of 15 to 25 percent of any recovery plus attorneys' fees. More than 500 suits have been filed, with total recoveries of $400 million, and whistle-blowers received an average of $1 million. In one case, a whistle-blower stands to win as much as $25 million for exposing "yield burning" improprieties in muni-bond underwriting to federal regulators.[20]

Whistle-blowing displays the classic conflict between the high ethical standards of individuals and the often lower morality found in the business world. The ultimate answer may occur when more firms set up formal internal mechanisms so that employees with moral problems to report are not ignored or punished.

GOVERNMENT REGULATION

When business fails to operate in an ethical manner, there is usually a public outcry for more *government regulation*. Thus one of the basic roles of government is to set minimum standards of business morality and then to enforce the rules. The judicial branch of government settles disputes over the interpretation of the regulations, and Congress writes new rules as they are needed. Some of the first government regulations in the United States affecting business were designed to protect the public from noncompetitive activities. The types of activities laws are designed to prevent include a scheme by Archer-Daniels-Midland Co. to rig the worldwide market for lysine, a livestock feed additive, with four Asian competitors. In this case, ADM paid a $100 million antitrust fine, and two executives were fined $350,000 each for price fixing and sentenced to two years in prison.[21]

Consumer Protection

A number of federal laws have also been passed to set ethical standards for transactions between manufacturers and the consumer. For example, the common practice of dealers inflating the prices of new cars was stopped by the Automobile Information Disclosure Act, which requires manufacturers to attach labels to car windows that show the suggested price for the car, accessories, and transportation. Deceptive packaging has been attacked with the Fair Packaging and Labeling Act, which calls for standard package sizes and disclosure of the manufacturer's name or the distributor. Attempts by loan companies and retailers to mislead consumers on interest rates have led to the enactment of the Consumer Credit Protection Act. *Truth in lending* laws require full disclosure of annual interest rates and other charges on loans and credit sales. More recently, the Magnuson-Moss Warranty Act has increased the FTC's power to regulate product warranties. New FTC rules require full disclosure of warranty terms and reduce the use of warranties as promotional gimmicks.

Why Are Regulations Needed?

Government often gets involved in business ethics when the problem is too big for individual firms to handle. For example, automobile exhaust is a major cause of air pollution, but it is difficult for an individual firm to solve the problem. If one company feels it is morally correct to install air pollution equipment on their cars, their costs will be higher than those of the competition. Thus the cars of the ethically lazy firm will be cheaper and more powerful, and they will literally run off with the market. In this situation, government regulation allows the well-intentioned business to be the good citizen it wants to be.

Although there are many arguments for a minimum of government regulation of business, there are also other problems with regulation. Businesspeople generally dislike government controls because they rob them of the flexibility needed to respond to changing conditions. Government rules established to solve problems in one decade are often obsolete by the next decade. For instance, the federal government got into the regulation of natural gas prices because gas is often shipped through interstate pipelines. As might be expected, the government tended to set low gas prices for maximum political gain. However, the drillers were more rational, and they slowed their search for new gas. As a result, the supply of natural gas declined until the price controls were removed.

We believe there should be a balance between too little government ("yield burning" in muni-bond underwriting) and too much regulation (as occurred in the natural gas industry) where business was strangled by endless rules and red tape.

BUILDING A SALES ETHICS PROGRAM

The moral climate of a business reflects the words and actions of its top executives. If management tolerates unethical behavior in the sales force, then there is little a member of the organization can do about it. Superiors set the moral climate and provide the constraints within which business decisions are made. Thus, the best way for a manager to build a strong sales ethics program is to get the backing of the board chairperson and the president of the company (Table 6-1). When this support is not available, there are sure to be ethical violations.

Codes of Ethics

Once a sales manager gains the support of top management, the next step is to prepare a written sales *ethics policy statement* that indicates to the sales force that the company believes in playing fair with customers and competitors. Research has shown that senior executives believe the adoption of a corporate code of ethics is the most effective way to

TABLE 6-1 Eight Ways to Keep Your Sales Force Honest

1. Get support from top management showing that they expect you to follow the spirit and letter of the law.
2. Develop and distribute a sales ethics policy.
3. Establish the proper moral climate. If the bosses follow the rules, then the troops are likely to do the same.
4. Assign realistic sales goals. People who try to meet an unfair quota are more likely to rationalize their way to a kickback scheme.
5. Set up controls when needed. Watch people who live above their income.
6. Suggest that salespeople call for help when they face unethical demands.
7. Get together with your competition if payoffs are an industry problem.
8. Blow the whistle if necessary.

encourage ethical behavior. A survey of 218 salespeople indicated that field reps want written policies that help them perform their jobs ethically.[22] Also, the policies need to be monitored on a regular basis to make sure that they are germane to the current selling arena. The advantage of a written ethics policy is that it allows the firm to be explicit about what activities are permissible and what actions violate company standards. This can be useful when customers, suppliers, or your boss ask you to participate in some unethical activities. If your company has a code of ethics, you can reply, "I'm sorry, but company policy forbids that," and graciously end a conversation about a shady deal. The vast majority of firms that were involved in foreign payoff scandals had no written policies on commercial bribery. Today most firms claim to have formal ethics codes, but only half ask employees to acknowledge or sign them.[23] This suggests some firms need to make reps more aware of the company's ethical standards.

An example of what a written code of ethics should look like is provided by General Motors. GM's policy is a 12-page document complete with instructional scenarios featuring fictional characters.[24] One scenario has a purchasing employee visiting the home office of a possible supplier where he was offered a ticket to a Rams football game and to mingle with top executives. This opportunity should be turned down. In another scenario an investment banking firm that helped with an acquisition for GM invites several GM employees to New York for a dinner and the gift of a mantel clock. In this case the dinner and the clock should be refused. GM's policy provides some wiggle room for employees outside the United States. Workers in certain countries may accept meals, gifts, or outings to comply with local business practices and to avoid being placed in a competitive disadvantage. Also GM employees can continue providing gifts and meals to their customers, but only within limits. The most expensive restaurant in town is no longer appropriate. GM's policy requires GM employees to avoid violating the customer's gift policy.

Sales managers should also be prepared to enforce company policies on bribery. This means it pays to keep tabs on salespeople who appear to live beyond their income. It also means setting reasonable sales goals so that salespeople will not be tempted to cheat to reach an unfair quota. Salespeople should be encouraged to ask for assistance when they encounter unethical situations. If payoffs become too widespread, the sales manager should meet with the competition to work out a set of standards for the industry.

Ethics Training

Our discussion has shown that field salespeople are involved in a variety of competitive situations that may tempt reps to engage in unethical behavior to reach company or personal goals. However, research has revealed that only 44 percent of firms include ethics as a topic in their sales management training programs.[25] This suggests that more attention to ethics training is needed to help salespeople function in today's business environment.

You should remember that simply publishing a sales ethics code does not guarantee that it will be followed by field sales representatives. Companies should offer classes to make sure employees know what to do in morally ambiguous situations. In the case of pharmaceutical salespeople, research has shown that reps should stress the importance of long-term relationships with doctors and develop training classes that enhance product and customer knowledge. Reps with the greatest expertise tend to act more ethically in their relationships with doctors.[26]

Research has confirmed that younger sales managers are less idealistic and more relativistic in their ethical decision making.[27] These findings suggest the importance of adjusting training program content to meet the needs of different age groups. New hires and younger managers, for example, should be given material that emphasizes the importance of company ethical norms and values.

Honeywell revamped employees' training and replaced a vague policy manual with a detailed handbook. Some of the unacceptable practices spelled out in the handbook include catcalls, sexual jokes, and staring. Nearly three-quarters of DuPont's 90,000 U.S. staffers have taken harassment-prevention training dubbed "A Matter of Respect," and sexual harassment suits involving the company have diminished. Corning is testing its first workshops on ethics, because people who feel harassed on the job aren't productive workers.[28]

These programs bring groups of employees together with an instructor to find solutions to simulated moral dilemmas. By working through a number of scenarios, employees learn how to recognize problems, assemble facts, consider alternatives, and make decisions. They can also pick up some tips on how the company expects them to operate. At one session a salesperson asked, "When I check in at a motel, I get a coupon for a free drink; can I use it?" The correct answer was that it would be acceptable to use the coupon, but it would be wrong to accept $50 to stay there in the first place. At DuPont the course offers advice on what women should do when a male customer makes a pass and puts his hand on the saleswoman's knee. In this case she should firmly remove his hand and say, "Let's pretend this didn't happen." Some firms also include training sessions for men on how to avoid crude jokes and other forms of intimidation when dealing with women buyers. The idea behind ethics training is to make sure employees are equipped to handle real-world issues they are likely to encounter when calling on customers.

SUMMARY

Sales ethics provides a moral framework to guide salespeople in their daily contacts with customers. Ethical dilemmas are common in selling because salespeople often have to make decisions in the field in response to customers' demands and competitive offers. This chapter has attempted to equip you with the following skills:

1. **Explain the moral bases for business ethics.** Sales ethics form a code of moral conduct that guides sales managers and salespeople in their everyday activities. Ethical decisions can be based on different moral rules including idealism, relativism, the self-interest of Social Darwinism, the unscrupulous expediency of Machiavellianism, or conventional morality.

2. **Understand how to make decisions that involve ethical problems.** Managers who score high on idealism tend to make the most ethical decisions. Perhaps the best way to solve ethical problems is the pragmatic approach, which involves an objective analysis of relevant facts and leads to more rational decisions.

3. **Recognize the issues of common sales ethics.** Areas in which the sales manager is likely to confront difficult ethical situations involve hiring, house accounts, whistleblowing, expense accounts, requests for payoffs, and customer gifts and entertainment.

4. **Discuss how to build a sales ethics program.** Building a good company sales ethics program would include the following: getting support from top management, developing and distributing a sales ethics policy, establishing a proper moral climate, assigning realistic sales goals, setting up controls when needed, suggesting that salespeople call for help when faced with unethical demands, and blowing the whistle when necessary.

KEY TERMS

Bribes

Business ethics

Consumer protection

Conventional morality

Deceptive sales practices

Ethics policy statement

Foreign Corrupt Practices Act

Gifts for buyers

Government regulation

Job description

Kickbacks

Machiavellianism

Relativism

Role morality

Self-regulation

Sexual harassment

Situation ethics

Social Darwinism

House accounts

Idealism

"When in Rome"

Whistle-blowing

DEVELOPING YOUR COMPETENCIES

1. **Strategic Action.** In 1996, a report prepared by insurance regulators from 30 states revealed that management at Prudential Insurance Co. of America knew of sales abuses by agents and in many cases failed to adequately investigate and impose effective discipline. The report cited cases where agents with "significant complaint histories" were promoted to sales and general managers, with supervisory and training responsibility over agents. Prudential's negligence in its accountability for its agents was particularly noticeable with regard to "churning." This is a practice where agents withhold information or use deceptive sales pitches to persuade customers to use the built-up cash value of older policies to finance new, more expensive ones. As a result of Prudential's lack of control over its sales force, the company was forced to pay hundreds of millions of dollars in fines and restitution to its customers. In addition, a new chairman had to clean house and fire hundreds of agents and sales managers. The insurance regulator's report suggests that Prudential was following an unwritten strategy of allowing its agents to engage in activities that helped the company at the expense of its customers. Why did Prudential permit and even encourage its agents to employ unethical sales practices? What actions should Prudential take to prevent these practices from being used by its agents in the future?

2. **Self-Management.** A stockbroker pleaded guilty to conspiracy charges in San Diego for accepting $500,000 in bribes to promote the sale of certain stocks. The bribes amounted to 15 percent of the value of stock sold to clients and were paid in cash. In this case, the stocks were recommended to customers regardless of whether they fit the investment needs of the client. How should firms structure their self-management programs so that employees will be better able to resist bribes when they are offered? Can employees be trained to refuse payments for unethical conduct?

3. **Technology.** The Internet has proved to be extremely helpful to field salespeople who use e-mail to communicate with customers and their corporate colleagues. Also, Web sites on the Internet allow customers to check product availability and place routine reorders. Although the Internet is a technological marvel, some employees use it to further their own unethical activities. At one company, an employee set up a fake Web site and posted false information on the firm. The Web site was so professional that many outsiders used the false information in buying and selling the company's stock. It appeared that the fake Web site was set up to help the employee make money for his own brokerage account by selling when false rumors drove up the price of company stock. At another firm an employee sent out phony e-mail messages concerning alleged racial discrimination to enhance the chances for a bigger settlement from the firm. What should companies do to make sure that technological innovations are used ethically and not for personal gain?

4. **Global Perspective.** A United Technologies employee has charged that the company's Sikorsky division offered two Saudi princes a "bonus" of 3 to 5 percent of a $130 million portion of a $6 billion potential Blackhawk helicopter order. Payments to foreign intermediaries to gain orders are illegal under the U.S. Foreign Corrupt Practices Act. The employee is seeking $100 million in damages from United Technologies. Under the U.S. False Claims Act, whistle-blowers are also entitled to 25 percent of any money the government recovers from defendants in cases of fraud. What seems to be the employee's motive in this case and why are such "commissions" so common in foreign sales agreements? How should the company handle these demands for special favors?

5. **Team Building.** A stockbroker at Merrill Lynch & Co.'s office in Cape Coral, Florida, complained to the company that a branch manager was soliciting business and making trades before his license had been transferred to the firm. Later a replacement branch manager asked the broker to oversee things while the new manager was on vacation. The manager had made no arrangements to distribute holiday paychecks, so the broker opened a letter addressed to the manager to get some information on employee pay levels. He then matched this information against the checks and handed them out. For this, the broker was fired and told to pack his things and leave. As soon as the broker left the office, the manager divided up the broker's $82 million of accounts among himself and other brokers in the office. The manager and the brokers stayed late at the office so they could immediately call all the customers to say their broker was no longer with the firm and urging them to stay with Merrill Lynch. The largest portion of the broker's accounts went to the manager who would now receive commissions on all trades made for these accounts. The unethical practice of firing successful stockbrokers so managers can increase the assets under their own control is more widespread than the industry acknowledges. What can brokerage firms do to encourage more teamwork at their branch offices? Should successful brokers be dismissed for minor offenses so branch managers can make more money?

IN-CLASS EXERCISE

6-1: Special Support

Assume you have taken over the territory of Henry Perkins, who has retired after 30 years with your firm. Henry was well liked by everyone and earned $60,000 in commissions on printing sales in his last year. You are having dinner with one of the best customers in the territory, Mary Stevens. Mary bought $100,000 in printing services from your company in the past year, and this business earned Henry $6,000 in commissions. You have been emphasizing to Mary how you plan to continue to provide the same high-quality service that Henry was providing. Mary responds that she has recently talked to several other quality printers who also provide good service, and she wonders if you intend to continue Henry's special support activities. You say that you are not sure what special support Henry has been providing. Mary indicates that Henry paid $2,000 for a trip to Jamaica each winter to help relieve her arthritis.

Questions

1. Discuss how you would respond in this situation in small groups in your class for seven minutes.

6-2: "Customer Gifts versus Company Policy"*

George Freitag, a salesperson at Steel International, is a professional at relationship building. His customers are the grateful recipients of cards for every occasion, tickets to sporting and

---

*Contributed by Eli Jones, University of Houston.

entertainment events, even trinkets from Freitag's road trips. Any time he sees "the perfect gift" for one of his customers—whether it is a book on their favorite subject or some nifty gadget that's made just for their hobby—Freitag buys and sends the gift.

Freitag's manager, Jesse Webster, enjoys seeing the pleasure Freitag and his customers get from the gifts—especially since Freitag always makes his quota, and the prices of the gifts are always low enough to squeeze into his Travel and Expense (T&E) budget. Unfortunately, Steel's new CEO has recently introduced a strict "No Gifts" policy—right before the holiday season. Webster has learned through the grapevine that Freitag plans to send holiday gifts to his customers anyway, and work them into his T&E budget as other expenses, such as "breakfast meetings."

Webster is in a tough situation. He wants to keep Freitag and his customers happy, but he knows that he should follow the CEO's policy.

Questions

1. What should Webster do now?
   - Should he pretend as though he didn't hear the rumor and let Freitag send his gifts?
   - Should he discuss the situation with the CEO?
   - Should he simply tell Freitag, "Sorry, but this is now the policy"?
   - Which option is best, or is there another, better choice?
2. If you were the sales manager, what would you do about the following:
   a. Handling the rumor, that Freitag plans to disregard the new company policy.
   b. Keeping Freitag motivated despite the new policy.
   c. Teaching Freitag alternative methods of building customer loyalty.
3. Is there a high probability of Freitag losing customers because of the new policy?
4. What are the possible reactions of Freitag's customers?
5. Given the precedent that Freitag has set with his customers by supplying them with a continuous flow of gifts, what is going to happen when Freitag stops giving gifts and his competition continues?

6-3: "Ethics"*

Ken Rowland, a regional manager for General Corporation, was leaning comfortably back in his airplane seat. He was returning from his industry's annual conference. His head was full of new marketing strategies, so instead of napping, he pulled out his laptop and started jotting notes to himself. A short while later there was a break from the hum of the airplane. "I think it's time for a price cut," the man in front of him said to his seatmate. Rowland paused; he listened for what would come next.

As it turns out, the two men seated in front of Rowland were the vice president of sales and the president of General's largest competitor. They were flying from the conference to a customer meeting in Rowland's territory. They spent an hour discussing an upcoming pricing strategy, with Rowland feverishly taking notes the entire time. Rowland couldn't believe his luck. Not only did he make a significant number of contacts at the show, he now had at his fingertips the competition's entire pricing strategy for the second quarter of the year. *This is too good to be true,* he thought.

The next morning in his Boston office, Rowland wrote a memo outlining all of the key points of the competition's pricing strategy. He sent the memo via e-mail to all of General's sales managers and regional managers, the vice president of sales, Nicole Hobbs, and the company president, Jacob Pierce. Hobbs was dumbstruck when she read the e-mail. She was shocked that Rowland would send the e-mail without first consulting her on the appropriate

---

*Contributed by Eli Jones, University of Houston.

action. Rowland's decision to e-mail sensitive information without checking with her first could have any number of repercussions.

Questions

1. What is Hobbs' (the vice president of sales) course of action now?
2. How should Hobbs handle Rowland? Should she reprimand him, or congratulate him for being alert to the competition's moves?
3. What are the possible reactions from the field to Rowland's information?
4. What are the ethical issues involved in this case?
5. What is an "ideal" course of action given all of the issues involved?
6. Write a brief step-by-step plan to handle this situation.

CASE 6-1   TEXXON OIL COMPANY

The retail gasoline marketing strategy of the major oil companies first began to develop in the early 1930s. Before 1910 gasoline was sold by livery stables, garages, and hardware, grocery, and general stores. However, by the mid-1920s, with the dramatic growth of automobile registrations, a clear need emerged for a new type of outlet. The result was the development of the gasoline service station, which quickly dominated the sale of gasoline.

HISTORY OF GASOLINE MARKETING

Gasoline Service Stations

The initial demand for service stations was met by independent businesspeople who were eager to capitalize on the profit opportunity in this important venture. The result was intense competition among the major oil companies for exclusive representation by the higher-quality, independently owned retail outlets. This competition had two consequences for quality representation. First, the price of quality representation became quite high. Second, frequent brand switching by the independently owned outlets often disrupted major oil company coverage in an area.

For these and other reasons, the major oil companies began to integrate forward to control their key marketing facilities, either by outright ownership or by long-term leases. Forward integration also ensured that the outlets would sell only the brand of the owning company. It also permitted greater control over station appearance and operation. Such control is very important in the development of a favorable brand image for an unpackaged product like gasoline.

While the ownership and control of stations permit employee operation, most major companies have chosen to use independent dealers to run their service stations. Under this arrangement, the major oil company is both landlord and supplier.

This was not always so. Initially, it was quite common for the major oil companies to operate their stations with company employees. For a number of reasons, including the avoidance of chain store taxes, most majors moved away from direct station operation by the mid-1930s. The threat of unionization, as well as the desire to shift the burden of the often low returns from retailing to others, also entered into this decision.

Franchised Station Operation

The franchise relationship in the petroleum industry is unique in that the franchiser not only grants the franchisee the use of his trademark but often controls, and leases to the franchisees, the retail facility used by the franchisee. In addition, the franchiser is almost always the primary supplier of the franchisee's principal sale item: motor fuel. This relationship is often complex and is sometimes characterized by competing interests. There is also a substantial disparity of bargaining

---

This case was prepared by James M. Patterson.

power between the supplier and the dealer. This disparity results in standard franchise agreements that translate into the dealer's continuing vulnerability to the demands and actions of the supplier.

The natural tensions that are created by this relationship have led to numerous complaints by dealers of unfair terminations or nonrenewals of their franchises by their supplier/landlords. Allegations have been made in court and before congressional committees that the refiner/landlord uses terminations and nonrenewals to compel franchised dealers to comply with the marketing policies of the franchiser, even though they are often at odds with the dealers' own economic interests.

While the relationship of the parties in a motor fuel franchise agreement is basically contractual, the franchiser often avoids the normal remedies for violations of the provisions. Moreover, the disparity of bargaining power that disadvantages the franchisee in negotiations leading to the execution of the agreement often manifests itself in one-sided remedies for contract violations. In addition, the franchiser is able to capitalize on this disparity in bargaining power to obtain greater flexibility with respect to his or her right to terminate the contractual relationship. As a result, termination of franchise agreements for contract violations has been repeatedly utilized, often for what to many seem to be minor infractions.

Franchiser/Franchisee Conflict

As in other franchise relationships, the parties to a motor fuel franchise believe the relationship will be a continuing one. This expectation is often fostered by the nature of the actions and sometimes by the statements of the franchiser. It is clearly in the dealer's best interest to build customer goodwill for the location and for the franchiser's brand and to develop customer loyalty for the services and products he or she offers. Consequently, the nonrenewal of a motor fuel franchise relationship can be almost as punitive as a termination during its term. In the case of nonrenewal, the reasonable expectations of the franchisee are destroyed. This loss is made even more severe in the case of the lessee/dealer since the dealer loses not only the goodwill generated for the franchiser's brand, but also the goodwill generated for service at a specific location. By contrast, landlord/suppliers are able to convert most of the goodwill generated by dealers to their own use. The losses from nonrenewal, therefore, fall more heavily on the lessee/dealer.

Disparity of bargaining power at the start of a franchise relationship may manifest itself in the use of ter-

mination as a remedy for contract violations. In addition, the prospect of nonrenewal of a franchise relationship may be used to coerce the dealer into accepting the franchiser's marketing policies against his or her better judgment. Threats are not even essential to the leverage that nonrenewal provides a franchiser over the activities of the dealer. The prospect is ever present, and the lessee/dealer can readily imagine and comprehend the implications of departing from the marketing policies of the franchiser, even if they are contrary to the dealer's own economic interests. This problem is made even more severe when the franchiser uses shorter franchise periods.

Congress enacted the Petroleum Marketing Practices Act in 1978.[1] The purpose of the law was to ensure that the grounds for termination and nonrenewal were not so broad as to deny dealers meaningful protection from arbitrary or discriminatory terminations and nonrenewals. The law also sought to establish uniform guidelines regarding the franchise relationship.

The drafters of the law also sought to accommodate the legitimate needs of a franchiser to terminate or not renew a franchise relationship by reason of certain serious specified actions of the franchisee.[2] The intention was to provide adequate flexibility so that franchisers might respond to changing economic conditions and consumer preferences.

Divorcement/Anticonversion Legislation

During this same period, Maryland enacted legislation to prevent refiner/marketers from taking back their dealer stations and operating them as company stores with their own employees. This reintegration was a natural outgrowth of the changes that were taking place in the marketing of gasoline during the 1970s. High-volume, self-service, gasoline-only stations were the wave of the future. Unlike the traditional low-volume, full-service station, these new express stations could be operated with employees or contract labor as opposed to dealers. Moreover, the traditional dealer

---

[1] Petroleum Marketing Practices Act, 15 U.S.C. 2801.

[2] The following are grounds for termination or nonrenewal of a franchise relationship: (1) failure to comply with reasonable and material provisions of the contract; (2) failure of the dealer to exert good faith efforts to carry out the provisions of the franchise; (3) the occurrence of an event that is relevant to the franchise relationship; (4) agreement between the parties; and (5) a determination made by the franchiser in good faith and in the normal course of business to withdraw from the retail marketing of motor fuel in the relevant geographic area.

margins, which were based on low-volume full-service stations, were out of line with what was required for the new retail operations. Many dealers were getting rich at oil company expense. In fact, some dealers were making more money than the oil company managers supervising them.

Initially, this dealer-inspired divorcement legislation merely prohibited refiner/marketers from operating stations with their own employees. But since the refiners immediately challenged these laws on constitutional grounds, the dealers got their friends in the state legislature to enact legislation that would make it illegal for any service station that had been offering automotive repair service to continue to operate as a service station without also continuing to provide this service. No longer could a traditional station be razed and converted to an express, gas-only operation. Ultimately, both laws withstood constitutional challenge and were upheld as valid exercises of the state's police power.

These anticonversion laws served the dealers' goal of self-preservation because very few stations offering automotive service had ever been successfully operated by the refiners. Automotive service operations were too hard to control from headquarters. They required continuous, detailed supervision and local initiative for them to be profitable. As a result, the dealers knew that if automotive service at a location had to be continued by law, lessee/dealers would continue to be used to operate the station at that location.

Richie Highway Texxon Station

Governor Richie Highway is a true "gasoline alley." This highway is a major north–south four-lane road that runs from Baltimore to Annapolis. There is hardly a stretch along its 25 miles where a gasoline service station is not in sight. The road is a classic strip-retailing commuting corridor interspersed with several large shopping centers. The highway is heavily traveled, almost to the point of congestion. Most major brands, from Amoco to Sun, are represented on this highway. There is no significant private brand presence, but Crown, a strong regional marketer that prices with the majors, has a strong presence. Prices are very competitive, since commuters driving to work notice the range of posted prices and fill up at the lowest-priced station on the way home.

Compared with the new, attractive stations, Texxon (MD–73) is an old-timer, having been built in 1969. The retail configuration is traditional. The building is a red brick colonial with two service bays and an automotive rollover car wash. The station has three pump islands with mechanical pumps and no canopy. The lighting and signage are old-fashioned. Nevertheless, the station has experienced good volume since the Texxon brand and credit card are well received. Texxon is one of the top gasoline marketers in Maryland and has nearly 200 stations statewide. Operating data for MD–73 appear in Exhibits 1 and 2.

Ron Kile, the most recent lessee/dealer to operate MD–73, took over the station in November 1992, and operated it under a succession of standard Texxon dealer agreements until the last one expired in November 1996. Kile paid $123,000 to the former dealer to acquire the business and goodwill of MD–73. Kile, as well as his father and brother, are personally obligated on the loans obtained to finance this business at MD–73.

At the time Kile acquired MD–73 in 1992, Texxon approved Kile as the Texxon franchisee. Texxon was also aware that Kile, who had previously managed MD–73 for the former dealer, had paid a substantial sum to acquire the business at MD–73.

Prior to the time that Kile acquired the business of MD–73, the dealer rep advised him informally that Texxon intended to renovate the station and convert it to an advanced marketing facility with an overhead canopy, computerized gasoline pumps, sales kiosk, and upgraded service bays. This understanding, however, was never put in writing and was not part of the franchise agreement.

Upon acquiring the business, Kile spent a great deal of effort and money to improve the premises, promote the sale of Texxon gasoline and products, and otherwise comply with the written franchise agreements.

The New Texxon Express Station

Shortly before Kile became the Texxon franchisee at MD–73, Texxon's real estate department acquired an older Hess-brand, gas-only station located approximately 1500 feet south of MD–73 on the same side of the highway. The Hess station (which did not offer automobile repair service) was in plain sight of MD–73. Kile knew of this acquisition but was unclear about Texxon's plans for the Hess property.

In the spring of 1993, Texxon razed the Hess property and constructed a new state-of-the-art gasoline express station. The new outlet is operated by another Texxon franchisee, in compliance with the Maryland divorcement law, and is in direct competition with MD–73.

Shortly after the new express facility opened, Kile's business at MD–73 began to deteriorate rapidly. Gasoline sales at MD–73 dropped from 2,405,890 gallons in 1992 to 1,564,330 gallons in 1993. Moreover,

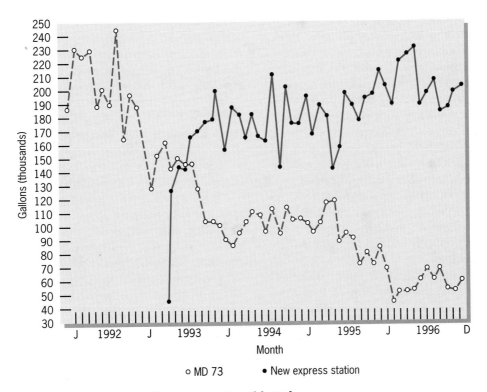

○ MD 73   ● New express station

EXHIBIT 1   Texxon Oil Company, Monthly Volume

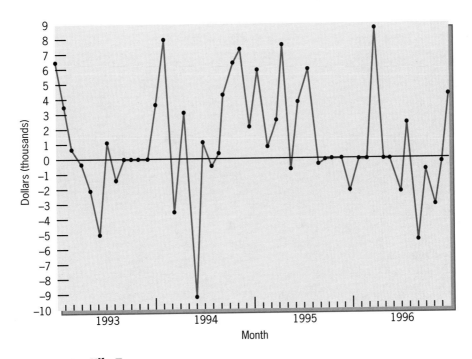

EXHIBIT 2   Kile Texxon

despite repeated requests from Kile, Texxon refused to upgrade MD–73 or to give Kile any additional retail marketing tools or subsidies to compete with the new express station. Rather, the opposite was the case. Between 1993 and 1996, Texxon raised the rent on MD–73 from $1,992 to $3,371 per month.

The new express station, which opened in April 1993, prospered during this same period. From 1,371,000 gallons in 1993, its gallonage grew to 2,415,000 in 1996 (Exhibit 1). Initially, Kile sought to meet the competition of the new express station by cutting his price, but when this measure failed to slow down the loss of gallonage, he raised his price and sought to offset the loss of volume with a higher margin. But this strategy also failed, and operating profits continued their nosedive.

As a result of his concern over the deteriorating business and Texxon's failure to provide him with assistance, Kile began to experience considerable emotional distress. Increasingly, he withdrew from day-to-day operations and left the management of the facility to his employees. Since this withdrawal led to a deterioration in the appearance and quality of service at the station, it soon became a bone of contention between Kile and the Texxon station rep. Kile was cited several times by the rep for sloppy operations.

Obviously, Texxon knew that the new facility would be in direct competition with MD–73. However, it was Texxon's stated position that it would be "up to the market" to determine which location would survive. Kile was to be on his own in this struggle.

Consulting Report

In the summer of 1995, Texxon commissioned a study of MPSI Americas, Inc., a well-regarded Tulsa retail consulting firm, to examine the implication of an upgrade of MD–73. The proposed tactic would be to add a canopy and a 600-square-foot mini-convenience store and to upgrade the pumps and other equipment. The MPSI computer model showed that this tactic would increase MD–73's gallonage by 29,000 gallons per month but would cut into the gallonage at the new Texxon express station by 2,500 gallons per month. The improvements would cost on the order of $160,000 to $175,000. Earlier, in November 1994, an MPSI study examining the consequences of closing MD–73 had estimated that Texxon would keep only 22,500 gallons of MD–73's then 137,664 monthly gallonage and would lose the rest to competitors up and down the street (Exhibit 3).

After three years of competition between the two stations, and after Kile's volume had fallen to an all-

EXHIBIT 3 **MPSI Study of the Impact of Closing MD–73**

Outlet Number	Brand Name	Tactic Results			
		Tactic Increase	Tactic Decrease	Base Volume	Total
1	Amoco	3401		220,958	224,359
2	Merit	2472		133,368	135,840
3	Texxon	3411		171,898	175,309
4	Mobil	7438		138,247	145,685
5	BP	6177		187,552	193,729
6	Gulf	3542		124,004	127,546
7	Exxon	3081		105,760	108,841
8	Texxon	3407		118,468	121,875
9	Texaco	2177		70,071	72,248
10	Shell	2721		48,604	51,325
11	Mobil	3210		49,171	52,381
12	Gulf	5279		63,459	68,738
13	MD–73		137,664	137,664	0
14	New Express Station	12209		158,596	170,805
15	Exxon	3997		48,146	52,143
16	Sunoco	4492		53,931	58,423
17	Crown	17415		226,585	244,000
18	Texxon	3502		42,223	45,725
19	Amoco	5598		94,949	100,547
20	Shell	2584		210,661	213,245
21	BP	2422		152,217	154,639

time low of 35,000 gallons in February 1996, Texxon made the decision to abandon MD–73 and not to renew the franchise relationship with Kile at the expiration of the current agreement ending in November 1996. Kile, however, was not advised of this abandonment decision at that time.

With full knowledge that the franchise relationship would not be renewed, and possibly with an intent to circumvent Kile's potential purchase rights under the Petroleum Marketing Practices Act (PMPA),[3] Texxon began to document a case that would justify the termination of Kile's franchise prior to abandonment. Whether or not it was Texxon's intention to circum-

---

[3] The act states that if a determination is made by the franchiser "in good faith and in the normal course of business ... to convert the leased premises to a use other than the sale or distribution of motor fuel ... or to sell the premises ... or to materially alter or replace the premises ... or if the renewal is likely to be uneconomical, the franchiser must first make a bona fide offer to sell, transfer or assign to the franchisee such franchiser's interests in such premises, or offer the franchisee the right of first refusal" 15 U.S.C. 2801, Section 102 D.

vent Kile's purchase rights under PMPA, the fact remains that it was clearly not in Texxon's interest to have the MD–73 site remain a gas station after taking down the Texxon sign. Accordingly, on July 30, 1996, Texxon advised Kile that his franchise relationship was terminated and would not be renewed at the expiration of his lease on November 11, 1996. The grounds for termination involved such alleged infractions as failure to remain open for the full number of hours specified in the agreement; failure by Kile to operate the premises in a clean, safe, and healthful manner; and finally, failure by Kile to exert good faith efforts to carry out the provisions of the franchise by virtue of his high-price, low-volume policy.

In October 1996 Kile contracted for the sale of the business at MD–73. As part of this proposed sale, Kile was to assign the lease agreement for MD–73 to the prospective purchaser. However, Texxon refused to consent to the proposed sale, transfer, and assignment on the ground that Kile had already been notified of Texxon's proposed termination. On January 15, 1997, Kile relinquished possession of MD–73, and the station has been boarded up ever since.

CASE 6-2   DAVE MacDONALD'S ETHICAL DILEMMAS

The following situations are real events experienced by the case writer. Only the names have been changed.

HALCO MANUFACTURING

Dave MacDonald was excited when he got the unexpected phone call from Nicki Steele, a senior buyer from Halco Manufacturing.

"I know it's a year since we bought that prototype reel from you, but we just got a contract from the government to build 10 more 'bear traps' and we desperately need to hold our price on these units. Could you possibly sell us 10 new reels at the same price you charged last year?" Nicki inquired.

"I'll see what I can do and call you back today," Dave replied.

Dave immediately retrieved the file from the previous year and saw that they had supplied the reel for $6,990.00 F.O.B. the customer's warehouse. There was a breakdown of the pricing on the file:

Manufacturer's list price	$4,000.00
Special engineering charge (25%)	1,000.00
Total list price	5,000.00
Distributor discount (20%)	1,000.00
Distributor net cost	4,000.00
Estimated currency exchange (8%)	320.00
Estimated duty (22½%)	972.00
Estimated freight	245.00
Estimated brokerage	55.00
Estimated distributor cost, F.O.B. destination	5,592.00
Markup (25%)	1,398.00
Selling price, F.O.B. destination	$6,990.00

There were some notes on the file that Dave reviewed. The reel was designed as part of a "bear trap" on Canadian navy ships. These bear traps would hook onto helicopters in rough weather and haul them safely onto landing pads on the ship decks. The reel was really a model SM heavy-duty steel mill reel, except that some of the exposed parts were to be made of stainless steel to provide longer life in the saltwater atmosphere. There was a special engineering charge on the reel, as it was a nonstandard item that had to be specially engineered. The manufacturer had suggested at the time they quoted that Dave could keep the full 20 percent discount, as they thought there was only one other manufacturer capable of building this unit, and their price would likely be much higher.

When Dave got a price from the manufacturer on the 10 new units, he was surprised that they quoted a price of only $3,200.00 each, less 40/10 percent. When he asked that the price be verified, the order desk clarified the pricing. First, there had been a 20 percent reduction in all SM series reels. That made the manufacturer's list price only $3,200.00. Then, because there was a large quantity, the distributor discount was increased to less 40/10 percent instead of the 20 percent that was given on the original reel.

As Dave estimated his cost, things got better. The original reel was imported from the United States at 22½ percent duty as "not otherwise provided for manufacturers of iron or steel, tariff item 44603-1." In the interim, the company Dave worked for had gotten a duty remission on series SM steel mill reels as "machinery of a class or kind not manufactured in Canada, tariff item 42700-1," and the duty was remitted (and the savings supposedly passed on to the end customer). The currency exchange rate also improved in Dave's favor, and the estimated freight and brokerage charges per unit dropped considerably because of the increased shipment size. Dave estimated his new cost as follows:

Manufacturer's list price	$3,200.00
Distributor discount (40/10%)	1,472.00
Distributor net cost	1,728.00
Estimated currency exchange (2%)	35.00
Estimated duty (remitted)	0.00
Estimated freight	85.00
Estimated brokerage	14.50
Estimated distributor cost, F.O.B. destination	1,862.50

This case was prepared by H. F. MacKenzie of Memorial University of Newfoundland, St. John's, Canada. The case was prepared as a basis for class discussion and is not intended to illustrate effective or ineffective handling of a management situation. All names in the case have been disguised. Copyright © 1994 by H. F. MacKenzie, Memorial University of Newfoundland, Faculty of Business Administration, St. John's, Newfoundland A1B 3X5. Reproduced by permission.

Now that he had all the figures, Dave had to decide what the selling price should be to his customer.

CROWN PULP AND PAPER LTD.

Bill Siddall had been promoted to the position of salesperson, and he was pleased when he received an order for nearly $10,000 for stainless steel fittings from the new pulp mill being built in his territory. Unfortunately, he quoted a price that was 40 percent below his cost.

"We have to honor the price quoted," Bill insisted.

"I know if you let me talk to Rory, he'll let us raise the price," replied Dave MacDonald, the Sales Manager. "Rory used to be the purchasing agent at one of my best accounts before he came to the mill."

"No. You gave me responsibility for this account, and I want to build a good relationship with Rory myself. He gave us the order over two weeks ago. He can't change suppliers now because he needs the material next week, and I don't want to put him on the spot now because it would be unfair. Since this is our first order, I would like to supply it without any problems. We'll get back the money we lost on this order many times if we can get their future business. This material is needed for a small construction job, and they haven't even started to consider their stores inventory yet."

After much discussion, it was agreed that the order would stand, but Dave would call the fitting manufacturer's Sales Manager, Chuck Knowles, as the two men were good friends.

"We need some help on that last order we placed with you. Bill sold it at 40 percent below our cost," said Dave.

"How could that happen?" Chuck seemed amazed.

"Well," replied Dave, "you give us a 25 percent distributor discount, and we gave 10 percent to the customer due to the size of the order. What we forgot was to double the list price because the customer wanted schedule 80 wall thickness on the fittings instead of standard schedule 40. This was Bill's first large inquiry, and he made an honest mistake. He doesn't want me to get involved with the customer, and I don't want to force the issue with him, so I'm hoping you can help us on this one order. We expect to get a lot of business from this account over the next few years."

"I'll split the difference with you. What you're selling now for $0.90, you're paying $1.50 for, and if I give you an additional 20 percent discount, your cost will come down to $1.20. Can you live with that?" Chuck asked.

"It's a help. We appreciate it. We'll see you on your next trip to our territory, and I'll buy lunch."

"A deal. See you next month." The conversation ended.

When it was over, Dave was feeling reasonably satisfied with himself, but he still felt somewhat uneasy. He promised not to call Rory, and he promised not to interfere with the account, but he still thought something could be done.

On Saturday morning, Dave went to the Brae Shore Golf Club. He was confident that Rory would be there. Sure enough, at 8:00 A.M., Rory was scheduled to tee off. Dave sat on the bench at the first tee and waited for Rory to appear. Promptly, Rory arrived with Bob Arnold, one of his senior buyers. The three men greeted each other pleasantly, and Rory asked who Dave was waiting for.

"Just one of my neighbors. He was supposed to be here an hour ago, but I guess he won't show."

"Join us. We don't mind. Besides, we might need a donation this fall when we have our company golf tournament. We'll invite you, of course, and we'll invite Bill if he plays golf."

"He doesn't play often, but he's pretty good. Beat me the last time we played. How is he doing at your mill? Is everything okay?" Dave asked.

"Checking up on him? Sure. He's fine. He made a mistake the other day when he went to see our millwright foreman without clearing it through my office first, but he'll learn. He'll do a lot of business with us because we want to buy locally where possible, and you have a lot of good product lines. I think he'll get along well with all of us as well. He seems a bit serious, but we'll break him in before long. We just gave him a big order for stainless fittings a few weeks ago, but we told him to visit at ten o'clock next time and to bring the doughnuts."

"I know," replied Dave. "Unfortunately, we lost a lot of money on that order."

"Your price was very low. I couldn't understand it because I knew your material wasn't manufactured offshore. Did you quote the cheaper T304 grade of stainless instead of the T316 we use?"

"No. We quoted schedule 40 prices instead of schedule 80. The wall thickness for schedule 80 is twice as thick, and the price should have been double as well."

"Heck. Double the price. We'll pay it. I'll make a note on the file Monday. I know you're not trying to take us, and I can appreciate an honest mistake. At double the price, you might be a bit high, but you know we want to place the order with you anyway because you're local. Eventually we'll want you to carry some inventory for us, so we might just as well make sure we're both happy with this business."

STRAIT STRUCTURAL STEEL LTD.

Dave MacDonald was sitting in the outer office waiting to see Stan Hope, the purchasing agent for Strait Structural Steel, a new account that had just begun operations in a remote coastal location about 40 miles from the nearest city. Stan had telephoned Dave the previous week and had an urgent request for four large exhaust fans that were required to exhaust welding fumes from enclosed spaces where welders were at work. The union had threatened to stop the project unless working conditions were improved quickly, and although Dave didn't sell fans at the time, he found a line of fans and negotiated a discount from the manufacture, along with an agreement to discuss the further possibility of representing the fan manufacturer on a national basis.

When Stan gave the order to Dave for the fans, the two men discussed other products that Dave sold. Dave sold products for a company that was both a general-line and specialty-line industrial distributor. Included in the general-line products were such items as hand and power tools, cutting tools (drills, taps, dies), safety equipment, wire rope and slings, fasteners (nuts, bolts), and fittings (stainless steel, bronze, and carbon steel flanges, elbows, tees). Included in the specialty-line products were such items as electric motors and generators, motor controls, hydraulic and pneumatic valves and cylinders, rubber dock fenders, and overhead cranes. When the men finally met, they were almost instantly friends, and it was obvious that the opportunities for them to do further business were great. "One item that really interests me," said Stan, "is PTFE tape. We need some, and we will be using a lot of it."

"We have the largest stock of PTFE tape in the country," replied Dave. "We import it directly from Italy, but it's high quality and is the same standard size as all others on the market; $1/2$ inch wide, .003 inch thick, and 480 inches long. How much are you interested in?"

"Let's start with 400 rolls," Stan suggested.

PTFE tape was a white, nonadhesive tape that was used as a pipe thread sealant. It was wrapped around the threads of pipe or fittings before they were screwed together to make a leakproof seal. The tape first came on the market in the late 1960s at prices as high as $3.60 per roll, but since then prices had dropped con-

siderably. North American manufacturers were still selling the tape for list prices near $1.80 and were offering dealer discounts of between 25 and 50 percent, depending on the quantities that dealers bought. Dave was importing the tape from Italy at a landed cost of $0.17 per roll.

"We have a standard price of $1.00 per roll as long as you buy 200 rolls," Dave offered.

"No question. You have an excellent price. How much would you charge M H Sales?"

"I don't know. Who is M H Sales?" asked Dave.

"A small industrial supply company located in my basement. The 'H' is for Hope. I share the company with Bruce Malcolm, the 'M,' and he's in purchasing at Central Power Corporation. M H Sales is a small company, and we are looking for additional products to sell. Between Strait Structural and Central Power, we could sell several thousand rolls of PTFE tape each year."

McCORMICK GLEASON LIMITED

Dave MacDonald telephoned Clarey Stanley, a Senior Buyer at McCormick Gleason Limited. "Clarey, I'm calling about that quote we made on Lufkin tapes. Can we have your order?"

"Sorry. Your price was high. I gave the order to Ken Stafford. You need a sharper pencil."

"How much sharper?" Dave asked.

"I can't tell you that. But you were close," Clarey replied. "By the way, Kenny called me from the stores department this morning, and he has a large shipment of electric relays that was delivered yesterday. They weren't properly marked, and he can't identify the ones with normally open contacts from the ones with normally closed contacts. Do you want them returned, or can someone see him and straighten it out here?"

"Tell him I'll see him immediately after lunch. I can tell them apart, and I'll see they get properly identified."

When the conversation ended, Dave made a note to see Clarey about the tapes. There was a problem somewhere. Dave knew his cost on Lufkin tapes was the lowest available, and he quoted 12 percent on cost because he really wanted the order. The order was less than $1,500, but it meant that Dave could place a multiple-case order on the manufacture and get the lowest possible cost for all replacement inventory. That would increase the margin on sales to other customers who bought smaller quantities. There was no possibility that Stafford Industrial, a local, one-person, "out-of-the-

basement" operation that bought Lufkin tapes as a jobber, not as a distributor, could match his price.

That afternoon, while waiting to see Ken MacKay,
the Stores Manager, Dave noticed a carton from
Stafford Industrial Sales being unloaded from a local
delivery van. Although he knew that Stafford supplied
quite a few maintenance, repair, and operating (MRO)
supplies to this customer, Dave decided to play igno-
rant.

"What do you buy from Stafford Industrial?" he
asked the young stores clerk who was handling the
package.

Opening the carton, the clerk read the packing slip.
"It says here we ordered 144 measuring tapes, $3/4$
inches wide by 25 feet long."

"Are those things expensive?" Dave asked.

"Don't know. There's no price on the packing slip.
Clarey Stanley in purchasing ordered them. You could
talk to him." The clerk continued to unpack the shipment. As he did, Dave noticed that the tapes were
manufactured offshore and were poor in quality compared to the Lufkin tapes that he sold and that he
quoted to Clarey Stanley the previous day.

"Aren't those supposed to be Lufkin tapes?" Dave
asked.

"Not that I know. The packing slip just says tapes.
Wait, and I'll haul our copy of the purchase order."
The clerk went to a filing cabinet next to his desk and
returned with a carbon copy of the purchase order.
"No, it just says tapes. It doesn't specify any brand."

There was something wrong, and Dave was determined to get an answer.

ESTIMATING POTENTIALS AND FORECASTING SALES

> The pace of events is moving so fast that unless we can find some way to keep our sights on tomorrow, we cannot expect to be in touch with today.
>
> DEAN RUSK

Chapter Consultant:
Beth Forbes, Director of International Results & Analysis, GTE International

LEARNING OBJECTIVES

After studying this chapter, you should be able to:

→ Estimate market potentials.

→ Understand judgmental forecasting.

→ Calculate naive, moving average, and exponential smoothing forecasts.

WHY FORECAST?

One of the keys to sales management success is knowing where customers are located and being able to predict how much they will buy. Firms have found that potentials data are indispensable in setting up territories, assigning quotas, and comparing sales performance of individual salespeople. Sales forecasting is so important that more than 50 percent of firms include this topic in their sales manager training programs.[1]

Inaccurate demand predictions can have disastrous effects on profitability. For example, a few years ago Hewlett-Packard was unable to predict the proper mix of products demanded by its customers for two quarters in a row. Demand for low end printers and workstations was high and demand for commercial computers was low. As a result, earnings were 14 percent less than analysts expected. The stock market was dismayed with Hewlett-Packard's forecasting problems and knocked the company's stock down 5 percent in one day.[2] This example demonstrates the importance of being able to measure the size of market opportunities. In this chapter, we will show you how to measure demand for today and how to forecast sales for tomorrow.

WHAT IS MARKET POTENTIAL?

Market potential is an estimate of maximum demand in a time period based on the number of potential users and the purchase rate. Actual industry sales are usually less than market potential, as shown in Figure 7-1. For instance, the U.S. market potential for digital video disc players could be defined as the total number of households with television sets based on

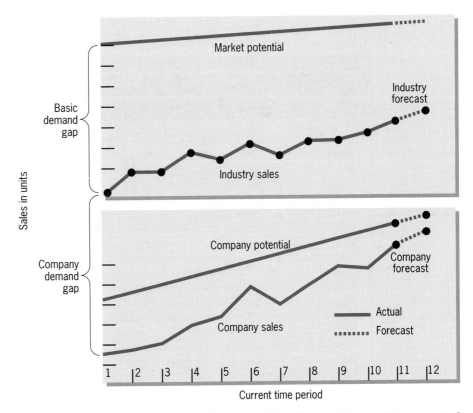

FIGURE 7-1   **Relations Among Market Potential, Industry Sales, and Company Sales**

typical purchases of one unit per family. Actual sales are less than potential because it takes time to convince people to buy expensive items such as digital video disc players, and because some can't afford them. The industry purchase rate is a function of price levels, promotional expenditures, and the number of stores stocking the machines.

Company *sales potential* is a portion of total industry demand. It is the maximum amount a firm can sell in a time period under optimum conditions. As Figure 7-1 suggests, company sales will generally be lower than industry sales. The ratio of company sales to industry sales is a measure of the market share of the organization.

An example showing how Duracell converts industry demand for batteries into sales forecasts is described in the Strategic Action Competency box.

In your position as sales manager, you will be asked to estimate current values for market and company potential for products assigned to your care. This can be tricky because the number of users and the purchase rate change over time. Also, price declines, industry promotions, and changing economic conditions can influence the size of the market. Besides measuring current levels of demand, you will be required to forecast into the future. These predictions are shown as the dashed lines for period 12 in Figure 7-1. Our discussion begins with demand measurement and shifts to the issue of forecasting later in the chapter.

Estimating Potentials

All estimates of potential are based on two key components—namely, the number of possible users of the product and the maximum expected purchase rate. Sometimes you can get estimates of these numbers from trade associations or commercial research associations, but you have to come up with your own potential figures broken down by geographical area, industry, and customer type.

STRATEGIC ACTION COMPETENCY
Forecasting at Duracell

Duracell, a division of Gillette, is the world's leading alkaline battery manufacturer. Every month, five standard alkaline battery sizes are built into thousands of stock-keeping units that are shipped to customers. Forecasting's mission at Duracell is to provide management with forecasts to help prepare strategies and set goals. The basic formula at Duracell is that Shipments = Retail Market × Market Share +/– Changes in Retail Inventories. Thus forecasts are a function of the size of the market times anticipated market share with an adjustment for inventory changes. The company currently uses six different statistical models to determine market size. Marketing executives estimate market shares based on plans for advertising, product enhancements, distribution strategies, and pricing. Changes in retail inventories are the most difficult to estimate. Duracell uses five forecasting cycles: competitive view, strategic business plan, tactical plan, latest estimate (monthly), and supply chain management (weekly). To ensure coordination of resources, marketing, finance, and production planning activities all use the same forecasts. Their forecasting toolbox includes judgmental, time series, and causal model approaches. No single procedure meets all forecasting needs and Duracell selects methods that best suit the situation. This often means using simple naive methods for tactical forecasts of less than one year. They also use linear regression, optimized exponential smoothing, moving averages, and causal models for long-term situations. Causal models are sometimes based on nonlinear multiple regressions. Duracell often selects forecasting methods on the basis of those that tests show to be the most accurate with company data.

The easiest way to estimate the number of buyers is to use secondary sources. A wide variety of commercial data are available that provide the potential number of buyers, size of firms, age of consumers, income levels, and locations. Dun's Marketing Services and *Sales & Marketing Management* magazine sell these data on diskettes for use with personal computers. You can also access potential data banks through computer networks on a fee basis. Large firms often have their own data banks that can be mined for potential information.

Purchase rates are usually derived from trade organizations or government publications. For existing products, you can use the ratio of current sales to the number of households or sales per person. These ratios can be obtained from trade publications such as those from the Conference Board, or calculated from published data. For example, average demand per household could be derived by dividing total industry sales for an area by the number of households. In the case of new products, managers may estimate conversion rates from experience with other items. If a similar product was sold to 4 percent of U.S. households during the first year, this rate could be applied to obtain demand estimates for new merchandise.

Buying Power Index Method

Market potentials for consumer goods are usually estimated by constructing indexes from basic economic data. Perhaps the most popular multifactor index of area demand is the Buying Power Index (BPI) published each August by *Sales & Marketing Management* magazine. This index combines estimates of population, income, and retail sales to give a composite indicator of consumer demand in specific states, metropolitan areas, counties, and cities in the United States.

Data used to calculate the Buying Power Index for the Atlanta, Georgia, area are summarized in Table 7-1. The figures show that Atlanta Metro area has 1.524 percent of the U.S. income, 1.532 percent of retail sales, and 1.391 percent of the U.S. population. These three numbers are weighted to give a Buying Power Index for Atlanta Metro of 1.498.

Thus, an area with only 1.391 percent of the U.S. population has 1.524 percent of the national income and 1.532 percent of retail sales. This suggests that income for the Atlanta Metro area is above average. When retail sales for an area are greater than the income and population, as in this example, there is strong evidence that people are driving in from surrounding counties. This suggests that managers must spread their promotional dollars over a fairly wide area if they expect to reach all the customers who shop in the Atlanta area.

Buying Power Index values are used to help managers allocate selling efforts across geographic regions. That is, the Buying Power Index suggests that Atlanta Metro, with 1.498 percent of the U.S. sales potential, should receive about 1.498 percent of the personal selling and advertising budgets for products in national distribution.

TABLE 7-1 Data Used to Calculate Buying Power Index

	1999 Effective Buying Income		1999 Total Retail Sales		1999 Estimated Total Population		Buying Power Index
	Amount ($000,000)	Percentage of United States	Amount ($000,000)	Percentage of United States	Amount (000,000)	Percentage of United States	
Total United States	$4,621,491	100.0%	$2,852,429	100.0%	273,537	100.0%	100.0
Atlanta Metro	70,465	1.524%	43,703	1.532%	3,807	1.391%	1.498

NAICS Method for Business Markets

Business market potential can be built up from data made available through the U.S. *Census of Manufacturers*. The Census of Manufacturers is available every five years, and combines businesses into North American Industry Classification System (NAICS) codes according to products produced or operations performed.

The first step in estimating potentials from census data is to identify all the NAICS codes that make use of the product or service. This is usually accomplished by selecting industries that are likely customers, using judgment to pick codes from the NAICS manual, and running surveys of different types of firms to see where products are employed. Next, the firm must select an appropriate database for estimating the amount of the product that will be used by each NAICS code. A food machinery manufacturer, for example, could review past sales data to determine the relationship between the number of its machines in use and the number of production workers in a particular industry. If the manufacturer found that 8 machines were used for every 1,000 grain milling employees, 10 for every 1,000 bakery workers, and 2 for every 1,000 beverage workers, then the market potential for North Carolina could be determined as shown in Table 7-2. The 1992 Census of Manufacturers showed that North Carolina actually had 2,300 grain milling workers. If 8 machines were used per 1,000 workers, the market potential would be 2.3 × 8, or 18.4 machines. Similar calculations for other codes yield a total market potential of about 141 machines for the state of North Carolina. The potential built up for North Carolina would then be added to estimates derived for other states to give national figures. These figures can be converted into annual measures of market potential by adjusting for the average life of the machines. If the machines last an average of 10 years, then 10 percent of the North Carolina potential of 141 units, or 14 machines, would be replaced each year. Estimates of company potential would be derived by multiplying annual demand potential by the firm's current market share.

QUALITATIVE SALES FORECASTING

Sales forecasting is concerned with predicting future levels of demand. These projections are vital for budgeting and planning purposes. For new products, a few simple routines can be employed. The absence of past sales means that you have to be more creative in coming up with predictions of the future. Sales forecasts for new products are often based on executive judgments, sales force projections, surveys, and market tests. We will begin our discus-

TABLE 7-2   Estimating the Market Potential for Food Machinery in North Carolina

Code	Industry	(1) Production Employees (1000)[b]	(2) Number of Machines Used per 1000 Workers[a]	Market Potential (1 × 2)
204	Grain milling	2.3	8	18.4
205	Bakery products	11.9	10	119.0
208	Beverages	1.9	2	3.8
				141.2

[a] Estimated by the manufacturer from past sales data.
[b] The production employee data are from the 1992 Census of Manufacturers, Geographical Area Series, North Carolina, p. NC 11. The codes are the old SIC codes that were used in the 1992 Census of Manufacturers. More recent data from the 1997 Census of Manufacturers using the new NAICs codes will be available sometime in the spring of 2000.

sion of forecasting techniques by focusing on subjective methods that are based on interpretations of business conditions by executives and salespeople.

Sales Force Composite

A favorite forecasting technique for new and existing products is the *sales force composite* method. With this procedure, salespeople project volume for customers in their own territory, and the estimates are aggregated and reviewed at higher management levels. Sales force composite forecasting is the most popular method and is used by 45 percent of the firms in a U.S. survey (Table 7-3). This technique is favored by industrial concerns because they have a limited number of customers and salespeople are in a good position to assess customers' needs. This technique was adopted by a medical products subsidiary of American Home Products.[3] Previously the sales forecast came down from headquarters and now the forecast is built up from estimates prepared by 120 field reps. When salespeople provide input they buy into the forecast and are more likely to achieve their sales quotas. The net result at the medical products firm has been improved sales forecast accuracy.

Jury of Executive Opinion

This technique involves soliciting the judgment of a group of experienced managers to give sales estimates for proposed and current products. The *jury of executive opinion* was used by 37 percent of the firms described in Table 7-3. The main advantages of this method are that it is fast and it allows the inclusion of many subjective factors such as competition, economic climate, weather, and union activity. United Parcel Service forecasts are prepared by a group of senior executives using economic indicators such as the Consumer Price Index, historical sales data, and other trends. These forecasts are then compared with predictions developed by salespeople and the differences are reconciled.

The continued popularity of jury of executive opinion shows that most managers prefer their own judgment to other less well-known mechanical forecasting procedures. However, available evidence does not suggest that the jury of executive opinion method leads to more accurate forecasting. Perhaps the main problem with the method is that it is based on experience, and it is difficult to teach someone how to forecast using this method.

TABLE 7-3 **Utilization of Sales Forecasting Methods by 134 Firms**

Type	Method	Percentage of Firms that Use Regularly	Percentage of Firms No Longer Used
Subjective	Sales force composite	44.8	13.4
	Jury of executive opinion	37.3	8.2
	Intention to buy survey	16.4	18.7
	Industry survey	14.9	17.9
Extrapolation	Naive	30.6	9.0
	Moving average	20.9	15.7
	Percent rate of change	19.4	14.2
	Leading indicators	18.7	11.2
	Unit rate of change	15.7	18.7
	Exponential smoothing	11.2	19.4
	Line extension	6.0	20.9
Quantitative	Multiple regression	12.7	20.9
	Econometric models	11.9	19.4
	Simple regression	6.0	20.1
	Box-Jenkins	3.7	26.9

Leading Indicators

Where sales are influenced by basic changes in the economy, *leading indicators* can be a useful guide in the preparation of sales forecasts. For example, 19 percent of the firms in Table 7-3 regularly use leading indicators in sales forecasting. The idea is to find a general time series that is closely related to company sales, yet is available several months in advance. Changes in the series can then be used to predict sales directly, or the series can be combined with other variables in a forecasting model. For example, General Electric has found that sales of dishwashers are closely related to the number of housing starts that occur several months earlier. Thus if GE observed a 4 percent increase in housing starts in California, they could expect demand for dishwashers to increase by about 4 percent two months later. Obviously, the key issue is finding indicators that have forecasting value for particular products. Some of the more useful leading indicators include prices of 500 common stocks, new orders for durable goods, new building permits, contracts and orders for plant and equipment, and changes in consumer installment debt.

Perhaps the greatest contribution of leading indicators is their ability to predict turns in a series. Most of the mechanical forecasting techniques that we will discuss do a very poor job of telling managers when a series is going to change direction. Leading indicators are sensitive to changes in the business environment, and they often signal turns in the economy months before they actually occur.

When Should Qualitative Forecasting Methods Be Used?

Qualitative methods are often used when you have little numerical data to incorporate into your forecasts. New products are a classic example of limited information, and qualitative methods are frequently employed to predict sales revenues for these items. Qualitative methods are also recommended for those situations where managers or the sales force are particularly adept at predicting sales revenues. In addition, qualitative forecasting methods are often utilized when markets have been disrupted by strikes, wars, natural disasters, recessions, or inflation. Under these conditions, historical data are useless and judgmental procedures that account for the factors causing market shocks are usually more accurate. Managers should calculate and record the forecasting errors produced by the qualitative techniques they employ so they know when these methods are best employed.

QUANTITATIVE SALES FORECASTING

We now shift our focus from qualitative based methods to quantitative techniques. These procedures are based on manipulations of historical data. Quantitative methods are more number oriented than those that use the qualitative approach.

Seasonal Adjustments

Before we discuss data-based forecasting techniques, it's important to understand how seasonal factors influence predictions of the future. Sales forecasts are often prepared monthly or quarterly, and seasonal factors are frequently responsible for many of the short-run changes in volume. Thus, what may appear to be a good forecast may turn out to be a poor one because of the failure to consider seasonal factors. When historical sales figures are used in forecasting, the accuracy of predictions can often be improved by making adjustments to eliminate seasonal effects.

The first step in seasonally adjusting a time series is to collect sales figures for the past several years. Next, sales for months or quarters are averaged across years to build a seasonal index. In Table 7-4 four years of quarterly sales are averaged to give a rough indica-

TABLE 7-4   Calculating a Seasonal Index from Historical Sales Data

Quarter	Year				Four-Year Quarterly Average	Seasonal Index
	1	2	3	4		
1	49	57	53	73	58.0	0.73[a]
2	77	98	85	100	90.0	1.13
3	90	89	92	98	92.3	1.16
4	79	62	88	78	76.8	0.97

Four-year sales of 1268/16 = 79.25 average quarterly sales

[a] Seasonal index is 58.0/79.25 = 0.73.

tion of seasonal effects.[4] The quarterly averages are then divided by mean sales for all quarters to give seasonal index numbers. For example, when average sales of 58.0 for quarter 1 are divided by the mean for all quarters of 79.25, a seasonal index of 0.73 is obtained. This number indicates that seasonal factors typically lower first-quarter sales by 27 percent. Computer programs used in sales forecasting take these indexes and make forecasts for future periods. For example, the Technical Competency box describes how Nabisco calculated seasonal indexes for use in forecasting the sales of new cookie and cracker products. In this case, Nabisco found that seasonal indexes based on Nabisco weekly shipment data reduced forecasting errors by up to 21 percent compared with forecasts made with indexes based on national store scanner data.

Some students assume that because seasonal adjustments complicate the forecasting process, they are not worth the time and effort required. However, there are two truths about seasonal adjustments that you should remember:

1. Seasonal adjustments are widely used in business.
2. Seasonal adjustments reduce forecasting errors.

Technology Competency
Computer Forecasting at Nabisco

Nabisco Biscuit Company uses computer programs to forecast sales of new cracker and cookie brands soon after they have been introduced. Because new products have no sales history, Nabisco's program uses an exponential smoothing approach that can start forecasting with only two periods of data. The first six weeks of sales figures are discarded in the Nabisco model because these shipments are used to build store and warehouse inventories. Then the program de-seasonalizes the sales figures using weekly seasonal factors from a similar product, brand, or category. Nabisco initially used seasonal indexes based on retail store scanner data supplied by the independent marketing research firm IRI. However, these indexes did not significantly reduce forecasting errors, so Nabisco decided to calculate the indexes from Nabisco weekly shipment data. These indexes led to a 14 percent reduction in forecasting errors for four-week projections for cookies and 21 percent reductions in errors for crackers. The Nabisco forecasting program also includes adjustments for trend and sales promotions. Nabisco's new computer forecasting program led to 34 percent overall reductions in errors in national weekly projections and a 53 percent reduction in errors in four-week projections compared to their old method. Nabisco's program has been employed successfully for several years and has been adapted for use with existing products that have been hurt by new items or have been affected by mergers or acquisitions.

Naive Forecasts

Time series forecasts rely on past data to provide a basis for making projections about the future. The *naive forecast* is the simplest numerical forecasting technique and is often used as a standard for comparison with other procedures. Thirty percent of the firms in Table 7-3 use naive forecasts on a regular basis. This method assumes that nothing is going to change and that the best estimate for the future is the current level of sales. For example, actual sales of 49 units observed in quarter 1 in Table 7-4 can be used to predict sales in quarter 2. Naive forecasts for the last three quarters of year 1 would be

	Quarter			
	1	*2*	*3*	*4*
Actual sales	49	77	90	79
Naive forecast		49	77	90

The error in the naive forecast for quarter 2 is the difference between 49 and 77. A formula for the *percentage forecasting error* is

$$Percentage\ forecasting\ error = \frac{forecast - actual}{actual}$$

This means the percentage error for the naive forecast in quarter 2 is

$$Percentage\ error = \frac{49 - 77}{77}$$

$$Percentage\ error = 36\%$$

If the data were seasonally adjusted, the forecasting error for quarter 2 would be only 1.3 percent. This example shows that seasonal adjustments can lower forecasting errors for simple naive forecasts.

MAPE

When you want to compare forecasting accuracy across several time periods, the *mean absolute percentage error* (MAPE) is the method used by most forecasting professionals.[5] The formula for calculating MAPE is:

$$MAPE = \frac{\sum_{i=1}^{n} (forecast - actual) / actual}{n} \times 100\%$$

where *n* is the number of forecasts to be made. MAPE calculates the percentage forecasting error for each period without regard to whether the errors are positive or negative, adds up the errors and divides by the number of periods being forecast. The main advantage of MAPE is that it allows easy comparison of forecasting errors across product categories and companies.

Trend Projections

The use of *trends* to project sales is a popular technique among business firms. With this method, the analyst estimates trends from past data and adds this figure to current sales to obtain a forecast. For example, in Figure 7-2 sales increased from 10 units in period 2 to 20

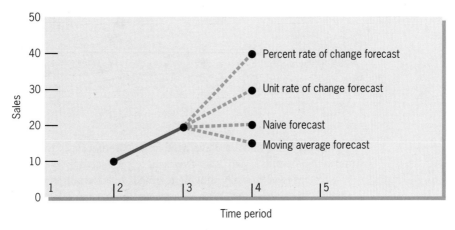

FIGURE 7-2 **Comparing Trend Forecasting Methods**

units in period 3, suggesting a trend of 10 units per period. A *unit rate of change* forecast for period 4 would combine current sales of 20 plus 10 units of trend for a total of 30. Trends can also be expressed as a *percentage rate of change*. With this method the 10 units of trend would be divided by the base of 10 units of sales to give a 100 percent growth rate. A 100 percent growth rate applied to current sales of 20 units would give a forecast of 40 units for period 4. Note that the percentage rate of change method and the unit rate of change procedure give different sales forecasts. When sales are increasing, forecasts prepared with the percentage rate of change approach will normally be higher than those obtained by other projective techniques. Research reported in Table 7-3 shows that the percentage rate of change method is the most popular projective forecasting technique, followed by the unit rate of change. Trend projections are often combined with exponential smoothing and moving average forecasts to help improve forecasting accuracy.

Moving Averages

With the *moving average* method, the average revenue achieved in several recent periods is used as a prediction of sales in the next period. The formula takes the form

$$F_{t+1} = \frac{S_t + S_{t-1} + \ldots + S_{t-n+1}}{n}$$

where

F_{t+1} = forecast for the next period

S_t = sales in the current period

n = number of periods in the moving average

This approach assumes that the future will be an average of past achievements. For example, if sales in the last two periods went from 10 to 20, then a two-period moving average forecast would be 15 (Figure 7-2). Thus, when there is a strong trend in a time series, a moving average forecast without a trend adjustment lags behind. However, this lag can be an advantage when sales change direction (suddenly increase or decrease). If actual sales decline to 17 units in period 4, as shown in Figure 7-2, then the moving average forecast will be more accurate than the trend projection methods.

Students must remember that a moving average really does move. For example, sales data from Table 7-4 can be used to make two-period moving average forecasts as follows:

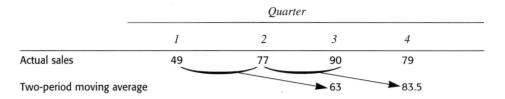

	Quarter			
	1	*2*	*3*	*4*
Actual sales	49	77	90	79
Two-period moving average			63	83.5

Thus periods 1 and 2 are averaged to give a forecast of 63 for period 3. Then period 1 is dropped and periods 2 and 3 are averaged to produce a forecast of 83.5 for period 4.

A crucial issue in using moving averages is determining the ideal number of periods *(n)* to include in the average. With a large number of periods, forecasts tend to react slowly, whereas a low value of *n* leads to predictions that respond more quickly to changes in a series. The optimum number of periods can be estimated by trial and error or with computer programs.

A characteristic of moving averages that distracts from their ability to follow trends is that all time periods are weighted equally. This means that information from the oldest and newest periods is treated the same way in making up a forecast. A popular technique that overcomes this problem is exponential smoothing.

Exponential Smoothing

An important feature of *exponential smoothing* is its ability to emphasize recent information and systematically discount old information. A simple exponentially smoothed forecast can be derived using the formula:

$$\overline{S}_t = \alpha S_t + (1 - \alpha)\overline{S}_{t-1}$$

where

$\overline{S}_t$ = smoothed sales for period t and the forecast for period $t + 1$

α = the smoothing constant

S_t = actual sales in period t

$\overline{S}_{t-1}$ = smoothed forecast for period $t-1$

The formula combines a portion (α) of current sales with a discounted value of the smoothed average calculated for the previous period to give a forecast for the next period.

An example using data from Table 7-4 is shown below with a smoothing constant of .4.

	Quarter			
	1	*2*	*3*	*4*
Actual sales	49	77	90	79
Smoothed forecast			60.2	72.1

The forecast for period 3 is obtained by multiplying .4 times the current sales in period 2 of 77 plus .6 times 49, which is the estimate of smoothed sales for the prior period [(.4 × 77) + (.6 × 49) = 60.2]. A forecast for period 4 would be obtained by multiplying .4 times the period 3 sales of 90 plus .6 times the smoothed forecast for period 3 [(.4 × 90) + (.6 × 60.2) = 72.1].

The major decision with exponential forecasting is selecting an appropriate value for the *smoothing constant* (α). Smoothing factors can range in value from 0 to 1, with low values providing stability and high values allowing a more rapid response to sales changes. Using a smoothing constant of 1.0 gives the same forecasts that are obtained with the naive method.

Forecasts produced with a low smoothing constant, such as 0.2, lag behind, and forecasts generated with high values, such as 0.8, will likely overestimate sales at turning points. When historical data are available, analysts should search for the optimum smoothing constant by trying out different α values to see which one forecasts best. In the case of two consumer products, a smoothing constant of 0.2 produced the lowest MAPE values.[6] Regression techniques have advantages in situations in which managers wish to incorporate other variables in their forecasting program.

Linear Regression

In *simple linear regression,* the relationship between sales *(Y)* and some independent variable *(X)* can be represented by a straight line. The equation of this line is *Y = a + bX,* where a is the intercept and *b* shows the impact of the independent variable. The key step in deriving linear regression equations is finding values for the coefficients *(a, b)* that give the line that best fits the data. The best fit can be obtained by employing a *least squares* procedure (as illustrated in Figure 7-3), where sales *(Y)* have been plotted against time *(X).* The equation *Y = 63.9 + 3.5X* indicates that sales are 63.9 plus a trend of 3.5 for every unit of time. Two variable regression equations can be easily calculated using some pocket calculators or desk and laptop computers using Excel or other programs.

A limitation of simple regression forecasting is the assumption that sales follow a linear pattern. Although this may hold for some series, others have cyclical patterns that are hard to track with linear equations. In this case, the analyst can base the forecasting equation on the logarithms of the time series data to produce improved forecasting equations.

Another problem is knowing how much past data to include in the calculation of the forecast. Usually all past data points are used to provide greater stability. Sometimes shorter regressions will do a better job of tracking changes. The Global Perspective Competency box explains how Procter & Gamble forecasts detergent sales in Italy using three years of historical data.

The simple regression equations that have been described use time as the independent variable, which is common in sales forecasting. With time as the independent variable, a regression approach becomes a trend forecast. Other variables such as income or the rate at which products are sold for junk, could be used if they are found to be closely related to sales. When sales seem to be associated with several independent variables, multiple regression procedures can be used to build a forecasting model.

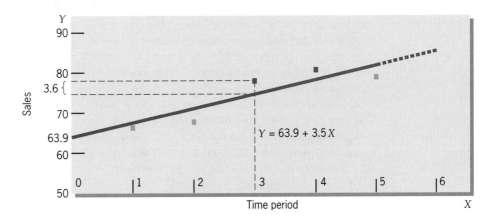

FIGURE 7-3 Fitting a Trend Regression to Seasonally Adjusted Sales Data

GLOBAL PERSPECTIVE COMPETENCY
Forecasting at P&G in Italy

Procter & Gamble's Italian division produces powdered and liquid detergents with a staff of 400 employees. Their annual sales volume is about $385 million per year. They regularly prepare sales forecasts for two powdered detergents and one liquid detergent for use with washing machines. In addition, P&G prepares sales forecasts for one powdered and one liquid detergent used to hand wash cloths. For established products, P&G Italy looks at the history of a product, adjusts for advertising effects, and employs a computer program to prepare sales forecasts. Normally, they use three years of historical data to prepare these forecasts. Forecasts for new products are based on estimates of expected market shares. Sales forecasts at P&G Italy are medium to long term, and their most detailed forecasts are for three years. P&G Italy has difficulty in forecasting liquid detergents because they are new and they do not have an established sales history. Forecasting errors at P&G Italy are usually a few percentage points and the company is fully satisfied with their sales forecasting efforts. Assignments in the sales forecasting area at P&G Italy help sales and marketing people climb the corporate promotion ladder.

Multiple Regression

With *multiple regression*, a computer is used to build forecasting models based on historical relationships between sales and several independent variables. Sales managers first have to find an appropriate set of independent factors that are related to the series being predicted. Some of the best variables for multiple regression equations are leading indicators such as housing starts, new orders for durable goods, and contracts for plant and capital equipment. These variables have the advantage that current values can be plugged into multiple regression equations to predict the future. However, if your regression model is based on income, interest rates or population figures, then you have to predict these factors for future time periods before loading them into the forecasting equation.

The decision whether to use a simple or multiple regression forecasting model often depends on the values of three statistics that are calculated by your computer forecasting program. For example, if the R^2 value was .70, your equation explained 70 percent of the variation observed in your data. Forecasting equations with high R^2 are generally preferable to equations that explain only 5 to 10 percent of the variation. The standard error of the estimate tells you the range within which you can expect to find the true value of the variable you are predicting. Also the errors in the coefficients for the variables in your equation should be smaller than the coefficients. If the errors are larger than the coefficients, then there is good reason to drop that variable from your forecasting equation. With regression forecasting, you need five observations for every independent variable in your equation. Thus an equation with 1 predictor variable would need 5 observations and an equation with 3 variables would need 15 observations. If your data set does not meet these requirements, then another forecasting method should be selected.

Despite the complexities of multiple regression forecasting, this technique was the most popular of the quantitative methods reported in Table 7-3 and was used regularly by 13 percent of the firms. A real data set that you can use to build a multiple regression forecasting equation is included with problem 6 (Table 7-6) later in this chapter.

TABLE 7-5 Commercial Forecasting Programs

Vendor	Package	Description	Price
Applied Decision Systems	SIBYL	18 distinct time series forecasting techniques.	$495
Delphus, Inc.	The Spreadsheet Forecaster	Curve fitting, seasonal decomposition, exponential smoothing, regression for monthly and quarterly data.	$79
Delphus, Inc.	Autocast II	Built-in expert forecasting system tests seasonality, outliers, trends, patterns, and automatically selects best forecasting model from nine alternatives.	$349
SmartSoftware, Inc.	SmartForecasts II	Expert system graphics and data analysis; projects sales, demand, costs, revenues; time series analysis, multivariate regression.	$495

Turning Points

The numerical forecasting methods we have discussed make projections from historical data, and most of them do a poor job of predicting turning points in a time series. Percentage rate of change, unit rate of change, and two-variable regression are all notoriously poor predictors of series that change direction. Naive, moving average, and exponential smoothing are somewhat better, because they tend to lag and then adapt to new information. If the identification of turning points is important to you, then the use of qualitative procedures is often the best approach. These methods can pick up environmental cues that signal turning points frequently missed by numerical methods. Sometimes leading indicators can be included in multiple regression equations to help predict turning points.

When Should Quantitative Forecasting Methods Be Used?

Quantitative forecasting techniques are best employed in situations where you have access to historical numerical data. Also it is helpful if the time series you are trying to forecast are stable and do not often change direction. Quantitative methods have distinct advantages in situations where you must make frequent forecasts for hundreds or thousands of products. Because of the large number of calculations required by quantitative forecasting procedures, analysts need access to computers and appropriate forecasting software. The successful use of quantitative forecasting methods demands that analysts be well versed in the statistical procedures used by these techniques. In addition, quantitative techniques are most useful in firms where management understands and endorses their application to sales forecasting problems.

SELECTING FORECASTING PROGRAMS

Most initial sales forecasts today are prepared with computer programs. A recent survey of 207 firms revealed that 76 percent of the companies allowed managers to make adjustments to computer generated forecasts with judgmental procedures.[7] This same study showed that the average firm uses 1.8 sales forecasting computer systems. Management believes that more than one computer system can help reduce forecasting errors. More than half of the companies use customized forecasting software.

When selecting a commercial software package you need to find a program that works for the time series you plan to predict. Features to look for include an ability to plot data, seasonally adjust data, and measure percentage forecasting errors. Also look for a program that includes naive, moving average, exponential smoothing, simple regression, and multiple regression procedures. An ideal program would also find optimal lengths for moving averages and optimal exponential smoothing constants based on an analysis of past data. The four forecasting programs described in Table 7-5 are only a small sample of the many commercial programs available.

Once you have selected a forecasting program, remember that simple procedures such as naive, moving averages, and exponential smoothing often have lower forecasting errors than other more complex methods.[8] This suggests you should start with the basic procedures and move on to more complex models only when they are needed. It is rare that one technique is best in all situations, so you may want to base your predications on the average of several methods to help reduce forecasting error.

Finally you must select techniques that can be sold to management. If managers cannot understand how forecasts are prepared, they are likely to reject the techniques in favor of their own judgmental forecasting methods.

SUMMARY

An important part of your job as sales manager is to prepare estimates of current market potential and to make forecasts for the future. After studying this chapter, you should be able to:

1. **Estimate market potentials.** Estimates of potential are based on projections of the number of users and the expected purchase rate. Geographical measures of potential can be obtained by using the Buying Power Index and NAICS Code procedures. Sales forecasts are key inputs for business planning, so you must know how they are prepared.

2. **Understand judgmental forecasting.** Forecasts of the future may be extensions of historical data or, in the case of new products, based on judgement. Examples of qualitative forecasting methods include sales forecast composite, jury of executive opinion, customer surveys, and leading indicators.

3. **Calculate naive, moving average, and exponential smoothing forecasts.** A variety of numerical sales forecasting techniques are available, and you need to understand how they work and where they should be employed. Detailed explanations have been presented for naive, moving average, exponential smoothing, and regression procedures. Your choice among these and other methods is a function of the length of the forecast, pattern of the data, cost, accuracy, and ease of understanding. The ideal forecasting procedure is likely to combine a numerical analysis of past data with your own interpretation of current developments.

KEY TERMS

Buying Power Index (PBI)
Exponential smoothing
Jury of executive opinion
Leading indicator
Mean absolute percentage error (MAPE)
Moving average

Multiple regression
Naive forecast
North American Industry Classification System (NAICS)
Percentage forecasting error
Percentage rate of change forecast
Sales force composite

Sales potential
Seasonal forecast adjustments
Simple linear regression
Smoothing constant
Trend
Unit rate of change

PROBLEMS*

1. Using the following sales data, forecast revenue for periods 4 through 7, using naive, trend projections, moving average, and simple exponential smoothing. Compare MAPEs across methods for time periods 4 to 7. What length of moving average and smoothing constant works best? What are your forecasts for periods 8 and 9?

Period	1	2	3	4	5	6	7	8	9
Sales	12	15	17	14	16	19	18	?	?

2. Quarterly sales (thousands of dollars) for the Chester Furniture Company for the past four years have been as follows.

			Year		
Quarter	1	2	3	4	5
1	230	240	264	328	?
2	245	266	290	344	?
3	193	259	221	275	?
4	174	218	202	281	?

Calculate seasonal indexes and adjust the data. Run seasonally adjusted naive, moving average, exponential smoothing, and linear regression forecasts through the data to see which method has the lowest MAPE. Select the best method and forecast sales for quarters 1 through 4 in year 5.

3. Sales (in thousands of dollars) for the Busy Bee Bakery for the past 15 time periods have been:

Period	Sales	Period	Sales	Period	Sales
1	2005	6	2360	11	3442
2	2150	7	2354	12	2948
3	1940	8	2682	13	3020
4	1770	9	2504	14	3079
5	2285	10	2329	15	3275

Prepare sales forecasts for periods 6 through 15 using the naive, projection, moving average, exponential smoothing, and regression techniques. What length of moving average and smoothing constant work best? What method does the best job of tracking the data over periods 6 through 15? What is your forecast for periods 16 through 24?

4. The following table shows the first six years of sales of retail optical scanners in the United States. What forecasting method seems to track quarterly sales best over the period from quarter 4 of year 1 through quarter 3 in year 6? What is your forecast for the number of scanners installed in the fourth quarter of year 6?

		Quarter		
Year	1	2	3	4
1	0	1	3	1
2	3	4	7	12
3	10	15	17	19
4	27	25	31	23
5	47	67	95	137
6	173	196	235	?

Excel spreadsheets for working on these problems are available at www.wiley.com/college/dalrymple. Go to "Student Resources."

5. You are the sales manager for a manufacturer and you have been asked to forecast company sales for the next six months. You have collected data on company sales and other variables for the last 38 semiannual time periods (Table 7-6). In addition, you have estimates for period 39 for most of your variables. Using the Excel spreedsheet file accompanying this text or another multiple regression program, calculate a correlation matrix and explain what it tells you about your variables. Create an equation to predict sales using all or a subset of your variables. Explain why you have included each variable and discuss the power of your equation. Forecast sales for period 39 using your multiple regression model.

TABLE 7-6   Company Sales and Other Variables (Semiannual)

Period	Company Sales (thousands of dollars)	Personal Disposable Income (millions of dollars)	Dealer's Allowances (thousands of dollars)	Price (dollars)	Product Development Budget (thousands of dollars)	Capital Investments (thousands of dollars)	Advertising (thousands of dollars)	Sales Expenses (thousands of dollars)	Total Industry Advertising Budget (thousands of dollars)
1	5540.39	398	138	56.2058	12.1124	49.895	76.8621	228.80	98.205
2	5439.04	369	118	59.0443	9.3304	16.595	88.8056	177.45	224.953
3	4290.00	268	129	56.7236	28.7481	89.182	51.2972	166.40	263.032
4	5502.34	484	111	57.8627	12.8916	106.738	39.6473	258.05	320.928
5	4871.77	394	146	59.1178	13.3815	142.552	51.6517	209.30	406.989
6	4708.08	332	140	60.1113	11.0859	61.287	20.5476	180.05	246.996
7	4627.81	336	136	59.8398	24.9579	−30.385	40.1534	213.20	328.436
8	4110.24	383	104	60.0523	20.8096	−44.586	31.6456	200.85	298.456
9	4122.69	285	105	63.1415	8.4853	−28.373	12.4570	176.15	218.110
10	4842.25	277	135	62.3026	10.7301	75.723	68.3076	174.85	410.467
11	5740.65	456	128	64.9220	21.8473	144.030	52.4536	252.85	93.006
12	5094.10	355	131	64.8577	23.5062	112.904	76.6778	208.00	307.226
13	5383.20	364	120	63.5919	13.8940	128.347	96.0677	195.00	106.792
14	4888.17	320	147	65.6145	14.8659	10.097	47.9795	154.05	304.921
15	4033.13	311	143	67.0228	22.4940	−24.760	27.2319	180.70	59.612
16	4941.96	362	145	66.9049	23.3698	116.748	72.6681	219.70	238.986
17	5312.80	408	131	66.1843	13.0354	120.406	62.3129	234.65	141.074
18	5139.87	433	124	67.8651	8.0330	121.823	24.7122	258.05	290.832
19	4397.36	359	106	68.8892	27.0486	71.055	73.9126	196.30	413.636
20	5149.47	476	138	71.4177	18.2208	4.186	63.2737	278.85	206.454
21	5150.83	415	148	69.2775	7.7422	46.935	28.6762	207.35	79.566
22	4989.02	420	136	69.7334	10.1361	7.621	91.3635	213.20	428.982
23	5926.86	536	111	73.1628	27.3709	127.509	74.0169	296.40	273.072
24	4703.88	432	152	73.3650	15.5281	−49.574	16.1628	245.05	309.422
25	5365.59	436	123	73.0500	32.4918	100.098	42.9984	275.60	280.139
26	4630.09	415	119	74.9102	19.7127	−40.185	41.1346	211.25	314.548
27	5711.86	462	112	73.2007	14.8358	68.153	92.5180	282.75	212.058
28	5095.48	429	125	74.1615	11.3694	87.963	83.2870	217.75	118.065
29	6124.37	517	142	74.2838	26.7510	27.088	74.8921	306.80	344.553
30	4787.34	328	123	77.1409	19.6038	59.343	87.5103	210.60	140.872
31	5035.62	418	135	78.5910	34.6881	141.969	74.4712	269.75	82.855
32	5288.01	515	120	77.0938	23.2020	126.420	21.2711	328.25	398.425
33	4647.01	412	149	78.2313	35.7396	29.558	26.4941	258.05	124.027
34	5315.63	455	126	77.9296	21.5891	18.007	94.6311	232.70	117.911
35	6180.06	554	138	81.0394	19.5692	42.352	92.5448	323.70	161.250
36	4800.97	441	120	79.8485	15.5037	−21.558	50.0480	267.15	405.088
37	5512.13	417	120	80.6394	34.9238	148.450	83.1803	257.40	110.740
38	5272.21	461	132	82.2843	26.5496	−17.584	91.2214	266.50	170.392
39	?	485	125	81.6257	20.0000	40.000	85.0000	275.00	180.000

PARKER COMPUTER

Two engineers, Bill Parks and Anne Smith, founded Parker Computer in 1983. The company specialized in the manufacture of high-end personal computers and low-priced workstations for product design and other business applications. Bill was chairman of the board, and Anne was director of research and development. For the first 10 years of its life, Parker enjoyed steady growth in sales and profits. Parker's success was based on providing customers with superior computer performance at prices slightly above average. However, in 1997 aggressive price cutting by large competitors began to erode sales growth. Parker's revenue peaked in 1998 at $75 million.

SOLVING PARKER'S PROBLEMS

Although customers were willing to pay for high-quality computers in the 1980s, this strategy did not attract many buyers in the cost-conscious 1990s. Bill Parks realized that the company had to do a better job of both marketing and cost reduction. The company currently employed a small sales force but relied primarily on a network of local dealers to sell its computers to the business market. Bill knew that the company needed a stronger customer focus, so he hired a CEO with a marketing background. As a result, the company started to pay more attention to marketing activities and began to prepare detailed marketing plans for each product line. Jane Austin, a recent business graduate, was hired as a marketing assistant to help with the planning.

Part of Jane's responsibility was to estimate sales for the PC220 and PC440 computers for the next year.

In the past, these forecasts had been developed using judgmental procedures. Jane knew that the CEO expected a more thorough analysis of sales trends for the 2000 marketing plan. When she was in school, Jane had become familiar with the use of computers to predict future sales. This seemed to be a good time to make use of her computer expertise.

ENTERING THE DATA

Jane entered the quarterly sales data for PC220 from Exhibit 1 in the first 12 spaces on her spread sheet. Sales for 1997 were entered as observations 1 through 4, sales for 1998 were entered as observations 5 through 8, and sales for 1999 were entered as observations 9 through 12. Sales figures for PC440 were entered in a separate column.

As a first step in analyzing the data, Jane thought she would plot the sales figures to see what trends were evident. Sales were placed on the Y axis and time was plotted on the X axis. Next she decided to calculate some quarterly seasonal indexes for the two products to see if seasonal adjustments were needed.

SELECTING FORECASTING METHODS

The first method Jane tried with the computer sales data was the naive approach. Sales in quarter 1 were used to predict sales in quarter 2, then sales in quarter 2 were used to predict sales in quarter 3 and so on until all the periods had been predicted. Once she had forecasts for 11 periods, she could calculate the average

EXHIBIT 1   Quarterly Sales for the PC220 and PC440

	1997		1998		1999	
Quarter	PC220	PC440	PC220	PC440	PC220	PC440
1	1950	770	3150	545	2924	350
2	2920	620	2600	450	3380	420
3	2560	623	3002	400	2554	310
4	3330	830	4250	639	2800	775

This case was prepared by Douglas J. Dalrymple of Indiana University.

forecasting error for the naive method using the formula for MAPE.

The second method Jane decided to use was the moving average. With this technique, sales in several periods are averaged to give a forecast of sales in the next period. To use this method, she had to decide how many periods to include in her forecast. She decided to start with a 2 period moving average and compare her results with those from 3 and 4 period moving averages. Her decision on the length of moving average would then be made on which method produced the lowest average forecasting error.

Jane knew that a variation of the moving average known as exponential smoothing would sometimes produce lower forecasting errors than the moving average procedure. However, with this method she would have to select an appropriate value for the smoothing constant. These constants could vary in size from 0.01 to 1.0 with low values giving forecasts that lagged the data and high values that were similar to naive forecasts. She decided to try out smoothing constants of different sizes to see which one gave the lowest MAPE.

The fourth method Jane selected was simple regression. This approach calculates a trend line equation that can be used to forecast the four quarters of 2000. While this method does well when there is a trend in the sales data, it can lead to large forecasting errors when there are changes of direction. The R statistic printed out by her computer program would give her some idea of how well the regression equation fit the computer sales data.

Once Jane had run her four methods through the historical sales data in Exhibit 1, the MAPE values that she had calculated would help her select a method to predict computer sales in 2000. This choice was complicated by the need to decide whether to seasonally adjust the sales data for either the PC220 or PC440 computers.

Another issue that Jane was concerned about was whether to report one set of quarterly forecasts for 2000 for each computer line or to average the forecasts of the best two methods. Although her computer allowed Jane to try many different forecasting techniques, it did not tell her which forecasts to include in her report. On the other hand, Jane knew the computer was fast and it would take her several hours to forecast quarterly computer sales for 2000 using a pocket calculator.

CASE 7-2 BATES INDUSTRIAL SUPPLY

*P*hil Harper had been recently appointed marketing manager for Bates Industrial Supply. Bates was a regional wholesaler of industrial cleaners and related chemicals. Phil directed the field sales force and was in charge of reordering stock for the warehouse. Recently, the company had been having trouble balancing orders against inventory. Customers were complaining about late shipments and items being short on delivery. The company president asked Harper to look into the problem and come up with some recommendations.

Phil realized that establishing direct computer links with manufacturers who supplied them with chemicals could reduce their out-of-stock problem. However, it would take months to buy the necessary equipment and debug the programs. Anticipated costs for direct computer links would be several hundred thousand dollars. A simpler approach would be to study the variations in sales of inventoried items to see if improved demand forecasts would help. Phil decided to call up some sales figures for four popular industrial cleaners on his desktop computer (Exhibit 1). The numbers on the screen represented three years of monthly sales for the four items. Several series seemed to exhibit seasonal patterns, and others were dominated by trends and unknown components. Bates normally prepared fore-

This case was prepared by Douglas J. Dalrymple of Indiana University.

EXHIBIT 1   Monthly Sales of Four Industrial Cleansers

Time Period	SH60	PN25	SX80	TL75	Time Period	SH60	PN25	SX80	TL75
1	3848	362	5666	885	19	4667	1132	6104	884
2	4024	346	5405	870	20	3555	1360	6812	878
3	3416	382	5001	866	21	3101	1589	8367	874
4	3671	526	4688	859	22	3507	1137	8130	865
5	3762	675	5492	862	23	3131	1739	7525	868
6	4444	440	5231	855	24	3639	1380	6918	855
7	5375	547	4813	857	25	2762	1366	6737	857
8	3752	655	4780	839	26	2929	915	6900	865
9	2884	313	4611	847	27	3137	1651	6112	861
10	3324	555	5201	836	28	2975	1282	6717	853
11	3133	806	5136	876	29	3274	1128	7937	860
12	3048	678	5124	873	30	3422	1397	7647	863
13	3163	568	6149	865	31	4507	1102	6993	882
14	3217	741	6202	860	32	4054	769	8089	876
15	3106	631	5808	846	33	4426	1412	9279	883
16	3196	1006	5572	839	34	4083	1161	9547	875
17	3118	1216	7069	852	35	3924	1210	8064	861
18	3305	862	6839	864	36	4274	1133	8188	864

casts for each inventoried item 12 months into the future so that purchase discounts could be taken and delivery charges minimized. The usual procedure was to use simple projection methods to obtain the forecasts.

Computer forecasting offered several advantages over the current methods. First, the computer would make it easier to seasonally adjust the data to help improve forecasting accuracy. Also the computer would make it simpler to calculate MAPEs to see which techniques worked best. Computers were fast and they would allow Phil to try out more forecasting procedures.

Phil thought he should run naive, moving average, exponential smoothing, and simple regression forecasting techniques on his four time series. Since regression required five periods of data to get started, forecasts for all of his methods should start in period 6 and run through period 36. This would make it eas-

ier to compare the MAPE values for each method because they would all be based on forecasts for the same time periods.

Phil decided to start with the sales data from SH60 to see if he could find the best forecasting technique for this series. Then the computer could be used to project sales for periods 37 through 48. One issue Phil was not sure about was whether the technique that worked best for SH60 could be used to forecast sales of the other chemicals. Certainly, it would save him a lot of time if he used the same forecasting procedure for all the products. He also wondered whether seasonal adjustments were worth the bother. Once he had some results for the four chemicals, he would be in a better position to decide whether improved forecasting procedures would solve the out-of-stock problem. Since it was getting late, Phil decided he better get started.

ORGANIZATION

> The same old way doesn't work anymore.
>
> ANONYMOUS

Chapter Consultants:
Russel Donnelly, Sales Manager, Central Region, Ericsson Inc.
B. J. Polk, Customer Business Development Manager, Procter & Gamble

LEARNING OBJECTIVES

After studying this chapter, you should be able to:

→ Describe the guiding principles underlying all sales organizations.

→ Explain the various ways by which sales forces can be organized as specialists.

→ Explain what a Strategic Accounts Management program means.

→ State the reasons for the growth in telemarketing and the obstacles to be overcome.

→ Tell why and when sales agents are utilized.

HEWLETT-PACKARD REORGANIZES

Before the sales force reorganization, a salesperson for Hewlett-Packard's Computer Systems Organization (CSO) would jump from customer to customer within a defined geography. That meant that one day a salesperson could be working with a clothing manufacturer, the next with a government agency, and the next with a securities firm. After the reorganization, a salesperson might call on only banks, for instance. This helps the salesperson become a specialist in the information problems of a particular industry. The changes seem to have impressed customers, who say that H-P salespeople ask more thoughtful questions about customer needs and implementation of computer systems, questions customers say they don't get from H-P's competitors. Success of the reorganization is also reflected in H-P's CSO sales, which now exceed $7 billion compared with only $4.7 billion in 1991.

In part, a technological revolution in computing drove the need for a sales reorganization. H-P anticipated that the reduced instruction set computing (RISC) chip would lead the industry away from proprietary systems to open systems where customers could mix and match components from several vendors. As a result, computer hardware would no longer be the main discussion point; now, whether "you can solve my business problems" would be the center of discussion.

H-P's sales effort is divided into red, blue, and green teams. The red team represents the heart of H-P's sales force, with salespeople specializing in either financial services, federal government and discrete manufacturing, or telecommunications, media, and utilities. The green team represents channel partners, such as VARS (Value-Added ReSellers) and independent agents, whom the company relies on to sell to smaller firms. The blue team includes telemarketing and geographically organized accounts that don't fall neatly into any of the strategically targeted industries on which H-P focuses.[1]

As the Hewlett-Packard example illustrates, changes in the competitive environment may require reorganization of the sales force. When the way your customers purchase changes, sales organization issues usually arise. Issues include how many salespeople are needed (see Chapter 2), how they should work together, and how they should be organized to ensure both efficiency and effectiveness in accessing an identified customer base. In addition, lines of authority and areas of responsibility must be defined so that all sales activities are properly coordinated.

The discussion in this chapter is organized as follows. First, we review a set of principles that should be considered in building any sales organization. Second, the question of sales force specialization and major accounts is addressed. This is followed by a discussion of the advantages and pitfalls of telemarketing and independent agents, alternatives to the traditional field sales force. The chapter closes with a discussion of emerging sales organization issues such as accessing global markets, working with sales partners, and sales teams.

ORGANIZATIONAL PRINCIPLES

Although responding to market changes and opportunities is important, some basic organizational principles should always be considered when building and evaluating a sales orga-

Unity of Command	Each person should report to only one boss.
Hierarchy of Authority	A clear and unbroken chain of command should link every person in an organization with someone at a level higher.
Stability and Continuity	Activities should be assigned to a position based on the goals and strategies of the company.
Coordination and Integration	Activities of salespeople should be integrated with customer needs, coordinated with activities of other departments, and coordinated with tasks of all salespeople.

FIGURE 8-1   Fundamental Organization Principles

nization. Although discussion of these principles is beyond the scope of this book, they are summarized in Figure 8-1.

Three additional issues are particularly prominent in current sales force organizational decisions—span of control, centralization versus decentralization, and cross-functional coordination. These issues are discussed in the following sections.

Span of Control

Span of control refers to the number of subordinates who are supervised by each manager. Ratios of 1 manager for every 10 salespeople are typical for many American firms.[2] Narrow spans of control are more common in small firms and with high-tech products such as aerospace equipment (7:1). Narrow spans of control are also appropriate when salespeople are inexperienced; new salespeople benefit greatly from one-on-one coaching in the field from sales management.

Although the narrow span of control used by many American companies allows closer control, it also tends to complicate the communication process, to isolate management from grass-roots operations, and to increase operating costs. These problems occur because a narrow span of control requires more layers of supervision, which add to selling expenses and separate management from the final consumer.

A recent article suggests that today's salespeople are better educated (65 percent have college degrees), know more about their customers' business, are more comfortable with technology, and can function with wider spans of control. For example, Caradon Everest, a British maker of replacement windows, has equipped its reps with laptops loaded with software that allows them to configure customized products on the spot and calculate their prices.[3] These changes allow firms to move to wider spans of control in the range of 10 or 20 salespeople. For example, a Dartnell survey shows insurance firms have average spans of control of 16:1, food products companies 14:1, real estate 14:1, and paper products 13:1.[4] These ratios lead to fewer levels of management, which forces sales managers to become facilitators of change, coaches, and visionaries. Procter & Gamble has recently eliminated three levels of management to make the company a swifter global marketer. A wider span of control also requires organizations to delegate more responsibility and authority to the lowest level.

Centralization versus Decentralization

A recurring point of discussion in sales management is to what extent control and authority over the sales force should rest in the hands of top management versus field sales managers (e.g., regional or district managers). In a completely decentralized organization, field sales managers have the resources and responsibility for performing recruiting, selecting, training, compensating, motivating, and evaluating salespeople. In a highly centralized operation, these activities are mostly controlled by central headquarters. In addition to its potential economies, highly centralized decision making is believed to be one way to encourage coordination and integration of salespeople's behaviors and efforts. It also helps to ensure uniformity in an organization's product and service offerings and consistency with the marketing plan.

Despite the possible benefits of centralized decision making, the trend is toward greater decentralization. This is occurring in part to meet the needs of a more diverse customer and to address local competitive conditions. This was part of Hewlett-Packard's motivation to reorganize.

Virtual Offices   Advances in technology, especially communications technology, are also making decentralization more feasible while not sacrificing the greater control and internal communications associated with centralized organizations. "Virtual offices" are being created with the use of laptop computers that can wirelessly tie into corporate Local Area Networks (LANs). In addition, wireless telephone technology has further evolved with the features required to support business applications such as call transfers, e-mail, speakerphones, and Internet access. Some large companies such as IBM, AT&T, Xerox, and ADP have moved toward greater use of virtual offices for some time now. Cost savings in real estate and office leasing are significant in this decision.

Many firms attempt to combine the advantages of centralized and decentralized sales organizations. They may use sales offices to provide service to customers but centralize part of the training and recruiting functions to increase efficiency. Companies such as IBM, Alcoa, and Xerox use line managers from local sales offices to recruit from nearby areas and corporate staff recruiters to travel across the country looking for prospects. These firms do some training at sales branches to reduce fixed overhead and encourage on-the-job contact. They also use centralized training facilities where new employees can be brought in for short, intensive training sessions using specialists and equipment not available at the sales branches.

Cross-Functional Coordination

The traditional flow of communications in most organizations has been directed outward from the organization to the customer through the sales force. While the sales force had some interaction among other functional areas—R&D, production, logistics, and accounting and finance—the need for coordination was limited owing to the mostly one-way flow of communications out to the sales force.

With an increased focus on solving customers' problems, the flow of communications between sales and other departments is becoming more of a two-way communications flow. The sales force now communicates customers' needs and expectations back to the organization. Wal-Mart's and Procter & Gamble's teams have constructed a formal, written code of conduct, for instance, in which each has agreed to be the other's advocate within their respective firms. If both teams agree that a particular type of promotion would work best in Wal-Mart, for example, then the P & G sales team is responsible for selling the program inside P & G. To facilitate more honest and candid exchange of information between functional areas, some companies are turning to networked personal computers to facilitate consensus building and brainstorming.[5]

With which functional areas is the sales force most likely to interact? Depending on the organization and situation, sales will often need to work harmoniously with the following departments to successfully address customer needs.

- **Engineering**—new product and product modification ideas
- **Marketing**—advertising themes and media, cooperative advertising efforts, development of sales aids, channel issues, competitive pricing, and competitive market information

- **Production**—product availability, sales forecasting, production scheduling, technical product information, special product features and characteristics, and delivery schedules
- **Accounting and Finance**—special pricing and credit schedules, customer credit information, budgets and quotas, compensation programs, and control of expenses
- **Operations/Customer Service**—equipment installation, customer training, equipment upgrades, ordering problems, warranty servicing, and emergency needs of customers

According to a recent survey by Andersen Consulting, front-line sales are most likely to interact with operations and customer service, followed by product development.[6] Ensuring proper coordination and communications between sales and these functions is often difficult. It may involve adjustments in training programs, communication technology, compensation, and perhaps reorganization. Nevertheless, the benefits of a coordinated effort to address customer problems are often worthwhile.

SPECIALIZATION

Sales forces are usually assigned geographic areas. In addition, sales organizations are increasingly specializing their sales efforts by organizing their sales force into customer, product, or functional specialists.[7] Figure 8-2 presents the results of a recent survey indicating how sales forces are organized today and how they are likely to be organized in the future. Notice that sales managers are expecting big changes with many anticipating their sales force being organized around type of customers. At the same time, fewer organizations are expecting to be focused on all customers within a geographic area without further specialization. Specialization, however, presents important challenges in terms of coordination, integration, and, most important, higher expenses. In general, geographic specialization tends to focus on reducing expenses, while other forms of specialization are intended to increase salespeople's expertise with the customer. A review of the advantages and possible pitfalls of the most common types of sales force specialization follows.

Geographic Specialization

The most common and least complicated way to organize a field sales force is by geographic territories, with a salesperson assigned to sell all products to all customers within a specified

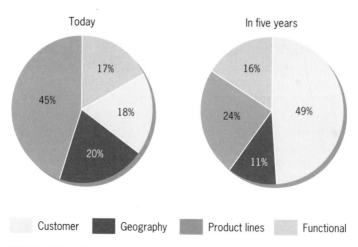

FIGURE 8-2   How Sales Forces Are Organized

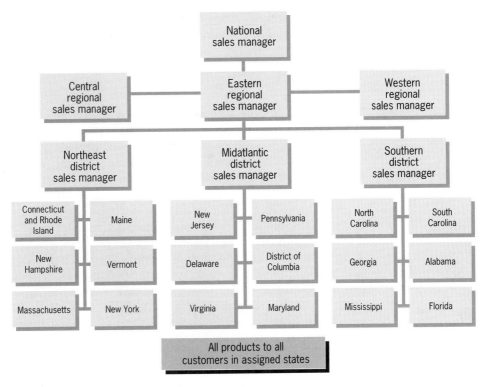

FIGURE 8-3 Geographical Sales Organization

geographic area. For example, Figure 8-3 shows the eastern third of the United States divided into 18 sales territories, where each salesperson sells to all customers and prospects located within a designated state. The 18 territories are grouped into three geographic districts, each headed by a district sales manager. In this case, all the territories, districts, and regions are based on specific geographic (i.e., state) boundaries.

An important advantage of changing from a completely open sales force structure to *geographic specialization* is that travel time and expenses are reduced. Customer service may also improve because the number of customers to be serviced is limited and geographically concentrated. This organization also minimizes conflict over who is responsible for getting the job done in each area. A geographic organization works best when the product line consists of related products or services that appeal to a rather homogeneous group of buyers.[8]

Serious shortcomings may arise, however, when salespeople sell a company's entire line of products to all types of customers. Salespeople may find themselves at a competitive disadvantage if they are asked to sell many diverse products or if customer problems and needs are diverse and complex, as was the case with Hewlett-Packard in the opening vignette of this chapter. When salespeople sell many products, they tend to degenerate into order takers, and brands can turn into commodities. There is also the risk that salespeople will spend too much time with customers who are easy to sell but who are not necessarily profitable or high-growth opportunities. With more mergers and acquisitions resulting in customer consolidation, another problem arises with geographic sales force organizations. Although a customer's headquarters may be located in one territory, they may have stores or plants in other territories. If in-store or in-plant support is needed for the sale, how should you split sales credit among the salesperson who calls on the headquarters and the other salespeople who service the local stores in their territories? These problems can be partially overcome by providing close supervision, giving incentives to perform strategic activities, and hiring better than average candidates and supporting them with extra training and technical support. Ultimately, many organizations have decided that they needed to specialize beyond simple geography.

Product Specialization

There are 164 operating companies at Johnson & Johnson producing and selling products such as orthopedic implants, pharmaceuticals, and sutures. How could one person know enough about each product line? The answer is they couldn't, so J&J has organized its sales force around defined product lines. An organization of salespeople by products is shown in Figure 8-4. In this organizational structure, each salesperson specializes by selling only a few of the products in the organization's total product portfolio.

Companies may switch to product specialization for one of several reasons. For instance, salespeople may need greater product knowledge to sell technologically complex product lines. Another common reason is because new products may be added (either through new product development or acquiring another company), which are quite different from existing product lines or are sold to a different customer segment. Not wanting to distract their current sales force from pushing existing lines was the reason that Harford Steam Boiler Inspection and Insurance Company (HSB), for example, added a specialized sales force to sell its new product, called All Systems Go. Customers for this product were much smaller than those purchasing policies for heavy machinery and atomic power plants.[9]

While *product specialization* allows salespeople to become experts in a particular product line and selling process, this type of organization is likely to be more expensive than a simple geographic organization. This is one reason Colgate-Palmolive Company recently combined its two main sales forces, household products and personal care products, into a single sales force. Both product lines are now serviced during a single store visit, and if one buyer is busy, the Colgate-Palmolive salesperson can speak with the person in charge of the other product line. As usual, other facets of sales management had to be adjusted accordingly. Both the sales force training program and compensation plan were altered to fit the new organization.

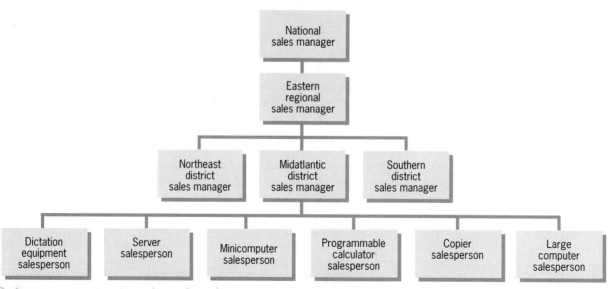

FIGURE 8-4   Product Specialized Sales Force

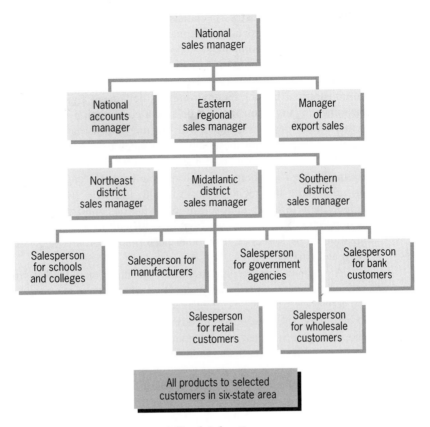

FIGURE 8-5 Customer Specialized Sales Force

High overhead costs were also a driving force behind Procter & Gamble's recent reorganization of its sales force. An internal study discovered that P&G had the highest overhead costs in the business. It is no wonder. Its sales force had five divisions with three sales layers organized around product groups, selling more than 2,300 stock-keeping units in 34 product categories. The quarterly sales promotion plan for health and beauty products, for instance, exceeded 500 pages and was sent to every salesperson. P&G has reorganized around 35 specific customers that account for nearly 80 percent of its sales.

Duplication of calls on customers may also become a problem. Separate sales forces frequently do not coordinate their customer contacts and sometimes compete for the same purchasing budget. This was the reason 3M recently reorganized its almost 50 division sales forces into customer-focused teams it refers to as its Integrated Solutions program. The Hyatt Hotel sales situation before reorganizing represents an extreme example of duplicate sales calls. It was discovered that one customer was called on by 63 Hyatt salespeople. This happened because each Hyatt resort property had its own sales force, before Hyatt reorganized into central sales offices with assigned customer accounts.

Customer Specialization

In *customer specialization,* which is also referred to as *vertical marketing,* each salesperson or sales team sells the entire product line to select types of buyers. Thus the six salespeople in Figure 8-5 are assigned to banks, retailers, and other types of customers, instead of to geographic regions or product lines, as before. IBM recently reorganized its sales force into industry specialists. With personal computers becoming commodities, profits in the business computer market have migrated to the services needed to support the use of personal computers. According to a recent study, the computer itself represents only 18 percent of the costs associated with business use of computers. Eighty-two percent of the cost is in such services as technical support, network equipment, support and administration. In such an environment, delivering a great product is not enough to gain customer loyalty. You have to deliver a combination of services that minimizes a customer's total costs associated with owning and using the product. IBM has shifted its emphasis to providing these support services to its business customers. To do so, IBM has had to understand its customer's needs much more intimately than when it was only selling "boxes." To help their salespeople become "customer experts," IBM reorganized its sales force to specialize according to industry. IBM believes that this change has helped them to better spot selling opportunities and to increase customer satisfaction. It is important to note, however, that it is difficult to isolate the effects of sales force organization on performance from other performance drivers (e.g., market growth, new products, and competition).

A customer-focused organizational structure is more market driven. This type of organizational structure is particularly attractive when buyers are geographically concentrated, as are aerospace firms in Los Angeles and auto assembly plants along route I-75 from Detroit to Memphis. The most important advantage of customer specialization is that it allows salespeople to gain a better understanding of the customer's special needs and problems and become experts in a particular industry. A customer specialization organization may result in an important selling advantage when an organization wishes to execute a consultative or enterprise level relationship strategy with its customers.

Salespeople must be well supported to be customer experts, which may even influence hiring practices. Nike often hires ex-athletes to sell to colleges and universities. To support its focus on the education market, Apple Computer hires former teachers as sales representatives because of their excellent rapport with user customers. As with other forms of sales force specialization, costs and coordination are potential problems. The sharing of information across various specialized sales forces of a company can also be problematic.

Functional Specialization

A fourth type of specialization in sales organizations, *functional specialization,* focuses on the jobs or functions performed by customer contact people (Figure 8-6). American Express profits by having some salespeople generating initial sales and others servicing the account later. Gillette has also organized its sales force according to functional specialty. One set of salespeople, sometimes known as "hunters," sell and market the company's products to the retail trade, while a separate group of merchandisers perform point-of-sale activities such as shelf management, setting up displays, and other in-store activities. The skills needed to sell Gillette's products are believed to be quite different from those needed for in-store merchandising support. Instead of paying people with selling skills to spend a significant portion of their time in merchandising activities, Gillette decided to develop separate, but coordinated, sales forces. Some sales consultants warn, however, that customers may be vulnerable to competitor raids at the point when the "hunter" passes the customer along to the maintenance sales force.

There is no one best way to organize the sales force, and companies are experimenting with many different forms in order to compete profitably. A company should start by examining its customers and looking at its organization from the customer's position. Research suggests that when superior selling skills are required, some form of specialization works best; however, there is some danger of role stress and job ambiguity.[10]

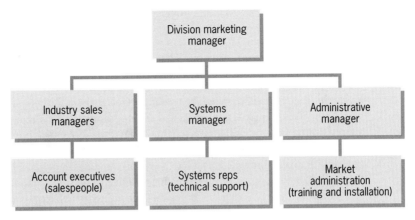

FIGURE 8-6   Functional Specialization

STRATEGIC ACCOUNT MANAGEMENT PROGRAM

Regardless of whether the sales force consists of specialists or generalists, many organizations find it necessary to develop a strategic account management program in addition to their regular sales force. Also known as key, national, major, and global accounts programs, a *strategic account management program* (as already mentioned in Chapter 5) is more than a selling strategy. It is a marketing philosophy directed at a select group of customers that account for a disproportionately large share of the seller's total revenues. These customers have been selected for special attention because they put more emphasis on value-added options such as education, electronic data interchange, and management information system compatibility. As a result, strategic account programs are established to give these customers more management attention to coordinate strategies, greater resource commitment to grow revenues, and customized solutions built around individual customer needs. In this way, strategic account programs are different from other account programs and represent how organizations execute their enterprise account relationship strategy, discussed earlier in Chapter 2.

Despite the potentially significant benefits to strategic accounts, companies often encounter problems in setting them up. In a recent survey of 220 organizations with strategic account programs, only 45 percent rated their programs as being successful.[11] Two problems have been particularly problematic—account selection and organizational structure.

Strategic Accounts Selection

An important issue to be addressed is which customers, if any, should be treated as a strategic account. There is often a tendency to focus on customer size. If purchasing is negotiated at each of many locations, however, then even a large customer may not be appropriate. See the Strategic Action Competency box for a discussion of how one company discovered that size was not a good indicator of account profitability, and did something about it. Major account programs are usually quite expensive. Many companies initially choose too many accounts to participate in the program, resulting in an overworked major account sales force and underserviced customers.

The emerging view is that customers who qualify for a strategic account program are those who purchase a significant volume and exhibit one or a combination of the following characteristics:

- Involve multiple people in the buying process
- Purchase centrally
- Desire a long-term, cooperative working relationship
- Expect specialized attention and service

Kinko's Inc., a California-based chain of printing and computer centers, is a good example of how a company might use other factors in addition to size to identify its strategic accounts. When Kinko's Inc. launched its program in 1992, the company first attempted to identify large Fortune 500-type accounts. They then looked for companies that had divisions or operations in all 50 states, as well as a large mobile sales force that could be serviced by multiple Kinko's branches. But most important, the accounts had to have characteristics similar to Kinko's—fast-growing business with a similar entrepreneurial spirit.

As with many marketing decisions, deciding which company should be a strategic account depends on learning the customer's needs. Trane, a leading manufacturer of heating and air conditioning, designed a process for selecting strategic accounts, which attempts to assure that Trane clearly understands the account's current and desired situation. The unique aspect of Trane's account selection process is that throughout the process, both parties sign documented agreements, which outline commitments to meeting the customer's objectives. Trane has found that this process aids in its strategic thinking and planning. In summary, strategic accounts are those that are seeking better service on a national or global basis. The characteristics listed above are indicators that a customer may desire and need special attention.

How to Organize?

Companies have taken a variety of approaches in organizing their strategic accounts programs. What works for one company and is appropriate for one situation may not work in another. The major organizational alternatives are as follows.

Existing Sales Force   As an initial effort, companies often rely on their existing sales force to service the national account customer. This strategy has the advantage of being less risky and less expensive than setting up a separate sales force. On the other hand, the relationship with these strategic accounts may not be very different from that with regular accounts, thus raising the question of whether a national accounts program is needed. There is also some

---

STRATEGIC ACTION COMPETENCY
CRI: Eliminating Some Customers

Custom Research Inc. (CRI) is a national market research firm. In the late 1980s, it was earning $10 million in revenues from 157 customers. After a thorough revenue and profitability analysis of all 157 customers, CRI was disturbed to find that only 10 customers fell in the high revenue/high profit category and that customers they thought were profitable were adding little if anything to the bottom line. What made this discovery more interesting was that many of these customers were in the Fortune 500. It's rare for a firm to even determine its individual customers' profitability; it's even rarer for a firm to act on that knowledge. Over the next several years, CRI stopped doing business with more than 100 of its customers so it could focus on what it called its "core partners." In 1998, CRI earned $30 million from 80 customers, 35 of which were core partners. In 10 years, through exceedingly disciplined strategic account management, CRI tripled its revenues and doubled its margins.

evidence that salespeople will focus mostly on closing orders and securing revenue rather than building relationships.[12] A short-term focus is especially likely when the sales force is under constant quota pressure such as when there is a monthly quota target.

Management A step up from this initial organization is to assign strategic account responsibility to management. Computer Task Group, Inc., an Atlanta-based software services firm, assigns a strategic account to each of the top 25 executives in the company. In addition to being relatively inexpensive, executives are likely to have the authority and power to meet special customer needs. An additional advantage is that it keeps management close to the customer.

Separate Sales Force Where the need for a strategic accounts program is greatest, a separate sales force devoted strictly to strategic accounts often evolves. The Gold Bond Building Products division of National Gypsum is organized in this manner. Successful field salespeople are promoted to the strategic accounts sales force. These people report to a strategic accounts manager, who in turn reports to the national sales manager. Hewlett-Packard, Xerox, MCI, and other companies have similar arrangements.

Sales Teams Where the selling process is very complex, sales teams may be assigned to strategic accounts. AT&T has more than 370 such strategic account teams; each team is headed by an account manager with broad product and account knowledge. Providing technical support to the team are two or three product specialists and staff technical specialists. IBM and Pitney Bowes also employ national account teams. The major drawback to this type of organization is its expense. A recent two-day planning meeting for just one national account cost AT&T $5,000.

Strategic account management represents a significant opportunity for many companies to grow through meeting the needs of their customers. We have just noted two of the important problems associated with establishing these programs. In addition you should be aware of the potential risks even when a program has been successfully established. These customers often represent such a large percent of a supplier's total sales that there is a significant risk to the business when one of these customers is lost to a competitor. From 1985 to 1995 the number of periodicals wholesalers has dropped from 205 to 100 in the United States. One reason for this consolidation is that retail book chains have become so large that the wholesaler who loses a contract for a retailer's business would often sell out to the contract winner.[13] The stakes are high should you choose to play in this game. In many industries a company has no choice but to play the game if it wants to be one of the big players in the industry.

TELEMARKETING

Customers are demanding more attention just when many companies—including Apple Computer, IBM, Merck, and Procter & Gamble—are reducing their sales forces. Strategic account programs may pay off for large customers, but few companies have the time or money to offer these kinds of services to all customers. An increasingly popular and cost-effective way to serve small and even medium-sized customers is with a telemarketing support system. *Telemarketing* refers to customer contacts utilizing telecommunications technology for personal selling without direct, face-to-face contact. Business-to-business telemarketing is growing at a rate of 30 to 40 percent a year and generated sales in excess of $240 billion in 1997 (the latest year for which information is available).[14] That total represents 44 percent of all business-to-business direct marketing sales, including in-person visits, mailings, faxes, and e-mail. More than two million people are employed in consumer

TABLE 8-1 Doing the Math on Account Management

	Field Rep	Telemarketing
Sales calls per day	5	25
Sales calls per quarter	325	1,624
Sales calls per year	1,300	6,500
Salespeople required	6.5	1.2
Cost per sales call	$250	$15
Cost per year	$1,998,750	$117,000

and business-to-business telemarketing operations. The effectiveness and opportunity that telemarketing represents are shown by the $1,000 value of the average business-to-business telemarketing sale. Corporations such as IBM, Procter & Gamble, Chase Manhattan Bank, and Union Pacific Railroad have all developed telemarketing systems.[15]

Advantages

One reason for the growing popularity of telemarketing is that it allows companies to make cost-effective sales calls, especially on smaller customers. Telemarketing is 5 to 15 times more efficient and 70 to 95 percent less expensive than field sales because telemarketing representatives cover their territory using the telephone instead of battling traffic.[16] See Table 8-1 for a comparison of field sales and telemarketing costs.

The situation at the Medical and Surgical Products Division of 3M is typical of that found in many firms. The company determined that it cost $200 for each call by field salespeople. Because each sale required 4.3 calls, the selling cost per sale averaged $860. Small hospitals did not generate enough sales to cover this cost, and about half of the hospitals serviced by 3M's salespeople were considered small. To address this imbalance, 3M instituted a telemarketing program. Because telemarketing reps can make many more calls per day than field salespeople, the average cost of a telephone sales call is $25.

A second reason for telemarketing's popularity is that many business customers like it. With increasing demands on their time, purchasing agents often appreciate the speed of telephone purchasing. A study of the wholesale distribution industry conducted by Arthur Andersen and Company predicted that in the near future half of the average wholesaler's sales force would be telemarketers.[17] The demand for field sales reps dropped to eighth place in the study (Table 8-2).

Scope

The role of telemarketing may differ considerably from one business to the next. Some of the more common roles for telemarketing are to provide customer service, prospect and lead qualification, account management, and promotion support.

TABLE 8-2 Ranking of Customers' Wants

	1970	1980	1990
Contact with outside salesperson	1	3	8
Frequency and speed of delivery	2	1	2
Price	3	2	4
Range of available products	4	5	3
Capable inside salesperson	5	4	1

Customer Service   Companies provide customers with a number they can call if they have any questions. General Electric built what is referred to as the "Answer Center" in Louisville, Kentucky, to answer questions about products 24 hours a day, 7 days a week. Reps answer up to 5,000 calls per day, using information in a computer database on 120 product lines with 85,000 models and 1,100 operating and repair procedures.[18]

Prospecting and Lead Qualification   Instead of simply waiting for prospects to call, some firms are taking a proactive approach to prospecting by having telemarketers call prospects or qualify them for face-to-face selling. AT&T built its National Sales Center to house and train telemarketers in lead generation and qualification. Prior to using telemarketers to qualify prospects, the national closing ratio on sales visits by AT&T salespeople was 1 in 10. After only one year of the telemarketing program, the close ratio was improved to 6.5 in 10. The Center handles more than 300,000 contacts a year. Other companies have reported having success with telemarketing in developing leads for their field sales force.

Account Management   Many companies find it economical to service small customers and sell peripheral or secondary product lines by phone, thereby freeing their salespeople to concentrate on key customers and strategic product lines. In a recent Hewitt Associates survey of 165 firms, 62 percent of respondents anticipated shifting responsibilities now handled by field reps to inside resources via phone, mail, and electronic commerce by the year 2000.[19] IBM uses telemarketing to sell computer supplies and equipment through their IBM Direct operation. A. B. Dick is a prime example of using telemarketing to maintain contact with more than 100,000 small accounts whose average order ($50.00) is too small to cover the cost of a sales call ($66.88).

Promotion Support   Today it's common to see newspaper and magazine ads that feature either a local or an 800 number to get information or to place an order. Merrill Lynch, Chevron, and Blue Cross–Blue Shield are among the many companies that rely heavily on this approach.

Challenges

Despite considerable merit, telemarketing presents several unique management challenges. Among these are gaining acceptance for telemarketing by the field sales force and managing telemarketers.

Acceptance   Integrating telemarketing with a traditional sales force can be challenging, because many field salespeople feel threatened by telemarketers. Even when a company continues to pay salespeople a commission on sales made by telemarketers to their accounts, salespeople often fear that management will eventually cut their commissions on these. As a result, salespeople may withhold critical customer information and refuse to integrate fully telemarketers into the selling process.[20]

Management   Hiring the right person for telemarketing can be a potential problem area. The type of individual needed is one who combines some of the attributes of a good customer service person with those of a successful salesperson. The best telemarketers are concerned with details and possess the positive outlook and aggressiveness of good salespeople. However, customer service people are often reluctant to make the first call, and salespeople tend to prefer one-on-one relationships and are likely to spend a lot of time on the phone with one account. Many firms find it necessary to look outside the firm for the right person.

Motivation and retention are also potential problem areas. Telemarketers do not have the freedom of movement of field salespeople and may be required to make 20 to 30 calls per hour. Adding to the problem is lower pay than outside salespeople and the status of second-class citizens relative to salespeople. Average compensation for telemarketing reps is just over $25,000.[21] Companies have tried to provide telemarketers with significant bonuses based on performance, greater training, and increased interaction with salespeople and customers. In general, motivation and retention continue to be problems.[22]

Internet   As always, the key Internet question is whether the Internet replaces or enhances current sales and marketing efforts. Although still not entirely clear, there are indications that the Internet has the capability to greatly enhance company telemarketing efforts. This is because the Internet or corporate extranets give telemarketing the visual supports not otherwise available when talking to customers. If you have Internet capabilities, then when ordering a new computer from Dell for instance, you can see the computer alternatives you might be considering purchasing and have a telemarketer there to answer your questions. This has been referred to as *permission marketing,* which means that the customer asks for the information before it is provided. Notice in the Dell example that the customer initiates the contact, that is, gives the company permission to provide them with additional information instead of having it forced on the consumer. The advantage of permission marketing is that it increases the efficiency with which information is broadcasted. Instead of sending it out to a large group of people who the marketer thinks will be interested in the information, the customer tells the marketer that he or she is interested. The Internet and telemarketing are ideal media for this process.

Airlines, on the other hand, appear to be pursuing a strategy of replacing telemarketers with the Internet, by encouraging people to make airline reservations over the Internet and by offering discounts to those who do so. Here the emphasis seems to be on reducing labor costs by having the consumer perform part of the labor. Regardless of the strategy pursued, the Internet offers companies additional choices as to how to best access their customers.

Organizational Structure Summary

Sales management is much more complex and exciting in today's environment. In organizing the sales effort, a large number of specialized sales options are now available, including inside telemarketing specialists, pure product or system specialists, vertical market or customer specialists, and strategic account specialists. Deciding when and how to specialize is not easy because of the trade-offs that are present. The attractiveness of specialization will depend on a firm's objectives, strategies, capabilities, and external environment. Some points to consider when evaluating specialization options are the following:

- If a company's objective is to reduce costs, then full-line salespeople and telemarketing are the best low-cost options.
- If a company's objective is to increase revenue, then specialization (product, customer, functional, and major accounts) supported by telemarketing should be considered.
- Exceptional training capabilities are frequently critical to the success of specialized salespeople. Specialization by itself is rarely sufficient to produce exceptional results; development of specialized skills must be fostered and enhanced by appropriate training programs.
- When specializing, a firm must have the capability of developing new products and modifying existing products for individual product lines and/or markets. Sales force reorganization cannot solve a product problem.
- If your market is susceptible to demand or margin downturns, then specialists may prove too expensive and too difficult to redeploy.

These factors are likely to vary with the products/markets in which an organization competes. Thus, many large companies combine a variety of specialized sales force structures within their overall selling organization. This also suggests that there is no optimal way for all companies to organize.

INDEPENDENT SALES AGENTS

Up to this point, we have focused on how to organize a company sales force in which all the salespeople and managers are employees of the firm. An important alternative is to hire *independent sales agents* (sometimes referred to as manufacturers' reps) to perform the selling function. Sales agents are not employees, but independent businesses given exclusive contracts to perform the selling function within specified geographic areas. They take neither ownership nor physical possession of the products they sell and are always compensated by commission. Agents are often used to develop new markets through a combination of persuasive selling skills and technical competence. This technical competence exists in part because agents usually handle five to eight noncompeting but related product lines that they know fairly well and sell to similar types of buyers.

When to Use Sales Agents

An estimated 45,000 to 50,000 U.S. manufacturers sell through sales agents.[23] While agents may be the only sales force for a smaller manufacturer, large manufacturers such as ITT, Corning, Monsanto, Teledyne, and Mobil Oil may supplement their own sales force by contracting with sales agents in secondary markets. Xerox, for instance, sells strictly through agents in rural areas and recently switched to selling smaller metropolitan accounts through agents.

The decision to pay sales agents to cover a particular product/market is not easy to make or to implement. Management should consider three factors: (1) economic consequences, (2) level of control, and (3) competitive market environment.

Economic Consequences   The economic issue centers on the fixed-cost nature of a dedicated sales force versus the largely variable cost associated with sales agents. A simplified representation of cost differences between sales agents and a company sales force with a straight salary compensation plan is shown in Figure 8-7. Although there may be some fixed costs associated with sales agents, sales administration costs are usually a relatively small

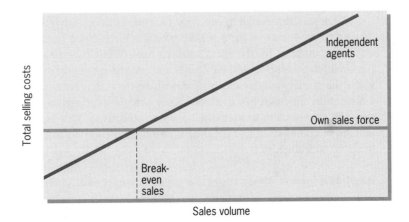

FIGURE 8-7   Total Costs of Independent Agents vs. Own Sales Force

proportion of total selling costs. Additionally, agents receive neither salary nor reimbursement for travel and entertainment expenses. Because agents are paid strictly on commission, costs rise as sales volume increases. Consequently, there is a break-even sales volume below which sales agents are less expensive and above which a company sales force costs less. These economic factors are one reason agents may be used by small companies and in secondary markets.

Suppose that independent sales agents receive a 5 percent commission on sales and administrative overhead costs $50,000. Company sales personnel receive a 3 percent commission plus a salary. Total salary and administrative expenses are estimated at $550,000. At what sales level would the cost of a company sales force equal that of sales agents? This question can be answered by setting the cost equation for both types of sales forces equal to each other and solving for the sales level amount as follows:

$$\text{Cost of company sales force} = \text{Cost of sales agents}$$
$$0.03x + \$550,000 = 0.05x + \$50,000$$

where x is the break-even sales volume.

Solving for x, we see that break-even sales volume equals $25 million. If sales are expected to be below $25 million, then sales agents are less expensive. The cost of a company sales force is less when sales exceed $25 million.

While Figure 8-7 accurately depicts the essential economic relationships when comparing agents with a dedicated sales force, the situation is often more complicated than one might expect. Adding new salespeople to produce greater volume, for instance, results in fixed costs increasing in a stair-step fashion. Thus, there may be multiple break-even points at ever-increasing levels of sales. Another cost consideration is that reporting and documentation expenses tend to increase as the number of employees increases beyond a certain threshold number. Companies using sales agents are often able to avoid these government-related costs since sales agents are not employees. On the revenue side of the issue, agents may be able to pick up a competing line of goods, thereby reducing actual sales volume below that expected when switching to a dedicated sales force. These and other considerations can make the decision to build a dedicated sales force far less clear-cut than may first appear.

Level of Control   Costs are not the only consideration. Managers can control a company sales force through the selection, training, and supervision of salespeople; establishment of operating policies and procedures; and various evaluation and reward programs. Salespeople who are part of an in-house sales force spend 100 percent of their time on the company's products.

When selling through agents, you face competition at two levels: manufacturers selling competing products and firms selling products through the same agents. In other words, the company competes for the agent's selling time. While management should try to establish a personal relationship with their agents and sell the agents on the company's marketing program, the primary control mechanism with agents is the commissions paid on sales.[24] This is a market-driven control method, and agents can be expected to spend their time in a manner that will enable them to meet their income objectives. That is, they will evaluate both the amount of commission and the time it will take to earn the commission when deciding how to spend their time.

Additional Issues   When speed and timing are important, such as when you need to enter a new geographic area or product market quickly, sales agents may be the best alternative. Sales agents have an established relationship with customers in a geographic area and offer quick access to targeted buyers. They will still need to learn about the product, but they

GLOBAL PERSPECTIVE COMPETENCY
DHL: Segmenting Global Accounts

DHL operates the world's leading international air express network, linking 80,000 destinations in 227 countries. The scope of DHL's operations is matched by the diversity of global accounts that DHL serves. In 1996, DHL's Global Accounts Management Team recognized that account management resources were being monopolized by a small number of demanding high-value clients, preventing other critical accounts from receiving the attention they needed or desired. In response to this problem DHL developed and implemented a global accounts segmentation strategy. DHL's global accounts are now segmented into four groups, based on customer need rather than geographic location, product usage, or arbitrary revenue plateau. DHL through its tiered segmentation and value delivery approach is now better able to meet the needs of all its global accounts. See *www.dhl.com.*

should already be familiar with the general product line, because they are selling related items. Manufacturers competing in high-risk industries with short life cycles or rapidly changing technologies will often rely on sales agents to preserve their flexibility and minimize the downside losses from the expense of an in-house sales force. It may cost $75,000 a year, for example, to keep an in-house salesperson on the road.[25]

Agents' contracts are usually signed annually. Contracts generally require 30 day notice, so agents can be dismissed relatively quickly. Despite the tenuous nature of the relationship, sales agents have maintained a strong presence in the distribution of both consumer and industrial products. According to U.S. Department of Commerce statistics, sales agents have accounted for approximately 10 percent of all domestic sales in the United States since 1972.[26] One study found that companies are reluctant to switch from sales agents to an in-house sales force because of the difficulty in setting up a new system. An equally important consideration should be the potential difficulties of dismantling the existing sales agent system.[27]

EMERGING SALES FORCE ORGANIZATION ISSUES

Three issues related to sales force organization are getting increasing management attention—global sales organizations, sales teams, and selling partners.

Global Sales Organizations

Firms operating in other countries, referred to as *global sales organizations,* must decide how to organize their selling efforts across national boundaries. While there is added complexity in organizing and managing multinational sales efforts (see the Global Perspective Competency box), the basic questions to be answered are the same as those faced in domestic markets: Should we use independent agents? Should we have a general sales force or specialists? Should we organize by geography, products, customers, or functions?

A recent study of multinational corporate practices sheds some light on how companies are organizing their sales forces.[28] Approximately 25 percent of the companies used independent agents, about the same as in the United States. Independent agents were most likely to be used in countries where sales are relatively small and geographically dispersed. Agents are more likely to be used in Canada, Brazil, and Mexico, for instance, where company salespeople are uneconomical in outlying areas. This is consistent with the earlier discussion

---

TEAMWORK COMPETENCY
Procter & Gamble and Black & Decker

"What more can we do for you?" This is an often asked question, but increasingly the answer requires more than one person and people from other functional areas besides sales, as the following examples illustrate.

Procter & Gamble planted a crop of executives in Arkansas to work with Wal-Mart on a daily basis. The team consists of sales managers, but also of managers from other areas of the company—marketing, finance, distribution, and operations. This team works on such problems as reducing the cost of warehousing Pampers and planning new-product introductions. Together, P&G and Wal-Mart developed a data highway that linked P&G data to Wal-Mart data, driving down costs and sharing information to meet the consumer's needs. Wal-Mart had scanners in all of their stores to track, measure, and analyze their business. Wal-Mart collected its own data, then analyzed the results. P&G also had data about the consumer that was used to make product decisions. Combining these databases into a data highway allowed P&G and Wal-Mart to create joint business scorecards and support replenishment, EDI, customer table checking, and category management efforts. While playing an important role in the development of the data highway, the sales force could never have done this on its own. Wal-Mart is now P&G's largest account, bigger than its total business in every country outside of the United States except Germany. See *www.pg.com* and *www.wal-mart.com*.

Black & Decker went so far as to set up Home Depot divisions to cater specifically to those fast-growing accounts. In each account, a vice president oversees a group composed of salespeople, marketers, an information systems expert, and a financial analyst. This gives the team the capability of designing promotion programs specifically for the account, including package redesigns. The payoff for such expensive efforts had better be huge. Sales of Black & Decker products sold to Home Depot have climbed almost 40 percent. See *www.blackanddecker.com* and *www.homedepot.com*.

---

of independent agents in the United States. A consideration not discussed earlier is language. In multilingual markets (as in Sri Lanka, Thailand, and Singapore), companies tend to hire agents with the language and dialect skills appropriate to a particular region. Slightly less than half (48.5 percent) of the firms surveyed used some kind of specialized sales force organization. The reasons given for specializing and the type of specializing indicate that multinational firms resolve organizational issues largely the same way they do in the United States.

Sales Teams

Today's customers have increasingly customized and complex needs—needs that frequently cannot be met by individual salespeople. In these situations, success depends on the ability to marshal resources effectively across a range of buying locations, buying influences, product lines, and internal organizational boundaries. Now, companies such as AT&T, Baxter, Dun and Bradstreet, and Procter & Gamble are discovering that meeting customer procurement requirements and perfecting the overall customer interface requires a customer-focused *sales team* consisting of salespeople, customer service, technical specialists, and other functional areas. The objective of these teams is to consolidate greater knowledge and skills to focus on a more creative and complete solution to a customer's needs in order to build stronger customer relationships.

Dun and Bradstreet recently formed teams to concentrate on meeting with D-B's top 50 accounts. Previously, multiple salespeople representing D-B's different divisions would all call on the same customers. The switch to teams was made to streamline the organization, to present a more unified image to customers, and to increase revenue with a focus on building business with existing customers.[29] Xerox has used a team approach for some time, utilizing the slogan "Team Xerox." The account team is comprised of an account representative, a high-speed duplicating specialist, an electronic printing specialist, an office systems and networking specialist, an electronic keyboard and workstation specialist, a copier specialist, and an account manager.

Sales teams need not be limited to in-house personnel. MCI's team (now WorldCom) made a presentation to a company about setting up a data application network together with representatives of IBM and Rohm. MCI provided the information on data communication, IBM on computer hardware and software, and Rohm on switching equipment.[30]

Coordination is critical to the success of sales teams. Three issues are of particular importance in the coordination of sales team efforts: the reward system, the goal-setting process, and staffing and training. Compensation must be flexible, focus on the results of the team rather than the individual, and focus on a longer time frame since the selling cycle is usually longer. The goals of the team and the individuals on the team need to be clarified with respect to each person's responsibilities and the desired team accomplishments. Disseminating information about company strategy helps to clarify team sales goals and the effort top management expects. Teamwork in sales is the sum of individual efforts working cooperatively toward a common goal. This means that recruiting people with the aptitude for teamwork and developing skills such as delegating responsibility and working with and through others are important. Today's sales strategy is quite different from the past, where sales was the vocation of a single, energetic, persistent individual. Selling skills and product

---

SELF-MANAGEMENT COMPETENCY
Emerging Sales Competency Study

One important aspect of self-management is a willingness to relearn continually and revise as changing situations call for new skills and perspectives. With all the changes occurring in relationships between organizations, the skills needed to be successful are also changing. This prompted MOHR, a sales training and consulting firm, to investigate the skills related to sales effectiveness in today's selling environment. They examined the following skills:

- **Aligning strategic objectives** by identifying new opportunities and applications that add value for customers and enhance the value of the relationship for the salesperson's organization.
- **Understanding the financial impact of decisions** on both organizations and quantifying and communicating the value of the relationship.
- **Orchestrating organizational resources** by identifying key contributors, communicating relevant information, and building collaborative, customer-focused relationships.
- **Consultative problem solving** to create new solutions, customized products and services, and paradigm changes while being willing and able to work outside the norm when necessary.
- **Building strategic plans** for account penetration by mapping the process for doing business with customers.
- **Utilizing basic selling skills** including establishing rapport, uncovering needs, relating benefits to product features, handling objections, and closing.

Considering this list of six skills, rate each according to (1) importance to the relationship, (2) need of improvement, and (3) relationship to salesperson effectiveness ratings.

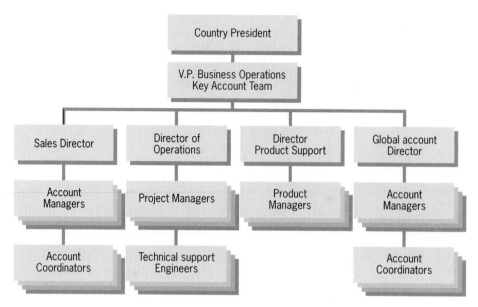

FIGURE 8-8   Sales Team Organization at Ericsson Inc.

knowledge are still important, but additional skills are also needed for sales teams to function effectively.

Figure 8-8 illustrates how part of Ericsson's Key Account sales force is organized. The account manager for a major customer can call on the expertise and support of the account coordinator, a project manager, and a technical support engineer. If the situation is appropriate, the team may also call on additional technical expertise of the specific product manager. If the customer has international operations, then a global account manager will also work with the team to coordinate their effort worldwide. In Ericsson, Key Account sales teams are responsible for building on existing customer account relationships, while the National Account Team (not shown in Figure 8-8) is responsible for finding new business with totally new customer accounts. Ericsson, as in many large companies, incorporates aspects of different types of sales force organization discussed in this chapter: geographic territories, product specialization, customer specialization, and functional specialization, as well as major accounts and selling teams.

Selling Partners

With the shift to direct channels and the need to customize solutions to individual customers, companies are finding it necessary to market through "selling partners." These are salespeople who are not on the payroll, and who not only sell, but provide technical and operating support. An example is Siebel Systems Inc., a San Mateo, California-based software provider, which uses partner companies to customize its software for large- and medium-size customers. Siebel provides the software code, and the selling partner provides the consulting and systems integration services to install the software in a company. To get the software product to market, Siebel needs value-added selling partners that actually implement the software package. This arrangement raises many strategic issues for Siebel. It does not have to shoulder all the selling costs involved in getting the attention of the final customer, but it also has almost no control over the selling process. Perhaps more important, Siebel may have very little brand or company equity with the final customer because they are dealing with the selling partner, not with Siebel. If a conflict arises with its selling partners, will Siebel have the power to influence its resolution?

SUMMARY

Changes in the competitive environment and in the way your customers want to purchase often require a reorganization of the sales force. Decisions must be made about how many salespeople are needed, how they should work together, and how they should be organized to ensure both efficiency and effectiveness in accessing an identified customer base. These decisions are likely to have a profound effect on the performance of the sales force and the organization as a whole.

1. **Describe the guiding principles underlying all sales force organizations.** Span of control refers to the number of people reporting directly to any one manager. Unity of command refers to the concept that each person should report to only one boss. Hierarchy of authority suggests that there be a clear and unbroken chain of command linking every person with someone at a level higher in the organization. Stability and continuity refers to the practice of assigning activities to a position. Coordination and integration refers to the integration of salespeople's activities with customer needs and coordinating with the activities of other departments.

2. **List the various ways by which sales forces can be organized as specialists.** Almost all sales organizations use some sort of geographic breakdown to help control the costs and activities of field salespeople. Firms with diverse lines of high-technology products often can improve their sales performance by specializing selling efforts by product. Where buyers have special needs, customer specialization can improve efficiency by eliminating duplication of calls and by more effectively identifying and meeting customers' needs. With complex products, the sales organization may be divided along functional lines into initial contact people and account maintenance people.

3. **Explain what a strategic accounts management program means.** This is a marketing philosophy directed at a select group of customers that account for a disproportionately large share of the seller's total revenues and have complex needs and problems. These customers have been selected for special attention because they put more emphasis on value-added options such as education, electronic data interchange, and management information system compatibility.

4. **State the reasons for the growth in telemarketing and the obstacles that must be overcome to implement a successful telemarketing program.** Telemarketing refers to customer contacts utilizing telecommunications technology for personal selling without direct, face-to-face contact. One reason for the growing popularity of telemarketing is that it allows companies to make cost-effective sales calls, especially on small customers. Another reason for its success is that many customers prefer this method of communications owing to time pressures. The primary obstacles to successful implementation of telemarketing are resistance by field salespeople and the special management issues associated with hiring, motivating, and retaining telemarketers.

5. **Describe what is meant by an independent sales agent.** Independent sales agents are not employees, but independent businesses given exclusive contracts to perform the selling function within specified geographic areas. They take neither ownership nor physical possession of the products they sell and are always compensated by commission.

KEY TERMS

Affordability approach	Decentralization	Global sales organization
Centralization	Functional specialization	Hierarchy of authority
Customer specialization	Geographic specialization	Incremental approach

Independent sales agents
Major account program
Major accounts
Product specialization

Sales teams
Span of control
Stability and continuity
Telemarketing

Unity of command
Vertical marketing
Workload approach

DEVELOPING YOUR COMPETENCIES

1. **Self-Management.** The world of business-to-business management is changing, radically and permanently. New selling methods, especially national accounts programs and telemarketing, have altered the role of traditional face-to-face selling. The role of the traditional field sales force has shrunk, while telemarketing focuses on small customers and national accounts programs sell to the largest customers. How do you think these developments will affect the role of the traditional sales manager and the skills required for the position? How does the sales manager's role compare with the roles of national accounts managers and telemarketing managers?

2. **Strategic Action.** Corporate restructuring is becoming an everyday occurrence in today's business environment. Such restructuring may happen when one company acquires another or picks up a new product line. It may also occur in the process of divesting a business or product line or when merging several product lines, each with its own sales and distribution forces, into a single division. Restructuring offers opportunities and also poses threats to sales force management. If, for example, a national company decides to combine its separate housewares and audio business sales forces, what issues must be considered? What kinds of analysis would you do prior to any reorganization? How would you execute a merger between these two sales forces?

3. **Technology.** The 3M Company offers an 800 number to assist its telecommunication equipment customers. The 3M National Service Center, located in St. Paul, Minnesota, is staffed 365 days a year, 24 hours a day, with skilled technicians and coordinators. Through systematic questioning and a variety of facsimile, ASCII communication terminals, the latest monitoring and testing equipment, and a sophisticated on-line computer system, the staff can isolate an equipment problem or operator error. The 3M Center has found that in more than 30 percent of the calls, the equipment failure can be corrected in minutes, without dispatching a service technician. Considering the other possible telemarketing roles besides customer service, what are other possible applications of technology in telemarketing?

4. **Global Perspective.** The goal of Oracle's Global Account Management Program (GAMP) is to dramatically improve international customers' ease and effectiveness of doing business with Oracle. To accomplish this goal, Oracle uses its own database technology to support a worldwide GAMP information networking system. In addition to the customer having access to the database, any Oracle employee supporting an account can access the system. What are the possible risks and uses for such a database? *www.oracle.com.*

5. **Team Building.** Minneapolis-based ADC Telecommunications strategically uses suppliers as part of its sales team to support its account management efforts. A variety of consulting and training firms serve as resources to address strategic account issues. These firms are brought together on an as-needed basis to address issues collectively, rather than independently. By using this approach to address customer needs and issues, ADC has an opportunity to bring additional value to its customers. Additionally, the practice has been found to improve customer relationships and generate new revenue opportunities. A number of issues are critical to the success of this teamwork effort. For instance, how does ADC ensure the quality of advice given by these outside firms? How does

ADC coordinate the efforts of these partners with their own efforts? What are some other issues critical to the success of this program and how might an organization address these issues? *www.adctelecom.com.*

6. **Coaching.** American Electric Power recognized the need to strengthen the financial measures of its sales performance and how its customer management program contributed to the firm's bottom line. AEP tested profitability modeling based on revenue generated by individual "deals," but found that this approach did not provide AEP management with the total long-term value of the account relationship. This led AEP to a dramatic leap in quantifying returns on relationship management investments. AEP's Customer Asset Management Accounting (CAMA) software package is based on the premise that account relationships are assets. CAMA allows AEP to quantify the contribution of individual accounts to its bottom line and provides a powerful tool for selecting strategic accounts and allocating sales resources. It has also proven to be a powerful internal marketing tool as well, used to justify internally investments in individual accounts. The value of CAMA depends on the inputs provided by the salesperson.

Assume you are a regional manager with AEP and a new salesperson has raised concern about the use of his time to supply this information. How would you respond to his questioning of this use of his time? Also, explain the asset management focus of the system, as opposed to an individual "deal" or sales approach to evaluating the financial value of a customer.

PROBLEMS*

1. Your company currently generates $200 million in revenue selling through 50 independent sales agencies. The agencies are paid a flat 5 percent commission on sales they generated. You are wondering whether it would be less expensive to develop your own dedicated sales force. Your industry's trade association conducts an annual compensation survey, which indicated that the average salary for salespeople is $60,000 including benefits. In addition, an incentive compensation of 0.5 percent (i.e, one-half of one percent) of sales was also typical. You estimate that you would need to hire 100 salespeople to replace the sales agents. Given the information provided, which would cost you less at $200 million in revenue—your own dedicated sales force or independent sales agents? What is the break-even sales volume for your company; that is, when do the two sales force alternatives cost the same?

2. Upon further reflection on the previous problem, you realize that you have neglected to consider several relevant costs in your calculations. You have one national sales manager and a marketing manager who presently interface with the independent sales agents, but additional management levels will be needed to train and manage the number of sales people you are anticipating hiring. First, you have decided to divide the nation into two regions with a regional sales manager in charge of each. According to industry sources, a regional sales manager's average salary is $12,000. Second, a number of district managers will be needed to manage directly the salespeople. A span of control of 10:1 (10 salespeople to 1 manager) is believed to be necessary. Salaries for district managers averages $90,000. Incentive pay for managers, both regional and district, is expected to be 0.35 percent of sales. Third, it should cost $120,000 to recruit and train each salesperson. Finally, management wants sales to grow by 10 percent next year to $220 million, so more than 100 salespeople will need to be hired. Average sales per salesperson are expected to be $2 million. Given this new information, which type of sales force will be less expensive? What is the break-even sales volume now?

Excel spreadsheets for working on these problems are available at www.wiley.com/college/dalrymple. Go to "Student Resources."

IN-CLASS EXERCISES

8-1: Damage Control

Six months after joining Pilot Pen Corporation, the national sales manager is informed by the president that the company has decided to switch to an in-house sales force of 40 salespeople instead of having independent sales agents sell the company's product line of pens, pencils, markers, and accessories.

Pilot Pen's sales are headed for $57 million this year. It has sold through sales agents throughout its 32-year history. Sales have grown rapidly over this time, and 100 sales agents currently represent the product line to Pilot's customers. The agents sell directly to retailers and to office product distributors, who, in turn, sell office products to retailers such as college bookstores, office supply stores, drugstores, and grocery stores. The marketplace is changing as large discounters such as Wal-Mart and K-mart are growing. The fastest-growing market force is the large office product stores such as Office Max, which sell to businesses as well as to the walk-in retail trade.

In addition to the national sales manager, there are two regional sales managers at Pilot Pen, a subsidiary of Japan's Pilot Corporation. Along with the national sales manager, the regional managers are responsible for recruiting high-quality sales agents and working with them to ensure that Pilot gains full line distribution. The sales manager will need their help to put together an in-house sales force and to undertake damage control when the sales agents are informed of the new organization.

After briefly discussing some current sales issues, the president informs the sales manager that Pilot wants to change from independent agents to an in-house sales force. Among other reasons for the change, the company has decided to open its first U.S. manufacturing facility next year and wants to leverage its production capabilities as soon as possible. The president also mentions that he believes the sales agents have grown "older and wealthier" and are losing the "energy and drive" of earlier years.

The sales manager's reaction is one of surprise, followed by a realization of the magnitude of the undertaking. The president informs the sales manager that he has two months to complete a plan for starting the new sales force. The sales manager says that he had better get started right away and suggests that he meet with the two regional sales managers this week.

In the initial meeting with the two regional sales managers, the sales manager informs them of the impending change in organization. After expressing their surprise, the regional sales managers focus on their concern with agents' reactions. They say there is no way that this plan can be kept a secret until it is implemented and that the agents are likely to be angry about losing the 20 percent commissions they have become used to receiving over a long period of time. During this discussion, possible retaliatory actions by the agents are discussed. At the conclusion of the meeting, the vice president suggests that they all think about how to "ease out" the 100 agents without suffering undue economic recriminations and calls a meeting for next week to discuss alternative plans.

Questions:

1. As national sales manager, how would you conduct the meeting with the two regional sales managers?
2. What issues would you have to address in starting your own sales force?
3. How would you attempt to control the potential economic damage that may occur when switching from sales agents to your own sales force?

4. What would you suggest doing if one of your agents asked you whether it was true that Pilot Pen was going to release all its agents and switch to a dedicated sales force?

8-2: A Global Account Assignment*

Mark Fisher, global sales director for Global Access Communications in California, needs to fill a sales slot in Bath, England. He has the perfect candidate: Grace Bowens, a strategic account manager. The problem is, can Mark convince Grace to take an international assignment given Global's expatriate policy?

The policy is this: Global pays relocation expenses for a contracted two-year-or-more assignment, but offers no base pay increase for time abroad. Management believes that an expatriate assignment should be treated the same as any in-country relocation. Otherwise, the company would have to pay too many people a percentage increase, because Global has salespeople and managers in more than two dozen countries.

Trying to convince Grace to take the assignment is complicated by the fact that she is married to a successful graphic designer, who probably wouldn't give up his job and lucrative salary.

Mark would like Grace to take the expat assignment for three years, then bring her back to the States and promote her to head up a top-five global account based in the United States. He knows he needs a creative solution, but what it is, he isn't sure.

Questions:

1. What actions would you recommend Mark take?
2. How would you negotiate with Grace Bowens?
3. Should Global be responsible for finding an equitable position for Grace's husband?
4. Do you agree with Global's policy regarding expatriate assignments?

---

*Contributed by Eli Jones, University of Houston.

CASE 8-1 SALES TEAMS AT LEXMARK CANADA INC.

When Gord MacKenzie, Vice President of Sales at Lexmark Canada Inc., checked his voice-mail on Wednesday morning, April 9, 1997, he realized that the Quebec sales team situation was at a critical point. The message said that resistance to the new sales team approach had just resulted in the loss of a second Account Manager in Montreal. Yves Gagnon, the Quebec Team Leader, now was faced with trying to rebuild his team while continuing to manage his own accounts. Gord needed to enhance the implementation of the sales team approach or scrap the sales teams in favour of some other approach to deploying and organizing Lexmark's salespeople. Another option might be to go back to an individual-focused structure.

The sales organization that Gord inherited with his promotion had recently changed from an *individual-based* structure to a *sales team-focused* structure. The sales teams were composed of Account Managers, or sales representatives, located in specific geographic regions. The Account Managers were empowered to manage their regions through decisions made by the team. They had to plan how they would approach their marketplace as a *team*. For example, they had to decide who would focus on specific accounts, and specific industries, and who would perform specific marketing activities. This had a major impact on the sales organization across Canada; some sales teams fully embraced the concept while others resisted. The introduction of the sales team approach resulted in many changes.

A significant change was to the Account Manager's compensation plan. The Account Manager's previous compensation plan was a combined salary/incentive program with a target compensation package that consisted of 50 per cent salary and 50 per cent incentive. The incentive component was based on the achievement of a predetermined sales quota. This sales quota was set each year by the Sales Manager based on previous sales results and revenue targets. The incentive portion was paid quarterly based on actual desktop printer sales relative to printer quota goals. For example, Account Managers targeted to make $100,000 would be paid $50,000 in salary and $50,000 in incentive if they achieved their sales quota. If an Account Manager only achieved 50 per cent of his or her quota, she or he would only receive $25,000 incentive compensation. However, if Account Managers over-achieved their target by 50 per cent, they would receive $75,000 in incentive compensation. In addition, they were motivated to achieve their sales quota to win the "Winner's Circle Award," an all-expense paid vacation for the sales quota winners of the year and their spouses.

Under the sales team approach, the incentive portion of an Account Manager's compensation would now be based on the achievement of a joint sales team quota rather than her or his own individual quota. Account Managers would be eligible to win the "Winner's Circle Award" if the sales team met its quota. To some this would take glory away from outstanding individual Account Managers.

Coming from an International Business Machines Corporation (IBM) sales background, Gord was familiar with the sales team concept. However, he realized that its implementation within Lexmark would be challenging. Since he was essential to implementation success, Gord quickly began to gain knowledge of the benefits and challenges involved with using sales teams. However, he had not expected to lose Account Managers over the team concept and certainly did not want to lose any more. Taking a deep breath, Gord dialled the Montreal office to return Yves's phone call.

LEXMARK INTERNATIONAL

Lexmark International Group, Inc. was a fast-growing, integrated, global developer, manufacturer and supplier

This case was prepared by Karen Boehnke under the supervision of Professor Don Barclay solely to provide material for class discussion. Certain names and other identifying information may have been disguised to protect confidentiality. It is not intended to illustrate either effective or ineffective handling of a managerial situation. Ivey Management Services prohibits any form of reproduction, storage, or transmittal without its written permission. This material is not covered under authorization from CanCopy or any reproduction rights organization. To order copies or request permission to reproduce materials contact Ivey Publishing, Ivey Management Services c/o Richard Ivey School of Business, The University of Western Ontario, London, Ontario; Canada, N6A 3K7; phone (519) 661-3882; fax (519) 661-3882; e-mail cases@ivey.uwo.ca. One time permission to reproduce granted by Ivey Management Services on November 3, 1999.

of printer solutions and products. Products included laser, inkjet, and dot matrix printers and associated consumable supplies for the office and home markets. Lexmark competed primarily in the laser and color inkjet printer markets—two of the fastest-growing printer categories. Every sale of a Lexmark printer started the flow of consumable supply sales including toner, photoconductors and ink technologies. Lexmark also manufactured after-market cartridges for laser printers and typewriters. Driven by its printers and associated supplies business and aggressive cost management, Lexmark continued to achieve strong revenue and earnings growth, despite an unusually challenging environment.

An enabling factor for this success was Lexmark International's strong global presence. Lexmark employed approximately 7,000 employees worldwide. The company had executive offices and its largest manufacturing center in Lexington, Kentucky. Other manufacturing centers were in Boulder, Colorado; Juarez, Mexico; Rosyth, Scotland; Orleans, France; and Sydney, Australia. With more than 50 per cent of revenues derived from sales outside the United States, Lexmark's products were sold in more than 150 countries around the world. The company also had more than 50 sales offices globally and thousands of resellers and retail locations worldwide. Although Europe continued to be Lexmark's top international market, it was making significant gains in the Asia/Pacific and Latin American regions. As Lexmark expanded, it focused on establishing and strengthening new global partnerships and alliances. Lexmark was joint marketing internationally with companies such as Fujitsu, Samsung, Unisys and Sun Microsystems.

Lexmark was the only significant focused and fully integrated printer solutions company in the world. The Lexmark team earned a global reputation for leadership as a provider of high-value, innovative products as demonstrated by its success in winning 160 product awards worldwide (Exhibit 1). This technical leadership, plus Lexmark's relentless pursuit of exceeding customer expectations and maintaining a lifelong relationship with customers, enabled the organization to compete successfully in a marketplace characterized as highly competitive and brand loyal. Hewlett-Packard Company (HP) was the market share leader with over 60 per cent of the worldwide market. Customers had been loyal to HP products due to their exceptional reliability. Lexmark had the second highest share of the market with approximately 12 percent. Other competitors included Xerox, Epson, Brother, Canon, QMS, and IBM who re-entered the market after the Lexmark/IBM contract expired in 1996.

IBM One Day, Lexmark the Next

Lexmark was formed in March 1991 when IBM sold its Information Products business to the investment firm of Clayton, Dubilier & Rice Inc. This "spin-off" enabled a division within IBM to successfully transform itself into an independent company with its own line of products, its own sales and marketing relationships, and its own development and manufacturing processes. Although Lexmark used the IBM logo in the company's early stages, a brand transition strategy was implemented resulting in Lexmark-branded products and the elimination of the IBM logo. Important achievements since 1991 included reducing cycle time for most new product developments from 24 to 12 months, reducing debt from $940 million to $180 million, and achieving a position of technological leadership in laser printers. This success enabled Lexmark to move from a privately owned company to a publicly traded firm. Lexmark went public on November 15, 1995. Since many Lexmark employees had participated in a stock option plan, this was an exciting time at Lexmark. The shares were listed on the New York Stock Exchange under the symbol LXK (Exhibit 2).

Lexmark developed and owned most of the technology for its laser printers and consumable supplies. This differentiated the company from a number of its major competitors, including Hewlett-Packard, which purchased laser engines from a third party. Lexmark's integration of research and development, manufacturing and marketing enabled the company to design laser printers with features desired by specific customer groups. This resulted in substantial market presence for the company within certain industry sectors such as banking, retail/pharmacy and health care. The company's control of critical technology and manufacturing also allowed Lexmark to carefully manage quality and to reduce its typical new product introduction cycle time to one of the shortest in the industry. Lexmark believed that these capabilities contributed to its increasing market share.

THE DESKTOP PRINTER INDUSTRY

Two of the fastest-growing printer categories in the desktop printer industry were the color and monochrome desktop Laser Printers and Color Inkjet Printers. Laser printer growth was being driven by the migration from large mainframe computers for offices to local area networks that linked various types of computers using a variety of protocols and operating systems. This shift

What the industry thinks about Lexmark printer solutions ...

LEXMARK™
ADVANCING THE ART OF PRINTING
1-800-358-5835
http://www.lexmark.com

EXHIBIT 1

... **you get the idea**

EXHIBIT 1   (Continued)

EXHIBIT 2   Financial Data

(In millions, except share data) Statement of Operations Data:	1996	1995	1994	1993	1992
Revenues	$2,377.6	$2,157.8	$1,852.3	$1,675.7	$1,763.9
Cost of revenues	1,630.2	1,487.9	1,298.8	1,107.4	1,130.5
Gross profit	747.4	669.9	553.5	568.3	633.4
Research and development	123.9	116.1	101.0	111.7	135.7
Selling, general and administrative	388.0	359.1	292.9	322.0	367.9
Option compensation related to IPO[a]	—	60.6	—	—	—
Amortization of intangibles[b]	5.1	25.6	44.7	64.0	89.2
Operating income[c]	230.4	108.5	114.9	70.6	40.6
Interest expense	20.9	35.1	50.6	63.9	70.7
Amortization of deferred financing costs and other	7.9	10.1	13.6	13.1	16.5
Earnings (loss) before income taxes	201.6	63.3	50.7	(6.4)	(46.6)
Provision for income taxes	73.8	15.2	6.1	3.0	10.7
Earnings (loss) before extraordinary item	127.8	48.1	44.6	(9.4)	(57.3)
Extraordinary loss[d]	—	(15.7)	—	—	—
Net earnings (loss)	127.8	32.4	44.6	(9.4)	(57.3)
Earnings (loss) per common share before extraordinary item[e]	1.68	0.64	(0.46)	(0.34)	(1.12)
Net earnings (loss) per common share[e]	1.68	0.43	(0.46)	(0.34)	(1.12)
Shares used in per share calculation	76,221,843	74,932,103	61,430,896	61,458,241	61,419,631
Statement of Financial Position Data:					
Working capital	$ 343.8	$ 227.7	$ 237.5	$ 293.6	$ 347.5
Total assets	1,221.5	1,142.9	960.9	1,215.0	1,440.2
Total long-term debt (including current portion)	165.3	195.0	290.0	650.7	759.2
Redeemable senior preferred stock[f]	—	—	—	85.0	85.0
Stockholder's equity[f]	540.3	390.2	295.5	173.7	197.4
Other Key Data:					
Operating income before amortization and unusual item[g]	$ 235.5	$ 194.7	$ 159.6	$134.6	$ 129.8
Earnings (loss) per share before unusual item[h]	$ 1.68	$ 1.16	$ 0.49	$ (0.34)	$ (1.12)
Cash from operations[i]	118.0	307.5	361.9	176.4	102.1
Capital expenditures	145.0	106.8	58.1	62.4	57.8
Debt to total capital ratio	23%	33%	50%	72%	73%
Return on average equity before unusual items[j]	27%	25%	21%	(6%)	(23%)
Number of employees	6,573	7,477	5,934	5,885	5,738

[a] The Company recognized a non-cash compensation charge of $60.6 ($38.5 net of tax benefit) in the fourth quarter of 1995 for certain of the Company's outstanding employee stock options upon the consummation of the initial public offering.

[b] Acquisition-related intangibles were fully amortized by March 31, 1996.

[c] Operating income in 1992 is net of a $40.0 provision related to the Company's restructuring of its operations.

[d] Represents extraordinary after-tax loss caused by an early extinguishment of debt related to the refinancing of the Company's term loan in April 1995.

[e] Earnings (loss) per common share are net of dividends of $11.8, $11.5 and $11.5 paid on the Company's redeemable senior preferred stock in 1994, 1993, and 1992. Earnings attributable to common stock in 1994 are also net of a $61.3 preferred stock redemption premium related to the exchange of redeemable senior preferred stock for Class A common stock on December 30, 1994.

[f] Redeemable senior preferred stock with a liquidation preference of $85.0 was exchanged for 9,750,000 shares of Class A common stock on December 30, 1994.

[g] Unusual item in 1995 reflects the non-cash compensation charge discussed in (a) above.

[h] Unusual items in 1995 includes the non-cash compensation charge discussed in (a) above and the extraordinary after-tax loss discussed in (d) above. The unusual item in 1994 represents the preferred stock redemption premium discussed in (e) above.

[i] Cash flows from investing and financing activities, which are not presented, are integral components of total cash flow activity.

[j] Unusual items in 1995 include the non-cash compensation charge discussed in (a) above and the extraordinary after-tax loss discussed in (d) above.

created strong demand for medium-speed (7 to 14 pages per minute) to high-speed (15 to 30 ppm) laser printers with network connectivity attributes (Exhibit 3).

The color inkjet printer market, the fastest-growing segment in the personal printer market, was expanding rapidly due to the growth in personal computers and home offices, and the development of easy-to-use color inkjet technology with good quality color print capability at low prices. According to industry analysts, the inkjet market was expected to grow from 6 million

Lexmark Laser Printers

Today's business leaders demand high-quality documents, and the versatile, speedy, reliable printers that can produce these documents on an array of media in a wide variety of environments.

Lexmark develops, manufactures and markets superbly engineered printers, network print servers and software tools to ensure that when you need a document printed, it gets printed—quickly, efficiently and with the kind of quality that you demand.

To help you get the most from these products, Lexmark offers a superior level of customer support. A World Wide Web site, an on-line bulletin board and a technical support hotline allow you to contact Lexmark when you need help or information.

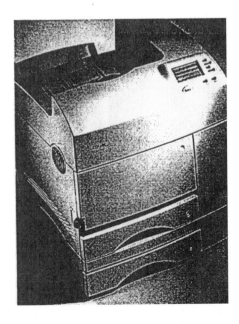

Lexmark Product Guide Winter 1997

EXHIBIT 3

units in 1994 to more than 25 million units in 1999. This market growth was attributed to a shift in customer preferences from monochrome to color, with inkjet printers continuing to replace low-speed laser printers.

LEXMARK'S STRATEGY

Lexmark's laser printer strategy was to target the fast-growing segments of the network printer market and to increase market share by providing high quality, technologically advanced products at competitive prices. To enhance Lexmark brand awareness and market penetration, Lexmark identified and focused on customer segments where Lexmark could differentiate itself by supplying laser printers with features to meet specific customer needs. With its new line of Optra plus 16 ppm laser printers, a majority of the company's laser printers were in the high-speed range, an area which the company believed would be one of the most important segments of the laser printer market. During 1995 Lexmark announced its first color laser printer, the Optra C, and in 1996 its first 24 ppm monochrome laser, the Optra N.

The company's inkjet strategy was to generate demand through retailers for Lexmark color inkjet printers by offering high quality products and providing retailers with the opportunity to earn higher margins on Lexmark products than on competitors' models. Lexmark introduced its first color inkjet printer using its own technology in 1994 and experienced strong sales growth, particularly in retail channels. Lexmark had a presence in more than 12,000 retail stores worldwide. As a result, the company made substantial capital investments in its inkjet production capacity to meet the growing demand for its color inkjet printers. Lexmark developed the new 2055 Color Jetprinter specifically focused on the needs of small business as well as 1020, 2030, 2070 Jetprinters for the home marketplace (Exhibit 3).

In addition to its core printer business, Lexmark developed, manufactured and marketed a broad line of other office imaging products, including supplies for IBM-branded printers, after-market supplies for original equipment manufacturer (OEM) products, and typewriters and typewriter supplies sold under the IBM trademark. These products required little investment but provided an important source of cash flow. Lexmark also introduced after-market laser cartridges for the large installed base of HP and other OEM laser printers. The potential for additional after-market laser cartridge business was significant.

Lexmark's distribution strategy involved a partnership between Lexmark's sales force and the dealers and distributors in the market chain. Lexmark Account Managers worked with these dealers and distributors to fulfill end-user customer requirements (Exhibit 4).

Lexmark's network printer sales strategy was to generate sales directly by calling on end-user customers. Lexmark's sales team continuously focused on delivering solutions to customers that met their needs and improved their businesses. Although Lexmark generated end-user sales, Lexmark did not sell directly to end-user customers. The product was distributed through the distributor and dealer channel. Lexmark sold products to distributors that, in turn, sold Lexmark product to dealers ranging from large corporate-focused dealers to small retail-focused dealers. These dealers fulfilled end-user customer orders generated by Lexmark Account Managers and their own sales representatives.

Lexmark's retail and supply products were also marketed through these channels. In addition, specific market chain members in the area of retail and supply products worked with Lexmark to deliver their products to end-user customers.

LEXMARK INTERNATIONAL 1996 RESULTS

In 1996, Lexmark International announced record revenues of $ 2.6 billion, record net earnings of $235 million, and a record increase in net earnings per share from $1.16 to $1.68. These numbers represented a 10 per cent increase in revenue, a 21 per cent increase in operating income and a 45 per cent increase in net earnings per share for 1996.

> "We are very pleased with our performance this year," said Marvin L. Mann, Lexmark Chairman and CEO, "particularly in light of our exit from the keyboard business at the end of the first quarter, significant inkjet printer price reductions, a new laser product announcement by Hewlett-Packard in April, IBM's re-entry into the desktop laser market in June, and a less favorable IBM supplies distribution agreement." The company's operating margins strengthened as we continued to provide highly competitive printer solutions while aggressively managing both manufacturing costs and operating expenses.

Lexmark's ability to achieve strong growth, in spite of the factors mentioned, was the result of excellent performance of our printer and associated supplies business. Revenues from this core business increased 24 per cent and contributed 77 per cent of the corporation's revenues in 1996 versus 69 per cent in 1995.

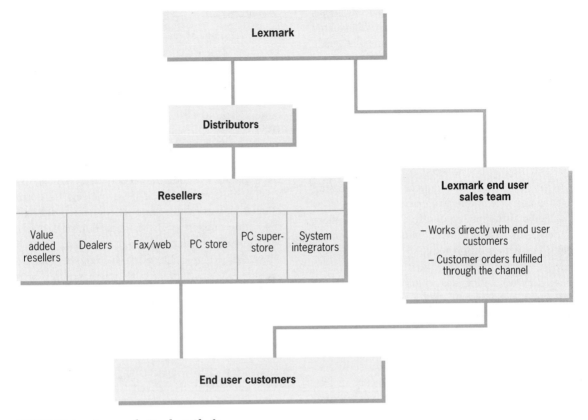

EXHIBIT 4   Lexmark Market Chain

During 1996 the company's achievements also included continued development of international markets, particularly in the Asia/Pacific region. A number of product introductions and enhancements, including the new Optra E and Optra N laser printers, and the Color Jetprinter 2030 and Color Jetprinter 2050, extended the range and competitiveness of Lexmark's printer solutions.

LEXMARK CANADA INC.

Lexmark Canada Inc., with headquarters in Markham, Ontario, was a wholly owned subsidiary of Lexmark International Group, Inc. The Canadian subsidiary was very successful in growing the business from a $40 million revenue company in 1991 to $100 million in 1996. It was often referred to as a model for other Lexmark subsidiaries around the world. The Canadian firm was well known for its creativity in approaching the marketplace.

First, Lexmark Canada early on changed the nature of the business by opening up new distribution channels via partnerships with distributors such as Merisel, Globelle and Ingram Micro. This gave Lexmark Canada a first-mover advantage over its competitors and this remained a cornerstone of its business. The approach was transferred and successfully implemented across the Lexmark worldwide organization.

Another innovation developed by Lexmark Canada was a change in its sales approach to the marketplace. Initially, the Lexmark sales organization worked with the dealer channel to push the sales of Lexmark printers. Lexmark Canada, however, had implemented a direct corporate sales force that focused on generating the business from end-user customers and then pulling the sale through the dealer channels. This idea was also shared with the other geographies. In addition, Lexmark Canada was considered a leader in cost-saving programs within the global operation as demonstrated by its exceptional expense/revenue ratio of 15 per cent.

LEXMARK CANADA'S SALES ORGANIZATION

Lexmark Canada Inc.'s prime mission was marketing and selling Lexmark products throughout Canada. As a result, the development of customer interface strategies and the deployment of the sales force were considered strategic boardroom issues. When Lexmark Canada was established, only IBM Marketing Representatives were hired. They used their IBM expertise to focus on generating business from their previous IBM accounts and also on generating new business. Their title became Account Manager although their job responsibilities were similar to their role at IBM. They were responsible for managing customer relationships with Lexmark, acting as consultants to solve customers' business problems, and most importantly, increasing the revenue and gross profit to Lexmark.

Located in different regions across Canada, there were two sets of Account Managers—Channel Account Managers and End-User Account Managers:

- The main task of Channel Account Managers was to motivate distributor and dealer representatives to sell Lexmark rather than competitors' products by using marketing incentives and generating strong customer relationships.
- End-User Account Managers focused on selling to large end-user customers in specific industry sectors such as government, education, health, automotive, banking, insurance and financial services. Using industry expertise, the Account Managers provided unique, value-added solutions to their customer sectors. Gord MacKenzie managed End-User Account Managers.

A Typical End-User Relationship

The end-user customer sales process was highly consultative which depended on an Account Manager's ability to build strong relationships. Account Managers met directly with senior level management to understand the client's business and technology strategy and resulting printing needs. They worked with the MIS Director of the organization to understand the technical environment and customer needs. Lexmark System Engineers—highly focused, technical members of the Lexmark team were often brought into the planning process. As a team, the Account Manager and Systems Engineers worked with the MIS Director and his/her department to solve business problems using printing technology. The Account Manager closed the sale by delivering a solution to the customer that improved their business success. Once the sale was completed, the Account Manager worked with selected channel dealers to fill the order and provide ongoing customer support and relationship management for the customer.

The Transition

Many Account Managers saw the move from IBM to Lexmark as a welcome change. They were able to be more creative in a less bureaucratic environment. There was also a sense of ownership in building this business. The Lexmark stock option plan, and the entrepreneurial nature of those who left the security of IBM to join Lexmark, further reinforced this feeling. They still had the support of Systems Engineers who would handle technical issues and system support for their clients. System Engineers were critical to successful implementation of large projects for corporate clients. However, the Account Managers did lose the marketing support of IBM, and additional marketing responsibilities were assigned to the Account Managers. For example, Lexmark was not yet geared up to provide extensive direct mail, telemarketing, or product launch support. Some of these activities were time-intensive and took away from the focus on customer calls. In effect, the Account Managers were responsible for initial customer contact through to training, to successful installation, to follow-through. Since the company was growing, this approach appeared to have been successful. However, when less experienced Account Managers from non-IBM backgrounds joined the organization, a need for change became evident.

Options considered to deal with the issue included training the new employees, coaching by sales managers, and setting up a mentoring system. Training was provided for new Account Managers at "Printer University" in Lexington, Kentucky. This training focused primarily on product knowledge and basic selling skills. Lexmark Canada could introduce consultative selling skills training to further enhance these skills. Coaching could be provided by the VP of Sales and by the more experienced Account Managers. However, since management time was limited and the experienced Account Managers were focused on achieving their individual quotas, this option would be difficult, although worthwhile considering. Another option was to start again to hire experienced salespeople with computer industry backgrounds. However, Lexmark Canada would need to aggressively step up recruiting efforts and this option would require very high compensation packages. With Lexmark's focus on aggressive cost management, this was something it hoped to avoid.

The Sales Teams

The option chosen to deal with the new, inexperienced Account Managers was the *sales team* concept. There were strong benefits anticipated from the new sales team approach. The approach seemed like a way to generate high performance from the sales organization at a time when the industry was becoming more demanding and competitive. It would encourage the experienced Account Managers to share their knowledge with the "rookies" and promote coaching and mentoring within the team. Competitively, this would enable Lexmark to respond more quickly to tenders and customer requests since a team with its diverse skills could get a proposal together more quickly than could a single Account Manager. In addition, it was perceived that the customer would benefit from the new sales team approach with increased customer service by having more than one person familiar with the customer.

The sales team approach was implemented just before Gord entered his new position. Based on geographic regions, the Account Managers were put into teams and assigned a team quota to achieve. Fifty per cent of their compensation depended on achieving a team quota rather than making an individual quota; 50 per cent was salary. A team would receive increased administrative and marketing support from headquarters. As well, Systems Engineers were assigned to specific teams with hopes of increasing response time and customer focus. Although assigned to sales teams, the Systems Engineers continued to report formally to Systems Engineering Managers. Account Managers faced the same issue they had faced before the sales team approach, which was struggling to gain access to a scarce resource—Systems Engineers, over whom they had no formal control. Was this really a team?

When the plan was announced, it received mixed reviews. Although team training and a well-planned selection of team leaders accompanied the rollout, this was a significant change. For years many Account Managers had controlled their compensation individually, and had not worked extensively on teams. Some Account Managers embraced the idea while others felt it would negatively impact their compensation (Exhibit 5).

THE QUEBEC SALES TEAM

Yves Gagnon joined Lexmark after working for IBM for eight years. He had extensive experience in marketing to banks and insurance corporations within the Montreal region. The role of Team Leader was new for Yves and would be performed in conjunction with his current responsibilities as an Account Manager. The team would consist of three Account Managers and one Systems Engineer who would cover the Quebec territory. When the concept was introduced, the other two Account Managers were negative. They felt that they could not control their compensation and both were disappointed that Yves had been selected over them as the Team Leader. They both left Lexmark within two months of the announcement despite strong attempts by management to get them on board.

At this point Yves placed his call to Gord and started thinking about his new team. How would he

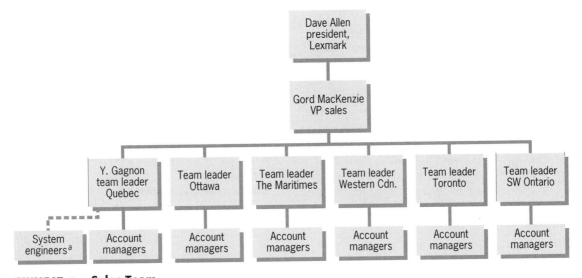

EXHIBIT 5   **Sales Team**
[a] Structure similar for other Teams

recruit new people with the skills necessary to make the Quebec team successful? Currently, he had one Systems Engineer on his team and two or three openings for new Account Managers. There were high expectations for Quebec. At the current rate it did not look as if they would make their quota target.

WHAT NOW?

Gord MacKenzie had two issues to work through. First, he had to figure out how to respond to Yves's call. What could he do for a Team Leader with no team? Was there conceivably a short-term fix?

Second, Gord had worked hard to implement the sales team concept. He believed it could be successful and could truly empower the sales force to grow the business in their regions. Some teams had already demonstrated increases in performance with the implementation of the concept. They had developed joint marketing programs and had won contracts by working together effectively. The concept certainly had strong potential. Specifically, it seemed to Gord that the team approach should help Quebec which had its own unique selling needs such as French documentation and marketing materials. However, other teams, in addition to the Quebec team, were not demonstrating success. They attempted to act as a team but were really not changing their behavior. A team would basically divide the region and the team quota among team members and proceed as they had in the past. They hoped that the sum of the individual efforts would add up to the team quota.

Gord had to think about his options and whether or not to continue with the sales team concept at Lexmark Canada Inc. Possibly there could be other ways to enhance teamwork within the sales organization that would not impact the sales force structure or the compensation plan. It was important for Gord to make a decision soon because Lexmark International continued to have high expectations of Lexmark Canada. This decision would be seen clearly by the rest of the corporation.

CASE 8-2 JEFFERSON-PILOT CORPORATION

On February 28, 1993, Roger Soles, Jefferson-Pilot's (J-P) President, Chairman of the Board, and Chief Executive Officer for the last 25 years, retired. J-P Corporation had 1992 revenues of $1.2 billion from its four business segments (individual, group, casualty and title insurance; and a communications group) and from investment income.

Soles had used a strong leadership style to guide J-P during his tenure. Decision-making and management had a top-down focus, and Soles exercised a high level of control. Despite J-P's success under Soles' leadership, however, revenues had been basically flat for the last five years (1988–92). Low interest rates, which affected investment earnings, and declining life insurance sales contributed to the sluggish revenues and earnings. The corporate culture also seemed resistant to change and fixed on retaining the status quo—the traditional way of doing things.

J-P's Board of Directors felt the company needed aggressive new leadership if the company were to be a market leader. In order to provide for a smooth transition following Soles' retirement, the Board selected David A. Stonecipher to become President-elect and brought him on board in September 1992. Stonecipher had been the president and CEO of Life of Georgia, an Atlanta-based insurance company. He also served as President of Southland Life Insurance Company and had recently become President of Georgia US Corporation, the parent company of both Life of Georgia and Southland Life.

Stonecipher had a reputation as an aggressive, outgoing leader who was willing to change and try new things. He realized that increased sales would be the

This case was prepared by Dr. Lew G. Brown, Associate Professor, and Michael Cook, MBA, of the University of North Carolina at Greensboro. The authors express their appreciation to Jefferson-Pilot Corporation for its cooperation in development of this case. Copyright © by Lew G. Brown and the North American Case Research Association. Reproduced by permission.

key to J-P's revenue growth and that he needed a strong management team if he were going to make the necessary changes. With that in mind, one of his first acts was to appoint Kenneth Mlekush as Executive Vice President of Individual Insurance. Mlekush, who had previously served as President and CEO of Southland Life, brought over 30 years of experience to the position and specialized in marketing individual life and annuity products. Mlekush later asked Ron Ridlehuber, who had worked with him at Southland, to join J-P as Senior Vice President for Independent Marketing. Ridlehuber had 18 years of experience in marketing and field sales management. Stonecipher also promoted Bill Seawell from his position as an agency manager in J-P's career sales force to serve as Senior Vice President for Ordinary Marketing. Seawell had been with J-P since 1976 and had managed the Greensboro agency since 1981. During that time, the Greensboro agency had consistently been among J-P's leading agencies.

A STRATEGIC REVIEW

After assembling his management team, Stonecipher asked a major consulting firm that specialized in working with life insurance companies to conduct a strategic marketing review of the firm. Now, in early 1993 Stonecipher had assembled the new team in a conference room in the firm's corporate offices in Greensboro, North Carolina, to hear the consultant's report. He knew this report would provide a basis for the strategic decisions the group would have to make if the company were going to meet the Board's and the shareholders' expectations. The managers knew that a key focus of the report and of the decisions facing them would be how J-P should structure and manage its sales force because life and annuity sales would need to grow dramatically in order to increase revenues significantly.

J-P'S SALES FORCE

J-P distributed its individual insurance products through three separate systems: career agents, independent producing general agents, and financial institutions. J-P hired career agents and provided them with extensive training, an office, and full staff support. The company paid the agents a salary subsidy during their training year and then changed them to a commission-only basis. The agents earned a commission on the premiums each policy generated. The agent earned a

higher commission rate on the first-year premium and then earned a lower commission rate on renewal premiums thereafter as the policyholder renewed the policy year after year. The career agents were very loyal. In fact, the company was very selective in choosing career agents. Becoming one was difficult, and those who were successful were very proud of their position. But growth based on a career system was slow, and the costs of maintaining the sales force were high.

In early 1993, J-P had approximately 800 career agents. They sold about 90 percent of its life insurance policies. Agents on average during 1992 wrote about 30 policies and earned about $26,000 in first-year commissions (the commissions paid on the policy's first-year premium). The first-year commission rate averaged 50 percent of the first-year's premium. The average career agent earned total income, including commissions on renewal policies, in the high $40,000 range. Bill Seawell was responsible for managing the career sales force.

At the beginning of 1993, there were approximately 1,400 independent personal producing agents (PGAs) distributing J-P's life and annuity products. Twelve salaried regional directors recruited about 15 to 20 PGAs each year, seeking agents who were already established in the insurance business. Although the independent agents did not work directly for J-P, the company provided extensive training and support. The PGAs allowed J-P to extend its marketing operations (in a limited way) beyond its core geographic distribution areas. Although there were more PGAs than career agents, many of them sold few J-P policies each year. They had contracts with J-P as well as with other insurance companies and could sell policies offered by any company they represented. First-year commission rates on policies sold PGAs by were in the 80–85 percent range. These rates were higher than those for career agents because J-P did not pay any of the PGAs' expenses, as it did for career agents. Ron Ridlehuber was responsible for managing the independent sales force.

J-P also used an additional distribution channel consisting of 19 relatively small community banks and savings institutions that contracted to distribute life and annuity products. J-P designed the annuity products for these institutions and controlled pricing. Jefferson-Pilot financial data are presented in Exhibits 1 and 2.

THE CONSULTANTS' PRESENTATION

David Stonecipher glanced around the conference room to make sure everyone was ready. "Well, gentlemen, let's begin." Aaron Sherman and Larry Richard-

EXHIBIT 1   Consolidated Statements of Income

(Dollar Amounts in Thousands Except Per Share Information)	Year Ended December 31		
	1990	1991	1992
REVENUE			
Life premiums and other considerations	$238,326	$230,369	$230,034
Accident and health premiums	375,872	382,624	383,552
Casualty and title premiums earned	$47,078	45,270	44,815
Total premiums and other considerations	661,276	658,263	$658,401
Net Investment income	342,053	352,772	360,882
Realized investment gains	28,201	33,963	48,170
Communications operations	127,330	125,045	129,734
Other	3,753	3,433	5,142
Total Revenue	1,162,613	1,173,476	1,202,329
BENEFITS AND EXPENSES			
Death Benefits	111,444	104,131	105,013
Matured endowments	5,223	4,455	4,576
Annuity benefits	13,903	14,912	15,054
Disability benefits	1,224	1,151	1,185
Surrender benefits	59,297	47,174	38,485
Accident and health benefits	322,922	318,876	317,350
Casualty benefits	34,605	36,657	30,025
Interest on policy or contrast funds	89,651	93,995	94,106
Supplementary contracts with life contingencies	4,997	5,346	5,637
(Decrease) in benefit liabilities	(10,050)	(764)	(1,292)
Total benefits	633,216	625,933	610,139
Dividends to policyholders	16,950	16,598	16,997
Insurance commissions	63,396	57,237	54,382
General and administrative	125,101	124,470	128,501
Net (deferral) of policy acquisition costs	(15,745)	(12,214)	(11,536)
Insurance taxes, licenses and fees	22,750	24,351	24,660
Communications operations	95,356	92,334	93,560
Total Benefits and Expenses	941,024	928,709	916,703
Income before income taxes	221,589	244,767	285,626
Income taxes (benefits):			
Current	68,031	77,839	88,889
Deferred	(4,079)	(8,759)	(6,501)
Total Taxes	63,952	69,080	83,388
Net Income	$157,637	$175,687	$203,238
Net Income Per Share of Common Stock	$2.94	$3.42	$3.99

Source: Jefferson-Pilot 1992 Annual Report.

son, who directed the project for the consulting firm, began the presentation.

"Gentlemen, I have given each of you a detailed report summarizing our findings. We wanted to meet with you today to present an overview of the key points and to answer any questions you have," Aaron Sherman began. "As you are aware, we began this process by holding a workshop with J-P's executives at which we asked them to rate issues the company faces. The number one issue they identified was that your total annualized premium income has declined during the past five years while most of your major competitors' revenues have grown. Although J-P has an excel-

lent core of field and home-office people and is in excellent financial condition, our analysis highlights areas where you need to take action.

Target and Managerial Peer Companies

"In conducting our analysis, we looked at a group of 13 companies, 7 of which we call 'managerial peers' and 6 of which we call 'target companies.' The target companies are those you face on a day-to-day basis in competing for policyholders and new agents. Some of these operate using a 'general agent,' that is an independent agent who is not a company employee. The managerial peer companies are those you compete with

EXHIBIT 2   Jefferson-Pilot Segment Information

	(Dollars in Thousands)		
	1990	*1991*	*1992*
REVENUE			
Life insurance	$946,262	$956,426	$965,862
Other insurance	55,164	53,472	53,907
Communications	127,330	125,045	129,734
Other, net	33,857	38,533	52,826
Consolidated	$1,162,613	$1,173,476	$1,202,329
INCOME BEFORE INCOME TAXES			
Life insurance	$179,725	$202,349	$217,635
Other insurance	6,575	919	7,820
Communications	16,902	18,023	24,262
Other, net	18,387	23,476	35,909
Consolidated	$221,589	$244,767	$285,626
IDENTIFIABLE ASSETS AT DECEMBER 31			
Life insurance	$4,132,811	$4,535,398	$4,817,482
Other insurance	136,449	147,309	158,741
Communications	111,130	102,836	99,938
Other, net	74,518	139,677	159,676
Consolidated	$4,454,908	$4,925,220	$5,235,837
DEPRECIATION AND AMORTIZATION			
Life insurance	$5,031	$5,741	$6,055
Other insurance	155	209	194
Communications	9,980	10,013	8,425
Other, net	324	327	172
Consolidated	$15,490	$16,290	$14,846

Source: Jefferson-Pilot 1992 Annual Report.

when you sell policies or recruit agents, but all of them use a career system like J-P, with agency managers who are responsible for the agents who work out of their offices. J-P has the highest rating in terms of claims-paying ability from both A.M. Best and Standard and Poor's rating services. Only 5 of the 13 peer companies have similar ratings. Some of your agents see the company's financial strength as a competitive weapon, while some others question whether the company has been too conservative.

Performance Analysis

"This overhead (Exhibit 3) presents a summary of your operating performance over the 1987–91 period as compared with the 13 target and managerial peer companies. As you can see, premium income and net gain before dividends have grown more slowly than the target group's average but faster than the managerial peers' average. Over this same period, the number of J-P's career-ordinary life agents has shrunk from 1,186 to 546. As a result, you have seen a decline in the percentage of your total premium income coming from

life insurance. This results also from a decline in the number of policies written and in the face amount per policy. It also appears that the productivity of your agents has lagged behind competitors. You also rely heavily on the business you develop in North and South Carolina and Virginia, as this overhead indicates (Exhibit 4).

Customer Analysis

"Next, we looked at your customers. This overhead (Exhibit 5) first compares J-P and the peer groups on the basis of premium per policy and average size per policy. Then, we break down your customers into male, female, and juvenile groups. As you can see, J-P has a lower premium per policy, average size policy, and premium per $1,000 coverage than do the peer companies. Like the peers, however, your typical customer is a male, under 35 years old who is employed in a professional or executive position. Your career agents sell 91 percent of your policies, but the policies they sell are smaller in terms of size and premium than those sold by your PGAs.

EXHIBIT 3   Jefferson-Pilot's Summary of Operations 1987–1991 (Dollar Amounts in Millions)

	1987	1988	1989	1990	1991
Premiums & annuity considerations	$648.1	$718.0	$716.3	$727.2	$768.9
Net investment income	250.1	295.3	313.0	326.6	338.7
Other income	32.0	25.8	24.1	28.0	26.8
Total income	930.2	1,039.1	1,053.4	1,081.8	1,134.4
Total expenses	802.3	916.8	890.0	896.9	930.6
Net gain before dividends	127.9	122.3	163.4	184.9	203.8
Dividends to policyholders	18.8	25.3	24.7	23.8	22.5
Net gain after dividends	109.1	96.9	138.7	161.1	181.3

	Change from 1987–1991			Average Annual Percent Change		
	JP	Target Group Average	Managerial Peers Average	JP	Target Group Average	Managerial Peers Average
Premium & annuity considerations	$120.8	$850.9	$3,182.0	4.4%	7.5%	11.7%
Net investment income	88.6	371.7	723.4	7.9%	9.1%	6.2%
Total income	204.2	796.5	3,590.1	5.1%	4.7%	8.6%
Deductions	(128.3)	(528.9)	(3,337.8)	(3.8)%	(3.5)%	(8.8)%
Net gain before dividends	75.9	267.6	252.3	12.4%	14.4%	6.3%

Source: Jefferson-Pilot.

EXHIBIT 4   Jefferson-Pilot 1991 Market Share for Selected States

	JP Share of Ordinary Life Insurance			JP's Ordinary Life Premiums (000)
	% Premium	% Issues	% In-Force	
Core Southeasten states:				
North Carolina	3.97%	2.86%	3.57%	$63,794
South Carolina	2.08	1.62	1.86	15,884
Virginia	0.94	0.54	0.88	13,017
Other major Southern states:				
Texas	0.58	0.36	0.50	19,368
Florida	0.37	0.19	0.35	10,268
Georgia	0.59	0.39	0.55	8,785
Tennessee	0.57	0.30	0.52	5,865
Louisiana	0.51	0.52	0.55	4,352
Alabama	0.36	0.07	0.28	3,108
Mississippl	0.63	0.29	0.68	2,794
Kentucky	0.33	0.35	0.31	2,181
Outside the South:				
Virgin Islands	3.73	0.60	3.28	433
Puerto Rico	2.58	1.15	1.89	3,853
California	0.07	0.03	0.05	3,738
U.S.total	0.32%	0.20%	0.29%	$175,446

Source: Jefferson-Pilot.

EXHIBIT 5   Comparison of Premiums and Average Size Per Policy

Premium/Policy Size	Jefferson-Pilot	Target Group	Managerial Peers
Premium per policy	$889	$1,211	$966
Average size policy	$101,470	$126,940	$91,580
Premium per $1,000	$8.76	$9.54	$10.55

PERCENT OF POLICIES (PREMIUM PER POLICY)

Customer Demographics	Jefferson-Pilot	Target Group	Managerial Peers
Male	51% ($1,213)	57% ($1,567)	53% ($1,257)
Female	38 ($639)	33 ($879)	36 ($744)
Juvenile	11 ($233)	10 ($255)	11 ($303)

By Whom Sold	Full-Time Agents	PGAs
Percent of policies	91%	9%
Premium of policy	$837	$1,439
Average size policy	$100,920	$127,580
Premium per $1,000	$8.29	$11.28

Source: Jefferson-Pilot.

"Because adult males account for a little over half of your policies and 70 percent of your premiums, we wanted to look more closely at this group. This overhead (Exhibit 6) shows the occupation, age, and income distribution for your male customers and those of the peer companies. Although we saw earlier that your typical customer is under 35 years old, you will note that the peer companies have larger percentages of their customers in this group and that you have a higher percentage of your customers over 45 years old. This would suggest that you should have higher premiums per policy, yet your premiums per policy are lower in both the younger and older groups and overall. Our analysis indicates that your typical male customer has a median income of $37,500."

"Why do you think our premiums are typically lower than those of the peer companies?" Ken Mlekush asked.

"That's a good question, Ken," Larry Richardson responded. "Our feeling is that the lower premiums are the result of your company's concentration in the Southeast, where incomes are generally lower than in the Northeast. A number of the peer companies have a major presence in the Northeast. Also, some of your

EXHIBIT 6   Analysis of Adult Male Consumer by Occupation, Income, and Age

	Percent of Policies (Premium per Policy)		
Occupation	Jefferson-Pilot	Target Group	Managerial Peers
Executive	37% ($1,756)	36% ($2,003)	28% ($1,728)
Professional	33 ($1,234)	41 ($1,651)	28 ($1,492)
Blue Collar	21 ($710)	18 ($884)	38 ($772)
Clerical	9 ($866)	5 ($1,664)	6 ($734)
Income			
Under $25K	26% ($625)	14% ($582)	24% ($603)
$25K–49.9K	45 ($841)	41 ($811)	51 ($956)
$50K or over	29 ($2,421)	45 ($2,400)	25 ($2,541)
Age			
Under 35	39% ($561)	47% ($671)	47% ($688)
35–44	31 ($1,169)	32 ($1,647)	27 ($1,034)
45 or over	30 ($2,056)	21 ($3,536)	26 ($2,494)

Source: Jefferson-Pilot.

agents may not be capitalizing on the opportunities in their markets, but we believe the regional difference is the key factor."

Product Comparison

"If that answers your question, Ken, we'll move on to our discussion of your products," Aaron Sherman resumed. "Our next overhead (Exhibit 7) presents an analysis of J-P's product mix, based on first-year commissions, as compared with the peer companies. As the exhibit shows, J-P has been steadily selling less life insurance, down from 76 percent of first-year commissions to 63 percent, just since 1989. The other companies' life insurance shares have held relatively constant over this time. Your salespeople are selling considerably more disability income and health insurance and annuities than are the other companies."

"Why do you think our agents are selling more annuities and disability income policies?" David Stonecipher asked.

"Our experience indicates that agents find it easier to sell disability income and annuities as compared to life insurance," Aaron Sherman answered. "Consumers can understand these policies better and salespeople find them easier to explain. Thus, the salespeople go for the easy sale. What is more important to under-

stand, however, is that it is unusual for a company with a large career sales force to stress universal life. Whole life policies provide more support for the field sales force because consumers tend to keep the policies in force longer and the renewal premiums are higher."

Sales Force Comparison

"How do our salespeople feel about the products we give them to sell?" Bill Seawell asked.

Larry Richardson responded by presenting an overhead (Exhibit 8). "This overhead summarizes our findings on that question. As you can see, relative to the norm for other companies we have surveyed, your agents were less pleased with the variety of products and were significantly less pleased with new product development. They also seemed to feel that the company is not as market driven as it should be."

"Larry, while we are on the subject of how the salespeople feel, how did we stack up relative to recruitment and retention of the sales force?" Ron Ridlehuber wondered.

"That's an important question, Ron. Our study shows that only 35 percent of J-P's new agents made it through the first year, 15 percentage points below the industry average, and only 24 percent made it through

EXHIBIT 7   Product Mix Trends (Percent of First-Year Commission)

	1989	1990	1991
JEFFERSON-PILOT			
Life	76%	70%	63%
DI/health	9	12	12
Annuities	11	13	17
Investment Products	4	5	7
Group	0	0	0
Total	100%	100%	100%
TARGET GROUP			
Life	78%	75%	75%
DI/health	7	6	6
Annuities	4	6	7
Investment Products	5	6	8
Group	7	7	5
Total	100%	100%	100%
MANAGERIAL AGENCY PEERS			
Life	76%	78%	77%
DI/health	5	5	5
Annuities	8	9	9
Investment Products	3	3	4
Group	7	6	4
Total	100%	100%	100%

Source: Jefferson-Pilot.

EXHIBIT 8 Sales Force's Ratings of JP's Products (Percent of Agents Agreeing)

Agents' Overall Assessment of Companies' Products	Jefferson-Pilot	Norm
I am pleased with the variety of products our company offers.	66%	78%
I am satisfied with our company's development of new products.	33	65
Our company is market driven, responding to the needs of its target market with appropriate products and services.	25	66

Source: Jefferson-pilot.

the first two years. Moreover, only 7 percent stay more than four years.

"This overhead (Exhibit 9) summarizes your situation pretty well. The first part of the overhead shows that in 1991, recruits represented 48 percent of your base sales force, as compared with 29 percent and 38 percent for the two peer groups. Further, as we've

noted, your base sales force has been declining while your peers' sales groups have been stable or increasing. Likewise, your turnover rates have been consistently higher than your peers. Finally, the overhead shows that only 35 percent of your sales force has been with you more than 5 years as compared with 40 percent and 46 percent for the two comparison groups.

EXHIBIT 9 Sales Force Recruitment and Retention

RECRUITS AS A PERCENT OF BASE FORCE

	Jefferson-Pilot		Target Group	Managerial Peers
	Rate	No. of Recruits		
1991	48%	280	29%	38%
1990	58	378	31	41
1989	34	316	30	40
1988	40	459	30	45
1987	42	501	33	41

PERCENT CHANGE IN BASE FORCE

	Jefferson-Pilot[a]	Target Group	Managerial Peers
1991	−6%	−1%	−1%
1990	−11	b	2
1989	−31	b	1
1988	−2	b	9
1987	−2	1	6

TURNOVER RATE

1991	36%	24%	28%
1990	44	24	28
1989	48	23	28
1988	30	23	25
1987	31	24	25

DISTRIBUTION OF SALES AGENTS BY YEARS OF SERVICE
Years of Service

1	35%	24%	29%
2	15	14	15
3	10	9	9
4	5	7	7
5+	35	46	40

[a] The field force has declined from 1,161 to 546 full-time agents.
[b] Less than 1/2 of 1 percent

Source: Jefferson-Pilot.

And after five years, we expect agents to be in their most productive period."

"Larry, what did you determine about our agents' productivity versus the peer groups?" David Stonecipher asked.

"We looked closely at the issue of productivity. We found that J-P agents earned on average lower first-year commissions (not including renewal commissions) in each year as compared with the peers. Your base sales force had average first-year commissions of about $22,000 versus $31,000 for the target group and almost $25,000 for the managerial peer group. When we looked at number of policies sold, we also found that your agents sold fewer individual life policies."

"Do you have any ideas as to why our productivity is lower, Larry?"

"Yes, David. Although there are many factors that affect productivity, it seems to the project team that J-P's production standards are low compared to the peers' standards. This may cause more experienced agents to place less business with J-P. They may meet their performance goals with you and then place other business with other firms in order to meet goals there."

"There is also evidence that the agents feel that the production levels are too low. As this overhead (Exhibit 10) shows, your managers believe that they help agents set high but attainable goals, yet slightly less than half of the agents feel that way. In looking at the validation requirements, the performance standards that first-year agents must meet, 69 percent of the agents believed they were modest or too low. Finally, your agents had considerably less activities in direct mail, telephone prospecting, etc., than did agents from the peer companies. Many salespeople don't like to perform these activities, but experience shows that the activities are a key part of building a clientele.

"Your managers and agents also seem to have different perspectives on what is required of new agents. This overhead (Exhibit 11) indicates that over 90 percent of your managers felt they give a realistic picture of an agent's career to an agent they are recruiting, yet only 32 percent of the agents felt that way. Moreover, when we asked the managers which activities they required of a new agent prior to signing a contract with them, we got a very different set of responses than we got when we asked the new agents the same question. Seventy-three percent of your new hires have not been

EXHIBIT 10   Results of Agent Survey—Production Goals

In our agency, a good job is done of helping agents set challenging but attainable production objectives:	Percent Agreement
Agency Manager	88%
Sales Manager	73
Agent	49
Norm for FT agent	52%

If validation requirements were a production level goal toward which I was working, I would see it as:	Jefferson-Pilot	Target Group	Managerial Peers
Challenging	30%	40%	48%
Modest	51	35	33
Too low	18	23	14
Too high	1	2	5

In the past month, how many:	Jefferson-Pilot	Target Group	Managerial Peers
Prospects have you mailed to	99	231	278
Prospects have you phoned	113	211	147
Cold calls have you made	41	74	63
Appointments have you had	29	49	41
Fact-finders have you completed	22	17	17
Closing Interviews have you done	17	18	18

Source: Jefferson-Pilot.

EXHIBIT 11   Results of Agent Survey—Precontract

In our agency, new agents are given a realistic picture of the agent's career:	
	Percent Agreement
Agency Manager	100%
Sales Manager	93
Agent	32
Norm for FT agent	39%

Managers: Which activities do you typically require of producers prior to contract?			
	Jefferson-Pilot	*Target Group*	*Managerial Peers*
Learn a sales talk	100%	63%	83%
Make joint calls	93	57	60
Market opinion surveys	93	74	78
Complete sales	81	57	53
Basic insurance knowledge	70	79	77
Become licensed	59	82	93

Agents: Which of the following activities were you required to complete prior to being contracted?			
Market opinion surveys	64%	24%	39%
Basic insurance knowledge	51	54	51
Become licensed	49	62	66
Complete sales	47	28	27
Learn a sales talk	39	36	40
Make joint calls	30	19	18
None	8	17	12

Source: Jefferson-Pilot.

full-time life agents previously, so it is not hard to understand that they might not fully understand what being a career agent requires."

Marketing Costs

"How did we compare as far as marketing costs, Aaron?"

"Ken, our analysis indicates that your marketing costs are generally in line with the managerial peer group. As you know, because of the one-time cost of issuing a policy and the high first-year sales commission, it costs J-P about $1.65 for each $1.00 of premium income in the first year. In other words, you lose $.65 for every dollar of premium income in the first year. That's why it is so important to keep policies on the books. It takes into the second or third year before the company makes any money on the policy.

"Your $1.65 figure compares with $1.66 for the managerial group, but it is higher than the target group's average of $1.45. We think that comes from your having more smaller offices. When we controlled for office size, your costs seemed to be in line. This overhead (Exhibit 12) shows the elements of your costs as compared with the peer companies. Your costs are higher for both producer (agent) compensation and management compensation due to your competitive bonus structure and your agent financing plan. Your home office expenses are probably higher simply because you are a smaller company than some of the peers, and there are certain fixed costs you have to bear. You should be able to grow and spread those fixed costs. To help you compare your agencies' costs with the peer group's, I prepared this overhead (Exhibit 13). It shows that your agencies are on average about one-third the size of the average peer agency."

"How do our agents feel about their compensation, Larry?"

"Bill, I prepared this overhead to summarize our findings on that point (Exhibit 14). As you can see, your full-time agents are below the norm in every category for all agents in our survey. On the other hand, your managers are above the norm in each category except for how secure they feel about their income.

"David, I think that about covers the points we wanted to present at this time. We will, of course, be

EXHIBIT 12   Components of Marketing Costs: 1991 (Per $100 of Weighted New Premiums)

	Jefferson-Pilot	Target Group	Peer Group
Producer Compensation[a]	$61	$55	$62
Management Compensation[b]	26	23	19
Field Expenses Paid by Company[c]	37	36	43
Field Benefits	17	17	24
Sub-Total	141	131	148
Home Office Marketing Expenses	24	14	18
Total	$165	$145	$166

[a] Includes all compensation *other than* renewal commissions; includes first-year commissions on management personal production.
[b] Includes compensation paid to agency managers and second-line supervisors.
[c] Includes all operating expenses paid by Company (e.g., clerical salary, rent, postage, telephone, etc.).

Source: Jefferson-Pilot.

EXHIBIT 13   1991 Average Agency Characteristics

	Jefferson-Pilot	Peers
Manager Income[a]	$100,913	$150,145
Agency first-year commission revenue	$247,941	$778,431
Managers' years of service	9.9	6.1
Number of agents	11.1	32.9
Number of recruits	5.7	11.2
Number of 2nd-line managers	1.5	2.2
2nd-line manager income[a]	$23,489	$52,075
Number of agencies	35	473

[a] Excludes personal production.

Source: Jefferson-Pilot.

EXHIBIT 14   Attitudes Toward Compensation

Full-time Agent Responses (Percent Agreement)		
	Jefferson-Pilot	Norm
I have a secure income.	39%	46%
I have a good compensation plan.	46	58
My compensation plan is competitive.	38	49
My compensation plan is clear and understandable.	51	53
I have good fringe benefits.	51	64
Managers' Responses		
	Jefferson-Pilot	Norm
I have a secure income.	33%	58%
I have a good compensation plan.	67	65
My compensation plan is competitive.	56	55
My compensation plan is clear and understandable.	66	57
I have good fringe benefits.	44	73

Source: Jefferson-Pilot.

available to answer additional questions you have as you proceed with your planning." Larry concluded.

"Thank you, Larry and Aaron. Your work will be very helpful. We'll let you go now while we continue our discussion."

OPTIONS

"Well, I don't know that any of the consultants' findings surprised us, but hearing them all together is certainly sobering," David began. "We've got our work cut out for us if we are going to achieve the growth and profitability goals the Board has set. It wants us to grow earnings per share by 10 percent per year and achieve above average returns on capital. Ken, what do you think our options are?"

"David, even if we choose the option of continuing to have the same kind of company we've had, that is one focused primarily on using the career agent to sell our products, we've got to make a number of changes to address the issues in the report. We seem to be in a cycle of declining performance. Fewer agents lead to less new business. This causes an expense problem. Due to that problem, we don't do the things we need to do to develop competitive products. It's a vicious cycle. Don't you agree, Bill?"

"Yes, Ken. But I think it is important for us to remember that our career-agent system is our key strength. We are known as a company because of that system. We have many long-term, loyal agents. As you know, my father worked here and was in charge of our career agents. We need to improve the quality of our recruits, train them better, and keep them with us. If we can do those things, we will grow faster and be more profitable."

"That's true, Bill," Ron joined in, "but it seems to me that we need to look more closely at complementing the career system by increasing our emphasis on the independent agent. We have many independent agents now, and the report shows that they are very productive. But they have never been the focus of our system. Under a new system we would contract with existing insurance agents, allowing them to offer our products. This avoids the problem of having to hire and train new recruits, and it would allow us to expand our geographic coverage more quickly. Further, we would not have to pay the office costs and associated salaries. We could pay these independent agents on a comission-only basis. Instead of using our 12 regional directors to recruit, we could license independent marketing organizations to recruit for us, with them earning an override commission on sales their agents made."

"Ron, I know you used this kind of system at Southland, but it would be such a radical change for J-P," Bill responded. "If you increased the size of our sales force substantially by using independent agents, I'm not sure how our career force would react. I'm afraid they'd be terribly threatened. And the folks in the home office are used to working with career agents. The independents would not be loyal to the company. We would have less control over what they sell and over the quality of their work with policyholders. And can you imagine what will happen the first time one of our career agents runs into an independent agent trying to sell the same product to the same customer!"

"David, you asked about options," Ken continued. "I guess this exchange points out that we could continue with a predominantly career-based system, move to a predominantly independent system, or have a combination of the two approaches. We're going to have to make significant changes under any of the options, and I'm sure there will be problems we'll have to address. A final growth option, of course, is to acquire other insurance companies. We certainly have the financial strength to do that, but even then we are going to have to address the issue of how we distribute, how we sell, our products to our policyholders."

"Yes, Ken, distribution is a key issue. I can see that there are many issues we need to think carefully about before we make a decision. Here's what I'd like for you to do. I'd like for each of you independently to consider our situation and develop recommendations as to how we should proceed. I'd like to meet again in two weeks to hear your presentations. I'll call you to set up a specific time once I check my calendar."

CASE 8-3　SHANANDOAH INDUSTRIES (B)

*I*n November 1986, Shanandoah merged with Lea-Meadows Industries, a manufacturer of upholstered furniture for living and family rooms. The merger was not planned in a conventional sense. Charlton Bates's father-in-law died suddenly in August 1986, leaving his daughter with controlling interest in the firm. The merger proceeded smoothly, since the two firms were located on adjacent properties and the general consensus was that the two firms would maintain as much autonomy as was economically justified. Moreover, the upholstery line filled a gap in the Shanandoah product mix, even though it would retain its own identity and brand names.

The only real issue that continued to plague Bates was merging the selling effort. Shanandoah had its own sales force, but Lea-Meadows Industries relied on sales agents to represent it. The question was straightforward, in his opinion: "Do we give the upholstery line of chairs and sofas to our sales force, or do we continue using the sales agents?" John Bott, Shanandoah's sales vice president, said the line should be given to his sales group; Martin Moorman, national sales manager of Lea-Meadows Industries, said the upholstery line should remain with sales agents.

LEA-MEADOWS INDUSTRIES

Lea-Meadows Industries is a small manufacturer of upholstered furniture for use in living and family rooms. The firm is over 75 years old. The company has some of the finest fabrics and frame construction in the industry, according to trade sources. Net sales in 1986 were $3 million. Total industry sales of 1,500 upholstered furniture manufacturers in 1986 were $4.4 billion. Company sales had increased 15 percent annually over the last 5 years, and company executives believed this growth rate would continue for the foreseeable future.

Lea-Meadows Industries employed 15 sales agents to represent its products. These sales agents also represented several manufacturers of noncompeting furniture and home furnishings. Often a sales agent found it necessary to deal with several buyers in a store in order to represent all lines carried. On a typical sales call, a sales agent would first visit buyers. New lines, in addition to any promotions being offered by manufacturers, would be discussed. New orders were sought where and when it was appropriate. A sales agent would then visit a retailer's selling floor to check displays, inspect furniture, and inform salespeople on furniture. Lea-Meadows industries paid an agent commission of 5 percent of net company sales for these services. Moorman thought sales agents spent 10 to 15 percent of their in-store sales time on Lea-Meadows products.

The company did not attempt to influence the type of retailers that agents contacted. Yet it was implicit in the agency agreement that agents would not sell to discount houses. All agents had established relationships with their retail accounts and worked closely with them. Sales records indicated that agents were calling on furniture and department stores. An estimated 1,000 retail accounts were called on in 1986.

SHANANDOAH INDUSTRIES

Shanandoah is a manufacturer of medium- to high-priced living and dining room wood furniture. The firm was formed in 1902. Net sales in 1986 were $50 million. Total estimated industry sales of wood furniture in 1986 were $7.1 billion at manufacturers' prices.

The company employed 10 full-time sales representatives who called on 1,000 retail accounts in 1986. These individuals performed the same function as sales agents but were paid a salary plus a small commission. In 1986 the average Shanandoah sales representative received an annual salary of $50,000 (plus expenses) and a commission of 0.5 percent on net company sales. Total sales administration costs were $112,500.

The Shanandoah sales force was highly regarded in the industry. The salespeople were known particularly for their knowledge of wood furniture and their willingness to work with buyers and retail sales personnel. Despite these points, Bates knew that all retail accounts did not carry the complete Shanandoah furniture line. He had therefore instructed John Bott to "push the group a little harder." At present, sales repre-

Prepared by Professor Roger A. Kerin of Southern Methodist University. Reproduced by permission.

sentatives were making 10 sales calls per week, with the average sales call running three hours. Remaining time was accounted for by administrative activities and travel. Bates recommended that the call frequency be increased to seven calls per account per year, which was consistent with what he thought was the industry norm.

MERGING THE SALES EFFORT

In separate meetings with Bott and Moorman, Bates was able to piece together a variety of data and perspectives on the merger question. These meetings also made it clear that Bott and Moorman differed dramatically in their views.

John Bott had no doubts about assigning the line to the Shanandoah sales force. Among the reasons he gave for this approach were the following. First, Shanandoah had developed one of the most well-respected, professional sales groups in the industry.[1] Sales representatives could easily learn the fabric jargon, and they already knew personally many of the buyers who were responsible for upholstered furniture. Second, selling the Lea-Meadows line would require only about 15 percent of present sales call time. Thus he thought the new line would not be a major burden. Third, more control over sales efforts was possible. He noted that Charlton Bates's father-in-law had developed the Shanandoah sales group 25 years earlier because of the company commitment it engendered and because it provided customer service "only our own people are able and willing to give." Moreover, "our people have the Shanandoah 'Look' and presentation style that is instilled in every person." Fourth, he said it wouldn't look right if we had our representatives and agents calling on the same stores and buyers.

He noted that Shanandoah and Lea-Meadows Industries overlapped on all their accounts. He said, "We'd be paying a commission on sales to these accounts when we would have gotten them anyway. The difference in commission percentages would not be good for morale."

Martin Moorman advocated keeping sales agents for the Lea-Meadows line. His arguments were as follows. First, all sales agents had established contacts and were highly regarded by store buyers, and most had represented the line in a professional manner for many years. He, too, had a good working relationship with all 15 agents. Second, sales agents represented little, if any, cost beyond commissions. Moorman noted, "Agents get paid when we get paid." Third, sales agents were committed to the Lea-Meadows line: "The agents earn a part of their living representing us. They have to service retail accounts to get the repeat business." Fourth, sales agents were calling on buyers not contacted by Shanandoah sales representatives. He noted, "If we let Shanandoah people handle the line, we might lose these accounts, have to hire more sales personnel, or take away 25 percent of the present selling time given to Shanandoah product lines."

As Bates reflected on the meetings, he felt that a broader perspective was necessary beyond the views expressed by Bott and Moorman. One factor was profitability. Existing Shanandoah furniture lines typically had gross margins that were 5 percent higher than those for Lea-Meadows upholstered lines. Another factor was the "us and them" references apparent in the meetings with Bott and Moorman. Would merging the sales efforts overcome this, or would it cause more problems? Finally, the idea of increasing the sales force to incorporate the Lea-Meadows line did not sit well with him. Adding a new salesperson would require restructuring of sales territories, potential loss of commission to existing people, and "a big headache."

---

[1] Additional background information on the company and industry can be found in case 2-2, Shanandoah Industries (A).

CHAPTER 9

TERRITORY DESIGN

> Remember that time is money.
>
> BENJAMIN FRANKLIN

Chapter Consultant:
David Pinals, President, TTG, Incorporated

LEARNING OBJECTIVES

After studying this chapter, you should be able to:

→ Explain when sales territories should be used.

→ List the advantages of sales territories.

→ Design territories using the workload and buildup methods.

→ Understand how computers programs can help build sales territories.

WHY USE TERRITORIES?

In the previous chapter on designing sales force organizations, we mentioned that one of the most common sales force specialization methods is to assign salespeople all accounts in a particular geographic area. Even when sales forces are organized according to other specialties (e.g., products, customers, or functions), salespeople's responsibilities are often restricted to a particular geographic boundary or territory. The purpose of this chapter is to discuss processes for designing geographic territories and issues when assigning salespeople to a particular territory.

A *territory* is defined as customers located in a geographic area that are assigned to an individual salesperson. Thus, although territories are often referenced in geographic terms, the defining element of a territory is the set of customers in the geography. The primary benefit of using sales territories is improved market coverage—which usually means better customer relations. Having each field rep assigned to a specific group of customers and prospects enables the salesperson to know each customer for which they are responsible, which, in turn, is likely to lead to improved service on orders and delivery. Many customers prefer building an enduring relationship with a single field rep rather than having to get acquainted with a new person on each call. In this section, the reasons for assigning salespeople to territories are discussed.

Motivation and Cost Savings

The use of territories benefits salespeople. When salespeople know that they are responsible for all of the customers in an area, they are more likely to put forth extra efforts to satisfy their customers' demands. This sole responsibility for a territory increases salespeople's involvement and pride in their jobs. They participate in goal setting and have benchmarks by which they can evaluate their own success. Hiring salespeople to match customers' requirements in each territory can greatly improve the effectiveness of the sales force.

Sales territories can be justified economically because they help reduce marketing costs. When only one person covers each geographic area, duplication of sales calls and related travel costs are eliminated. Salespeople in well-designed territories spend less time traveling and more time selling, resulting in lower sales costs as a percentage of sales.

Evaluation and Control

The performance of individual salespeople can be more easily controlled and evaluated with sales territories. When territories are well balanced in terms of potential, differences across territories can be attributed to the abilities of individual salespeople. Thus when salespeople have their own areas, performance can be more easily compared across time, and against sales potential and sales quotas. The Strategic Action box discusses how even smaller companies are finding that well-designed territories are important, and that mapping software can be helpful in designing sales territories.

When Are Territories Unnecessary?

Although sales territories have many benefits, companies that sell directly to consumers, such as real estate brokers, stockbrokers, insurance salespeople, and some door-to-door salespeople, do not have assigned territories. Territories are not essential when salespeople contact customers infrequently and spend most of their time prospecting for new clients. For example, one salesperson sold an amazing $1.3 million of Mary Kay Cosmetics to friends in Minneapolis in a calendar year. This feat would not have been possible had Mary Kay restricted its consultants to specific areas.

STRATEGIC ACTION COMPETENCY
Helping Smaller Companies to Be Competitive

Dividing up sales territories is an infrequent event because of the complexity of the task. Today, however, even small firms are able to employ computer mapping software to simplify the process. For example, a sporting goods rep organization with seven salespeople used a program offered by GeoQuery of Naperville, Illinois, to create sales territories. When the company plotted the location of its 200 top accounts on the territory maps, they found examples of overlapping coverage and misallocated resources. The maps were so vivid and convincing that the salespeople voluntarily adjusted their account assignments with little or no hassle.

Western Sales Company, a rep firm that sells to 300 plumbing distributors, used mapping software to help fuel a 20 percent sales increase in a 40 percent down market. Their objective was to divide up the workload of four outside salespeople to create equitable territories and increase sales. Western begins with the selection of an arbitrary geographic area near the salesperson's home. The accounts and contacts from the company database are displayed on GeoQuery maps. The territories are each reviewed to be sure a salesperson can write enough business to justify the territory's existence. If it is too big it is divided or shared with another salesperson. Even before hiring is done, an area can be plotted to see whether there is enough volume for another rep. Now the company can try out territories in a few minutes where before it would have taken 90 days.

The other frequent exception to assigning people sales territories is in the case of strategic accounts. In a strategic accounts program, managers are assigned a limited number of accounts, perhaps only one. The headquarters of these accounts may be in geographic proximity, but the discussion of the benefits of geographic specialization and the methods discussed in this chapter for designing territories are not applicable.

TERRITORY DESIGN PROCEDURES

The effective design of sales territories is basically a six-part decision process (Figure 9-1). A variety of events can trigger adjustments in field sales territories. When two firms merge, it is often necessary to combine sales forces to save money and to ensure adequate market coverage. Territories are also redesigned when sales in an area grow to the point where the existing salesperson is unable to handle the business. Sometimes territories are revised to take into account product line changes or relocation of the company's or customer's plants. Each step in the territory design process can be done manually or with the help of a computer. We will start by discussing each step and then describe how territories can be designed using computer programs.

Select Control Units

The first step in the process is to select an appropriate *geographic control unit,* which is a unit of geography that can be combined to form sales territories. Control units must be small enough to allow flexibility in setting boundaries but not so small as to require massive data manipulation. These units also must have less area than a territory and clearly recognized boundaries. Examples of commonly used geographic control units are described in Table 9-1. At first glance, countries would seem to be too large a unit for designing sales territories. However, a firm that is exporting goods to Europe might combine several small countries

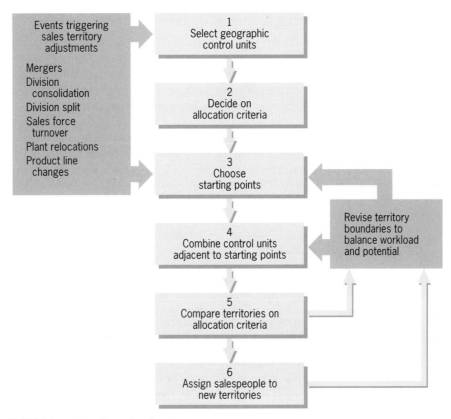

FIGURE 9-1   Territory Design Process

such as Holland, Belgium, and Luxembourg into one territory. States or provinces may also appear to be too big for combination into territories. States are most often used as control units when a firm attempts to cover a whole country with a few salespeople. Small states such as Rhode Island, Connecticut, Massachusetts, and New Hampshire are frequently combined to create a single territory.

When a firm does a lot of urban business, cities or metropolitan areas can be desirable control units. Firms that divide up cities into several sales territories often rely on zip codes or census tracts as control units. The ultimate control unit involves building territories by combining groups of customers. This approach is seldom used because the computational burden becomes excessive. Only when a company has a very limited number of large customers can accounts serve as territorial design control units. The most common approach in the United States is to build up territories using counties. They are small enough to expedite territory construction, and potential data are routinely published for these units.

TABLE 9-1   Geographic Control Units Used in Territory Design

Countries	Cities
States or provinces	Zip codes
Counties	Census tracts
Metropolitan areas	Customers

Decide on Allocation Criteria

A variety of criteria such as *equality of opportunity,* number of current customers, and sales potential can be employed to combine control units into viable sales territories. The idea of building sales territories to ensure equality on some dimensions has great appeal to both sales managers and salespeople. Equality among territories should provide a sense of fair play, because every salesperson has a chance to earn equal pay.

A company may not want its territories designed equal in potential, for instance, when it wants a career ladder for its salespeople that does not require them to become managers. A career ladder concept provides people with the opportunity to assume increased responsibilities and rewards in order to recognize their professional success and to provide them with an opportunity for continued growth. As a result, some companies have different grades or levels to which salespeople can be promoted, which include greater responsibilities and also the opportunity for greater rewards. In such a system, the company will be more interested in equalizing territories within the same sales grade on the career ladder, rather than equalizing all sales territories.

Quantitative Factors   Three basic allocation criteria include:

1. Number of current customers.
2. Potential (number of possible accounts or Buying Power Index).
3. Size (square miles or square kilometers).

The current customer base provides a good estimate of the present workload. It is desirable to include some existing customers in each sales territory you create, because having some regular customers helps boost sales force morale and provides a minimum income for reps paid on commission. Current dollar sales in an area should not be used as the sole allocation criterion, because it ignores future potential. Furthermore, a salesperson who has worked hard to build up a territory will be quite unhappy if his or her territory is split up on the basis of current sales and a new person reaps the benefits of those past labors.

Potential is an important design factor because sales managers are interested in new business growth. Potential can be measured as the number of customers who could use your product or as an index such as the Buying Power Index. When potentials are poorly allocated across territories, salespeople often spend too little time opening accounts. Balancing territories on the basis of geographic size has a direct impact on sales force efficiency. When some territories are much larger than others, salespeople will spend excessive time traveling between accounts and not enough time closing sales. Remember that when you make territories compact, you also help reduce travel expenses.

Additional Factors   Other factors that influence the design of sales territories include the location of rivers, lakes, bridges, mountains, and roads. Sales managers often keep relief maps in their offices so that they can see how topographical features will influence sales force travel patterns. The availability of bridges and superhighways often influences how boundaries are drawn for sales territories. Sometimes information on the special needs and requirements of large accounts can impact territory design.

Choose Starting Points

The third step in territory design is to select geographic locations to serve as *starting points* for new territories. Since geographic control units are combined to form territories, one control unit must be chosen around which to combine the additional control units. This control unit is referred to as the starting point. The significance of this point is that the starting point that is chosen often determines the geographic boundary of the territories.

A common choice is the salesperson's present home, because the cost of relocating salespeople can be avoided and representatives remain near family and friends. Another popular *starting point* is a large city. Salespeople in urban locations usually have access to a large number of customers, and there is less need for extensive travel. An alternative method is to design the sales territory around the needs of major clients. In this case, the location of the largest customer in an area might be selected as the home base for the salesperson, and other areas might be added to complete the territory. Occasionally a starting point will be a central geographic location, and the preferences of the salesperson or the presence of a city is disregarded. This approach assumes that a place can be found for the salesperson to live after the territory has been created.

The problems of finding starting points for sales territories can be illustrated by looking at a map of the state of Kentucky (Figure 9-2). This map shows the location of counties, major cities, and county population as a measure of potential. If two salespeople are placed in Kentucky, one would probably be located in Louisville to cover the western half of the state, and the second would be placed in Lexington to handle the east. Neither location is very good because they are on the extreme northeastern or northwestern edges of the two territories. In addition, the Lexington-based salesperson would have to travel to the northern tip of the state to cover Covington, which is across the Ohio River from Cincinnati. The heavy concentration of business in the Cincinnati area would probably lead this salesperson to neglect some of the mountainous areas in the southeastern part of the territory. One possible solution would be to give Boone, Kenton, and Campbell counties to the Cincinnati-based salesperson.

If three salespeople are assigned to Kentucky, then the third territory would be placed in the western part of the state. Possible starting points for this territory would be Bowling Green, Owensboro, and Paducah. Owensboro has the disadvantage of being on the northern edge of the territory, and Paducah is too far to the west. A Paducah location would require extensive travel in an east-west pattern. Also, the north-south orientation of Kentucky Lake and Lake Barkley further complicates travel patterns in the area. One solution would be to carve off the seven most westerly counties and give them to a salesperson in another state. This example shows how difficult it is to find starting points for sales territories when you have an irregularly shaped state bounded by rivers and containing noncentral population clusters. You can also see why some firms use independent agents to cover sparsely populated areas.

Combine Adjacent Control Units

Once starting points have been selected, the next step is to begin combining control units. The most popular way of doing this is known as the *buildup method*. To be effective, you need to keep running totals on the allocation criteria for each new territory. If number of customers per county is the criterion, you first combine the counties adjacent to each starting point and keep track of the total number of customers in each territory. Then you assign counties between different starting points to territories to balance the number of customers across the new territories. The process of allocating counties to starting points continues until all control units are assigned to individual salespeople.

An example of three sales territories that were built up around the suggested starting points for Kentucky is shown in Figure 9-3. The territories were constructed using the county population figures shown in Figure 9-2. Note that the solution was simplified by including the three northernmost counties in the Cincinnati territory. Territory 2 turned out to be the smallest because of the heavy population concentration in the Louisville-Frankfort area. Territory 1 is large and ungainly, but it can be covered quite well from Bowling Green using Route 64, Cumberland Parkway, Kentucky Parkway, and the Green River Parkway. Routes 64 and 75 are available to travel the northern and western parts of

The numbers in each county are
population figures and are
a measure of potential.

FIGURE 9-2   **Kentucky Counties, Major Cities, and Population Centers**

territory 3. However, the rest of territory 3 is mountainous and will be extremely difficult to cover.

Compare Sales Territories   After you make an initial allocation of control units to starting points, you need to compare territories using other criteria. For example, if a set of territories has the same number of customers, you would then calculate the square miles in each territory to see how the territories compare in size. If there is an imbalance, look at counties on the borders of the territories to see if some switching could improve the initial allocation. The solution may be to shift a large county with few customers from the largest to the smallest territory. Unfortunately, large and small territories are not always contiguous, and switches often must be made across several territories. *Balancing territories* on several important criteria, such as customers, potential, and size, is often very difficult.

A comparison of three sales territories created for Kentucky (Figure 9-3) is shown in Table 9-2. The three territories are well matched in terms of potential as measured by population. The largest and smallest territories vary less than 1 percent on this dimension. In terms of size, however, territory 2 is only 60 percent as large as the other territories. This means that territory 2 would be relatively easy to cover, whereas the others present some problems. With the present boundaries, the salesperson in territory 3 has to cross part of territory 1 to get to Whitley County in the south (Figure 9-3). If the salesperson has to cross Laurel County, why not shift Laurel from territory 1 to territory 3? Although this move would help balance the territories in terms of size, it would lead to greater imbalance on potential. The salesperson in territory 1 would have to give up potential represented by 38,982 people. In this particular case, territory 1 might be willing to give up Laurel County because the Cumberland Parkway stops in neighboring Pulaski County. Given the uneven distribution of potential across Kentucky, there is no way that the three territories can be perfectly balanced on both size and potential.

FIGURE 9-3 **Three Kentucky Sales Territories**

The problem of designing three territories for Kentucky gets more complicated when you introduce a third allocation factor, such as the number of customers. Because many salespeople receive commission income, it is important to balance territories based on existing customers so that wages do not get out of line. However, keeping track of three allocation variables as you move counties back and forth among territories gets rather confusing. One solution that we will discuss later is to use a computer to help you design sales territories.

A Workload Approach

An alternative to the traditional buildup method of creating territories is the *workload approach.* The basics of this technique were presented in Chapter 2 when discussing alternative methods for determining the desired size of the sales force. The workload approach focuses on the development of territories that are equivalent in terms of the work to be performed. The key step is the determination of the optimum call frequency for particular classes of customers. Present and potential customers are located on a map, and the number of firms in each class is multiplied by the theoretical call frequencies to give a total number of planned calls for each area. Adjacent areas are then combined to create territories with a proscribed number of annual sales calls. An example of how the workload approach was successfully employed is presented in the Coaching Competency box.

TABLE 9-2 **Comparing Three Kentucky Sales Territories**

Territory	Potential as Measured by Population	Number of Counties
1	1,124,897	47
2	1,129,290	27
3	1,131,137	43

COACHING COMPETENCY
Eastman Kodak Company

Kodak's experience with territory redesign in its professional imaging division is a example of the workload approach to territory design, and also illustrates how territories can be combined with other forms of sales force specialization. Kodak was experiencing problems with customers because salespeople had to call on a wide variety of clients and sell a vast array of products. Sally Malloy had to sell film and paper to portrait and wedding labs, commercial color labs, and professional resellers. Each type of customer had special needs and Sally had to be familiar with more than 60 types of film. To improve customer service, Kodak shifted from straight geographical territories where reps had to sell everything to everyone, to customer-oriented territories that recognized the special skills of each salesperson. The new territories were created with a geographic mapping program. This showed the locations of different types of customers on a computer screen and the home bases of each salesperson. Annual call frequencies were developed for each account and the special selling skills of the 300 salespeople were identified. The sales force was reorganized into three groups for commercial services and six for portrait/wedding and photographer/resellers. Sally Malloy is now assigned to a new territory in Chicago where she calls exclusively on commercial photo labs. Sally's dollar volume is less and her customer base has dropped from 500 to 60. However, Sally is a lot happier, her compensation has remained the same, and her new territory allows her to do a better job of solving customers' problems. A workload approach to territory design was successful for Kodak because salespeople are paid salaries and are not compared on the basis of sales volume. For more information on Kodak, see *www.kodak.com*.

While the workload method focuses on the number of sales calls required for a set of accounts, revenue and profit potential need not be forgotten when developing territories. W.W. Grainger Inc., a $3.5-billion distributor of maintenance and repair supplies, divides its account list among its 1,400 salespeople using what it calls an alignment index. An alignment index is assigned to each account based on its revenue history and workload. Workload is measured as the number of service hours devoted to each account. Whether a salesperson manages four small accounts or one large account, the alignment index should total approximately 1,000 points.

Dividing a Large Territory

A common problem encountered by sales managers is how to divide a territory that has too many present and/or potential customers for one person to handle. A map of an area to be divided into two sales territories is shown in Figure 9-4a. The map shows the present number of customers per county for one salesperson working the territory from Brockton. A logical home base for the second salesperson is Hillsdale, located in the west-central part of the territory. If these two cities are used as starting points, new territories can be constructed by adding and subtracting adjacent counties until all counties are assigned and the number of customers is the same for both territories.

Proposed new territories are shown in Figure 9-4b. Note that the heavy concentration of customers in the Brockton area has produced one small territory in the eastern region and one very large territory in the west. Although the two new territories have the same number of customers (225), the western territory requires considerable travel because the customers are more scattered. This solution may be acceptable if the current salesperson is located in Brockton and has reached an age where a smaller geographic territory would be appreciated.

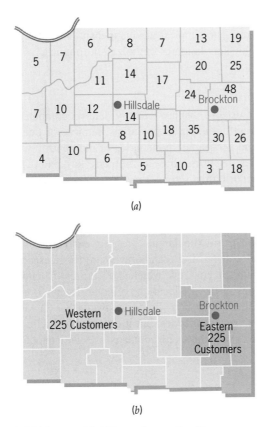

FIGURE 9-4   Dividing a Large Territory

An alternative solution is to divide the area into northern and southern territories, with Brockton located at the boundary between the two. While the size of the territories, number of customers, and travel time would be equalized, the territories would be wide and narrow. If both salespeople were traveling west from Brockton, travel expenses would be greater than the solution shown in Figure 9-4b.

The next step in the buildup process is to consider sales potential figures for each county. The western territory has more undeveloped potential than the eastern region, and the two new territories would be more balanced on size and potential if four or five western counties are shifted to the Brockton territory. Unfortunately, the current workload is then out of balance, since the eastern territory would have about 50 more customers. The example shows that variations in the dispersion of customers and potential across areas make it extremely difficult to construct territories that are equivalent in terms of travel time, number of present customers, and sales potential. Since both the buildup and workload methods create territories by combining geographic areas according to a set of rules, computers can be employed to speed the search for the most efficient territory boundaries.

DESIGNING TERRITORIES BY COMPUTER

Computer software programs are now routinely used to help design sales territories. Sales managers can save a great deal of time by building territories with computer programs. In one firm it took up to a day to redefine boundaries for a single territory, whereas the whole job can now be done in a few hours on a computer.[1] Territory design programs function by automating some or all of the design processes shown in Figure 9-1. There are three basic types of design programs. The simplest are inexpensive mapping programs; the more complicated programs employ simulation or optimization routines.

Territory Mapping Programs

Mapping programs are used to display territory data on computer screens. First, you enter into the program basic information on potentials, number of present accounts, home locations of salespeople, and geographic boundaries of the control units. Then you draw tentative territory boundaries, using a mouse or numeric key pad. The program displays your planned territories in color on the screen, together with summary data on potentials, current accounts, and geographic size. Through an interactive process of trial and error, you reallocate control units to balance your territories.

STARmanager Advanced Edition, published by TTG, Inc., is an example of a commercial mapping program. This microcomputer program can be purchased for under a thousand dollars and used to reallocate territories and draw maps for salespeople. In this program, territory maps are tied in with spreadsheets, which show current potentials, sales, and target number of calls. Any changes made in allocations of control units to territories are automatically reflected in the spreadsheet data. You should be aware that STARmanager is an interactive program that helps you create territories, but it does not find an optimum design. The Technology Competency box shows how one company uses an interactive mapping program.

Simulating New Territories

A more advanced approach to territory design employs computer simulation procedures. With simulation, you set up an objective function and attempt to minimize it, subject to a set of constraints. Some computer programs use an objective function designed to ensure com-

---

TECHNOLOGY COMPETENCY
Perdue Frederic Pharmaceuticals

Dividing up sales territories is a headache for most companies. Stephanie Thompson, manager of marketing programs at Perdue Frederic Pharmaceuticals, recalls: "We used to sit down with our district sales manager for days and do a ton of manual calculations to put together our territories." As the company grew in size, they found they could no longer manage their territories by hand, and they turned to a computer software package. The mapping software allowed Thompson to reconfigure regions in just half a day instead of the several days she previously needed.

The interactive computer program selected uses data on zip code locations of physicians, current call activities, and major highway routes to build territories. As the territories are put together, they are shown as maps on a computer screen and summarized on spreadsheets. This allows managers to balance territories on potentials and other variables. The computer-generated territories are fine-tuned during meetings with regional and district managers. Although "the software is a wonderful thing, nothing takes the place of a district manager's knowledge."

Perdue Frederic believes the computerized system works better than the old approach. Salespeople can see that new assignments are fair because objective criteria are used. The company no longer makes the arbitrary assignments of physicians that were common under the old plan. Also, salespeople now get printed maps and lists of physicians to be called on. This was not available with the manual program.

pactness, called the moment of inertia. This is simply the sum of the squares of distances from the control units to the trial territory centers weighted by the potential in each area. The smaller the moment of inertia, the greater the compactness of the territories that make up the sales district.

Simulation leads to improved territory designs because the computer examines more combinations than a manager is likely to review using an interactive mapping program. However, simulation does not produce the best possible or optimum territories, and multiple runs are needed to find a good solution.

Optimizing Territory Design

The most sophisticated design programs balance territories that are financially optimal, using a customer response to selling effort and minimizing driving time. These optimizing programs are quite complicated and must be run on high-powered computers. TerrAlign, published by Metron, Inc., requires a Windows operating system, and costs $20,000 and up.[2] Tactics International, Ltd., offers a territory modeling program called Heavy Duty Tactician for $9,995.[3] The high cost of *optimizing programs* suggests that they are most appropriate for firms with large numbers of field salespeople.

Guiding Reps to Clients

Computers can also be used to guide salespeople to the location of customers within the territories you have created. Cars can be equipped with a radio that communicates with a Global Positioning System (GPS) satellite and an onboard computer with detailed maps. The salesperson simply enters the location in the territory that he or she wants to visit, and the computer provides on-screen directions.[4] The GPS system locates the car within a few feet and can even tell you what lane to be in to make a turn. These systems are available on Avis rental cars in many cities and can be purchased as an option on some new cars.

Limitations of the Computer Approach

Computers are being used successfully to build territories and guide reps to customer locations. However, they sometimes make mistakes when they don't know about traffic congestion, the location of rivers, and other natural barriers. One computer-designed sales territory was split down the middle by the Appalachian Trail. This meant that the salesperson would have to spend a great deal of time traveling up and down narrow mountain roads to get from one half of the territory to the other. To avoid these problems, the computer either has to be told about the barriers or managers must make manual adjustments.

TERRITORY ASSIGNMENTS

The last step in our territory design process is to assign salespeople to individual territories (Figure 9-1). This task is usually completed by district sales managers. The decisions are made by matching the background and needs of salespeople with the opportunities in each geographic area. Factors considered include the present home location, age, and experience of salespeople; the size of the territories; and the customer mix located in each area. For example, some firms try initially to place newly hired young people in territories near areas where they have grown up or gone to school. This makes it easier for new reps to get started and can reduce first-year turnover. Conversely, experienced salespeople may be given more remote territories that are full of undeveloped sales potential.

You should realize that territory boundaries do not last forever, and you have to adjust them regularly to resolve local issues (Figure 9-1). These include situations where salespeople encounter personal problems and are unable to handle all their accounts. Also, you may have a situation where the special needs of a customer require a more experienced rep. Often these problems can be resolved by assigning a few accounts to salespeople in adjacent territories. The idea is to fine-tune territory boundaries without having to go through a complete redesign that would upset everyone.

SUMMARY

Sales territories are the group of customers located in a geographic area that are assigned to individual salespeople. Territories are frequently used in combination with other forms of sales specialization such as product, customer, and function.

1. **Explain when sales territories should be used.** Sales territories are likely to be used in any industry, although they are less likely to be used when the sales force is contacting consumers infrequently and spending most of their time prospecting for new customers, as in the case of Mary Kay Cosmetics, Tupperware, insurance, and other direct marketers. Geographically defined territories are also of less relevance for the management of strategic accounts.

2. **List the advantages of sales territories.** Well-designed sales territories should increase salespeople's motivation and involvement, while helping to control sales costs and evaluate the performance of individual salespeople.

3. **State the steps in designing territories using the workload and buildup methods.** The steps are (1) select a geographic control unit, (2) decide on an allocation criteria, (3) choose a starting point, (4) combine control units adjacent to starting points, (5) compare territories on allocation criteria and perhaps return to step 3 and choose a new starting point, and (6) assign salespeople to individual territories.

4. **Describe how computer programs can help in building sales territories.** Three types of computer software are available for designing sales territories. Mapping programs allow sales managers to combine geographic control units on a map while the program calculates the statistics for the design. Simulation programs attempt to minimize an objective function based on the geographic distance and potential of the territories. Optimizing programs are based on modeling the response function of customers to different amounts of sales effort and attempting to optimize the financial results of the territories.

KEY TERMS

Allocation criteria	Equality of opportunity	Optimizing program
Balancing territories	Geographic control units	Starting points
Buildup method	Mapping programs	Territory
Duplication of opportunities	Moment of inertia	Workload approach

DEVELOPING YOUR COMPETENCIES

1. **Technology.** Market Statistics, which produces the Survey of Buying Power, is now offering a computer program to help design sales territories. The basic program sells for $5,950 and includes some on-site training. A county data file to use with the program costs $6,950, zip code data sell for $11,950, and both files are priced at $12,950. Major

highway data are available for $450. The program displays county and zip code borders on a computer screen and allows you to draw lines to create sales territories. In addition, the program keeps running totals on several control factors. Additional training and support for the program can be purchased for $600 a day plus travel and expenses. How can sales managers justify expenditures of this size to the presidents of their companies? How will you know whether you have an optimum solution with this program? What determines the amount of money you can spend on computer programs to design sales territories?

2. **Self-Management.** Often the size and potential of their assigned territories directly affect the success and income of salespeople. However, it is difficult to create territories that are equivalent in terms of potential and travel time. The three Kentucky sales territories shown in Figure 9-3 are a case in point. Louisville is clearly the best territory, and the sales manager has to decide who gets this plum. Some managers solve this problem by giving the best territories to their best salespeople or as a reward to a favorite salesperson. Should the person who sold the most in the previous period always be the one considered for the best territory? What ethical issues might arise in such a situation and how should they be resolved?

3. **Coaching.** FiberTech Medical Inc.'s process for opening new territories is a good example of not doing what most other people do. When FiberTech Medical Inc. opens a new sales territory, it doesn't look to its current salespeople or hire a new salesperson to oversee the new territory. In fact, the seller responsible for the new territory most likely is an independent sales agent who sells a number of different companies' products and services. Why would FiberTech, a Baltimore-based company that services endoscopes and other medical accessories, give the responsibility of growing a new territory to an independent sales agent? Are there any other alternatives to your own salespeople opening a new territory?

4. **Strategic Action.** Peckham Boston Advisors shows how strategy affects the need for territories. Jack Peckham, a commercial real-estate broker and president of Peckham Boston Advisors, isn't big on face-to-face meetings with prospective clients. So how was Jack able to clinch a recent $28 million sale of an office building located in Marlborough, Massachusetts? Simple: He does all his selling in cyberspace. In the past two and a half years, Jack has sold commercial real estate almost exclusively online. He lists properties for sale on his company's Web site, sends e-mails highlighting new listings, and negotiates and closes deals via e-mail, and occasionally by telephone. Speaking of the $28 million sale, Peckham says, "In all, this deal took about 14 weeks. If we hadn't used cyberspace, a normal deal like this could take six months or more." In addition to apparently reducing the selling cycle, how else does the Internet help Peckham? Are there any limitations to using the Internet as a substitute to face-to-face selling? In which types of selling situations would cyber-selling likely not be as successful?

5. **Global Perspective.** Territory alignment and assignments seem to get even more complicated in an international setting. Consider the following situation. Debbie Smith has had enough of Rome, Madrid, and Berlin. Enough of trains and planes. And enough of language barriers. Her boss, Claire Williams, vice-president of international sales for Luxury Resorts, is rarely available for advice. With Smith based in Paris and Williams in Los Angeles, communication is a real challenge. Although conversant in French, she doesn't know enough of the European languages, customs, and etiquette to successfully sell to the high-end executives her company targets for its resort properties in the United States. Basically, Smith feels that she has no support, and has been shipped off to Europe to sink or swim. Tired of being ignored, Smith called James Cook, Luxury's worldwide director of sales and marketing. She requested a position back in the States, and offered to remain in her position until Cook could find a replacement. His initial reaction was to try to con-

vince Smith to stay on in Europe, but she said she would only do so if she could report directly to Cook—and that she would leave the company altogether if she couldn't have one of those two options. He said he'd get back to her within the week. Cook does not want to lose Smith or upset Williams. What would you advise Cook to do?

6. **Teamwork.** When you consider your company's customer list to be like a pie and sales territories are an effort to cut the pie into pieces, you realize that territory realignments have the potential to undermine the cohesion and effectiveness of your sales team. Suppose you are a regional manager and one of your salespeople has left the company on short notice. You have to quickly assign that salesperson's 50 accounts to another salesperson before you start losing sales to your competition. On the one hand, you might consider giving the accounts to a veteran salesperson in your region because it is an easy transition. You feel comfortable that the senior salesperson will properly service these accounts. On the other hand, you wonder if you should give these accounts to a new salesperson that you hired just two weeks earlier. This would help the new salesperson build his account list. Further, let's say that both salespeople feel that they deserve the accounts for the same reasons that you do. Finally, add to this that all the accounts are in one county, but it's farthest from the office from which you and your salespeople work. What's the best solution for the company and to keep both salespeople happy?

IN-CLASS EXERCISES

9-1: Strike Three

Walker Computer Systems manufactures and sells office computer systems and word processors. It has enjoyed double-digit growth over the past decade because of the growing demand for office automation. Advances in technology have resulted in increased capacity and lower prices in office PCs. As a result, the demand for office automation equipment has exploded as smaller businesses have begun to automate their offices.

One of the consequences of this growth is that Walker has constantly had to increase its sales force, to the point where there are now more than 400 salespeople servicing the U.S. market. This has meant constant adjustments to territories, with the result that salespeople are usually given a reduced geographic area to cover. Another adjustment has been in the sales force compensation program because of increased competition and the need to reduce costs. At the same time, the selling cycle time has been decreasing steadily as primary market demand increased and people became more familiar with office automation technology. Just six months ago, Walker introduced a new sales compensation plan designed to place more emphasis on strategic product lines as opposed to total sales volume.

Kim Bryant is the district sales manager for the Texas district. Kim joined Walker six years ago and was promoted to district manager after four years in sales, the last two as the top salesperson in the Southern Region. Kim manages seven people who are located in Dallas, Houston, Austin, Amarillo, and San Antonio. The last person was added just nine months ago in Austin. Owing to increased demand, Kim is being asked to add another person to the Dallas-Fort Worth area. Kim's idea is to have the new person cover the Fort Worth area, while Aaron Hughes, the current Walker rep in the area, continues to service the Dallas and mid-cities (cities located between Dallas and Fort Worth) area. This is the second reduction in Aaron's area in the past year, so Aaron will not be pleased to hear of the change. This area, however, is believed to have a lot of untapped potential and more demand than one person can cover.

Aaron Hughes currently services the Dallas-Fort Worth area for Walker Computer Systems. For the past three years, Aaron has been the top rep in the Texas district and is one of the top 10 salespeople in the company in terms of total sales volume. Aaron has turned down opportunities for promotion to management on several occasions. One reason for the decision is that Aaron would have to take a pay cut over the short term. Last year Aaron earned just over $160,000 in commissions.

Aaron's Response

"What do you mean 'redesigning' my territory?" bellows Aaron. "Don't you really mean 'reducing' my territory? First, you take Waco away from me. That's strike one. Then you change the compensation plan so that I have to work twice as hard to make as much as I did last year—strike two. Now you want to 'redesign' my territory. That's strike three and I'm out—as in out of this company."

Kim tries to calm Aaron down and tells Aaron that he has no choice in this matter. The order came from headquarters. Aaron is not buying this and replies, "There are a lot of office companies that would like to hire the top Walker rep in the South."

Kim does not want to lose Aaron or have a disgruntled former star salesperson in the district. She is convinced that adding another person to the Dallas-Fort Worth area is the right thing to do for the business. Remember that she is the district sales manager, not the regional or national sales manager. Break into small groups and discuss how Kim should resolve this problem.

Questions:

1. Why do companies redesign territories?
2. What mistakes were made in the Walker territory realignment?
3. What options are available to make territory changes work?
4. Should the company give in to Aaron and not change his territory?

9-2: Selling a New Sales Alignment Idea

Mike Clayton, a salesperson for Hull Systems, was recently promoted to a Southeastern regional manager, overseeing four area salespeople. Part of his promotion was transfer from Dallas to Atlanta. The Southeastern region was the poorest performing region in the country. Clayton's job? Boost sales and profitability.

Prior to his move to Atlanta, Mike spent a month studying the Southeastern region: its past performance, sales potential, and staff. After much consideration, Mike decided that the problem was in the territory alignment. The business climate in the southeastern states was changing, but the territories were not changing with it. For example, one salesperson based in Charlotte, North Carolina was assigned to cover Tennessee, South Carolina, and the burgeoning business in North Carolina. Mike felt that he needed one rep to cover North Carolina exclusively, and move South Carolina and Tennessee to other territories.

Mike concluded that he should realign three of the four sales territories and hire three new salespeople. Now he just had to convince company management of the soundness of his plan, and get his three salespeople, none of whom would have to move, to buy in to the plan. He knew that management would be concerned about added costs in a poorly performing area, and that his salespeople would worry that their compensation potential would be threatened. As a first-time manager, he was torn on how he should approach the situation.

1. Should he now call a meeting with management?
2. Should he seek the salespeople's opinions, so they feel that they are part of the decision process? If so, should he do this before or after his meeting with management?
3. Are there other alternatives to hiring three new salespeople that Mike should consider?

CASE 9-1   D. F. HARDWARE COMPANY

The D. F. Hardware Company was a hardware wholesaler/distributor located in Cleveland, Ohio. The company handled hardware products for a number of manufacturers, selling primarily to retail hardware stores in the greater Cleveland area. Sales were made by a company salesperson, Ted Tyler, who called on the local retailers. D. F. Hardware Co. trucks later delivered the purchased products to these retailers. Tyler reported to Matt Simmons, the company's General Manager, who also acted in the capacity of D. F. Hardware's sales manager. With only one salesperson, this position did not occupy much of Simmons' time.

One of D. F. Hardware's most valued suppliers was the Livingston Tool Corporation, a large manufacturer of hand and power tools. Livingston Tool sold its products in many markets, one of which was retail hardware stores such as were sold by D. F. Hardware. In this particular market, Livingston Tool used selective distributors, since most of the stores were small and widely distributed. D. F. Hardware had functioned as a distributor for Livingston Tool for a number of years in the Cleveland marketplace. The association between the two companies was very amiable; D. F. Hardware valued the Livingston Tool distributorship and its line of high quality products, and Livingston Tool was also pleased with D. F. Hardware's performance in the marketplace.

In April 1978, Cecil Andrew, the national sales manager of Livingston Tool, approached Simmons with an interesting offer. Livingston Tool was revising its policy on its distributor network. Instead of using several distributors to cover a market area, Livingston Tool was consolidating and attempting to cover the same area with an exclusive distributorship. In Ohio, for example, Livingston Tool had been using distributors in Columbus, Toledo, Cincinnati, and Steubenville in addition to D. F. Hardware in Cleveland. Andrews wanted to replace the five with a single distributor that would be granted the exclusive right to sell Livingston Tool products in the state of Ohio. He offered the exclusive Ohio distributorship to Simmons and D. F. Hardware.

THE DILEMMA

The Livingston Tool offer was an exciting one for Matt Simmons. As was stated, D. F. Hardware had been pleased with the Cleveland area distributorship, and the thought of having this position for all of Ohio really excited Simmons. The Livingston Tool product line was of high quality, profitable, and fast moving, and Simmons saw it as a major profit maker for D. F. Hardware.

As inviting as the Livingston Tool offer was, Simmons knew its acceptance would involve profound change for his company. The new franchise would necessitate an expansion of D. F. Hardware's sales force, with the establishment of sales territories and sales quotas in the entire Ohio market area. Ted Tyler could continue to sell the Cleveland area, but he could not be expected to cover the entire state of Ohio. In addition, Simmons knew that an acceptance of the Livingston Tool offer would involve changes in his company's physical distribution network, inventory policy, credit policies, and other such related areas.

Simmons found none of these changes formidable enough to warrant the rejection of the Livingston Tool offer. The prospect of having the profitable Livingston Tool franchise for all of Ohio seemed to overshadow any possible obstacles. In addition, he felt that such a move would be the first his company might make in regard to increasing its market penetration and its size. He envisioned that D. F. Hardware would someday be a large regional distributor and that this move was but the forerunner of several similar ones. After weighing all the pros and cons, Simmons accepted Andrews' offer as Livingston Tool's Ohio exclusive distributor. Andrews then informed the other four Ohio distributors (in Columbus, Toledo, Cincinnati, and Steubenville) of Livingston Tool's decision and told them that as of June 1, 1978, D. F. Hardware would serve as exclusive distributor in the Ohio market area.

After signing the contract, Simmons felt that his first task was to develop sales territories and quotas and determine how many salespersons the company would need to adequately serve the newly enlarged market area.

This case was prepared by Robert W. Haas of San Diego State University. From Robert W. Haas, *Industrial Marketing Management,* 3rd ed. (Boston: Kent Publishing Company, 1986), pp. 522–528. © 1986 by Wadsworth, Inc. Reprinted by permission of Kent Publishing Company, a division of Wadsworth, Inc. An adaptation of a publication of the U.S. Government Printing Office.

MARKET CHARACTERISTICS

Not long after the contract was signed, Simmons met with Andrews. This meeting was set up so that Andrews could provide Simmons with market characteristics and other information that would help D. F. Hardware in its new territory. In addition, the meeting was intended to establish the sales volume performance that Livingston Tool expected from D. F. Hardware in Ohio for the coming year. More specifically, Andrews informed Simmons of the following:

1. D. F. Hardware was to sell the Livingston Tool products *only* to retail hardware stores in the Ohio area. Although Livingston Tool products were distributed through other retail outlets such as discount houses, department stores, and farm equipment dealers, the company used other channels to reach these types of customers. Livingston Tool wanted its distributor to cover basically the retail hardware store marketplace.

2. Total U.S. shipments by hand and power tool manufacturers, such as Livingston Tool, had been $2,196.6 million in the previous year, according to data generated by the *Survey of Industrial Purchasing Power.* In that same year, Livingston Tool's shipments amounted to $140.6 million, or 6.4 percent of total shipments. Andrews thought that this 6.4 percent market share estimate was appropriate for the state of Ohio.

3. Andrews estimated that 21.8 percent of hardware store retail sales were accounted for by products similar to those manufactured by Livingston Tool, based on analyses his company had conducted over time. This percentage would give Simmons a good idea of the size of the Ohio retail sales market for the types of products D. F. Hardware would distribute.

4. Andrews expected sales of Livingston Tool products in Ohio to increase by 3.75 percent over the previous year because of increased sales effort due primarily to consolidation of distributors and expected D. F. Hardware's increased sales performance. Livingston Tool would provide D. F. Hardware with sales materials and would participate in cooperative advertising with the distributor to assist in reaching this 3.75 percent objective.

5. Andrews had determined that a typical distributor salesperson could average about 5 sales calls per day, or approximately 1,250 calls in a 250-day work year, based on past experience with other successful distributors across the country. He believed these figures to be appropriate for Ohio but cautioned Simmons to make certain that sales territories were drawn on the basis of both the number of calls to be made and an equal distribution of the total company's sales quota. If these points were not adequately considered, salesperson dissatisfaction would occur and problems would develop. Simmons understood and agreed.

6. Andrews also had determined that a distributor salesperson should call at least once every month on the larger retail accounts (20 or more employees) and at least once every three months on the smaller ones (fewer than 20 employees). He recommended that this would be a good rule of thumb for Simmons to follow, at least initially, in setting up his sales force.

Simmons found the meeting with Andrews to be quite helpful. After their meeting, Simmons began to outline the approach he would use to develop sales territories and quotas and then to determine the optimum number of salespeople for D. F. Hardware to employ. He immediately recognized the need for pertinent data on his Ohio marketplace. The next morning, he visited the library of a large local state university to seek out the data he required. Using such sources as the U.S. Department of Commerce's *County Business Patterns* and the *Census of Retail Trade,* he developed Exhibits 1, 2, and 3. He also located a map of Ohio that outlined

EXHIBIT 1 Estimated Total Retail Sales by Hardware Stores SIC 5251 in Ohio by SMSA

SMSA	Estimated Total Retail Sales ($000)	Number of Establishments
Akron	$ 11,797	59
Canton	13,837	49
Cincinnati	31,635	133
Cleveland	39,901	191
Columbus	23,595	93
Dayton	20,139	79
Hamilton–Middletown	4,510	19
Huntington–Ashland	10,037	41
Lima	7,808	36
Lorain–Elyria	6,555	27
Mansfield	2,695	14
Parkersburg–Marietta	2,310	17
Springfield	3,843	16
Steubenville–Weirton	5,300	15
Toledo	16,963	84
Wheeling, W. VA–Ohio	3,531	21
Youngstown–Warren	14,837	40
Total	$219,293	934

Source: U.S. Census of Retail Trade, 1977.

EXHIBIT 2　Estimated Total Retail Sales by Hardware Stores SIC 5251 in Ohio by Counties Not Included in SMSA Classifications

County	Estimated Total Retail Sales ($000)	Number of Establishments
Ashtabula	$ 3,456	17
Columbiana	5,437	18
Erie	D[a]	5
Hancock	1,383	13
Huron	2,157	12
Licking	D	9
Marion	1,601	11
Muskingum	910	8
Ross	D	5
Sandusky	D	6
Scioto	D	6
Seneca	2,186	4
Tuscarawas	D	10
Wayne	4,839	17
Total	$21,969	141

[a] D indicates counties where retail sales were withheld to avoid disclosing data for individual companies.

Source: U.S. Census of Retail Trade, 1977.

all standard metropolitan statistical areas (SMSAs) and showed their relationships to all other Ohio counties. This map is shown in Exhibit 4. Since these data were published in the previous year, 1977, Simmons believed they were reliable enough to use in any calculations he might want to make. From these sources, he estimated there were more than 1,000 hardware retail stores in his new market area with total estimated retail sales exceeding $240 million.

With these data, Simmons believed he had sufficient information to determine sales territories and appropriate quotas and decide on the optimum number of salespeople to employ.

EXHIBIT 3　Number of Hardware Stores SIC 5251 by Size in Each SMSA and Other Counties in Ohio

SMSA	Outlets with Less Than 20 Employees	Outlets with More Than 20 Employees
Akron	58	1
Canton	45	4
Cincinnati	133	0
Cleveland	186	5
Columbus	88	5
Dayton	75	4
Hamilton–Middletown	18	1
Huntington–Ashland	41	0
Lima	36	0
Lorain–Elyria	26	1
Mansfield	14	0
Parkersburg–Marietta	17	0
Springfield	15	1
Steubenville–Weirton	14	1
Toledo	83	1
Wheeling	21	0
Youngstown–Warren	34	6
Other Counties Outside SMSAs		
Ashtabula	16	1
Columbiana	18	0
Erie	5	0
Hancock	13	0
Huron	12	0
Licking	9	0
Marion	11	0
Muskingum	8	0
Ross	5	0
Sandusky	6	0
Scioto	6	0
Seneca	3	1
Tuscarawas	10	0
Wayne	16	1

None of the remaining counties show retail hardware outlets.

Source: Adapted from Census of Retail Trade, 1977, and *County Business Patterns,* 1977.

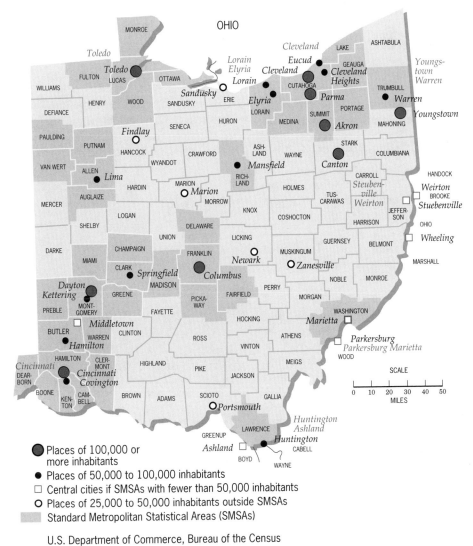

EXHIBIT 4   **Standard Metropolitan Statistical Areas for Ohio**

CASE 9-2 | KENT PLASTICS

The regional sales manager for Kent Plastics, Jill Hayes, was considering how to reorganize the Indiana district. This area had been divided into two sales territories in the past, with Bill Hicks covering the northern half of the state from Kokomo and Sally Hall covering the southern counties from Columbus (Exhibit 1). However, market growth suggested that four salespeople were now needed. Company policy stated that, when sales in an area exceeded $900,000 per territory, the district had to be divided into smaller segments. Sales in Indiana were currently running $3 million per year.

The Kent Plastics Company began operations as a supplier of plastic parts to manufacturers, but it had expanded into selling plastic bags and meat trays to retailers. Sales personnel were paid a salary plus an annual bonus based on district performance and achievement of territory sales quotas. Travel expenses were paid by Kent, and each salesperson was supplied with a company car.

Jill Hayes wanted to create four compact territories in the state of Indiana that would be similar in terms of sales potential and work load. She felt that equal-opportunity territories would improve morale and make it easier to compare the performance of individual salespersons. Travel expenses would be lower if the territories were designed to minimize the distance from the salespersons' home to different customers' locations. Jill realized, however, that the job of selecting home bases for salespeople was complicated by the heavy concentration of customers located in Marion County in the center of the state.

Counties seemed to be the most logical control units for building new territories, and Jill quickly assembled some statistics for Indiana from secondary sources (Exhibit 2). She obtained the location of each county and major population centers from maps supplied by the Indiana Highway Department (Exhibit 1).

As Jill Hayes looked over the available figures, she wondered what factor or factors would make the best allocation criteria. Jill had recently obtained a copy of a territory design program published by TTG. Perhaps it was time to call this program up on her computer to help redesign the Indiana district. She knew she had

only a few days left to carve out four new territories from the Indiana district before she presented the plan to the sales force at the annual convention. She also had to decide which of the new territories to assign to Bill and Sally.

EXHIBIT 1   Current Sales Territories and Location of Indiana Counties and Major Cities

---

This case was prepared by Douglas J. Dalrymple of Indiana University.

EXHIBIT 2   Selected Statistics for Indiana Counties

County	Number of Retail Stores	Number of Manufacturing Firms	Value Added by Manufacturing (millions)	Buying Power Index (BPI)	Number of Kent Customers	Kent Sales (thousands)	Square Miles
Adams	273	46	82	.011	3	15	345
Allen	2,187	421	832	.150	50	140	671
Bartholomew	542	70	327	.029	10	35	402
Benton	128	5	2	.005	2	3	409
Blackford	174	32	57	.006	2	6	167
Boone	301	38	19	.015	4	8	427
Brown	105	3	1	.004	5	2	319
Carroll	141	19	21	.007	10	16	374
Cass	429	61	88	.019	4	15	415
Clark	642	78	221	.042	32	61	384
Clay	249	13	11	.010	2	6	364
Clinton	307	43	65	.004	10	11	407
Crawford	90	6	3	.005	3	1	312
Daviess	283	38	30	.010	9	18	430
Dearborn	259	30	159	.012	15	24	306
Decatur	213	27	49	.009	8	12	370
DeKalb	324	60	82	.013	22	17	366
Delaware	1,153	185	275	.060	21	68	396
Dubois	309	102	101	.012	3	7	433
Elkhart	1,229	609	751	.070	15	91	468
Fayette	244	35	99	.012	2	4	215
Floyd	449	73	80	.025	10	21	149
Fountain	257	27	37	.008	3	5	397
Franklin	127	14	9	.006	3	7	394
Fulton	207	40	29	.007	12	13	368
Gibson	313	35	16	.013	15	26	498
Grant	769	120	330	.037	5	45	421
Greene	304	35	15	.011	30	31	549
Hamilton	513	68	55	.029	11	28	401
Hancock	299	39	20	.019	17	27	305
Harrison	175	22	16	.008	8	15	479
Hendricks	381	32	8	.027	23	52	417
Henry	505	55	111	.024	10	17	400
Howard	790	92	535	.047	16	43	293
Huntington	349	71	65	.016	9	32	369
Jackson	331	59	65	.015	7	8	520
Jasper	246	22	95	.010	3	10	562
Jay	239	31	69	.010	12	16	386
Jefferson	279	37	59	.012	4	13	366
Jennings	153	15	14	.008	7	6	377
Johnson	551	55	49	.031	17	49	315
Knox	457	48	49	.018	7	20	516
Kosciusko	564	144	164	.023	24	23	540
LaGrange	203	50	44	.010	5	10	381
Lake	3,746	387	1,874	.267	93	310	513
LaPorte	933	169	293	.051	28	63	607
Lawrence	363	60	66	.017	17	18	459
Madison	1,281	146	603	.069	8	52	453
Marion	6,259	1,178	2,297	.422	173	527	392
Marshall	428	111	75	.017	3	27	443
Martin	113	12	25	.004	4	6	345
Miami	348	53	46	.015	15	17	377
Monroe	671	60	321	.041	27	54	386
Montgomery	394	41	80	.016	3	11	507
Morgan	352	38	12	.020	19	21	406

(continued)

EXHIBIT 2   (Continued)

County	Number of Retail Stores	Number of Manufacturing Firms	Value Added by Manufacturing (millions)	Buying Power Index (BPI)	Number of Kent Customers	Kent Sales (thousands)	Square Miles
Newton	147	13	8	.017	1	6	413
Noble	370	84	76	.013	2	8	412
Ohio	35	2	1	.002	4	2	87
Orange	182	25	23	.006	3	7	405
Owen	121	10	4	.005	1	4	389
Parke	151	8	4	.005	8	9	445
Perry	208	30	51	.007	7	11	384
Pike	149	18	7	.005	3	5	335
Porter	631	69	293	.045	11	63	424
Posey	198	12	8	.008	4	6	412
Pulaski	145	17	12	.003	1	4	433
Putnam	255	25	42	.011	17	21	490
Randolph	321	68	86	.012	15	24	457
Ripley	234	29	77	.010	3	8	442
Rush	196	28	17	.008	7	12	409
St. Joseph	1,915	388	486	.109	42	189	466
Scott	153	11	4	.007	2	5	193
Shelby	307	58	68	.012	19	18	409
Spencer	188	7	2	.007	3	11	396
Starke	204	28	12	.009	4	4	310
Steuben	344	45	36	.012	8	14	309
Sullivan	188	29	9	.007	5	6	457
Switzerland	57	8	8	.004	1	2	221
Tippecanoe	871	95	258	.052	51	88	500
Tipton	138	21	16	.006	4	5	261
Union	56	5	1	.003	1	3	168
Vanderburgh	1,547	243	523	.077	62	172	241
Vermillion	202	15	81	.007	3	9	263
Vigo	994	143	266	.056	26	99	415
Wabash	363	74	107	.015	19	17	398
Warren	58	7	3	.008	2	5	368
Warrick	233	19	21	.012	14	24	391
Washington	165	27	25	.007	7	7	516
Wayne	726	125	212	.038	3	58	405
Wells	205	36	66	.010	4	13	368
White	276	31	18	.009	8	7	497
Whitley	236	49	41	.010	4	3	337

RECRUITING AND SELECTING PERSONNEL

Chapter Consultants:
Howard Stevens, Chairman, The H. R. Chally Group
John Schreitmueller, Partner, Ray & Berndtson

LEARNING OBJECTIVES

After studying this chapter, you should be able to:

→ Discuss how to plan for recruiting and selection.

→ Identify relevant hiring criteria for sales jobs.

→ Identify the different sources of recruits.

→ Understand the selection and validation process.

PRUDENTIAL'S RECRUITING PROCESS

Hiring the right people at Prudential Financial is critical to the firm's success, which is why Prudential invests a significant amount of time and money to get it right the first time. The recruiting process begins with the district sales manager identifying key people in the community—such as important business leaders, or college faculty. The district sales manager will then meet with these key people to discuss potential candidates who are likely to fit the 12-point profile of successful Prudential agents. Once identified, candidates are invited to an informal discussion of the job opportunity with the district sales manager. The purpose of this step is to provide candidates with a realistic job preview and to determine whether there is a mutual interest in pursuing the opening.

If a mutual interest is established, candidates will visit the Prudential office and take an analytical and personality profile to assess their fit to a composite of highly successful Prudential agents. If a fit is determined, the candidate will then meet with a human resource specialist for a structured interview. The purpose of this interview is to assess the candidate's ability to think quickly and creatively. The third step is a role-playing interview with the district manager to determine the candidate's baseline selling competency. The fourth step is a meeting with the agency's managing director who provides details of the training programs, products, and a vision of the candidate's future career. The fifth step is the extension of a formal written offer of employment. Finally, Prudential offers an optional "VIP Interview" where the candidate can bring a friend, spouse, or parent(s) to the office for additional input into the candidate's decision. An additional benefit to such an intense hiring process is that it helps Prudential screen through those applicants who do not have the stamina or discipline to make it through the entire process. Prudential estimates its first-year investment per hire to be between $60,000 and $100,000. While the expense of Prudential's multi-step recruiting process is one of the highest in the industry, the investment has more than paid for itself. The first round of advisers hired using this process greatly exceeded expectations by generating an average of $14.5 million of client assets each.[1]

As a first-line sales manager you will likely have the ultimate responsibility for recruitment and selection of your sales staff. How effective you are in attracting, matching, and motivating the right people could determine your success as a sales manager. Let's face it, regardless of how well you train, motivate, coach, or counsel your sales staff or develop your sales and marketing strategy, without properly qualified people, you are in the same predicament as a great basketball coach with a team of six-footers who can neither run, jump, shoot, nor rebound.

The costs associated with a poor hiring decision are significant. An often-quoted figure is that out-of-pocket costs associated with recruiting and selection range from 20 to 80 percent of a salesperson's annual salary. Costs go up dramatically, however, when a poor hiring decision is made. Costs associated with a poor hiring include (1) initial training and subsequent training costs needed to overcome deficiencies; (2) costs of absenteeism, poor customer service, and excessive expense account spending associated with gradual withdrawal from the organization; and (3) the opportunity cost associated with lost profits that a qualified person would have generated during the time a poor hire occupies a territory. Experts estimate that the costs of firing an employee, and hiring and training a new one, can run as high as 150 percent of the fired employee's salary.[2]

In addition to the costs involved in a poor hiring decision, the impact of such a decision on the organization cannot be exaggerated. Especially in the case of a termination, employee morale, productivity, and client relationships potentially suffer. In the past decade, the frequent downsizings and layoffs have been much more damaging to organizations than anticipated, including negative press, litigation, and other serious issues. Thus, effective sales managers will be especially aware of the total costs, both direct and indirect, of poor hiring decisions.

Despite these costs, recruiting tends to be an area of underinvestment by most companies, perhaps because so many of the expenses are so difficult to quantify. It has been estimated that more than half of all people in sales positions are not suited for such a career.[3] Selection of good salespeople obviously represents an important opportunity to gain a competitive advantage. Why is the selection of good salespeople so difficult? One reason is the pressure to fill open territories. When unemployment is at a historical low, finding and hiring good performers are challenges for managers in every industry. On the other hand, when unemployment is high, managers are vulnerable to making a hiring mistake from the large number of applicants they receive. According to many sales managers, lack of time is responsible for most of their hiring mistakes.[4] Recruiting and selection are also difficult because many companies fail to provide effective interviewing training for key line managers who complete the interviewing process.

Our discussion of the recruiting and selection process is based on the following model that emphasizes proper planning. First, the number of people to be recruited must be determined, together with an analysis of each sales job. A careful review of the activities to be performed by salespeople helps sales managers prepare a list of specific job qualifications, which can then be used to build a profile to guide the search for successful recruits. Next, management must decide where to look for recruits. From a pool of recruits, sales managers then must select job candidates. We start our discussion with the planning phase of the recruiting process.

PLANNING PROCESS

The recruiting planning process should include a preliminary analysis of personnel needs, a job analysis, and a review or creation of a job description and job qualifications. Based on the results of these analyses, sources of sales recruits and selection procedures should be planned. Proper planning will help ensure the success of the recruiting process and provide more time for locating the best candidates.

Personnel Needs

The number of new salespeople needed will depend on several factors, including sales growth targets, distribution strategies, changes in sales force organization, and sales force turnover. For example, AT&T's consumer direct sales division continually reassesses open territories to determine if any economic changes have occurred that may have affected previous sales growth estimates. Based on this reassessment, AT&T might combine an open territory into existing territories and not hire a new salesperson, or split the territory and fill it with multiple hires, depending on the reassessed growth estimates.[5] Additional analyses, therefore, may be necessary when determining the number of new salespeople needed.

There are a number of reasons for salesperson turnover. Examples include resignation because of poor performance, resignation for another job, retirement, or promotion. To calculate an estimate of the rate at which salespeople leave requires an estimate of the *sales force turnover rate*. The rate is calculated by dividing the number of separations during a year by the average size of the sales force. Thus, if 15 people leave each year and the size of the sales force is 150, the turnover rate would be

$$\text{Turnover rate} = \frac{\text{Separations per year}}{\text{Average size of the sales force}} = \frac{15}{150} = 10\%$$

Because of the recruiting and training expenses incurred, sales managers often try to keep turnover as low as possible. The average sales force turnover rates for service, consumer, and industrial goods companies are illustrated in Figure 10-1. Notice that turnover is highest among service companies. Many service sales positions are in industries where it is very difficult for new salespeople to build a list of clients. In the insurance industry, for example, the first-year retention rate is just a little over 50 percent.[6] The somewhat higher turnover rate among consumer goods companies may be due to the faster promotion tracks of these companies. In the Personal Products Division of International Playtex, for example, new college recruits are expected to be promoted to sales managers or a staff position within 12 to 20 months. Some turnover, therefore, is not dysfunctional.

Turnover can be too low as well as too high. A well-entrenched sales force may be unable to adjust to a changing environment. While promoting company loyalty, low turnover may also indicate a lack of career growth opportunity by promotion or lateral movement. It is interesting to note that as organizational structures become flatter, and more decentralized, there are often fewer opportunities for advancement, which could lead to increased turnover. However, flatter organizations do give individual reps more responsibilities. This suggests that turnover is not something to be minimized or maximized; rather, it is a useful guide for administrative action. The objective is to have enough turnover so that new personnel and enthusiasm can be added to the sales force, yet not so much that sales managers spend all their time recruiting and training new employees.[7] See the Technology Competency box for an example of how Lanier Corporation solved its high turnover problem with a sales force automation solution.

Company Culture

In addition to the preliminary analysis of personnel needs and other factors, a specific definition of the organization's culture is necessary for the planning cycle's validity. The process of aligning a company's recruiting strategies to its core culture should help attract and retain higher performing salespeople as compared with those companies whose recruiting processes are reactive and culturally disconnected.[8] A well-educated, high-energy, articulate candidate, for example, might seem like a superb addition to the sales team. However, if a recruit does not perceive the company's cultural needs and demands as a match with his or her values, the potential for turnover increases dramatically. For instance, some people

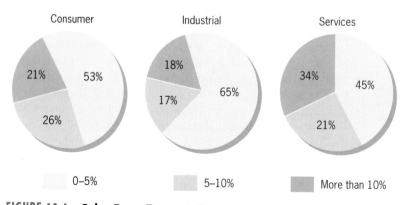

FIGURE 10-1   **Sales Force Turnover Rates**

TECHNOLOGY COMPETENCY
Minimizing Turnover with Sales Force Automation

Lanier Worldwide, Inc. was recently facing a number of challenges. The most urgent was the 100 percent turnover in its sales force every six months. Salespeople were leaving the company, frustrated because they were making too many cold calls and were unable to close deals. The cycle continued with new reps because they had few qualified leads to pursue and had little or no contact information about existing accounts. What's more, customer surveys revealed dissatisfaction among some of Lanier's clients, primarily because they had to rehash information about their product requirements, budget, and buying schedule every time they met with a new salesperson. Lanier turned to sales force automation to help solve these problems. While technology pundits often cite a 55 percent failure rate of sales force automation projects (based on a Gartner Group report), Lanier Worldwide, Inc. is an example of what can happen when everything goes right. The software program was intended to assist Laniers' reps to sell more consultatively by providing survey questions that assess customer needs. In addition, the program maintains case histories of clients and allows managers to track salespeople's activities. Shortly after installing the software, Lanier saw a drastic reduction in turnover and an increase in revenue produced per rep. An added benefit is that automation has made recruiting easier because Lanier is now differentiated from its competitors.

For more information about Lanier, visit their homepage at: *www.lanier.com.*

thrive in a highly competitive environment, while others abhor it. The fact that cultures are likely to vary from one sales branch to another even within the same company, makes the task more difficult but even more necessary. The importance of cultural "fit" between the company and the recruit is tremendous. As the Strategic Action Competency box illustrates, Cisco Systems maintains its competitive advantage through an innovative hiring process geared toward finding not only the most talented people, but also those that fit with Cisco's culture.

Job Analysis

Before managers can effectively recruit new salespeople, they must clearly understand the activities, tasks, and responsibilities of their sales representatives. A *job analysis* is a systematic way to describe how a job is to be performed, as well as the tasks that make up the job. Keep in mind, though, that there are a number of different procedures for performing a job analysis. One is the *job analysis interview,* whereby in-depth interviews are conducted with management and salespeople. Management would be queried, for instance, about the sales and marketing plans of the company so as to clarify the role of the sales force. Salespeople would be interviewed to determine how they see their role and how much time they spend on particular activities. In addition to the interviews, the sales force may be sent questionnaires in which they indicate the frequency of performance as well as the importance of each task in their job. Standard questionnaires are available for this task, such as the Position Analysis Questionnaire (PAQ), which lists 194 items describing behavior at work.

While considering management's plans, a job analysis should focus on those critical success tasks high-performing salespeople spend their time on and compare those with the lower-performing salesperson tasks. This can serve as a "reality check" on management's assumptions. For example, a sales manager might describe a job as the merchandising of sales promotions to store managers. However, if more effective salespeople actually spend their time stocking shelves and checking inventory, those salespeople hired to sell to store

STRATEGIC ACTION COMPETENCY
Finding and Attracting the Best at Cisco Systems

Effective high-tech sales professionals in Silicon Valley are fueling the growth of the high-flying companies. One of the highest flyers is Cisco Systems, the leader in computer networking. Cisco believes the secret to its success is its ability to identify exactly the person the company should hire, determine how they do their job hunting, and provide an innovative hiring process to attract them. According to CEO John Chambers:

> Cisco has an overall goal of getting the top 10% to 15% of people in our industry. Our philosophy is very simple—if you get the best people in the industry to fit into your culture and you motivate them properly, then you're going to be an industry leader.

Cisco believes that the best people already have good jobs and are often happy with their employers. Instead of targeting the pool of applicants that are actively looking for work, Cisco targets what it calls passive job seekers. To find out how to attract these passive job seekers, Cisco first had to learn how they spend their free time. It used focus group discussions with ideal recruitment targets from competitors to determine that potential applicants are not reading the want ads. They're more likely spending time surfing the Internet, attending art fairs, or home and garden shows. At such events, Cisco recruiters work the crowds, collect business cards, and provide informal information about the company. Cisco also uses a "friends" program where potential prospects are paired up with current employees with similar backgrounds and skills to help answer questions and provide a realistic description of the working environment. The program has been advertised on its web page and in local theaters and so far has been very successful. To maintain employee enthusiasm about the program, Cisco has instituted a generous referral fee and a free-trip lottery ticket if employees befriend someone who is eventually hired.

To learn more about Cisco, visit their homepage at: *www.cisco.com.*

managers are likely to be unhappy when they discover that the job is really that of a glorified stock clerk. In short, job analyses must incorporate the unpleasant as well as the attractive aspects of the job.

One of the best ways for a company to analyze a selling position is to send an observer into the field. The observer can record the differences in the amount of time higher- and lower-performing salespeople spend talking to customers, traveling, record keeping, setting up displays, and attending meetings. Additional information concerning sales jobs can be obtained by interviewing customers, using daily diaries, and reading sales reports to pinpoint critical incidents that spell the difference between success and failure. Written customer ratings of the sales force have been noted to be particularly important in identifying salesperson critical success factors.[9] It is interesting to note that a recent study reports that sales excellence (as perceived by the customer) is inversely related to the sophistication of the product. For example, salespeople who sell more commodity-type products, which have little differentiation among competitors, tend to do better focusing on customer needs than sales people selling more sophisticated products.[10]

Job Description   Information from the job analysis should be used to produce a *job description,* which is a written document that spells out the job relationships and requirements that characterize each sales position. The job description explains (1) to whom the salesperson reports, (2) how the salesperson interacts with other staff marketing people, (3) the customers to be called on by the salesperson, (4) the specific tasks to be carried out, (5) the mental and physical demands of the job, and (6) the types of products to be sold.

Position Title			Pos. No.	
Armstrong Marketing Representative (all levels)			_____	
			Date: 8/99	
Incumbent	*Plan/Dept.*	*Writer*	Approved	
			S.A.D.	MGR.
As assigned	Floor division	J.A. Gingrich		

Job Function:
Under general supervision of the District Manager or Assistant District Manager, the position is responsible for developing and achieving maximum profitable sales volume of Division products in an assigned territory.

Dimensions

Sales Volume—ranges from $1–7 million.

Territory—the District is typically divided into geographic areas, with this position responsible for one of those areas; additionally, the position will be given direct responsibility for 1–4 Armstrong wholesalers.

Product Line—consists of a wide range of resilient flooring products including Corlon and Solarian sheet flooring; resilient tile; vinyl sheet flooring; and adhesives and sundries.

Distribution—is achieved by sales to wholesalers, who in turn sell to flooring specialty stores, flooring contractors, furniture stores, department stores, building supply stores, and home improvement centers.

Major Emphasis—is directed toward developing and improving the wholesalers in all their functions through such means as training and assisting wholesaler salespeople, helping these people make specific sales, developing new business, and generally contributing to the effectiveness of their operations.

Organization Supervised   None

FIGURE 10-2   Job Description for a Field Sales Representative

An example of a job description for a field sales position at Armstrong World Industries is presented in Figure 10-2. Notice that the job description states that the field representative works under the district manager and is responsible for achieving maximum profitable sales within an assigned territory. In this example, the major emphasis is placed on improving the operations of wholesalers. The field representative is expected to work closely with wholesalers to implement promotional programs, train salespeople, and expand coverage of retail accounts. The Armstrong representative is also expected to make regular calls on key retailers, control expenses, handle complaints, and keep the district and Lancaster offices advised on competitive conditions, product needs, prices, and market conditions.

Job Qualifications

While a job description focuses on the activities and responsibilities of the job, *job qualifications* refer to the aptitudes, skills, knowledge, and personality traits necessary to perform the job successfully. A statement of job qualifications would typically include education,

---

Principal Activities

1. Develops and achieves maximum sales volume consistent with realistic sales projections within assigned territory. Controls expenditures within approved expense budget.

2. Develops and maintains favorable wholesale distribution of entire Division line within assigned territory. Recommends on the addition or termination of wholesalers. Develops thorough familiarity with wholesaler's business, sales activity, potentials, and requirements.

3. Closely oversees operations of assigned wholesalers. Advises or assists them in such areas as inventory selection and control, service to customers, profit opportunities and rations, etc. Investigates and corrects problem situations such as duplication of orders, receipt of poor quality goods, etc. Draws on Armstrong staff services as special assistance is indicated.

4. Translates promotional goals into concrete plans and assignable responsibilities determining what is to be done and achieved, and who is to achieve it.

5. Identifies the work which must be done to achieve intended results. Divides this work into parcels that can be performed by single individuals.

6. Maintains proper relationships and interrelationships to assure teamwork and a unified effort between wholesaler and retailer.

7. Promotes Armstrong product line and its features and sales points, and an understanding of Armstrong policies and procedures, among the entire wholesaler organization. Keeps personnel informed on new products, price changes, and related concerns. Adapts Lancaster promotional services to local needs and conducts sales meetings to explain the same, follows through on all promotions.

8. Assists wholesalers, sales personnel in concerned territory in their selling efforts, and trains same through promotional meetings, traveling with each person on a regular basis, helping in making specific sales, and developing new business.

9. Plans territory coverage. Regularly calls upon key retail accounts (current and prospective). Takes orders, promotes the marketing and display of Armstrong products, encourages dealer to capitalize on Armstrong's advertising and promotional efforts, introduces new materials, trains counter personnel, provides literature and samples.

10. Investigates and evaluates field complaints; recommends disposition of complaints accordingly.

11. Keeps District Manager's Office and Lancaster advised on matters of specific business interest such as market conditions, competitive situations, product needs, etc. Consults with District Manager's Office concerning matters of policy, unusual situations, pricing, etc.

FIGURE 10-2　Continued

previous work experience, technical expertise, aptitudes, and interests. These qualifications, based on the job description, serve as a set of selection criteria that will help sales managers choose the best prospects from among those who apply. Typical of many other companies, the Invacare Corporation, a manufacturer of wheelchairs and other medical products, looks for people with drive, interpersonal skills, common sense, intelligence, and experience in selling.[11] It is important to note, however, that every company should be able to demonstrate to the Equal Employment Opportunity Commission that their job qualifications are required for the job.

In addition to creating a job description, some large firms evaluate the personal histories and skills of current salespeople to build a profile of the successful salesperson with their company. Edward Jones, a financial services company, recently did this with the help of the Gallup Organization's management consulting unit. Through focus groups with top salespeople and sales managers, Gallup created a composite profile that identified three key success traits: strong work ethic, high degree of motivation, and the ability to build rapport. To assess candidates' qualifications, a Gallup consultant would ask 60 questions aimed at uncovering the three traits. Based on this new selection process Edward Jones's attrition rate has fallen from 21 to 9 percent.[12]

Research   Almost everyone has a stereotyped image of the kind of person who will be successful at sales. A review of more than 400 studies of the relationship between personal characteristics and salesperson performance found some interesting results and drew the following conclusions:[13]

- Sales aptitude, personal characteristics (e.g., physical traits, experience), selling skills, role perceptions, and motivation are not consistently related to sales performance.
- Personal variables such as family background, personal history, and current marital and family status are some of the best predictors of sales performance among the many personal characteristics examined. However, it is generally illegal to ask these sorts of question.
- General time and territory management skills, such as organization skills, are critical to success in personal selling.
- Educational level, intelligence, and sociability are not consistently related to sales performance.

In the aggregate, these results suggest that widely held stereotypes of what is needed to be successful in sales are often inaccurate. Part of the problem may be that different kinds of personalities may be successful in different kinds of sales positions.[14] In addition, this study concluded that developmental characteristics such as specific selling skills, motivation level, and role perceptions are generally more closely related to performance than are lasting, innate characteristics. This suggests that sales managers can and do have an important influence on the performance of a sales force.

On the other hand, it is important to understand that the hiring manager's perceptions play an absolutely critical role in the hiring decision.[15] Ultimately, regardless of education, experience, or any other tangible qualification, it is often the hiring manager's impression of "fit" that stacks the deck in favor of a particular candidate. This underscores again the role of culture in the process, and places a significant burden on the applicant to understand it.

Buyer's Perspective   A survey of 205 purchasing agents concluded that the most valued traits of salespeople were those shown in Table 10-1. The results suggest that sales managers should hire people who are loyal to the customer, willing to fight for them, detail oriented, and able to follow through on promises. Although product knowledge was fourth on the list, it is usually not a key hiring criterion because deficiencies can be addressed during sales training.[16] An important area of concern for purchasing agents, not included in the table, is that salespeople must able to understand the customer's business. In fact, purchasing agents frequently cite this as an important area for salesperson improvement.[17] Note that these preferred traits are not those easily discerned from a resume.

Today some people are taking a different approach to identifying desirable personality traits in sales candidates. Instead of identifying personality traits associated with overall performance, they are looking for traits related to desirable selling abilities, such as the ability to adjust sales behaviors based on the nature of the selling situation. Sales adaptiveness, for example, has been found to be associated with an internal locus of control (i.e., performance is caused by behavior, not luck), empathy, self-monitoring (i.e., sensitivity to other people's behavior), and androgyny (i.e., both assertive and yielding).[18] This approach is new but

TABLE 10-1   What Purchasing Agents Like About Salespeople

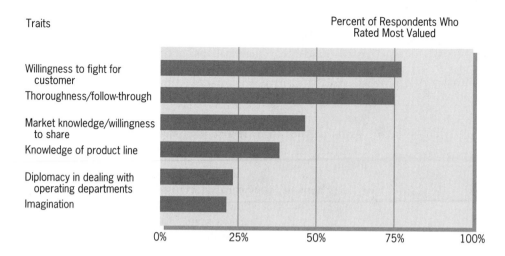

holds promise for improving sales force selection. Another example of using personality traits as selection criteria is described in the Self-Management Competency box.

Sales versus Technical Skills   One of the perennial dilemmas for sales managers is whether to hire technicians and teach them to sell or to hire experienced salespeople and teach them the technical aspects of the job. Either strategy can succeed; the key factor is the company's approach to selling and the training capability of the firm. Pharmaceutical giants Bristol-Meyers, Eli Lilly, SmithKline, and Parke-Davis prefer candidates with a science or health care background. Eli Lilly, for example, only hires people with technical degrees, and only 20 percent of its sales force has a business degree.[19] Other leading health care companies such as Pfizer, Merck, and Baxter-Travenol, on the other hand, do not require technical backgrounds for their sales applicants. There appears to be no clear consensus as to whether a technical background is needed in sales.

SELF-MANAGEMENT COMPETENCY
Understanding Your Tendencies

It is part of personal selling's conventional wisdom that optimists perform better than pessimists. Now there is research indicating why this might be true. It appears that people who are optimists (people who expect the best possible outcome) handle stress differently from pessimists. When given a challenging objective, optimists believe it is possible to achieve the goal, and focus their attention on devising strategies for achieving it. Pessimists, on the other hand, think there is little chance of achieving the goal, so they believe they can only endure the situation. As a result, they focus their attention inwardly, in an attempt to assuage their own negative feelings, instead of developing a strategy for meeting their goals. Based on this notion, a company in the United Kingdom has introduced a psychometric questionnaire for its recruitment procedures for sales personnel. An increase in sales confirmed the research findings and the questionnaire has been made a standard component of the selection process for sales personnel.

Legality of Job Qualifications

Although lists of qualifications are useful in recruiting for sales positions, they must be employed with caution. The main concern is to avoid employment discrimination caused when qualifications are used to exclude some individuals from certain jobs. The Civil Rights Act of 1964 was the first of several laws designed to prevent illegal employment discrimination. This was followed in 1967 by the Age Discrimination in Employment Act and in 1973 by the Vocational Rehabilitation Act, which was designed to protect the rights of the handicapped. These laws make it illegal to use as job qualifications any attributes that result in discrimination against persons of a given race, religion, nationality, sex, or age. The only exception occurs when the employer can show that the characteristic is essential to the successful performance of the job.

Guidelines explaining the discrimination laws have been issued by the Equal Employment Opportunity Commission (EEOC) and the Office of Federal Contract Compliance (OFCC). The regulations issued by the EEOC apply to firms with 25 or more employees. The OFCC rules apply to companies with 100 or more employees that have contracts with the federal government.

Legal guidelines and laws affecting recruiting and selection are constantly evolving and changing. A particularly important federal civil rights law is the Americans with Disabilities Act (ADA), which became effective in 1992.[20] This law makes it illegal to discriminate in employment against qualified individuals with disabilities. Disabilities covered by the law include visual, speech, and hearing impairment, human immunodeficiency virus infection, cancer, mental retardation, emotional illness, drug addiction, and alcoholism. Although originally protected by the law, illegal drug users are not currently protected.

The law also specifies that employers have an obligation to make reasonable accommodation to the known physical or mental limitations of an individual. Examples of accommodations include making facilities available, restructuring jobs, reassignment, modifying work schedules, modifying equipment, and providing readers or interpreters. The implications of this new law are clearly far-reaching. It is important to point out, however, that employers can take action on an unproductive person and still be in compliance with the ADA. For example, it is well within the employer's right to terminate, or refuse to hire someone, if the employee cannot perform the minimum job requirements, such as a having a valid driver's license.

RECRUITING

The goal of recruiting is to find and attract the best-qualified applicants for sales positions. The number of applicants needed to meet personnel requirements will be larger than the number of people to be hired. Not every applicant will have the job qualifications, and not everyone offered a job will accept the offer. The number of applicants needed can be determined by using a simple formula based on the company's experience from past recruiting efforts. The number of recruits (R) is

$$R = \frac{H}{S \times A}$$

where

H = required number of hires
S = percentage of recruits selected
A = percentage of those selected who accept

Thus, if a company needs to hire 10 people and expects to select 10 percent of those applying, and if 50 percent of those offered a position typically accept, then $R = 10/(0.10 \times 0.50)$ or 200. Therefore, the company needs to plan its recruiting process so as to attract 200 applicants.

Notice that the number of recruits *(R)* can be reduced by either increasing the percentage of people selected *(S)* or increasing the percentage of those selected who accept an offer *(A)*. You may wish to speculate as to whether increasing *A* and *S* in order to reduce *R* is necessarily beneficial to an organization. What else must be considered besides reducing recruiting time and costs?

Sources of applicants vary widely, depending on the job to be filled and past hiring success. For example, educational institutions and employment agencies are the most popular sources for sales trainees. On the other hand, present employees and personal referrals of people working for other firms in the industry are good sources for sales jobs involving technical product knowledge and industry experience. Companies rarely rely exclusively on only one source for sales applicants, because each source has advantages and limitations. These sources are discussed in the following sections.

Classified Advertising

Classified advertisements in newspapers and trade journals are often used to attract salespeople. One advantage of classified ads is their ability to attract a large number of applicants. *The Wall Street Journal* and trade journals such as *Women's Wear Daily* are full of ads for experienced sales reps, sales managers, vice presidents of sales, and general sales managers. Classified ads have the advantage of reaching a wide audience and may attract candidates who are not actively looking for a job. One way to narrow the reach of a classified ad is to advertise in trade publications. Some companies are now using humor to make their ads stand out. For example, Signal Corp., an information-technology services provider in Fairfax Virginia, used a picture of a messy-faced manager shortly after taking part in a company pie-eating contest with the tag line "And you should see us on casual day."[21]

Advertising's strength in attracting job applicants may also be its greatest drawback. There is a tendency to overburden the selection process with underqualified applicants, resulting in an extensive and costly screening process, which produces a high cost per hire despite a low cost per applicant.

Present Employees

Present employees often make good candidates for sales jobs, because they are familiar with the company's products and procedures and do not require as much training as prospects recruited from outside sources. They have established job histories with the firm and can be observed in action when evaluating their potential as sales representatives. People usually consider a transfer to the sales department to be a promotion because of the job's independence and frequently higher earnings potential. Results of a recent survey also suggest that these people tend to perform well, as one third of the top-performing reps surveyed previously held non-sales positions within the same firm.[22]

Candidates for major account sales positions are also most likely to come from company sources. Sources of candidates for these sales positions are likely to differ from those of regular sales positions because of the differences in the responsibilities in major account sales. For example, Banta Corporation, a printing company, has been very successful in hiring its customer service employees for its major account sales force. One reason why Banta targets its customer service employees is because they tend to work on cross-functional teams involving logistics, purchasing, and accounts payable, which gives them a basic understanding of how these functions interact to affect the customer. In addition, Banta has found that their customer advocate role has prepared these employees to provide the high level of service and attention a major account requires.[23] The Banta example, however, is not the norm, because most companies (90 percent) recruit major account salespeople from among the regular salespeople with the firm, with 44 percent also considering referrals from their major account salespeople.[24]

Hiring from within the company has potential pitfalls. Bad feelings may arise, for example, if managers think that their best people are being pirated by the sales force. In addition, some companies find that employees may harbor hidden prejudices about sales and rely too heavily on their previous experience. Engineers, for example, may tend to use facts and figures, whereas customer service people may find it hard to take a tough negotiating stance.

Referrals/Networking

Another major internal source of recruits is recommendations by present employees. Statistics prove networking and informational interviewing to be among the top conduits for effective recruiting in today's workplace. Well-informed students and graduates in entry-level positions learn each day the values of networking with other sales professionals, executives, senior executives, faculty members, and others whose daily routines immerse them in the business community. Because the informed interviewee has probably gained significant grasp of the company's cultural, ethical, and business issues, these individuals often make superb candidates for sales representatives, and at reduced risk for the company.

References from managers and salespeople are particularly valuable because these persons tend to have wide social contacts and often meet individuals who make good prospects for the sales team. Company executives understand the needs of the sales program and are in a good position to convince others of the merits of a sales career. Moreover, they are likely to know when people are looking for new jobs and to have some personal knowledge of their qualifications. A number of companies are also providing financial incentives for employee referrals. Cisco Systems, Inc., for example, provides a referral fee starting at $500 and a lottery ticket for a free trip to Hawaii for each "friend" who is hired (see the Strategic Action Competency example). Some fast-growing companies, such as I-Cube of Cambridge, Massachusetts, encourage repeat participation in their referral program by giving progressive and changing incentives. For example, in one program, anyone who makes eight successful referrals in one year is awarded a new Jeep Wrangler.[25]

Employment Agencies

Employment agencies are a frequently used source of salespeople. One-third of the companies responding in one recent survey reported depending on agencies to help fill the vacancies in their ranks.[26] Employment agencies are popular because they can save busy sales managers time and money. The agencies advertise, screen resumes, interview prospects, and present qualified applicants to the client. At this point, the sales manager chooses candidates for further interviews. A private agency is paid only when a person is actually hired. Employment agencies that charge applicants a placement fee must be given a detailed set of specifications, because they tend to refer candidates on their current lists. Agencies that charge the employer a fee are more likely to find recruits who match a particular job. Often firms find that the best agencies with which to work are those that specialize in finding sales recruits, such as SALESworld and Sales Consultants. Sales Consultants, for example, advertises that it places more sales management talent than any other organization.

School and Colleges

Perhaps the best source of sales trainees is educational institutions. For some firms, such as Dresser Industries, a manufacturer of power transmission equipment, and Hewlett-Packard, colleges are the focal point of their total hiring process. Armstrong International, for instance, hires 60 percent of its new sales personnel from college graduates.[27] Digital Equipment Corporation (DEC) has switched from relying on transfers from engineering to enthusiastic college graduates as their primary source of sales candidates.[28] Recognized for recruiting the best salespeople in the pharmaceutical industry, 50 percent of Merck & Company's new salespeople came from its college recruiting efforts.

College graduates are an attractive source of salespeople for a number of reasons. Graduates tend to be more easily trained and are often more poised and mature than those without college training. Successful college students typically know how to budget their time and, perhaps most important, have the perseverance needed to get jobs done.[29]

College students, however, usually lack sales experience and require considerable training and one-on-one coaching before they become productive salespeople. Many expect to be promoted rapidly to positions in management and become impatient if promotion opportunities are not soon forthcoming. Philip Morris, for instance, has found that college graduates become bored calling on retail stores to set up displays and sell cigarettes, and has reduced turnover by hiring people with three to five years of retail selling experience.

Customers, Suppliers, and Competitors

Customers and suppliers may also be a source of good recruits. They know the business, are familiar with the company, and may know what is expected of a salesperson. Care should be taken to ensure that the customer or supplier is aware of the recruiting process and is willing to cooperate.

Hiring competitors' salespeople is particularly attractive when a firm's training capabilities are limited, when customers are loyal to the salesperson and will therefore buy from the new company, and when new salespeople must be productive in a short period of time. When it decided to sell to large corporate accounts, Apple Computer targeted experienced salespeople with IBM, DEC, and Data General in its recruiting. Competition is the source for about 80 percent of new salespeople hired by Wang.[30] This practice is also common among insurance firms, stockbrokers, office equipment suppliers, and clothing representatives.

Hiring competitors' salespeople and customers' employees is controversial and gives rise to ethical and legal issues when the suspicion of divulging company secrets is involved. Retaliation and lawsuits are often the reaction of firms in industries where salesperson raiding is not common. Furthermore, because people rarely leave a job they like strictly for financial reasons, the new company may "buy" an unhappy employee. Only 10 percent of firms responding to a recent survey, for example, listed competitors as the best source of sales candidates.[31] A study in the pharmaceutical industry concluded that although salespeople hired from competitors produced the highest initial sales volume, the higher costs associated with attracting these people more than offset their higher productivity, making this source of sales candidates the least profitable.[32]

SELECTING PROSPECTS

After recruiting a pool of sales candidates, managers must screen out candidates who do not meet the *hiring criteria*. The procedure for selecting prospects is a sequential filtering

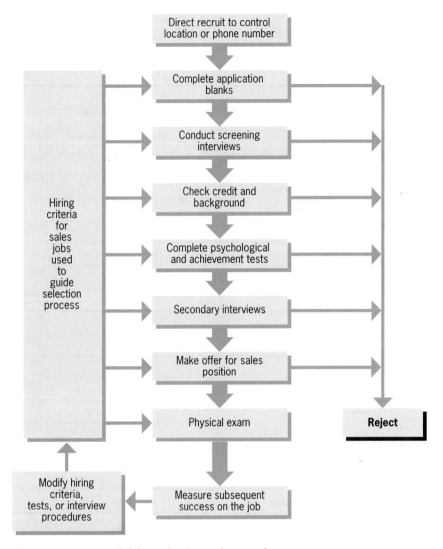

FIGURE 10-3 A Model for Selecting Salespeople

process, as depicted in Figure 10-3. The recruiter begins the selection process by evaluating application blanks and resumes and proceeds to interviews and background checks. In this way, obviously unsuitable prospects can be eliminated with low-cost methods, and the more expensive testing procedures can be saved for a smaller group of promising candidates. Each of the major selection tools is discussed in this section.

Application Forms

A popular way to gather personal history data is to have candidates fill out an *application blank*. It is easy to administer and requires very little executive time because the information is in a standardized format, as opposed to a resume. The basic purposes of application forms are to (1) provide information, gathered in a standardized manner, that is useful in making a selection decision, and (2) to obtain information that may be needed during an individual's employment.

Sales managers are primarily interested in several types of information found on application blanks. First, the sales manager wants information about the candidate's educational

Form 350- R24

PRE-EMPLOYMENT APPLICATION

An Equal Opportunity Employer
Male and Female

OWENS-ILLINOIS

Date _____

Personal Data

Name	(Last)		(First)		(Middle)	Social Security Number

Permanent Address	(No. & Street)		(City)	(State)	(Zip Code)	Telephone

Present Address	(if different from above)		Until What Date	Telephone

Age (if under 18)	Have you worked for Owens-Illinois before? ☐ Yes ☐ No If Yes, what location	Date available for work

Position for which you are applying

Application received from	Location	Date

Educational Background
Complete all sections applicable

Job Category				From	Major or Specialization
High School	Name			From	Major or Specialization
	City			To	Received Diploma ☐ Yes ☐ No
College	Name			From	Major Specialization
	City			To	Type of Degree Received
College	Name			From	Major or Specialization
	City			To	Type of Degree Received
Graduate School	Name			From	Major or Specialization
	City			To	Type of Degree Received
Other	Name			From	Major or Specialization
	City			To	Type of Degree Received

Stenographic And Clerical Applicants

What types of office machines can you operate

Do you take shorthand ☐ Yes ☐ No	Please indicate any other clerical skills or qualifications

U. S. Military Service

Date Entered	Date Discharged	Branch of Service	Highest Rank	Military Job

Affirmative Action Assistance
Vietnam Era Veterans, Disabled Veterans & Qualified Handicapped

As a government contractor, we are required to take affirmative action to employ and advance in employment Veterans of the Vietnam Era, Disabled Veterans, and qualified Handicapped. If you feel that you qualify under this program, please tell us on a voluntary basis if you would like to be considered under the Affirmative Action Program.

Name   *FOR OFFICE USE ONLY*

FIGURE 10-4   Application Form Used by Owens-Illinois

Employment Record (Begin with most recent)
Include prior employment with Owens-Illinois and part time work if college student

1.

Employer	Job Responsibilities
Address (No. & Street) (City & State)	
Date Began / Date Left / May we contact ☐ Yes ☑ No	
Immediate Supervisor's Name / Ending Rate of Pay	Reason for Leaving

2.

Employer	Job Responsibilities
Address (No. & Street) (City & State)	
Date Began / Date Left / May we contact ☐ Yes ☐ No	
Immediate Supervisor's Name / Ending Rate of Pay	Reason for Leaving

3.

Employer	Job Responsibilities
Address (No. & Street) (City & State)	
Date Began / Date Left / May we contact ☐ Yes ☐ No	
Immediate Supervisor's Name / Ending Rate of Pay	Reason for Leaving

4.

Employer	Job Responsibilities
Address (No. & Street) (City & State)	
Date Began / Date Left / May we contact ☐ Yes ☐ No	
Immediate Supervisor's Name / Ending Rate of Pay	Reason for Leaving

Qualifications And Achievements
Please tell us about your personal qualifications for the work for which you have made application. Use additional sheet if necessary.

The applicant herein authorizes the Company to investigate information supplied by him or her and to inquire further in regard to the applicant's background including academic, occupational and health records in its consideration of him or her as a prospective employee. In making this application for employment, it is understood that an investigation may be made whereby information is obtained through personal interviews with your neighbors, friends or others with whom you are acquainted. This inquiry includes information as to your character, general reputation and general characteristics. You have a right to make a written request within a reasonable period of time for a complete and accurate disclosure of the nature and scope of this investigation. It is understood that as part of our Health Program each applicant is required to complete a health examination.

I verify that the above information is true and that I have read and understand the last paragraph of this application.

Form 350- R24 (back)   Signature of Applicant _____

FIGURE 10-4 (Continued)

background. A second category of information is the past employment record. Sales managers are looking for any employment gaps and prefer candidates whose employment records show a natural progression in job responsibilities and wages. One study found that high-performing salespeople with a high propensity to remain with the firm have a job history of extensive selling experience on their resume, and view sales as a career position rather than as a stepping stone to another position.[33]

Noticeably absent from the application blank in Figure 10-4 are questions about marital status, gender, religion, race, handicaps, and age exceeding 18 years. These questions have been removed from employment applications for fear that the answers would be used by recruiters to discriminate against certain candidates. Some applicants may include extraneous information about themselves on an application so they can later claim they were rejected for unlawful reasons. Thus, all application forms should include a statement that indicates any applications with unrequested information will be automatically rejected.[34] Most application forms ask for data on military service, so that the firm can comply with affirmative action regulations on the employment of veterans.

Personal Interviews

The *personal interview* is a crucial part of the selection process for all sales positions, because interpersonal skills are so important in sales. Interviews are typically conducted at two levels. The first interview is used primarily to inform the candidate about the job and look for *knockout factors,* which are characteristics that would eliminate a person from further consideration, such as poor speech patterns, unacceptable appearance, or lack of necessary maturity. This initial interview is followed by the main interview, in which candidates are screened in order to identify people who best match the job's qualifications. The main interviewing process may include a series of interviews with sales managers, typically including the person to whom the candidate would report. After an initial interview with a divisional manager, Hewlett-Packard holds a series of five or six more interviews at the regional sales office where the job opening exists. SmithKline Beecham uses a "team interview" process where the candidate meets with a team of managers including the appropriate sales manager, service manager, sales director, and technical director. They switched to this format because previous candidates had learned the "right" answers by the end of a series of interviews.[35]

One of the benefits of interviews is that managers can follow up on information obtained from application blanks. For example, candidates can be asked to explain gaps in their employment or educational record and defend decisions to leave previous employers. A second advantage of interviews is that they allow sales managers to assess the applicant's level of interest and desire for the job. Interviews also allow managers to observe a candidate's conversational ability and social skills. One of the problems with the personal interview, however, is that managers fall into a trap of assessing how easy the candidate would be to manage, instead of assessing how effective the candidate would be in selling. In addition, recruiters must avoid asking questions during the personal interview that can be used to discriminate by hiring on the basis of race, sex, religion, age, and national origin. This is sometimes easier said than done, because some seemingly innocent questions can be viewed as attempts to gain information that might be used to discriminate against a candidate.

Figure 10-5 includes some typical questions asked in sales interviews. The candidates for any professional selling position should be prepared to present their background and career goals in a capsulation of approximately two minutes. This is often referred to as a "Two-Minute Drill," and responds to the question most typically asked at the beginning of the interview cycle, "Tell me about yourself."

Interviewing is a subjective process, so there are bound to be a few mistakes. Substantial evidence indicates that applicant ratings based on personal interviews vary dramatically among interviewers (Table 10-2). Worse yet, studies have found that personal interview rat-

---

Why should we hire you?

Regardless of the company and type of sales position for which you may interview, there are some interview questions that are typically asked. You may not be asked each of these questions in every interview, but you should be prepared to answer them all. After reading each question, think about what the interviewer's purpose may be in asking the question. What is he or she trying to determine? What should your response be to each question?

- What was the most monotonous job you ever had to do?
- In thinking about the people you like, what is it you like most about them?
- Up to this point in your life, what do you consider to be your biggest disappointment?
- How willing are you to relocate? To what extent are you willing to travel?
- How do you feel about the way your previous employer treated you?
- What are your long-term financial objectives, and how do you propose to achieve them?
- What was the most difficult decision you ever had to make as a leader?
- Why should we hire you?
- Sell me this pen.

FIGURE 10-5   Typical Interview Questions

ings are a very poor predictor of subsequent job success. One laboratory study, for instance, found that experienced interviewers incorrectly interpreted smiling, gesturing while talking, and talking more than other applicants as indicators of motivation.[36] Because of the personal nature of selling, the interview has remained the preferred selection tool of most sales managers. One way to minimize selection mistakes is to train sales managers on what questions to ask, how to ask each question, and how to rate applicants. SmithKline recruiters, for example, are required to be certified by their internal recruiting program so they can consistently apply their standard process around the world.[37] Another, more informal way to improve the interviewing process is to inform recruiters on a regular basis about the progress of candidates previously hired. Feedback on successes and failures can be a tremendous help in refining or improving interviewing techniques.

Patterned Interviews   There are several types of interviewing styles from which to choose. One type of interview is a *patterned interview,* in which the sales manager asks each

TABLE 10-2   Validity of Predictors for Entry-Level Jobs

Predictor	Validity
Ability composite (tests)	.53
Job tryout	.44
Biographical inventory	.37
Reference check	.26
Experience	.18
Interview	.14
Training and experience ratings	.13
Academic achievement	.11
Education	.10
Interest	.10
Age	.01

prospect a set of questions and records the responses on a form. The primary advantage of such structured interviews is that they facilitate comparison of candidates when more than one person is conducting screening interviews. When different questions are asked of each candidate, a comparison of candidates is often based on impressions rather than on recall of relevant information.

Semistructured Interviews   A completely structured interview may not always be appropriate for choosing among candidates. When interviewing veteran salespeople for a major account sales position, an interviewer may be looking for someone who will take control of the situation, because this is expected of the individual. In such a situation, it may be more appropriate to use a *semistructured interview* that is intended to gather critical pieces of information, but the questions are not repeated word-for-word and the candidate is expected to take a more active role in the direction an interview takes. An example of a form used to record information from semistructured interviews is shown in Figure 10-6. The key section of the form requires that the interviewer rate each candidate on education and training, work experience, skills and abilities, and career interests, using a scale from 1 to 5. These ratings are based on responses given by the candidate.

Field Observation   A special kind of interview that has proven effective for some organizations is *field observation,* which includes taking candidates out to observe a day of field sales work. The prospect travels with a salesperson, making calls on regular customers. The major benefit of the field interview is that prospects are shown exactly what the job entails, and those who feel they aren't likely to meet the challenge can eliminate themselves before being hired.

Follow-up

The interview does not end when the face-to-face discussion has ended. Sales management should track the timely response of candidates for sales positions by their responses in the forms of letters, notes, or other means. This tends to correlate to on-the-job accountabilities, where the most successful sales professionals typically have penchants for following up on their telephone and face-to-face encounters with customers, suppliers, and other key contacts.

Background and Credit Checks

How honest are people about their educational and employment histories? In a review of records from the past 20 years, one executive search firm found that almost half of all job applicants lie about their salaries and job responsibilities with previous employers. The message is clear: Don't assume that people are telling the truth. While an in-depth probe of a large number of references can be time-consuming and costly, failure to check resumes may result in hiring overpaid and unqualified salespeople. Scientific Data Systems, for example, found that 30 percent of their sales force had faked either their educational or work experience.[38] They also found that typically the top performers had told the truth and the bottom performers had lied.

Credit checks are commonly used to assess the financial responsibility of applicants, since financial responsibility goes hand in hand with job responsibility. Although no research has verified this relationship, Equifax, Inc., of Atlanta, claims it sold 350,000 of its credit reports to 15,000 employers in one year. Under the Credit Reporting Act of 1971, applicants must be told that a credit check is being conducted, and they must be given the name and address of the source if the check results in the rejection of a candidate.

Form 2680-R3

HR SELECTION, RECRUITMENT &
EMPLOYMENT
QUALIFICATION SUMMARY

Social Security Number	Insert Letter in box at right				
	A = College Recruit	B = Write-In	C = Employment Agency	D = Other	
Surname	First Name	Initial	Interview Date (mo., day, year)	Date Available for Employment	
Street Address	City		State	Zip Code	Telephone
College / University	Major		Degree B, M or D	If degree M or D, denote undergrad course and college	
Graduation Date (mo., year)	Grade Point Average		Geographic Preference		

Education and Training	
Work Experience	
Skills and Abilities	
Career Interests	
Overall Rating	
Remarks (if any)	

Insert Number in boxes at right   1st ☐   2nd ☐

1 = Corporate Comptroller Training Program	7 = Industrial Engineering	13 = Research & Development
2 = Financial (Accounting, Auditing, etc.)	8 = Plant Engineering	14 = Manufacturing Supervision
3 = Purchasing	9 = Manufacturing Engineer	15 = Adv. Degree Program
4 = Information System / Data Processing	10 = Product Engineer	16 = Other (list below)
5 = Sales / Marketing	11 = Package Engineer	
6 = Personnel / Ind. Relations	12 = Ceramic / Material Sci. Engineer	

☐ Refer   ☐ Reject

Division	Location	Date Referred	Division	Location	Date Referred
Division	Location	Date Referred	Division	Location	Date Referred
Was candidate given an O-I application and return envelope ☐ Yes ☐ No	Interviewing Staff or Division	Interviewer		Location	

Source: Owens-Illinois, Inc.

FIGURE 10-6   Interview Evaluation Form

Testing

Today, some form of testing is being used more often than in the past to help select field salespeople. Tests often provide more objective information than can be obtained from subjective conversation. Interviewers frequently reject prospects on the basis of personal biases and whims. Candidates have been rejected after interviews for such minor matters as speech accents or wearing short-sleeved shirts, short socks, or light-colored suits. These biases can be offset by the use of valid and reliable tests. Referring once again to the results in Table 10-2, notice that testing was found to be the most reliable predictor of entry-level job success, nearly three times as valid as interviews.

Three types of tests are being used in sales force selection: (1) intelligence, (2) personality, and (3) aptitude tests.

Intelligence Tests   These tests measure the degree to which a candidate has the minimum mental capabilities to perform the job. As such, the test is used as a knockout factor; that is, not meeting a minimum level will eliminate a candidate, but scores beyond the minimum will not determine the final candidate selection. *The Wonderlic Personnel Test* is a widely used general intelligence test because it is short and it has been extensively validated. It consists of 50 items and requires only about 12 minutes to complete.

Personality Tests   General *personality tests,* such as the *Edwards Personal Preference Schedule,* evaluate an individual on numerous personality traits. Unfortunately, such generalized tests may provide some traits that are irrelevant for evaluating future salesperson success. However, some companies develop specialized tests designed to measure specific personality traits felt to be important in a sales position, such as teambuilding. Such tests are generally thought to be a weaker approach than the others mentioned here, but could provide useful information about candidates if properly validated by careful job analysis, as is done at Pfizer.[39]

Aptitude Tests   These tests are designed to determine whether a candidate has an interest in certain tasks and activities. The *Strong Vocational Interest Blank,* for example, asks respondents to indicate whether they like or dislike a variety of situations and activities. Creating or tailoring tests to company specific requirements is also recommended. It is possible that top performers selling different product lines within the same company may have different critical success skills.[40] Responses can be compared with those of successful people in a certain type of sales position to determine if the candidate will be successful in the position. The Self-Management Competency example presented earlier in the chapter explains how aptitude tests are being used in the United Kingdom to select sales talent.

Recommendations   One common error made by recruiters is to adopt some readily available intelligence or psychological test that may be inappropriate for selecting field salespeople. Better results are achieved when tests are tailor-made by testing experts and human resource specialists for the needs of a particular firm or industry. It is also important to base the test on an analysis of the job in question and to validate the relationship between test scores and subsequent job performance. Comparing scores of the most successful and least successful salespeople currently employed by the firm is a frequently used validation method. A word of caution is recommended, however. Such tests should only be used as a part of the selection process, not as the sole decision criterion. There is little statistical evidence of these tests successfully discriminating between future high- and low-performing salespeople. One reason may be that candidates provide responses they think management wants, and thus their answers may not be an accurate reflection of the person's feelings or behaviors.

Physical Examination

Traditionally, the last step in the selection process for salespeople has been a routine physical examination (which typically includes testing for illegal drugs). Field selling is strenuous, often involving extensive travel and hauling sample cases into and out of customers' offices. Because salespeople typically must endure a lot of stress and frustration, the sales manager wants to be certain that the candidate has the stamina needed for the job, as well as to avoid costly medical bills.

With passage of the ADA, preemployment medical examinations have been prohibited.[41] Examinations are permitted once an employment offer is made and prior to commencement of the job. An employer could therefore make a job offer contingent on successful completion of the physical. However, questions about whether the person has a disability, and the nature and severity of the disability, are prohibited.[42]

Additional Selection Tools Some companies are using additional selection tools to help choose the right sales candidate. One such tool is the *assessment center,* in which candidates participate in job related exercises. Assessment centers were first used by the German military to select officers during the 1930s.[43] Merrill Lynch uses a sales simulation process in the selection of account executives. At one brokerage house, candidates are asked to sell a particular stock to a prospect, who is really a psychologist hired by the firm. The prospect greets the telephone caller, saying how busy he is at the moment. In this simulation, the employer is assessing the candidate's persistence, an important attribute to the job.

More and more companies are using *internship* programs, not only to determine if the person has selling skills, but also to see if he or she fits in with the company culture. With an internship, an individual is hired for a limited period of time, during which he or she is asked to perform certain tasks and gets the chance to observe and work with others in the company. Each year Northwestern Mutual Life recruits approximately 500 sales interns, called college agents. The internship program is also considered a major part of the recruiting process at Dow Chemical Company. Dow finds that it can attract good people at an early stage of their college careers and that it operates as a screening device for choosing the best people. The majority of salespeople hired at Dow have previously worked as interns.[44] The next section discusses some common hiring mistakes and gives ideas on how to avoid them.

Nine Mistakes and How to Avoid Them

Mistake 1: Relying solely on interviews to evaluate a candidate The typical interview only slightly increases a company's chances of selecting the best candidate. Experts offer three reasons why interviews are such poor predictors of sales success and why they remain the most common selection technique:

- Most managers do not take the time to structure an interview beforehand and determine the ideal answers to questions.
- Candidates do much more interviewing than most managers and are more adept at presenting themselves than many managers are at seeing through their "front."
- A typical interview helps managers evaluate personal chemistry and determine how well candidates might work together with others.[45]

Mistake 2: Using a generalized "success" model for selection While measuring the success characteristics of top performers may seem like a good idea, understanding differences between top performers and low achievers is more important for developing a selection model. Also, validating the critical success skills by comparing large enough samples of top performers and weak performers will help you determine the factors that consistently distinguish the winners from the "also rans." Duplicating success may seem like a good idea, but the reasons people succeed cannot be determined simply by measuring the characteristics of top performers. Otherwise, you may select well-spoken, energetic candidates who fail quickly, but with style.

Mistake 3: Too many criteria   Avoid getting caught up in looking for a large number of success factors. Be sure to validate those that you do select. Usually, the most critical factor for predicting success in a particular job is as important or more important than all other factors combined. To hire winners, decide on six to eight factors that separate them from losers. Ignore those factors that are not validated, or you may end up hiring nice guys who finish last.

Mistake 4: Evaluating "personality" instead of job skills   Although certain personality traits—high energy, honesty, a solid work ethic—seem to practically guarantee success, they don't. Many consultants and distributors of preemployment tests claim that certain personality factors help ensure management or sales success and offer psychological theories to support that belief. However, solid statistical research from many objective sources shows little correlation between any one personality factor and sales. You might enjoy knowing your sales candidates have self-confidence and energy, but knowing whether they can answer objections and close sales is probably more important.

Mistake 5: Using yourself as an example   Your own sales success might lead you to believe you can spot candidates with potential, but don't count on it. Many managers who reached their position by virtue of their sales success believe they can instinctively recognize a good candidate, when they are unconsciously just using themselves as a template. In these instances, one's ego often gets in the way, which can "bias" or skew one's objectivity in judging others.

Mistake 6: Failure to use statistically validated testing to predict job skills most critical to success   In some companies, committees use deductive reasoning or brainstorming to identify criteria for candidate selection. While this technique may encourage cooperation and participation, it has the potential to result in too many nonessential success characteristics. In other words, using statistically validated selling skills and ability should be the goal. Often, committees and commonsense attitudinal and personality criteria are used because these are easier to use than measuring candidates' skills. Gauging skill levels requires carefully developed tests or on-the-job trials many managers are unwilling or unable to conduct.

Mistake 7: Not researching why people have failed in a job   The reasons why people fail in a job are often different from the criteria used to select them. Most managers can list the most common reasons why people have failed, yet they seldom incorporate the information into developing new criteria for future candidates. There would be a significant reduction of hiring mistakes if managers would incorporate the identified "failure points" into the selection process. In most competitive sales situations, for example, the average prospect buys from a new salesperson only after six contacts. The average unsuccessful salesperson tends to give up after three contacts. Although some of that salesperson's techniques may be adequate, the tendency to give up after three rejections is not easily uncovered or evaluated.

Mistake 8: Relying on general "good guy" criteria   Everyone may want to hire good people, but being a good person does not ensure success on the job. You may be able to get away with using broad "good guy" criteria for entry-level hiring, but more specialized criteria is needed for those sales positions that require experience or specialized sales skills.

Mistake 9: Bypassing the reference check   Various recruiting and placement agencies report a fairly high percentage of false information presented in resumes and job applications. In fact, as many as 15 to 20 percent of job applicants provide false information on their resumes. To find out who's pulling the wool over your eyes, make the extra effort to verify the information your applicants provide. An individual who twists the facts to get a job is likely to bend the rules on the job. Checking references may seem tedious, but it beats the frustration and cost of hiring someone you have to fire in two weeks.

An Issue of Integrating Diversity

It should come as little surprise that America is becoming more diverse. The problem is not the changing composition of the workforce itself, but the difficulties companies are having in integrating and utilizing a truly heterogeneous workforce at all levels in the organization. Consider the following trends.[46]

- Analysis indicates that 65 percent of new jobs created during the 1990s will be filled by women.
- By 2050, one-half of the U.S. population will be African American, Hispanic American, Native American, and Asian American.
- The median age of the U.S. population is projected to rise from the current 32 years to 36 years by 2000 and to 39 years by 2010.

Companies that attempt to address diversity issues by meeting hiring quotas are unlikely to be successful. Changes must be made in the way corporations work. Though the solutions are not clear, some of the problems companies are grappling with include the following:

- Identifying and eliminating discrimination in hiring and management based on age, sex, and ethnicity.
- Developing creative ways to encourage productive people to stay in the workforce longer by offering part-time, flexible schedules and retraining to upgrade skills.
- Recognizing the concerns of men and women with different family structures and family responsibilities by addressing the issue of family care.

One reason why it is important for corporate America to address these concerns is that, unless employee differences are taken into account, companies will be unable to attract a sufficient number of qualified people to meet their needs. Another reason is that the markets for products are becoming more diverse, and it is necessary to have an in-depth understanding of those markets that may be facilitated by employee diversity. As a result, managers are faced with a number of challenges in leading newly diversified sales organizations to optimal performance.[47] Not only are we faced with challenges at home, but throughout this text there are examples of how global companies must recognize and adjust to cultural differences in other countries. It is at least as important that companies make similar adjustments in dealing with employees at home. Some of the international issues are discussed in the Global Perspective Competency box.

VALIDATING THE HIRING PROCESS

The last step in the hiring process involves validating the relationship between the selection criteria used by the firm and job success. Validation is generally most useful in large samples where information is collected on the progress of sales personnel and is fed back

GLOBAL PERSPECTIVE COMPETENCY
"Whom Should We Hire in Belgium?"

Hiring successful salespeople becomes much more complicated when American corporations go overseas. The numerous social differences between the United States and foreign markets complicates the process. Following are some examples of the social class, religious, and ethnic differences affecting salesperson selection:

- Latin American cultures are largely stratified into high and low, with a very small middle class. Respect is automatically given to superiors. Lighter-skinned groups are generally ascribed higher social status.

- While Europeans on the surface appear to be similar to Americans, there are a number of subtle differences. In Germany, ethnic biases favor hiring native Germans over those of Turkish or Yugoslav origin. Belgium is ethnically and linguistically split between Flemish and French. About 150 families control much of Belgian commerce.

- Malaysia has U.S.-style affirmative action laws to encourage the participation of native Malays (55 percent of the population) but not for the Chinese (33 percent). Malay society is highly stratified. How a person is treated depends on background, family, and social status.

into the system to modify the factors considered in the hiring process. Validation requires that managers specify exactly what distinguishes top performers from poor performers.

A new insurance salesperson, for instance, might have to meet the following criteria by the end of the first year of work: sales premiums of $120,000; renewal of policies at a rate of 60 percent or more; and submitting orders, reports, and paperwork that are legible, accurate, and timely. Those who achieved the standard would be examined carefully to see what common traits they share. The common traits of those who failed to meet the standard would also be examined to determine differences. The objective of the validation process is to build a profile of the successful performer that can be used to select additional salespeople.

Suppose that an analysis of 50 first-year insurance salespeople reveals that the typical successful salesperson has more than six months' prior sales experience, a score of 65 or better on the Selling Aptitude Test, and a college degree. These results could then be used to help standardize the hiring criteria to screen applicants. Persons who did not have a college degree or six months' sales experience could be weeded out on the basis of information supplied on their application forms. Those who survive the initial screening hurdles would have to take the Sales Aptitude Test. Candidates who scored below 65 on the test would be dropped before the final interviews.

Validation seeks to build a set of hiring criteria that filters out poor prospects and makes offers to those who have a high probability of success. No system can be 100 percent correct, but a carefully designed program can improve the ratio of successful hires to failures. The stringency of the hiring criteria will depend on the type of sales job for which the person is being recruited. For some routine sales jobs, a set of fairly easy hiring criteria may be adequate. In more specialized industrial selling jobs where a heavy investment in training is required, a more rigorous set of experience and educational criteria may be justified. The goal of validation is to learn what factors are related to success so that they can be used to select new additions to the sales force.

SUMMARY

The recruitment and selection of salespeople constitutes one of the primary responsibilities of field sales management. A poor hiring decision will not only increase out-of-pocket costs but, in some instances, damage employee morale, productivity, and client relationships. After reading the concepts discussed in this chapter you should be able to:

1. **Discuss how to plan for recruiting and selection.** Proper planning for recruiting is essential. To aid in planning, a multi-stage model for recruiting and selecting salespeople is presented. First, the number of people to be recruited is determined. The sales manager then prepares a thorough analysis of each sales job. A careful review of the activities to be performed by salespeople helps the sales manager in preparing a list of specific job qualifications. These job qualifications can then be used to build a profile to guide the search for successful recruits. Next, management must decide where it will look for recruits. From a pool of recruits, sales managers then must select job candidates. Finally, validating the hiring process helps to modify the hiring process for continued success.

2. **Identify relevant hiring criteria for sales jobs.** Job qualifications refer to the aptitudes, skills, and knowledge necessary to perform the job successfully. These qualifications should be the basis for the posted job opening and serve as a set of criteria that will help limit the number of applicants and help sales managers choose the best prospects from among those who apply. Research suggests that there is no natural-born salesperson, so an important criterion should include customer-focused selling abilities, such as a willingness to follow-through for the customer and the ability to adapt to the selling situation.

3. **Identify the different sources of recruits.** Depending on the type of job to be filled and company policy, the sales manager should seek applicants through various sources—educational institutions, other departments within the firm, present employees, employment agencies, classified advertising, competing or customer firms, and even Internet-based sources.

4. **Understand the selection and validation process.** Managers must evaluate the pool of applicants in order to select the most promising candidates. The selection process involves the use of application blanks, interviews, background and credit checks, and examinations in order to identify those persons who meet the job qualifications. Then the sales manager must decide which, if any, of the candidates should be offered selling positions. Hiring criteria should be validated by identifying traits associated with success on the job and including these traits as screening criteria for new candidates.

KEY TERMS

Application blanks
Aptitude tests
Assessment centers
Classified advertisements
Credit checks
Drug testing
Employment agencies
Field observation
Hiring criteria

Informational interview
Intelligence tests
Internship
Job analysis
Job analysis interview
Job description
Job qualifications
Knockout factors
Networking

Patterned interview
Personal interview
Personality tests
Recruiting
Selecting prospects
Semistructured interview
Turnover
Validation

DEVELOPING YOUR COMPETENCIES

1. **Strategic Action.** Representatives in the pharmaceutical sales industry deal with two distinct groups. They call on physicians, attempting to convince them of the product's superior quality, and they call on pharmacists, who must be persuaded to stock the product instead of a competitor's products. In recruiting salespeople, some firms hire only pharmacy school graduates, whereas others hire business or liberal arts majors and put them through an intense training program. What are the advantages and disadvantages of each method? What implications might this have for sales management? Will there be a difference in the number or type of persons moving into middle and upper management?

2. **Coaching.** The first few days on the job can be very important in determining how quickly the new salesperson gets started in the territory. How would you answer the following questions about the initial socialization of salespeople into the company? Should new people set their own pace during their first week on the job? Should new salespeople be asked to assess their territory before taking it over?

3. **Team Building.** SmithKline's "team interview" process requires that each candidate meet with a team of managers including a sales manager, service manager, sales director, and technical director. To make an offer of employment, the team must approve an applicant. What are the advantages to using the team approach to interviewing? What types of problems could occur by using such a team?

4. **Self-Management.** The pressure to fill an open sales position frequently leads to situations in ethically gray areas. Earnings potentials may be slightly inflated, or optimistic three-year predictions may be based on one high performer, whereas the average earnings are much lower. Relating how one person was promoted in only 18 months, even though this was highly unusual, may lead the candidate to believe that quick promotion is very probable. What if your company is in a changing industry in which the role of the salesperson is likely to be quite different in the near future and the earnings potential limited? What if you, the interviewer, are thinking of quitting? Should you let the candidate know? Should candidates be informed when it is likely the organization will go through a downsizing event sometime in the foreseeable future?

5. **Global Perspective.** The Czech economy is booming and many American companies with facilities there are hiring. The challenge is that the local workforce is steeped in the traditions of socialism and no one has a track record in selling and servicing in a free market economy. Companies such as Warner Lambert, Kmart, and Amway have turned to Caliper Corporation, a recruiting firm, for help. How should Caliper choose the right person the for job?

6. **Technology.** Peoria Resin and Plastics is a regional manufacturer of special grade plastics that are used as a key component in manufacturing a wide assortment of molded plastic products. The company is located in the three Midwestern states of Illinois, Indiana, and Michigan, but is planning to expand its current regional focus to include the adjoining states of Ohio on the east, Kentucky to the south, and Missouri to the southwest. You have been asked to develop an estimate of the number of additional salespeople who will be required to support this expansion. In carrying out your assignment, you have elected to use the "workload approach" discussed in Chapter 2. Analysis of your sales management database provides you with the following information:

   (a) on average, each one of Peoria Resin and Plastics salespeople can make 500 sales calls annually;

   (b) each prospect/customer account served requires an average of 25 sales calls over the course of any given 12-month period; and

(c) the company's sales force turnover has averaged 18 percent over each of the previous five years.

Access the Big Yellow Pages Web site at the URL: **<http://s13.bigyellow.com>** and search for the number of firms in each of the three new states that are active in the manufacture of molded plastic products. Next, enter the industry descriptor **<molded plastics>**, select one of the states of interest, and click on **<Find It>**. Do this for each of the three states of interest and record the number of plastic molding firms active in each state. Sum these individual state figures to determine the total number of firms actively involved as manufacturers of molded plastics products in the three new states. Using the "workload approach," incorporate this total number of firms in the three states with the previous information produced from the company's sales management database to derive an estimate of the number of new salespeople who will be required to support the expansion.

IN-CLASS EXERCISES

10.1: "Turnover: Counter-Offers"*

George Austin's jaw dropped. His top account executive, Angela Harris, just finished telling him that his best customer, Bernard Wells, president of Sterling Corporation, made her a generous offer to come sell for him. Although Harris hadn't agreed yet to take the position, she was tempted. She would receive a 15 percent increase in base pay, keep the three weeks vacation she had accumulated working seven years for Austin's ad agency, and could earn a year-end bonus of up to 25 percent of her total compensation. In addition, she knows the customer's company as well as she knows Austin's agency (since Sterling has been her client for six years).

Austin asked Harris to give him a few hours to compose himself, and then they would talk more. She agreed.

As soon as Harris closed the door behind her, Austin slumped into his chair, elbows on his desk, face buried in his hands, shaking his head. He could wish her well and let her go, but would her other accounts look for new agencies because their key contact at Austin Advertising left (he knows very well that advertisers can be a fickle bunch)? Or, should he counter the offer (he could)? She was well worth it. However, this might upset Bernard Wells and his best customers, causing him to look elsewhere for his advertising services. He was so exasperated he could only draw a blank.

Questions:

1. Should Austin make a counteroffer?
2. Is Harris a loyal employee?
3. Is Harris easily replaced?
4. Will Austin lose a great deal of business if Harris leaves?
5. Will Sterling actually change agencies based on a battle for this employee?

10.2: "Hiring Pressures"*

Jerry Silver, the general sales manager for the $500 million Pendulum Enterprises Corp., recently had to fire one of his three regional sales managers because of a consistently underperforming territory. In seeking to fill the position, he wanted to promote from within—and

---

*Contributed by Raymond Rody, Loyola Marymount University.

put on the list three reps who have solid sales performance and the skills and personality traits necessary to succeed as a manager. However, before he could arrange to meet with those reps to discuss the situation, the company president, Howard Stressler, gave Silver an order: Do whatever it takes to rehire Susan Kelleher. While a manager at Pendulum, Kelleher had increased the revenue and profitability of her territory by 47 percent. Two years ago she left the company to move to a competitor. Stressler's mandate was so firm it implied that Silver's own job would be in jeopardy if he couldn't convince Kelleher to rejoin the firm.

During the next few days, as Silver prepared an offer to woo back Kelleher, two of the reps he was initially considering approached him to apply for the job. Now he was feeling the pressure.

Questions:

1. What do you think Silver should do?
   - If he didn't at least meet with these reps, would he lose them—either physically (to the competition) or mentally (the reps might be disappointed because they were not considered for the spot)?
   - If he does meet with them, how does he conduct the interviews when he knows that he has only one true choice to fill the spot?
   - Should Silver take a huge risk and confront Stressler with a detailed explanation of why he should promote from within rather than rehire Kelleher?

CASE 10-1　FORTRESS ELECTRICAL TAPE COMPANY

Ralph Harris, sales manager of the Fortress Electrical Tape Company of Boston, Massachusetts, was attempting to select one candidate among three to fill an opening in his sales force. Fortress executives had for some time retained the services of a psychologist, Dr. Robert Gold, to assist them in selecting new employees. Dr. Gold's reports on these three candidates were available to Harris.

COMPANY BACKGROUND

Fortress's 1992 sales were in excess of $100 million. The company manufactured and marketed rubber and plastic electrical tapes. These tape products were sold by a sales force of five industry specialists to utilities, transportation firms, industrial plants, and electricians through a network of approximately 3,000 independent distributors. These latter were serviced by 27 manufacturers' representative organizations ("reps"). Exhibit 1 shows a partial organization chart of the sales operation.

The industry specialist's job was to acquaint end users with the specific technical advantages of Fortress electrical tape. The specialist also had to learn each customer's splicing requirements and other technical problems to be able to develop new applications for Fortress tape. The specialist actually spent only one-fourth of his or her time working directly with present or potential end users, however. Most of the specialist's time was spent working with the reps, arranging and conducting frequent regional sales meetings to pass on new information. The industry specialist also attended similar regional meetings held by the rep groups for their distributors. Typically, the specialist

This case was prepared by Derek A. Newton. The case was written as a basis for class discussion rather than to illustrate effective or ineffective handling of an administrative situation. Copyright (c) 1993 by the University of Virginia Darden School Foundation, Charlottesville, VA. All rights reserved. To order copies, send an e-mail to dardencases@virginia.edu. No part of this publication may be reproduced, stored in a retrieval system, used in a spreadsheet, or transmitted in any form or by any means—electronic, mechanical, photocopying, recording, or otherwise—without permission of the Darden School Foundation.

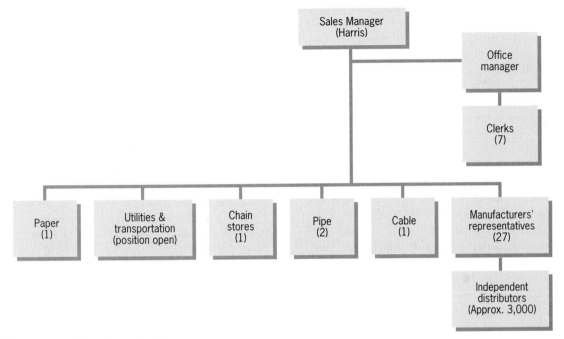

EXHIBIT 1   Sales Organization

spent one-half of his or her time away from the main plant in Boston.

The industry specialists were typically in their thirties and earned about $60,000 a year. All had previous sales experience. According to company executives, the most desirable background for an industry specialist would include a college degree and selling experience. Fortress executives also looked for candidates familiar with the Fortress product line or with a group of Fortress customers, and who could handle a fast-paced work schedule and a good deal of traveling.

During the past few years, a sharp increase in business—especially in small orders—from the public-utility and transportation industries led Harris to believe that his company could support a full-time specialist serving these markets. This new position would free the paper-industry specialist, who currently served the public utility and transportation markets, to develop the considerable potential in the paper industry.

Harris planned to have the new specialist report directly to him, as did the other industry specialists. The specialist would be based in Boston and would travel at least three-fourths of the time. He or she would initially assist the reps by making missionary and follow-up sales calls on large-volume prospects. After two years, Harris believed, this missionary selling activity could be reduced. The new industry specialist could then give more effort to maintaining a few key customers and guiding the reps.

This job could lead to the position of assistant sales manager to Harris, or to the position of regional sales manager, a post that Fortress sales executives planned to create within a few years to provide independent representatives and distributors with better supervision and assistance. A candidate's promotability, then, was important to Harris in determining which applicant to select.

THE SELECTION PROCEDURE

Harris and other Fortress executives were dissatisfied with interviews, résumés, and references as means of evaluating candidates. Harris felt that hiring judgments based on interviews were often subjective. While résumés provided concrete data, such information was often difficult to interpret. And Harris had never seen a negative reference. Moreover, most candidates requested that their present employers not be contacted, so Harris felt that the most pertinent information about their job histories was not available to him.

To make better hiring decisions, Fortress executives employed a psychologist, Dr. Robert Gold, to gather and assess more information about prospective employees. Dr. Gold's qualifications included a B.S. and an M.A. in Psychology and Sociology from Tufts University and a Doctor of Education degree in Psychology from Boston University. He had an established practice in Brookline, Massachusetts, was on the faculty of a local college, and had done consulting work for various businesses and public-school systems. Dr. Gold was widely regarded as an expert in dealing with psychological variables in normal and abnormal human functioning. Dr. Gold charged Fortress $1,500 per candidate. In return for this fee, Fortress executives received an interpretation of the applicant's personal history and a discussion of the applicant's qualities for the position.

Among the tests used by Dr. Gold were the following standard individually or self-administered psychological tests: Wechsler Adult Intelligence Test; Reading Comprehension Test; FACT Arithmetic Test; FACT (verbal) Expression Test; FACT Judgment and Comprehension Test; Sales Comprehension Test; Strong Vocational Interest Test; and various projective personality tests. Dr. Gold also used special performance situations and his clinical judgment to assess other personal qualities, such as emotional stability, mental organization, resourcefulness, flexibility, tact, creativity, and motivation.

During the past several months, Harris had interviewed more than a dozen people for the position of industry specialist in the public-utility and transportation industries. He had chosen three candidates to receive psychological testing. His impressions and those of other Fortress personnel are presented below, together with excerpts from the reports submitted by Dr. Gold on each of the three candidates.

Joseph Waring

Joseph Waring had been referred to Harris by the company's largest distributor, who was enthusiastic about Waring's selling and managerial abilities. Although Waring was not actively seeking a job, he was interested enough in the opportunity at Fortress to arrange an interview.

Harris believed that Waring made a good appearance and would probably be an excellent salesman, although he tended to be "a little cocky." Waring knew Fortress's customers very well and had experience calling on these customers, especially the larger distributors. He also responded very well to several questions about the electrical-tape industry.

Harris recalled meeting Waring at a trade show earlier in the year. They had a mutual interest in sailing, and Harris believed that he would enjoy working with Waring. The office secretarial staff was also favorably impressed with Waring.

During a luncheon with Fortress top management, Waring impressed these executives with his selling ability, but they wondered whether he had the capacity to assume a management position at a later date. This doubt was generated largely by Waring's comments about the problems of dealing with excessive paperwork.

Dr. Gold interviewed the candidate and reported the following information about Mr. Waring's background and personal history:

> Waring is the youngest of four children; he has one older brother who is an engineer; his two older sisters are married. His father put himself through engineering college and owned a small company. Waring characterized his childhood as excellent, but says that he has not struggled as hard as his father did. He has been married for eight years. His wife is one year younger than he. They have a good marriage, according to him. They have three children, all boys, and there are no problems. His hobbies include boating, other water sports, hunting, fishing; his wife loves boating. He enjoys an occasional drink. He was in the Army Reserves for a little more than 10 years before resigning.
>
> Waring has a long history of not applying himself, and his academic background and work history underscore this pattern. He was a fair-to-poor student in elementary and high school because, as he states, he did not "get kicked hard enough." He attended a local university for one year in the school of business administration, where he did fair work and, again, did not apply himself. He then moved to another local university "because of the school-work program." However, because the work program required very long hours (7 P.M. to 7 A.M., six days per week), he decided to leave school and work full time at this job (a government project). He remained in this position for four years; his work was largely technical, but he also did some work for the purchasing director. He felt that he was getting good experience, but the job offered little chance for advancement. He then worked for two years with a builder-realtor.
>
> Waring ran a branch office and supervised construction as well as property sales. He left because he preferred "more technical sales and getting around more." He then sold diesel motors for a large distributor for a year, but "the money wasn't there." His most recent job has been with a small company where he began as a product manager, then became an assistant sales manager, and then assistant to the vice president. He was let go along with many other administrative personnel during a company downsizing. He has been without work since last April. He does not need to make a hasty decision about future employment because he runs a two-boat business with his brother. He stated that he is interested in Fortress but is considering another job as well.

After reviewing the test results, Dr. Gold submitted his assessment of Waring's abilities and potential.

Waring's reaction to the assessment procedures was only fair. He complained about the tests to my assistant and also told her that he does not like to take tests. He has a tendency to talk a lot, but he expresses himself well and has a good sense of humor. He was well groomed. He had previously taken an extensive battery of tests for a position with another company. Only one of the present tests was a repetition, however.

Waring has excellent practical reasoning ability. He approaches problems well and thinks before he acts, and his thinking is organized, flexible, and resourceful. He is above average in judgment and comprehension. His vocational preferences and work history show strength in business and sales. He performed at an average level in reading comprehension, arithmetic ability, and sales comprehension. He shows fairly good tact and fair creativity.

In general, Waring has good basic intelligence. He apparently has not done too much with it, however. He lacks self-discipline and the ability to apply himself consistently to the tasks at hand. This lackadaisical quality prevents him from fully using his talents. He also has difficulty making decisions; he procrastinates and avoids responsibility. He needs outside direction, but he has good interpersonal relationships with authority figures, so he is able to take direction well. He is emotionally immature but basically stable. He shows real warmth in his relationships with other people.

Robert Mann

Mann was referred to Harris by a well-known personnel-placement agency in downtown Boston. The agency was especially enthusiastic about Mann and convinced Harris to come to their offices to interview him. After a very successful interview, Harris invited Mann to Fortress to visit the plant and meet other company executives. Harris enjoyed Mann's sense of humor and believed that the candidate would work out well at Fortress. Harris especially liked Mann's initiative in working his way through college and his general desire to move ahead. Harris also believed that Mann knew as much about Fortress's customers and products as some of the present industry specialists—his answers to questions on technical aspects of electrical tape were flawless. His previous experience seemed to be ideal preparation for the job.

During a luncheon with Fortress top management, Mann made a favorable impression and managed to keep the conversation relaxed with several humorous stories. The only reservations that the executives later expressed stemmed from some dissatisfaction with Mann's appearance and from some perplexity over his lack of progress in his career.

Dr. Gold's interview with Mann produced the following information about his personal history and background:

He grew up in greater Boston and attended public schools. He stated that his marks in high school were below average: He had good marks in English and social sciences, but passed by "the skin of my teeth" in other subjects. He also stated that he did very well in grammar school. After high school he worked for a year as a clerk with a supermarket chain; he felt that he was good with the customers. He then had a short enlistment in the Navy, where he went to electronics school and college preparatory school, and achieved the rank of seaman 2nd class. He hated the Navy saying "they wouldn't let you think." He then spent one year at a junior college where he did very well; following that he spent three years at a local university and finished with a low "B" average. While at college, he worked a full nightshift to pay for his college career; he lost a great deal of weight because of overwork.

Following college he worked for the telephone company for three years as a communications consultant; he left for more money. He then spent seven years with a local company. He trained inside for a year, then moved to outside sales; he left for more money. He then spent seven weeks with a small company and left because it was an "impossible situation and the wrong place": apparently, the job had been misrepresented to him, for it turned out to require 100% travel. He then worked for a large company in selling for two years; he was asked to resign, and he is not sure why. He is presently selling computer software; he is leaving because "Every order I have sold has been fouled up." "The quality is adequate, but I am used to selling the best." He also says, "There is no place to go." He is currently interested in more responsibility. He feels that he is a proven salesman; he is now looking to make his last move. He feels that Fortress is a dynamic company and says "I have a real solid feeling" toward Fortress.

Mann is the second of four boys; he characterizes his childhood as happy. As a child he had a temper, and he correlates his red hair with his fighting to defend himself. Both of his parents are living; his father has been a jobber and real-estate salesman; his brothers are in sales and marketing. Mann has been married 12 years. His wife graduated from high school and secretarial school. They have three children: The oldest is a girl who is a good student, the next is a boy who is bright but has no motivation for school, and the youngest is a girl who is not yet school age. He states that he has an excellent marriage and that his physical and emotional health are excellent. He mentioned that he had an ulcer at age 30, due to tension. He feels that he has done a good job as a father in that he represents security to his children; that is, he does not vary in his discipline. His hobbies are fixing up around the house, reading, coaching a Little League team, and fishing; he and his wife do not go out very much. He is a beer drinker—three or four in the evening, and apparently each evening. He has an occasional highball with customers but says that he does not like to drink at noon.

After reviewing Mann's test results, Dr. Gold submitted the following report:

> Mann reacted well to the assessment procedures. He was alert, fresh, and motivated both at the beginning and at the close of the evaluation sessions. He stated that he had taken such tests on two previous occasions. He makes a good impression, speaks well, but he has a tendency to wander from the subject under discussion. He appeared to be tense, and he exhibited a constant small-amplitude hand tremor; the tremor did not vary even under stress. He has a ruddy complexion, and he chain-smokes cigarettes. He tended to try to impress me about the way he handles himself in selling situations.
>
> Mann's vocational preferences suit him for work in sales, personnel, and public administration. Mann's mental performance was very high in nearly all the skill and ability tests: basic intelligence, reading, verbal expression, business judgment, and sales comprehension. Only in mathematical ability is he merely a little above average. He is very good in practical and abstract reasoning. He catches on quickly, thinks clearly, and approaches problems well in that he figures things out before responding. He does not become rattled under pressure. He also performed well in the tests for mental organization, resourcefulness, flexibility, tact, and creativity.
>
> Emotionally, he is expansive, optimistic, motivated, and generally mature. He also has a good sense of humor. However, all of the personality tests showed that he is defensive—he held back in his responses, making them difficult to analyze. His defensiveness suggests that he may be hiding some emotional problem. He is tense, has constant hand tremors, and had an ulcer at age 30. Clinically, I wonder if he may be an alcoholic. An essential feature of his overall performance was his excellent stamina. We can infer that this stamina would carry over to the work situation. On the other hand, if he does in fact have some basic emotional disturbance and/or is an alcoholic, he would not be able to cover up his problems indefinitely.

John Turner

The third candidate, John Turner, was referred to Harris by a small suburban sales-placement agency. Harris went to the agency for a morning of interviews, and Turner was by far the best of the candidates. He was currently working for an ashtray manufacturer, and during the interview he showed his selling process by picking up the table ashtray, selling it to Harris. He cleverly described product differences among various

ashtrays and convincingly demonstrated superior features of a particular style of ashtray. His relaxed and positive manner during this sales presentation convinced Harris of his natural sales ability. Turner also mentioned that he had traveled to Europe some years ago, working his way across the Continent. He had also worked his way through college. This initiative also impressed Harris, and he invited Turner to Fortress for a plant tour.

Turner arrived early in a Mercedes-Benz and accidentally met Harris in the parking lot. They walked into the Fortress building together. Turner made a noticeable impression on the Fortress receptionist and displayed a very winning manner to Harris's office staff. As a result, the entire office staff believed that Turner would make a valuable and personable contribution to the sales force.

Although Turner knew very little about Fortress products or customers, he assured Harris that he would have little difficulty in this respect. Turner said that it had taken him less than two months to learn the specifics in his present position.

At a luncheon with top company executives, he impressed the group so favorably that they later decided that he did not have to be assessed psychologically. However, Harris had already scheduled the evaluation procedure and could not cancel it.

Dr. Gold reported the following information about Turner's personal history:

> Turner has one younger brother who sells electronic calculators. He described his family as close, saying that "we have a great deal of fun together." He characterized his father as strong willed but said that he and his brother "survived" and now have a good relationship with him. Turner has been seeing a woman for two and a half years and has plans to marry her. She has a staff position at a university. He has not been engaged previously. His hobbies are skiing, scuba diving, and tennis. He describes himself as having been a "hard drinker" while in the service, but he has cut down a great deal since then; he now rarely drinks during the week.
>
> He lived in many parts of the country while he was growing up because his father was a salesman. He describes himself as an erratic student in the various public schools that he attended. He went to prep school for three years, where his performance was also erratic; at one point he won a prize for raising his average more than any other student in the space of one year. He then went to college for one year with the hopes of studying to be an industrial engineer, but he found engineering courses uninteresting. He left college to join the Marine Corps, where he remained for two years, elevating himself to private 1st class. He then attended a business college here in

Massachusetts. He said that the courses made sense to him and he did well the first year, although his grades went down the second year. Following his junior year, he left to tour Europe for six months. He states that he always worked during his schooling, primarily cutting trees on a contract basis. He stresses his need for money and his desire for the "finer things in life," and the fact is that he did make good money. When he returned to school, he achieved average grades.

After graduation he worked for a brokerage firm in New York for 20 months. Because he still wanted to do industrial sales, he left the brokerage firm and went to work for his father as a manufacturer's representative. He left this job after three and a half years because the "rep business folded" (apparently only for him, not for his father). He did not like the work because, as he says, "you had to be less than honest in getting in to see a person" and "you had to wrench the customer's money away from other things he wanted to spend it on." Thus, he says, "I could only go so far and not quite far enough to close the sale." He left the job after six months.

He has been looking for a new position for more than a month now, but says that he is not looking too actively because he wants to make sure that he is going into the right thing. He went to a prominent national personnel-counselling firm for evaluation. He was told that he should aim for management through sales and marketing. He has found that he should stick to selling, and to tangible products. He states that he has had a couple of "interesting offers," but that he is favorably disposed toward Fortress. He feels that he is too "fidgety" to take an office job at this time. He also states that his value is a little higher than most companies are willing to pay for.

After testing Turner, Dr. Gold submitted the following assessment of the candidate's strengths and weaknesses:

Turner's reaction to the assessment procedures was fairly good at the outset. Initially, he seemed quite alert, peppy, interested. He showed a good command of the English language and generally spoke well, except that he tended to ramble and his explanations were not always to the point. He displayed a fairly good sense of humor and was at times quite definitely flip. However, about two-thirds of the way through the tests and interviews he began to wilt. He was visibly tired and was comparatively unkempt in appearance and demeanor. It appeared that he had put up a front at the beginning of the assessment but had lost it by the end. He stated that he had not previously taken so extensive a battery of tests.

In general, the test results showed that Turner has very high intelligence, verbal expression, reading ability, and judgment and comprehension, although his sales comprehension was well below average. His vocational preference is for work requiring verbal expression.

Analysis of his intellectual behavior shows that he has excellent practical and abstract reasoning abilities. He thinks well on his feet and was not visibly bothered by pressure; he did not become rattled when he was obviously having difficulty with a task. He was methodical in his approach to problems, yet his thinking was resourceful, flexible, and creative. However, his performance was sometimes erratic, probably due to periodic lapses of interest. His performance was relatively weaker on tasks calling for immediate effort.

Emotionally, Turner is immature, egotistical, selfish, and spoiled. He seems to have little emotional interaction with others, although he presents himself well in interpersonal encounters. He projects a need for nurturance from father figures. He avoids responsibility and decision making, although he can evaluate situations quite well up to the point of making decisions. He is a talker rather than a doer. His behavior is generally erratic, and there seems to be no stable pattern to his life.

Harris wanted to add the needed sales support as soon as possible, and he did not believe that further searching would glean any better candidates than these. He now had to decide which of the three people would be the best addition to his sales force.

CASE *10-2*   ADAMS BRANDS

Ken Bannister, Ontario Regional Manager for Adams Brands, was faced with the decision of which of three candidates he should hire as the key account supervisor for the Ontario region. This salesperson would be responsible for working with eight major accounts in the Toronto area. Bannister had narrowed the list to the three applicants and began reviewing their files.

COMPANY

Warner-Lambert, Inc., a large, diversified U.S. multinational, manufactured and marketed a wide range of health care and consumer products. Warner-Lambert Canada Ltd., the largest subsidiary, had annual sales exceeding $200 million. Over one-half of the Canadian sales were generated by Adams Brands, which focused on the confectionery business. The major product lines carried by Adams were:

1. Chewing gum, with brands such as Chiclets, Dentyne, and Trident.
2. Portable breath fresheners including Certs and Clorets.
3. Cough tablets and antacids such as Halls and Rolaids.
4. Several other products, including Blue Diamond Almonds and Sparkies Mini-Fruits.

In these product categories, Adams Brands was usually the market leader or had a substantial market share.

The division was a stable unit for Warner-Lambert Canada, with profits being used for investments throughout the company. Success of the Adams Brands was built on:

1. Quality products.
2. Strong marketing management.
3. Sales force efforts in distribution, display, and merchandising.
4. Excellent customer service.

Adams was organized on a regional basis. The Ontario region, which also included the Atlantic provinces, had 46 sales representatives whose responsibilities were to service individual stores. Five district managers coordinated the activities of the sales representatives. As well, three key account supervisors worked with the large retail chains (e.g., supermarkets) in Ontario and the Atlantic area. The key account supervisor in the Toronto area had recently resigned his position and joined one of Adams's major competitors.

THE MARKET

The confectionery industry comprised six major competitors that manufactured chocolate bars, chewing gum, mints, cough drops, chewy candy, and other products. The 1993 market shares of these six companies are provided in Exhibit 1.

In the past few years, total industry sales in the confectionery category had been flat to marginally declining in unit volume. This sales decline was attributed to the changing age distribution of the population (i.e., fewer young people). As consumers grew older, their consumption of confectionery products tended to decline. While unit sales were flat or declining, dollar sales were increasing at a rate of 10 percent per annum as a result of price increases.

In the confectionery business, it was critical to obtain extensive distribution in as many stores as possible and, within each store, to obtain as much prominent shelf space as possible. Most confectionery products were purchased on impulse. In one study it was found that up to 85 percent of chewing gum and 70 percent of chocolate bar purchases were unplanned. while chocolate bars could be viewed as an indirect competitor to gum and mints, they were direct competitors for retail space and were usually merchandised on the same display. Retailers earned similar margins from all confectionery products (25–36 percent of the retail selling price) and often sought the best-selling brands to generate those revenues. Some industry executives felt that catering to the retailers' needs was

---

This case was prepared by Gordon McDougall, Wilfrid Laurier University, and Douglas Snetsinger, University of Toronto.

EXHIBIT 1   Major Competitors in the Confectionery Industry

Company	Market Share (%)	Major Product Lines	Major Brands
Adams	23	Gum, portable breath fresheners, cough drops	Trident, Chiclets, Dentyne, Certs, Halls
Nielsen/Cadbury	22	Chocolate bars	Caramilk, Crunchie, Dairy Milk, Crispy Crunch
Nestlé Canada	15	Chocolate bars	Coffee Crisp, Kit-Kat, Smarties, Turtles
Hershey	14	Gum, chocolate bars, chewy candy	Glossette, Oh Henry, Reese's Pieces, Lifesavers
Effem Foods	11	Chocolate bars, chewy candy	Mars, Snickers, M&M's, Skittles
Wrigley's	9	Gum	Hubba Bubba, Extra, Doublemint
Richardson-Vicks	2	Cough drops	Vicks
Others	4		

Source: Company records and industry data.

even more important than understanding the ultimate consumers' needs.

Adams Brands had always provided store display racks for merchandising all confectionery items, including competitive products and chocolate bars. The advantage of supplying the displays was that the manufacturer could influence the number of prelabeled slots that contained brand logos and the proportion of the display devoted to various product groups such as chewing gum versus chocolate bars. The displays were usually customized to the unique requirements of a retailer, such as the height and width of the display.

Recently, a competitor, Effem, had become more competitive in the design and display of merchandising systems. Effem was regarded as an innovator in the industry, in part because of their limited product line and their new approach to the retail trade. The company had only eight fast-turnover products in their line. Effem had developed their own sales force, consisting of over 100 part-time merchandising salespeople and 8 full-time sales personnel, and focused on the head offices of "A" accounts. "A" accounts were large retail chains such as 7-Eleven, Beckers, Loblaws, A&P, Food City, Shopper's Drug Mart, K-Mart, Towers, and Zellers. Other than Adams, Effem was one of the few companies that conducted considerable research on racking systems and merchandising.

THE RETAIL TRADE

Within Adams Brands, over two-thirds of confectionery volume flowed through wholesalers. The remaining balance was split between direct sales and drop shipments to retailers. Wholesalers were necessary because, with over 66,000 outlets in food, drug, and variety stores alone, the sales force could not adequately cover a large proportion of the retailers. The

percentage of Adams sales through the various channels is provided in Exhibit 2.

The volume of all consumer packaged goods sold in Canada was increasingly dominated by fewer and larger retail chains. This increased retail concentration resulted in retailers becoming more influential in trade promotion decisions, including dictating the size, timing, and number of allowance, distribution, and coop advertising events. The new power of the retailers had not yet been fully wielded against the confectionery business. Confectionery lines were some of the most profitable lines for the retailer. Further, the manufacturers were not as reliant on listings from any given retailer as were other food and household product manufacturers.

The increased size of some retail chains also changed the degree of management sophistication at all levels, including that of the retail buyers—those individuals responsible for deciding what products were carried by the retail stores. At one time, the relationship between manufacturers' sales representatives and retail buyers was largely based on long-term, personal associations. Usually the sales representative had strong social skills, and an important task was to get along well with the buyers. Often when the representatives and buyers met to discuss various promotions or listings, part of the conversation dealt with making plans for dinner or going to a hockey game. The sales representative was the host for these social events.

More recently, a new breed of buyer had been emerging in the retail chains. Typically the new retail managers and buyers had been trained in business schools. They often had product management experience, relied on analytical skills, and used state-of-the-art, computer-supported planning systems. In some instances, the buyer was more sophisticated than the sales representative with respect to analytical

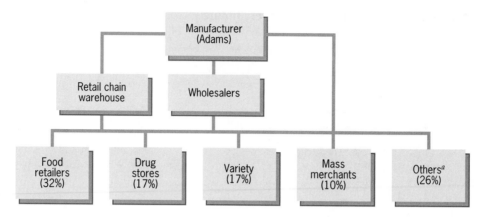

EXHIBIT 2   Adams Brands Sales by Distribution Channel

a Consists of a wide variety of locations, including vending machines, restaurants, cafeterias, bowling alleys, and resorts.

approaches to display and inventory management. The buyers frequently requested detailed plan-o-grams with strong analytical support for expected sales, profits and inventory turns. The buyer would also at times become the salesperson. After listening to a sales presentation and giving an initial indication of interest, the buyer would attempt to sell space, both on the store floor and in the weekly advertising supplements. For example, the buyer for Shopper's Drug Mart offered a dump bin location in every store in the chain for a week. In some instances, both the buyer and the representative had the authority to conclude such a deal at that meeting. At other times, both had to wait for approval from their respective companies.

The interesting aspect of the key account supervisor's position was that the individual had to feel comfortable dealing with both the old and new schools of retail management. The task for Bannister was to select the right candidate for this position. The salary for the position ranged from $31,000 to $54,200, depending on qualifications and experience. Smith expected that the candidate selected would probably be paid somewhere between $38,000 and $46,000. An expense allowance would also be included in the compensation package.

THE KEY ACCOUNTS SUPERVISOR

The main responsibility of the key accounts supervisor was to establish and maintain a close working relationship with the buyers of eight A accounts whose head offices were located in the Toronto area. An important task was to make presentations (15 to 30 minutes in length) to the retail buyers of these key accounts every

three to six weeks. At these meetings, promotions or deals for up to five brands would be presented. The supervisor was responsible for all Adams brands. The buyer might have to take the promotions to the buying committee, where the final decision would be made. In addition, the representative used these meetings to hear about and inform the buyer of any merchandising problems occurring at the store level.

Midyear reviews were undertaken with each account. These reviews, lasting for one hour, focused on reviewing sales trends and tying them into merchandising programs, listings, service, and new payment terms. Another important and time-consuming responsibility of the key account supervisor was to devise and present plan-o-grams and be involved with the installation of the displays. The key account representative also conducted store checks and spent time on competitive intelligence. Working with the field staff was a further requirement of the position.

Bannister reflected on what he felt were the attributes of the ideal candidate. First, the individual should have selling and merchandising experience in the retail business in order to understand the language and dynamics of the situation. On the merchandising side, the individual would be required to initiate and coordinate the design of customized display systems for individual stores, a task that involved a certain amount of creativity. Second, strong interpersonal skills were needed. The individual had to establish rapport and make effective sales presentations to the buyers. Because of the wide range of buyer sophistication, these skills were particularly important. Bannister made a mental note to recommend that whoever was hired would be sent on the Professional Selling Skills course, a one-week program designed to enhance listening, selling, and presentation skills. Finally, the candidate should possess analytic skills because many of the sales and performance reports (from both manufacturers and retailers) were or would be computerized. Thus, the individual should feel comfortable working with computers. Bannister hoped that he could find a candidate who would be willing to spend a minimum of three years on the job in order to establish a personal relationship with the buyers.

Ideally, the candidate selected would have a blend of all three skills because of the mix of buyers he or she would contact. Bannister felt it was most likely

that these characteristics would be found in a business school graduate. He had advertised the job internally (through the company's newsletter) and externally (in the *Toronto Star*). A total of 20 applications were received. After an initial screening, three possible candidates for the position were identified. None were from Warner-Lambert (Exhibit 3).

In early August 1994, Bannister and a member of the personnel department interviewed each of the candidates. After completing the interviews, brief fact sheets were prepared. Bannister began reviewing the sheets prior to making the decision.

EXHIBIT 3 Lydia Cohen

Personal:	Born 1963, 168 cm; 64 kg; Single
Education:	B.B.A. (1985), Wilfrid Laurier University, Active in Marketing Club and intramural sports
Work:	1992–94 Rowntree Macintosh Canada, Inc.–District Manager
	Responsible for sales staff of three in Ottawa and Eastern Ontario region. Establish annual sales plan and ensure that district meets its quota.
	1985–91 Rowntree Macintosh Canada, Inc.–Confectionary Sales Representative
	Responsible for selling a full line of confectionary and grocery products to key accounts in Toronto (1990–91) and Ottawa (1985–89). 1991 Sales Representatives of the Year for highest volume growth.
Interests:	Racquent sports
Candidate's Comments:	I am interested in working in the Toronto area, and I would look forward to concentrating on the sales task. My best years at Rowntree were in sales in the Toronto region.
Interviewer's Comments:	Lydia presents herself very well and has a strong background in confectionary sales. Her record at Rowntree is very good. Rowntree paid for her to take an Introductory course in Lotus 1-2-3 in 1991, but she has not had much opportunity to develop her computer skills. She does not seem to be overly ambitious or aggressive. She stated that personal reasons were preeminent in seeking a job in Toronto.

John Fisher

Personal:	Born 1967, 190 cm; 88 kg; Single
Education:	B.A. (Phys. Ed.) (1992), University of British Columbia
	While at UBC, played four years of varsity basketball (team captain in 1990–91). Assistant Coach, Senior Basketball, at University Hill High School, 1988–92. Developed and ran a two-week summer basketball camp at UBC for three years. Profits from the camp were donated to the Varsity Basketball Fund.
Work:	1987–93 Jacobs Suchard Canada, Inc. (Nabob Foods)
	Six years' experience (full-time 1992–93, and five years part-time, 1987–92, during school terms and full-time during the summers) in coffee and chocolates distribution and sales; two years on the loading docks, one year driving truck, and three years as a sales representative. Sales tasks included calling on regular customers, order taking, rack jobbing and customer relations development.
	1993–94 Scavolini (Professional Basketball)
	One year after completing studies at UBC, traveled to Western Europe and Northern Africa. Travel was financed by playing professional basketball in the Italian First Division.

Candidate's Comments:	I feel the combination of educational preparation, work experience, and my demonstrated ability as a team player and leader make me well suited for this job. I am particularly interested in a job, such as sales, that rewards personal initiative.
Interviewer's Comments:	A very ambitious and engaging individual with a good record of achievements. Strong management potential is evident, but interest in sales as a career is questionable. Minored in computer science at UBC. Has a standing offer to return to a sales management position at Nabob.

Barry Moore

Personal:	Born 1954, 180 cm; 84 kg; Married with two children
Education:	Business Administration Diploma (1979), Humber College
	While at school, was active participant in a number of clubs and political organizations. President of the Young Liberals (1978–79).
Work:	1991–94 Barrigans Food Markets—Merchandising Analyst
	Developed merchandising plans for a wide variety of product categories. Negotiated merchandising programs and trade deals with manufacturers and brokers. Managed a staff of four.
	1988–91 Dominion Stores Ltd.—Assistant Merchandise Manager
	Liaison responsibilities between stores and head office merchandise planning. Responsible for execution of merchandising plans for several food categories.
	1987–Robin Hood Multifoods, Inc.—Assistant Product Manager
	Responsible for the analysis and development of promotion planning for Robin Hood Flour.
	1982–87 Nestlé Enterprises Ltd.—Carnation Division Sales Representative.
	Major responsibilities were developing and maintaining sales and distribution to wholesale and retail accounts.
	1979–82 McCain Foods Ltd.—Inventory Analyst
	Worked with sales staff and head office planning to ensure the quality and timing of shipments to brokers and stores.
Activities:	Board of Directors, Richview Community Club
	Board of Directors, Volunteer Centre of Etobicoke
	Past President of Etobicoke Big Brothers
	Active in United Way
	Yachting—CC 34 Canadian Champion
Candidate's Comments:	It would be a great challenge and joy to work with a progressive industry leader such as Adams Brands.
Interviewer's Comments:	Very articulate and professionally groomed. Dominated the interview with a variety of anecdotes and humorous stories, some of which were relevant to the job. Likes to read popular books on management, particularly books that champion the bold, gut-feel entrepreneur. He would probably earn more money at Adams if hired.

CHAPTER

11

SALES TRAINING

> The problem with experience is that the test comes before the lesson.
>
> ANONYMOUS

Chapter Consultants:
George Pettegrew, Senior Sales Training Manager, Johnson & Johnson Medical
Jerry Willett, National Sales Manager, Software Spectran

LEARNING OBJECTIVES

After studying this chapter, you should be able to:

⟶ Determine specific training needs for a sales force.

⟶ Discuss the topics to include in a training program.

⟶ Describe the advantages to centralized and decentralized training.

⟶ Understand the use of line, staff, and outside trainers.

⟶ Recognize the value of alternative training methods and media.

⟶ Describe the different methods for evaluating training results.

SALES TRAINING AT LUCENT TECHNOLOGIES

Lucent Technologies, a leading telecommunications company, recently remade its sales training program in an effort to improve its effectiveness. Lucent once required all salespeople to attend a yearlong series of training seminars at its Sales Academy, which didn't necessarily cover the areas in which reps most needed training. Lucent's new sales training philosophy requires each member of its 2,400 network sales force to have a personal development plan. The customized plan approach is designed to improve reps' competencies in the areas where they showed weaknesses. Through intensive phone interviews, sales managers assessed the sales reps' experience, skills, and knowledge in order to get a clear picture of where every member of the sales organization stood. With the interview results, Lucent managers formulated individual development plans with the sales rep. The development plans included training at the Sales Academy, nontraining developmental options, recommended readings, and Web sites. Sales training at Lucent now focuses on the areas where each account executive needs help, thereby increasing training effectiveness.[1]

National surveys of sales and marketing executives consistently indicate that good salespeople are made, not born. Research results also indicate that characteristics that can be developed—such as selling skills, motivation, and role perceptions—are more closely related to sales performance than enduring traits like appearance, aptitude, and personality.[2] This is one reason why sales training is such a booming business today. U.S. companies, for example, spent $8.6 billion for sales training in 1998.[3]

Training requirements and spending are closely related to other management decisions such as recruiting and selection procedures. If a firm believes it needs to hire young, aggressive people with little prior sales experience, then training of new recruits takes on special significance. For example, nearly every one of Armstrong World Industries' salespeople has been recruited right out of college. Initial training is conducted at Lancaster, Pennsylvania, near company headquarters. Trainees live in a dormitory-style building called The Manor. Although the total cost of recruiting and training is quite high, Armstrong believes the benefits of hiring people without industry-related biases and conflicting opinions are worth the cost.

If a firm hires mostly veteran salespeople from within its industry, then training of new salespeople is less expensive and generally focuses on company procedures. DuPont usually hires people with technical backgrounds, and although their compensation is higher than that of trainees with a nontechnical background, the training period is shorter (only a couple of weeks) and focuses on "people sensitivity." There are also obvious differences in the type and level of compensation plans that are appropriate for each situation. The point is that the various management decisions are related and must be compatible. Spending less in one areas often means spending more in another area.

The main sales training issues covered in this chapter are highlighted in the following diagram. Deciding whether a sales training program is needed often involves balancing training costs against alternative methods of obtaining effective field sales coverage. As illustrated in the Lucent example, managers frequently find that not all salespeople need the same kind of training. If a training program is recommended, sales managers must decide what topics will be covered, where the training sessions will take place, who will conduct the sessions, and what methods of instruction will be employed. Although most formal training programs are designed for newly hired personnel, sales managers must also schedule periodic retraining sessions for experienced salespeople because the environment, products, and marketing programs change over time. The manager of sales training activities must then evaluate the contributions of the training program. The primary concerns are to ensure that training objectives are met and to determine whether programs are cost-benefit justified.

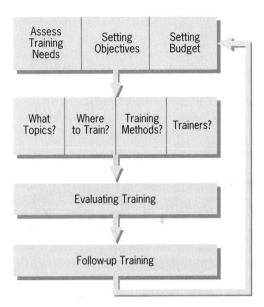

WHY TRAIN SALESPEOPLE?

Sales executives and purchasing agents generally agree that inadequate training of salespeople is one of the most common problems they encounter. When asked what qualities make a top salesperson, purchasing agents frequently mention qualities that can be influenced by training, which is why some of the most respected companies are willing to spend a great deal on sales training. Consider the following examples:

- Xerox spends $100,000 for salary and training during a salesperson's first year on the job.
- IBM budgets more than $1 billion per year for training. Moreover, IBM pulls its best salespeople from the field to help conduct the company's training programs.[4]

These companies consider training costs as an investment in the future success of the firm rather than simply as a current expense.

What are some of the benefits that these and other organizations hope to realize from their sales training programs?

Increased Productivity

The ultimate objective of any training program is to produce profitable results. The Nabisco Biscuit Company recently estimated that they realized a return of 122-to-1 on a program that teaches salespeople to plan for and make professional sales presentations to retail customers. Nabisco paid $1,008 to put each salesperson through the program and preliminary results equate to an increase of $122,640 in sales per year per salesperson.[5] While money spent on poorly conceived and executed training programs is largely wasted, the Nabisco example illustrates the potential for significant returns on money spent on training. Sales trainers report that companies are increasingly requiring this type of sales justification from training investments.

Reduced Turnover

Turnover is the ratio of the number of people who leave to the average size of the sales team. Salespeople who go into the field without adequate training typically find it difficult to see buyers, answer questions, or close orders. The resulting confusion and disappointment often cause novices to quit before they have a chance to learn how to sell effectively. A study of the insurance industry found that the likelihood of turnover peaks at 15 months of employment and is highest among low-productivity agents.[6] However, results of a multiple industry study revealed that management may be able to reduce job stress (an indicator of turnover intentions) and increase management satisfaction by providing new agents with a quality sales training program.[7]

Improved Customer Relations

Industrial buyers, in particular, complain that too much of their time is wasted in dealing with untrained salespeople. Buyers do not like to spend their time counseling salespeople on market conditions and product needs. They prefer to work with trained salespeople with a thorough knowledge of the industry, their firm's business, and their own product lines. Companies are attempting to respond to these concerns. "We train our sales force to understand why customers buy our products," says Pat Dalton, business operations manager for Caterpillar's North American commercial division. "We want them to know what their needs are, the importance of follow-up, the need to let a customer vent his anger, and how to help a customer resolve problems without passing the responsibility on to someone else in the company."[8]

With more and more buyers requiring vendors to provide a total business solution, the number of a sales rep's contact points within the buying firm is also increasing. Today's sales training programs are responding by providing information about the buying motives for other potential key influencers, such as finance executives, operating officers, and accountants. Tellabs salespeople, for example, are now trained to discuss strategic growth and capitalization requirements with a prospect's senior executives.[9]

Better Morale

Sales training increases product knowledge and improves selling skills; it also builds self-confidence and enthusiasm among the sales force. When salespeople know what is expected of them, they are in a better position to withstand the disappointments and meet the challenges of a sales career. Trained salespeople start producing orders faster, and the increased earnings help boost morale. The significance of this objective is reinforced by a recent study of sales trainees, in which attitude was the most frequently mentioned characteristic of successful salespeople. When brought together for training, people get a sense of belonging to a team in which they can exchange successful selling techniques and ideas.

Improved Time and Territory Efficiency

Enhancing salesperson time and territory management skills is important for all sales organizations. Salespeople are constantly faced with time pressures that make it difficult to effectively allocate resources. Frequently it is difficult to determine what is really important and what only seems important. Understanding the difference, however, is often what separates the stellar from the average performer.

The use of technology to improve time and territory management efficiencies has had a tremendous impact over the last few years. Sales force automation has been estimated to boost productivity by as much as 20 to 40 percent.[10] Pitney-Bowes, for example, put 3,000 of its salespeople through a sales automation training program to teach them how to use specific account management software. The results not only improved salesperson productivity by 30 percent, but also improved customer satisfaction ratings.[11]

PLANNING FOR SALES TRAINING

Planning for sales training involves three related processes: (1) assessing sales training needs, (2) establishing specific objectives for the training program, and (3) setting a budget for the program. Each of these processes is discussed in this section.

Assessing Training Needs

Without oversimplifying the issue, sales force productivity needs generally break down into one of three elements. The sales force either does not know what to do, or how to do it, or why they should do it. A training needs analysis is a process for determining where problems and opportunities exist and whether training can best address the issues. A complete training needs analysis includes a review of the firm's strategic objectives, management observation and questioning of salespeople, customer input, and a review of company records.

Management Objectives   An organization's strategic programs frequently focus on certain products, customers, and customer relationships. Because Caterpillar embraces a corporate strategy of selling premium products at a premium price, its selling process emphasizes total customer value. As a result, Caterpillar trains its people in consultative selling requiring intimate customer knowledge, including costs, benefits, and profits. DuPont's salespeople are taking more courses in international areas, in addition to technical and product-oriented courses, as a result of changes to its marketplace. These examples illustrate the necessity of identifying training needs as a result of changes in strategy, market environment, and competitive environment. This recommendation is reinforced by surveys of sales management practices, which indicate that judgments of upper management and sales management are considered most important in determining sales training needs.[12]

Sales Force Observation and Survey   Observation of salespeople is an excellent way to identify shortcomings, especially when successful and unsuccessful sales calls and salespeople are compared. Observation of sales calls of a company selling auto parts, for example, revealed that the discussion during successful sales calls focused on which products the customer should order. Less successful salespeople spent far more time waiting or talking about nonbusiness subjects. This type of salesperson observation often identifies areas that need improvement. For example, it was also discovered that sales managers needed to be better in coaching salespeople.[13]

Customer Information   Sending customers questionnaires can also be quite revealing. Questions to be asked may include: What do you expect from a salesperson in this industry? How do salespeople disappoint you? Which company in the industry does the best job? In what ways are its salespeople better? An alternative to surveys is to conduct a series of focus group sessions with 6 to 10 customers. A focus group is essentially a meeting with a group of customers to elicit specific information, in this case information on training needs. See how 3M incorporates customer input into its training program in the Strategic Action Competency box.

Company Records   Companies with a degree of computer sophistication may have a great deal of useful data for analyzing training needs, especially if call reports are available. Cross-tabulating performance records may also be helpful in identifying which salespeople need what type of training. Cross-tabulation involves examining performance by certain sales force characteristics, such as years of experience, geographic area, or area of specialization.

STRATEGIC ACTION COMPETENCY
Getting Customers into the Act

In an effort to align its sales force with its strategic direction of "the voice of the customer," 3M revised its training program for veteran salespeople by asking customers to tell 3M where salespeople needed to improve skills and get additional training. Although 3M had been surveying its customers before, the questions had been too general and tended to focus on product quality and technical values rather than on personal selling skills. Corporate training developed a questionnaire to assess skills in six areas—knowledge of products and services, strategic skills critical to leveraging time with the customer, interpersonal selling, sales negotiations, internal influence and teamwork, and customer-focused quality. Salespeople or their managers deliver questionnaires to six customers, chosen by the salesperson, who assess the importance of each skill to the selling relationship, and the salesperson's application of each skill. With the feedback report in hand, salespeople and their managers determine a training curriculum focusing on the salesperson's three most significant gaps according to the customer survey. Following the voluntary sales training, sales managers are expected to follow up with reinforcement and field coaching, while salespeople return to the customers who received the survey to review the composite results and to ask for additional direction in closing the gap. Divisions of 3M participate in this program on a voluntary basis, but it has been 3M's experience that veteran salespeople will pay more attention to what the customer says than what other people may say. Overall, linking the customer to specific training needs has had a tremendous impact on the performance of 3M's salespeople.

For more information about 3M, visit *www.3M.com*.

Table 11-1 illustrates how a cross-tabulation may be useful in identifying training needs. Three intermediate measures of performance are crossed with two characteristics of the sales force—years of experience and geographic region. Experience was chosen as a characteristic based on management concerns that both new and senior salespeople were thought to be having difficulties. Regional differences were also of interest because managers had considerable latitude in the training of salespeople and complete responsibility after the initial six-week training of new salespeople.

The results in Table 11-1 suggest that there may be a problem with both new and senior salespeople. New salespeople have the lowest average order size and lowest total number of customers, which may suggest that new salespeople need more training in how to increase business with existing customers. At the same time, senior salespeople with more than 10 years' experience appear to have a problem with prospecting for new customers. There also seem to be difficulties with the Southwest region, because it has the lowest average order size and total customers per salesperson.

What's the next step? Design a training program on prospecting for senior salespeople? Implement a whole set of training programs for the Southwest region? The answer is no because we have not yet investigated the needs of the sales force in sufficient depth. Cross-tabulating experience with regions may reveal that the Southwest region has mostly new salespeople. There may be competitive reasons for the results. There may be demand and economic differences between the various regions. In short, the needs analysis should return to a dialogue with salespeople and sales managers to identify the causes of the problems. This hypothetical situation points out an important principle when investigating training needs: Use multiple sources of information and cross-validate the information whenever possible.

TABLE 11-1 **Cross-Tabulations from Company Records**

	Average Order Size per Salesperson	New Customers per Salesperson	Total Customers per Salesperson
Experience			
Less than 2 years	392	21	86
2–5 years	593	29	145
5–10 years	565	5	152
More than 10 years	470	8	139
Regions			
Northeast	528	6	140
Southeast	520	8	161
Midwest	512	18	107
Southwest	421	26	111
West	544	21	131

Setting Objectives

After assessing the training needs of the sales force, specific sales training objectives should be established and put in writing. Like all good objectives, training objectives should be specific enough and measurable so that the extent to which they have been met can be evaluated following the training program. This will also help avoid the problem of training for training's sake. Written objectives are also helpful in gaining top management's commitment and willingness to provide budget support for training. As one sales training consultant noted, "I've seen excellent programs fail—and poor programs succeed. The difference has always boiled down to one thing—*management commitment*."[14]

Setting a Training Budget

New Salespeople Companies spend millions of dollars every year on new salesperson training. Table 11-2 shows the average cost of training new salespeople, including salary during the training period. It also shows the average length of formal training for sales trainees. It should come as no surprise that the more technically oriented industrial and service industries spend more money and take more time to train new salespeople. Intel, for instance, almost exclusively hires engineers for sales positions, and puts them through a two-year training program before deploying them to its field offices.

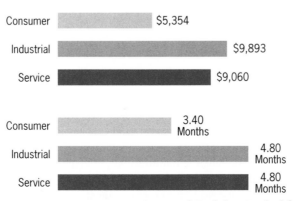

TABLE 11-2 **Average Cost and Training Period for Sales Training**

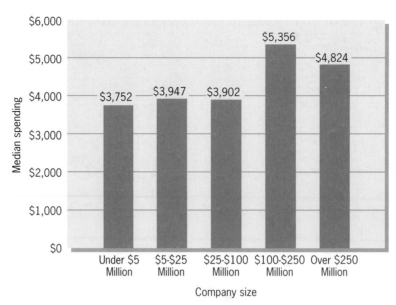

TABLE 11-3   Average Cost and Company Size for Veteran Salespeople

Although the overall numbers indicate a relationship between time to train and cost of training, this is not necessarily the case for individual organizations. A study of paper and plastics wholesalers found that top-performing sales forces took more time to train salespeople, but did not spend more money for training than their low-producing counterparts.[15]

Retraining Veteran Salespeople   Most managers believe that the need to learn is never-ending and that even the most successful sales representatives can benefit from refresher training. Products change, markets shift, territories are reorganized, and salespeople need additional training to help adjust to these new environmental situations. Table 11-3 indicates how much various types of companies are spending on training experienced salespeople. Burlington Industries' training for experienced salespeople is typical of that offered by many firms. Each division's salespeople meet four times a year for one-day sessions, in which sales and products are reviewed against the competition, and selling skills are honed. Bell Atlantic had taken a different approach. At Bell, 60 top salespeople from a sales force of 250 representatives were chosen for an intense 13-week course that examined emerging technologies in the communications-information services complex.[16] Veteran salespeople at Owens-Corning participate in seminars on such topics as time and territory management, problem solving, and consultative selling.[17] In general, retraining veteran salespeople is not easy, and experts suggest using adult learning principles, which emphasize a significant amount of training time on interpersonal interaction and role-playing.

DEVELOPING THE TRAINING PROGRAM

After determining the needs of the sales force, and setting specific objectives and a budget for training, a number of decisions critical to the success of the individual training program must be addressed. These decisions include (1) what topics to cover, (2) where to conduct the training, (3) who should do the training, and (4) what training methods to use. These four decisions are interrelated so that one decision will impact the others. We will take a close look at each decision in this section to get an understanding of the trade-offs that are made.

Training Topics

The choice of subjects to be covered in a sales training program depends on the products to be sold, purpose of the training, and the background of those being trained. Firms that sell complex products, of course, must include more material in their programs than firms selling less complex products or services. Val-Pak, which distributes home-delivered coupons of local retailers, recruits on college campuses and puts new hires through a 17-week training program where they learn about direct mail and selling. Eastman Chemical's training program lasts six to nine months and requires trainees to spend several weeks in technical service labs learning to process chemicals, plastics, and fibers. The purpose of training may be to provide initial training for new hires, continuing development, or training for a specialized situation. Similarly, initial training may vary depending on the selling experience of the new salespeople. Now let's take a look at the topics typically included in training programs.

Product Knowledge A common misconception is that sales training is designed primarily to improve the selling skills of sales representatives. While selling skills are important, more sales training time, usually about 40 percent, is spent presenting product information. This information is frequently related to the introduction of new products. Merck, a multi-billion-dollar pharmaceutical company, has a short time to bring a new product to market following FDA approval. In just one week, Merck's 3,000 salespeople will attend an off-site training session where—with the help of physicians and computerized product information—they learn about the new product and become familiar with the disorder it treats. Six weeks after product introduction, salespeople are brought together once more to solidify their product knowledge. Product understanding is considered essential if sales representatives are to communicate effectively and address customer needs, and has been found to be closely related to product success in the marketplace.[18]

Selling New recruits must be familiar with how the sales process works before they can be effective and productive field representatives. Even recruits with previous selling experience need this training because selling approaches may differ from one company to the next. Veteran salespeople will also benefit from training in how to sell in specific situations and when presenting new products.

Supporting this notion that even experienced salespeople can benefit from learning new selling skills is research on cognitive selling scripts. A script is the knowledge an expert, such as an effective salesperson, possesses based on remembered similar experiences. Experts are said to possess two types of knowledge. The first type of knowledge, referred to as declarative knowledge, permits them to recognize a selling situation requiring a somewhat unique selling process. The other type of knowledge is called procedural knowledge. This knowledge consists of the process or sequence of behaviors that are necessary to achieve a successful conclusion in a particular sales situation. Research techniques have been recently developed to determine knowledge structures of experts for developing customized expert training systems.[19] The implications for sales training are significant. Both novices and experienced salespeople can be taught how to identify selling situations and customer types and what approaches are likely to be successful based on the knowledge of company experts. These techniques also capture the expert's knowledge base indefinitely, in case he or she ever leaves the company.

Improving Teamwork As sales organizations focus on developing more enterprise relationships (as discussed in Chapter 2), sales training has also begun to focus on training salespeople as members of cross-functional sales teams. Sales teams are generally composed of a group of specialists, each of whom contributes different skills to deliver a system-oriented solution to customer problems. In these situations a salesperson may not only be responsible for maintaining the customer relationship, but also for motivating and coordinating the sales team. Working in teams, therefore, requires new competencies from people who are used to working independently of other employees. Procter & Gamble, for instance, found that people needed to be trained in such skills as how to evaluate other team members, coordinate projects, arrive at mutually agreed-upon objectives, settle disputes within the team, and provide feedback to team members. Notice that many of these topics were once the concern of management personnel only.

Increased interaction with other functional areas within a company has also meant a change in training methods. Eastman Chemical's 500 salespeople are responsible for more than $4 billion in sales, and often find themselves in the position of coordinating many of Eastman's 18,000 total employees in team efforts focused on improving customer relationships. Eastman realized that they needed to give their salespeople greater working knowledge of the company, its products, and how these products were produced than was previously required. A "working" knowledge is just what Eastman provides. Part of the six- to nine-month basic training of all Eastman Chemical salespeople is an extended stint in the technical services labs, where salespeople learn to use the same equipment that their customers use to process Eastman chemicals, plastics, and other products. This allows salespeople to talk with the technical people and to communicate customers' problems more effectively inside Eastman.[20] Thus, although product knowledge and generic sales skills training remain important, shared account situations also require skills training that focuses on the teamwork and coordination needed to work effectively across functional groups, product lines, sales forces, or even across nationalities with different cultural orientations. For an example of an innovative and enjoyable new sales-training program, see the Self-Management Competency box.

Customer and Market Information   Training time is also devoted to giving recruits customer information and the general background on the market for the goods and services pro-

SELF-MANAGEMENT COMPETENCY
Whirlpool Gets Real with Customers

Whirlpool, the home-appliance giant, has initiated a cutting-edge sales-training program called Real Whirled that's part MTV, and part collegiate home economics. Eight twenty-something sales trainers—the people who go out in the field and teach clerks at places like Home Depot and Sears how to sell Whirlpool products—are thrown together in a seven-bedroom retro-decor house near a Lake Michigan beach. They spend two months living, baking, washing, cooking, and cleaning with the products their company sells. They then take what they've learned as real-world consumers, and use those insights and experiences to train Whirlpool retailers to sell products in terms that buyers can understand. It's not all fun and games, however. The trainees have to work as a team by making sales pitches to one another, studying appliance features together, and discussing the cool time-saving features they discovered. Not only does this program provide real stories about how products work, but Real-Whirleders are able to *show* retail salespeople how the products solve real problems. It provides a much more compelling case of why Whirlpool products are different. According to Josh Gitlin, formerly national director of sales operations, a co-developer of the program, "Trainers are the brand ... They are Whirlpool." While watching some recent graduates make a sales pitch, he is amazed at their professionalism and how consistent their message is. "I don't know how we survived before this program."

duced by the firm. This information not only helps salespeople identify prospects that need the firm's products and services, but also helps salespeople offer innovative solutions to customer problems. Sales recruits are given facts about the size and location of present customers, their buying patterns, needs, and technical processes. Trainees who understand their customers are in a better position to identify customer problems and to discuss how they can solve the buyer's problems.

Pitney Bowes, a leading manufacturer of mailing equipment, understands the importance of this skill and has developed a rigorous training program designed to help salespeople offer innovative solutions to their customers' mail processing needs. Just to enroll in the program, the rep must complete several prerequisites. The prerequisites include everything from working in a postal distribution center, to passing a computer test on postage-meter security. Once enrolled, reps receive a three-inch-thick manual that covers every aspect of the U.S. Postal Service. Sales reps must pass a 50-question written exam with a minimum score of 49 to move on to the oral exam where they must ace three open-ended questions. Upon successful completion of the program, a Pitney Bowes salesperson is designated as a "Certified Postal Consultant." Interestingly, this program is completely voluntary, but designed to provide a basis for sales reps to become experts at solving their customers' mailing problems.[21]

Company Orientation   Salespeople who represent a company to the outside world must be well-versed in the company's history, organization, and policies, as well as having an understanding of corporate citizenship and building core workplace competencies. Salespeople must have pride and confidence in their company and its offerings. Training sessions include policy discussions on returns and warranties, credit arrangements, production sources, and sequencing of orders. Trainees must know about exclusive merchandise, price guarantees, discounts, and latitude on pricing. When customers are desperate for an order, salespeople must know how to expedite delivery. Dow Chemical Company's initial sales training program, for example, "aims to produce a fully balanced seller, not just someone trained in product knowledge."[22] During its yearlong program, trainees work on three related training projects involving such things as working in Dow's customer service center taking customers' calls and orders, or producing an in-depth marketing study involving customers or new markets.

Other Topics   Owing to changes in technology and the marketing environment, new topics are finding their way into sales training programs. Many companies now require their salespeople to use personal computers (PCs) to plan sales calls, check on orders, prepare presentations and proposals, aid in presentations, check on inventories, and place orders. Computer software training is needed to ensure the use of PCs in the field, which is why Northwestern Mutual Life trained its agents on how to use its LINK system, a computer network that ties agents directly to the home office in Milwaukee.

Other topics in which some salespeople are receiving training include time and territory management, handling price objections, and resolving legal and ethical issues. Some of the more exotic topics on which salespeople may be trained include reading body language, understanding eye movement, and identifying people's decision-making styles. Opinions differ as to the effectiveness of some training, and companies should establish for themselves the costs and benefits of these programs.

Where to Train

Having determined training topics, a company must still decide where and how training will be conducted and who will lead the training sessions. Although the decisions are interrelated, we discuss alternative locations for training salespeople in this section. First, we look at whether training should be centralized or decentralized.

Centralized versus Decentralized Training   One of the recurring controversies in sales management is whether sales training should be centralized or decentralized. Some managers contend that centralized training leads to greater efficiency, whereas others insist that training should be done in the field where skills are used.

Centralized training occurs when all the salespeople to be trained are brought to one central location—a plant, the home office, or a training facility. A major advantage of centralized training is the quality and consistency of training. Quality is enhanced through the use of specially trained instructors, custom designed materials, and audiovisual equipment such as closed-circuit television systems. Furthermore, communications and coordination are enhanced when everyone receives the same training. It is also possible to give trainees exposure to top-level managers and other specialists, which can help boost morale and provide valuable insights into sales procedures and customers' needs.

On the negative side, centralized training is very costly and time consuming. Because training facilities and equipment are expensive, and trainees have to be reimbursed for travel to the central site and for lodging, managers usually attempt to keep these sessions fairly short. In an effort to offset high costs, Xerox now offers its training facilities, once confined to its own sales force, to all kinds of organizations. Hewlett-Packard, Aetna Life & Casualty, and even the U.S. Navy are among those that have decided to learn Xerox's brand of salesmanship at Xerox Document University in Leesburg, Virginia.

Some companies are attempting to reduce the cost while preserving the advantages of centralized facilities by broadcasting training sessions from headquarters' facilities. This is fairly new technology, however. A recent survey found that fewer than 20 percent of respondents utilized videoconferencing or teleconferencing (audio only) to train salespeople.[23]

Decentralized training of salespeople is usually done in field or regional sales offices, which moves the learning process closer to the customers and directly involves field sales management. New recruits are able to observe top salespeople selling to customers similar to those they will encounter in their own nearby territories. Location of the training at sales branches also reduces travel and instructional expenses. At Allegiance Healthcare, for example, region and branch offices share ongoing sales training responsibilities. New hires spend time in the region office to understand how the business works, what role that office plays, and the administrative requirements. The branch level puts together programs on their marketplace with a major focus on specific products, systems, or services required for customers within that particular territory.[24]

Despite these advantages, there are a number of potential problems. Perhaps the most common one is that sales managers are so busy supervising the existing sales force that they fail to take the time needed to train new recruits. Sales managers whose income is based on a percentage of their salespeople's commissions (called *commission overrides*) are likely to be most concerned about current income and may give training of new employees a low priority. As a result, the content and quality of the training process may vary widely across the branches.

A common resolution of the centralized versus decentralized training issue is to use some combination of the two approaches. Xerox, for example, brings new recruits into the branch offices for a few weeks of familiarization with company procedures and products. With this background orientation, the novice salespeople are then sent to a central facility for a short session of intensive training. This program allows those who are not committed to the company to drop out before the expensive portion of the program begins. After completing the centralized training, Xerox salespeople go back to the field for more practical experience and coaching by their sales managers. At the end of six months of sales experience, the new salespeople return to the central facility for another week of advanced training.

Field Training   Field or *on-the-job training* (OJT) is the most widely used method of sales training for new recruits. According to a recent survey, 82 percent of responding firms indicated using this method of training. Small companies especially rely on this method of training new salespeople because of the high cost of developing alternative training methods when only a few people need to be trained.

The basic idea of on-the-job-training is that every time salespeople call on customers, they should learn from the experience. To facilitate and encourage learning, new salespeople are often paired with successful veterans. Georgia Pacific and Ortho Pharmaceutical's Biotech Division, for instance, take this approach to OJT. Another alternative is to have the immediate supervisor travel with the new salesperson and observe sales calls.[25]

Although this experience is important and people should be taught to learn from their experiences, OJT should not be relied on as the sole means of learning. First, experience is costly; while salespeople are gaining experience, sales are lost and relationships may be strained. Second, the quality of training is likely to be uneven; some people are simply better trainers than others. More important, the new salesperson may pick up the bad habits of the veteran salesperson, resulting in a lack of consistency in how salespeople are going to market. It was precisely for this reason that Johnson Controls, Inc. established a six-month training program for new salespeople. The best means of development is not experience alone, but experience in combination with a planned program.

Training Media

A variety of media are used by companies for sales training. Cost reductions in technology are making it possible to use alternative media, regardless of the training location. Table 11-4 lists the five most frequently used training media according to a recent survey. As the percentages in the table indicate, most companies rely on a variety of media for sales training. Although many people are quite familiar with the videotape and case study methods of learning, the use of role-plays, games and simulations, and audiotapes as instructional media may not be as familiar. Some emerging technology-based training methods are also discussed.

Role-Playing   *Role-playing,* typically of simulated sales presentations, is quite common in sales training (49 percent). Merck and Company relies heavily on role-playing to train new salespeople in how to sell pharmaceuticals.[26] One Cleveland radio station instituted daily role-playing exercises for its sales representatives. This technique is quite effective when used to reinforce information presented in videos and lectures by requiring active participation and practice. Role-playing helps to determine if the trainee can apply the information. Video cameras are often employed to capture role-plays on tape so that they can be reviewed for critique and self-observation.

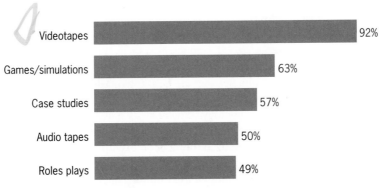

TABLE 11-4   Instructional Methods Used in Training

Despite its wide use, role-playing has some pitfalls. The biggest concern is the stress caused by the videotaping. People may be unable to focus on the subject to be learned when under too much stress. One way to reduce the stress is to conduct a critique immediately following the role-play, emphasizing positive points and encouraging self-analysis: What did I do right? What will I do differently next time?[27]

Games and Simulations   One of the fastest-growing sales training media are simulations designed to encourage the learning of specific behaviors. Behavioral simulations use business games, simulations, case studies, and role-playing in which trainees assume a specified role in a selling situation. Companies such as Chase Manhattan Bank, BMW's Motorcycle Division, Caterpillar, and Ford's Heavy Truck Division regularly use games to encourage the learning of product knowledge.

Microsoft has new sales hires participate in games that include props and facilitators who play roles and dress in costumes. In "Gold of the Desert Kings," for instance, teams compete to manage their resources and limited supplies to successfully cross a harsh desert, mine for gold, and return home with the most gold. The game is designed to teach the importance of planning, teamwork throughout the organization, and communication. Many companies believe this type of learning takes more creativity and makes them more receptive to the information than simply by talking to them.

Another popular game is the quiz-show format, in which teams of salespeople compete on stage, complete with emcee and electronic scoreboard. Customized questions deal with realistic selling situations and product knowledge. This quiz-show format in sales training is used by such companies as Coca-Cola, Sherwin-Williams, Minolta, Nabisco, and Shearson Lehman Hutton.[28]

Audiotapes   Audiotapes are an effective way to present and reinforce selling and product information because of the time salespeople spend traveling and waiting. More than 500 exhibitors of audiocassette training material attended a recent national meeting for the American Society of Training and Development. Tape Rental Library (TRL) has over 2,000 titles for sales training, which it offers to clients such as Pfizer Labs, Moore Business Forms, Scott Paper, Johnson & Johnson, and Gillette.[29] The biggest limitation to audiotapes as a training medium is their inability to get and hold the listener's attention for a significant period of time, which is why audiotapes are frequently used in conjunction with other training media and to reinforce previous training information.

Emerging Technology-Based Training Methods   As changing economic conditions have forced companies to seek cost-effective sales training for their worldwide sales force, more and more are turning to technology-based solutions. One pharmaceutical company, for example, estimated that it cost $7 million to bring all of their 6,000 salespeople together for training. Now, instead of bringing its sales force together from places like Kuala Lumpur for two annual sales meetings, it holds as many as 18 on-line worldwide sales training meetings.[30] By using Internet- or Intranet-based technology, managers can make sure their salespeople get the necessary information as soon as it's available without leaving their territories or customers. It's that flexibility that's fueling the growth of Internet training in the United States. One study estimates that the U.S. Internet-based training market will grow from $19 million in 1995 to approximately $2 billion by the beginning of the twenty-first century.[31] Of course, no new technology is without its drawbacks. Initial startup costs are high, class size should be considered to maximize individual attention, and distractions at the rep's location need to be minimized. For a good example of how Sun Microsystems has benefited from technology-based training, see the Technology Competency box.

Other popular technology-based training includes CD-ROM programs and interactive videos. IBM, for example, developed a CD-ROM *interactive* self-study system called Info

Window to aid in the redeployment of 11,800 employees in the field as marketing representatives and system engineers. Before attending classes in Atlanta, a sales trainee can practice making sales calls. The onscreen actor is programmed to portray a customer in a particular industry whose response depends on the sales trainee's behavior. Trainees can also film themselves as they interact with the actor. Some of the latest computer-based sales training programs include Nintendo-like graphics. Reuters salespeople, for example, train with customized computer programs of football players and race-car drivers in a video-game format to role-play effective and ineffective customer calls.[32]

Interactive videos are used by companies such as Warner-Lambert to train their veteran salespeople without pulling them out of their field sales offices. Although the videos may cost $50,000 or more to produce, which is prohibitive to many companies, their customization to specific needs provides an extended shelf life. Hewlett-Packard uses interactive TV/satellite training sessions to help regional sales groups whose customers might benefit from new H-P products.[33]

Who Should Train

The three most popular types of sales trainers are regular line executives, staff personnel, and outside specialists. Because each has certain advantages, it is not unusual to find organizations using all three types. The selection of trainers for individual firms depends on where the sessions are held, the size of the firm, the characteristics of the product line, and the focus of the training.

Staff Specialists   When centralized sales training is used, companies often have staff specialists prepare the materials and conduct the classes. Staff trainers must not only be good teachers, but also experts in selecting the proper methods and audiovisual equipment needed to meet program objectives. If sales training is conducted on a decentralized basis, staff specialists in the central office usually prepare the program materials, and the instruction is carried out by line managers.

There are some disadvantages to using staff trainers. One complaint is that despite their teaching skills, they often lack experience in realistic field-selling situations, making it difficult for trainees to apply the classroom instruction to real-world customer contacts. In addi-

---

TECHNOLOGY COMPETENCY
Intranet Savings in Sales Training

Technology-based sales training is upon us and the salespeople at Sun Microsystems Computer Company in Mountain View, California, are already learning about it firsthand. Lifecycle Selling, Inc., a sales training firm, recently developed an intranet version of its training program for Sun. Sales reps just log onto a centralized server and call up a browser that takes them through the Lifecycle Selling application. The benefit to Sun is that reps can now learn about new product lines and sales strategies outside of the classroom, so they can now spend more time in the field. The time savings have added up for Sun. For example, to provide training to its 2,000 direct salespeople and 5,000 distributors in a classroom of about 25 to 30 trainees would take more than a year. Sun estimates it has shortened the sales training time by about 75 percent, which translates into a three-month rollout of a new product instead of a year. Sun has plans to expand the program to CD-ROMs and the Internet. For more information about Sun, visit *www.sun.com.*

tion, a staff trainer's salary commonly runs up to $50,000 or more, and small firms simply cannot afford this cost.

Outside Specialists   The employment of outside specialists to conduct sales training is a fairly common business practice. In fact, it is estimated that only 16 percent of companies develop and deliver *all* training in-house.[34] Outside consultants may be entirely responsible for the training programs or brought in to conduct specific sessions within a total training program. More effective sales consultants usually tailor their training programs to meet the special needs of individual firms and industries. Large companies tend to use outside specialists more than small companies and report being very satisfied with their experience.[35] The main attraction of outside trainers is the variety, inspiration, and excitement they can bring to the training program. Some companies have taken a different approach by inviting customers to be present at their sales training sessions.

The potential problems with outside specialists are similar to those of staff specialists. In addition, outside trainers may be unfamiliar with a company's selling situation (lack of familiarity with industry jargon, customers, and competitors). For example, a trainer may discuss price discounting in a presentation when the company is emphasizing value-added selling to avoid price discounting. Salespeople may disregard the training altogether as a result or, even worse, be misled.

Line Executives   Using line executives (usually sales managers) as sales trainers lends credibility to the program because these people have successful sales backgrounds and salespeople are more likely to recognize their knowledge base.[36] They know how to sell, and they know what skills trainees need in order to perform well in the field. The scheduling of line executives for sales training sessions enables these managers to become better acquainted with the entire sales force. When sales managers who actually supervise the salespeople do the training, new recruits are more likely to put the ideas into practice.

Line executives are not always asked to lead sales training for a variety of reasons. Although line managers know a great deal about selling, they may not be trained in how to communicate the information to a group of people in a classroom setting. Furthermore, line executives are usually preoccupied with current sales problems and may not have time to do a good job of training. Solutions to these problems include giving managers "release time" so that they can prepare for their training classes, and instructing the managers in better communication techniques. Smaller firms, in particular, must deal with these problems, because many cannot afford staff trainers and are forced to use line executives or outside specialists. The Team-Building Competency box provides a good illustration of how a team of in-house executives is used to reinforce training content.

EVALUATING SALES TRAINING

Because the costs of training are substantial, sales managers must continually determine whether this investment is paying off. However, it is not easy to establish clear-cut relationships between initial sales training and sales performance. A number of environmental and marketplace factors affect a salesperson's job. As a result, training managers have often relied on instinct to determine if the training was worthwhile. According to industry experts, this attitude has changed in many companies to one in which management is asking, "What did we get from our training dollars?" This change in attitude came immediately after the recession of the early 1990s, when trainers became the victims of corporate budget cutting. Figure 11-1 describes the four levels on which sales training can be evaluated.

Despite the emphasis on showing demonstrable results from training, as presented in Table 11-5, most companies are likely to use trainee feedback to evaluate training pro-

TEAM-BUILDING COMPETENCY
Getting Past the Review Board

Headquartered in Southfield, Michigan, Federal-Mogul is an automotive parts manufacturer that believes teamwork helps make sales training stick. After its sales reps completed a value-based selling course two years ago, Federal-Mogul established an opportunity review board. The committee is made up of 10 executives from departments both in and outside of sales. When business development sales reps decide to go after a prospect that may require special efforts, they present their plan to the review board. Members of the review board quiz reps on their strategies, asking such questions as: What presentation strategies are you planning to use? Are you sure you are talking to the decision maker? What do you think you will need to do to close this sale? Federal-Mogul believes that the team process not only provides different view-points in dealing with a prospect, but also continually reinforces the value-based selling culture the company wants. The review board also decides early on if it's even worthwhile to pursue certain business, and discourages reps from selling to prospects that may not be profitable for the company. One business development rep discovered the benefits of presenting to the review board when he was working with a problematic prospect. The prospect had asked the rep to make an exception from its usual policy and sell parts directly, instead of through one of its distributors. Although the business would have been worth about $500,000, the review board pointed out that selling direct would jeopardize Federal-Mogul's relationships with its current distributors, and advised the rep to sell through one of them. The rep agreed, "We would have ruined our credibility by taking business away from existing accounts." The business development reps have grown accustomed to presenting to the board. According to one executive, "They know what questions will get asked; they know they better have their i's dotted and their t's crossed." For more information on Federal-Mogul, see *www.federal-mogul.com*.

grams. Sales management's appraisal of the trainees' behavior following the training is also often used for training assessment, as is a salesperson's evaluation of his or her own behavior.

Level One:	Reactions	Are trainees satisfied with the training? This also provides information so that the parts they don't like can be improved.
Level Two:	Learning	Did the training change attitudes, increase knowledge, or improve the skills of the trainees? This usually requires testing before and after training.
Level Three:	Behavior	Are salespeople using their knowledge and skills on the job? This may be measured in a variety of ways: asking salespeople, sales manager observation of salespeople, and questioning customers.
Level Four:	Results	What effect does the training have on the company? The bottom-line results of training can include increased sales; higher profits, more new customers, and reduced costs.

FIGURE 11-1   **The Four Levels of Training Evaluation**

TABLE 11-5   Sales Training Evaluation Practices

Measure	Criteria Type	Importance Rank
Trainee feedback	Reaction	1
Supervisory appraisal	Behavior	2
Self-appraisal	Behavior	3
Bottom-line measures	Results	4
Customer appraisal	Behavior	5

Bottom-line measures of performance (e.g., sales and profits) were ranked only fourth in frequency of use. One problem with using sales as a performance measure is that sales may change as a result of factors outside the salespeople's control. One way to overcome this problem is to compare the results of those who completed a training program with those who did not but who are in otherwise similar situations. The Nabisco estimate of a 122-to-1 return on its sales training program, discussed at the beginning of this chapter, was based on the sales results of the 104 salespeople who completed the training compared with 386 salespeople in the same region who were not trained.

Field experiments to control for outside influences on sales are not easily designed or conducted. People with similar experiences, previous performance, and other characteristics, for instance, should be assigned to both the control group (salespeople not given training) and the group of salespeople given training. Results must usually be measured shortly after training, as well as several months later, to enable comparison between short-term and long-term effects. Similarly, outcomes should be measured before training to determine the extent of the change that can be attributed to training. These are just some of the issues that must be considered.[37]

FOLLOW-UP

Regardless of management's philosophy toward the training issues discussed in this chapter, one of the biggest mistakes management can make is failure to follow up on training. One-shot training is a proven formula for failure and a big waste of company money. No one can train salespeople once a year at the annual sales meeting. According to a study at Xerox, 82 percent of skills learned in a training session are lost if not reinforced. Training efforts are most successful when training is scheduled at regular intervals throughout the year. At American Bankers Insurance Group, for instance, the sales force goes to Miami twice a year for a weeklong training session. Also, salespeople meet for a full day once every two weeks with their regional managers to review what was taught in the training sessions. Consistent, ongoing training and reinforcement lead to development and improvement as part of an organization's culture. This obviously must start with top management's support and participation. American Bankers demonstrates this commitment when the chairman, vice chairman, or national sales manager holds quarterly meetings with each salesperson.

ADDITIONAL SALES TRAINING ISSUES

Developing Salespeople

Salesperson development involves helping people develop goals, skills, and habits beyond those necessary for the present job. Many experts feel that developing personnel is the most important and most difficult responsibility of first- and second-line sales managers. This process, sometimes referred to as *career planning,* often involves retraining salespeople to expand their responsibilities. As companies move toward flatter organizational structures, career planning for salespeople can become even more difficult because of fewer advancement opportunities.

Being stuck in a job in which there is little or no opportunity for further personal development can be very demotivating. Most people are stimulated by new challenges and the possibility of having an important impact on the performance of the organization. Salespeople who face a future of no new responsibilities beyond their present territory are likely to be less motivated and less committed to the organization than those who have these prospects. Their sales performance may also level off or decline.

What can first- and second-line sales managers do to help salespeople develop their full capabilities and prevent career stagnation? Here are a few suggestions:

1. Help salespeople gain a realistic understanding of the process and of their chances of getting promoted. This should begin with the initial socialization of the new salesperson into the organization and continue with veteran salespeople.
2. Give people opportunities to develop new skills within their present job. For example, a veteran salesperson with the appropriate skills and desire may be asked to train a new salesperson or to open a new territory.
3. Be creative in letting veteran salespeople know that they are successful and important to the company even if they are not in management. Recognition is particularly effective in this regard. For example, an expensive gift could be awarded for achieving a particular sales level.
4. Be constantly alert for salespeople with the skills and desire for management or other advanced sales positions. Watching how other salespeople react to the individual in an informal setting is particularly important. Periodic checking of the person's career aspirations is also necessary, because these may change, especially as an individual's family situation changes.
5. Design a program for developing salespeople for their next assignment either in management or in an advanced sales position. Like the sales training program, this program should begin with the tasks to be performed in the next position that can be practiced and modeled in the current position. For example, a salesperson could be given responsibility for designing and conducting part of the next district sales meeting.

For a career development system to be effective, a company must reward managers for developing its employees. In some companies, this is part of the regular evaluation process of sales managers. Without such rewards, managers often tend to hold on to good representatives rather than develop them for their next position.

SUMMARY

Initial and refresher training sessions are vital to the success of any field sales organization. Sales personnel must understand their products, their customers, and the marketing program of the firm. This chapter has introduced a number of sales force training issues so you can now:

1. **Determine specific sales force training needs.** A training needs analysis is a process for determining where problems and opportunities exist and whether training can best address the issues. A complete training needs analysis includes a review of management objectives, surveys and observation of the sales force, customer input, and a review of company records. Each of these sources of information should be cross-validated whenever possible.
2. **Discuss the topics to include in a training program.** The choice of subjects to be covered in a sales training program depends on the products sold, training purpose, and personnel background. However, the topics typically covered in training programs include:

product knowledge, selling skills, teamwork, customer and market information, company orientation, among others. Some recent training developments include sales force automation and Web-based topics.

3. **Describe the advantages to centralized and decentralized training.** An advantage to centralized training is the high quality and consistency of the training. In addition, communications and coordination are enhanced when everyone receives the same training. It can also boost salesperson morale by giving trainees exposure to top-level managers and other specialists. Decentralized training, on the other hand, provides a learning environment closer to the salesperson's customer base. Trainees participate in programs that incorporate customer issues similar to those they will encounter in their own nearby territories. It also tends to reduce travel and instructional expenses.

4. **Understand the use of line, staff, and outside trainers.** Training can be conducted by staff specialists, line managers, or outside consultants. Staff specialists are usually involved with centralized training activities and the preparation of classroom materials. First-line sales managers are more likely to conduct one-on-one training. This method allows sales managers to take immediate corrective action to improve the skills of those working under their supervision. Outside consultants provide a degree of variety, inspiration, and excitement to the training program.

5. **Recognize the value of alternative training methods.** Company-run training programs generally are the best way to instill the necessary knowledge; a variety of teaching methods can be used, including lecturers, case studies, videotapes, and programmed instruction. Role-playing exercises and one-on-one coaching are also a good way to teach sales skills. Filming and videotaping of trial presentations help to increase participation and to polish skills during training sessions.

6. **Describe the different methods for evaluating training results.** Sales training requires substantial investment in facilities and materials, and sales managers must continually justify these expenditures. Training programs should be evaluated on a regular basis to measure their impact on sales force turnover, morale, product knowledge, and sales revenues. Knowing the results of training efforts can help managers refine these programs for maximum efficiency and effectiveness. Remember, a firm must follow up on training in the field, where sales occur.

KEY TERMS

Behavioral simulations
Centralized training
Cognitive selling scripts
Commission overrides
Cross-tabulation

Decentralized training
Declarative knowledge
Interactive system
On-the-job training (OJT)
Procedural knowledge

Role-playing
Salesperson development
Training needs analysis
Turnover

DEVELOPING YOUR COMPETENCIES

1. **Strategic Action.** As the marketing manager, you are very excited about a new product R&D that has been developed, which will eventually take your company in a new strategic direction. You know it will sell because you have tons of market research data to back it up. You are also painfully aware that the product and its benefits are complex to the customer, so that it will take significant sales force backing to make it successful. No matter how often you tell the sales department how great this product is, you know that their instinct for selling won't automatically translate into a passion for selling this prod-

uct. You decide to present your product to the sales force at the next sales training meeting. You are nervous because you realize that sales support is absolutely critical if the product is to succeed. The sales force must put significant time behind it. What directions would you give the marketing manager in preparing for the training session? What are the alternative training approaches (e.g., lecture) that you could use in this training session? What will salespeople want to know about the new product?

2. **Team Building.** It is estimated that about one-third of the nation's major firms have formal mentoring programs, with senior managers providing personal counseling and career guidance for younger employees. However, a mentoring program is difficult for salespeople who spend a lot of time on the road. Georgia Pacific has tried to resolve this problem by using the salesperson's immediate superior as the mentor for the new salesperson. The company has also created some literature that offers advice which is sent directly to the field reps. What do you think of this program? Do you see any problems? Would you like to see anyone else in the mentoring position? For more information about Georgia Pacific, see their Web site at *www.gp.com*.

3. **Technology.** Westvaco uses the computer to augment its sales training program. Sales managers are given data on costs, profit, volume, and other information and asked to make recommendations on business alternatives. The computer responds with estimated results for sales dollars, profits, and inventories. The simulation is set up as a game, with managers competing against other managers. List the possible benefits of this unique program. To learn more about Westvaco, visit their Web site at: www.westvaco.com

4. **Coaching.** As the sales manager for a medium-sized industrial firm, you have just finished reading an article in a business journal that praised the benefits of providing field sales training for experienced salespeople as a refresher. The author claimed that a sales manager observing the calls of veteran salespeople spotted and eliminated bad habits and techniques. When you suggested doing the same thing, your sales force strongly objected. One salesperson feared it would look bad to have the manager come along on calls. Another said that after 10 years on the job, he didn't need any further training. You are still convinced that there would be some benefits to this type of training. Would you go ahead with the program, despite the objections? If you do, how do you plan to convince the sales force that there is a need for such a program?

5. **Self-Management.** As discussed in the chapter, the sales manager plays an integral part in the training process. However, one aspect of sales training is to take charge of one's own self-development process. One popular method is the use of audiocassettes. Using audiocassettes as a sales training tool has attracted sales trainers for many years because of the amount of time salespeople spend traveling between accounts. (The history of recorded sales materials can be traced back to 1959, when Bob Stone and Don Reaser started The Business Man's Record Club.) Most companies, however, have been unable to sustain a regular schedule of tapes to the field beyond a few months or, in some cases, only three or four basic tapes. The greatest difficulty has been to produce material that salespeople will find worthwhile and to which they will be willing to listen. Reflect on what would be necessary for you to listen to a tape, enjoy it, and learn from it. What would you recommend to someone producing sales training tapes for a field sales force to ensure that the salespeople will listen to and learn from the tapes?

6. **Global Perspective.** Computer Associates trains its international sales force using weekly conference telephone calls. It may have as many as 3,000 reps worldwide on one conference call. For example, it would not be unusual for one person in France to dial in and have as many as 60 people listening in the room. One benefit is that a phone call isn't as expensive as pulling everyone out of the field and training them for four days. Do you see any problems with this international training program? What would you do dif-

ferently? To find out more about Computer Associates, visit their Web site: *www.cai.com.*

IN-CLASS EXERCISES

10.1: "Sales Training for Profits"*

Patrick McKnight just became vice president of sales for General Industries, overseeing 150 salespeople and 10 sales managers. General's sales were solid, but profit margins were abysmal. General's president charged McKnight with correcting the situation.

During the first few months of McKnight's tenure, he spent much of his time on the road with his salespeople, visiting customers. His mission was twofold: introduce himself to General's customers, and observe the selling styles of his reps. He discovered that price cutting was rampant. McKnight's predecessor, he learned, had managed with the credo "sales at any cost." Unfortunately for General, the practice cost the company profits.

McKnight has to devise a turnaround strategy. His biggest challenge will be to get 150 salespeople to drastically adjust the way they have been selling for the past four years under the former sales VP. And, he must get his 10 sales managers to support and encourage the change. McKnight knows that his toughest challenge will be managing the drop in sales that may result from his new mandate of "sell on value, not on price cuts." But he's also worried that many of his reps will leave the company, fearful that their commissions will be reduced in the short term.

Questions:

1. How can he introduce his new policy without creating resentment among the reps?
2. What would you focus on in the "retraining" program?
3. What could you do to minimize the financial impact to the sales force when they lose accounts because of the increased prices?

10.2: "Training Woes"*

It was the first day of Penton Group's three-day sales training meeting. The company's 10 salespeople talked excitedly during breakfast about the upcoming events: a few rounds of golf, some whitewater rafting, an awards dinner at which the annual incentive contest winners would be announced. They even looked forward to the three 5-hour intensive training session (one each day) that had been billed as unique and transforming. Also attending the meeting were Penton's two sales managers and Constance Frazier, the company's vice president of sales and marketing, who were quietly listening to the rep's banter.

At 7:45 A.M., the salespeople got up from their tables and walked down the Colorado Highland Resort's hallway to its meeting rooms. Finding the Mountainview Room, the reps took their seats. At 8 A.M. sharp their instructor, Tom Baker, walked in and began the session. Five hours later the salespeople emerged and reconvened in the Snowdrift Café for lunch. They were soon joined by the managers, who had attended leadership training conducted by the same company.

The moment they sat down the rep's ranting began: "This was the worst training I've ever attended." "It was tedious." "I could've learned more in my sleep." The managers were surprised, because their session was excellent. The reps, however, were so perturbed that

---

* Contributed by Raymond Rody, Loyola Marymount University.

they didn't want to sit through the two remaining sessions. "Ten more hours would be pure torture," one salesperson insisted.

Frazier suggested to the reps that they focus on enjoying that afternoon's activity, rafting, then excused herself to handle the situation. She said she would have a resolution by the time she rejoined them for dinner. Frazier didn't want this meeting to turn out to be a bust; she also didn't want to squander the company's investment in the sales meeting and training sessions. As she sat in the lobby awaiting the two instructors from the training company, she tried to devise a solution.

Questions:

1. What steps should Frazier take to resolve the situation? (Canceling the remaining sessions is not an option.)
2. How can Frazier avoid this situation in the future?

CASE 11-1 WESTINGHOUSE ELECTRIC CORPORATION

*B*ob Ray, the marketing manager for the Overhead Distribution Transformer Division (OHDT) of Westinghouse Electric Corporation, was concerned about his field sales engineers. It had been four years since OHDT had initiated any sort of formal training program directed at the field sales force. Company information revealed that the sales force had an annual turnover of 10 percent. His concern for newer salespersons' depth of training was paralleled by his conviction that the veteran sales engineers would benefit from more exposure to product knowledge, especially in light of recent innovations. Interpretation of direct and indirect feedback revealed that both groups were reaching for more depth in product knowledge.

WESTINGHOUSE ELECTRIC CORPORATION

Westinghouse was the world's oldest and second largest manufacturer of electrical apparatus and appliances. Founded by inventor George Westinghouse in 1886, the corporation marketed some 300,000 variations of about 8,000 highly diversified basic products ranging from a simple piece of copper wire to a complex commercial nuclear power plant. The firm employed over 145,000 men and women in laboratories, manufacturing plants, sales offices, and distribution centers from coast to coast and around the world.

Over 1,800 of its scientists and engineers were actively engaged in research and development activities. The corporation had more than 160,000 stockholders.

Because of its size and the diversity required to serve a variety of markets, Westinghouse was organized into four companies operating within the corporation. The companies were Power Systems; Industry and Defense; Consumer Products; and Broadcasting, Learning and Leisure Time.

Each company was headed by a president, who had full responsibility for designing, building, and selling the company's products and services throughout the world. Each company had its own staff of specialists in certain fields. It also could draw on corporate resources for additional specialized support in fields such as marketing, manufacturing, engineering, design, research, personnel and public affairs, finance, and law.

The basic organizational unit of the company was the division, each with its own line of products and services. Each division, in turn, was grouped with a number of other divisions with related products and services, such as major appliances, construction products, or power generation equipment.

Combined sales before taxes were $5.1 billion. The Power Systems Company was the leading contributor to income after taxes, with a 43 percent contribution.

This case was prepared by Norman A. P. Govoni, Babson College; Richard R. Still, Florida International University; and Kent Mitchell, the University of Georgia. Copyright @ by Joseph C. Latona. Reproduced by permission.

The Power Systems Company was divided into two main areas: the Power Generation Group and the Transmission and Distribution Division located in Athens, Georgia.

OVERHEAD DISTRIBUTION TRANSFORMER DIVISION (OHDT)

OHDT considered itself first in facilities, developments, and service; and rightfully so, for it had led the nation in overhead distribution transformer sales since 1971, with a fairly consistent market share of about 23 percent. Industry sales were projected to be nearly $900 million by the early 1980s.

Since 1958, all Westinghouse overhead distribution transformers were designed and manufactured in the Athens plant. The previous manufacturing site was in Sharon, Pennsylvania. OHDT was particularly proud of its engineering leadership. In the past few years, Westinghouse had expanded its staff and facility in a time when others were cutting back. Bob Ray was instrumental in making this crucial marketing decision and was later honored with the Corporation's highest award, "The Order of Merit," an award given to three employees each year. In the capacity over demand ratio, the company had been 131 percent, 85 percent, and 88 percent, respectively, for the past three years.

COMPETITION

Westinghouse had been recognized for several decades as the primary innovator in the distribution transformer industry. Four other companies, each of which had active R&D facilities, were considered major innovators: General Electric, RTE, Allis-Chalmers, and McGraw-Edison. Other strong companies among the 29 national competitors were Wagner, Kuhlman, and Colt.

The Westinghouse product was generally ranked tops in its field, representing true value for dollar investment. Some competitors, though, had been successful in promoting a less expensive product.

THE CUSTOMER AND PRICING

The electric utility companies were the consumers for distribution transformers, and they were divided into three major classes: investor-owned utilities, rural electric cooperatives, and municipalities. There were approximately 300 investor-owned utilities, which accounted for about 80 percent of consumption. The coops and municipalities numbered about 920 and 2,000, respectively, and together accounted for the remaining 20 percent. With the increasing migration of families and industries to metropolitan outskirts, the coops were expected to represent a considerably larger share of consumption in the years to come. There were about 33 million overhead distribution transformers across the nation. Sales in this market represented about 60 percent changeouts (i.e., replacements in an area where power consumption had increased) and 40 percent new development units.

In pricing, the major utilities negotiated year-long purchasing commitments during November–December of each year. Fierce price competition was prevalent among the investor-owned utilities, and large discounts off list prices were normally expected. Pricing for the coops and municipalities was more stable, with smaller discounts from list being offered. The method of negotiation was small orders throughout the year for the smaller utilities and the sealed bid method for the publicly owned companies.

PROMOTION

Westinghouse advertised its electrical transmission, generation, and distribution equipment in leading electrical trade journals. Additionally, it was a member of the National Electrical Manufacturers Association (NEMA), which set standards for the industry. NEMA issued monthly reports to its members which included total market volume and member market share information. Distribution was by a field sales force selling direct to customers.

MARKETING MANAGEMENT

The marketing department of OHDT consisted of a marketing manager, a marketing services manager, and four area sales managers who were assisted by a staff of their own. The sales areas were divided geographically. Almost all personnel in the marketing department had an engineering background, which was considered a must in this complex field. The department had ultimate responsibility for the success of its product. They were particularly proud that Westinghouse had been number one in market share of transformer sales each year since 1971.

The marketing department had been located in Athens since 1968, when it moved down from Sharon, Pennsylvania. Exhibit 1 shows where the marketing department fit into the organization of the Athens firm.

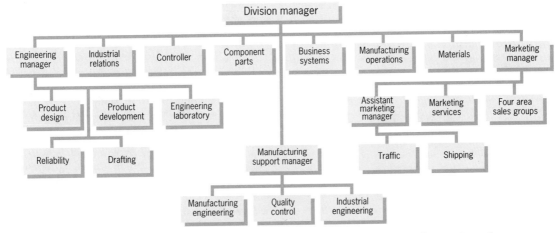

EXHIBIT 1   Westinghouse Electric Corporation Marketing Department—Athens, Georgia

THE FIELD SALES FORCE

Overhead distribution transformers were sold through two of the four Westinghouse companies: the Power Systems company and the Industry and Defense company. Each company had its own sales network, as shown in Exhibit 2.

There were over 300 Westinghouse corporate field sales engineers, district managers, and zone managers located throughout the country handling OHDT accounts. In addition to being loaded with OHDT products, the salespeople were responsible for other Westinghouse utility products. For example, they represented the Electrical Relay Division, the Circuit Breaker Division, and the Electric Meter Division, each of which was managed through other corporate channels. The field sales engineers, in serving several product divisions, reported to district managers for product loading.

The area sales managers and their staffs (of OHDT) served the field sales engineers by taking and expediting product orders, answering product questions, and collecting feedback. Additionally, they traveled into the field to hold training seminars and to assist salespeople on important sales. Bob Ray often got involved in following through with especially important customers.

TRAINING A FIELD SALES ENGINEER

Westinghouse sales engineers were required to have a Bachelor of Science in Engineering. When brought into the corporation, the new recruit was first sent to Pittsburgh for a basic 3-week orientation to the Westinghouse company. The recruit was then assigned to a corporate "graduate studies program" which lasted from 3 to 12 months, depending on his or her skills. Upon completion, he or she was assigned to the field as an assistant sales engineer to serve a training tenure, which lasted anywhere from 6 to 24 months, again depending on individual requirements. During this period, the person would travel for a 2-week period visiting the various manufacturing plants he or she would later serve. Each plant gave the future salesperson a 2-day training and orientation seminar. Ideally, the sales engineers were supposed to return to these parent manufacturing divisions annually for refresher training. Additionally, they would attend district or zone training seminars held by representatives of the parent divisions.

A sales engineer, depending on experience and length of service to Westinghouse, drew a base salary averaging about $35,000 a year, not including the bonus. The number of calls and the type of customer were established according to ability, experience, and product loading. It took, on the average, about $500,000 worth of sales to support a sales engineer in the field.

THOUGHTS OF AN OHDT AREA SALES MANAGER

Marvin Jones was one of the four area sales managers for the OHDT division. Prior to his present assignment, he was a field sales engineer for over 12 years. Reflecting on his days in the field, he remembered quite well the difficulties involved in attending training seminars held by the various divisions. Salespeople recognized that training was essential, that effective selling required sound training, and that a person's

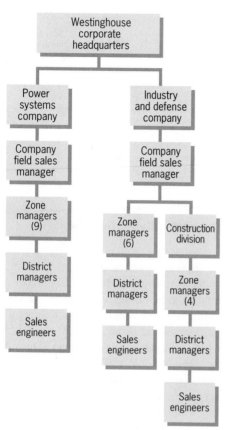

EXHIBIT 2   Westinghouse Electric Corporation Sales Organization Chart

potential (not to mention the quota) really could not be realized without training. However, getting a salesperson to a training seminar was a difficult task, because when there was a sale to be made, there wasn't time for training. The training, as important as it was, would have to wait. At least this was the common thing when attendance at refresher training was more or less left to the individual sales engineer.

THE NEED TO TRAIN

Bob Ray was very concerned about the field sales force's depth of knowledge about overhead distribution transformers, especially in light of fairly recent innovations (a trend which would be expected to continue). He knew Westinghouse had become the leading producer of transformers, but he attributed this more to excellent engineering, excessive demand, and the expertise of his department.

As questions were coming in to the area sales managers at a slightly higher than normal rate, he pinpointed the problem to training. He also knew that the economy might be expected to take a slight decline. With the growing threat that demand might slacken in the months to come, he felt that competition would really start getting rough. In addition, he realized that an unprepared sales force might not fare so well when the time came to give more in-depth and high-quality sales presentations. And it had been a while since Athens had initiated a formal training program. The previous program, which was considered a success, consisted of a campaign to inform the sales force about the overhead distribution transformer, and, as a gimmick, miniature transformer parts were sent to the salespeople.

Unfortunately, a salesperson's time was an extremely valuable commodity, and Bob Ray knew it. Training in any organization was one of the most difficult tasks to pull off effectively, even when the trainees were geographically close to management; but the Westinghouse field sales force, scattered across the nation, was another matter. Making the training task even more burdensome was the fact that these sales engineers had more than just the OHDT account to worry about. It was realized that Athens would have to compete for both time and attention.

FROM IDEAS TO ACTION

With the facts on the table, Bob Ray called on Larry Deal, who headed Marketing Services, and his assistant, Glynn Hodges, who at that time was involved with marketing communications. Hodges was sent to Pittsburgh a few times to work jointly with Earl Swartz the corporate contact to the ad agency used by Westinghouse. By June, Hodges had the layout completed for the proposed solution to the training problem—a training campaign to be called "The Problem Solvers." Bob Ray liked it. It was estimated that the campaign would ultimately cost about $20,000 representing a large slice of the OHDT marketing budget. Exhibit 3 gives an idea of the estimated costs.

ABOUT "THE PROBLEM SOLVERS" CAMPAIGN

An overview of "The Problem Solvers" appears in Exhibit 4, which contains the following: background, problem objectives, program implementation, elements of the program (Stages 1 and 2), and a summary of elements and timing.

EXHIBIT 3   Westinghouse Overhead Distribution Transformers: "The Problem Solvers" Promotion

General
   This document summarizes various elements of the "Problem Solver" promotion. The costs are based on quotations from suppliers who have seen initially prepared layouts.

Puzzles
   Five puzzles will be purchased directly from supplier by Westinghouse.

Shipping Boxes for Puzzles
   Five puzzles each of the five different size boxes plus one 6"-by-6" envelope (for crossword puzzles and brochure mailing), each to be printed in two colors using the same "Problem Solver" design. (Suggestion: each box to have a different color on the design.)
   Delivery time: six weeks from receipt of order.
   Cost: including converting boxes, design preparation, color plates and printing: $2,500.

Crossword Puzzle
   To be completed by salesperson and submitted with photo to get personalized jigsaw puzzle prize.
   Timing: Six weeks from receipt of words and clues from Westinghouse. Puzzles to be printed in simple 4-page format and inserted in envelope along with cover letter and brochure.
   Cost: $800.

Jigsaw Puzzle
   One 11"-by-14" puzzle will be sent to every salesperson submitting photo along with completed crossword puzzle. Photos will be held and sent in bulk to puzzle manufacturer, who will then send completed puzzle directly to each salesperson along with the original photo.
   Timing: four weeks delivery from receipt of photographs.
   Cost: $1,300.

Cover Letters
   Total of five (one for each puzzle mailing), 400 copies of each.
   Cost: including artwork for masthead, copy editing, typesetting, and printing: $600.

Brochures
   One brochure will accompany each of the five puzzle mailings. Each brochure will focus on one aspect of the overhead transformers. The cover will have a full color cover of the puzzle being sent; inside pages will be black and white and use existing line art.
   Cost: including photos, typesetting, tissue layout and key art, copy editing, and production supervision for five 20-page booklets: $12,000.
      Total Cost: up to $20,000.

To catch the salesperson's attention, the proposed campaign would consist of expensive, eyecatching adult games which emphasized puzzle problems. The games would cost $4–$5 each; a good example was a three-dimensional tic-tac-toe game made of three clear plastic decks mounted on top of each other. Each player was represented by either clear blue or yellow marbles about an inch in diameter each. The game could be won horizontally, vertically, or diagonally.

Along with the mailing of each game would be a cover letter and an information bulletin emphasizing a particular feature of the overhead distribution transformer. As the salesperson reads each information bulletin, he or she would fill in "clues" to a master crossword puzzle. When the mailings were completed, the salesperson would send in the completed crossword puzzle and picture of himself or herself (along with the rest of the family if desired) to the marketing department in Athens. Athens would have the picture made into a jigsaw puzzle and return it to the participant a few weeks later.

THE MARKETING SERVICES DIVISION—A SPECIAL PROJECT

Larry Deal's Marketing Services Division had been assigned the responsibility of supporting the ad agency by providing the technical information necessary for turning "The Problem Solvers" idea into a manageable campaign. Brian Kennedy, assigned to marketing communications, and assistant Jody Unsler had been asked to design the instruction brochures and crossword puzzle. Also, coordination with Earl Swartz had resulted in the initial selection of a container for the games. The

EXHIBIT 4   Westinghouse Overhead Distribution Transformers: An Overview of "The Problem Solvers"

Background

The total market for overhead distribution transformers is very good. For Westinghouse, it is excellent. While Athens is producing at full capacity and the current problem is meeting demand, there still remain several conditions with which Athens must cope if it is to achieve its long-range potential:

1. Many Westinghouse and agent salespeople do not understand the advantages of Westinghouse transformers.

2. There are competitors who manufacture and sell transformers at a cheaper price. These transformers are inferior to those at Westinghouse. The Westinghouse story, which must be communicated through sales personnel to customers, is a *value* story.

3. The present sales boom cannot be expected to continue indefinitely, and the sales force must be prepared to conduct tougher, more effective sales presentations.

Program Objectives

The object of this program is to make Westinghouse and agent sales personnel more effective representatives for Athens by showing them why Westinghouse is the value leader and by giving them the information and tools needed to make more effective presentations.

By accomplishing these objectives, the sales representatives will become more confident of their abilities—and the Westinghouse line. This growing confidence will, in turn, create even greater success.

Program Implementation

This is a two-stage program. The Stage 1 phase, the more important, is directed to the Westinghouse sales force and includes an explanation of the program, a summary of the transformer market (and the profit contribution made by Westinghouse transformers), and detailed instructions on transformers (using the theme "The Problem Solvers") along with unique mailings.

The Stage 2 phase is the person-to-person contact between salespeople and customers. Having been effectively indoctrinated into the advantages of Westinghouse transformers, the salespeople are now supplied with effective sales presentation material, which will make contact between sales representatives and customers more productive for the Athens division.

Elements of Program—Stage 1

1. Cover letter No. 1 from Mr. Meierkord (general manager, OHDT) or Mr. Ray spelling out the theme "The Problem Solvers" and the purpose of the program.

2. Instruction brochure No. 1 on Cover and Bushing Assembly along with puzzle.

3. Cover letter No. 2 from Meierkord or Ray.

4. Instruction brochure No. 2 on Tank Assembly along with puzzle.

5. Cover letter No. 3 from Meierkord or Ray.

6. Instruction brochure on Core Assembly along with puzzle.

7. Cover letter No. 4 from Meierkord or Ray. Letter to state that crossword puzzle answers are found in instruction booklet. If salesperson returns completed crossword puzzle along with any photograph of his or her choice, Athens will return a custom-made jigsaw puzzle made out of the photo.

8. Instruction brochure No. 4 on CSP (completely self-protected transformer) features along with crossword puzzle. Crossword puzzle will contain such clues as:

   CSP Transformers (OUTLAST) conventional types by 60 percent.

   CSP arresters (LOWER) discharge voltage on high surge currents.

   After overload trips breaker, breaker can be reset to (TEN) percent more capacity.

Elements of Program—Stage 2

After salespeople have studied the four bulletins, they are better prepared to make more effective presentations to their customers. To help them in their calls, they will be furnished with the following:

1. Cover letter (No. 5) again from Meierkord or Ray, reiterating the profitability of transformers, that they are great "Problem Solvers," and that the salespeople (the ultimate "Problem Solvers") are now well prepared to communicate to their customers why Westinghouse transformers are truly tops in the field. Cover letter will dwell on the importance of customer presentations, preparation, and follow-through.

2. Flip chart presentation entitled "Westinghouse Distribution Transformers: `The Problem Solvers.'" The presentation will summarize the most important "Features/Functions/Benefits" from the four technical bulletins. The presentation will be designed in a horizontal format so that the pages are adaptable for photographic slide or strip film production.

3. Customer booklet to be prepared using same text and artwork from the presentation flip chart. Booklet will be left with the customer as a reminder of what was presented and as a source document for later reference.

4. Capabilities brochure, about to be produced, can be an added ingredient to the presentation. While it emphasizes Athens' manufacturing capability—as opposed to the engineering emphasis of the presentation—the booklet is prestigious and will reflect Westinghouse distribution transformers as being a value line.

EXHIBIT 4   **(Continued)**

If not used as part of the presentation, the capabilities brochure would make an impressive mailing to the customer, along with a "thank you" letter for listening to the presentation.

Summary—Elements and Timing

Stage 1

First Mailing:	Cover Letter No. 1 (Program Summary)
	Bulletin No. 1 Cover and Bushing
	Puzzle No. 1 (Adult Game)
	Master Crossword Puzzle
Second Mailing:	Cover Letter No. 2
	Bulletin No. 2 Tank Assembly
(Two months later)	Puzzle No. 2
Third Mailing:	Cover Letter No. 3
	Bulletin No. 3 Core and Coil Assembly
(Two months later)	Puzzle No. 3
Fourth Mailing:	Cover Letter No. 4
	Bulletin No. 4 CSP Features
(Two months later)	Puzzle No. 4

Stage 2

Fifth Mailing:	Cover Letter No. 5 (Customer Presentations)
	Flip Chart Presentation
(Two months later)	Presentation Summary for Customer
	Athens Capability Brochure
	Puzzle No. 5

container was a cardboard box with a design of jigsaw puzzle parts; each part had a letter on it, which when put together spelled out "The Problem Solvers." Kennedy put in long hours working on the instruction brochures. In explaining the various components of the transformer, he had decided to set a conversational sales presentation scene between a Westinghouse salesperson and a purchasing agent. The salesperson, who was "Mr. Problem Solver" or "Ms. Problem Solver," was smoothly answering the questions asked by a purchasing agent, who was appropriately labeled "Mr. A. Gent" or "Ms. A. Lady."

EARLY NOVEMBER

One morning in early November, Bob Ray was relaxing at his desk sipping a cup of coffee. He was thinking about "The Problem Solvers" campaign. Things were moving along pretty well. At the present rate, he would be able to meet the January 15 target date for the first mailing. He knew $20,000 was a lot of money for OHDT to spend on a training campaign of this type, but he was confident in the overall idea and felt it was the best way to reach such a broad and isolated

target. However, a few decisions remained. There was some question about the two-month interval between each of the five mailings. He definitely wanted the sales force ready for November–December when the big utilities would negotiate year-long contracts for the following year. In a way, he wanted the campaign to last a good while, as it represented a big chunk of the budget, but he wondered whether the field sales force's attention would be held over such a period. Another thought entered his mind about the effectiveness of the campaign's feedback mechanism. He remembered Glynn Hodges saying he anticipated a 65 percent response. Another point that was undefined in the campaign was what stand OHDT should take on the future newcomers to the field sales force. Since the previous campaign, the new people learned through OJT (on-the-job-training) and sales materials, as well as by picking up what they could from OHDT bulletins. However, this provided only short-range coverage and would break down in the long run or when making sales got tough. This had been one of the factors contributing to the present situation.

With those thoughts in mind, Bob Ray decided to call a division head meeting that afternoon.

CASE *11-2*   SANDWELL PAPER COMPANY

George Murphy, Sandwell Paper Company's Bakersfield branch manager, undertook a careful study of his operation. The study was in keeping with his philosophy of having an alert, informed management, and it dealt with both the managerial and sales aspects of the distribution center.

COMPANY BACKGROUND

The Sandwell Paper Company, a large paper wholesaler, originated in Omaha, Nebraska, in the 1890s. During its early years, the firm was involved mainly in sales and distribution to final users and bought its paper from other wholesalers. However, as sales grew, the Sandwells soon began a warehouse operation of their own. The product line was quite diversified and included both printing (fine) and industrial (wrapping) grades of paper. Paper merchants carrying both product lines became known as *dual distributors*. To meet the rapid growth of markets on the West Coast, the company established several divisions in that area. Murphy's operation was the Bakersfield branch of the Los Angeles division. There were two other California divisions located at San Diego and San Francisco.

Murphy was quite pleased with the decentralized profit center arrangement of Sandwell and the independence it afforded him. He felt that the challenge of earning a satisfactory rate of return on investment for the branch provided sales incentive for his organization.

George Murphy was in his early fifties and had been in paper sales work for the past 25 years. He had graduated in business administration from the University of Southern California and had gained sales and management experience with two other firms (a paper manufacturer and another paper wholesaler) before joining Sandwell.

The Bakersfield sales force under Murphy consisted of three salespeople of fine paper and two of industrial paper. The division had formerly prepared its salespeople in a special sales trainee program that had consisted of daily classroom instruction in products and methods of selling. The instruction involved lectures, cases, and role playing. Regular written homework was required of all trainees. However, because of the company's high turnover of sales personnel, Murphy had terminated this formal method of training. The new method required sales trainees to work at various warehouse jobs, thereby learning firsthand about the products and problems of the business.

According to Murphy, about one-third of his time was spent dealing with problems of warehousing, accounting, and credit extension and about two-thirds with sales meetings, forecasting quota setting, and actual selling to his own accounts.

PRODUCT LINE

Sandwell Paper had always been a dual house supplying both printing (fine) and industrial (wrapping) paper goods. In addition to traditional paper goods, the company stocked plastics and other nonpaper items to promote unitized selling.

The objective of unitized or packaged selling was to enable the salesperson to supply all customer needs, thereby simplifying customer ordering and billing and maximizing selling efficiency. Sandwell had been concentrating its unitized sales effort in the meat market and custodial service or janitorial supply areas.

The Sandwell paper product line was divided into two sections—printing and industrial. The fine (printing) paper line (Exhibit 1) represented the more specialized and profitable of the two sections. Printing grades had the best gross trading margin for the Bakersfield branch. Printers did not want to maintain large inventories, yet they wanted quick delivery on the many grades listed in their sample books. They were willing to pay a premium to wholesalers for maintaining inventories of wide ranges of grade sizes, weights, and colors. In the printing paper field, Sandwell Paper was a franchised distributor for Medallion Paper Company, a large, recognized manufacturer of printing paper. In areas serviced by more than one wholesaler, Sandwell had exclusive sales of the Medallion paper

This case is reproduced with the permission of its author, Dr. Stuart V. Rich, Professor of Marketing, and Director, Forest Industries Management Center, college of Business Administration, University of Oregon, Eugene, Oregon.

EXHIBIT 1   Printing Grade Categories

Categories	Percent Sales
Bond–Ledger	40
Bond	
Ledger	
Flat writing	
Safety papers	
Mimeograph	
Duplicator	
Index–Bristol	20
Index	
Bristol	
Blotting	
Boards	
Cardboards	
Cut cards	
Tags	
Information	
Book–Cover	20
Book	
Cover	
Envelopes	
Specialty	20
Announcements	
Thin papers	
Gummed	

EXHIBIT 2   Industrial Grade Categories

Categories	Percentage of Sales
Bags (cellophane, bakery, grocery, department)	20
Industrial (towels, tissue, wrap, lumber wrap)	21
Packing (filter, wadding, corrugated)	3
Waxes, glassine, parchment	6
Boxes, cases, board	7
Food containers, plates, napkins	20
Twine, ribbon, tape	14
Sanitary tissues	9

line. As a result of handling the complete line, ordering and inventory problems were minimized. Uniform quality could be depended on. Although competitive price inroads were being made on some of Medallion's grades, Murphy and other company managers had elected to continue to carry the line since Medallion's trade name commanded such recognition of excellence.

The Sandwell industrial paper line consisted of those paper goods utilized by manufacturers in making wrapping or in transporting their products. Exhibit 2 lists those items carried by the branch. Industrial grades were characterized by volume selling and price competition, and these grades greatly overtaxed warehouse space. Murphy indicated that industrial sales out of stock were 72 percent and that direct mill shipments (orders taken by the wholesaler) were 28 percent. Also, because of Sandwell's policy of selling its customers unitized service, many other nonpaper items were carried in stock. Goods such as cleaning fluid, floor wax and waxing machines, light bulbs, and polyfilm and plastic containers were coupled with paper goods to make up unitized or packaged sales to meat markets, building custodial firms, and other user groups.

George Murphy also commented that the branch's inventory turnover rate was 5 to 6 times per year, while the national average for dual houses was 4.5 times.

NATURE OF SALES ACTIVITIES

According to Murphy, Sandwell Paper divided its customer market into three parts—printing, industrial, and resale (retail). The resale market consisted mainly of retail grocery stores and variety stores. The majority of paper wholesalers did not sell directly to this market but let the regular grocery and dry goods wholesaler serve it. Murphy felt that this was a growing market and wanted his salespeople to spend more time developing it.

Company sales to each market segment were as follows: printing, 13 percent; industrial, 62 percent; resale, 25 percent. The same items might be sold to all three customer types. The market segments differentiated the customer, not the type of paper commodity.

Murphy continually had to make decisions on the performance of his salespeople, market trends, price changes, and quotas. He gleaned much of this information from month-old sales invoices, informal talks with salespeople, and quick calls to the divisional sales manager.

In 1995 the Los Angeles division decided to reevaluate its present sales position and effectiveness. As illustrated by Exhibit 3, the sales volume had continued to expand, while the gross trading margin had declined. Both gross margin and net profit were below the industry average (Exhibit 4). The problems observed by the division, according to Murphy, were present on the branch level and had in part caused the present study to be done. The pricing in the industrial grades had become very competitive, and warehouse space was critical. Murphy felt that expansion of the

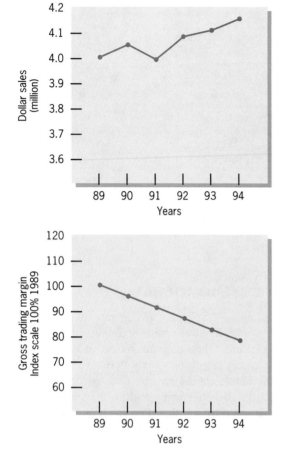

EXHIBIT 3   Company Trend in Sales and Gross Margin

Each salesperson had an established monthly draw (salary). The draw was an advance in anticipation of the coming month's sales. The sales quota was set in profit dollars—that is, dollars above item and operating costs. The salesperson had to cover the draw for the month. Because the draw was a minimal amount, once the draw was covered, the salesperson could keep 15 percent of each additional dollar of profit.

George Murphy pointed to the schedules of his salespeople, "They've got as many calls crammed into a day as possible," he said. "They really use their effective selling time [i.e., time with the buyer]." Murphy pointed out that certain aspects of paper selling, especially in selling printing grades, were highly technical in nature. Printers could put an inexperienced salesperson on the spot.

Murphy discussed what he felt was very important in selling—talking to the person who was responsible for the buying. He also pointed out that those who used the paper could help influence the buyer.

As was noted earlier, industrial grades had become quite competitive. Murphy stated that competitors often engaged in price cutting to secure new customers. However, it had been Sandwell's policy to maintain their price against competitive inroads and defend their position by supplying "quality service and good will." This policy was still upheld, with the exception of some large-volume competitive goods like toweling and freezer wrap.

New product items were continually being added to the product line, two or three items quarterly. The division headquarters had tried to encourage sales of new items by organizing sales contests. These attempts had been partially successful. Some salespeople had immediate success with a new item, whereas others were unable to move it. With the next new item the success situation might be reversed.

George Murphy decided that the best way to study the selling techniques of his salespeople was to have Phil Edwards, a sales promotion staff member from the Los Angeles division headquarters, accompany the salespeople on calls. Phil had planned on making such

warehouse was not economically feasible because of the low profit margin in industrial grades.

Despite the apparent downturn in trading margin, the number of accounts in the resale area was increasing. Murphy noted that customers were continually calling in orders and requests for service even though branch salespeople were constantly on the go, many times calling in their orders instead of dropping them off at the warehouse (as they had once done).

EXHIBIT 4   Gross Margin and Profit Performance (figures represent percentages)

	Industry Average (NPTA)		Sandwell	
	Warehouse	Direct	Warehouse	Direct
Gross trading margin	22.3	8.5	20.1	8.1
Total expense	19.7	6.5	18.1	7.0
Net profit (before tax) as percent of sales	2.6	2.0	2.0	1.1

a tour for general information and could combine the two projects.

PRINTER SELLING

Mason Printers was a medium-sized printing account specializing in offset and letterpress printing. The business was located on Eleventh Street just off the main business section of Bakersfield. Bud Williams, who had been with Sandwell for three years, was precise in his call schedule and arrived at the shop at 10:30 A.M. each Thursday. While walking to the shop, Bud discussed the account with Phil Edwards.

BUD: Roy Mason is a real artist. When a job is running smooth, he's as agreeable as all get-out. Other times—look out. Sometimes he's out and I waste time just sitting out front waiting for him. He knows I'll be here, so he sometimes leaves an order or note for me. He's the fellow that buys and I sell him Medallion paper on price, quality, and press runability.

EDWARDS: I hear Mason's shop is one of only two in town that has a multisection offset press in operation.

BUD: I know they are making some expensive additions. I try to keep up on the technical stuff, but it's really complicated. Sometimes Roy starts in on what's wrong with an order of paper we sent, and I just can't defend it at all.

The two arrive at the shop and go in. Roy Mason is in the front office (the print shop is in the rear) and makes a gesture of setting his watch at Bud's approach.

BUD: Good morning, Roy.

ROY: Right on time.

BUD: Roy, this is Phil Edwards of our L.A. sales staff. They've sent him over to visit some of our good customers.

EDWARDS: Pleased to meet you, Roy.

BUD: What's up for today, Roy?

ROY: Oh, things are okay. That offset grade you sent over for our regular Smith Company job is going all right. I wish you fellows hadn't run out of that light pink coated cover we always use.

BUD: *(with "Well, so long as it's going through the press okay" relieved look):* Have you got enough of your other stock grades to keep you through the week?

Maybe I should check inventory. I know how you like to keep the bare minimum in there.

ROY: We're all set. We have a special job to do for the city. I got out the sample books, and we picked out this grade and color (shows sample). They'd like it with this textured finish. How do you think that will reproduce on the offset press?

BUD: Perfect reproduction! Medallion always runs good.

ROY: I thought it'd be okay, but Ed, my pressman, didn't like the look of it.

BUD: I think it'll be all right. The mill rep is in town, so I'll check with him and let you know.

ROY: Okay, but I'll be in and out all afternoon.

BUD: Say—you know that 25-pound letterpress grade you've been buying from Mentons [another wholesaler]?

ROY: Yes?

BUD: Well, we've got the same color and weight made by Simplin at 5 percent off because the sheet didn't pass the mill quality control specifications. The jobs you use that grade for don't demand quality, so you could use up this off-quality stuff and make yourself a good margin.

ROY: Do you think it will give Ed any trouble on the press? You know he gets pretty angry when a sheet picks, lints or is so porous that the vehicle (ink solvent) carries the pigment into the sheet.

BUD: It shouldn't give you any trouble.

ROY: All right, we'll order it from you this month.

(Glancing quickly at his watch, Bud saw he was going to be late for his call at Fan Fair Supermarket.)

ROY: You know, with this new press we just put in, we're trying to compete for some big accounts. I've got some notes and questions here; maybe we could go over some of them.

BUD: I'll tell you what, Roy, the Simplin rep will be here till next Tuesday. Maybe he and I could get in here Monday morning and talk about your plans.

ROY: Okay, fine by me.

A call from the press room ends the discussion. Roy bids good-bye and Bud and Edwards leave. They walk quickly to the car.

BUD: I'm a little late for Fan Fair. Even though they're a small outfit, their school supplies section really sells the paper. Did you want me to drop you at the office?

EDWARDS: Yes, I've got to meet with Jane Austin (one of two industrial account salespeople) after lunch.

The two drive off.

INDUSTRIAL SELLING

Jane Austin stopped by the office (adjacent to the warehouse) and picked up Edwards. Jane had been selling at the branch for about a year. She started work, as did most prospective Sandwell salespeople, in the warehouse. After four months she had moved to the office order desk, where orders were called in by customers and salespeople. This procedure had been used to prepare Jane for field selling.

Edwards got into the car, and Jane drove out of the parking area.

EDWARDS: Where are we headed?

JANE: Sun Fair Market. I've got to check with the meat department manager. I think he left an item off his order list. And if he runs out of board trays on a weekend, we'll be sure to get the blame for it. This unitized selling puts a lot of pressure on the salespeople.

EDWARDS: I can't think of a quicker way to lose a market customer than to have him come up short of wrapping film or trays on a busy weekend. What calls do you regularly make on Thursday?

JANE: Well, last year, when I started out, Thursday afternoons were for my three big department store accounts. Ted Richards and I—you remember Ted, he's the rep for Thall's Specialty Bag Company—we used to spend a lot of time with store managers laying out the designs for their store merchandise bags. Things have really picked up this year, though. I'll make about eight calls this afternoon, it's a real clockwork schedule. In a way it helps, because people know when you'll be in and they plan on it.

They arrive at the market and walk to the meat department. The man behind the counter waves and points in the direction of the cutting area.

JANE: Jack must be doing some cutting.

They turn the corner and see Jack Wilson.

JACK: What in the world are you doing here today?

JANE: Want to double-check your order for the weekend. You don't have any meat trays down.

JACK: Sure I do! Let's see.

Jack looks at the order sheet developed by Sandwell and Sun Fair executives for ease of ordering.

JACK: Well, I'll be …! Guess I don't. Boy, that would have finished us.

JANE: Jack, this is Phil Edwards, one of our staff salespeople from L.A.

EDWARDS: Pleased to meet you, Jack.

JACK: The same.

JANE: Say, Jack, remember you asked me why we didn't carry the new polyvinyl wrap for chicken? Well, I received a sales bulletin from the division office, and not only do we carry it, but the price is below that of the film you're buying now.

JACK: That's a good one. You guys sell so much, you don't have time to find out everything you're selling. Next time we'll switch over to that new wrap. I hope it "breathes" good and lets the tissue gases escape. We had 50 chickens spoil last month, you know.

JANE: Don't worry! It won't cause any spoilage.

JACK: Well, I better get to work. Thanks for catching my error.

JANE: Okay, Jack. We'll see you.

The two leave, walk to the car, and drive away.

JANE: Now I'm going up to South Eleventh to call on the manager of the New Towers Building. I'm trying to get him to purchase our new custodial service unit. This unit selling works fine sometimes—like at the market—but other times these people don't want to buy everything from you. Are you going to come in?

EDWARDS: No, Jane, I'll sit here and catch up on my study notes.

JANE: Okay.

She parks the car and goes in to see the manager. Twenty minutes later she returns.

JANE: I don't understand it. I've talked with that fellow about using our service on three separate occasions. He's real interested, listens, asks questions, but when I try to get an order all he says is, "I'll check into it." I wish he'd let me know one way or the other.

EDWARDS: Who's next on your call schedule?

JANE: Dairy O, that high-volume hamburger and milkshake outfit. Ed Stenuf is the manager.

EDWARDS: Let's go.

They arrive at the Dairy O, and Austin and Edwards go in. Ed Stenuf is out front waiting on customers.

JANE: Hi, Ed.

ED: Hello, Jane.

JANE: Ed, this is Phil Edwards from our L.A. headquarters.

EDWARDS: Good to meet you, Ed. Jane tells me you've got a good business here.

ED: Oh, we're doing pretty good.

JANE: Well, Ed, can we stock up your bag, napkin, and container-cup inventories?

ED: Well, you know, your competition was in yesterday offering prices below yours. So if you people can't match 'em, we'll have to switch over.

JANE: Well, Ed, Sandwell likes to be as competitive as the next guy. We give our customers quality goods with the best service of any other supplier. We keep track of your supplies, and you never have to worry about being short.

ED: I know, Jane, but these fellows are offering a good hard dollar-and-cents deal. Those shake containers go for $12.70 a three-gross box, and they're offering the same for $12.00.

JANE: I'll have to check at the office tomorrow, and I'll come out and talk price with you.

ED: Okay, Jane. Excuse me, I've got a customer.

JANE: See you tomorrow, Ed.

They walk out to the car.

JANE: There goes some good business. Do you think we can match their price?

EDWARDS: We just can't let everyone who wants a little more business scare us into dropping our prices, after all we've done to stabilize our price level. You better check with George [Murphy] this afternoon and see what develops.

JANE: You bet! Now comes the big push—I call on all my Dairy Queen stores. My big accounts take a lot of time. These little stores don't seem to be worth the time the other fellows give them. Say, it's about 2:30. Did you want to go back to the office?

EDWARDS: Yes, I've got to see George about a warehouse mix-up. Medallion sent out the wrong paper in a carton with proper order labels on it.

Jane drops Edwards off and starts her calls on the Dairy Queen stores.

RESALE SELLING

Edwards had told salesperson Bob Thomas to pick him up before making calls Friday morning. Bob had been with Sandwell for four years, selling mainly industrial goods to resale dealers or retail merchants. Before joining Sandwell, Bob had been employed as a salesperson for a grocery products company. He was to meet Edwards at the office at 8:30 A.M.

EDWARDS: Who do we see today?

BOB: I'm after my resale picnic supply outlets [independent retail stores and chain supermarkets]. The sales department finally got out the new picnic supplies display rack. I guess there was quite a battle deciding what suppliers would get on it.

EDWARDS: Yes, that's an excellent point-of-sale display.

BOB: Do you think the division is going to make the quota for the salmon-fishing trip?

EDWARDS: The way we're going, it'll be close. You guys have got to dig in.

BOB: What about the new bakery bag order I called Murphy about yesterday? There's good profit in those white multisized baked-goods bags. I don't see all the fuss about whether to put them on an open account so they'll have credit till the end of the month.

EDWARDS: We don't know much about the outfit You know the policy on doubtful accounts. You guys get big orders with these accounts, but the office has to collect them.

BOB: Well, we need orders to make the quota. It doesn't make much difference to me whether they wait till the end of the month to pay.

EDWARDS: Spoken like a true salesperson. Say, George tells me he's got you fellows keeping a list of all the prospective customers you've called on about the new polyvinyl strapping for unitized lumber.

BOB: Yes, I called on the Medford and the Sellers Lumber Companies Monday. Put on a little demonstration for their salespeople. I'm afraid the introduction fell a little flat, though I told them that the vinyl was stronger than the steel strapping they're now using to hold their unitized lumber packets together during shipment … but they started asking some technical questions about strength and shipping and I was having enough trouble getting the band taut and crimped around the lumber unit.

EDWARDS: George said they think this item should be very competitive. The vinyl is 8 to 20 percent cheaper, yet performs as well as steel strapping. It's sure to click.

They arrive at the Careways Market and enter the store. Bob approaches Joe Martin, a buyer for the Careways chain. Introductions are made.

BOB: Say, Joe, it's about time you started stocking up on picnic items.

JOE: How much markup can we expect to get this year?

BOB: Fifteen percent on most.

JOE: How fast did they move last year?

BOB: Stores that got their display racks out near the cash registers, and other good selling points, ordered weekly.

BOB: We've rearranged and substituted some of the items on the rack for maximum sales effect. This year should be the best yet.

JOE: Some of the stuff on the rack we already have in stock from other suppliers. I don't think I'll use the rack. You go ahead and see what we need from the

inventory listing, and I'll check back with you in a few minutes to see what you have.

Joe walks off. Bob checks inventory figures and writes up an order for various tissue and toweling items.

BOB: Phil, the pricing on these consumer products is really getting ridiculous. With so many distributors handling them at such low margins, we'll all be out of business. Every day someone is cutting the price, or a manufacturer is handling the account direct or something!

EDWARDS: Yes. Pricing on those high-volume consumer items is a problem.

The two return to Joe Martin.

JOE: Let's see what you came up with. Yes, that's about right. The toweling and napkins stay about the same. Send eight cartons of plates, instead of six. Same for the cold cups. Oh, and we won't need any of the plastic knives. They aren't used as much as the forks and spoons.

BOB: All right, Joe. We'll have this order delivered tomorrow.

JOE: Good. So long.

As they leave the store and walk to the car, Bob wonders how he can change Joe's mind on installing some display racks.

BOB: I'll get that rack in there. I'll get back to see him Monday for a little chat. I've got lots of accounts to call on, but I have a flexible schedule, so I can put in a little extra selling effort when I think it's worthwhile.

EDWARDS: A few racks in that Careways chain would really up sales.

BOB: I'll say. I'm going to Smith Company. Did you want to go up there too?

EDWARDS: Well, if you could drop me off at the office on your way up there, it would be convenient for me. I'm supposed to see George at 11:00.

BOB: Okay, fine.

Back at the office, Phil Edwards talked with George Murphy about the weaknesses of the three salespeople and how additional sales training could remedy the problems.

CHAPTER 12

LEADERSHIP

> Of the best leader, when he is gone, they will say: we did it ourselves.
>
> CHINESE PROVERB

Chapter Consultant:
Carol Caprio, Software Business Unit Executive, IBM

LEARNING OBJECTIVES

After studying this chapter, you should be able to:

→ Explain what is meant by leadership.

→ Understand how leaders manage change.

→ Determine the appropriate leadership styles for a particular situation.

→ Know when and how to coach salespeople.

→ Discuss what is involved in planning and conducting a sales meeting.

→ Recognize common people problems.

WHERE IS RICHARD WAXLER?

"Where is he now?" Sales managers want to know where their staff is, but there is always one person who marches to the beat of a different drum. In this case his name is Richard Waxler—whereabouts unknown.

He operates as though he hasn't a care in the world. Company policy requires planned itineraries, but you never know when he will roll into the office. He has made the best of a slow territory, so what's the gripe? Richard is popular and well-liked by the rest of the sales team, but he is not turning in the documents needed for lost-sales reports. You can't tell where the market is going when you have only half of the information. The usual procedures have been tried, but Richard goes his own way, merrily or otherwise. Now is the time to do something about it, but you don't want to smother his high energy. You must make him realize that he is part of a team.

You are considering several options. Which is the best choice?

1. Set an exact time and place to meet with Richard. At this meeting, tell him that he will not leave the office without first filing an itinerary with you. Also tell him that you expect a written sales report within three days of his return. If he does not abide by these rules, you will not consider him a candidate for bonuses.
2. Tell other salespeople about the problem and ask them to try to get Richard to fall into line with your policies and procedures.
3. At the next sales meeting, have a major discussion concerning the need for the information that Richard has been omitting. Don't mention any names, but be sure that everyone knows the consequences of not filling out and submitting the proper reports. The guilty should get the hint.
4. Tell Richard that you need to travel with him for a week in order to better critique his methods. Have him prepare the itinerary and include all the details of the upcoming trip.

The most important assets of every company walk out the door each day at 5 P.M. Developing and protecting this highly mobile asset is more demanding for sales managers than for other managers. Salespeople may not even come into the office in the morning. They're out in the marketplace every day, and your best salespeople are subject to all sorts of attractive temptations from other companies. Important as money is in ensuring sales force performance, it alone does not inspire loyalty. In fact, results of a recent survey suggest that dissatisfaction with a salesperson's manager (not money) is the number-one reason for voluntary salesperson turnover.[1] This is just one of many reasons why leadership and supervision are critical.

Which option do you favor to persuade Richard Waxler to complete his written reports? Some of the options are better than others. Each option is discussed in this chapter.

LEADERSHIP

Leadership is defined as the ability to influence and inspire the actions of people to accomplish worthwhile goals. Leaders inspire trust and loyalty, and they understand how to direct the talents of others toward achieving important objectives. Sales leadership requires more intuition and foresight than just supervising the day-to-day activities of the sales force. Effective leaders create an atmosphere of change to deal with the realities of the marketplace and provide a realistic vision for the future.

Research on leadership indicates that salespeople have better attitudes toward their jobs, greater commitment, less job stress, more attachment to the job, and improved performance when managers clarify sales roles, demonstrate difficult tasks, and clearly define how sales-

FIGURE 12-1 **Leadership Skills**

people are rewarded for their efforts.[2] Great leaders are able to identify sales force needs and show reps the benefits of accomplishing individual and corporate objectives.

Skills

Joe Clayton, Vice President of Sales for Thomson Consumer Electronics, describes leadership as "partly ingrained and partly learned. Experience, both successes and failures, provides the intuition needed for successful leadership. To me, leadership is the ability to influence the decision-making process or change the course of events."[3]

Research suggests that there are five skills that the best leaders develop during their careers (see Figure 12-1).

1. *Empowerment* refers to a leader's ability to share power with others by involving them in setting objectives and planning. This requires spending time with salespeople, particularly top people.
2. *Intuition* refers to the ability to anticipate change and take risks. Although experience helps to develop a sense of intuition, inexperienced sales managers can build a sense of intuition by actively seeking information from customers, salespeople, sales support personnel, company records, and any other source that could serve their ultimate purpose.
3. *Self-understanding* implies a willingness to receive and understand both positive and negative feedback from others, including subordinates. It also means knowing how it feels to lead and coping with those feelings. One manager said, "You have to recognize that every 'out front' maneuver you make is going to be lonely, but if you feel entirely comfortable, then you're not far enough ahead to do any good."[4]
4. *Vision* is the ability to conceive what may impact a business in the future and what changes are needed for it to prosper. A successful vision exists when you can envision where the sales organization needs to go, communicate that belief throughout the organization, get endorsement from all levels, and then execute plans to get there.
5. *Value congruence* means that everyone in the organization is striving for the same business objectives. Achieving it requires good communication skills, as well as the ability to convince others that certain ideas are worth implementing. Value congruence allows a leader to delegate to others the authority to run their own operations.

Companies can speed the process of leadership skill development through sales management training. Unfortunately, many sales managers fail to receive such training. To help you get the most out of management training so you can succeed as a leader, see the Self-Management Competency box.

SELF-MANAGEMENT COMPETENCY
Sales Management Training for Sales Managers

Results of a recent study indicate that more than 50 percent of the sales mangers surveyed say their company failed to provide them with sales management training after their selection to sales manager. Among those who did receive training, more than 40 percent reported that they received training only after they had risen to senior sales management positions (e.g., regional or national sales manager). While some companies consider training and additional education the employees' responsibility, many companies offer training reimbursement plans, in-house training programs, and other expense reduction programs. If your company has a policy of paying for training, then we recommend a few tips to ensure that you get the necessary training to adequately prepare you for the skill sets of a sales manager:

1. Request sales management training upon first being selected to sales manager and periodically thereafter as your knowledge and skills need updating.

2. Resist temptations to remain heavily involved in personal selling so you can focus on "managing" instead of "selling."

3. Request financial data that will allow you to make profitability analyses by product, customer, territory, and salesperson so that you can manage the sales staff more efficiently.

4. Subscribe to sales and marketing publications to keep abreast of the latest research findings and the availability of formal training courses.

5. Send key articles on sales management to senior management at your company to help them understand how a sales manager's use of financial data and sales management training can improve the company's profits.

Power

Power is the ability to influence the behavior of others. All sales managers use power, but effective sales managers know how to use it wisely. Power is critical to leadership because it reveals why subordinates follow leaders. The five sources of power are legitimate, reward, coercive, referent, and expertise.[5] Effective leaders may have to use a combination of all five types of power at different times.

- *Legitimate power* is based on the manager's position in the organization. Salespeople put extra effort behind products that a sales manager has targeted for special promotion because they think the manager has a right to expect this effort. In the case of Richard Waxler, the second option, which asks other salespeople to help solve the problem, undermines your legitimate power as district sales manager. To some degree, you are transferring your role as manager to your salespeople, and this may make you appear weak.

- *Reward power* relies on a leader's ability to award subordinates for outcomes that they value. For example, salespeople may put extra effort behind a particular product because the sales manager has offered to pay a bonus for each unit sold over a three-month period. This power depends on the size of the bonus and the importance of extra compensation to the salesperson.

- *Coercive power* leads to compliance due to fear of punishment. Salespeople who believe that they could be fired will spend extra time prospecting for new customers. However, if the person is already thinking of quitting, then the power of this threat is minimal. This leadership style is rapidly losing favor and the role of today's manager is to support the efforts of the team, not to control and direct. The option of setting up a meeting with Richard Waxler and requiring an itinerary is an example of coercive power. This option is loaded with threats. Keep in mind that withholding bonuses could be illegal, depending on employment contract terms.

- *Referent power* is the leader's influence on others because of friendship with the leader. Salespeople comply because they feel that friends help friends or because they so admire the manager that they want to emulate him or her.
- *Expertise power* is based on the perception that a manager has special knowledge, usually based on past success. Thus, new salespeople may put extra effort into targeted accounts because a sales manager has told them that this is the key to future success and because the manager has a long and distinguished district sales record.

Any of the five power bases can lead to desired behavior by subordinates, but salespeople are more satisfied with supervision when they feel a sales manager is particularly knowledgeable and makes good decisions and suggestions (expert power), and when they identify closely with the sales manager (referent power). Although rewarding salespeople for good performances can be an effective use of power, too much reliance on reward power leads to a mercenary attitude among salespeople rather than a commitment to the overall vision of the organization. Coercive power leads to mere compliance, but employees lack the enthusiasm that accompanies commitment to a course of action. This commitment is usually critical because sales involves more than avoiding mistakes.

To illustrate how some of these forms of power are more useful than others, let's consider the situation at Mary Kay Cosmetics. In this company the sales consultants work for themselves and are fully empowered. From the CEO on down, the company's national and local sales directors realize that their role is to keep the entire team motivated to achieve personal and overall performance goals. Mary Kay's unique approach and use of the five types of power is illustrated in the Strategic-Action Competency box.

Change Management Process

As you may have noted in the leadership skills section, one important characteristic that today's leaders possess is their ability to deal with change. Customer expectations for new products, and changes in the competitive environment are forcing many managers to change their sales strategies and tactics. A recent study of 259 marketing executives reported that 84 percent had at least one change initiative going on in their organization.[6] Although many people thrive on change, others have a low tolerance for the uncertainty and ambiguity of change. According to experts, only 20 percent of the employees in an organization are likely to be change-friendly whereas 50 percent will be "fence sitters," and 30 percent will resist or even deliberately try to make the initiative fail.[7] How then does a sales manager succeed in getting all salespeople to implement a change initiative? One thing is certain, salespeople with greater trust in the sales manager will be more accepting of the anticipated changes, especially in the longer run.[8] Effective sales managers today, therefore, not only recognize the need for change, but also excel in implementing changes.

While leading change is a complex process with many possible avenues for success, research suggests that successful change programs tend to use a five-step process: assessment, redesign, measurement, sales support programs, and implementation.[9]

1. *Assessment.* In the assessment phase of a change management project, sales managers typically engage in reexamining the customer environment(s) in which the company operates. Pharmaceutical manufacturer and marketer, The Upjohn Company, noticed that the pharmaceutical decision makers were changing, but the company's traditional selling process addressed only prescribing doctors. Upjohn ignored the changes related to managed care organizations that use different purchase criteria. Based on this assessment, Upjohn's sales force eventually had to develop new skills and new strategies to meet the needs of the large and growing managed care market.

STRATEGIC-ACTION COMPETENCY
Power to the People

The goal of Mary Kay Ash, founder and now chairman emeritus of Mary Kay Cosmetics, was to provide women with an unlimited opportunity for personal and financial success. The company was set up so that every Mary Kay Beauty consultant works as an entrepreneur who buys products from Mary Kay and then sells them to customers. The most successful consultants advance to become sales directors for a group of consultants, and eventually national sales directors.

In a company where everyone's her own boss, how do Mary Kay and sales directors influence and motivate the others to work as hard as they do? What types of power are used? With everyone as her own boss, legitimate power is irrelevant. Coercive power is contrary to the company's use of the Golden Rule—"Do unto others as you would have them do unto you"— as its guiding philosophy. Thus, coercive power is not allowed. Reward power is used on many occasions. Mary Kay is well-known for their extravagant annual sales meetings to recognize outstanding achievements. In these partylike atmospheres, trips, office equipment, cash, and even cars are given away. Pink cars are considered the signature award—a pink Cadillac in the United States, a pink Mercedes-Benz in Germany, a pink Toyota in Taiwan, and a pink Ford in Argentina.

Expert power is considered particularly important within Mary Kay. From the beginning, Ash understood that training is vital to improving sales figures. Sales directors hold weekly meetings with consultants who pass along proven selling techniques. Good sales techniques, along with a strong sense of motivation, have been the driving force behind the company's success. The high motivation level has also been attributed to referent power of Mary Kay Ash. The nearly half a million Mary Kay Beauty consultants around the world admire the company's founder and are eager to use her as their role model. Lisa Madson expressed the inspiration Mary Kay gave her: "I was a secretary. I was not voted most likely to succeed in high school. But she reaches so many people by talking about the living potential that everyone has inside. And she's the living example." For 10 consecutive years Mary Kay consultants have set new sales records, selling more that $2 billion worth of products in 1997 alone. The consultants continue to show a strong commitment to their retired leader and her original goals.

Visit *www.marykay.com* for more information about Mary Kay.

2. *Redesign.* In the redesign phase, change initiatives are made in three areas: (a) customer orientation, (b) sales strategy, and (c) selling processes. To redesign a sales staff's *customer orientation,* not only does the sales manager need to be knowledgeable of their customers needs and wants, but they must align their sales force's selling strategies and tactics with customer buying processes. Many customers, particularly the larger ones, may have new and stringent requirements for suppliers. These include a broader range of salesperson skills, such as financial, communications, and consensus building within and across organizations.

Once the customer orientation is assessed, the second step is to develop a *sales strategy* that defines how the company deploys its sales resources. One way to do this is to segment the market, which means emphasizing customizing strategic selling approaches to better fit the buying processes and relationship requirements of targeted customer segments or even individual accounts. This approach offers excellent opportunities to grow revenues and increase productivity, since selling efforts are tailored to customer segments with higher potential.

The final step in sales managers' redesign efforts includes implementing changes in the *sales processes* of the sales force. To accomplish the change initiatives, the sales manager may need to redesign the tactics used in selling present customers, new customers, or both. Often the changes in the sales process include a need to redefine the sales job.

3. *Measurement.* Once the design is in place, the next step is to measure indicators of successful change. Sales force change management programs typically measure revenue growth in new strategic areas, such as new customer acquisition or new product placements, greater sales productivity, improved customer coverage, or customer retention.

4. *Sales Support Programs.* Sales support programs are important drivers of successful long-term change initiatives. Sales managers can provide a number of supporting programs to energize and direct continued performance. Examples include: training, compensation, rewards and recognition, sales automation, and supervision. Allegiance Healthcare's recent change initiative toward team selling, for example, required knowledge and skill development programs to foster a willingness and capability of the sales force to change and learn to work together in teams.

5. *Implementation.* How quickly the changes are implemented will be a function of the sales organization's size and complexity. However, one method that has been proven to speed implementation is a pilot test. Many companies undertake a pilot test of their proposed change program so they can experiment with aspects of change in one geographic area or with a particular industry or company type. Upjohn, for example, began its change management program in one state, Minnesota. To sustain sales force morale and motivation, a manager may need to align compensation incentives with the change initiative and continually update the sales force about the future and the challenges ahead.

LEADERSHIP STYLES

When trying to influence and change the behavior of others, you need to think about your leadership style, which is defined as the pattern of behaviors that others perceive you to use when trying to influence their behavior. While your perceptions of your own behavior are important, these are not useful unless they match the perceptions of others.

Every sales manager has his or her own leadership style when dealing with a sales force. Research has shown significant correlations between the type of leadership style employed by first-line field sales managers and their performance ratings.[10] Managers who are fair in rewarding their sales reps' efforts and do not intervene in their lives unless there are problems, tend to get higher evaluations.

Situational Leadership

A *situational leadership* model with four types of leadership styles is shown in Figure 12-2. These leadership styles are based on two characteristics: directive and supportive behavior. *Directive behavior* is the extent to which a leader engages in *one-way* communications, spelling out what, where, when, and how to do it. Performance is closely supervised and controlled by the leader. The canned sales presentation is an example of this behavior. *Supportive behavior* is the extent to which a leader engages in *two-way* communication involving listening and providing support and encouragement. With supportive behavior, a sales manager involves the salesperson in the decision process. Participation in quota setting often involves supportive behavior. It is important to note that the situational leadership emphasizes that a leader's style must be flexible to adapt to changing situations and maturity level of the salesperson.

Four Leadership Styles

The four leadership styles shown in Figure 12-2 are referred to as telling, selling, supporting, and delegating. Each style results from a combination of high or low supportive and directive behavior. When the manager provides low supportive behavior, but high directive behavior, he or she is using a *telling style*. In this style of leadership, managers tell a salesperson what, when, how, and where to do various tasks. Identifying the problem and stating how the salesperson will accomplish the goal are initiated by the manager. Communication is largely one way. For example, a sales manager establishes a call frequency pattern for all the customers in a salesperson's territory. No deviations from the pattern are permitted.

A *selling style* is when the manager provides high supporting behaviors and also high directive behaviors. Leaders using this style tend to provide a great deal of direction with their own ideas, but also solicit salespeople's ideas. In this case, the sales manager may ask the salesperson for a reaction to the call frequency schedule and will consider exceptions to the general policy that the salesperson feels are justified.

A *supportive style* is characterized with highly supportive behaviors, and low amounts of directive behaviors. Essentially a supportive style calls for a shift of day-to-day problem solving from the sales manager to the salesperson. The sales manager's role is to provide recognition, to listen actively, and to facilitate problem solving by the salesperson. For example, with a supportive leadership style, management decides that a call schedule is required but allows the salesperson to devise a call plan. The sales manager may provide past call report information and, if necessary, suggest changes in the schedule.

Finally, a manager providing low supportive and low directive behaviors would be using a *delegating style*. Sales managers using this style tend to discuss problems in the territory with the salesperson. Decision making is then delegated to the salesperson, who

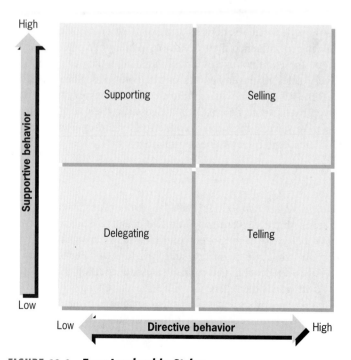

FIGURE 12-2   Four Leadership Styles

decides how a problem is to be handled. The focus of the sales manager–salesperson inter-action is to reach agreement on the cause of a problem. The salesperson may decide that a revised call pattern, for example, is the answer to a problem of small orders in the territory.

TEAM BUILDING

Teamwork in sales organizations has become much more important in recent years as shown by the following quotes.

- "I called our district manager in Phoenix and explained that I was preparing an important proposal for this big account, and would he please help with the part having to do with an account located in his district. He reluctantly agreed, but I haven't seen anything yet, and he hasn't returned my last two phone calls."
- A sales rep selling equipment, while salespeople in another sales force sell related supply items to the same accounts, comments: "Many customers want to coordinate their pur-chases of equipment and supplies because of the impact they have on their production processes. I meet a lot with my supply brethren because while we share all of our accounts, what's often not shared or clear are our individual goals."[11]

The most common reasons cited for a lack of sales team cooperation include such things as rewards and compensation that focus on individual performance rather than team efforts. Also information systems often do not keep team members supplied with perti-nent data. Another problem is that organizational structures foster internal competition rather than cooperation. Finally the mind-set of some people makes them unwilling to set aside position and power for mutual gains.[12] The job of the sales manager is to help break down these barriers and reduce destructive competition among reps. A good exam-ple of the type of problems faced by sales managers is illustrated in the Team-Building Competency box.

The job of getting individual members of a sales organization to work together to form a functioning and supportive team is made easier when you have a better understanding of how groups operate. One of the most useful ways to describe how groups function is the Homans system model, developed by George Homans.[13]

The Homans System

Homans thinks of a group as an interacting system of activities, interactions, sentiments, and norms (Figure 12-3).

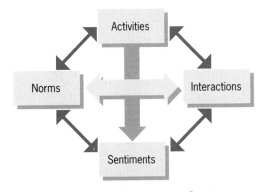

FIGURE 12-3   Internal Systems of a Group

Activities   Activities include many types of behaviors. In Tom Plankton's case (see "The Case for Effective Team Building" in the Team-Building Competency box), it includes developing formal bids. Other tasks may include analyzing problems, evaluating alternatives, making decisions, and writing proposals. These task-related activities will occupy most of the salesperson's time and are likely to be of primary interest to the group members, rather than social activities such as coffee breaks, talking, and playing cards.

Interactions   Interactions are generally defined as the communications that occur between two or more people. The amount of interaction may be identified by answering the following questions:

- With whom do the salespeople talk?
- How often do they talk to one another?
- How long do they talk?
- Who starts the conversation?

In "The Case for Effective Team Building," what would you guess is the level of interaction between the sales force and engineers in the factory? between the sales force and customer service personnel?

Sentiments   Sentiments reflect the emotional climate of a group. They may be described in terms of day-to-day feelings, such as anger, happiness, and sadness, as well as deeper feelings, such as trust, openness, and freedom. Deeper sentiments are important because the more these positive sentiments are present, the more likely it is that the group will be effective and productive. Negative sentiments of distrust and lack of interdependence are implicit in the service manager's statement in the Team-Building Competency box.

Norms   Informal rules of behavior that are widely shared and enforced by groups are referred to as norms. Norms of a work group may define how much work members should do, how they interact with other departments, how they feel about the organization, how they act around the manager, and even what they wear.

   Norms develop in one of three ways.[14] (1) Sales managers or salespeople explicitly state what should or shouldn't occur. For example, Fred may have unwittingly established the norm for not helping a fellow salesperson by telling reps during evaluations that salespeople are responsible for their sales results. (2) Events in a sales department's history also lead to the development of norms. These events frequently occur early in the formation of a group or when a new sales manager takes over. In Fred's example, he may have encouraged salespeople to review all bid specifications with him in an effort to get to know each salesperson in the Central Region. (3) A carryover of norms from past experiences may influence the formation of norms in new situations. Perhaps a regional sales manager who preceded Fred discouraged salespeople from helping each other in developing formal bids because one salesperson was being asked to do too much of the work. Obviously, it would be helpful if Fred knew how the norms evolved in order to address the team-building issue.

External Conditions   A number of outside conditions can also influence how sales teams operate. These include such factors as organizational structure, technology, and management values. For example, Fred may want to evaluate his sales force compensation program, because commission plans often fail to reward teamwork or encourage salespeople to help each other. Alternatively, Fred may wish to devise an incentive or recognition program to reward team efforts.

   Unlike many other leadership situations, key activities and even the location of the field sales offices are geographically separated from company headquarters. This spatial isolation raises the importance of leadership activities of local sales managers. Two key leadership activities of sales managers that may help are one-on-one coaching and conducting sales meetings.

COACHING

As discussed in Chapter 1, an important function of first-line sales managers is to develop the skills of the sales team through coaching. In fact, research suggests that sales manager coaching provides a significant opportunity to influence salesperson performance.[15] Given the uncertainty associated with a field sales job, managers are often needed to define and clarify the salesperson's role. Poor coaching can seriously affect salesperson job satisfaction, which can lead to increased turnover and ultimately affect customer service. *Coaching* is essentially a sequence of conversations and activities that provides ongoing feedback and encouragement to a salesperson or sales team member with the goal of improving that person's performance. Coaching sessions may take place in the office, but most sales coaching is done in the field during visits by sales managers. It consists of three components: (1) positive feedback, (2) role modeling, and (3) trust. Although the three components are interrelated, we will discuss each in turn.

Feedback

Although feedback is used in basically all facets of a salesperson's job, we will focus our attention on feedback of selling effectiveness. To provide effective and useful feedback, it is important to be aware of sales force behaviors that detract from sales effectiveness. Questions that can be used to elicit this information are:

TEAM-BUILDING COMPETENCY
The Case for Effective Team Building

Fred Kennedy is regional sales manager for Mebco Equipment Company. His operation covers a 50-mile radius and includes five salespeople, two secretaries, and two planning and layout specialists. Also sharing the office is the regional service manager.

Fred has been reviewing negotiations with young Tom Plankton. Fred says, "I'm sorry I had to be downstate when the Hillman job broke for you. Did you get your bid in as we discussed?"

"I made it," replies Tom. "And by the skin of my teeth. I couldn't get hold of anyone at the factory who could fill in the spec data, for one thing —"

Dan breaks in. "What about Ralph here in the office? He's sold so many of those drives that he knows more about them than the engineers."

"I asked him if he would help, but he said he had to work on another job of his own," says Tom.

"I had to estimate the installation figures," Tom continues. "Our illustrious service manager said he was too busy and we would probably lose it anyway. I ended up typing it myself at the last minute. The typists said they had to get their invoices out because it was the end of the accounting period."

After Tom leaves, Fred thinks about what had just been said. "It's a good office, with highly capable people," he muses, "except that they're all a bunch of individualists going in their own directions instead of pulling together to the same drumbeat."

What steps could Fred Kennedy take to increase teamwork?

To learn more about Mebco, visit their Web home page: *www.mebco.com.*

- **Planning.** Includes setting territory and call objectives, routing of sales calls, and use of time. "Before we go in, what is your objective for this call? What do you specifically want to achieve?"
- **Attitude.** Includes the attitude toward products, specific customers, the company, the salesperson's career, company programs, and company policies. "I have the feeling you didn't care for that assistant buyer. Your attitude is pretty evident."
- **Knowledge.** Includes product-related, customer business and specific industry issues, competition, territory, company, and policies. "I liked the angle you took on describing the product benefits, but let me ask you, what other approach could you have taken with this product?"
- **Selling skills.** Includes prospecting, selling steps, handling objectives, buying-center roles, negotiating skills, including helping set customer expectations for investment returns. "Let's talk about the timing when you ask for the order." "Who else in a key buying position are you familiar with at this account?"

The best time for feedback is just prior to and following a sales call. This takes advantage of the important learning principle of recency, which suggests that feedback should be given immediately after the behavior. The type of feedback also matters. Research suggests that positive feedback provides both information and motivation, whereas negative feedback communicates only information. It is not surprising, therefore, that positive feedback has a greater impact on performance and satisfaction than negative feedback.[16] The key to effective sales coaching is not in negative feedback, but discussions of why the behavior was not correct, how a better response could have been made, and why this response would lead to the desired outcome.

When a manager accompanies a salesperson to a sales call, the manager must also remember to let the salesperson control the situation. At times, a manager may be called on to address a particular issue, but should keep his or her remarks focused on that issue while giving the salesperson responsibility for the overall call. Otherwise, the salesperson will turn sales calls over to the manager whenever a tough issue arises. When coaching is the reason for being together, sales calls should not become a team selling effort. The manager is there to observe the salesperson's selling skills. Prior to the call, the manager should make it clear that the salesperson is making the call and that the manager will not interfere with the selling process.

Another important factor to consider when providing feedback is the maturity level of the salesperson. With a mature, experienced salesperson, it is probably most useful to use the post–sales-call phase of coaching to identify strengths, build on them, and challenge salespeople to excel in the areas where they do their best work. Any correcting may be accomplished prior to the next call, using the methods described earlier. For less mature salespeople, the post–sales-call phase of coaching may be best used to establish and reinforce self-evaluation of his or her performance. Questions that may be asked include: "How do you think it went?" "What went well?" "What could you have done differently?"

Role-Modeling

The second component of effective coaching is role modeling. *Role-modeling* is when a salesperson perceives a sales manager's behavior as being consistent with both the values the sales manager upholds and the goals of the organization. While role-modeling can take many different forms, a recent study suggests that positive role-modeling behaviors include: (1) personally demonstrating proper selling technique to salespeople; (2) being on time to meetings and appointments; (3) conducting oneself in an honest, moral manner; (4) always presenting a professional image through appropriate dress and grooming; (5) listening to salespeople (so salespeople will listen to customers); (6) being a team player; and (7) never asking salespeople to do things that the manager would not do.[17]

Trust

The final component to sales coaching is a salesperson's trust in and respect toward a manager. In order for a sales force to *trust* a sales coach, they must respect and have confidence in the manager's integrity, reliability, and competency. According to one sales manager:

> [Sales managers] … need to be respected. Part of that respect is being a role model. The conduct of being a "role model" garners respect and enhances a manager's leadership status. If as a leader you don't set a good example, you are never in a position to earn the respect of your team. Without respect you cannot get the job done.[18]

Indeed, research suggests that without trust, role-modeling has no effect on salesperson job satisfaction or performance.[19] Attempts at coaching salespeople without trust are likely to fall on deaf ears. The bottom line is that a salesperson is likely to listen and respond to a sales manager's coaching attempts only if the manager is respected and trusted.

By now you may have recognized that the last option in the Richard Waxler case is an example of coaching. Because coaching takes place one-on-one, Richard is not as likely to be defensive as in a more social situation. By instructing Richard in preparing an itinerary and a call report, you are giving him an important and specific demonstration of how to manage his time and territory. This is a positive approach with a high probability that the lessons learned will be retained. Coaching is the option with the highest probability of success.

SALES MEETINGS

Coaching is best suited to individual training and motivational issues. When a sales team needs help on how to sell a new product, for example, it is often better to address the need in a group setting. A common method for motivating and communicating with the sales team is the sales meeting. One reason why companies hold sales meetings is so the sales manager can be sure that everyone is exposed to the same message. They also make effective use of speakers, training films, and special entertainment. However, keep in mind that meetings eat into selling time and hurt short-term sales revenues. Prior to organizing a meeting, sales managers should ask, "Do we need to meet at all?" Could this information be *effectively* communicated through a memo or by e-mail? If so, a meeting may not be necessary.

If you need to organize a sales meeting, however, plan to organize around three key factors: meeting objectives, budgets, and location and timing. Planning a sales meeting without proper attention to these factors could cause some headaches, as illustrated by a quote from a frustrated sales manager:

> Planning a sales meeting [was] a horror show. You're hounded for weeks by countless phone calls and faxes. You battle constant budget headaches. What's more, you have to coordinate far-flung reps, who dread being taken out of the field. And then, when the meeting starts, a host of potential disasters await. Is this what [I] became a manager for?[20]

Let's see how we can avoid these problems.

Meeting Objectives

Every sales meeting should have a set of meaningful objectives, the most common involving communication, reward, encouragement, and training. Decisions about the objectives will dictate where and how long the meeting will last. For example, if a meeting is strictly for educating reps on products, then a location for a quick arrival and departure is important. Conversely, if the primary objectives are to provide recognition and to motivate, then the location becomes more important. In this case, more upscale properties are likely to be considered (depending on the budget). Some examples of specific meeting objectives might include the following:

- Present restyled, redesigned, or new products.
- Explain new marketing and advertising programs.
- Train salespeople in advanced selling methods.
- Motivate salespeople through interaction with senior executives and celebrities, such as TV or movie personalities who promote a product.
- Recognize contest winners or superior performers.
- Elicit sales force feedback.

The most popular topic covered in sales meetings—sales force feedback—comes as a surprise to many readers. Meetings are usually thought of as a way to provide information, but effective sales managers also consider them a good opportunity to learn about conditions in the field. According to one marketing VP: "At a sales meeting ... we get a chance to talk informally... The truth of the matter is that we get some of our best ideas in these informal sessions. And we discover things informally that no one would think of asking formally."[21]

Objectives of meetings should be relevant to all salespeople. In the case of Richard Waxler, one of the options was to hold a sales meeting, and in this situation, itinerary reports were an issue only with Richard. It is helpful to review reporting requirements with the sales team, but it may not be wise to state the dire results one can expect for not fulfilling the requirements. People who have already completed the reports are likely to wonder why the manager is being so negative, and veiled threats could ultimately lower the productivity of the sales team. On the other hand, sales meetings should be viewed as occasions for providing personal rewards. Never miss the opportunity to recognize people.

Meeting Budgets

Annual budgets for sales meetings (excluding travel) typically range from $10,000 to $70,000. A two-day meeting for 48 people in New Orleans, for example, is estimated to cost $41,213, or $858 per person.[22] Most businesses cannot afford to spend a lot of money, so they hold meetings locally at company sites. Sales managers must control expenses without sacrificing effectiveness. A few firms are trying to reduce costs by using teleconferences or on-line meetings. Others are stretching their budgets by having fewer meetings or shorter meetings, by doubling up on room assignments, or by cutting back on hospitality suite time.

Locations and Timing

Pulling salespeople away from their territories for meetings means that some sales opportunities will be lost, but this problem can be minimized by careful scheduling. Sales meetings are usually held during slack times so that they will not interfere with normal customer contacts. Typically, sales meetings are classified as local, regional, or national.

Local Sales Meetings   Local sales meetings are usually run by field managers and are held frequently, perhaps as often as every week, month, or quarter. These meetings are informal and take place in a conference room at the branch sales office or in a nearby motel. With advances in video technology, involvement of home office personnel in local meetings is enhanced.

Regional Sales Meetings   Regional sales meetings include salespeople from several states and are usually held quarterly or less often. These meetings are more structured and often feature presentations by sales executives and training specialists from headquarters. With regional meetings, personnel from the head office do most of the traveling, which can save time and reduce expenses for salespeople.

National Sales Meetings　　National sales meetings bring the entire sales force together at a central location, and usually occur once a year or less. These meetings require higher travel expenditures, and firms tend to stage more elaborate speeches, presentations, and entertainment at these events. A typical objective of national meetings is to boost the sales force's morale and promote "psychic bonding" among salespeople so that they feel more like a team.[23] At a national sales meeting at the Seth Thomas Company, for example, the baseball theme "Covering All the Bases" was used. The top salesperson was named "Most Valuable Performer," and the meeting culminated with attendance at the opening home game of the Atlanta Braves, with T-shirts and baseball caps for all. When the Travelers Insurance Company Asset Management Division was depressed about low sales, two vice presidents in black suits stepped to the microphone at the annual sales meeting and lip-synched the Blues Brothers' song "Soul Man." This was followed by acts from other regional sales offices. The enthusiasm from the entertainment boosted spirits and made the rest of the meeting more successful.[24]

Common Problems

Interest　　The most damning outcome of a sales meeting is when participants find it boring and a waste of time. Unproductive meetings are demoralizing and worse than no meeting at all. Surveys have shown that salespeople expect sales meetings to be exciting and fast-paced and to make good use of the time available. Providing information about new products or services is a good way to avoid the lack-of-interest problem. Problems can also be partially avoided by careful scheduling, hiring inspirational speakers, and using films, slides, and other audiovisual equipment.

Participation　　Another common complaint about sales meetings is that salespeople spend most of their time listening and do not get a chance to participate and interact with management. Encourage audience participation by keeping the meeting groups small so that each speaker leads a discussion rather than presents a formal talk. Also, make sure some informal socializing sessions are planned.

Follow-Up　　Problems can also result from a failure to determine whether salespeople have actually learned the information provided during the multi-day sales meeting. EMC Corporation, for example, uses a multiple-choice exam to test reps in the meeting's final session. The results are used to determine if a follow-up session is needed.[25] Sales managers should also give participants materials to take with them so that they can review the information and use it in their day-to-day activities. Moreover, there should be reminder letters and checks by local managers to ensure that new procedures are being implemented by salespeople.

SALES FORCE PERSONNEL ISSUES

Sales managers face difficult personnel issues in their development of effective selling teams. Several of these problem areas are reviewed and suggestions are made on ways to manage these situations.

Plateauing

Plateauing occurs when people stop growing as sales professionals. They reach a stage where they are just holding their own or are underperforming. Perhaps they have even stopped showing an interest in the job itself. Sales managers report that 15 percent of the typical sales force is plateaued and that the percentage may be as high as 40 to 50 percent in some sales organizations.[26] Plateauing is most likely to occur when salespeople are in their forties, but it may occur even during their thirties.

Causes of Plateauing   The primary causes of plateauing among salespeople are shown in Table 12-1. Notice that the number-one reason for plateauing is the lack of a clear career path for salespeople. This reinforces our discussion of the benefits of developing a career path for salespeople who do not want to go into management. It also reinforces the suggestion made in Chapter 10 that a realistic picture of the sales position and future opportunities be presented to all recruits.

Sales managers believe there are some differences among sales forces in terms of the causes of plateauing. The most important reason for women is burnout (Table 12-1). Burnout is also an important cause of plateauing among salespeople on commission. Other common reasons for commission salespeople to plateau is that their economic needs have been met or that they have not been managed adequately. These results suggest that there are limitations to compensation plans and that people want more from their jobs once their basic compensation needs are satisfied.

Business strategy also influences the incidence of sales force plateauing. Only about 7 percent of salespeople are plateaued in companies that emphasize growth through the development of new products. Within companies defending market share in low-growth markets with commodity-like products, the incidence of plateauing is 34 percent.[27] This suggests that people can be left in a job too long, and that a highly structured job is more likely to lead to plateauing.

Signals of the early stages of plateauing should warn managers that this process is happening. Sales managers say the most important early signal is when salespeople do not prospect hard enough. Other signals are a lack of follow-through in customer servicing and working fewer hours.

Signals of plateauing appear even when interviewing persons for a sales position. For example, people who subsequently plateau are more likely to mention circumstances beyond their personal control for leaving their previous job. Conversely, among people who do not plateau, the two most common reasons cited for changing positions are better compensation and a new opportunity.[28]

Solutions to Plateauing   Managers need to respect the experience that plateaued salespeople have and at the same time find ways to get them to try new approaches to serving customers. Frequently mature salespeople resist change because they do not want to make mistakes and appear foolish. One manager gets his reps together and places a $100 bill on the table. He then says: "I'm going to tell you about a mistake I made last week and what I learned from it. The $100 is for anyone who can top it."[29]

Another way to prevent plateauing and possible turnover is to develop alternative career paths. These positions should provide new challenges to salespeople in order to help them develop professionally. National Semiconductor of Santa Clara, California, for example, instituted a dual-career path for salespeople with nonmanagement positions ranging from marketing engineer to senior marketing technician. An important reason for National's organizational change was that the cost of replacing one salesperson ranged from $125,000 to $175,000.[30]

Another suggestion is to confront plateauing as soon as indicators suggest that it may be occurring. Sales managers should look for ways to enrich current sales positions. For example, plateaued salespeople could be trained to help coach new salespeople, to help introduce new products, or to develop key customer accounts. Another alternative is to give these salespeople responsibility for gathering competitive intelligence. Tough-to-crack new

TABLE 12-1   Sales Managers' Rankings of the Causes of Plateauing Among Salespeople

	Overall	*Mostly Women*	*Commission Only*
No clear career path	1	2	4
Not managed adequately	2	4	1
Bored	3	3	5
Burned out	4	1	2
Economic needs met	5	7	3
Discouraged with company	6	5	6
Overlooked for promotion	7	6	8
Lack of ability	8	9	7
Avoiding risk of management job	9	10	9
Reluctance to be transferred	10	8	10

accounts could be reassigned, together with the award of valuable and unusual prerequisites if the salesperson is successful (e.g., vacations and bonuses). The number of job-enrichment solutions is limited only by the sales manager's imagination.[31]

Termination of Employment

Termination of salespeople should be considered an option of last resort. At some point in their career managers will find it necessary to terminate a rep. After this decision has been made, termination should be performed in a humane manner, with concern both for human feelings and avoiding lawsuits.

Court dockets today are crowded with wrongful termination suits charging broken promises, invasion of privacy, violation of public policy, and failure of good faith. Former employees are suing—and winning—millions of dollars in damages. Awards are high because a company may have to pay for past and future wages and lost benefits, as well as mental and emotional suffering. In this environment, one misstep by a small company could drive it out of business.

There is no way to eliminate the chance of a lawsuit, but several steps should be followed prior to terminating a salesperson. The first step is to establish a paper trail. The trail should begin with employee manuals that spell out specific company policies and procedures. Performance reviews should occur on a regular basis, be documented in writing, and include both positive and negative elements. The written reviews should be accompanied by a candid discussion between the manager and the salesperson in unambiguous language.

Legal aspects of termination are important, but humanitarian issues are of major concern. One suggestion for softening the blow is to offer an attractive benefit package to terminated employees. This may include an outplacement service to help the person focus on the future and a sizable severance pay, which may range from one to four weeks of pay for each year of employment.

Firing sessions should be brief because neither side gains from a lengthy discussion. Also, the firing session should take place at the beginning of the week—never on a Friday. This allows people to get an immediate start on their future rather than spending the weekend reflecting on the past. Never terminate anyone over the phone, and always do it in a way that preserves the person's dignity.

Sexual Harassment

Women occupy 24 percent of all sales positions (Table 12-2). In some industries, such as educational services, the majority of the salespeople are women. Studies indicate few gender

TABLE 12-2 Women in Sales: Percentages by Industry

Industry	Percent of Women in Sales Force
Banking	24.7
Business services	30.3
Chemicals	9.1
Communications	34.7
Educational services	50.4
Electronics	19.6
Food products	28.5
Health services	45.1
Insurance	27.4
Miscellaneous manufacturing	17.6
Office equipment	24.1
Printing/publishing	38.9
Retail	20.0
Rubber/plastics	17.7
Transportation equipment	23.9
Wholesale (consumer)	19.5
Average	**24.3**

differences in job attitudes and performance, but the issue of *sexual harassment* is becoming more common.[32] Although no information exists on its incidence in sales compared with other occupations, many sales jobs place people in a position where sexual harassment is possible. A client may misinterpret sales enthusiasm as personal attraction. Many positions call for extensive overnight travel, and social interaction is frequently required. Results of a recent study also suggest that sexual harassment tends to be more frequent and more serious as the customer's power increases.[33]

The Equal Employment Opportunity Commission (EEOC) has stated sexual harassment is the "fastest growing employee complaint," citing a 150 percent increase in cases filed between 1990 and 1996. The EEOC cites 15,342 claims filed in 1996.[34] Discussions with female salespeople suggest that women will experience some form of sexual harassment—physical, verbal, nonverbal, intentional, unintentional—at some point, and that it is more likely to occur early in their career.

Women who have had such experiences in sales have several suggestions to offer when confronted with this situation:[35]

- **Direct approach.** The direct approach can be the most effective, especially with established customers. This technique may be as simple as looking the person in the eye and saying, "Don't you ever do that again."
- **Consequence approach.** Most people agree that humor is often the best tactic. For example, say, "If I kiss you, I expect you to drop your wife."
- **Leave.** Many women prefer to avoid confrontations, especially if they are alone with someone with whom they are not familiar. Thus, they immediately leave.
- **Aftereffects.** If it is impossible to avoid the offender in the future, then it is best to get back to the person as soon as possible about some work-related matter. This eases the tension for both people and doesn't jeopardize the business relationship.

Saleswomen surveyed all agreed that the best advice is to avoid potentially embarrassing situations in the first place. They offered several suggestions:

- Conduct yourself professionally.
- Dress appropriately.
- Be cautious in drinking at business functions.

- Don't listen to sob stories.
- Avoid being alone in a one-to-one situation when possible.
- Use independent transportation.

Although sexual abuse is most often discussed from a female viewpoint, men may also experience subtle or explicit instances of sexual abuse. The influx of women into sales, sales management, and buying positions makes this even more likely today. The possible reactions and preventive suggestions discussed are just as appropriate for men as for women.

Companies can help prevent sexual harassment by having a written policy with examples of illegal behavior and by including the subject in its initial employee training and socialization program.[36] It should be made clear what constitutes sexual harassment, what procedures a victim of sexual harassment should follow, and the consequences of offensive behavior.

As a sales manager, what should you do to help salespeople deal with harassment? First, recognize that your salespeople may not tell you about an incident because they are embarrassed and may feel that they are taking a risk by going to the boss. Rather than advising you of the situation, they may ask to drop a particular account, request a transfer within the company, or ask for general advice on how to handle such situations. Most important, do not dismiss the problem. Second, you may offer the alternatives discussed above. If appropriate, you may share some of your own experiences and tips. If the offender is a colleague, the manager should confront the person directly. If the offender is a customer, the manager should offer to join the salesperson on the next call. You must be careful, however, to avoid giving the customer the impression that the salesperson cannot handle the situation alone. You should also be aware of your legal responsibilities to the employee. According to the law, if managers have knowledge of an alleged incident, they must investigate and resolve the matter, or liability can fall on them.

Alcohol and Chemical Abuse

There is no evidence that alcohol and chemical abuse are more prevalent among salespeople than among people in other occupations. However, alcohol and chemical abuse is a national concern, and there is no reason to believe that it is less prevalent among salespeople. Estimates suggest 5 percent of the nation's workforce are addicted to alcohol, and another 5 percent are serious alcohol abusers. Salespeople spend a lot of time on the road, which is conducive to escape behaviors, including alcohol and drug abuse.

Most sales managers realize that salespeople will drink socially with some of their customers as part of the personal relationship-building process. While this is generally considered an acceptable activity, managers know that salespeople are exposed to the potential of alcohol abuse. It is often difficult to detect when a salesperson is a social drinker or has a problem. Detection of alcohol problems is generally done through personal observation or information from fellow salespeople. Although companies can fire a person for using illegal drugs, very few firms have a company or a division-wide policy for dealing with alcohol abuse. The most common reaction of sales managers is to engage in informal counseling with the abuser. Another is to refer the salesperson to an alcohol abuse program and to terminate, either after a warning or immediately.

In most cases, the responsibility for determining alcohol and chemical abuse (including the abuse of legal drugs) rests with the sales manager. Where there is no formal company policy, a sales manager is advised to develop one and ensure that all salespeople understand exactly what the policy is. You should not ignore or tolerate the signs of abuse among your salespeople. It is also advisable to resist the temptation to engage in informal counseling with the problem drinker or chemical abuser. Alcohol and chemical abuse is a complicated psychological and physical problem that requires the intervention of trained professionals.

Finally, sales managers must lead by example. They should ensure that they are sending the right signal by carefully watching their own alcohol consumption, both on and off the job.

SUMMARY

Leadership is essential to maintaining a high-performing sales force. A sales manager's leadership responsibility is multifaceted and affects every aspect of a salesperson's job. This chapter has introduced you to a number of topics and issues facing sales leaders. You should now be able to do the following:

1. **Describe the basics of leadership.** Leadership is defined as the ability to influence the behavior of other people. Research suggests that there are five skills that the best leaders develop during their careers: empowerment, intuition, self-understanding, vision, and value congruence. Leaders also rely on five types of power to exert influence: legitimate, reward, coercive, referent, and expert. The most effective use of power results in salespeople who are committed to the manager's goals. Although combination of power types may be appropriate at certain times, salespeople tend to be more satisfied with supervision when they feel a sales manager is particularly knowledgeable and makes good decisions and suggestions (expert power), and when they identify closely with the sales manager (referent power).

2. **Describe the process involved in managing change.** Effective sales force change management programs tend to use a five-step process: assessment, redesign, measurement, sales support programs, and implementation. Assessment is the examination of the customer environment in which the company operates. Redesign change initiatives are made in three areas: (a) customer orientation, (b) sales strategy, and (c) selling processes. Measurement involves measuring indicators of successful change. Sales support programs energize and direct performance for the long term. Finally, the implementation process will be a function of the size and complexity of the organization.

3. **Explain the different leadership styles.** Based on the combination of two behavior characteristics (directive and supportive) we discuss four leadership styles: telling, selling, supporting, and delegating. In telling style (low supportive/high directive), managers tell a salesperson what, when, how, and where to do various tasks. In selling style (high supportive/high directive), leaders provide a great deal of guidance with their own ideas, but salespeople's ideas are solicited. A supportive style (high supportive/low directive) calls for a shift of day-to-day problem solving from the sales manager to the salesperson. A delegating style (low supportive/low directive) has the sales manager discussing problems in the territory with the salesperson. An important concept of the situational leadership model is that a leader's style should be flexible in order to adapt to changing situations.

4. **Know the principles involved in coaching salespeople.** Coaching consists of three components: (1) positive feedback, (2) role-modeling, and (3) trust. The best time for coaching is before and after actual sales calls. Immediate comments on the salesperson's behavior can be effective in improving the selling and territory management skills of the salespeople. Managers must be careful, however, to always emphasize the things salespeople do well and to praise them for their accomplishments.

5. **Discuss what is involved in developing teamwork and organizing sales meetings.** High performance depends on cooperation between salespeople and others within the company. One of the responsibilities of a sales manager is to develop a team effort emphasizing mutual support and respect. In order to develop effective teams, sales managers must understand how groups function. One of the most commonly used methods

for influencing the sales team is through sales meetings. Planning effective sales meetings is based on three key factors: meeting objectives, budgets, and location and timing.

6. **Understand common people problems.** In today's environment, sales managers are likely to encounter a number of personnel issues that can reduce the effectiveness of selling teams. Chief among these issues are plateaued salespeople, management development problems, termination practices, sexual harassment, and alcohol and chemical abuse. Managers must develop policies to handle them when and if they arise.

KEY TERMS

Coaching	Leadership style	Self-understanding
Coercive power	Legitimate power	Selling style
Change management process	Local sales meetings	Sexual harassment
Delegating style	National sales meetings	Situational leadership
Directive behavior	Norms	Supportive behavior
Empowerment	Plateauing	Supportive style
Expertise power	Power	Telling style
Homans system	Referent power	Value congruence
Intuition	Regional sales meetings	Vision
Leadership	Reward power	

DEVELOPING YOUR COMPETENCIES

1. **Strategic Action.** Effective leaders make sure that they inspire vision and instill confidence about the organization's ability to achieve that vision. Many corporate annual reports include a vision or mission statement. Look at the annual reports of three companies you would like to work for upon graduation. Based on the vision statement and any other information contained in the annual report, what type of leadership style does the CEO of the company seem to have? Would you want to work for this person? Why, or why not?

2. **Technology.** Sales technology has continued to advance at such a rapid pace, the popular and highly recognized journal, *Sales & Marketing Management* has begun publishing a special supplement, *Software Directory,* that is dedicated to the discussion and application of selling technology. Reflecting the popularity of its focus on technology issues, *Software Directory* is now available in an on-line version via the *Sales & Marketing Management* Web page located at the URL: *http://www.salesandmarketing.com.* Access Sales and Marketing Management Online and select an interesting technology product from any link within the Web site. Access the on-line article and study what it is saying. What are the implications of this technology issue for sales manager leadership (e.g., how does it influence access and communications flow; more efficient use of time; enhanced information regarding salesperson performance; allow more timely feedback and control; etc.)?

3. **Coaching.** Julie has the talent and experience to greatly improve sales in her territory. A veteran 15-year salesperson with the company, Julie has been a top performer in the past, but just gets by now. Her husband is a doctor and their children are on their own, so Julie's financial needs are fully met. Julie's sales volume is third in the district of five people, so it's not that she doesn't sell, it's just that her sales volume has not increased much in the past three years and you believe there is opportunity for greater sales out of her territory. Your company has recently downsized and budgets are tight. It's time to do

something about Julie. How would you address this situation without losing a strong salesperson?

4. **Team Building.** As companies recognize that sales involves the ability to work in teams, more and more companies are seeking salespeople with demonstrated leadership capabilities. Choose an industry of interest to you and explore the job announcements. Are companies looking for salespeople who can demonstrate their effectiveness as leaders? Does leadership seem to be more important for some companies than others? Several Web sites provide extensive listings of job openings, including job listings from classified newspaper ads, which can be found at:

www.monster.com

jobs posted by hundreds of companies at:

www.jobfind.com

and the job seekers Web site of the National Association of Colleges and Employers at:

www.jobweb.org

5. **Global Perspective.** The Global Leadership and Organizational Behavior Effectiveness Research Program (GLOBE) is a comprehensive worldwide study of leadership. The GLOBE project seeks to address several interesting questions about the nature of leadership in organizations throughout the world. One key question under investigation is whether some leader behaviors are considered effective by managers worldwide. While preliminary research results suggest some leadership patterns are universally considered positive or universally considered negative, there are important cultural-based differences with some leadership behaviors. Japanese leaders, for example, tend to be more effective using a supportive style. Assume that you are working for a company that has recently begun selling in the Japanese market. You have been asked to travel to Japan and work with their sales force. Up to now you have been successful using the telling leadership style with U.S. salespeople. What types of behavior changes would you need to make to be effective in dealing with the Japanese salespeople?

6. **Self-Management.** Consider the following situation described by an executive with the Aurora-Baxter Corporation, a company that makes construction materials:

> A couple of years ago, following a scandal in the awarding of highway contracts, the state legislature enacted some very stiff laws forbidding state purchasing officers from accepting any gifts—even free lunches. This can be a little awkward in certain respects. When our marketing guys are in the middle of negotiations with them it's natural to go out with the buyers for drinks and a nice meal. Everybody knows that each person there is supposed to pay for his or her own meal. Our guys are told that they have to make that clear. So at some point one of them will say, "Okay, everybody, chip in. You know the rule." Maybe there are five of them and three of us and say the bill is $300. When the meal's over they've put in $2 each and we pick up the rest of the tab.[37]

If you were the sale manager in charge of this situation, what would you do?

IN-CLASS EXERCISES

12.1: "Thanks for the Memories"*

Luxury Airlines recently added a direct route from Chicago to Paradise Island. To celebrate, Luxury's vice president of sales, Jacob Rikker, asked each of his 10 reps to invite their three

---

* Contributed by Raymond Rody, Loyola Marymount University.

best Midwest customers for a four-day weekend trip, compliments of the airline. Each customer was invited to bring one guest.

After a successful weekend of golf, extravagant meals, and dancing till dawn, Luxury's customers left happy and ready to increase their business with the airline. Rikker was so pleased with the results, he decided to send handwritten thank-you notes to the homes of each of the guests.

Approximately two weeks after he mailed the notes, he got a call from one of his reps, Sue Shafer. Apparently, one of her customers brought someone other than his spouse to the weekend trip. As a result, the customer's wife is threatening divorce; she'd already asked her husband to move out.

Rikker was dumfounded. He never imagined something like this would happen. How should he handle it?

Questions:

1. Did Rikker do anything wrong?
2. How should Rikker handle things from this point on?

12-2: "Confidential Documents"*

Joe Brennan, the global sales director for Amstar Partners, recently hired Mark Martin as a regional sales manager. Martin was a top manager at Amstar's competitor Locklear International. Under Martin's direction, Locklear's western region grew about 35 percent annually over the past three years; Amstar's western region has grown only about 12 percent annually during that same time.

Brennan thought that hiring Martin was a tremendous coup. He's well-known in the industry, has an invaluable contact list, and easily ingratiated himself with his team at Amstar. Best of all, within his first three months, Amstar's western region sales increased 25 percent.

Now Brennan was wondering if he made the right choice after all. Earlier today, when Brennan left a proposal on Martin's desk (Martin was out on a sales call), Brennan noticed some partially hidden papers with the Locklear logo on them. Curiosity getting the best of him, Brennan took a look. The papers were confidential Locklear sales information: pricing, marketing strategies, forecasts, and more. Brennan assumed that Martin used this information to formulate his current tactics with Amstar, to Amstar's benefit.

Brennan was torn. On one hand, sales are way up and he was never meant to see those documents. On the other hand, using a competitor's confidential documents has both ethical and legal ramifications. What's more, if Brennan confronted Martin, would Martin leave and take Amstar's confidential information to the next competitor? Brennan was unsure how to proceed.

Questions:

1. What should Brennan do?
   • Should he forget what he saw? Confront Martin? Or is there another solution?

---

* Contributed by Raymond Rody, Loyola Marymount University.

CASE 12-1   FIRST NATIONAL BANK

"I'm concerned about Karen," said Margaret Costanzo to David Reeves. The two bank officers were seated in Costanzo's office at the First National Bank's branch in Federal Square.

Costanzo was a vice president of the bank and manager of the Federal Square branch, the third largest in First National's 92-branch network. She was having an employee appraisal meeting with Reeves, customer service director at the branch. Reeves was responsible for the Customer Service Department, which coordinated the activities of the customer service representatives (CSRs, formerly known as tellers) and the customer assistance representatives (CARs, formerly known as new accounts assistants).

Costanzo and Reeves were discussing Karen Mitchell, a 24-year-old customer service rep, who had applied for the soon-to-be-vacant position of head CSR. Mitchell had been with the bank since graduating from junior college with an associate in arts degree three and a half years earlier. She had applied for the position of what had then been called head teller a year earlier, but the job had gone to a candidate with more seniority. Now that individual was leaving—his wife had been transferred to a new job in another city—and the position was once again open. Two other candidates had applied for the job.

Both Costanzo and Reeves were agreed that, against all criteria used in the past, Karen Mitchell would have been the obvious choice for head teller. She was both fast and accurate in her work, presented a smart and professional appearance, and was well liked by customers and her fellow CSRs.

However, the nature of the teller's job had been significantly revised nine months earlier to add a stronger marketing component. (Exhibit 1 shows the previous job description for teller, Exhibit 2 shows the new job description for customer service representative.) CSRs were now expected to offer polite suggestions that customers use automatic teller machines for simple transactions. They were also required to stimulate customer interest in the broadening array of financial services offered by the bank. "The problem with Karen," as Reeves put it, "is that she simply refuses to sell."

THE NEW FOCUS ON CUSTOMER SERVICE AT THE FIRST

Although it was the largest bank in the state, the "First" had historically focused on corporate business, and its share of the retail consumer banking business had declined in the face of aggressive competition from other financial institutions. Three years earlier, the Board of Directors had appointed a new CEO and given him the mandate of developing a stronger consumer orientation at the retail level. The goal was to seize the initiative in marketing the ever-increasing array of financial services now available to retail customers. The new CEO's strategy, after putting in place a new management team, was to begin by ordering an expansion and speed-up of the First's investment in electronic delivery systems. The bank had tripled the number of automatic teller machines in its branches during the past 18 months, and was engaged in an active branch renovation program. One year ago, the First had also joined a regional ATM network, which boasted freestanding 24-hour booths at shopping centers, airports, and other high-traffic locations.

These actions seemed to be bearing fruit. In the most recent six months, the First had seen a significant increase in the number of new accounts opened, as compared to the same period of the previous year. And quarterly data released by the Federal Reserve Bank showed that the First was steadily increasing its share of new deposits in the state.

Customer Service Issues

New financial products had been introduced at a rapid rate. But the bank found that existing platform staff—known as new accounts assistants—were ill-equipped to sell these services because of lack of product knowledge and inadequate training in selling skills. Recalled Costanzo:

> The problem was that they were so used to waiting for a customer to approach them with a specific request, such as a mortgage or car loan, that it was hard to get them to take a more proactive approach that involved actively probing for customer needs. Their whole job seemed to revolve around filling out forms.

This case was prepared by Christopher H. Lovelock. Copyright © by Christopher H. Lovelock. Reproduced by permission.

EXHIBIT 1 First National Bank: Position Description for Teller

FUNCTION
Provides customer services by receiving, paying out, and keeping accurate records of all monies involved in paying and receiving transactions. Promotes the Bank's services.

RESPONSIBILITIES
1. Serves customers
   Accepts deposits, verifies cash and endorsements, and gives customers their receipts.
   Cashes checks within the limits assigned or refers customers to supervisor for authorization.
   Accepts savings deposits and withdrawals, verifies signatures, posts interest, and balances as necessary.
   Accepts loan, credit card, utility, and other payments.
   Issues money orders, cashier's checks, traveler's checks, and foreign currency and issues or redeems U.S. savings bonds.
   Reconciles customer statements and confers with bookkeeping personnel regarding the discrepancies in balances
      or other problems.
   Issues credit card advances.
2. Prepares individual daily settlement of teller cash and proof transactions.
3. Prepares branch daily journal and general ledger.
4. Promotes the Bank's services:
   Cross-sells other bank services appropriate to customers' needs.
   Answers inquiries regarding bank matters.
   Directs customers to other departments for specialized services.
5. Assists with other branch duties:
   Receipts night and mail deposits.
   Reconciles ATM transactions.
   Provides safe deposit services.
   Performs secretarial duties.

As the automation program proceeded, the mix of activities performed by the tellers started to change. A growing number of customers began to use automatic teller machines for cash withdrawals and deposits, as well as for requesting account balances. The ATMs at the Federal Square branch had the highest utilization of any of the First's branches, reflecting the large number of students and young professionals served at that location. Costanzo noted that customers who were older or less well educated seemed to prefer being served by "a real person, rather than a machine."

A year earlier, the head office had selected three branches, including Federal Square, as test sites for a new customer service program. The Federal Square branch was in a busy urban location, about one mile from the central business district and three blocks from the campus of the state university. The branch was surrounded by retail stores and close to commercial and professional offices. The other two branches were among the bank's larger suburban offices and were located in a shopping center and next to a big hospital, respectively. As part of the branch renovation program, each of these three branches had previously been remodeled to include no fewer than four ATMs (Federal Square had five), a customer service desk near the entrance, and two electronic information terminals that

customers could activate to obtain information on a variety of bank services. The teller stations were redesigned to provide two levels of service: an express station for simple deposits and for cashing of approved checks, and regular stations for the full array of services provided by tellers. The number of stations open at a given time was varied to reflect the volume of anticipated business. Finally, the platform area in each branch was reconstructed to create what the architect described as "a friendly, yet professional, appearance."

HUMAN RESOURCES

With the new environment came new training programs for the staff of these three branches and new job descriptions and job titles: customer assistance representatives (for the platform staff), customer service representatives (for the tellers), and customer service director (instead of assistant branch manager). The head teller position was renamed head CSR. Position descriptions for all these jobs are reproduced in Exhibits 2, 3, 4, and 5. The training programs for each group included sessions designed to develop improved knowledge of both new and existing retail products. (CARs received more extensive training in this area

EXHIBIT 2   First National Bank: Position Description for Customer Service Representative

FUNCTION
Provides customers with the highest quality services, with special emphasis on recognizing customer needs and cross-selling appropriate bank services. Plays an active role in developing and maintaining good customer relations.

RESPONSIBILITIES
1. Presents and communicates the best possible customer service.
   Greets all customers with a courteous, friendly attitude.
   Provides fast, accurate, friendly service.
   Uses customer's name whenever possible.
2. Sells bank services and maintains customer relations.
   Cross-sells retail services by identifying and referring valid prospects to the customer assistance representative or customer service director. When time permits (no other customers waiting in line), should actively cross-sell retail services.
   Develops new business by acquainting noncustomers with bank services and existing customers with additional services that they are not currently using.
3. Provides a prompt and efficient operation on a professional level.
   Receives cash and/or checks for checking accounts, saving accounts, taxes withheld, loan payments, Master Card/Visa, mortgage payments, Christmas clubs, money orders, traveler's checks, cashier's checks, premium promotions.
   Verifies amount of cash and/or checks received, being alert for counterfeit or fraudulent items.
   Accepts deposits and withdrawals, verifying signatures where required by policy.
   Cashes checks in accordance with bank policy. Identifies payees; verifies signatures; checks dates and endorsements; compares written dollar and figure amounts; ensures that numbers are included on all counter checks, deposit slips and savings withdrawal and deposit slips; watches for stop payments and holds funds per bank policy.
   Where applicable, pays credit card cash advances and savings withdrawals. Accepts credit merchant deposits. Receives payment for collection items, safe deposit rentals, and other miscellaneous items.
   Confers with head CSR or customer service director on nonroutine situations.
   Sells traveler's checks, money orders, and cashier's checks and may redeem coupons and sell or redeem foreign currency.
   Handles sale and redemption of U.S. savings bonds.
   Sells monthly transit passes.
   Ensures timely batching and preparation of work for transmittal to proof department.
   Prepares coin and currency orders as necessary.
   Services, maintains, and settles automatic teller machines as required.
   Ensures that only minimum cash exposure necessary for efficient operation is kept in cash drawer; removes excess cash immediately to secured location. Ensures maximum control over cash drawers and other valuables on hand throughout daily operation.
   Prepares accurate and timely daily settlement of work.
   Performs bookkeeping and operational functions as assigned by customer service director.

than did CSRs.) The CARs also attended a 15-hour course, offered in three separate sessions, on basic selling skills. This program covered key steps in the sales process, including building a relationship, exploring customer needs, determining a solution, and overcoming objections. The sales training program for CSRs, by contrast, consisted of just two 2-hour sessions designed to develop skills in recognizing and probing customer needs, presenting product features and benefits, overcoming objections, and referring customers to CARs.

All staff members in customer service positions participated in sessions designed to improve their communication skills and professional image: clothing and personal grooming and interactions with customers were all discussed. Said the trainer, "Remember, people's money is too important to entrust to someone who doesn't look and act the part!" CARs were instructed to rise from their seats and shake hands with customers. Both CARs and CSRs were given exercises designed to improve their listening skills and their powers of observation. All employees working where they could be seen by customers were ordered to refrain from smoking, drinking soda, and chewing gum on the job.

Although First National management anticipated that most of the increased emphasis on selling would fall to the CARs, they also foresaw a limited selling role for the customer service reps, who would be expected to mention various products and facilities offered by the bank as they served customers at the teller window.

EXHIBIT 3   First National Bank: Position Description for Head Customer Service Representative

FUNCTION
Supervises the customer service representatives in the designated branch office, ensuring efficient operations and the highest quality service to customers. Plays an active role in developing and maintaining good customer relations. Assists other branch personnel on request.

RESPONSIBILITIES
1. Supervises the CSRs in the branch.
    Allocates work, coordinates work flow, reviews and revises work procedures.
    Ensures that teller area is adequately and efficiently staffed with well-trained, qualified personnel.
    Assists CSRs with more complex transactions.
    Resolves routine personnel problems, referring more complex situations to the customer service director.
    Participates in decisions concerning performance appraisal, promotions, wage changes, transfers, and terminations
        of subordinate CSR staff.
2. Assumes responsibility for CSRs' money.
    Buys and sells money in the vault, ensuring adequacy of branch currency and coin supply.
    Ensures that CSRs and cash sheets are in balance.
    Maintains necessary records, including daily branch journal and general ledger.
3. Accepts deposits and withdrawals by business customers at commercial window.
4. Operates teller window to provide customer services (see Responsibilities for Customer Service Representative).

For instance, if a customer happened to mention a vacation, the CSR was supposed to mention traveler's checks; if the customer complained about bounced checks, the CSR should suggest speaking to a CAR about opening a personal line of credit that would provide automatic overdraft protection; or if the customer mentioned investments, the CSR should refer him or her to a CAR who could provide information on money market accounts, certificates of deposit, or the First's discount brokerage service. All CSRs were supplied with their own business cards. When making a referral, they were expected to write the customer's

EXHIBIT 4   First National Bank: Position Description for Customer Assistance Representative

FUNCTION
Provides services and guidance to customers/prospects seeking banking relationships or related information. Promotes and sells needed products and responds to special requests by existing customers.

RESPONSIBILITIES
1. Provides prompt, efficient, and friendly service to all customers and prospective customers.
    Describes and sells bank services to customers/prospects who approach them directly or via referral from customer
        service reps or other bank personnel.
    Answers customers' questions regarding bank services, hours, etc.
2. Identifies and responds to customers' needs.
    Promotes and sells retail services and identifies any existing cross-sell opportunities.
    Opens new accounts for individuals, businesses, and private organizations.
    Prepares temporary checks and deposit slips for new checking/NOW accounts.
    Sells checks and deposit slips.
    Interviews and takes applications for and pays out on installment/charge card accounts and other credit-related
        products.
    Certifies checks.
    Handles stop payment requests.
    Responds to telephone mail inquiries from customers or bank personnel.
    Receives notification of name or address changes and takes necessary action.
    Takes action on notification of lost passbooks, credit cards, ATM cards, collateral, and all other lost or stolen valuables.
    Demonstrates automatic teller machines to customers and assists with problems.
    Coordinates closing of accounts and ascertains reasons.
3. Sells and services all retail products.
    Advises customers and processes their applications for all products covered in CAR training programs and updates.
    Initiates referrals to the appropriate department when a trust or corporate business need is identified.

EXHIBIT 5   First National Bank: Position Description for Customer Service Director

FUNCTION
Supervises customer service representatives, customer assistance representatives, and other staff as assigned to provide the most effective and profitable retail banking delivery system in the local marketplace. Supervises sales efforts and provides feedback to management concerning response to products and services by current and prospective banking customers. Communicates goals and results to those supervised and ensures operational standards are met in order to achieve outstanding customer service.

RESPONSIBILITIES
1. Supervises effective delivery of retail products.
    Selects, trains, and manages the customer service representatives and customer assistance representatives.
    Assigns duties and work schedules.
    Completes performance reviews.
2. Personally, and through those supervised, renders the highest level of professional and efficient customer service available in the local marketplace.
    Provides high level of service while implementing most efficient and customer-sensitive staffing schedules.
    Supervises all on-the-job programs within office.
    Ensures that outstanding customer service standards are achieved.
    Directs remedial programs for CSRs and CARs as necessary.
3. Develops retail sales effectiveness to the degree necessary to achieve market share objectives.
    Ensures that all CSRs and CARs possess comprehensive product knowledge.
    Directs coordinated cross-sell program within office at all times.
    Reports staff training needs to branch manager and/or regional training director.
4. Maintains operational adherence to standards.
    Oversees preparation of daily and monthly operational and sales reports.
    Estimates, approves, and coordinates branch cash needs in advance.
    Oversees ATM processing function.
    Handles or consults with CSRs/CARs on more complex transactions.
    Ensures clean and businesslike appearance of the branch facility.
5. Informs branch manager of customer response to products.
    Reports customer complaints and types of sales resistance encountered.
    Describes and summarizes reasons for account closings.
6. Communicates effectively the goals and results of the bank to those under supervision.
    Reduces office goals into format which translates to goals for each CSR or CAR.
    Reports sales and cross-sell results to all CSRs and CARs.
    Conducts sales- and service-oriented staff meetings with CSRs/CARs on a regular basis.
    Attends all scheduled customer service management meetings organized by regional office.

name and the product of interest on the back of a card, give it to the customer, and send that individual to the customer assistance desks.

In an effort to motivate CSRs at the three test branches to sell specific financial products, the bank experimented with various incentive programs. The first involved cash bonuses for referrals to CARs that resulted in the sale of specific products. During a one-month period, CSRs were offered a $50 bonus for each referral leading to a customer's opening a personal line of credit account: the CARs received a $20 bonus for each account they opened, regardless of whether or not it came as a referral or simply a walk-in. Eight such bonuses were paid to CSRs at Federal Square, with three each going to just two of the seven full-time CSRs, Jean Warshawksi and Bruce Greenfield. Karen Mitchell was not among the recipients. However, this program was not renewed, since it was felt that there were other, more

cost-effective means of marketing this product. In addition, Reeves, the customer service director, had reason to believe that Bruce Greenfield had colluded with one of the CARs, his girlfriend, to claim referrals which he had not, in fact, made. Another test branch reported similar suspicions of two of its CSRs.

A second promotion followed and was based upon allocating credits to the CSRs for successful referrals. The value of the credit varied according to the nature of the product—for instance, a cash machine card was worth 500 credits—and accumulated credits could be exchanged for merchandise gifts. This program was deemed ineffective and discontinued after three months. The basic problem seemed to be that the value of the gifts was too low in relation to the amount of effort required.

Other problems with these promotional schemes included lack of product knowledge on the part of the

CSRs and time pressures when many customers were waiting in line to be served.

The bank had next turned to an approach which, in David Reeves' words, "used the stick rather than the carrot." All CSRs had traditionally been evaluated half-yearly on a variety of criteria, including accuracy, speed, quality of interactions with customers, punctuality of arrival for work, job attitudes, cooperation with other employees, and professional image. The evaluation process assigned a number of points to each criterion, with accuracy and speed being the most heavily weighted. In addition to appraisals by the customer service director and the branch manager, with input from the head CSR, the First had recently instituted a program of anonymous visits by what was popularly known as the "mystery client." Each CSR was visited at least once a quarter by a professional evaluator posing as a customer. This individual's appraisal of the CSR's appearance, performance, and attitude was included in the overall evaluation. The number of points scored by each CSR had a direct impact on merit pay raises and on selection for promotion to the head CSR position or to platform jobs.

To encourage improved product knowledge and "consultative selling" by CSRs, the evaluation process was revised to include points assigned for each individual's success in sales referrals. Under the new evaluation scheme, the maximum number of points assignable for effectiveness in making sales—directly or through referrals to CARs—amounted to 30 percent of the potential total score. Although CSR-initiated sales had risen significantly in the most recent half-year,

Reeves sensed that morale had dropped among this group, in contrast to the CARs, whose enthusiasm and commitment had risen significantly. He had also noticed an increase in CSR errors. One CSR had quit, complaining about too much pressure.

Karen Mitchell

Under the old scoring system, Karen Mitchell had been the highest-scoring teller/CSR for four consecutive half-years. But after two half-years under the new system, her ranking had dropped to fourth out of the seven full-time tellers. The top-ranking CSR, Mary Bell, had been with First for 16 years but had declined repeated invitations to apply for a head teller position, saying that she was happy where she was, earning at the top of the CSR scale, and did not want "the extra worry and responsibility." Mitchell ranked first on all but one of the operationally related criteria (interactions with customers, where she ranked second) but sixth on selling effectiveness (Exhibit 6).

Costanzo and Reeves had spoken to Mitchell about her performance and expressed disappointment. Mitchell had told them, respectfully but firmly, that she saw the most important aspect of her job as giving customers fast, accurate, and courteous service.

> I did try this selling thing [she told the two bank officers], but it seemed to annoy people. Some said they were in a hurry and couldn't talk now; others looked at me as if I were slightly crazy to bring up the subject of a different bank service than the one they were currently transacting. And then, when you got the odd person

EXHIBIT 6 **First National Bank: Summary of Performance Evaluation Scores for Customer Service Representatives at Federal Square Branch for Two Half-Year Periods**

CSR Name[a]	Length of Full-Time Bank Service	Operational Criteria[b] (max: 70 points)		Selling Effectiveness[c] (max: 30 points)		Total Score	
		1st Half	2nd Half	1st Half	2nd Half	1st Half	2nd Half
Mary Bell	16 years, 10 mos.	65	64	16	20	81	84
Richard Dubois	2 years, 3 mos.	63	61	15	19	78	80
Bruce Greenfield	1 year, 0 mos.	48	42	20	26	68	68
Karen Mitchell	3 years, 7 mos.	67	67	13	12	80	79
Sharon Ronsky	1 year, 4 mos.	53	55	8	9	61	64
Naomi Rubin	7 mos.	–	50	–	22	–	72
Jean Warshawski	2 years, 1 mo.	57	55	21	28	79	83

[a] Full-time CSRs only (part-time CSRs were evaluated separately).

[b] Totals based on sum of ratings against various criteria, including accuracy, work production, attendance and punctuality, personal appearance, organization of work, initiative, cooperation with others, problem-solving ability, and quality of interaction with customers.

[c] Points awarded for both direct sales by CSR (e.g., traveler's checks) and referral selling by CSR to CAR (e.g., ATM card, certificates of deposit, personal line of credit).

who seemed interested, you could hear the other customers in the line grumbling about the slow service.

Really, the last straw was when I noticed on the computer that this woman had several thousand in her savings account, so I suggested to her, just as the trainer had told us, that she could earn more interest if she opened a money market account. Well, she told me it was none of my business what she did with her money, and stomped off. Don't get me wrong, I love being able to help customers, and if they ask for my advice, I'll gladly tell them about what the bank has to offer.

Selecting a New Head CSR

Two weeks after this meeting, it was announced that the head CSR was leaving. The job entailed some supervision of the other CSRs (including allocation of work assignments and scheduling of part-time CSRs at busy periods or during employee vacations), consultation on—and, where possible, resolution of—any problems occurring at the teller stations, and handling of large cash deposits and withdrawals by local retailers (see position description in Exhibit 3). When not engaged in such tasks, the head CSR was expected to operate a regular teller window.

The pay scale for a head CSR ranged from $7.00 to $12.00 per hour, depending on qualifications, seniority, and branch size, as compared to a range of $5.40 to $9.00 per hour for CSRs. The pay scale for CARs ranged from $6.20 to $10.50. Full-time employees (who were not unionized) worked a 40-hour week, including some evenings until 6:00 P.M. and certain Saturday mornings. Costanzo indicated that the pay scales were typical for banks in the Midwest, although the average CSR at the First was better qualified than those at smaller banks and therefore higher on the scale. Karen Mitchell was currently earning $7.80 per hour, reflecting her associate's degree, $3^{1}/_{2}$ years' experience, and significant past merit increases. If promoted to head CSR, she would qualify for an initial rate of $9.50 an hour.

When applications for the positions closed, Mitchell was one of three candidates. The other two candidates were Jean Warshawski, 42, another CSR at the Federal Square branch, and Curtis Richter, 24, the head CSR of one of the First National Bank's smaller suburban branches, who was seeking more responsibility.

Warshawski was married and had two sons in high school. She had started working as a part-time teller at Federal Square three years previously, switching to full-time work a year later in order, as she said, to put away some money for her boys' college education. Warshawski was a cheerful woman with a jolly laugh. She had a wonderful memory for people's names, and Reeves had often seen her greeting customers on the street or in a restaurant during the lunch hour. Reviewing her evaluations over the past three years, Reeves noted that she had initially performed poorly on accuracy and at one point, while still a part-timer, had been put on probation because of frequent inaccuracies in the balance in her cash drawer at the end of the day. Although Reeves considered her much improved on this score, he still saw room for improvement. The customer service director had also had occasion to reprimand her for tardiness during the past year. Warshawski attributed this to health problems with her elder son who, she said, was now responding to treatment.

Both Reeves and Costanzo had observed Warshawski at work and agreed that her interactions with customers were exceptionally good, although she tended to be overly chatty and was not as fast as Karen Mitchell. She seemed to have a natural ability to size up customers and to decide which ones were good prospects for a quick sales pitch on a specific financial product. Although slightly untidy in her personal appearance, she was very well organized in her work and was quick to help her fellow CSRs, especially new hires. She was currently earning $7.20 per hour as a CSR and would qualify for a rate of $9.10 as head CSR. In the most recent six months, Warshawski had ranked ahead of Mitchell as a result of being very successful in consultative selling (Exhibit 6).

Richter, the third candidate, was not working in one of the three test branches, and so had not been exposed to the consultative selling program and its corresponding evaluation scheme. However, he had received excellent evaluations for his work in the First's small Longmeadow branch, where he had been employed for three years. A move to Federal Square would increase his earnings from $8.20 to $9.10 per hour. Reeves and Costanzo had interviewed Richter and considered him intelligent and personable. He had joined the bank after dropping out of college midway through his junior year, but had recently started taking evening courses in order to complete his degree. The Longmeadow branch was located in an older part of town, where commercial and retail activity was rather stagnant. The branch had not yet been renovated and had no ATMs, although there was an ATM accessible to First National customers one block away. Richter supervised three CSRs and reported directly to the branch manager, who spoke very highly of him. Since there were no CARs in this branch, Richter and another experienced CSR took turns handling new accounts and loan or mortgage applications.

Costanzo and Reeves were troubled by the decision that faced them. Prior to the bank's shift in focus, Mitchell would have been the natural choice for the head CSR job, which, in turn, could be a stepping stone to further promotions, including customer assistance representative, customer service director, and, eventually, manager of a small branch or a management position in the head office. Mitchell had told her superiors that she was interested in making a career in banking and that she was eager to take on further responsibilities.

Compounding the problem was the fact that the three branches testing the new customer service program had just completed a full year of the test. Costanzo knew that sales and profits were up significantly at all three branches relative to the bank's performance as a whole. She anticipated that top management would want to extend the program systemwide after making any modifications that seemed desirable.

CASE 12-2 ROMANO PITESTI

Events had come to a head in Tickton-Jones Ltd. and the Marketing Director, Jack Simpson, had called in his Consumer Products Sales Manager, David Courtney, to sort out the problem.

"To come straight to the point, David," said Jack, "I'm about up to here with this sales rep of yours. Romano Pitesti... Am I sick of hearing the guy's name! Everywhere I go, someone bends my ear about him. Last week it was the receptionist complaining about his making personal telephone calls during company time. Yesterday it was the security people about his untidy parking habits. And this morning, the accounts department is abuzz with outrage over his expense returns. Quite frankly, David, these are not isolated instances—he's out of control and I want to know what you intend to do about him, before the whole company is in uproar."

BACKGROUND

Tickton-Jones Ltd. was formed two years previously, when Tickton Flexible Products Ltd. acquired Samuel Jones Ltd., a local family-owned company. At the time, Tickton's annual sales were approaching $12 million and they employed 230 people; compared with Jones' $4.5 million and 110 people, respectively. Tickton was well established as a compounder of polyurethane and rubber materials and had its own molding facility for a wide range of industrial compo-

nents. Jones, after years of steady business as a manufacturer of shoes, ladies' handbags, and travel goods, had recently moved successfully into sports shoes and for the first time had made an impact in the export field.

Ben Jones was the Chairman and majority owner of Samuel Jones Ltd. He was the grandson of the founder and the last of the Jones family line with an active participation in the business. At age 63, he wanted to sell out and retire to the Channel Islands with his wife, who had a health problem. The remaining two senior Directors were willing to accept early retirement on generous terms.

Ben Jones had been very happy to accept Tickton's offer and was satisfied that the new company would not involve too much upheaval for his employees. He was a paternal Chairman with a strong Protestant work ethic, but in recent years this had softened, and the organization had become somewhat looser in all aspects of its operations.

Not everyone on the Tickton Board had been in favor of the acquisition, largely because it represented a major diversification into consumer products. But the Managing Director had swayed the decision on grounds of too much current dependence on declining customer industries (e.g., motor vehicles, railways, general mechanical engineering). Jones was considered to have good products in growth markets. In the words

This case was prepared by A. F. Millman of the Coventry Polytechnic, England. Copyright © by A. F. Millman. Reproduced by permission.

of Tickton's Managing Director: "An opportunity like this might never pass our way again. Ben Jones assures me that he has a sound labor force and, like our own, they're not strongly unionized. The sports and leisure shoe business looks particularly attractive. Put our expertise in molding technology alongside their distribution network, and it could be one of our main product lines in five years. It's now or never—it would be virtually impossible to find equivalent facilities within a five-mile radius." Within four weeks, the acquisition was agreed upon.

Due to the departure of Jones's senior Directors, integration of managerial staff provided few problems. Jones's production manager, Bill Thompson, was retained and placed in charge of the Jones site, which was effectively reduced to a manufacturing operation. All nonproduction staff, including the sales manager, David Courtney, were moved to the Tickton site.

However, the absorption of middle/lower-level administrative staff had not been easy, and there were still cliques of former Jones employees who felt aggrieved. For example, certain secretaries had found themselves reporting to managers of lower status; friction in the sales administration office and accounts office caused internal divisions; and there was growing rivalry among the industrial sales engineers and the consumer sales representatives.

The organization of Tickton-Jones's marketing department is shown in Exhibit 1. From the marketing point of view, Jack Simpson had merely added another arm to his departmental organization—the Consumer Products Group under David Courtney.

Prior to the acquisition, David Courtney had been very much a field sales manager. He was responsible for the usual sales management tasks of forecasting and budgeting, and spent most of his time dealing with major existing accounts or on the road developing new accounts. David Courtney, Romano Pitesti, and Jim Wells were all paid a salary plus commission. The commission element accounted for 20–25 percent of their annual pay. On joining Tickton-Jones's salary structure they received salary only, though in money terms this did not constitute a loss of total pay.

On the question of company car policy and day-to-day business expenses, there were major differences. Indeed, since at Samuel Jones Ltd. they applied to so few people, there were no formal procedures and Ben Jones signed off on everything, almost without question. In contrast, Tickton had a written document clearly setting out the type of car applicable to particular grades; spending limits for travel and entertainment, and so on. There was also a handbook covering Tickton's general conditions of service, which automatically became the Tickton-Jones handbook.

ROMANO PITESTI

To say that Romano Cesare Pitesti was *different* from the industrial sales engineers would be an understate-

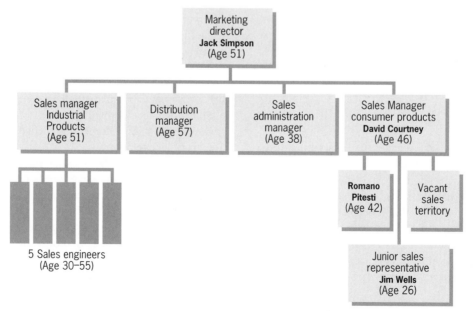

EXHIBIT 1   Organization of the Tickton-Jones Marketing Department

ment. While they "toed the line" and had quite similar training and attitudes, Romano "sailed close to the wind."

Romano liked to feel that he was an *individualist* and repeatedly proved disruptive in formal group situations. Though basically conscientious and hardworking, he operated in bursts of enthusiasm that usually came to nothing but sometimes, through sheer tenacity on his part, brought the company an important order.

He was the master of the *instant opinion* and often entered into conversation on a range of issues of which he had only cursory knowledge and experience. This led him into a number of embarrassing situations, reflecting his gullibility and boyish naiveté.

There were occasions when he could be charming, understanding, and a good listener, especially in female company. And even more so in the presence of Sheila Jones, his previous Chairman's wife! It was well known that she had a soft spot for Romano and had once saved him from serious trouble following an incident involving a secretary after the office Christmas party.

Romano was flamboyant in all things, yet beneath this facade lay a caring and deeply sensitive person. His colleague, Jim Wells, summed him up as "part hero, part villain, and part clown."

From the day he transferred to Tickton-Jones, Romano was regarded as a curiosity and a "figure of fun." The reasons were not hard to find. He dressed impeccably and in the height of fashion. Some would say that he overdid it for a 42-year-old, and he was soon dubbed "The Great Gatsby," "Peter Pan," and "The Aging Lothario."

In his first year with Tickton-Jones, Romano married Wendy Churchill, a 28-year-old set designer with a regional television company. This brought him in contact with numerous television personalities and turned him into a prolific name dropper. The stories he told provided unlimited ammunition for the industrial sales engineers, who cruelly taunted him at every opportunity. But Romano, unperturbed, shrugged off their remarks, usually with some witty return.

Despite all these oddities and eccentricities, Romano's sales performance was exemplary.

THE MEETING WITH DAVID COURTNEY

With Jack Simpson's words ringing in his ears, David Courtney summoned Romano to a meeting. Romano insisted that it would upset his call schedule, but after some cajoling agreed to attend the following morning.

David opened the meeting with firm words: "Romano, something has to be done about the way you operate in this company. It has been put to me that you are out of control. I'm taking the kicks at the moment and I don't like it! I've got a list of incidents to review with you—and you had better have good answers."

1. **David:** Your time-keeping leaves a lot to be desired, and you've been accused of wasting your own time and other people's. The normal starting time is 8:30 A.M. and not some time after 9:00 A.M. when you can make it!

   Romano: That's all very well, but I'm entitled to a little freedom on time. Only yesterday I left home at 6:00 A.M. to visit a customer and didn't return home until late in the evening. How many of those complaining about my time-keeping would be prepared to join me at such times of the day and night without overtime payments?

   David: And what about time wasting? You seem to spend a fair amount of time with secretaries and typists.

   Romano: No more than anyone else. It's just that other people spread their time over the week and mine's more concentrated. You know how much importance you attach to letter and report writing. Well, they all have to be typed.

2. **David:** That brings me to the time you claim to spend report writing. Taking Fridays off is a favorite for sniping by the industrial sales engineers.

   Romano: If you want me to write reports, you have got to allow me time to write them—it's as simple as that.

   David: The industrial sales engineers write their reports over their lunch break or between sales calls. Why can't you? There's a rumor circulating the company that you played golf last Friday.

   Romano: Yes, that's right. I played golf with Arthur Dixon—you know, Singleton's Purchasing Manager. I'm pretty close to a regular order from them. I'm playing with Arthur again on the 29th—should I cancel it?

   David: No, no—I only wish you to make yourself a little more *visible* on Fridays. Not every Friday, just now and then.

3. **David:** Are you aware that you have higher claims for replacement of damaged clothing than anyone in the company? Why?

   Romano: I can't help it if I wear trendy Italian

suits and shoes. That damaged briefcase I claimed last month really was two-tone crocodile skin and cost me $180. I can't visit my customers dressed like those scruffy *Herberts* in the Industrial Group. They wouldn't let me on the premises.

David: OK, OK, just try to moderate your claims in future. I'm the poor guy who has to sign them off.

4. **David:** The biggest problem, as always, surrounds your company car. It's like a big orange blotch on the company landscape!

Romano: I can't see what you have against my car, David. It's only a Ford Escort 1.3 and bought within the company rules. We have very little flexibility on choice of model. After all, it's my mobile office—I live in it for 15 hours per week.

David: Yes, but do you have to choose bright orange and add all those accessories? The industrial sales engineers all have more sober colors such as bottle green and navy blue. Do you really need two large spot lamps with checkered covers, a rear spoiler, and whiplash radio aerial?

Romano: I paid for the accessories myself. You could do the same if you wish. Incidentally, there's a nice vivid green in the Ford Sierra right now!

David: I can almost bear the color with my sunglasses on—but not when you park your car on the double yellow lines near the reception area.

Romano: I knew it! That receptionist has got it in for me. It would be her who complained and not the security people. I only popped in to the switchboard to collect my telephone messages from the overnight answering machine.

David: I can accept that as an isolated incident. But your car is so obvious—everywhere you go, it's instantly recognizable. Which leads me to a very serious issue—did you or did you not use your company car to ferry voters to the local Council elections?

Romano: Yes, I did. I had my doubts about it and was on the verge of opting out. Then I realized Bill Thompson, the Production Manager, was using his company car for the Labor Party, so I thought, what's good enough for Labor is good enough for the Liberals.

David: Perhaps I had better have a word with Bill about the matter. We'll pick this one up later.

5. **Romano:** You've mentioned all these minor irritations, David. Have you ever had cause to question my sales performance? I'm the best salesperson in this company, and you know it! When did I last fail to meet my targets? And have you received any complaints from customers? I was the same at Samuel Jones. Don't forget, we're a rep short at the moment. A few more salespeople like me and we would be a market leader in no time. Who was it who secured the Milan export order?

But at that particular moment there was an interruption. Romano's telephone paging beeper was signaling an incoming call, and he picked up David's telephone. It was Joe Pinkerton. Romano's number-two customer, with an urgent query.

Romano sat back in his chair, put his feet on David's wastepaper basket, and entered into a drawnout conversation. Twenty minutes later he was still engrossed in conversation. David shook his head and decided to abandon the meeting. Romano gave him a wry grin as he left the office.

MOTIVATING SALESPEOPLE

Success is often nothing more than moving from one failure to the next with undiminished enthusiasm.

WINSTON CHURCHILL

Chapter Consultants:
Liz Crute Vice President, Pitney Bowes Credit Corporation
Michael Mahar, Team Leader, IBM Global Services

LEARNING OBJECTIVES

After studying this chapter, you should be able to:

→ Define motivation and explain sales managers' concerns with motivation.

→ Tell how and why individual needs may differ.

→ Describe a basic model of the motivation process.

→ Discuss the different types of quotas and the administrative issues involved in using quotas.

→ Describe how to design incentive and recognition programs and their limitations.

THE PRESIDENT'S CLUB

Leo Kelly is a Philadelphia-based senior sales executive for the Business Systems Group of Xerox Corporation. Last year he finished at 247 percent of quota. In his 20 years with Xerox, Kelly has been a member of the President's Club 17 times. (This is the company's top incentive award, a four-day, first-class trip for a salesperson and spouse to a designated resort.) Says Kelly, "The President's Club is what we all strive for because it's how our success is measured within Xerox. I use it as a yardstick for minimum accomplishment. Other people might use 100 percent of plan; I would consider 100 percent of plan abject failure."

How does Leo Kelly feel about a turndown? "A no is like a buying signal to me," says Kelly. "I make money on no's. If a person is still talking to me, I'm still selling. I say, 'I'd appreciate it if you'd tell me where I have a problem—is the problem me, is the problem my product, or is the problem the way it was presented?' Then I shut up, sit back, and start taking notes—and I'm back in the sales call again."

What does Leo Kelly feel it takes to be a high performer? "The performers—the people who succeed—have tremendous discipline. There's always a reason not to call on someone. There's always a reason to go home early. There's always a reason not to come to work. Sales is a matter of being in the right place at the right time, and the only way you're going to be in the right place at the right time is if you're in a lot of places a lot of times. If you do that, you're going to be successful."[1]

A key management principle states that salespeople's performance is based on opportunity and on their level of ability and motivation. This principle is often expressed by the following formula:

$$\text{Performance} = (\text{opportunity} \times \text{ability} \times \text{motivation})$$

Although the combination of these factors limits overall performance, deficiencies in one factor may be offset by the others. With Xerox, Kelly enjoyed the opportunity to succeed with a great company, but just as important, he had the ability to sell and the motivation to be very successful.

This chapter is concerned with motivation and will follow the topical outline shown in the following diagram. First, we define motivation and discuss why sales managers are concerned with sales force motivation. Next, we discuss individual needs and how people's needs differ. This is followed by a model of motivation that identifies the factors which enhance salesperson satisfaction. Finally, we explain how to develop effective quota, incentive, and recognition programs. Although these programs are widely used to motivate salespeople, their limitations are also discussed.

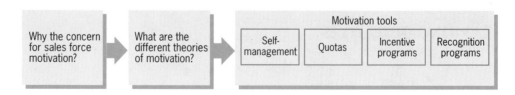

WHAT IS MOTIVATION?

Sales force motivation is a hot topic with sales managers. If the product or service is right and sales force selection, organization, and training are right, then motivation becomes the critical determinant of success. Another reason sales managers are concerned about motivation is the demanding environment in which salespeople operate. Field salespeople are continually going from the exhilaration of making a sale to the disappointment in being turned down. Salespeople frequently must talk with strangers who are not always ready or willing to buy what the salesperson has to sell. Some salespeople, furthermore, must routinely spend long hours on the road away from their families and friends. Faced with these conditions, it is understandable that salespeople may need extra support to do an effective job.

A second reason why motivation is critical is that most salespeople are not under direct supervision in the physical presence of their manager. Veteran salespeople often meet with their immediate sales managers fewer than six times a year. In the absence of direct supervision, self-motivation is critical.

Third, motivation not only affects what activities salespeople perform, but also their enthusiasm and the quality of their work. A salesperson's conviction that a product or service is best for the customer will have a profound influence on a customer's purchasing decision. Customers are unlikely to purchase if they feel the salesperson is not really interested in helping them.

What do sales managers mean when they talk about motivating a salesperson? We define *motivation* as an individual's willingness to exert effort to achieve the organization's goals while satisfying individual needs. Inherent in this definition are three components: effort, needs, and organizational goals. We have discussed typical sales force-related organizational goals—sales volume, market share, profits, customer retention, and so on—and will return to these goals when describing quotas later in this chapter. Let's focus for a moment on effort.

Effort

More than 25 years ago in a classic article on motivation, Herzberg noted that a KITP, which he coyly explained stood for "kick in the pants," may produce compliance, but it never produces motivation.[2] When describing someone as being motivated, sales managers are talking about three characteristics of effort:

1. **The drive to initiate action on a task.** A common concern among sales managers is to get salespeople to call on targeted prospects.
2. **The quality of effort on a task.** It's not enough to get people to call on prospects; they must also be motivated to put forth the effort to prepare to prospect properly and call on a potential customer.
3. **The persistence to expend effort over a period of time sufficient to meet or exceed objectives.** It is not enough to put forth the effort some of the time; high performers show up to win every time. Leo Kelly's discussion of what it takes to be a high performer ("There's always a reason not to come to work") is an excellent example of this drive.

Notice that all three of these dimensions of effort originate within the person. No one can motivate a salesperson to do anything, but a good sales manager can help salespeople to motivate themselves.

Behavior is not random; it is caused. What causes people to exhibit certain behaviors in defined circumstances? In addressing this question, we look at individual needs, what they are, and how they are related.

INDIVIDUAL NEEDS

In sales, the future of the business—and possibly even the sales manager's job—depends on managers' ability to understand the psychology of their salespeople. A good sales manager knows what his or her salespeople want—what drives them. If a sales manager feels that the

Sales Force Needs	Company Actions to Fill Needs
Status	Change title from "salesperson" to "area manager." Buy salespeople more luxurious cars to drive.
Control	Allow salespeople to help plan sales quotas and sequences of calls.
Respect	Invite salespeople to gatherings of top executives. Put pictures of top salespeople in company ads and newsletters.
Routine	Assign each salesperson a core of loyal customers that are called on regularly.
Accomplishment	Set reasonable goals for the number of calls and sales.
Stimulation	Run short-term sales contests. Schedule sales meetings in exotic locations.
Honesty	Deliver promptly all rewards and benefits promised.

FIGURE 13-1   Sales Force Needs and Ways to Fill Them

need for status, control, respect, and routine are most important, a number of actions can be taken to motivate a sales force, as shown in Figure 13-1.

A number of formal theories have been developed to understand differences in individual needs. Some of the classic theories include Maslow's needs hierarchy, Alderfer's ERG theory, Herzberg's motivation-hygiene theory, and McClelland's theory of learned needs. Because you have undoubtedly reviewed these theories in earlier courses, we assume you're familiar with them. Nonetheless, we've summarized them briefly in Figure 13-2. Keep in mind that these theories have very different implications for selling in other cultures. For example, the Global Perspective Competency box describes how Maslow's hierarchy of needs would apply in China.

Hierarchy of needs	Abraham Maslow	Physiological, safety, belonging, esteem, and self-actualization needs are ranked in a hierarchy from lowest to highest. An individual moves up the hierarchy as a need is substantially realized.
ERG theory	Clayton P. Alderfer	Hierarchically classifies needs as existence, relatedness, and growth needs. Like Maslow, suggests that people will focus on higher needs as lower needs are satisfied but, unlike Maslow, suggests that people will focus on lower needs if their higher needs are not satisfied.
Motivation-hygiene	Frederick Herzberg	Argues that intrinsic job factors (e.g., challenging work, achievement) motivate, whereas extrinsic factors (e.g., pay) only placate employees.
Theory of learned needs	David McClelland	Proposes that there are three major professional needs: achievement, affiliation, and power. A high need for achievement and affiliation has been related to higher sales force performance. A high need for power has been related to higher sales manager performance.
Equity theory	J. Stacy Adams	Proposes that people will evaluate their treatment in comparison to that of "relevant others" and that motivation will suffer if treatment is perceived to be inequitable.

FIGURE 13-2   Summary of Classic Motivation Theories

GLOBAL PERSPECTIVE COMPETENCY
The Chinese Needs Hierarchy

Maslow's hierarchy of needs is a peculiarly North American-based theory of needs. With the globalization of business, you should be aware of assumptions and perspectives that may not be valid in other nations and cultures.

Consider the Chinese culture and history. The importance of the group, rather than the individual, is a common thread running through Chinese culture and management concepts. It is consistent with the values of national loyalty, equity, communal property, reluctance to recognize personal accomplishment, and emphasis on motivating through group forces. A basic assumption of the Chinese culture is that a good member of society always places group objectives before individual needs. If, for example, you compliment a Chinese citizen on his or her accomplishment, the usual reply is, "I am only doing my job," or "It is my duty." Based on these cultural assumptions, the Chinese hierarchy of needs may look like the accompanying figure. Notice that self-actualization is in service to society rather than individual development. The Chinese stress loyalty and unity; Americans stress the integrity of the individual and individual achievement. Also, notice that affiliation is expected within the culture and consequently is considered a basic need. On the other hand, things that many people take for granted, such as food, clothing, and shelter, must be strived for in China.

These classic motivation theories are concerned with unique individual needs. Although each individual is unique, motivational and personality profiles of salespeople's wants and patterns of behavior have been identified. After 22 years and interviews with more than half a million salespeople, the Gallup Management Consulting Group's research has revealed that high performers tend to exhibit one of four personality types, each with different drives: the competitor, the ego-driven, the achiever, and the service-oriented.[3] Each of these is described in Figure 13-3. While no one is purely one type of personality, you might think about how you would motivate each type of person and identify the potential pitfalls associated with each type of person.

Career Stages

Experienced sales managers have long understood that motivation varies according to the age and experience of the salesperson. Career stages provide a framework to understand

The Competitor	This person not only wants to win, but derives satisfaction from beating specific rivals—another company or even colleagues. They tend to verbalize what they are going to do, and then do it.
The Ego-driven	They are not interested in beating specific opponents; they just want to win. They like to be considered experts, but are prone to feeling slighted, change jobs frequently, and take things too personally.
The Achiever	This type of person is almost completely self-motivated. They usually set high goals. As soon as they reach one goal, they move the bar higher. They like accomplishment, regardless of who receives the credit.
The Service-oriented	Their strengths lie in building and cultivating relationships. Winning is not everything to this person, but they do respond to feelings of gratitude and friendship from other people.

FIGURE 13-3   Sales Force Needs and Ways to Fill Them

how individual salespeople differ and how their approach to work is likely to change over time.

Jolson was the first to note that salespeople's performance resembled the four stages of the classic S-shaped curve of the product life cycle.[4] Later research suggested that, during their careers, salespeople go through four stages during which they focus on certain career concerns, developmental tasks, personal challenges, and psychosocial needs.[5] These are summarized in Figure 13-4.

Exploration Stage

Early in one's career, during the exploration stage, the overall concern is finding the right occupation—"What do I want to do for the rest of my life?" The stress associated with resolving this tough issue sometimes results in lower performance, especially among those unable to resolve this concern at an early age. The challenge facing management is to help people successfully address this concern. Managers should begin by giving realistic job and career opportunity descriptions during job interviews. Managers should also spend time with new people, providing feedback, reinforcing their accomplishments, and pointing out the long-term benefits associated with working for the organization.

Establishment Stage

Most people eventually change their focus from searching for the "best" occupation to committing themselves to getting ahead in their current jobs. People at the establishment stage of their careers are usually willing to put in long hours to improve their performance. For most people, settling down will occur sometime during the late twenties to early thirties.

One management concern is that the highest performers during this stage are most likely to change jobs. This is especially true if the rewards for high performance are not provided by their current organizations. In sales, the most obvious sign of getting ahead is promotion to sales management. Unfortunately, the downsizing of many organizations and the elimination of management layers to lower costs and get closer to the customer have

	Exploration	*Establishment*	*Maintenance*	*Disengagement*
Career Concerns	Finding an appropriate occupational field.	Successfully establishing a career in a certain occupation.	Holding on to what has been achieved; reassessing career, with possible redirection.	Completing one's career.
Motivational Needs Job Related	Learning the skills required to do job well. Becoming a contributing member of an organization.	Using skills to produce results. Adjusting to working with greater autonomy.	Developing broader view of work and organization. Maintaining a high performance level.	Establishing a stronger self-identity outside of work. Maintaining an acceptable performance level.
Personal Challenges	Establishing a good initial professional self-concept.	Producing superior results on the job in order to be promoted.	Maintaining motivation, though possible rewards have changed. Facing concerns about aging.	Acceptance of career accomplishments.
Psychological Needs	Support Peer Acceptance Challenging position	Achievement Esteem Autonomy Competition	Reduced competiveness Security Helping younger colleagues	Detachment from the organization and organizational life.

FIGURE 13-4 **Career Stage Characteristics**

reduced opportunities for advancement. Management's challenge in this case is to broaden salespeople's definition of success as something other than promotion to sales management.

The response to this situation by some companies has been to develop a "sales career path" for salespeople who do not want to pursue a management position. A typical sales career path might progress from sales rep to senior sales rep to executive rep to major accounts rep. This has retained senior people with higher base pay, healthier commissions, and a solid growth-oriented career path. This has motivated and will continue to motivate salespeople during their entire career.

Maintenance Stage

At some point, usually in their late thirties or early forties, people begin to reflect on their past accomplishments and reassess the career choices they have made. For many people, this coincides with the broader reassessment associated with the midlife crisis. Being turned down for promotion and realizing that future promotion opportunities are unlikely may trigger this reflective reaction in others. How people react to this reassessment of their careers is referred to as the maintenance stage.

People often have very different reactions when reflecting on their careers. Some people decide to switch occupations or organizations, whereas others choose to stay where they are. Similar to the stay-or-leave decision in the establishment stage, some people decide that sales is the best occupation for them, while others choose to stay in sales out of fear of change or because of other obligations, especially to their families. Still others choose to take a new direction, often pursuing a dream that had been set aside earlier in life.

Promotion to management is no longer as desired or valued by maintenance-stage people as it was during establishment. These people are most likely to be the backbone of the sales force and tend to have the highest sales volume. For most people, this stage will last for a long time, typically 15 to 20 years. The challenge for management is to maintain the high motivation and performance levels by encouraging people to use their knowledge in new ways. This also means introducing significant rewards for meeting new challenges and mastering them.

Disengagement Stage

Everyone inevitably withdraws from his or her job and career. The disengagement stage involves giving greater priority to issues other than work and career. For people facing imminent retirement, this transition period helps them to cope with the feeling of loss of focus and to face the fact they will no longer be making a contribution, which has been an important part of their careers.

For others, disengagement may occur as a gradual process, early in life, long before retirement. Some of these people are in their forties and early fifties and will remain on the job for some time to come. On-the-job reactions of these salespeople are quite dramatic. They tend not to be as involved in and challenged by their work, and, they are dissatisfied with many aspects of the job. The sales performance of these people suffers and is often significantly lower than that of people in the maintenance stage.

Attempts to motivate these people to achieve greater performance are often frustrating. Increased pay usually does not lead to sustained effort, and these people place less importance on management recognition than people in other career stages. Although they feel that it is important to meet sales quotas, they are not usually interested in opening new accounts. In short, their approach is one of achieving the minimum necessary to keep management off their backs.

Perhaps the best way for management to overcome this problem is to try to dissuade people from adopting this attitude when retirement is not imminent. The methods mentioned in this chapter for motivating salespeople can be useful. If results are not forthcoming, more drastic measures may be necessary, including termination.

A MODEL OF MOTIVATION

Even when organizations offer incentives, motivation may suffer. Sustained, productive effort requires more than offering the best rewards. Studies have shown that the amount of effort an individual will put into an activity depends on the interplay among three factors shown in Figure 13-5: (1) the relationship between effort and performance, (2) the relationship between performance and rewards, and (3) the importance of receiving more of a certain reward. This process model of motivation is referred to as expectancy theory.[6]

Effort-Performance Relationship

Expectancy refers to the salesperson's belief that greater effort will lead to greater performance. The more certain an individual is of this effort-performance relationship, the more effort will likely be expended.

Three aspects of this belief are significant to sales management. First, the strength of this belief (i.e., the degree to which an individual is certain of the effort-performance rela-

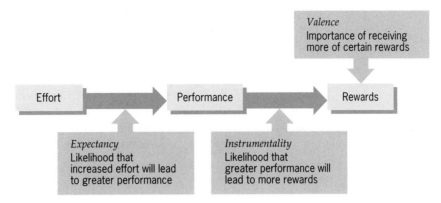

FIGURE 13-5 **Model of Motivation**

tionship) will influence one's willingness to "work hard." Leo Kelly at Xerox, for example, sounded very confident in his approach to handling customer rejection.

Second, management should be concerned with the accuracy of salespeople's role perception. Greater effort on the wrong activities will not lead to better performance, but it may lead to the conclusion that performance is not related to effort. Some refer to this as "working smarter." If a salesperson consistently uses an inappropriate selling strategy, for instance, sales call objectives are unlikely to be met. The individual may become frustrated, believing that no amount of effort will lead to better performance. This shows the interrelationship that exists among effective sales training, coaching, and motivation. No amount of incentive or cajoling will produce the desired level of performance in the absence of a certain level of skill and confidence in that skill.[7]

Finally, people want to know why something happens or doesn't happen and will make attributions about why a certain outcome occurs. *Attribution theory* suggests people are motivated to generate reasons for why an event occurred, especially when the outcome is unexpected (such as an underdog beating a heavy favorite), when the event generates suspicion, or when one fails to achieve something (such as not meeting quota). According to attribution theory, the type of attributions we generate will influence how we respond to the situation. For example, a salesperson may attribute failure to the sales strategy that was used, in which case a search for another sales approach may be undertaken in an effort to make the sale. The theory suggests that salespeople who attribute failure to meet sales quota to their own lack of effort are likely to make adjustments and increase their efforts to make quota in the future. Alternatively, people may attribute failure to factors external to themselves, such as the company, the product available to sell, or the competition. Salespeople who attribute failure to meet quota to circumstances perceived to be beyond their control are unlikely to make these adjustments and will probably decrease their efforts to meet quota in the near future.[8] This points out the need for managers to be in the field with the sales force to determine why salespeople believe they performed as they did. It also suggests that sales managers play an important role in coaching and training salespeople to generate performance-related attributions that positively impact expectancies.

Performance-Reward Relationship

The second element of the motivation process is the belief that a higher level of performance will lead to greater personal rewards. This element is referred to as *instrumentality*. When people are certain that their performance will be personally rewarding, their motivation will be higher. This is one of the reasons for the success of commission compensation plans. Salespeople know how much they will be paid for each sale and understand that their incomes will increase as a result of higher sales. This may also explain why limiting the number of winners in a sales contest may not motivate the average salesperson, whose expected performance level is not likely to be high enough to win.

For the past several years, the "pay-for-performance" sales compensation concept has been migrating to other parts of the organization. Marketing, accounting, human resources, virtually all departments, can enjoy additional compensation. Motivating this change in compensation practice, in addition to generating greater performance, is an organization's effort to foster increased customer and sales orientation among all functional areas.

Importance of Rewards

How much salespeople desire a particular reward will also influence their motivation to perform and is referred to as *reward valence.* Here we can see the connection between the previous need-based theories of motivation and expectancy theory. Both Maslow's and Herzberg's models suggest that there are limits to how much of any reward people will desire. Although many experts believe that salespeople place a high value on pay, this may not reflect a salesperson's day-to-day priorities. Some salespeople may feel that spending an afternoon with the family outweighs the possible financial loss. Understanding salespeople's desires for rewards becomes even more complex in an international setting.[9]

People don't simply look at their own rewards; they also make comparisons with other people's rewards. According to *equity theory,* people make inputs (e.g., effort, experience, territories) versus outcomes comparisons with relevant others to determine relative equity. One reaction to an inequitable situation (e.g., Bob puts in less effort but makes more money) is to reduce inputs. Their motivation is decreased. New sales managers are especially vulnerable to equity problems. In an effort to help one person, they may make exceptions or provide extra help. Other salespeople may see this as unfair unless they are also provided extra help in making the sale. This may eventually result in the sales manager doing the job of the salesperson and lead to lower overall performance.[10]

As a final point on rewards, it is important to remember that selling and effort are rewarding in and of themselves. People derive considerable rewards in the form of feeling good about themselves and their work. Organizations and sales management should do everything possible to reinforce these internal rewards and recognize their importance when communicating one-on-one with salespeople.[11]

Our model of motivation provides a framework for managers to understand the internal process by which people are motivated to put forth extra effort. Obviously, helping to motivate salespeople involves more than knowing what they want and need. A breakdown in any of the three dimensions of the motivation process will decrease overall motivation. Therefore, all three aspects of the process must be considered when trying to motivate someone to perform at the desired level.

How can sales managers put these theories to work? The remainder of this chapter looks at several tools available to sales managers to help salespeople put forth greater effort. Quotas, incentives, and recognition programs have been used successfully in a wide variety of organizations to motivate salespeople. A more recent approach, self-management, is gaining more popularity as companies embrace wider spans of control in which people are freed from traditional levels of supervisory control and monitoring. We will discuss this approach first.

SELF-MANAGEMENT

Salespeople typically work independently of direct supervision from their sales managers. In the wake of reengineering and reorganizing, which have eliminated layers of middle management, salespeople in many industries have learned to manage themselves. Companies that are increasingly encouraging self-management, with the sales manager playing a supporting role, are therefore particularly attractive. One approach to self-management is behavioral self-management (BSM), which consists of a series of steps involving monitoring, goal setting, rehearsal, rewards, and self-contracting. A summary of the techniques used in BSM is presented in Figure 13-6.

To better understand how BSM can be used in sales management, consider a situation in which you are attempting to increase the number of calls made each week on new accounts. Self-monitoring in this situation may mean recording the number of calls made on new customers over a four-week period. Having established the current level of effort, a goal is set for the number of new account calls that should be made each week. Stimulus cues may include such things as a small note placed on the dashboard of the car that says "Have You Met Someone New Today?" Alternatively, it may be a special notebook for recording the number of new-customer calls made each week. Consequence management may include stopping at a nicer place than usual for lunch when the weekly objective is met or skipping lunch if the objective is not met by a certain day of the week. Opening presentations with new accounts may be rehearsed in the car while driving to an account and scheduled for the same time each day. Finally, a contract specifying the criteria for rewarding success and punishing failure should be written and witnessed.

The sales manager plays an important role when salespeople use BSM. The manager may help salespeople set goals that are challenging and achievable, while at the same time being consistent with overall organizational goals. The manager can also be helpful in rehearsing desired behaviors through one-on-one coaching and can help reinforce rewards through recognition of successes and encouragement. Again, we can see the importance of having sales managers in the field and knowing what is going on in the territory so that they can encourage and facilitate the use of BSM.

An important step in BSM is self-set goals. Traditionally, however, goals are set by management for salespeople in the form of quotas. The next section discusses why quotas are used, different types of quotas, and administration issues.

QUOTAS

Quotas, which are one of the most widely used tools in sales management, are quantitative goals assigned to individual salespeople for a specified period of time. Sales of $150,000 in

Technique	Method	Tools
Self-monitoring	Observe and record behavior.	Can use diaries, counters, tally sheets, charts.
Goal setting	Establish behavior change objectives.	Should be specific and with a short time horizon.
Stimulus control	Modify antecedents to behavior.	May involve introducing or removing cues.
Consequence management	Modify antecedents to behavior.	May involve reinforcement, punishment, or extinction.
Rehearsal	Systematic practice of desired behavior.	May be overt or visualized.
Self-contracting	Specify the relationship between behaviors and their consequences.	May involve public commitment.

FIGURE 13-6 Self-Management Techniques

October is an example of a quantifiable goal for a specific period of time. This is the standard against which performance in October will be compared. Although quotas are often based on sales, they should not be confused with sales forecasts or sales potential. A sales forecast is an estimate of what a firm expects to sell during a time period using a particular marketing plan (see Chapter 7). Sales quotas may be set equal to, above, or below the sales forecast. Sales potential, on the other hand, is the maximum demand that a firm can possibly obtain. Potentials are useful for strategic planning and long-range forecasting. Sales quotas are related to sales forecasts and potential, but are used for entirely different purposes.

Three reasons for establishing quotas for salespeople are:

1. **To help management motivate salespeople.** Achievement-oriented people want specific and challenging goals, with regular feedback on their performance.
2. **To direct salespeople where to put their efforts.** When companies assign quotas for each product in their total line of products, they are trying to communicate to their sales force which products should be given priority. Often firms will adjust the sales quota according to product profitability or strategic intent. Salespeople have to meet three to four different sales volume quota categories. V. L. Service Lighting, for example, awards bonus points for each product line that salespeople can receive by exceeding biweekly and annual volume goals.
3. **To provide standards for performance evaluation.** Quotas lend themselves to *management by exception,* that is, focusing management's attention on the performance of people who are exceptionally above or below quota. Time can be spent with people whose performance is poor in order to determine if the salesperson is at fault or whether the poor results are due to factors outside the salesperson's control. At the same time, management may wish to spend time with high performers to identify key points that could be used to improve the performance of other salespeople.

Types of Quotas

There are three widely used types of quotas: sales volume, profits, and activity. Figure 13-7 shows the popularity of each type of quota among large and small firms. Sales volume quotas are the most widely used by both large and small companies. Profit-based quotas are far more common among larger firms, as are activity quotas. Each type of quota is discussed next.

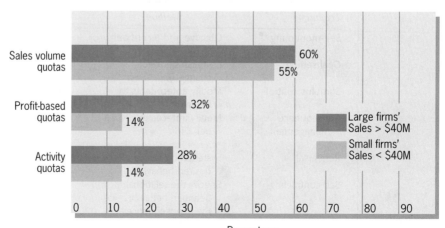

FIGURE 13-7   Use of the Various Types of Quotas

Sales Volume Quotas   Sales volume quotas are specific volume targets established for each territory, and possibly for each product line, for a specific period of time (usually a month, quarter, or year). The sales volume quota may be stated in a variety of ways, including dollar volume, unit volume, or a point system. A *dollar volume quota* is preferred when there is a large number of similarly priced items to sell (e.g., drugs to wholesalers), when prices reflect management's selling priorities (e.g., higher-priced products are more important than less expensive items), and prices are relatively stable. With *unit volume quotas,* sales objectives are stated in terms of the number of units of each product to be sold. Unit quotas are more popular in businesses that sell a limited number of high cost items (e.g., automobiles) and when price changes frequently. By stating quota in units, the effects of inflation are eliminated from the system. With a *point quota system,* the quota is stated as a certain number of points to be earned for selling each product. The point system provides greater management flexibility because points are assigned to the sale of each type of product. If management wishes to emphasize a new product, for example, they may simply increase the number of points awarded to the sale of the product.

Profit-Based Quotas   Profit-based quotas are similar to sales quotas, but focus on profits generated instead of just sales volume. Profit quotas are usually not based on bottom-line profits, but on gross margin (net sales minus cost of goods sold) or contribution margin (gross margin minus direct selling expenses). As such, they attempt to focus the salesperson's attention on profits as opposed to volume. As one sales manager put it, "There's shipping boxes, and there's shipping boxes at the right time to the right customer at the right cost, which is a far bigger idea."

Though more difficult to administer than sales volume plans, setting profit goals has become a growing trend in consumer goods organizations.[12] Profit-based quotas are most likely to be used when salespeople make decisions that dramatically affect the profits of the company. For example, salespeople may choose which of many products to push, or they may have some flexibility in setting prices. Profit contributions often vary considerably among different products. Unless salespeople are aware of these profit differences and know that they will be held accountable for profits, there is no incentive to sell the more profitable products. IBM has developed a special software program so that their salespeople have access to cost data, in order to determine the profitability of every transaction.

Activity Quotas   Too much emphasis on volume or profit quotas may lead to neglect of important nonselling activities and to lower long-run performance. This problem may be resolved by introducing activity quotas. Activity quotas set targets on specific activities that will help in meeting a firm's sales and profit objectives.

Activity quotas recognize the investment nature of selling; that is, salespeople must often perform activities that have the potential to produce significant sales volume sometime in the future. Some typical activity quotas include the following:

- Number of calls per day
- Display racks installed
- Calls on new accounts
- Dealer sales meetings held
- Proposals submitted
- Equipment test sites
- Product demonstrations
- Point-of-purchase displays

One important advantage of activity quotas is that they are based on behaviors that are largely under the control of the salesperson. As a result, a salesperson can be held more accountable for the results and will be more motivated to achieve these quotas.[13]

A serious disadvantage of activity quotas is that the information necessary to track activities is obtained from a salesperson's call reports. Not only does this require the salespeople to do more paperwork (usually on their own time), but there is also an opportunity for misrepresentation. As a result, activity reports may become an exercise in creative writing. Another drawback of activity quotas is that an overemphasis on quotas, such as number of calls per day, may result in salespeople giving management what it wants in calls per day, but sales performance may suffer. Large potential accounts on the fringe of a territory, for instance, may not be called on because of the travel time required.

When Are Quotas Effective?

A good place to start in answering this question is with goal theory. *Goal theory* examines the relationship between goal setting and subsequent performance.[14] This theory proposes that difficult goals, *if accepted,* will lead to higher performance than moderate or easy goals or no goals, such as "Do your best." This means that management must know what constitutes a difficult goal for a particular salesperson versus one that is easy or impossible. Underscoring the motivational influence of difficult goals is the experience of an electronic equipment manufacturer that had set challenging quotas on its data printer line. Although it took twice as long to sell a data printer compared to the other product lines, the data printer line was considered important to the future of the company. Some salespeople objected to the high quotas, however, so the company relaxed the quotas in six districts to see what the impact would be. A comparison of these six districts with comparable high-quota districts revealed that the high-quota districts outsold those with lower quotas. This led the company to conclude that many salespeople are "quota achievers" and that their motivation decreases if they are given quotas that are too easy to reach.[15] Experts also suggest that management should use a highly centralized quota (where sales quotas are specified for each customer and for each product line) with high quota levels for maximum effectiveness in motivating and channeling salesperson effort.[16]

For goal setting to be effective, management must play a much greater role than simply setting specific goals. For salespeople to accept the goals as their own, management must also be concerned with the following:

1. **Providing feedback.** Feedback, or knowledge of results, is necessary for goals to improve performance. Sales manager feedback is a very powerful force in shaping salespeople's performance. This suggests that management should give salespeople frequent feedback on their level of sales relative to the quota.[17]

2. **Gaining goal commitment.** Salespeople must consider the goal to be their own. This is what is meant by *goal commitment*—that is, a person's determination to attain a goal. Recall how Leo Kelly described the President's Club: "It is how our success is measured. … I use it as a yardstick." Leo has obviously committed himself to meet this objective. There are a number of ways to gain this commitment. One way is salesperson participation in goal setting. This explains why more than half of all firms using quotas ask their salespeople for estimates. It has also been found that salesperson estimates are just as likely to be high as they are to be low and that errors in either direction are 10 percent or less.[18] Another approach is to build team spirit and relate individual goals to the greater good of the team. What approach is effective will depend on the leadership style of the manager, the culture of the organization, and the individual salesperson's tendencies.

3. **Building self-confidence.** How people feel about their ability to perform certain behaviors successfully is very important to high performance. Recent research results indicate that salespeople who are confident in their sales ability set higher performance goals and perform better than those who are less confident.[19] This finding points out the considerable benefits of positive feedback and training, given that one's self-confidence can be

enhanced through experience of success, modeling oneself after successful performers, and verbal persuasion.[20]

This discussion suggests that it takes more than setting quotas to achieve maximum motivation and performance. Motivation is dependent on the total management system, and, therefore, several issues about quotas remain. The next section examines how to set equitable and fair quotas, how to evaluate performance when multiple quotas are considered, and the relationship between quotas and compensation.

Administering Quotas

Quotas are usually based on one or more of the following: past sales, forecasted sales, sales potential, and individual and salesperson territory adjustments. A "rough" method of determining a sales quota is simply to take sales in a territory for the past year (or an average of several years) and add a percentage based on the company's sales forecast. For example, if sales in territory B are currently $600,000 and the firm wants an 8 percent increase in company sales next year, the new quota would be $648,000. On the surface, this method appears to be equitable and fair. The problem is that past mistakes are likely to be perpetuated. If, in the past, for example, a salesperson has done a poor job covering territory B, then a quota based strictly on past performance will not reflect the true potential that exists in the area. The other problem is that historical sales figures may predate a recent industry slump, or they might fail to account for the product's being at a more mature stage in its life cycle, where the opportunities are different. To be realistic, quotas must also take into account local conditions.

A better approach is to compute sales potential in each territory and to consider this figure when setting quotas. (Procedures for estimating sales potentials are described in Chapter 7.) Suppose the Buying Power Index[21] shows that territory B has 5 percent of the total U.S. potential. If the firm plans to sell $17 million in total volume in the next year, then the quota for territory B would be 0.05 × $17 million, or $850,000. Note that the potential-based quota requires the salesperson to realize a sales increase of $250,000 for the year.

Basing quotas strictly on sales potential may not always be workable because it ignores past sales and assumes that all territories are the same with respect to the other factors that will determine the actual sales volume achieved. These include environmental factors (e.g., competition, size of customers), organizational factors (e.g., advertising support, proximity to warehouse and manufacturing facilities), and salesperson factors (e.g., experience, ability). Ignoring these factors may render the quota useless as a performance evaluation tool and for motivating salespeople. Thus, a quota of $850,000 may discourage rather than stimulate a salesperson when current sales in the territory are only $600,000. The best method, therefore, for setting quotas is to consider all three factors: past and forecasted sales, sales potential, and individual territory and salesperson characteristics. Setting quotas requires considerable judgment on management's part. It is easy to see why quotas are a potential bone of contention and why salesperson input can be beneficial.

TABLE 13-1   Evaluating Quota Performance in Territory B

Quota Factor	Three-Month Quota	Actual	Percentage of Quota Attained
Total sales volume	$83,000	$84,660	102%
Unit sales of Model 75	6	5	82
Point-of-purchase displays	25	17	68
Average calls per day	5	7	140
Percent store distribution	0.75	0.70	93
		Average:	97.2%

Another administrative concern of sales managers is how to evaluate performance when salespeople must meet several quotas. For example, Table 13-1 shows sales volume and activity quotas together with actual results for the salesperson in territory B. Note that although the overall sales goal was achieved, the salesperson was below quota on three of the five factors. Further, only about two-thirds of the allotted displays were achieved. The average quota achievement of 97 percent, however, appears to be good. It would be especially beneficial if all other salespeople in the company reached only 70 to 90 percent of their quotas. What should be this person's overall performance rating?

Although average quota achievement is a convenient summary figure, one potential problem is that "average performance" places equal weight on each element used to arrive at the average. In the example in Table 13-1, for instance, as much value is placed on point-of-purchase displays as on total sales dollar results. Some managers assign different weights to the various quota factors to handle this problem. Quota achievement is weighted by the importance of each quota factor, and the weighted ratings are added together to form an overall performance index. Care should be taken, however, not to create an overly complicated system.

Another important question is how high management should set the bar. Aiming high is laudable, but setting unattainable goals is a sure way to puncture a sales force's morale. Should a quota be set so that all people will likely exceed it, the top half, or only the few best salespeople? There is no clear-cut answer to this question. Practices vary from one company to the next. If bonuses for exceeding the quota are treated as a normal part of the salespeople's income, then achievable quotas should be set. Conversely, some companies try to challenge their people to greater performance by setting quotas at higher than expected levels and attach substantial and exceptional financial rewards to beating the quota. In this case, financial rewards for quota achievement may be treated as a way to retain top performers. The level at which a quota is set will depend on the role of quota achievement within the overall financial and nonfinancial rewards system of the organization.

When Not to Use Quotas

In certain circumstances, it is probably not advisable to use quotas. For example, when a significant portion of sales depends on cooperation between salespeople in different territories, individual quotas may either be unfeasible or discourage cooperation. This is likely to occur when third-party referrals involve prospects in other territories. The referral may not be passed along, especially if quota achievement is evaluated on a relative basis—that is, if bonus quota achievement is evaluated relative to how each salesperson performed.

Another situation not conducive to quotas is when sales are infrequent with a long selling cycle but the dollar value is very high. In this case, no sales may be recorded in a period, followed by extremely high sales volume in a subsequent period. Quota performance is relatively meaningless in such a situation.

INCENTIVE PROGRAMS

Incentive programs are short-term promotional events intended to inspire salespeople to a greater than usual performance level and provide them with rewards. Incentives are a proven motivational device with widespread acceptance. It is estimated that two-thirds of all consumer goods companies and more than half of all industrial goods companies have sponsored incentive programs. Incentive budgets are estimated to have ranged in size from under $5,000 to more than $1 million, with the average firm spending $97,800. In total, more than $6 billion is spent annually on sales incentive programs.[22] The large budgets and widespread acceptance of sales incentive programs may be explained by referring back to our model of motivation. Greater rewards will usually lead to greater motivation if the rewards are valued by the salesperson. Our model also explains why incentive programs are usually tied to special customer promotion efforts, a special low price, or premium offer, because these should help salespeople understand that their extra efforts will lead to higher performance. Recall that these estimates of success are critical to one's decision to put forth greater effort.

Goals and Timing

Incentives are not a giveaway. A generally accepted performance standard is to produce $4 for each $1 put into them. The objectives of a sales incentive program may include more than just producing overall increases in sales volume. Programs have goals such as finding new customers or boosting the sales of special items, counteracting seasonal slumps in sales, and introducing new items to customers. Less frequently used are objectives such as obtaining a better balance across product lines or encouraging dealers to build more in-store displays.

In addition to specific quantitative goals, incentive programs may be used to enhance qualitative goals such as team building. Basing rewards on department or team results is especially helpful in this regard. Approximately 48 percent of all companies with incentive programs, in fact, base rewards on team or non-sales position performance.[23] See the Teamwork Competency box as an example of using incentive programs for non-sales employees.

A sales manager should ask the following questions when deciding on the goal of the incentive program: Is it consistent with our overall marketing strategy? Can the program detract from long-run developmental concerns? Can the salesperson have an impact on the goal? Can the salesperson understand the goal? Can the company measure achievement of the goal? Unless a company can reliably track the money spent servicing each account, for example, profitability is not an appropriate objective. Another question a manager must ask is: What are some factors that will impact how salespeople respond to the incentive program? If, for example, your sales force is organized by territories, you may need to address the issue of a contest goal based on total dollar sales as compared with a contest goal based on performance of territory quota. The goal of total dollar sales may actually be demotivating for those salespeople, including top performers, with weaker territories. A contest goal of performance to territory quota, on the other hand, may be more motivating because of the adjustment for territory potential.

To maintain enthusiasm, sales incentive programs should be run for limited periods of time, because salespeople may lose interest in programs that last too long. The program may also detract from salespeople's other responsibilities if the program runs too long. A typical program lasts from one to three months, a period that allows salespeople to cover their territories completely and encourages maximum sell-through of the products. Better performance against objectives is generally achieved when the length of the incentive program is two months or less.[24] Salespeople are better able to maintain their focus and interest over this period of time.

An additional timing issue is the best time of year to hold a contest. No one answer is appropriate for all situations. Some programs are held during slow times to avoid a dramatic drop in sales. Others are held in peak sales periods because the potential for sales is greater if the sales force gives more effort. The correct timing depends on the company and the situation. You should not hold a contest at the same time each year. Salespeople may eventually consider the reward as normal income and may play games by withholding orders just prior to the contest.

Prizes

The success or failure of an incentive program often depends on the attractiveness of the awards offered to the participants. There are no firm rules for selecting prizes, except that

TEAM-BUILDING COMPETENCY
Sharing the Wealth

The sales role is not what is used to be. And neither is the sales incentive. What was once a way to reward top performers is now a sophisticated tool to motivate salespeople to be more team-oriented professionals rather than selling machines. "Today the salesperson functions as a resource coordinator, account strategist, and steward of the customer relationship," says Sandy Miller, a sales compensation consultant with Hewitt Associates. "As a result, more importance is being placed on account profitability, strategic achievements, effective account management, and customer satisfaction." All this is increasing the importance of teamwork in the sales process between salespeople and employees in non-sales positions. Today's effective incentive programs link the contributions of sales support staff and positions in other departments—such as customer service, technical support, and product specialists—to sales goals. Such programs enhance commitment levels of non-sales employees who generally don't see all the work the salespeople are doing, yet they feel they bear the burden of special handling, extra service, and last-minute rushes. Tying everyone together with shared incentive programs also helps all employees focus on the most important firm outcome—sales success.

To ensure that a shared incentive program will succeed, sales managers should plan ahead. First, choose a measurable objective that involves the greatest number of departments. For example, a measurement for the number of service contracts sold could be directly tied to the administrative staff's productivity goals for processing the contracts and benchmarks for field service reps. Second, create a potential list of sales force incentives and the investment required. One example might include rewards to customer service reps for passing on leads to the sales force. Third, meet with senior management for approval and request resources for the program. Finally, work independently with other departments to build a final program that retains an ultimate focus on sales with defining the role of other objectives (quality, productivity, safety, response time, etc.) in reaching a sales goal.

This program worked at Oakley Millworks of Frankfort, Illinois, where Glen Johnson, the company's president, instituted a shared, long-term incentive program to solve his problem of a glut of back orders. Initially, Johnson offered each of his 25 employees $10 for every day the company went without a back order. Ultimately, though, this became too expensive. So he offered a large travel incentive—a trip to Hawaii—to his whole staff if the company could go a year without a back order. The following year Johnson's staff was sipping piña coladas on the beach in Hawaii.

different prizes should be chosen for each contest and participants should find the prizes attractive. As indicated in Table 13-2, the most frequent awards are cash, followed by merchandise and trips. Cash is a popular award in sales contests, but cash prizes can be more difficult to promote to participants. A common solution to this problem is to offer cash as a substitute for merchandise or travel prizes. In this way, merchandise can be shown and promoted to the sales force, yet winners have the option of accepting cash if they do not want the merchandise. For example, one firm offered an antique car as a contest prize and the winner refused to accept it. Because the antique car would have been taxed as income to the salesperson at its fair market value, the contest winner was better off taking a smaller amount of cash and paying less income tax.

The advantages of merchandise awards are that tangible items can be displayed to the sales force and featured in promotional material. Furthermore, merchandise can be purchased at wholesale prices, giving the awards a higher value than they actually cost the com-

TABLE 13-2   Types of Incentive Awards Used by 168 Firms

Type of Award	Percentage of Firms Using
Cash	59
Selected merchandise	46
Merchandise catalog	25
Travel	22

pany to buy. However, merchandise prizes can lose their attractiveness if they duplicate things salespeople already own. Another drawback is that winners must pay income taxes on the merchandise that is won. One solution is to have the salespeople accumulate points that can be used to choose items from a catalog.

Travel awards add glamour and excitement to sales contests, and such awards are usually more appealing to older participants. Salespeople earning $50,000 a year are less likely to be interested in merchandise prizes, but a week's vacation in Hawaii can be very enticing. As a result, companies in the United States spend more than $3 billion annually on travel awards. However, travel awards are the least frequently used type of prize because their substantial cost limits the number that can be offered. In response to this situation, many companies are cutting back on the cost per trip by awarding less exotic trips to U.S. locales, such as San Diego, Chicago, and St. Louis. Moreover, the award winner can avoid paying taxes on the prize by combining the trip with a sales meeting.

Administration Issues

Although incentive programs have the potential to be very powerful motivators, they must be properly planned and executed. One of the keys to successful sales incentive programs is choosing a good theme for the contest. The theme is a unifying statement that ties together the business objective of the contest, the prizes, and the individual. Ideally, the theme will be simple, easy to execute, and something about which the participants can get excited. Common sales contest themes include sports (Super Bowl, World Series), travel locations, treasure hunts, gambling, and detective and mystery themes. These themes are used as reminders during the contest and may also be used to display current standings among the contestants.

A successful program should encourage the average salesperson to expend extra effort, because superior salespeople produce irrespective of the contest and people at the bottom are less likely to respond to any stimulus. Thus, success depends on setting the qualifications and rewards so that approximately the middle 60 percent of the sales force participates.[25] With this objective in mind, it is often advisable to have many prizes, instead of having one or two grand prizes that are likely to be won by the superstars. A sales contest can be set up, for instance, with several levels of achievement so that most people win something. One possible approach is to award salespeople who increase volume 10 percent during the program a $100 camera, whereas salespeople who achieve a 20 percent gain receive a portable TV set. A third level of achievement might reward the top overall producers with a trip to Las Vegas. A good rule of thumb is that half of the salespeople eligible for sales contests should win some sort of prize.

The incentive program should be highly promoted. Promotion informs salespeople of the incentive program and reminds them of the prizes to be won. A good way to build initial interest is to begin with a kickoff sales meeting in which the sales force can see the prizes and learn the details of the contest. This meeting should be followed by mailings, articles in the company newspaper, and trade advertising to maintain the attention and interest of the field reps. Because sales contests are short-lived, it is essential to issue frequent progress reports to let participants know where they stand and what they must do to qualify for an award.

RECOGNITION PROGRAMS

Without a doubt, recognition and prizes push people closer to their potential than envelopes stuffed with money. This is why almost all sales managers have some sort of recognition program. A recognition program is similar to incentives in that an individual or group of salespeople receive an award for exceptional performance. Recognition programs differ from incentive programs in several important ways. Although some monetary award may be involved, the primary award is recognition by management for exceptional performance. There are also timing differences. Where incentive programs are usually short in duration, a recognition program is usually based on performance over a year or longer. In addition, recognition programs usually focus on overall performance rather than the sale of targeted products.

Hewlett-Packard has one of the most professional and successful sales forces in the world. One key to its success is the company's many recognition programs. These programs are based on two principles: (1) generate enthusiasm and motivation for as many salespeople as possible, and (2) get useful feedback from the sales force to improve performance opportunities even more. Three of H-P's programs illustrate these principles:

- **The 100 Percent Club.** Each sales region sponsors a team-building and recognition program for all salespeople achieving 100 percent of the quota or better for the year.
- **Achiever's Club.** This club consists of the top 10 to 20 percent of salespeople in each region. They win a weekend vacation for two, which includes motivational and recognition activities.
- **President's Club.** This consists of the top 100 performers in the sales organization—85 salespeople and 15 district sales managers. Nominations are based on eight criteria: sales performance, customer satisfaction, resource management, sales planning, teamwork, leadership, enthusiasm, and role modeling. In other words, being a member takes more than simply producing the highest numbers.[26]

To be successful, recognition programs must become part of the company's culture; that is, they should be longstanding, anticipated, and have lasting value. As you can see, recognition programs focus on the third effort characteristic—the drive to persistently put forth exceptional effort (p. 433). Successful recognition programs appeal to the highest of Maslow's needs, self-actualization, which, you may recall, is never fully satisfied.

Why does recognition motivate salespeople? Part of the reason is that most people strive for recognition by management and peers, and most people cannot get enough recognition. For high performance to lead to positive job attitudes and subsequent high performance, individuals must have a positive emotional reaction to their performance.[27] A well-administered recognition program can help foster a strong, positive reaction to high performance.

Quality: Changes in Recognition Programs

TQM is having an important impact on what recognition programs reward and how the programs are conducted. One of the most important lessons for management is to ensure that the recognition system rewards what the organization values most. If a salesperson is given a large cash award for selling a product, for instance, but the person responsible for installing the product is given only a lapel pin, this quickly communicates how little the firm values customer service. The change in focus from selling to obtaining a customer for life based on satisfaction is forcing many companies to reevaluate their recognition programs to be sure that they communicate the right set of values.

As organizations embracing TQM expand employee empowerment, they are finding it practical to delegate recognition activities to them as well. What a change this is, given that historically all recognition program decisions were made by management! Delegating recognition increases the odds that the right people are recognized, because employees always know who really did the work. Instead of giving one salesperson a $10,000 award, for instance, a salesperson is given $10,000 or $15,000 to distribute among the team that made his or her achievement possible, with the salesperson sharing in the financial recognition.

Recognition programs also reflect TQM's emphasis on teams. Instead of recognizing the accomplishments of one salesperson, the entire sales unit is recognized for its overall accomplishments or for working together to close an important sale. Milliken and Xerox recognize teams by having them present the results of their work at Sharing Rallies in which they "pitch" their story to peers. One IBM organization awards a large silver medallion to team members, but only if another team nominates them for the award.

In summary, TQM has caused organizations to recognize more than volume and profit, to focus on teams as well as individuals, and to empower employees to recognize the accomplishments of other employees. Still, it is important that management never lose its focus on the individual as a team member. As one sales manager put it: "There still needs to be plenty of room for individual success and achievement. Otherwise, teamwork becomes an amorphous concept that can lead a group to underachieve in harmony."[28]

ETHICAL SITUATIONS

Despite their widespread use, ethical problems may arise with quota systems, contests, and rewards to motivate people on the job. Some people have questioned whether managers should administer rewards in ways that promote desirable behaviors from the organization's point of view and not worry too much about the individual's freedom to choose which behaviors to engage in to satisfy his or her own desires. When does a manager have too much power to manipulate people into doing what they would not otherwise do? There is also the issue of whether promising rewards detracts from the job. Does promising a reward for doing a job they already enjoy doing lead salespeople to view the reward as the motivation for performing the task, thus undermining their enjoyment of the job? For more on this subject, see the Coaching Competency box.

Poorly run or poorly conceived quotas and contests have high potential for fostering unethical behaviors by salespeople. When salespeople know that a contest is upcoming, for example, they may withhold orders prior to the contest in order to have greater volume during the contest. During a contest, "soft" orders, which will be totally or partially returned by the customer, may be submitted. If quotas are set on activities, such as calls per day, salespeople may be tempted to falsify call reports to avoid problems with an overzealous manager or to meet end-of-year objectives for which they are rewarded. If salespeople are rewarded for exceeding the quota, they may withhold additional orders during the reporting period in order to make their job easier during the next period. Some people have been known to start their own companies during the time they have available after meeting the quota. If a quota or contest is not designed or administered properly, people may easily justify unethical behavior. A good question to consider is how you would design a program in order to prevent or discourage each of these behaviors.

COACHING COMPETENCY
Why Incentive Plans Cannot Work

Some people argue that incentive plans do not work. They argue that incentives produce temporary compliance at best and that once the rewards run out, people revert to their old behaviors. They do not create an enduring commitment to any value or action. By contrast, training and goal-setting programs are believed to have a far greater impact on long-term productivity than any pay-for-performance plans.

Why do most executives continue to rely on incentive programs? Perhaps it is because the temporary benefits are much more noticeable than the long-run problems they cause. Moreover, we have been exposed to manipulation by rewards all our lives, so that incentives are now part of the fabric of American life.

In a *Harvard Business Review* article, Alfie Kohn offers the following reasons why incentives do not work:

- *Pay is not a motivator.* When people are asked what matters most to them, pay is usually ranked only fifth or sixth.
- *Rewards punish.* Not receiving a reward one had expected or thinks one deserves to receive is indistinguishable from being punished.
- *Rewards ignore reasons.* Managers often use incentive systems as a substitute for giving people what they need to do a good job—useful feedback, social support, and room for self-determination.
- *Rewards discourage risk taking.* When incentives are used to motivate, predictability and simplicity are desirable job features, since the objective is to get through the task expediently in order to get the reward. Exploration is therefore discouraged.

Assume you are a sales manager of a sales force that is compensated by a commission-based pay plan. What coaching activities could you do to overcome some of these criticisms?

SUMMARY

Role perceptions, skill levels, aptitude, and motivation all affect a salesperson's on-the-job performance. Salespeople need basic selling skills, but they also must be motivated to put forth the effort needed to achieve their objectives. Given the demanding environment in which salespeople operate, an effective motivator is often the only difference between a salesperson's success or failure. Sales managers who are able to motivate will be rewarded with a sales force that expresses little dissatisfaction and exerts high levels of effort. In order to be effective, however, managers must first understand the many factors that comprise motivation:

1. **Define motivation and explain how and why individual needs may differ.** Motivation is an individual's willingness to exert effort to achieve the organization's goals while satisfying individual needs. Sales managers should understand that people have different needs and that these needs change over a salesperson's career. The four basic career stages a salesperson experiences are: exploration, establishment, maintenance, and disengagement. Each of these stages has different career concerns, motivational needs, personal challenges, and psychosocial needs.

2. **Describe the expectancy theory of motivation.** Expectancy is the salesperson's belief that greater effort will lead to greater performance. Expectancy theory is based on three interrelated factors: (1) the relationship between effort and performance *(expectancies)*,

(2) the relationship between performance and rewards *(instrumentalities)*, and (3) the importance of receiving more of a certain reward *(valences)*. Salespeople estimate the chances that their actions will lead to specific goals and that goal achievement will lead to rewards, and they assess the desirability of the rewards offered for achieving those goals. If the objectives seem reasonable and the rewards sufficiently attractive, then salespeople will be motivated.

3. **Explain the different types of quotas and the administrative issues involved.** Quotas are widely used motivational devices that not only provide goals and direct salesperson efforts, but also set standards for evaluation of individual performance. The common types of quotas are: sales volume (which includes dollar volume, unit volume, and point quota systems), profit-based, and activity quotas. Management plays an important role in both setting quotas and ensuring that salespeople accept the goals. Quotas are usually set on one or more of the following: past sales, forecasted sales, sales potential, and individual and salesperson territory adjustments. For salespeople to accept the goals as their own, management should provide frequent feedback, have salespeople committed to the goal, and build salesperson self-confidence.

4. **Describe how to design incentive and recognition programs and their limitations.** Incentive programs are short-run promotional events that can stimulate salespeople to reach their quotas through the offer of prizes such as merchandise, cash, or trips. Recognition awards, such as "Salesperson of the Month" titles, trophies, and certificates are also effective motivational devices.

KEY TERMS

Activity quota	Goal commitment	Profit-based quota
Attribution theory	Goal theory	Quota
Behavioral self-management (BSM)	Hierarchy of needs	Recognition program
Disengagement stage	Hygiene-motivation factors	Reward valence
Dollar volume quota	Incentive program	Sales force segmentation
Equity theory	Instrumentality	Sales volume quota
Establishment stage	Maintenance stage	Self-efficacy
Expectancy	Management by exception	Unit volume quota
Expectancy theory	Motivation	
Exploration stage	Point quota system	

DEVELOPING YOUR COMPETENCIES

1. **Strategic Action.** Quotas at DSC Technologies are based on the average of sales over the past two years plus a 20 percent increase. The reason for the high increase in sales quota is that DSC manufactures and sells telephone switches in the communications industry, where new technologies are frequently introduced and industry growth over the past decade has averaged just over 20 percent a year. Bonuses are paid on the following schedule:

Bonus Percent	Percent of Quota
5	100–105
7	106–110
10	111–120

No additional bonus is given for windfall sales over 20 percent of the quota. What are the advantages and disadvantages of this approach? What is likely to happen? How would you change the method?

2. **Team Building.** Select another member of your class and use the expectancy theory of motivation to analyze this course. To what extent does the design of the course influence your expectancy, instrumentality, and valence perceptions? Discuss with each other how various elements of the course affect your perceptions of the three components of motivation.

3. **Global Perspective.** IBM's incentive programs are designed to include its worldwide sales force. A recent program dubbed "You Sell, You Sail," for its AS/400 computer sales force was one of the largest incentive contests ever run by a U.S. company. It included 7,000 participants. IBM believed it could communicate program goals, rules, and results directly to the 7,000 participants in 140 countries around the world using e-mail. However, making the contest meaningful and competitive was another challenge. What factors would you need to consider in order to have a meaningful competition for all 7,000 salespeople?

4. **Coaching.** You are a sales manager for an industrial manufacturer. The performance of one of your salespeople, James Weber, has slipped and he has achieved only 75 percent of his quota for the past six months. The average sales quota achievement in your district was 90 percent. Weber has worked for your firm for six years and has a bachelor's degree in business administration. Jim's territory is above average in potential but requires considerable travel. At the recent company picnic, Weber seemed depressed and spent his time drinking rather than interacting with the other salespeople. Weber is divorced, and his ex-wife lives in another city with their three children. You have decided that it is time to call in Weber for a conference. Develop a script for a meeting with Weber that will motivate him to work up to his potential. Be prepared to play the role of the sales manager or Weber in a meeting to be acted out in front of the class.

5. **Technology.** Sales and Marketing Management Online is a Web-based version on the highly respected selling journal *Sales & Marketing Management.* In the on-line journal is a special feature section entitled "What Would You Do?" that describes true-to-life experiences of field sales managers. Each month a different scenario is presented as a real-life case for the readers to respond and consider what they would do if they were in this situation. Access this special feature using the URL: *www.smmmag.com/what.htm*

   Study the situation as described and write a short paper summarizing: (a) what has happened? (b) what would you do? and (c) why you feel the selected response is proper. Check your answer with the correct answer in the following month's issue.

6. **Self-Management.** The following series of questions is designed to assess the needs that are important to you. There are no right or wrong answers. The best response to any item is simply the one that best reflects your feelings—either as you have experienced them or as you anticipate that you would experience them—in a work situation. Respond to the 20 statements by indicating the degree to which each is true for you. Use the following key and circle the number that best indicates how true and accurate the statement is.

     1 = Not true and accurate.
     2 = Slightly true and accurate.
     3 = Partly true and accurate.
     4 = Mostly true and accurate.
     5 = Completely true.

1. I believe that the real rewards for working are good pay, working conditions, and the like.   1 2 3 4 5

2. The most important thing to me in evaluating a job is whether it gives me job security and employee benefits.   1 2 3 4 5

3. I would not want a job in which I had no co-workers to talk to and share work stories with.   1 2 3 4 5

4. I want a job that allows rapid advancement based on my
own achievements.   1   2   3   4   5

5. Searching for what will make me happy is most important
in my life.   1   2   3   4   5

6. Working conditions (office space, equipment, and basic physical
necessities) are important to me.   1   2   3   4   5

7. I would not want a job if the equipment was poor or I was without
adequate protection against layoffs.   1   2   3   4   5

8. Whether the people I was going to work with were compatible
would affect my decision about whether or not to take a promotion.   1   2   3   4   5

9. A job should offer tangible rewards and recognition for a person's
performance.   1   2   3   4   5

10. I want a job that is challenging and stimulating and has
meaningful activities.   1   2   3   4   5

11. If I took a job in which there were strong pressures to rush and
little time for lunch, coffee breaks, and the like, my motivation
would suffer.   1   2   3   4   5

12. My motivation would suffer if my fellow employees were
unfriendly or held grudges toward me.   1   2   3   4   5

13. Being a valued member of the team and enjoying the social
aspects of work are important to me.   1   2   3   4   5

14. I'm likely to work hardest in a situation that offers tangible
rewards and recognition for performance.   1   2   3   4   5

15. Going as far as I can, using my skills and capabilities, and
exploring new ideas are what really drive me.   1   2   3   4   5

16. An important factor for me is that my job pays well enough to
satisfy the needs of my family and me.   1   2   3   4   5

17. Fringe benefits, such as hospitalization insurance, retirement plans,
and dental programs, are important to me.   1   2   3   4   5

18. I would likely work hardest in a job where a group of employees
discuss and plan their work as a team.   1   2   3   4   5

19. My accomplishments give me an important sense of self-respect.   1   2   3   4   5

20. I would work the hardest in a job where I could see the returns
of my work from the standpoint of personal interest and growth.   1   2   3   4   5

Scoring directions: In the following list, insert the number you circled for each of the 20 statements. Then add each column to get your summary scores.

	1. _____	2. _____	3. _____	4. _____	5. _____
	6. _____	7. _____	8. _____	9. _____	10. _____
	11. _____	12. _____	13. _____	14. _____	15. _____
	16. _____	17. _____	18. _____	19. _____	20. _____
Totals:	_____	_____	_____	_____	_____
Motives:	Basic Creature Comfort	Safety and Security	Social or Affiliation	Self-Esteem	Self-Actualization

Interpretation: For each of the five motives, there is a minimum of 4 and a maximum of 20 points. Scores of 18 or more are quite high and suggest that the motives measured by that scale are very important to you. Scores from 13 to 17 suggest that the motives measured are moderately important to you. Scores from 9 to 12 suggest that the motives are not especially important to you. Scores below 9 are quite low and suggest that the motives measured are not at all important to you.

IN-CLASS EXERCISES

13-1: "Motivation and Role Conflict"*

Jonathan MacMillan has worked as a rep for Crawford Industrial Products for almost three years. His first year he made 110 percent of quota, generating $750,000 in revenues. In year two he hit 120 percent of quota, a hefty $1.25 million. To do this, he worked 14-hour days during the week prospecting and meeting with customers, plus whatever weekend time was necessary to complete reports and write proposals. Keeping this pace, MacMillan was on target to reach this year's quota as well—that is, until he became a first-time father two months ago. He's now working only 50 to 60 hour weeks. The result is, of course, fewer sales.

Michael Gates, Crawford's national sales manager, is worried. Crawford is introducing three new products next month and has ambitious growth plans. Gates also had hoped to make MacMillan a member of the management team. But when talking casually with him about goals and future plans, Gates discovered that MacMillan is not interested in becoming a manager because at Crawford the big money is in sales. Even working fewer hours, MacMillan is earning a fat paycheck.

Gates is at a loss. He wants to get back the fiery, hard-charging MacMillan he hired, but he's not sure how.

Questions:

1. How can Gates remotivate MacMillan?
   - Does MacMillan need additional training, a new compensation program, more discipline, more recognition, etc.?
2. How should a manager deal with family role conflict?
   - Role conflict for someone's time is very common in sales. The family wants more of the salesperson's time. The manager wants more of the salesperson's time. Is there an answer to this conflict?
3. Is MacMillan now a slacker?
   - MacMillan is now only willing to work 50 hours a week and is not interested in changing. Is he going to be dead weight from now on? Is he worth the sales manager's time and effort if he won't work more than 55 hours per week? Should he be reprimanded?
4. How can Gates make MacMillan more efficient?
   - Productivity is often linked to efficiency. MacMillan has a history of productivity based on long hours. He may be very deficient in efficiency. How can Gates help MacMillan become more efficient (automation, staff support, etc.)?
5. Why is Gates so worried about MacMillan's lack of interest in management? Is this important?

13-2: "Sales and the Web"*

Countless Products Inc., a distributor of premiums and novelty items, recently began accepting orders via its Web site. The site features the company's entire product catalog and price list, including a volume discount calculator. Companies that order on-line are sent an invoice while their order is being processed. In the three months that on-line ordering has been available, more than 100 customers have used it.

Although the customers are happy with the site, Countless's 25 reps are not. Reps earn commission on orders from current customers processed via the Web, but orders from new

---

* Contributed by Raymond Rody, Loyola Marymount University.

customers have no commission. Reps feel that this cheats them out of commissions and sets up the Web site as competition to their efforts. The company president, Lynn Torre, feels that the Web is like another rep: The accounts that the site "sells" belong to it.

Caught in the middle is Brett Saber, Countless's vice president of sales. The reps are spending so much time complaining to him (and to each other) about the Web, that productivity and morale are suffering. The reps want commissions on sales made via the Web, period. A few reps have hinted at leaving if the situation persists.

Questions:

1. Is the Web an unfair competitor at Countless?
2. Can a compromise be reached?
3. How should the Web-based order entry system be positioned?
4. What changes can be made to the Web system to make it more salesperson friendly?

CASE 13-1   **HONGKONG BANK OF CANADA**

"We believe that it will be a very stimulating and productive meeting," said David Bond, Vice-President, Marketing and Public Affairs for the Hongkong Bank of Canada. It was mid-August 1991, and he was talking about a branch managers' meeting that would run early the following month. "Senior management decided in May that we would have a two-day branch managers' meeting and that it would be held at Whistler. They asked Steve Tait, our Vice-President, Human Resources, Jim Francis, our Assistant Vice-President, Training & Development, and myself to put together the meeting program. The 100-plus people that will be there include about 35 managers of the former Lloyds branches, the bank that we purchased and took over operations last year. The program that we have put together for them is very different from previous branch managers' meetings in that we're going to use it as the kickoff of a year-long contest."

THE HONGKONG BANK OF CANADA

In 1981, the Canadian federal government passed legislation which permitted banks with foreign ownership to operate in Canada. Several dozen banks started up operations in Canada. One of them was the Hongkong and Shanghai Banking Corporation (HSBC), headquartered in Hong Kong, which established a wholly owned subsidiary called the Hongkong Bank of Canada. The head office was established in Vancouver and operations started with one branch in that city in July 1981. The Hongkong Bank was one of the few new foreign-owned banks to open as a full-service bank, i.e., a bank that generated deposits and made loans to individuals as well as to organizations. This was in contrast to the vast majority of the foreign banks, who borrowed their loan funds from other financial organizations and confined their loan activities to commercial organizations. Management of the Hongkong Bank considered their full-service orientation as a natural extension of the operational philosophy of their HSBC parent.

Over the years the bank grew through a combination of additional business in existing branches, the opening of new branches, and an aggressive acquisition strategy. In 1985, they bought the Winnipeg and Halifax sites of the foundering Canadian Commercial Bank. The follow-

This case was prepared by Professor John Kennedy solely to provide material for class discussion. The author does not intend to illustrate either effective or ineffective handling of a managerial situation. The author may have disguised certain names and other identifying information to protect confidentiality. Ivey Management Services prohibits any form of reproduction, storage, or transmittal without its written permission. This material is not covered under authorization from CanCopy or any reproduction rights organization. To order copies or request permission to reproduce materials contact Ivey Publishing, Ivey Management Services c/o Richard Ivey School of Business, The University of Western Ontario, London, Ontario, Canada, N6A 3K7; phone (519) 661-3882; fax (519) 661-3882; e-mail cases@ivey.uwo.ca. Copyright © 1993 The University of Western Ontario. One time permission to reproduce granted by Ivey Management Services on November 3, 1999.

ing year they bought the financially troubled Bank of British Columbia, which had extensive retail operations in 38 branches in British Columbia and two in Alberta.[1] In 1988, the bank bought the Midland Bank of Canada which had operated primarily in the corporate lending market. This was followed in 1990 by the purchase of Lloyds Bank Canada with its 52 branches, most of which were in eastern Canada. Lloyds Bank Canada was the outcome of the Lloyds Bank of England purchase of the Continental Bank of Canada in 1986. There was speculation in the industry at the time of purchase that Lloyds had overpaid to get into the Canadian market. There was later talk that the English parent had never really "bought in" to the Canadian operation after its early discovery that it could make a far better return by investing incremental capital in England than it could in investing comparable funds in its Canadian subsidiary.

The Lloyds Bank Canada that Hongkong purchased was focused on the corporate market. The very limited amount of attention to the retail market was devoted exclusively to high net worth individuals. Small net worth customers were actively discouraged. Low Lloyds earnings in recent years had led to drastic reductions in the bank's renovations budget. As a result, many of the branch physical facilities that the Hongkong Bank acquired were worn and run down. Further, the physical layout in most branches was not appropriate for the Hongkong Bank's emphasis on retail banking. Finally, Lloyds Bank, by Hongkong Bank standards, was overstaffed. This resulted in the departure, in the months following the takeover, of close to 20% of the 1,500 former Lloyds employees.

The acquisition triggered a change in the operating structure of the Hongkong Bank. Four regions were created, Quebec and Atlantic Provinces, Ontario, Western, and B.C., with a senior vice president appointed to head each. One of the major tasks associated with bringing the Lloyds operations into the Hongkong Bank was the integration of computer systems. While substantial work had been accomplished since the merger, it was not expected that the system would be complete until October 1991.

THE 1990 BRANCH MANAGERS' MEETING

The 1990 branch managers' meeting was held in August, just a few months after the acquisition of

Lloyds Bank Canada. Thus, it was really the first large meeting of personnel of the two organizations. The day and a half meeting was held in facilities on the University of British Columbia campus, and started with a Thursday evening reception. "The Lloyds folks were understandably a bit wary to begin with," said a Hongkong Bank manager who had been an employee of the Bank of British Columbia at the time it was acquired by the Hongkong Bank. "But the fact that there was even a reception gave a message that most outsiders wouldn't think about. If you are part of a bank organization that is not doing too well financially, one of the first things to go is expenditure on what you might call employee social activities. I can remember back to the dark days of the Bank of BC, where you considered asking employees to pay for their own coffee during a meeting break."

The remainder of the meeting was virtually all one-way communication.

- Here are the Bank's products.
- Here is the way in which they are to be sold.
- Here is the operating system in which you are or will be operating.

"I think it was pretty apparent to everyone at the meeting," recalled another manager originally with the Bank of British Columbia, "that there was going to have to be a lot of work done on systems and organizational integration before we could really get down to the job of focused implementation across the organization."

PLANNING FOR THE 1991 BRANCH MANAGERS' MEETING

"When the three of us first got together," said David Bond, "we got talking about our personal experiences with managers' meetings, both here and in other organizations we had worked in. We concluded that they had been, for the most part, one-way communications by head office people designed to provide information and/or motivate the participants, together with some time for leisure and social activities. But when the meeting was over, that was it until the next one. No specific goals. No followup. No nothing! We decided that we wanted to break out of that pattern.

"From there, we spent some time thinking about the objectives we should set for the meeting. After a fair amount of discussion, we concluded that there should be three of them:

- "Stimulate growth of core deposits.

---

[1] In 1991, most of the British Columbia branches were still operating with signage that read "Bank of British Columbia" in large letters, followed underneath in smaller letters by the words "A Division of the Hongkong Bank of Canada."

- "Try to build some system to put together the good retailers in our organization with people that don't have those retail skills and abilities.
- "Integrate the Lloyds people into our value system, which is to treat every customer who walks in the door as if they are the most important person on earth.

"It was out of those three objectives that the idea of a contest evolved."

The contest concept and meeting program were fleshed out in a series of meetings which followed.

The Contest

The decision was made that the contest would focus on the growth of core deposits for the one-year period starting September 1, 1991. Core deposits were defined as personal GICs, RRSPs, demand deposits, and time deposits. Extensive discussion went into the development of the contest rules, which are given in Exhibit 1. A rule was developed to break a tie should one occur.

The Teams

After some discussion, the decision was reached to have five teams. Steve Tait, together with the bank's marketing department, assumed responsibility for putting the teams together, within the criteria that teams should be the same size, represent all regions, contain a mix of pretakover Hongkong branches and Lloyds branches, and be balanced in terms of size of existing personal core deposits, percentage growth over the previous year, and potential for growth over the next year. Steve went through a series of iterations in which he put teams together, shopped them around senior management asking for input as to team equivalence, and then made adjustments. The result of this process was the five teams outlined in Exhibit 2.

The Prize

Each branch manager of the winning team, together with a guest, would receive free round trip passage, five nights' accommodation, and a celebratory dinner in Hawaii in October 1992. Two business meetings would be held during the five-day period. Rules were developed to define manager eligibility.

The Meeting Program

"Putting the program together was a lot of fun," said Jim Francis. "We worked hard to get a sequence and mix of activities that would be most effective in development of the team spirit that is necessary not only for the contest but for the kind of organization we want to be. We concluded as well that the presentation of the meeting agenda should be a reflection of our operating style. Finally, we decided that we wanted to put a name on the event that described what we were trying to accomplish. We combined the ideas of the Whistler mountain resort where the conference was going to be, Diamond Head in Hawaii where the contest winners will stay, together with the meeting and contest objectives, to get the meeting title and theme, 'Peak Performance.'"

Arrangements had already been completed to provide each branch manager at the end of the meeting with a framed custom print of Whistler created by a well-known B.C. artist. The meeting schedule appears as Exhibit 3. This schedule had already been distributed to the meeting participants. The titles of the individuals named in the meeting agenda are given in Exhibit 4. While they were not explicitly identified on the schedule, two activities should be highlighted. The first of these would occur early on the morning of September 6. People were to meet in the hotel lobby as teams for the first time, and take a cable car up the mountain to a restaurant for breakfast. There, if the weather cooperated, everyone would be able to see the sun rise over Whistler mountain. Second, part of the Friday afternoon team activities would be devoted to competition on Whistler streets in a number of races, including a Chuckwagon Race in which the wagon would be a child's wagon.

Final Details

"To get the most out of the meeting, the branch managers will have to understand that they have to get actively involved in it," said David Bond. "At the same time, the head office participants in the Saturday morning sessions must understand that they have a specific role to play in those sessions. Therefore, we've put together two sets of instructions. The one for the participants[2] will be given out when the contest is introduced on the Friday[3] morning. The one for the head office people[4] has already gone out."

---

[2] See Exhibit 5.
[3] Friday, September 6.
[4] See Exhibit 6.

EXHIBIT 1   Core Deposit Campaign—Contest Rules

(1) The Bank's overall deposit target as defined by the 1992 business plan must be met in order for an overall award to be triggered.

(2) There must be a positive gain in core deposits by a branch on the winning team to be eligible to accompany the winning team to Hawaii.

(3) A Branch Manager on the winning team must be an employee in good standing at the time of the award allocation to be eligible.

(4) In the event a Manager is transferred from one branch to another and that branch is not within the same group but the original branch is among the winning teams, then if the Manager had been at the branch for the majority of the year and had accounted for a majority of the deposit growth, he or she will go on the trip. Otherwise, the new Manager will go.

(5) With the exception of St. Laurent, new branches which open during the campaign will not be included in the contest. Appropriate adjustments will be made to the deposit balances of existing branches which lose core deposits through transfer to a new branch during the first three months of operation.

(6) Points will be awarded as follows:

    (A) Team standing following "initiatives" at Branch Managers' Conference:

         1st–2.5 Pts
         2nd–2.0 Pts
         3rd–1.5 Pts
         4th–1.0 Pt
         5th–0.5 Pt

    (B) Greatest absolute dollar increase in core deposits:

         1st–10 Pts
         2nd–8 Pts
         3rd–6 Pts
         4th–4 Pts
         5th–2 Pts

    (C) Greatest percentage increase in core deposits:

         1st–5 Pts
         2nd–4 Pts
         3rd–3 Pts
         4th–2 Pts
         5th–1 Pt

    (D) Best all-around (i.e., most balanced) results (i.e., smallest percentage difference between largest percentage increase and smallest percentage increase on a team):

         1st–10 Pts
         2nd–8 Pts
         3rd–6 Pts
         4th–4 Pts
         5th–2 Pts

    (E) Largest percentage increase in number of new retail deposit accounts:

         1st–5 Pts
         2nd–4 Pts
         3rd–3 Pts
         4th–2 Pts
         5th–1 Pt

    (F) Highest absolute increase in net new retail deposit accounts (i.e., new accounts less closed accounts):

         1st–5 Pts
         2nd–4 Pts
         3rd–3 Pts
         4th–2 Pts
         5th–1 Pt

Winning = Highest Points of Sum of
A + B + C + D + E + F

(7) In cases of dispute, or extenuating circumstances, the judgment of the COO will govern.

EXHIBIT 2 Groups for Core Deposit Campaign

Group 1			Group 2			Group 3		
City/Branch	Prov	Origin	City/Branch	Prov	Origin	City/Branch	Prov	Origin
Brampton	Ont	LBC	Abbotsford	BC	BBC	Vancouver Broadway & Ash	BC	BBC
Calgary South	Alta	LBC	Calgary 5th Ave.	Alta	LBC	Campbell River	BC	BBC
Cranbrock	BC	BBC	Vancouver Cambie & 42nd	BC	HKBC	Chicoutimi	Que	LBC
Edmonton 101st Street	Alta	LBC	Vancouver Denman Street	BC	BBC	Edmonton Pacific Rim Mall	Alta	HKBC
Vancouver Georgia & Thurlow	BC	LBC	Vancouver Dundas Street	BC	HKBC	Halifax	NS	CCB
Hamilton	Ont	LBC	Edmonton Jasper Ave.	Alta	BBC	Vancouver Kingsway & Senlac	BC	BBC
Vancouver Hastings & Burrard	BC	BBC	Fredericton	NB	LBC	Markham	Ont	LBC
Lasalle	Que	LBC	Granby	QUE	LBC	Mississauga Golden Plaza	Ont	HKBC
Vancouver Lougheed & North Road	BC	BBC	Vancouver Granville & 12th	BC	BBC	Mississauga	Ont	LBC
Vancouver Main & Pender	BC	HKBC	Vancouver Hastings & Penticton	BC	BBC	Montreal Place Air Canada	Que	LBC
Montreal Place Victoria	Que	HKBC	Kelowna Richter Street	BC	LBC	Oakville	Ont	LBC
Montreal Rene Levesque	Que	HKBC	Vancouver Kingsway & Royal Oak	BC	BBC	Saint John	NB	LBC
Nanaimo	BC	BBC	Laval	Que	LBC	Saskatoon	Sask	HKBC
Ottawa	Ont	LBC	Red Deer	Alta	LBC	Sault Ste. Marie	Ont	LBC
Regina	Sask	LBC	Richmond Parker Place	BC	LBC	Scarborough Dragon Centre	Ont	HKBC
Richmond No. 3 & Park	BC	BBC	St. Catherines	Ont	LBC	Vancouver Sixth & Fifth	BC	BBC
Spadina	Ont	HKBC	Vernon	BC	BBC	Vancouver Main	BC	BBC
St. John's	Nfld	LBC	Victoria Fort Street	BC	BBC	Victoria 731 Fort Street	BC	HKBC
Surrey	BC	BBC	West Vancouver	BC	BBC	Victoria Douglas & Hillside	BC	BBC
Vancouver Tenth & Sasamat	BC	BBC	Windsor	Ont	LBC	Whitby	Ont	LBC
Trois-Rivieres	Que	LBC				White Rock	BC	BBC

(continued)

EXHIBIT 2 (continued)

Group 4 City/Branch	Prov	Origin	Group 5 City/Branch	Prov	Origin
Barrie	Ont	LBC	Calgary 8th Ave.	Alta	BBC
Chilliwack	BC	BBC	Calgary Good Fortune Plaza	Alta	HKBC
Edmonton South	Alta	LBC	Vancouver Columbia St.	BC	BBC
Vancouver Fraser & 48th	BC	BBC	Delta	BC	BBC
Haney	BC	BBC	Kelowna Bernard Ave.	BC	LBC
Vancouver Hastings & Gilmore	BC	BBC	Kingston	Ont	LBC
Kamloops	BC	BBC	Kitchener	Ont	LBC
Vancouver Kerrisdale	BC	BBC	Lethbridge	Alta	LBC
Langley	BC	BBC	Vancouver Main & Keefer	BC	BBC
London	Ont	LBC	Mississauga Chinese Cultural Centre	Ont	HKBC
Longueuil	Que	LBC	Mississauga North	Ont	LBC
Medicine Hat	Alta	LBC	North Vancouver	BC	BBC
Prince George	BC	BBC	Penticton	BC	BBC
Richmond Johnson Centre	BC	HKBC	Port Coquitlam	BC	LBC
Scarborough Eglinton Ave.	Ont	LBC	Saint Leonard	Que	LBC
Scarborough Milliken Square	Ont	HKBC	Sherbrooke	Que	LBC
Ste-Foy	Que	LBC	St. Laurent	Que	HKBC
Thunder Bay	Ont	LBC	Toronto Skyway Park	Ont	LBC
Timmins	Ont	LBC	Victoria Douglas & Johnson	BC	BBC
Toronto 70 York Street	Ont	HKBC	Willowdale	Ont	HKBC
			Winnipeg	Man	CCB

Legend:
HKBC = HongKong Bank of Canada
LBC = Lloyds Bank of Canada
CCB = Canadian Commercial Bank
BBC = Bank of British Columbia

**Hongkong Bank of Canada
1991 Managers' Conference**

September 5th

3:00 PM SHARP	Bus To Whistler Departs Vancouver	Head Office
6:00 - 7:00 PM	Reception	Ballroom
7:00 - 9:00 PM	Dinner	Ballroom
9:00 - 10:00 PM	Regional Meetings	TBA

September 6th

7:00 AM SHARP	1st Group Initiative	Lobby
7:30 - 8:30 AM	Breakfast	TBA
8:30 - 8:45 AM	Official Opening - Chris Crook	"
8:45 - 9:30 AM	The Opportunity - Clyde Ostler	"
9:30 - 9:40 AM	"A Moment With Mould"	"
9:40 - 10:00 AM	The Challenge - Chris Crook	"
10:00 - 11:00 AM	Team Activity - Name That Team	"
11:00 - 11:45 AM	Service Is The Key - Bill Dalton	"
11:45 - 12:15 PM	2nd Group Initiative	"
12:15 - 1:45 PM	Lunch - Hosted by Bob Hemond	Cheakmus
1:45 - 2:00 PM	"Another Moment With Mould"	Ballroom
2:00 - 2:45 PM	Team Activity - Brainstorming	"
2:45 - 3:15 PM	Merchandising Our Way - Chris Crook	"
3:15 - 5:00 PM	Team Activity - Strategy	Breakouts
5:00 - 5:30 PM	Free Time	Optional
5:30 - 6:00 PM	Reception	Ballroom
6:00 - 8:30 PM	BBQ - Hosted by John Ranaldi	"
8:30 - 9:00 PM	Team Activity - Presentations	"

EXHIBIT 3   Hongkong Bank of Canada 1991 Managers Conference

Conference Cont'd

September 7th

	Red	Blue	Yellow	Green	Pink	
7:15 - 8:20 AM	Breakfast - Hosted by Dewar Harper					Cheakmus
8:20 - 8:30 AM	"John Goes On!"					•
	Red	**Blue**	**Yellow**	**Green**	**Pink**	
	Diamond Head	Black Tusk	Board Room	Sutcliffe A	Sutcliffe B	Meeting Rooms
8:30 - 9:05 AM	CEO & COO	Back At The Branch	H.O. Panel	Local Marketing	Credit Connection	•
9:05 - 9:40 AM	Back At The Branch	H.O. Panel	Local Marketing	Credit Connection	CEO & COO	•
9:40 - 10:15 AM	H.O. Panel	Local Marketing	Credit Connection	CEO & COO	Back At The Branch	•
10:15 - 10:50 AM	Corporate Shuffle					TBA
10:50 - 11:25 AM	Local Marketing	Credit Connection	CEO & COO	Back At The Branch	H.O. Panel	Meeting Rooms
11:25 - 12:00 PM	Credit Connection	CEO & COO	Back At The Branch	H.O. Panel	Local Marketing	•
12:00 - 1:30 PM	Lunch - Hosted by Martin Glynn & Bruna Giacomazzi					Cheakmus
1:30 - 1:40 PM	"The Last Mouldy Moments"					Ballroom
1:40 - 2:30 PM	The Strategic Plan - Jim Cleave					•
2:30 - 3:15 PM	Team Activity - Strategic Plan					•
3:15 - 4:00 PM	Questions to Senior Executive					•
4:00 - 4:30 PM	Wrap-up and Farewell					•

EXHIBIT 3   **(Continued)**

EXHIBIT 4   Titles of Individuals Named in the Meeting Schedule

Name	Title
Chris Crook	Executive Vice President, Banking
Clyde Osler	A senior officer with the Wells Fargo Bank
John Mould	Sr. Vice President & Controller
Bill Dalton	Chief Operating Officer
Bob Hemond	Sr. Vice President, Quebec & Atlantic Provinces Region
John Ranaldi	Sr. Vice President, Western Region
Dewar Harper	Sr. Vice President, Ontario Region
Martin Glynn	Sr. Vice President, BC Region
Bruna Giacomazzi	Sr. Vice President, Special Credit
Jim Cleave	Chief Executive Officer

MEMBERS OF THE SATURDAY MORNING PANELS

Panel Name	Panel Member	Title
CEO & COO	Jim Cleave and Bill Dalton	
H.O. Panel	Steve Tait	VP Human Resources
	Jim Mayhew	AVP Human Resources
	Brian Salvador	AVP Compensation & Benefits
Local Marketing	Al Cummings	AVP Marketing
Credit Connection	Steve Wilson	VP Consumer Credit
	Bert McPhee	Sr. Vice President, Credit
Back at the Branch	Phil Scott	President, Scott Consulting Inc.

EXHIBIT 5   Instructions to the Branch Manager Participants

INSTRUCTIONS FOR FRIDAY AFTERNOON

You have a number of tasks to accomplish in a relatively limited time period.

You will be expected to present at dinner tonight a logo for your team and to have selected a theme song with appropriate words. The logos and the songs will be judged by the Fabulous Four* as to their appropriateness, suitability to the name chosen, ingenuity, originality, and presentation. The results of the judging will count toward the trip to Hawaii.

You will need to prepare yourselves to gain maximum benefit from tomorrow morning's activities. To do that you may wish to spend some time understanding the scope of the challenge that you face. What are the characteristics of the group? Just how daunting is the task ahead? What should be your major objectives and how do you plan to accomplish them? What are the strengths within the group and how can you capitalize upon them?

How will you communicate with each other and provide support to each other? The Bank will not pay for conference calls or travel, so what alternatives are available and how do they get organized and done?

Tomorrow morning between 8:30 and 12 noon you will have the opportunity to meet with five different groups or individuals. Each session is designed to provide you with some "tools" which you individually and as a team can use to help you get to Diamond Head. Each session has provided an outline of what they plan to discuss with you. You need to make sure that you gain the maximum benefit from these sessions with your group. What are the most important things for you to know with respect to each area? How will you organize to make sure that you accomplish your objectives for each of these consultative sessions?

* The "Fabulous Four" were the four senior officers of the bank:
James H. Cleave; President and Chief Executive Officer
William R. P. Dalton; Executive Director and Chief Operating Officer
Maurice R. Mourton; Executive Vice-President, Administration
Chris J. Cook; Executive Vice-President, Banking

EXHIBIT 6   Instructions to the Session Participants on Saturday Morning

The five teams will be meeting with five different groups for 30 minutes at a time. The purpose of these meetings is to give the individual teams information regarding the "tools" that they will be provided with during the year as they strive to win the trip to Diamond Head.

What you are asked to do is to provide, on one page maximum, an outline of the most salient information that you would be willing to provide to the group during your session. For example, the Marketing/Public Affairs group will be providing information on the detailed marketing campaigns planned for the year, and the type of support that will be provided for each branch.

Each group should be given the opportunity to ask you questions, and provide you feedback on what is of concern to them. Thus, any presentation should not be more than 15 minutes. If you wish, *at the conclusion of the session,* you can provide each manager with take-away material.

Thus, the challenge for the individual teams is to make sure that they have organized themselves to gain the maximum benefit from the opportunity of meeting with you. Your challenge is to present material in an interesting, informative, and inviting manner. Since the time is limited, you will be forced to concentrate on only the most essential matters. The draft of your material should be sent to Elaine Ranger no later than the 15th of August so that it can be reproduced and included in the Manager's packages.

CASE 13-2   GENERAL ELECTRIC APPLIANCES

*L*arry Barr had recently been promoted to the position of District Sales Manager (B.C.) for G.E. Appliances, a division of Canadian Appliance Manufacturing Co. Ltd. (CAMCO). One of his more important duties in that position was the allocation of his district's sales quota among his five salespeople. Barr received his quota for next year in October of the previous year. His immediate task was to determine an equitable allocation of that quota. This was important because the company's incentive pay plan was based on the salespeople's attainment of quota. A portion of Barr's remuneration was also based on the degree to which his sales force met their quotas.

Barr graduated from the University of British Columbia with the degree of Bachelor of Commerce. He was immediately hired as a product manager for a mining equipment manufacturing firm because of his summer job experience with that firm. Three years later he joined Canadian General Electric (C.G.E.) in Montreal as a product manager for refrigerators. There he was responsible for creating and merchandising a product line, as well as developing product and marketing plans. Two years later he was transferred to Coburg, Ontario, as a sales manager for industrial plastics. The next year he became Administrative Manager (Western Region) and when the position of District Sales Manager became available, Barr was promoted to it. There his duties included development of sales strategies, supervision of salespeople, and budgeting.

BACKGROUND

Canadian Appliance Manufacturing Co. Ltd. (CAMCO) was created under the joint ownership of Canadian General Electric Ltd. and General Steel Wares Ltd. (G.S.W.). CAMCO then purchased the production facilities of Westinghouse Canada Ltd. Under the purchase agreement the Westinghouse brand name was transferred to White Consolidated Industries Ltd., where it became White-Westinghouse. Appliances manufactured by CAMCO in the former Westinghouse plant were branded Hotpoint.

The G.E., G.S.W., and Hotpoint major appliance plants became divisions of CAMCO. These divisions operated independently and had their own separate management staff, although they were all ultimately accountable to CAMCO management. The divisions competed for sales, although not directly, because they each produced product lines for different price segments (Exhibit 1).

COMPETITION

Competition in the appliance industry was vigorous. CAMCO was the largest firm in the industry, with approximately 45 percent market share, split between G.E., G.S.W. (Moffatt & McClary brands), and Hotpoint. The following three firms each had 10–15 percent market shares: Inglis (washers and dryers only), W.C.I. (makers of White-Westinghouse, Kelvinator, and Gibson), and Admiral. These firms also produced appliances under department store brand names such as Viking, Baycrest, and Kenmore, which accounted for an additional 15 percent of the market. The remainder of the market was divided among brands such as Maytag, Roper Dishwasher, Gurney, Tappan, and Danby.

G.E. marketed a full major appliance product line, including refrigerators, ranges, washers, dryers, dishwashers, and television sets. G.E. appliances generally had many features and were priced at the upper end of the price range. Their major competition came from Maytag and Westinghouse.

THE BUDGETING PROCESS

G.E. Appliances was one of the most advanced firms in the consumer goods industry in terms of sales budgeting. Budgeting received careful analysis at all levels of management.

The budgetary process began in June of each year. The management of G.E. Appliances division assessed the economic outlook, growth trends in the industry, competitive activity, population growth, and so forth in order to determine a reasonable sales target for the next

---

This case was prepared by Richard W. Pollay, John D. Claxton, and Rick Jenkner. Copyright © by Richard W. Pollay, John D. Claxton, and Rick Jenkner. Reproduced by permission.

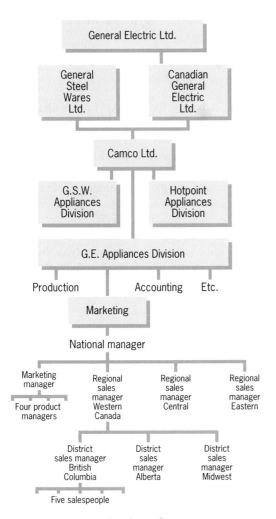

EXHIBIT 1 Organization Chart

year. The president of CAMCO received this estimate, checked and revised it as necessary, and submitted it to the president of G.E. Canada. Final authorization rested with G.E. Ltd., which had a definite minimum growth target for the G.E. branch of CAMCO. G.E. Appliances was considered an "invest and grow" division, which meant that it was expected to produce a healthy sales growth each year, regardless of the state of the economy. As Barr observed. "This is difficult, but meeting challenges is the job of management."

The approved budget was expressed as a desired percentage increase in sales. Once the figure had been decided, it was not subject to change. The quota was communicated back through G.E. Canada Ltd., CAMCO, and G.E. Appliances, where it was available to the District Sales Managers in October. Each district was then required to meet an overall growth figure

(quota) but each sales territory was not automatically expected to achieve that same growth. Barr was required to assess the situation in each territory, determine where growth potential was highest, and allocate his quota accordingly.

THE SALES INCENTIVE PLAN

The sales incentive plan was a critical part of General Electric's sales force plan and an important consideration in the quota allocation of Barr. Each salesperson had a portion of earnings dependent upon performance with respect to quota. Also, Barr was awarded a bonus based on the sales performance of his district, making it advantageous to Barr and good for staff morale for all his salespeople to attain their quotas.

The sales force incentive plan was relatively simple. A bonus system is fairly typical for salespeople in any field. With G.E., each salesperson agreed to a basic salary figure called "planned earnings." The planned salary varied according to experience, education, past performance, and competitive salaries. A salesperson was paid 75 percent of planned earnings on a guaranteed regular basis. The remaining 25 percent of salary was at risk, dependent upon the person's sales record. There was also the possibility of earning substantially more money by selling more than quota (Exhibit 2).

The bonus was awarded such that total salary (base plus bonus) equaled planned earnings when the quota was just met. The greatest increase in bonus came between 101 and 110 percent of quota. The bonus was paid quarterly on the cumulative total quota. A holdback system ensured that a salesperson was never required to pay back a previously earned bonus by reason of a poor quarter. Because of this system, it was critical that each salesperson's quota be fair in relation to those of the other salespeople. Nothing was worse for morale than one person earning large bonuses while the others struggled.

Quota attainment was not the sole basis for evaluating the salespeople. They were required to fulfill a wide range of duties including service, franchising of new dealers, maintaining good relations with dealers, and maintaining a balance of sales among the different product lines. Because the bonus system was based on sales only, Barr had to ensure that the salespeople did not neglect their other duties.

A formal salary review was held each year for each salesperson. However, Barr preferred to give his salespeople continuous feedback on their performances.

EXHIBIT 2   Sales Incentive Earnings Schedule: Major Appliances and Home Entertainment Products

Sales Quota Realization Percent	Incentive Percent of Base Salary Total	Sales Quota Realization Percent	Incentive Percemt of Base Salary Total
70	0	106	37.00
71	0.75	107	39.00
72	1.50	108	41.00
73	2.25	109	43.00
74	3.00	110	45.00
75	3.75	111	46.00
76	4.50	112	47.00
77	5.25	113	48.00
78	6.00	114	49.00
79	6.75	115	50.00
80	7.50	116	51.00
81	8.25	117	52.00
82	9.00	118	53.00
83	9.75	119	54.00
84	10.50	120	55.00
85	11.25	121	56.00
86	12.00	122	57.00
87	12.75	123	58.00
88	13.50	124	59.00
89	14.25	125	60.00
90	15.00	126	61.00
91	16.00	127	62.00
92	17.00	128	63.00
93	18.00	129	64.00
94	19.00	130	65.00
95	20.00	131	66.00
96	21.00	132	67.00
97	22.00	133	68.00
98	23.00	134	69.00
99	24.00	135	70.00
100	25.00	136	71.00
101	27.00	137	72.00
102	29.00	138	73.00
103	31.00	139	74.00
104	33.00	140	75.00
105	35.00		

Through human relations skills he hoped to avoid problems which could lead to dismissal of a salesperson and loss of sales for the company.

Barr's incentive bonus plan was more complex than the salespeople's. He was awarded a maximum of 75 annual bonus points broken down as follows: market share, 15; total sales performance, 30; sales representative balance, 30. Each point had a specific money value. The system ensured that Barr allocated his quota carefully. For instance, if one quota was so difficult that the salesperson sold only 80 percent of it, while the other salespeople exceeded quota, Barr's bonus would be reduced, even if the overall area sales exceeded the quota (Exhibit 3).

QUOTA ALLOCATION

The total sales budget for G.E. Appliances division for next year was about $100 million, a 14 percent sales increase over the current year. Barr's share of the $33 million Western region quota was $13.3 million, also a 14 percent increase over the previous year. Barr had two weeks to allocate the quota among his five territories. He needed to consider factors such as historical allocation, economic outlook, dealer changes, personnel changes, untapped potential, new franchises or store openings, and buying group activity (volume purchases by associations of independent dealers).

SALES FORCE

There were five sales territories within British Columbia (Exhibit 4). Territories were determined on the basis of number of customers, sales volume of customers, geographic size, and experience of the sales person. Territories were altered periodically in order to deal with changed circumstances.

One territory was comprised entirely of contract customers. Contract sales were sales in bulk lots to builders and developers who used the appliances in housing units. Because the appliances were not resold at retail, G.E. took a lower profit margin on such sales.

G.E. Appliances recruited M.B.A. graduates for their sales force. They sought bright, educated people who were willing to relocate anywhere in Canada. The company intended that these people would ultimately be promoted to managerial positions. The company also hired experienced career salespeople in order to get a blend of experience in the sales force. However, the typical salesperson was under age 30, aggressive, and upwardly mobile. G.E.'s sales training program covered only product knowledge. It was not felt necessary to train recruits in sales techniques.

Allocation Procedure

At the time Barr assumed the job of D.S.M., he had a meeting with the former sales manager, Ken Philips. Philips described to Barr the method he had used in the past to allocate the quota. As Barr understood it, the procedure was as follows:

The quota was received in October in the form of a desired percentage sales increase. The first step was to project current sales to the end of the year. This gave a

EXHIBIT 3   Development of a Sales Commission Plan

A series of steps are required to establish the foundation upon which a sales commission plan can be built. These steps are as follows:

Determine Specific Sales Objectives of Positions to Be Included in Plan

For a sales commission plan to succeed, it must be designed to encourage the attainment of the business objectives of the component division. Before deciding on the dimensions of a commission plan, you have to decide on which of the following objectives are important.

1. Increase sales volume
2. Do an effective, balanced selling job in a variety of product lines
3. Improve market share
4. Reduce selling expense to sales ratios
5. Develop new accounts or territories
6. Introduce new products

Although it is probably neither desirable nor necessary to include all such objectives as specific measures of performance in the plan, they should be kept in mind, at least to the extent that the performance measures chosen for the plan are compatible with and do not work against the overall accomplishment of the component's business objectives.

Also, the *relative* current importance or ranking of these objectives will provide guidance in selecting the number and type of performance measures to be included in the plan.

Determine Quantitative Performance Measures to Be Used

Although it may be possible to include a number of measures in a particular plan, there is a drawback to using so many as to overly complicate it and fragment the impact of any one measure on the participants. A plan that is difficult to understand will lose a great deal of its motivating force, as well as being costly to administer properly.

For components that currently have a variable sales compensation plan(s) for their sales, a good starting point would be to consider the measures used in those plans. Although the measurements used for sales managers need not be identical, they should at least be compatible with those used to determine commissions.

However, keep in mind that a performance measure that may not be appropriate for individual salespeople may be a good one to apply to their manager. Measurements involving attainment of a share of a defined market, balanced selling for a variety of products, and control of district or region expenses might well fall into this category.

The accompanying table lists a variety of measurements that might be used to emphasize specific sales objectives. For most components, all or most of these objectives will be desirable to some extent. The point is to select those of greatest importance where it will be possible to establish measures of standard or normal performance for individuals, or at least small groups of individuals working as a team.

If more than one performance measurement is to be used, the relative weighting of each measurement must be determined. If a measure is to be effective, it must carry enough weight to have at least some noticeable effect on the commission earnings of an individual.

As a general guide, it would be unusual for a plan to include more than two or three quantitative measures with a minimum weighting of 15–20 percent of planned commissions for any one measurement.

Establish Commission Payment Schedule for Each Performance Measure

Determine Appropriate Range of Performance for Each Measurement. The performance range for a measurement defines the percent of standard performance (R%) at which commission earnings start to the point where they reach maximum.

The minimum point of the performance range for a given measurement should be set so that a majority of the participants can earn at least some incentive pay, and the maximum set at a point that is possible for some participants to obtain. These points will vary with the type of measure used and with the degree of predictability of individual budgets or other forms of measurement. In a period where overall performance is close to standard, 90 to 95 percent of the participants should fall within the performance range.

For the commission plan to be effective, most of the participants should be operating within the performance range most of the time. If a participant is either far below the minimum of this range or has reached the maximum, further improvement will not affect his commission earnings, and the plan will be largely inoperative as far as he is concerned.

Actual past experience of R%'s attained by participants is obviously the best indicator of what this range should be for each measure used. Lacking this, it is better to err on the side of having a wider range than one which proves to be too narrow. If some form of group measure is used, the variation from standard performance is likely to be less for the group in total than for individuals within it. For example, the performance range for total District performance would probably be narrower than the range established for individual sales within a District.

Determine Appropriate Reward: Risk Ratio for Commission Earnings. This refers to the relationship of commission earned at standard performance, to maximum commission earnings available under the plan. A plan that pays 10 percent of base salary for normal or standard performance and pays 30 percent as a maximum commission would have a 2:1 ratio. In other words, participants can earn twice as much (20 percent) for above-standard performance as they stand to lose for below-standard performance (10 percent).

Reward under a sales commission plan should be related to the effort involved to produce a given result. To adequately encourage above-standard results, the *reward:risk ratio* should generally be at least 2:1. The proper control of incentive plan payments lies in the proper setting of performance standards, not in the setting of a

EXHIBIT 3   (Continued)

low maximum payment for outstanding results that provides a minimum variation in individual earnings. Generally, a higher percentage of base salary should be paid for each 1%R above 100 percent than has been paid for each 1%R up to 100%R to reflect the relative difficulty involved in producing above-standard results.

Once the performance range and reward:risk ratios have been determined, the schedule of payments for each performance measure can then be calculated. This will show the percentage of the participant's base salary earned for various performance results (R%) from the point at which commissions start to maximum performance.

Example: For measurement paying 20 percent of salary for standard performance:

Percent of Base Salary Earned	
1% of base salary for each + 1%R	0%
	20%
1.33% of base salary for each + 1%R	60%

Percent of Sales Quota
80% or below
100% (standard performance)
130% or above

Prepare Draft of Sales Commission Plan

After completing the above steps, a draft of a sales commission plan should be prepared using the accompanying outline as a guide.

Keys to Effective Commission Plans

1. *Get the understanding and acceptance of the commission plan by the managers who will be involved in carrying it out.* They must be convinced of its effectiveness in order to properly explain and "sell" the plan to the salespeople.

2. *In turn, be sure the plan is presented clearly to the salespeople* so that they have a good understanding of how the plan will work. We find that good acceptance

of a sales commission plan on the part of salespeople correlates closely with how well they understood the plan and its effect on their compensation. The salespeople must be convinced that the measurements used are factors which they can control by their selling efforts.

3. *Be sure the measurements used in the commission plan encourage the salespeople to achieve the marketing goals of your operation.* For example, if sales volume is the only performance measure, the salespeople will concentrate on producing as much dollar volume as possible by spending most of their time on products with high volume potential. It will be difficult to get them to spend much time on introducing new products with relatively low volume, handling customer complaints, etc. Even though a good portion of their compensation may still be in salary, you can be sure they will wind up doing the things they feel will maximize their commission earnings.

4. One solution to maintaining good sales direction is to put at least a portion of the commission earnings in an "incentive pool" to be distributed by the sales manager according to his judgment. This "pool" can vary in size according to some qualitative measure of the sales group's performance, but the manager can set individual measurements for each salesperson and reward people according to how well they fulfill their goals.

5. If at all possible, you should test the plan for a period of time, perhaps in one or two sales areas or districts. To make it a real test, you should actually pay commission earnings to the participants, but the potential risk and rewards can be limited. No matter how well a plan has been conceived, not all the potential pitfalls will be apparent until you've actually operated the plan for a period of time. The test period is a relatively painless way to get some experience.

6. Finally, after the plan is in operation, take time to analyze the results. Is the plan accomplishing what you want it to do, both in terms of business results produced and in realistically compensating salespeople for their efforts?

Tailoring Commission Plan Measurements to Fit Component Objectives

Objectives	*Possible Plan Measurements*
1. Increase sales/order volume	Net sales billed or orders received against quota
2. Increase sales of particular lines	Sales against product line quotas with weighted sales credits on individual lines
3. Increase market share	Percent realization (%R) of shares bogey
4. Do balanced selling job	%R of product line quotas, with commissions increasing in proportion to number of lines up to quota
5. Increase profitability	Margin realized from sales
	Vary sales credits to emphasize profitable product lines
	Vary sales credit in relation to amount of price discount
6. Increase dealer sales	Pay distributor salespeople or sales manager in relation to realization of sales quotas of assigned dealers
7. Increase sales calls	%R of targeted calls per district or region
8. Introduce new product	Additional sales credits on new line for limited period
9. Control expense	%R of expense to sales or margin ratio
	Adjust sales credit in proportion to variance from expense budget
10. Sales teamwork	Share of incentive based upon group results

EXHIBIT 4   G.E. Appliances—Sales Territories

Territory Designation	Description
9961 Greater Vancouver (Garth Rizzuto)	Hudson's Bay, Firestone, K-Mart, McDonald Supply, plus seven independent dealers
9962 Interior (Dan Seguin)	All customers from Quesnel to Nelson, including contract sales (50 customers)
9963 Coastal (Ken Block)	Eatons, Woodwards, plus Vancouver Island north of Duncan and upper Fraser Valley (east of Clearbrook) (20 customers)
9964 Independent and Northern (Fred Speck)	All independents in lower mainland and South Vancouver Island, plus northern B.C. and Yukon (30 customers)
9967 Contract (Jim Wiste)	Contract sales Vancouver, Victoria. All contract sales outside 9962 (50–60 customers)

base to which the increase was added for an estimation of the next year's quota. From this quota, the value of contract sales was allocated. Contract sales were allocated first because the market was considered the easiest to forecast. The amount of contract sales in the sales mix was constrained by the lower profit margin on such sales.

The next step was to make a preliminary allocation by simply adding the budgeted percentage increase to the year-end estimates for each territory. Although this allocation seemed fair on the surface, it did not take into account the differing situations in the territories or the difficulty of attaining such an increase.

The next step was examination of the sales data compiled by G.E. Weekly sales reports from all regions were fed into a central computer, which compiled them and printed out sales totals by product line for each customer, as well as other information. This information enabled the sales manager to check the reasonableness of his initial allocation through a careful analysis of the growth potential for each customer.

The analysis began with the largest accounts such as Firestone, Hudson's Bay, and Eatons, which each bought over $1 million in appliances annually. Accounts that size were expected to achieve at least the budgeted growth. The main reason for this was that a shortfall of a few percentage points on such a large account would be difficult to make up elsewhere.

Next, the growth potential for medium-sized accounts was estimated. These accounts included McDonald Supply, K-Mart, Federated Cooperative, and buying groups such as Volume Independent Purchasers (V.I.P.). Management expected the majority of sales growth to come from such accounts, which had annual sales of between $150 thousand and $1 million.

At that point, about 70 percent of the accounts had been analyzed. The small accounts were estimated last. These had generally lower growth potential but

were an important part of the company's distribution system.

Once all the accounts had been analyzed, the growth estimates were summed and the total compared to the budget. Usually, the growth estimates were well below the budget.

The next step was to gather more information. The salespeople were usually consulted to ensure that no potential trouble areas or good opportunities had been overlooked. The manager continued to revise and adjust the figures until the total estimate matched the budget. These projections were then summed by territory and compared to the preliminary territorial allocation.

Frequently, there were substantial differences between the two allocations. Historical allocations were then examined, and the manager used his judgment in adjusting the figures until he was satisfied that the allocation was both equitable and attainable. Some factors which were considered at this stage included experience of the salesperson, competitive activities, potential store closures or openings, potential labor disputes in areas, and so forth.

The completed allocation was passed on to the Regional Sales Manager for his approval. The process had usually taken one week or longer by this stage. Once the allocations had been approved, the District Sales Manager then divided them into sales quotas by product line. Often, the resulting average price did not match the expected mix between higher- and lower-priced units. Therefore, some additional adjusting of figures was necessary. The house account (used for sales to employees of the company) was used as the adjustment factor.

Once this breakdown had been completed, the numbers were printed on a budget sheet, and given to the Regional Sales Manager (R.S.M.). He forwarded all the sheets for his region to the central computer, which printed out sales numbers for each product line by salesperson by month. These figures were used as the salesperson's quotas for the next year.

Current Situation

Barr recognized that he faced a difficult task. He felt that he was too new to the job and the area to confidently undertake an account by account growth analysis. However, due to his previous experience with sales budgets, he did have some sound general ideas. He also had the records of past allocation and quota attainment (Exhibit 5), as well as the assistance of the R.S.M., Anthony Foyt.

Barr's first step was to project the current sales figures to end-of-year totals. This task was facilitated because the former manager, Philips, had been making successive projections monthly since June. Barr then made a preliminary quota allocation by adding the budgeted sales increase of 14 percent to each territory's total (Exhibit 6).

Barr then began to assess circumstances which could cause him to alter that allocation. One major problem was the resignation, effective at the end of the year, of one of the company's top salesmen, Ken Block. His territory had traditionally been one of the most difficult, and Barr felt that it would be unwise to replace Block with a novice salesperson.

Barr considered shifting one of the more experienced salespeople into that area. However, that would have involved a disruption of service in an additional territory, which was undesirable because it took several months for a salesperson to build up a good rapport with customers. Barr's decision would affect his quota allocation because a salesperson new to a territory could not be expected to sell immediately as well as the incumbent, and a novice salesperson would require an even longer period of adaptation.

Barr was also concerned about territory 9961. The territory comprised two large national accounts and seven major independent dealers. The buying decisions for the national accounts were made at their head offices, where G.E.'s regional sales had no control over the decisions. Recently, Barr had heard rumors that one of the national accounts was reviewing its purchase of G.E. appliances. If they were to delist even some product lines, it would be a major blow to the salesman, Rizzuto, whose potential sales would be greatly reduced. Barr was unsure how to deal with that situation.

Another concern for Barr was the wide variance in buying of some accounts. Woodwards, Eatons, and McDonald Supply had large fluctuations from year to year. Also, Eatons, Hudson's Bay, and Woodwards had plans to open new stores in the Vancouver area sometime during the year. The sales increase to be generated by these events was hard to estimate.

The general economic outlook was poor. The Canadian dollar had fallen to 92 cents U.S., and unemployment was about 8 percent. The government's anti-inflation program, which was scheduled to end next year, had managed to keep inflation to the 8 percent

EXHIBIT 5   Sales Results

Territory	Previous Budget (× 1,000)	Percent of Total Budget	Previous Actual (× 1,000)	Variance from Quota (V%)
9967 (Contract)	$2,440	26.5	$2,267	(7)
9961 (Greater Vancouver)	1,790	19.4	1,824	2
9962 (Interior)	1,624	17.7	1,433	(11)
9963 (Coastal)	2,111	23.0	2,364	12
9965 (Independent dealers)	1,131	12.3	1,176	4
House	84	1.1	235	—
Total	$9,180	100.0	$9,299	1

Territory	Following Year Budget (× 1,000)	Percent of Total Budget	Following Year Actual (× 1,000)	Variance from Quota (V%)
9967 (Contract)	$2,587	26.2	$2,845	10
9961 (Greater Vancouver)	2,005	20.3	2,165	8
9962 (Interior)	1,465	14.8	1,450	(1)
9963 (Coastal)	2,405	24.4	2,358	(2)
9965 (Independent dealers)	1,334	13.5	1,494	12
House	52	.8	86	—
Total	$9,848	100.0	$10,398	5

EXHIBIT 6   Sales Projections and Quotas

		Projected Sales Results, Current Year			
Territory	Current Year October Year to Date (× 1000)	Current Projected Total (× 1000)	Current Budget (× 1000)	% of Total Budget	Projected Variance from Quota (V%)
9967	$2,447	$3,002	$2,859	25.0	5
9961	2,057	2,545	2,401	21.0	6
9962	1,318	1,623	1,727	15.1	(6)
9963	2,124	2,625	2,734	23.9	(4)
9965	1,394	1,720	1,578	13.8	9
House	132	162	139	1.2	—
Total	$9,474	$11,677	$11,438	100.0	2

	Preliminary Allocation, Next Year		
Territory	Current Projection (× 1000)	Next Year Budget[a] (× 1000)	% of Total Budget
9967	$3,002	$3,422	25.7
9961	2,545	2,901	21.8
9962	1,623	1,854	13.9
9963	2,625	2,992	22.5
9965	1,720	1,961	14.7
House	162	185	1.4
Total	$11,677	$13,315	100.0

[a] Next budget = current territory projections + 14% = $13,315.

level, but economists expected higher inflation and increased labor unrest during the postcontrol period.

The economic outlook was not the same in all areas. For instance, the Okanagan (9962) was a very depressed area. Tourism was down, and fruit farmers were doing poorly despite good weather and record prices. Vancouver Island was still recovering from a 200 percent increase in ferry fares, while the lower mainland appeared to be in a relatively better position.

In the contract segment, construction had shown an increase recently. However, labor unrest was common. There had been a crippling eight-week strike recently and there was a strong possibility of another strike next year.

With all of this in mind, Barr was very concerned that he allocate the quota properly because of the bonus system implications. How should he proceed? To help him in his decision, he reviewed a note on development of a sales commission plan which he had obtained while attending a seminar on sales management the previous year (Exhibit 3).

COMPENSATING SALESPEOPLE

I've always been worried about people who are willing to work for nothing. Sometimes that's all you get from them, nothing.

SAM ERVIN

Chapter Consultants:
Randy Cimorelli, President/COO, Massey-Fair Industrial, Inc.
Robert C. Conti, Vice President, The Alexander Group, Inc.

LEARNING OBJECTIVES

After studying this chapter, you should be able to:

→ Balance the need for wages against company resources.

→ Select appropriate compensation methods.

→ Set pay levels.

→ Assemble a compensation plan.

COMPENSATION OBJECTIVES

Compensation is one of the most important tools for motivating and retaining field salespeople. However, compensation is a cost, and selling expenses have now increased to the point where they represent 10.0 percent of sales revenue.[1] Thus to maintain profitability, a sales manager must design compensation plans that encourage salespeople to work efficiently, which is not easy to do. Fifty-nine percent of the managers in a survey complain that their pay plans fail to motivate their staffs to make an extra effort, and 48 percent gripe that they overpay poor performers.[2] Part of the problem is that young firms often use the same commission rate for all products. Under these conditions, salespeople push low-margin products to maximize their income rather than higher-priced, high-margin, new items. If you want to sell new products, you have to reward salespeople for moving them.[3] One solution is to vary commission rates by item profitability so that salespeople are encouraged to sell a mix of products that maximizes overall company profits.

A good starting point is to define the goals of the company and how the sales force can support those goals. For example, do you want reps to sell more premium items in certain product lines? Increase customer satisfaction? Grow profits? For the past several years the sales compensation plan for Liberty Courier, Inc., a $1.3 million delivery company in Worburn, Massachusetts, had stunted the company's growth. Salespeople, who were paid a straight salary, expected a raise each time they increased their business. When the raise was not forthcoming, they began calculating what their earnings might look like if they worked for competitors, many of which offered commission-based plans. As a result, reps' motivation dropped and turnover increased. Liberty completely revamped the compensation plan to align it with its goal of increasing profits with the customers who were expected to produce the most revenue. Soon after the new plan was implemented, turnover dropped and Liberty's sales exploded to 130 percent from the previous year.[4]

This example shows that compensation plans must be custom designed to not only meet the goals of individual firms, but also provide competitive compensation packages to the marketplace. It also shows that the natural desire of salespeople to earn more money if left unabated could conflict with the firm's need to control expenses. This means that you have the difficult task of designing compensation programs that motivate salespeople to reach company goals and satisfy customers without bankrupting the firm. Because 30 to 40 percent of all sales reps are unhappy with their compensation plans at any one time, you may be constantly challenged to come up with a better program.

A useful tool to begin translating company objectives and the desired sales job into an appropriate compensation plan is to consider the Customer-Product Matrix introduced in Chapter 2. As shown in Figure 14-1, the Customer-Product Matrix divides sales opportuni-

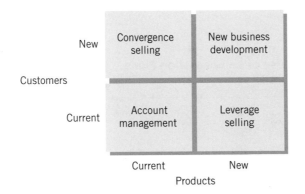

FIGURE 14-1 The Customer-Product Matrix

ties into combinations of new and old customers and products. In general, sales positions that focus primarily on New Business Development (upper right-hand quadrant) require a greater proportion of incentive (e.g., commissions and bonus) in the compensation plan than those sales jobs in the lower left-hand quadrant (Account Management). Sales jobs consisting primarily of Account Management involve a greater account servicing component and are therefore better suited to a salary form of compensation.

COMPENSATION METHODS

Several theories can guide you in designing sales compensation plans that fit the needs of a specific firm. Building a program is a combination of art and science, and sales managers often feel the need to review or alter compensation plans on a regular basis to increase their efficiency. By far the most common compensation plan combines a base salary with some type of incentives. Table 14-1 shows that approximately 83 percent of firms use combination plans for intermediate-level salespeople.

Straight Salary

Although a familiar form of compensation for most nonselling personnel, straight salary involves paying a fixed amount each pay period. *Straight salary* programs were used by approximately 17 percent of the firms reported in Table 14-1. The major benefits of salary are more control over wage levels and the ability to easily direct the sales force on non-selling/revenue generating activities. Such activities would include, for instance, taking orders for inventory replenishment, equipment installation and maintenance, and shelf-management programs. Salary is also helpful when a salesperson is responsible for covering an entire territory as opposed to a specific account list. In these situations, a manager can require a salesperson to call on all the accounts, not just the "best" accounts in a given region. This is an important issue in jobs where "blanket" coverage is expected, such as a manufacturer's rep. It is interesting to note that during the years 1996 to 1998, more firms began to use the salary compensation plan than any other plan.[5]

A Dartnell Compensation Survey showed that the average salary plan paid middle-level salespeople $38,900 per year compared with $51,400 for salespeople on salary plus incentive programs.[6] This does not necessarily mean that salary plans are inherently lower-paying compensation plans, but that the sales activities associated with most straight salary plans tend to be lower paying. Also, with a salary plan, wages are a fixed cost to the firm, and the proportion of wage expense tends to decrease as sales increase. Another advantage of salary is that it allows maximum control over salespeople's activities. Salaried employees can be directed to sell particular products, call on certain customers, and perform a variety of

TABLE 14-1   Use of Compensation Plans

	Percentage of Companies Using
Straight Salary	17
Straight Commission	20
Combination Plans (83%)	
Salary Plus Bonus	24
Salary Plus Commission	20
Salary Plus Bonus Plus Commission	18
Commission Plus Bonus	1
Total	100%

account servicing and other nonselling activities for customers. Because a salesperson's income is not tied to the volume of business done with specific customers, it is easier for the sales manager to divide territories and reassign salespeople to new areas. Further, salaried salespeople tend to exhibit higher loyalty to the firm than non-salaried employees. Because salary plans are fairly straightforward, they are also easy to explain to new employees.

Salary plans provide salespeople with security and a steady, predictable monthly income. Trainees, in particular, tend to favor this payment plan because they run the risk of having low incomes if they start out on a commission plan. The U.S. Chamber of Commerce pays new salespeople a salary for 90 days before moving them to a straight commission plan. Merrill Lynch, for example, has considered paying salaries to new brokers to reduce their temptation to boost commissions in ways that might conflict with client's interest.[7] Salary programs are also often preferred by customers, since they know salespeople are there to help rather than to load them with inventory.

Limitations   The most frequently heard criticism is that salaries do not provide strong incentives for extra effort. Even though salary adjustments are made to reward performance, these adjustments are usually annual and lack the more immediate reinforcement of alternative plans. As a result, some salespeople may not exert the extra effort to meet the needs of the company. Some experts argue that those who are allowed to "share the wealth" bring the most "help" to the buyer, which is why "account management" still needs to reward growth and discourage flat sales growth. Another problem is that salaried salespeople usually require much closer supervision by sales managers than salespeople who work under commission plans. Also, salary plans often overpay the least-productive members of a sales team and cause morale problems when new trainees earn almost as much as experienced salespeople.

Applications   Research has shown that salary is used more often in competitive labor environments, in situations where it is difficult to assess sales force activities and performance, and in companies where salespeople spend a lot of time on service and paperwork.[8] This suggests that salary is most appropriate in sales positions of Account Management when it is difficult to relate the efforts of individual salespeople to the size or timing of a sale. For example, the "detail people" for pharmaceutical companies are primarily engaged in missionary activities with doctors and do not sell directly to most of their customers. For years it was impossible to track drug orders prescribed by particular physicians. However, given the sophistication of today's information systems and the ability to calculate hospital and drugstore profitability across different product lines, the compensation plans of pharmaceutical sales forces are becoming more incentive oriented and salary is a lower percent of total compensation.

Salary is also used when team selling is important, as in the sales of complex aerospace products to airlines and the government. Salary is widely employed in nonferrous metals such as aluminum. Salespeople in this industry are technical advisers, and it may take years to convert a customer from one material to another. Salary is also appropriate in situations where the products are presold through advertising and the salesperson primarily takes orders. Liquor, for example, is largely presold through magazines and newspaper ads, and salespeople are mainly responsible for in-store merchandising and displays.

Straight Commission

Salespeople on commission are paid a percentage of the sales or gross profits that they generate. The *straight commission* plan rewards people for their accomplishments rather than their time or efforts. Straight commissions work on the principle that a salesperson will add value above his or her cost. Although this principle should be true for all compensation plans, this type of pay plan is ideal for those who are confident of adding value and want to be equitably rewarded for their efforts with commissions. On average, salespeople who are paid commissions make more money than those on other wage programs. A recent survey revealed that the average compensation of senior sales reps on straight commission is $122,900 per year compared with $73,500 for reps on salary plus incentive and $64,900 for those on straight salary.[9] It is possible that this high average is due to an outlier effect of really high producers. In general, however, higher wages tend to attract better-qualified applicants and provide a strong incentive to work hard. It is interesting to note that straight commission plans are used by a relatively small number of firms. As shown in Table 14-1, about 20 percent of the firms in the study reported using straight commissions.

Advantages   Straight commission plans foster independence of action and provide the maximum possible incentive. They are easy to understand, and it is fairly simple to calculate wages and administer the plan. Because the selling costs are entirely variable, the firm does not pay as much when sales decline or fail to meet growth objectives. When commissions are paid at the time revenues are received, there are definite cash flow benefits. It is also becoming more popular for firms to base commissions on the profitability of sales to motivate the sales force to focus on the most profitable products or customers. In these plans, the sales force would have a variable commission structure where relatively high commissions are paid for sales of the most profitable products or sales to the most profitable accounts. In addition, the variable rate plan can also be used to direct the sale force's efforts toward new strategic objectives, such as introducing a new product line.

The advantages of a 10 percent commission plan are shown graphically in Figure 14-2. Notice that when the sales per person figure is low, the costs of the commission plan are low. However, a *fixed cost* salary plan ($40,000) gives higher costs. Companies that want to minimize their financial risk can choose variable cost commission plans. Firms that want to minimize compensation costs as sales grow use fixed cost salary programs. Figure 14-2 shows that when sales are less than $400,000 per year, the salary plan is the high-cost method. But when sales exceed $400,000 per year, the straight salary plan results in lower total costs for the company in the example. Thus, small firms often start off using commission plans, then shift to salary when they grow. However, financial risk should not be the sole or even primary basis for choosing between a salary or commission compensation plan. The sales job to be performed should be the most important criterion. Note, for instance, that sales jobs with most new, small companies will fall in the New

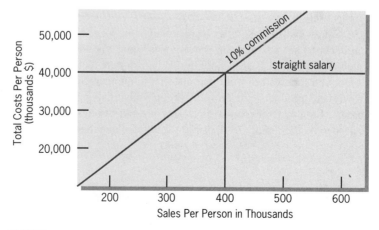

FIGURE 14-2   Comparing Salary and Commission Plans for Field Sales Representatives

Business Development quadrant of the Customer-Product Matrix, so compensation should include a significant incentive component.

Problems   Despite some advantages, straight commission has a number of drawbacks. The major problems are that sales managers have little control over commission salespeople and nonselling activities are likely to be neglected. Commission salespeople are tempted to sell themselves rather than the company, and to service only the best accounts in their territories. Because salespeople's wages are directly related to sales to particular accounts, salespeople are often reluctant to have their territories changed in any way. Turnover can become excessive among commission salespeople when business conditions are bad, because they often have little company loyalty. Wide variations in pay under commission plans may also lead to poor morale among lower-paid personnel, and highly paid salespeople may be reluctant to move into supervisory or managerial positions.

Examples   Straight commission works best when maximum incentive is needed and when a minimum of after-sale service and missionary work is required. This situation exists for most door-to-door organizations and many car dealerships, although this is changing somewhat as a result of Saturn's success with "no-haggle" pricing. Other types of businesses that use straight commission plans include life insurance, real estate, stock brokerage, printing, and wholesalers in many industries. Commission rates often range from 5 to 14 percent of sales.

Salary Plus Bonus

Recent data suggest there is a growing practice of paying salespeople a base salary with a bonus.[10] There are several advantages to this compensation plan. The base salary provides reps with income security, and the bonus gives added incentives to meet company objectives. Bonuses are discretionary payments for reaching specified goals and are usually paid annually. Reader's Digest, for example, found that by switching its compensation program from primarily a base salary (90 percent) to a salary (65 percent) plus bonus (35 percent) plan, it increased its advertising revenues 90 percent over the next four years.[11]

Salary plus bonus programs were the most preferred plan in Table 14-1, used by 24 percent of firms. The main advantage of salary plus bonus plans is that they balance the need to control selling expenses and provide extra rewards for added results. When products are largely presold by advertising, like many consumer items, it makes no sense to pay a salary plus a commission to get salespeople to push for added volume. Under these conditions, a salary plus a modest bonus is enough to get the job done.

Another possible advantage of salary plus bonus plans is they may lead to lower turnover among salespeople.[12] This is particularly important when buying cycles are long and reps must invest time to understand how customers do business. Business Wire, for example, has been able to quadruple revenues over four years using competitive salaries plus performance and year-end bonuses.[13] The security of a salary allows their reps time to both court prospects over a considerable period of time and to service existing customers. Business Wire also encourages longevity by gradually raising the share of bonuses and benefits to 60 percent of wages after six years. As a result, Business Wire's sales are up, and only two salespeople have left in the past four years.

Probably the most widely used basis for determining bonus pay is sales to quota. Another popular basis is average gross margin achieved by the rep. Other bonus factors are the number of new accounts, unit sales, and overall company performance. In some firms the size of the bonus may be arbitrary. Managers review sales results, customer relations, and after-sale service and then decide how much each person should receive. Managers who fail to communicate how bonuses are determined can lose some of their effectiveness as motivational devices. Salary plus bonus plans are commonly used by large food manufacturers, such as Quaker Oats and Procter & Gamble.

Salary Plus Commission

Industrial sales reps are frequently paid *salary plus commission* to give them the push needed to sell complex products or services. For example, Digital Equipment Corporation has converted its 10,000 computer salespeople from a straight salary plan to a salary plus commission program.[14] These plans pay a base salary plus a small commission of 1 to 6 percent of sales. Twenty percent of the firms in Table 14-1 employ salary plus commission programs. Salary plus commission plans are widely used by industrial firms selling building materials, machinery, electrical supplies, and paper products.

Although most firms start paying commissions on the first dollar of sales, approximately 40 percent establish *commission thresholds* that must be reached before the commissions apply. Often the commission rates vary, depending on sales volume. As an illustration, a salesperson might earn 4 percent on the first $20,000 of sales each month, 5 percent on the next $15,000, and 6 percent on anything over $35,000. Progressive commission rates are used when sales increases require extra efforts. Although progressive commission rates reflect the increase in selling effort, they may also increase sales expenses.

Commission rates can also be adjusted to promote the sale of individual products or to intensify efforts among specific market segments. Many firms vary commission rates according to the profitability of products. It is interesting to note that approximately 42 percent of firms have wage caps on the incentive portion of their compensation plans to prevent windfall earnings as a result of circumstances unrelated to salespeople's efforts.[15]

Commissions are usually paid monthly, providing almost immediate reinforcement for the salesperson's efforts. Some firms spread commissions over several months or years to smooth out the pattern of payments and to ensure that salespeople continue to service their accounts after the initial sale. Spreading commissions over a period of time also discourages a salesperson from leaving the firm once a large sale has been made.

The major drawbacks to salary plus commission plans are that they are more expensive and are costly to administer. Research has shown that the average maximum wages paid with a salary and commission program are higher compared with salespeople on salary plus bonus plans. However, firms that try to gain some control over the salary plus commission plan expense by imposing commission ceilings tend to dampen the enthusiasm and motivation of the sales force. In fact, 25 percent of the 305 salespeople who responded to a recent survey indicated that the incentive cap was one aspect of their firm's compensation plan with which they were most dissatisfied.[16] With an incentive ceiling, some salespeople could reach the earning maximum early in the year and then take it easy for the remainder of the year.

Salary Plus Commission Plus Bonus

The most comprehensive payment plans combine the stability of a salary, the incentives of a commission, and the special rewards of a bonus. Table 14-1 indicates that 18 percent of firms surveyed used this plan. The primary benefit of these plans is they allow the sales manager to reward virtually every activity performed by salespeople. Field representatives love these plans because there are so many different ways for them to make money. However, their complexity makes them difficult to administer.

IBM recently revised its *salary plus commission plus bonus* plan to make it more workable for its 14,000 reps around the world.[17] Under the old plan, reps earned most of their commission income in the fourth quarter of the year when business computers are usually delivered. The commission system paid lower rates for sales through distributors, and salespeople tended to ignore this important channel of distribution. A heavy reliance on contests under the old plan focused efforts on making the quick sale rather than finding solutions that fit customer needs. One of the most serious problems was that many IBM clients needed cooperation among sales reps from different states and countries to assure that equipment was installed correctly, and the reps were not financially rewarded for these activities. The old plan used 25 different performance factors to determine compensation, far too many for reps to oversee. IBM's new plan is simpler, using 10 performance factors to determine compensation. Also the commission structure was revised so that reps earn more selling to distributors. Now contest income is limited to 20 percent of incentive wages, and 20 percent is awarded for work team performance across geographic boundaries; these incentives are paid monthly. Sixty percent of incentive income is tied to personal performance on factors such as growth, customer solutions, channel partners, and profit contributions; this income is paid quarterly. The bonus portion of the plan, which is based on company profits and customer satisfaction, is paid annually. IBM also gives recognition awards in the form of trips and prizes that provide additional income for sales reps. This example shows that although salary plus commission plus bonus plans provide many ways to reward salespeople, they need to be modified periodically to ensure they are in tune with corporate objectives.

Communicating the reasoning behind a new compensation plan and the amount that above-average, average, and below-average salespeople can expect to earn will help maintain motivation and increase acceptance of the new plan. Thus, how you introduce a new compensation plan could spell the difference between a successful or unsuccessful transition. To learn how Allied Signal, Inc. implemented its new sales force compensation plan, see the Coaching Competency box.

COACHING COMPETENCY
Warning: Pay Change on the Way

Designing a new sales compensation plan requires a great deal of consideration and thought. Implementing it, however, is where the real difficulties lie. After all, compensation gets at the heart of what reps need, and changes are often met with some resistance. It takes a great deal of communication between the manager and sales reps to make the transition smooth. Letting reps know the compensation changes as far in advance as possible and providing detailed explanations of the reasoning behind the new plan will help with sales rep acceptance. If time permits, building in a transitional period for the new pay plan is also a good way to ease reps' anxiety about the new plan.

Allied Signal, Inc., for example, recently changed its sales force compensation plan, but gave its employees plenty of time to get used to the new one. The plan was implemented in four phases over two years. During the first six months (phase one) there was no change to salespeople's pay, but the pay statement indicated how much reps would have earned under the new plan. To entice reps to accept the new plan, Allied Signal paid reps the difference if they would have earned more with the new structure. During the next six months (phase two) Allied Signal instituted the new plan. However, during this six-month period, if salespeople were not making as much under the new plan, the company paid them the money to make up the difference in the form of a loan—and the loan was forgiven.

In the third phase, salespeople were still being paid the full amount of their previous salaries, but the company was maintaining true balances under the new version and working with reps to figure out how they would repay the company if they underperformed. The final step was full implementation. While this approach is very generous and time consuming, companies that do not have time to go through a similar process should, at a minimum, openly communicate how and why the new plan was developed.

See *www.alliedsignal.com* to learn more about Allied Signal.

Commission Plus Bonus

Another combination plan used by only 1 percent of the firms in Table 14-1 was the commission plus bonus program. This approach combines the incentives of a commission plus special rewards for meeting objectives. These plans are particularly well suited to a company that uses brokers or independent sales reps. They are also widely employed for stockbrokers and bond traders. For example, Merrill Lynch pays its brokers commissions plus cash bonuses and memberships in recognition circles. These clubs reward recipients with trips and deferred compensation worth tens of thousands of dollars each year. To maintain their club membership, brokers must sell 10 computerized financial plans a year. Tying the receipt of such perks to quotas on particular products doesn't appeal to every salesperson.[18]

Customer Satisfaction and Sales Force Compensation

Total quality management (TQM) focuses on delivering high-quality products to clients and making sure customers are satisfied. However, only 10 percent of 450 companies surveyed link some portion of sales force compensation with customer service.[19] Part of the problem is that firms have trouble measuring customer satisfaction and are afraid salespeople will manipulate the data to gain an advantage. Despite these problems, there is a growing trend toward tying compensation to customer contentment.

The most common objective in tying compensation to buyer satisfaction is to reduce the attrition of current customers. Companies that use surveys to measure satisfaction ask questions on sales force responsiveness, problem solving, after-sale service, and communication skills. This information is then used to modify some other sales force compensation factor or to calculate a percentage of base salary to award as a bonus. A typical firm assigns about 20 percent of total pay for achievements with customer satisfaction.

An example of a typical plan that ties customer satisfaction to sales force compensation is shown by Appleton Papers, Inc. The year-end bonus at Appleton is a significant portion of overall compensation and is based on volume, profit, and individual objectives. Forty percent of the bonus is awarded for objectives, and customer satisfaction is the leading goal. This means that at least 20 percent of the bonus is tied to customer satisfaction.

Team-Selling Plans

Because team selling is becoming more common in American business, firms must design their compensation programs to accommodate this trend. In its simplest form, team selling involves two salespeople in separate territories who need to coordinate their activities to complete the sale. The recommended solution is to establish a system for sharing commissions so that both reps will work for the order. A more complicated team-selling scenario has outside salespeople, technical specialists, service reps, and telemarketers all working together to make a sale. Because many firms are emphasizing organizational teamwork to improve sales and profits, compensation programs must be designed to reward other members of the selling team besides the outside salesperson. Since technical reps and service people are paid salaries, the usual approach is to share incentive payments with all members of the selling team.[20] Thus technical reps and service people on sales teams may be rewarded with small commissions, but more likely group bonuses. For example, Mine Safety Appliances pays its 28 sales teams a base salary, plus revenue-based and nonrevenue-based bonuses. Team members fill out questionnaires to help determine salary levels and discuss how to allocate bonuses for outstanding individual achievements.[21] Other firms, such as Xerox, have recently incorporated a new commission program geared toward motivating all front-line employees to enhance customer loyalty. To learn more about Xerox's new plan, see the Team Building Competency box.

TEAM-BUILDING COMPETENCY
Compensating for Customer Loyalty

Paul Allaire, Chief Executive Officer of Xerox Corporation (currently Chairman of the Board) realizes that customer lifetime value is enhanced through building relationships and teamwork. "Traditionally," Allaire says, "our company has been a box-oriented company, and therefore the sales force has been compensated mainly on equipment sales." Initial sales are only one component of revenues, which, according to Allaire, "represented less than half our total revenue stream, because we have service, supplies, and all these other factors that apply to the account side."

To motivate the sales force to build relationships with its most valuable customers, Xerox implemented a compensation program that ties commissions for *all* employees to customer-service goals. Most sales reps roll their eyes at a customer-focused compensation program because they feel that they have to give up today's income for the promise of tomorrow's potential gains. However, the unique feature of Xerox's program is that it gives an immediate payoff— leverage in closing more sales through building value.

Through customer input, Xerox provides salespeople a file with data including detailed installation information (Were all the parts there? Did the machine work properly upon startup? Who installed it? etc.). Xerox learns anything it has to in order to make the product work in the customer's environment. It then puts that information into every salesperson's laptop. Each rep learns whether there was a problem in site readiness, manufacturing, logistics, or performance, even whether the salesperson oversold the product. In short, customer interaction tells Xerox the current state of this customer's relationship and signals how and when to make the next sale.

Allaire says this system has built morale among his sales team as Xerox moves from a traditional distribution system to numerous sales channels, including telemarketing, and e-commerce. Reps now work "to bring in different equipment and different services, rather than just trying to do more of the same," Allaire says. Xerox's salespeople now have become agents of change. In addition, customer satisfaction goes straight to their paychecks while their new knowledge about customer relationships helps them make the next sale.

To learn more about Xerox, see its Web site: *www.xerox.com.*

Profit-Based Commissions

The main objective of compensation programs is to provide direction to the sales force to achieve the business' objectives. Unfortunately, this is not an easy task. For example, it has been shown that when incentive payments are based on a percentage of the sales of each product, as they are in 46 percent of firms surveyed, it is unlikely that salespeople will sell the mix of items that will lead to the highest profits.[22] Since salespeople rarely have data on costs and economies of scale, they will usually look only at the incentive rates and emphasize those items that are easy to sell and carry the highest commissions. One important factor in developing the ideal profit-based plan, therefore, is to make sure a system is in place for easy access to the necessary data to make informed decisions in the field.

An alternative approach is to pay commissions on the gross margin dollars on each product. With a *gross margin commission* plan, the company and the salesperson share the same pool of money (realized gross margin), so that both are interested in maximizing this amount. Theoretically when this occurs, the company makes more gross profit so they can share the increased profitability with the sales force, and the sales reps earn more money. Medical supply and retail automobile salespeople are paid a percentage of the gross margin on each sale so that they will negotiate with customers to obtain the highest possible profit for their employer and themselves. An example showing how a switch from sales commissions to gross margin commissions increased profits for Dell Computer is described in the Strategic Action Competency box.

Gross margin plans have not been successful in all situations. A problem with gross margin plans is the implicit incentive to work on larger, lower gross margin orders, instead of smaller, more profitable sales. Certain-Teed Corporation, for example, tried paying its building materials salespeople a commission on gross margin but was forced to shift to a salary plus incentive program because the salespeople were bringing in too many low-margin orders. The problem arose because the salespeople viewed a 10 percent gross margin on a $1 million order as equivalent to a 20 percent gross margin on a $500,000 order (Table 14-2). On both orders, the company makes $100,000 in gross margin and the salesperson collects $15,000 in commission. But if the selling time is similar, the salesperson is likely to work for the prestige of the $1 million order. However, the company is better off with the $500,000 sale, because the smaller order means lower inventory carrying costs and a reduced drain on raw materials and plant capacity. Perhaps a more appropriate plan would have been to pay commissions on a combination of gross margin and order size. The plan could have been designed to pay a lower commission rate when gross margin and the order size were smaller.

SETTING PAY LEVELS

Once a sales manager has selected a compensation method, the next job is to establish the best *wage level* for salespeople. At first glance, this task does not seem difficult, because there are only three options. The firm can pay the average prevailing wage, pay a premium, or offer less than the going rate. A premium wage level is appealing because it may attract

---

STRATEGIC ACTION COMPETENCY
Dell's Drive for Profits

Since 1984 Dell Computer has grown from sales of nothing to nearly $18 billion in annual revenue. This was accomplished by selling desktop personal computers at low prices directly to customers using telephone salespeople. Prior to the growth of Dell's Internet sales, 75 percent of Dell's sales were over the phone and only 10 percent through retailers. Dell's success was partially due to a system of paying sales commissions to its phone representatives. Although this approach allowed Dell to grow rapidly, the company had neglected some other areas of the business. Dell spends less on R&D than any of its major competitors. As a result, Dell's notebook PCs performed so poorly that Dell had to withdraw them from the market and take a $20 million charge in 1993. They were also late getting into the PC server market, and their control systems had been so weak that they had to take a $71 million inventory writedown in 1993. Also competitors started to narrow the price gap, and Dell was expected to report an annual loss for the first time. Dell realized it had to refocus on generating profits rather than just greater volume. To help make this possible, Dell calculated the profit margins on each of its products and switched its salespeople to a gross margin commission plan. Salespeople are now rewarded for selling the most profitable items instead of the low-margin PCs that salespeople pushed when they were paid on commission. Today, not only are Dell's average gross margins up, but the sales volume from telephone sales is 20 percent greater than the average sale made over the Internet without salesperson assistance. Visit *www.dell.com* to learn more about Dell.

TABLE 14-2   Comparing Gross Margin Commissions on Two Orders

Order Number	Percentage Gross Margin on Each Order	Size of Order	Gross Margin to Company	Percentage Commission on Gross Margin	Commission Paid to Salesperson
1	10	$1,000,000	$100,000	15	$15,000
2	20	$500,000	$100,000	15	$15,000

better salespeople and motivate them to sell high volumes. Paying higher than average wages makes it easier to recruit college-trained people who can be promoted into managerial positions later on. However, overpaying salespeople could cause resentment and low morale among the firm's other employees and executives when salespeople earn more than even top management. It is also not clear that offering unlimited opportunities to earn higher pay is always an effective method for continual motivation to increase sales effort. The results of one study showed that most salespeople will work toward a "satisfactory" level of compensation rather than to maximize their pay.[23]

Sales managers can obtain guidelines about current pay levels by reviewing surveys published by the Dartnell Corporation, the Conference Board, and trade and industry associations. For example, Table 14-3 shows typical 1998 pay levels for combination plans in sales organizations. Note that the highest pay goes to top sales executives followed by national account managers. First-level field sales managers ($84,800) earn more than the key account reps ($80,300). However, sales managers may earn less than the top rep in their district, especially when sales reps are on a commission-based plan. On the other hand, having positions such as key account rep in the middle of the compensation range provides incentives for trainees and telesales reps to move up the promotion ladder. Although sales trainees start with a base salary of only $29,700, they are often provided an opportunity to earn commissions or a bonus for a total compensation package of $43,100. In addition, new sales reps are often given a car and an expense account. In comparison, the relatively low pay of telesales reps ($33,400) and customer service reps ($25,200) could lead to morale problems and high turnover.[24] However, it is important to note that telesales revenues account for only 20 percent of total revenues on average, while field salespeople generate an average of 80 percent.[25]

The type of account relationship established by the salesperson also has significant implications for the amount of compensation rewarded. Table 14-4 illustrates how dramatic the differences can be. The top-level salesperson focusing on enterprise relationships earns, on average, $121,800, whereas the top-level salesperson using transactional relationships earns $83,300. The top-performing salesperson employing consultative relationships earns

TABLE 14-3   Compensation Levels for Firms Using Salary Plus Incentives, 1998

Position	Salary ($000)	Incentive ($000)	Total Compensation ($000)
Top Sales Executive	$91.0	$29.0	$120.0
National Account Manager	72.2	26.0	98.2
Regional Sales Manager	74.5	21.9	96.4
District Sales Manager	64.5	20.3	84.8
Key Account Rep	57.4	22.9	80.3
Senior Sales Rep	47.5	26.0	73.5
Intermediate Rep	36.1	15.3	51.4
Entry Level Rep	29.7	13.4	43.1

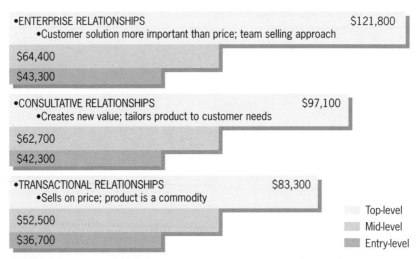

•ENTERPRISE RELATIONSHIPS $121,800
    •Customer solution more important than price; team selling approach

$64,400

$43,300

•CONSULTATIVE RELATIONSHIPS $97,100
    •Creates new value; tailors product to customer needs

$62,700

$42,300

•TRANSACTIONAL RELATIONSHIPS $83,300
    •Sells on price; product is a commodity
                                                                        Top-level
$52,500   Mid-level
$36,700   Entry-level

TABLE 14-4   Compensation Levels by Account Relationships, 1998

$97,100. This graphic clearly illustrates how compensation increases as the level of complexity and sophistication in the buyer-seller relationship increases.

EXPENSE ACCOUNTS AND BENEFITS

No discussion of sales force compensation would be complete without mention of expense accounts and other benefits. Almost all firms that pay straight salaries or some combination of salary, commission, and/or bonus cover expenses for salespeople. Typical expenses paid by firms include those for automobiles and other travel, tips, lodging, food, samples, telephone, postage, and tickets for sporting and theater events. A typical expense allocation reported in a recent survey averaged $16,000 per year.[26] These expenses run about $19,100 for industrial salespeople, and $11,500 for those selling consumer services.

Expense Reimbursement Programs

Three types of expense plans can be used: (1) unlimited, (2) per diem, and (3) limited repayment.

Unlimited Plans   One type of expense reimbursement plan has salespeople submit itemized forms showing their expenditures, and the firm simply pays all reported expenses. This approach allows salespeople wide discretion on where they travel and how they entertain customers. In addition, an unlimited expense plan is inexpensive to administer because no one regularly spends time checking expense accounts to see if they are overstated.

Unlimited expense plans are often favored by small firms that don't want to bother auditing expense accounts. They are also used by companies that sell expensive products such as airplanes and defense systems, where extensive entertainment of clients is routine. The main problem with these plans is some salespeople get too greedy and try to profit from their expense accounts. This forces management to occasionally fire reps who get out of line.

Per Diem Plans   A per diem expense plan pays the salesperson a fixed dollar amount for each day or week spent in the field. The amount is designed to cover food, gasoline, lodging, telephone calls, and other expenses. A major benefit of a per diem plan is that it is simple and inexpensive to supervise. However, salespeople may try to profit from the plan by spending less than the allowance, usually by cutting back on travel. Instead of driving to distant customers, salespeople could save money by concentrating on nearby prospects. Also, there is less incentive to entertain customers with a per diem plan than with an unlimited plan. These actions may keep salespeople under their expense allowance, but they may also cost the company sales revenues. Another problem is that per diem allocations have to be revised periodically to reflect inflation. Firms typically use per diem plans for routine reorder selling of standard items.

Limited Repayment Plans   With this approach the firm sets dollar limits on each category of sales expenses. For example, a firm might allow 33 cents a mile for travel, $8 for breakfast, $12 for lunch, $25 for dinner, and $70 for a room. These limits must reflect actual field experience, and they need to be adjusted frequently to reflect inflation. The objective of this plan is to make salespeople aware of what the company will pay and encourage them to control their expenses. The limited expense approach makes it easier to budget for sales costs and should reduce expense-account padding.

One problem with limited reimbursement plans is that new reps may be uncertain as to whether the firm will cover various miscellaneous expenses. Although 86 percent of companies pay for lodging, only 75 percent pay for entertainment, 63 percent pay a mileage allowance, 61 percent pay for car phones, 47 percent pay for home copiers, 31 percent pay for a leased auto, and 53 percent pay for home fax machines.[27] The net result of setting limits is that salespeople may spend their valuable time juggling expenses from one category to another or from one time period to another to make sure they cover their costs. This time could be better spent solving customers' problems.

Another issue with limited repayment plans is that they may be expensive to monitor. One large wholesaler hired 11 full-time clerks to check sales expense accounts. To help reduce expenses, the company stopped having reps fill out expense accounts and relied on a few experienced salespeople to keep track of their actual expenses for one week twice a year. These observed expenses were then used to set repayment rates for all reps. The new plan required only one clerk for administration and gave salespeople more time to sell, so that nine sales positions could be eliminated.[28] Another alternative would be to "spot-check" expense reports by randomly selecting expense reports to be verified.

Selecting Benefits

Benefits can be used to attract and reward salespeople. One study found that salespeople prefer benefits to recognition and incentive awards.[29] Benefit packages range from $4,300 for insurance salespeople to $21,000 for rubber and plastics reps, with a typical program costing $7,600.[30] These programs include a variety of hospitalization, insurance, and pension plans, as shown in Table 14-5. The recent explosion in medical care costs has made it difficult for many firms to control the expenses of benefit packages. One approach has been to raise the medical deductible levels so that employees pay more of the costs. Another popular solution is to allocate a certain number of benefit dollars to each salesperson and let them choose from a cafeteria line of possible benefits. This allows reps to select a benefit package that fits their individual needs.

You have to decide how much the salesperson should be required to contribute to the benefit program. If the salesperson is asked to pay a portion of the costs, the firm may give the person extra compensation to cover the contribution. However, this extra money is taxable and may even move the person into a higher income tax bracket. If the firm pays for these benefits directly so that salespeople receive the tax advantage, they may receive lower total wages than those offered by other firms, but they are ahead in the long run.

TABLE 14-5   Benefits Offered by Companies

Benefit	Percentage of Firms Offering
Hospital costs	90%
Life insurance	77
Dental plan	69
Long-term disability	56
Pension plan	55
Short-term disability	49
Profit sharing	44
Thrift savings	22
Employee stock purchase plan	21

Another recent trend is the opportunity for salespeople to negotiate stock purchase plans and stock options. Companies are offering salespeople an opportunity to buy stock shares at discounts from market prices, or, better yet, match the investment dollar-for-dollar or more. Of course, market risk is always a factor, but if the company is not high-risk or of questionable health, such purchase accumulation can be quite lucrative. Stock option plans are more likely to be offered by ambitious, fast-growing companies, or those that have only recently—or are about to—become publicly owned. Because such companies rapidly chew up capital, they often prefer to offer mixed compensation packages of cash, stock purchase opportunities, and long-term, far-above-the-market options. They may be more generous with this kind of compensation because it does not show up immediately on their expense sheets. Plus, the stock market does not seem to take them into consideration in the stock value dilution or in the potential dampening effect of buying back company stock. At the very least, this could be a factor in choosing employment, and in how people negotiate a new compensation package.

Expense accounts and benefit packages amount to a substantial portion of the costs of keeping a salesperson in the field. To some degree, cash wages, expense accounts, and benefits may be substitutes for one another, since they all provide rewards and incentives to salespeople. On the other hand, Maslow's Hierarchy of Needs theory would suggest that they address different needs.

ASSEMBLING THE PLAN

Sales managers are responsible for combining the various wage elements into an appropriate compensation plan and then predicting its effectiveness. This is not an easy task, and despite the advances in technology, firms have been slow to develop software that automatically calculates sales compensation plans. A recent listing of almost 300 software makers for sales force automation had only two software products specifically designed for calculating compensation plans.[31] Consequently, firms that have the in-house resources are developing their own software programs. See the Technology Competency box for an example of how Amdahl Corporation solved its worldwide sales compensation problems by developing its own compensation analysis program.

How Much to Pay?

In determining the appropriate level of wages to pay salespeople, a good starting point is the average wage paid by other firms of the same size in the industry. Other considerations might be the labor market where people are entering and leaving. Assume that comparable firms are paying their mid-level salespeople an average annual total compensation of

TECHNOLOGY COMPETENCY
Maximizing the Payoff from Information Technology

International business enterprises that sell an increasingly broad mix of products and services using direct sales personnel must have an effective compensation system. Amdahl Corporation, a $1.5 billion provider of enterprise computing products and services, has devised such a system to serve its 1,200 commissioned employees worldwide. The system, which links the firm's branches in North America, Asia, and Europe, uses object-oriented technology and can perform complex calculations involving various compensation and commission schemes. At last count, financial analysts were using the system to crunch numbers for 100 different compensation plans and more than 240 types of commissions and bonuses with few calculation errors. Prior to this, Amdahl employees spent more that six months on integrating the compensation plans. The new system has saved the company an estimated $1.5 million annually in reduced maintenance and administrative costs. And by giving sales managers the ability to quickly design compensation plans that reward desired behavior, company officials are convinced that the system is a competitive weapon that motivates salespeople. For more information about Amdahl Corporation, visit their Web site at: *www.amdahl.com*

$52,000. The sales manager now must split this total into salary, commissions, and a bonus. Based on an analysis of the sales job to be performed, the breakdown might be $38,000 for salary, $10,000 for commissions, and $4,000 for a bonus. The monthly salary of $3,167 provides stability of income and amounts to 73 percent of the wage package. For this company the commission rates could be set to vary from 1 to 4 percent of sales, depending on the profitability of the various products in the line and the source of the business. The following breakdown shows how the commission portion of the wage would be calculated:

Commission Rate	Type and Source of Business	Sales Achieved	Commission Amount
0.01	Reorders of supplies	$100,000	$1,000
0.02	New equipment sales	250,000	5,000
0.04	Sales to new accounts	100,000	4,000
Totals		$450,000	$10,000

Note that the compensation plan pays a fairly low commission rate of 1 percent on reorders of supplies that carry low profit margins. However, a 2 percent commission is paid on sales of the more profitable new equipment. Also, a 4 percent commission is paid on all sales to new accounts to encourage sales force prospecting.

The bonus portion of the plan is set up to pay 8.3 percent of salary and commissions to salespeople who exceed their annual quota for sales achieved. Assuming the salesperson met this quota, the bonus payment would be 8.3 percent of $48,000 ($38,000 in salary + $10,000 in commissions), or $4,000. The actual payment of the $4,000 bonus would be delayed until the end of the year. The total compensation for the salesperson in this case amounts to $52,000, which is about the average total compensation for an intermediate sales representative in Table 14-3 ($51,400).

The following list shows the addition of a car, other expenses, and benefits to the compensation program:

$38,000 Salary
10,000 Commission (1 to 4 percent of sales)
4,000 Bonus (8.3 percent of salary and commissions for exceeding new account quota)

7,500	Benefits
7,800	Car expense (24,000 miles at 32.5 cents per mile)
<u>10,000</u>	Lodging, food, and entertainment
$77,300	Total costs per salesperson

Although car expenses and payments for lodging, food, and entertainment are not part of real wages for salespeople, these expenditures do represent a growing proportion of the cost of keeping a salesperson in the field. Thus, as the price of lodging and entertainment increases, sales managers may have less money available for cash wages. While a current car expense of $7,800 seems high, this figure represents only 120 miles a day for a person who is on the road 200 days a year. Also, $10,000 a year for food and lodging seems adequate, but it amounts to only $50 a day for salespeople who are on the road four days a week. Unless sales managers can find ways to control escalating entertainment and travel expenses or increase sales volume or profits, they will have trouble keeping cash wages competitive.

Evaluating the Plan

After you have selected an appropriate compensation method and wage level, the plan must be evaluated to see how it will affect salespeople's wages and total costs. This evaluation usually involves taking sales figures from the previous year and calculating expected wages for a group of salespeople under the new program. These calculations are greatly simplified if you have an automated computer program like that described in the Technology Competency box. Your objective is to see how above- and below-average salespeople would fare under the new system. You want to avoid having salespeople reap windfall gains or suffer from unfairly low earnings. Caution should be used when introducing new compensation programs that pay lower wages than the current plan, because this often produces resistance among salespeople and can lead to higher turnover. In some situations, however, turnover may be welcome. Why?

SUMMARY

Compensation is one of the key factors in motivating salespeople to achieve the sales and profit objectives of the firm. However, the spiraling costs of compensating a sales force have made it increasingly important to be able to design a plan that encourages salespeople to work efficiently. After reading this chapter, you should be able to:

1. **Explain the need to balance wages against company resources.** Compensation plans should allow salespeople to reach their own income goals without overstocking customers or ignoring nonselling duties. However, it is difficult to design a compensation program that motivates salespeople to reach company goals and satisfy customers without bankrupting the firm. The Customer-Product Matrix is a useful tool for conceptualizing a compensation plan that matches company objectives with the desired sales job. Sales positions that focus primarily on new business development require a greater proportion of incentive (e.g., commissions and bonus) in the compensation plan than account management sales jobs. Account management-type sales jobs involve a greater account servicing component which is better suited to a larger component of salary compensation.

2. **Describe the various compensation methods.** Straight-salary plans and straight-commission plans represent two extremes in compensating salespeople. Straight-commission plans offer maximum incentives for performance, but little control over sales force activities. The opposite is true for straight-salary plans. The limitations of both plans have

made combination plans the most popular with sales organizations. The combination compensation plans discussed are: salary plus bonus, salary plus commission, salary plus bonus plus commission, and commission plus bonus. It is important that sales managers learn to combine salary, commissions, bonuses, and benefits so that both salespeople and the company benefit.

3. **Set pay levels.** Beyond the issue of what plan to use is the question of how much to pay. To determine the appropriate level of wages to pay salespeople, a sales manager could start with an analysis of competitors' compensation packages. The availability of qualified people in a tight labor market is also a consideration. Field sales reps are sometimes overpaid, and it is the job of the sales manager to balance constantly the costs against the benefits received for sales force expenditures.

4. **Assemble a compensation plan.** When properly conceived and implemented, a pay plan should offer a balance of control and incentive. Important considerations in obtaining such a balance include determining an expense reimbursement program, selecting a level of benefits to be offered, and evaluating the plan to see how it will affect salespeople's wages and total cost.

KEY TERMS

Benefits	Progressive commission rates	Team selling
Bonus	Salary plus bonus	Variable cost
Commission plus bonus	Salary plus commission	Wage caps
Commission threshold	Salary plus commission plus bonus	Wage level
Fixed cost	Straight commission	
Gross margin commissions	Straight salary	

DEVELOPING YOUR COMPETENCIES

1. **Strategic Action.** Assume you are a national sales manager for a large manufacturer of interconnectivity products for the Internet. The sales force is paid on a salary-plus-bonus arrangement. Currently, salespeople can earn up to 35 percent of their salary in annual bonus once they achieve their yearly sales quota. The current economic situation is very favorable to salespeople at your firm. You expect salespeople to easily exceed quota and earn a large bonus. The total average salesperson compensation next year, in your estimation, will be greater than your competitors. As a result, you are considering changing the compensation package because of the expected windfall earnings that you believe your salespeople will make. Your plan is to increase quota by 20 percent and cut the annual bonus to a maximum of 20 percent of salary. A few weeks prior to announcing your new compensation plan to the sales force, you overhear the following conversation between two of your salespeople:

   George: I'm looking forward to this year. I've really struggled the past two years to make only 80 percent of my quota. It's about time we get a break around here.

   Liz: I agree. If it wasn't for some unbelievable last-minute luck, I wouldn't have made quota last year either. I made it by the skin of my teeth.

   George: I was thinking about leaving the company if things didn't change and I came up short again. The salary is good enough to make ends meet, but when I get into the third quarter of the year, I realize I will not make quota and I just give up trying. What's the point?

Liz: The company gives us a very attractive incentive program, but they set quota so high that it's nearly impossible to achieve it. I agree with you, George, this year is going to be different.

Should you take into consideration this new information? What do you think needs to be done, if anything, about your plans for introducing the new compensation program?

2. **Team Building.** Designing compensation plans for team selling when the sales cycle is long and complicated is a difficult task. One consultant suggests dividing the selling job into parts, such as identifying the lead, qualifying the prospect, performing technical assistance, writing the proposal, and closing the sale. Then if a 20 percent commission was being paid, 4 percent would be allocated to team members who performed each of these tasks. If some tasks are more important than others, the 4 percent allocations could be changed to reflect these differences. What are the advantages and disadvantages of this system?

3. **Global Perspective.** As discussed in the Global Perspective Competency box in Chapter 13, culture has a powerful influence on an individual's values. A recent study of salesperson reward valences by Sandra Liu suggests that Chinese salespeople and their Hong Kong counterparts value rewards differently. Liu reported that Chinese salespeople attached the highest importance to managerial encouragement and support, followed by recognition for high performers, work-related factors, and finally individual incentives. Hong Kong salespeople, on the other hand, considered opportunities for career growth to be the most important factor, followed by incentives, support functions, and quotas. Assume you are the new International Sales Director for a multinational company with sales forces of both Hong Kong and Chinese salespeople. Using this new information, what would you do to design different compensation systems for each?

4. **Self-Management.** Different types of compensation plans fit different types of people. Northwestern Mutual Life is a marketer of permanent and term life insurance, disability income insurance, and annuity plans for the personal, business, estate planning, and pension markets. Northwestern's sales agents typically work on 100 percent commission. Visit Northwestern Mutual Life's home page at www.northwesternmutual.com. Once on the home page, click the box "Becoming an Agent," and explore the information about what Northwestern considers important traits for success. You can even take the on-line sales aptitude test (for interns) to see if you meet Northwestern's requirements to succeed in a 100 percent commission-based compensation environment. Would you like to work in this type of entrepreneurial culture? Why or why not?

5. **Technology.** Equity theory introduces the perception of fairness into sales force motivation and should be considered in the design and implementation of sales force compensation and reward plans. One concern regarding the equity of compensation stems from the fact that the cost of living varies from one location to another. Most compensation programs take these differences into consideration, and the calculation of these differences has been made much easier through the use of the Home Buyer's Fair site on the World Wide Web. One of the many popular features of this web site is its section that calculates the difference in the cost of living between virtually any two cities in North America.

As the National Sales Manager for The Big Cyclone Paper Company, headquartered in Kansas City, Kansas, you are designing a compensation system that will take into consideration the different cost-of-living figures for your Regional Dealer Account Managers in 10 cities across the United States: (1) Kansas City, KS; (2) Peoria, IL; (3) Louisville, KY; (4) Denver, CO; (5) Dallas, TX; (6) Los Angeles, CA; (7) Rochester, NY; (8) Orlando, FL; (9) Atlanta, GA; and (10) Cincinnati, OH.

As designed, your compensation plan is a hybrid system incorporating a mixture of fixed salary plus commission and incentive bonuses. The cost-of-living adjustments will be made through changes in the fixed salary component of the plan. That is, a base salary of $30,000 paid to salespeople in other locations will be increased (or decreased) according to the specific location's cost of living as compared to the Kansas City base figure. In this manner, all salespeople will be on an adjusted base salary equivalent to the $30,000 Kansas City figure.

Access the Home Buyer's Fair World Wide Web site at *http://www.homefair.com* and click on <The Salary Calculator> located on the left column titled Popular Exhibits. Determine the fixed salary for each of the locations that would be equivalent to the $30,000 base salary in Kansas City, Kansas. The initial salary must be entered first, followed by the proper states as called for in the instructions. With this information entered, click on the <Select Cities> button to activate the selection of cities available for each state.

Repeat this procedure to derive the proper adjusted fixed salary component for each of the subject locations:

Kansas City, KS	$30,000	Los Angeles, CA	_____
Peoria, IL	_____	Rochester, NY	_____
Louisville, KY	_____	Orlando, FL	_____
Denver, CO	_____	Atlanta, GA	_____
Dallas, TX	_____	Cincinnati, OH	_____

6. **Coaching.** As regional sales manager, you have to make salary recommendations for six district sales managers whom you supervise. They have just completed their annual appraisal period and are now to be considered for their annual raise. Your company has set aside 10 percent of salary costs for merit increases. Your total current annual salary cost is $297,300, which means that you have $29,730 for salary increases. There are no formal company restrictions on how you may distribute the 10 percent merit increase. Indicate the size of the raise that you would like to give each sales manager. All managers have the same job classification, and the salary recommendations are secret.

Employee Profile Sheet

- *John Smith* Age 30, three children, current annual salary $59,000, MBA, Harvard. John is married to the daughter of the chairman of the board and has been with the company five years, the last two as sales manager. He has one of the easiest groups to supervise, doesn't impress you as being very bright, but is a hard worker. You rated him as "slightly above average" (68 percent) on his last performance rating. You checked your opinion with others you respect; they, too, felt that he was less effective than other managers who work for you, but they reminded you of his potential influence.
- *Larry Foster* Age 27, single, current annual salary $38,300, BA, University of Maine. Larry has been with the company for four years, the last two as sales manager. He has a difficult group to supervise, is bright, often works overtime, and has "turned around" the group he supervises. You rated him as "an excellent manager with a good future" (89 percent) on his last performance rating.
- *Tim Hall* Age 44, four children, two in college, current annual salary $60,000 (three years of college, no degree). Tim has worked for the company for the past 18 years and has been in his current position for the past 8 years. He is unhappy that you were named regional sales manager because he was hoping to get the job. He is well-liked by all the other managers and by his employees. He rarely works on weekends, and he seems to be easygoing with his salespeople. However, his group had the second highest performance of the groups you manage. You rated him as outstanding (85 percent) on his last performance appraisal.
- *Ellen Panza* Age 30, married, two children, current annual salary $45,000, BA, City University of New York. Ellen has been with the company for two years and worked as sales analyst for the one year before being promoted to manager. You feel that she was given the job because she is a woman, and frankly, you resent it. In addition, you feel that her salary is too high compared with the salaries of others in the company. However, you must admit that she

has performed in an outstanding manner, since her group went from last to first place in performance this year. Her score on the rating sheet was 90 percent.

- *Otto Lechman* Age 36, married (wife works for the company as assistant personnel director), no children, current salary $55,000, MBA, University of Michigan. Otto has been with the company for nine years, the past six as manager. He is aggressive and hot-tempered, and though at one time you thought he was your best employee, during the past two years, you have found him to be a disappointment. You rated him as "slightly below average" (59 percent) on his last performance rating. You believe that one of the reasons Otto's performance has fallen off is that he has found out about John Smith's and Ellen Panza's salaries.

- *David L. Green III* Age 29, single, current annual salary $40,000, BA, Wayne State University. David has been with the company for six years and became the first black manager in your company five years ago. He has been instrumental in recruiting other blacks into the company and is often called on by the president to represent the company at civic and social events. You have found David's work to be marginal, and although you assigned him to manage the best group five years ago, the group's performance is not as high now. Based on the drop in performance, you rated David as "below average" (60 percent). Some people would like to get rid of him, but you don't know how you would replace him given his past success in recruiting minorities.

Your company has a secret pay policy. What information do you plan to share with your employees? What was your decision rule for administering the pay increases?

IN-CLASS EXERCISES

14-1: "Changing Sales Compensation Plans"*

Bob Grayson, vice president of sales for Widget Corporation, spent two weeks reviewing the company's current compensation plan. After deciding that the plan no longer matched the company's new objectives and attitude, he revamped it. Salespeople's commission would no longer be based solely on revenue generation. Now that the company was trying to be more customer-driven and give better service, 70 percent of the commission would be based on a sales quota, and 30 percent would be based on the quality of service given to current customers (which would be judged by repeat business and surveys). However, sales quotas for bringing in new business were increased to reflect the coming year's projected increase in business.

Three months after implementing the new compensation plan, Grayson noticed that sales were falling and that morale was low. When he met with his salespeople to discuss the problem, he found that they felt cheated: how could they meet their quota—necessary to keep their job—and still provide the kind of service needed to earn the same money they earned on their previous plan?

Questions:

1. Was the new compensation plan fair? Why or why not?
2. What advice would you give to help Grayson design a new compensation plan that a sales force will enthusiastically accept?

14-2: "The Elusive Commission: Now You See It, Now You Don't"*

Janice Stewart, the director of sales and marketing for Corporate Designs Limited, is appalled. Company President John Dancer again adjusted one of her sales rep's commissions. When the rep, Nancy Carr, finds out, she'll certainly quit.

---

*Contributed by Raymond Rody, Loyola Marymount University.

For the six months since CDL hired its first two sales reps, Dancer has skirted the issue of finalizing a compensation plan. Instead, he's assigned a commission percentage on a per-project basis. On several occasions, however, once the sale was made, Dancer decided the project didn't warrant the original commission and lowered it by whatever he felt was appropriate. In this case Dancer lowered the commission by $8,000.

Stewart did her best, as usual, to keep the commission as promised, but once Dancer's mind is made up, that is that. He feels that the handsome base salary and benefits package are more than enough to compensate for any discrepancies in commissions. When Stewart tells Carr about the commission change, Carr's response is as Stewart expected: Get my $8,000 back or today's my last day. Stewart doesn't want to lose half of her brand-new sales force.

Questions:

1. What could she do to broker a compromise between Dancer and Carr?

2. It is obvious that Stewart should try to change Dancer's mind about not having one standardized commission program. What would you recommend she do?

PROBLEMS*

1. You are considering the following three compensation plans for your sales staff. Which of these will be the most expensive? Which will be the least expensive? Which plan would you adopt for your sales staff? Why?

Plan A: Give each salesperson a salary of $35,000 a year and a bonus of 8 percent of all sales made over $360,000 each year.

Plan B: Give each salesperson a salary of $25,000 plus an 8 percent commission on all sales made each year.

Plan C: Give each salesperson a commission of 15 percent on the first $360,000 of sales made each year and 25 percent on all sales made over $360,000.

Below are the forecasted sales for next year. An excel spreadsheet is available to help you in your analysis. When using the excel spreadsheet, insert *only* next year's forecasted sales for each salesperson and Plan A and Plan B salary figures into the appropriate columns on the spreadsheet. The remaining columns have the necessary formula to calculate the compensation for each plan.

Salesperson	Forecasted Sales for Next Year
Munoz	$450,000
Pitt	$420,000
Jones	$400,000
Li	$380,000
Clancy	$380,000
Barone	$360,000
Dark	$360,000
Carter	$340,000
Doran	$340,000
Mickfly	$300,000
Total	$3,730,000

---

* Contributed by Avery Abernathy, Auburn University. Excel spreadsheets for working on these problems are available at www.wiley.com/college/dalrymple. Go to "Student Resources."

2. You own the XYZ Company and your goal is to maximize your before-tax profits. You currently pay salespeople a base salary and a flat 4% commission on sales. You sell three products. Following this question is an Excel spreadsheet printout titled "Current Situation" that gives the starting information.

Unit Costs do not include sales commission costs. You have 10 salespeople. You pay them $20,000 salary and $10,000 benefits each. This gives you $300,000 fixed sales costs. You have annual fixed costs of $1,200,000 (including fixed sales costs).

Unfortunately, your firm keeps losing the best salespeople. You are considering several options to retain your best salespeople. (1) Increase the commission to 6% or (2) alter the commission structure to reflect the profitability of each product. You think that if the total compensation plan is increased for the salesforce that your sales will increase 10% next year due to retaining the best people and increased motivation. Without this increase in sales compensation, you think that sales will increase 6%.

You might want to look at the potential financial impact of: (a) doing nothing, (b) increasing the commission from a flat 4% to a flat 6%, or (c) increasing the commissions in a manner that reflects the profitability of each product.

1. What was your total profit before taxes *this year*?
2. What is your expected total profit before taxes next year if the salesforce payment plan remains the same?
3. What is your expected total profit before taxes *next year* if you increase commissions to 6%?
4. If you raise your commissions to 6%, sales are expected to increase next year by 10% instead of 6%. Is this a reasonable expectation? What is the percentage increase in before-tax profit next year for a 6% commission compared to a 4% commission?
5. What were your unit contributions this year for products A, B and C?
6. Since your goal is to maximize before-tax profits next year, *specifically* how should you increase the commission structure to retain your best salespeople? Be sure to explain your answer.

A quick way to complete this exercise is to copy the first spreadsheet and then adjust the copied tables for the new information given above. Note that you will have to change the formulas in the cells titled "Commissions per Unit" and "Sales Commissions" to reflect the new adjustment on the commission increase. For example, to change the commission increase to 6%, you just multiply the unit sales by the new increase and change the sales commission percentage. Also, remember to change the units sold formula! The program *automatically* redoes all of the other calculations.

Current Situation ($30,000 and 4% Commission)

Unit Analysis	Product 1	Product 2	Product 3	Totals
Price per unit	$117.00	$29.00	$355.00	
Cost per unit	$55.00	$17.40	$195.25	
Commissions per unit	$4.68	$1.16	$14.20	
Contribution per unit	$57.32	$10.44	$145.55	
Aggregate Analysis				
Units sold	15,674	12,334	9,123	37,131
Dollar sales	$1,833,858.00	$357,686.00	$3,238,665.00	$5,430,209.00
Dollar costs	$862,070.00	$214,611.60	$1,781,265.75	$2,857,947.35
Sales commissions	$73,354.32	$14,307.44	$129,546.60	$217,208.36
Net contribution	$898,433.68	$128,766.96	$1,327,852.65	$2,355,053.29
Total net contibution	$2,355,053.29			
Total pretax profit	$1,155,053.29			

CASE *14-1* MADISON FIBER CORPORATION

*E*arly in February 1993, executives of the Madison Fiber Corporation of Baltimore, Maryland, were discussing some proposals to modify the company's sales-force compensation plan. The discussion had been prompted by the recent broadening of the product line and by widespread disenchantment with the current compensation plan, a straight salary system with an annual bonus set by means of subjective evaluations. Furthermore, Madison executives had recently reorganized the sales force. They believed that, if changes in compensation were to be made, now was the most appropriate time to make them.

COMPANY AND INDUSTRY BACKGROUND

Madison produced synthetic fibers, yarns, and fabrics. The company was founded in 1955 to serve a rapidly changing carpet-manufacturing industry. Subsequent to its founding, the firm made several major breakthroughs in synthetic fiber technology and production. These advances enabled Madison to become a significant supplier of synthetic carpet fiber as well as to make competitive entries into related fields.

Madison's three major product lines were synthetic carpet fiber, yarns, and industrial fabrics. Madison's synthetic carpet fiber—a monofilament—was used by leading carpet mills that produced tufted and needle-punch carpets for commercial and residential carpeting. The company manufactured synthetic yarns by twisting monofilament synthetic fibers into multifilament and ribbon styles for a variety of applications, including webbing in aluminum lawn furniture, grilles on high-fidelity speakers, and automobile seat covers. By weaving the yarns the company manufactured industrial fabrics used as bagging for such products as seeds, beans, fertilizer and minerals, and as sheeting for such applications as tents, swimming-pool covers, industrial wraps, and tarpaulins. Because monofilament fiber was the base material for carpet fiber, yarn, and fabric, companies competing in any one of the

above markets tended to compete in the others as well. Madison executives expected competitive pressure from industry overcapacity to become intense by the end of 1993. They ranked Madison fifth among its competitors in manufacturing capacity and estimated that the largest firm in the industry was four times Madison's size. Selected market estimates, forecasts, and sales data for carpet fiber and other Madison products are shown in Exhibit 1.

The Carpet Fiber Market

For many years the dominant materials used in carpet manufacturing were of natural origin such as wool. During the 1960s, synthetic fibers began to take a larger share of the market. Madison and its competitors moved quickly to increase their capacities for manufacturing synthetic fiber. By 1988 the synthetic-fiber industry was operating at capacity. During the period 1989–1991, however, the carpet-manufacturing industry experienced a period of stagnant sales growth. An upturn in 1992 signaled to Madison executives that the period 1993–1998 might promise a 4% annual increase in industry sales. Accordingly, using 1988 capacity as the base of 100, Madison executives were in the process of adding capacity to increase this figure to 115 by the end of 1993 and to 155 by the end of 1995. Most carpet customers (with a few notable exceptions) were located in the South; the majority were in or around Dalton, Georgia.

The Yarn Market

Because of the many potential applications for synthetic yarn and fragmented industry data, company executives could not estimate potential sales volume or Madison's share of the synthetic-yarn market. Company executives believed that Madison's sales were limited only by its ability to create customers and by available machine time. Currently, the company's backlog of firm orders extended into the middle of 1993. The available data indicated to company execu-

This case was prepared by Derek A. Newton. The case was written as a basis for class discussion rather than to illustrate effective or ineffective handling of an administrative situation. Copyright © 1993 by the University of Virginia Darden School Foundation, Charlottesville, VA. All rights reserved. To order copies, send an e-mail to dardencases@virginia.edu. No part of this publication may be reproduced, stored in a retrieval system, used in a spreadsheet, or transmitted in any form or by any means—electronic, mechanical, photocopying, recording, or otherwise—without permission of the Darden School Foundation. Reproduced by permission.

EXHIBIT 1   Sales Volume and Forecasts ($ million)

	Actual		Forecast		
	1991	1992	1993	1994	1995
Carpet-fiber industry (est.)	$829.7	$846.3	$880.1	$915.4	$952.0
Madison carpet-fiber sales	$87.1	$89.7	$96.8	$106.1	$116.1
Madison market share (est.)	10.5%	10.6%	11.0%	11.6%	12.2%
Madison yarn sales	$35.6	$38.3	$47.2	$57.9	$71.7
Madison fabric sales		$2.6	$12.9	$14.2	$15.6
Madison total sales	$122.7	$130.6	$150.6	$178.2	$203.4

tives that Madison had a small and spotty share of some of the applicable markets for synthetic yarns in 1992. For instance, they estimated they had 8% of the grille cloth market, 15% of the static automobile seat cover market, and 8% of the declining market for lawn-furniture webbing. Most of Madison's yarn customers were located near Chicago or other large industrial cities. Many potential yarn markets and customers were not being covered at all.

The Industrial Fabric Market

Because executives had waited to develop truly superior products, the firm was late in entering the industrial-fabric market. Madison fabric products were introduced during the last quarter of 1991. Demand for this material was so great in 1992 that the company was able to sell all of its limited production. There was no discernible geographic pattern among potential fabric customers.

MADISON'S MARKETING ACTIVITIES

Madison was organized into four departments: marketing, finance and administration, operations, and research and development. Each department was headed by a vice president, who reported to the company president. Three of the departments employed fewer than 60 people; operations employed more than 400. Reporting to the vice president for marketing were a customer-service manager, a sales manager, and three product-development managers (one for carpet fibers, one for yarns, and one for industrial fabric).

The customer-service manager handled telephone contacts with customers, solving customers' billing, delivery, and technical problems. She also served as an "inside" sales representative, referring sales leads and requests for product information to the appropriate sales rep. These inside sales activities, however, were always credited to the sales rep assigned to the account.

The product development managers helped sales reps and customers solve technical problems; analyzed the current and potential market for their products; suggested product-development or line-extension opportunities; developed specifications for new and proposed products; and forecasted demand for new, existing, and proposed products by making appropriate economic and profit analyses. The product-development managers were expected to be technically expert with regard to customers' manufacturing techniques, as well as familiar with the marketplace and likely prospects for new and existing product offerings. Unlike a typical "brand manager," the product-development managers had no responsibility for sales volume or profits.

The sales manager developed sales plans by product, territory, and account and also directed the sales force. The current sales manager had been promoted to his present position in January 1992, after ten years as a Madison sales rep. He was 42, a college graduate, and earned about $75,000 a year in salary and management bonus.

Because the equipment used to manufacture synthetic fibers, yarns, or fabric represented a substantial capital investment, the company's basic business strategy was to attempt to operate at full capacity (normally two shifts) at all times. Fluctuations in consumers' demand for carpeting and competitive or technological developments, however, often created undersold or oversold conditions.

Capacity-forecasting and profit problems led Madison executives to take steps to reduce the firm's heavy reliance on the carpet-manufacturing industry. Accordingly, they decided in 1990 to broaden research and development in yarn and fabric for other industries. In 1991 Madison diversified into industrial fabric and began a marketing strategy to increase the proportion of sales of products other than carpet fiber.

In the carpet market, Madison's new strategy was to increase its share of business with high volume accounts where it could become the primary supplier. Historically, Madison had been the secondary or tertiary supplier in such acounts, a condition that exacerbated the cyclicality of the business. A second objective was to reduce dependence on small accounts whose positions in the marketplace were marginal from the standpoints of credit and potential growth.

In the yarn market the strategy was to find new applications that would appeal to manufacturers with high poundage or high square-foot requirements. New customers had to be found beyond manufacturers of furniture, automobile seat covers, and grille cloth. Applications that would not generate significant volume were considered unattractive because of their low margins.

In the industrial-fabric market, the strategy was to provide improved material and new applications in volume for customers who were using or were likely to switch to superior synthetic fabric in some of their present or new end products. Examples of such products were specialty bagging (sacks, bales, bags), swimming-pool covers, tenting, tarpaulins, and industrial product wraps. Management estimated that much of the domestic market was concentrated in 100 large potential accounts. Major marketing efforts were to be undertaken at first, however, with only the largest potential customers with high-volume applications. This strategy required a very high investment in weaving and coating equipment. Madison was obliged to take heavy debt to enter this capital-intensive business.

SALES AND SALES MANAGEMENT ACTIVITIES

The job of the Madison sales reps was multifaceted. First, they were expected to service Madison accounts and obtain orders for all Madison product lines. By virtue of personal acceptability and technical competence, they were expected to assist customers in determining appropriate inventory levels, to monitor and correct possible problems as regards the quality of delivered products, to monitor and correct Madison's delivery service, to handle complaints, and to serve generally as on-the-spot trouble-shooters.

Second, the sales reps were expected to increase the proportion of business that Madison was obtaining from each account. Because most larger companies, particularly those purchasing carpet fiber, preferred to purchase from several sources, it was important that the sales reps penetrate past the customer's purchasing office and become influential with all important decision makers within the customer's operation.

Third, the sales reps were expected to work closely with the product-development managers to seek new applications for existing products and extensions of the product line, and to introduce new products to present and potential customers. In effect, between working with accounts and developing a close liaison with the product-development managers, a good part of the sale reps' job was to manage relations between the Madison plant and its customers.

Fourth—and increasingly important—given the company's efforts to reduce its dependence on carpet-manufacturing customers—the sales reps were expected to prospect for new accounts for yarns and fabrics. They were responsible for generating leads by observing, listening, reviewing such sources as the *Thomas Register,* and following up inquiries forwarded from the customer-service manager.

Thus, sales reps were required to call upon many different kinds of customers, ranging from large carpet manufacturers to small grille-cloth weavers to industrial packaging firms. They could experience considerable difficulty in determining who and where the likely prospects were for a number of quite different product applications. Finally, the company's marketing strategy was still in the process of evolving, forcing sales reps to tailor their activities by industry and by geographic area.

Late in 1991, the sales organization had been reduced from two regional managers supervising 14 Madison sales reps and four commission agents, to a single sales manager supervising 12 sales reps. This action had been taken after a detailed study of the sales reps' activities had revealed that the sales force was underutilized. As a consequence, each territory had been studied to determine the optimum number of calls per day from a well-planned itinerary. Each current account was analyzed to determine how many calls per year were required to offer the desired amount of service and selling time. A similar procedure was undertaken with respect to current and potential prospects. This analysis produced the current territory assignments and a concomitant increase in the number of required and actual sales calls per week. As Exhibit 2 shows, the dollar sales for 1992 were similar among the sales territories, except for the Atlanta territory with its large concentration of carpet manufacturers.

The current sales reps had been with Madison from four to twenty years. They had been hired as experienced sales reps and their ages ranged from 33 to 52. The company had no formal training program beyond a two-week tour in the plant to gather technical knowledge and a two-week tour in the field with an experienced sales rep to "learn the ropes."

In 1992, in recognition of the sales manager's increased span of control, three control forms were instituted to monitor the field activities of the sales force. The first was a weekly itinerary submitted by the sales rep to the sales manager. It listed the sales rep's planned calls by account and by day. It was faxed in to the sales manager on Friday to cover the following week. The second form was a trip report, which the sales rep filled out after each call. The sales rep listed the account's name, persons contacted, purpose of the call, results of the call, whatever marketing intelligence he or she had gathered, and whatever follow-up action should be taken by the sales rep or by the Madison plant. For a serious complaint, the sales rep was required to fill out a complaint report in seven copies, which were routed to various departments within Madison, depending upon the nature of the complaint. This form was also used to request price adjustments and to advise other Madison departments of problems with service, billing, pricing, delivery, and quality control.

The sales manager tried to maintain personal contact with each of the 12 sales reps by telephone at least once a week. His objective was to spend two and one-half to three days a week in the field working with the sales reps and calling on customers with them. This schedule permitted him to work in the field with each sales rep for two or three days in each quarter. An annual sales meeting, usually held in February, brought all the marketing and sales personnel together in Baltimore. This meeting, a combination of social and business activities, was the company's major opportunity to inform the sales force of technical developments in the Madison product line and to review marketing plans.

The sales manager conducted a formal performance review with each sales rep at the end of the year. The review took place either in the field or during a sales rep's visit to the Madison plant. The vehicle for performance appraisal was a two-page sheet that provided space for the sales manager to write a subjective appraisal and developmental action plan in each of six areas: technical knowledge, quality of work, quanity of work, initiative, relations with Madison personnel, and office procedures. These criteria were used throughout the company, and the form was standard for all departments and for all nonmanagerial employees.

The current compensation plan for the sales force paid a straight salary that, in 1992, averaged $50,000, plus a year-end bonus ranging from $4,000 to $6,000 per person. The size of the bonus depended on the collective subjective judgments of the sales manager, the marketing vice president, and the president. Seldom, according to the sales manager, was the size of the bonus related directly to sales dollars produced. In addition to earnings, the sales rep received all normal fringe benefits, plus a company car. He or she was reimbursed for all normal business expenses after submitting a monthly expense report.

THE COMPENSATION ISSUES

The first problem that senior executives had to deal with was the appropriate amount of compensation.

EXHIBIT 2   Individual Territory Results and Earnings–1992

Territory	Number of Actual and Potential Accounts[1]	Carpet Backing ($mm)	Yarn ($mm)	Fabric ($mm)	Total ($mm)	Salary	Bonus
Atlanta	42	$25.2	$1.9	$0	$27.1	$58,000	$5,200
Baltimore	40	8.3	1.8	0	10.1	49,000	4,000
Boston	38	1.9	6.6	0.2	8.7	51,000	4,200
Chicago	48	5.7	3.2	0.6	9.5	52,000	6,000
Cleveland	41	3.5	5.3	0.3	9.1	47,000	5,500
Detroit	50	2.8	6.6	0.4	9.8	48,000	5,000
Houston	44	8.8	0.7	0.2	9.7	44,000	5,700
Los Angeles	45	4.7	3.7	0.5	8.9	54,000	5,500
New York	44	9.5	0.3	0.1	9.9	57,000	4,700
Philadelphia	36	9.0	0.3	0	9.3	47,000	4,200
Pittsburgh	42	3.7	5.0	0.2	8.9	45,000	4,200
San Francisco	42	2.9	2.9	0.1	9.6	48,000	5,800
TOTAL	512	$89.7	$38.3	$2.6	$130.6	$600,000	$60,000

[1]Potential accounts referred to identified prospects whom the sales reps intended to call upon or had been called upon.

Madison executives estimated that the average sales rep's earnings in the industry were approximately $60,000 a year (including company car), although sales reps for two of Madison's larger competitors probably averaged about $75,000 a year. Earnings for the top sales reps in the industry appeared to be in the neighborhood of $80,000 to $100,000 a year.

The sales manager recognized that Madison sales reps' earnings were close to the industry average. But he argued that, because Madison was a small company relative to its major competitors, Madison should pay more than average compensation in order to attract and keep the best possible sales reps. The controller argued that, because turnover was almost nonexistent, there was no need to pay Madison sales reps more than they were already getting.

The second issue was the method of compensation. Firms in the industry exhibited considerable variety in methods of compensating their sales reps. Two of the large firms paid straight salary only. Some smaller companies used commissioned agents who paid their own expenses from a commission rate of one and one-half percent of their sales. Most of Madison's competitors, however, used a salary system with some form of bonus payment. Each of these methods had its adherents within Madison.

The president indicated that the decision of how the sales reps were to be compensated would be left up to the sales manager, the marketing vice president, and the company controller. He placed two constraints on their decision, however: (1) No sales rep doing a good job should suffer financially from a change in the pay plan and (2) if a bonus system was instituted, no sales rep could earn more than 50% of his or her salary in bonus, because the Madison managerial bonus plan had the same limit.

Accordingly, the marketing vice president, the sales manager, and the controller met to discuss the options they had studied over the past six months. These options are described below.

Straight Salary

The controller advocated paying sales reps a straight salary and basing future salary adjustments on past performance. He argued that a straight salary would give managers tight control over the sales reps' order taking and account servicing. Because much of the sales reps' success depended upon their ability to bring the internal resources of the company to bear on the solution of customer problems, the "credit" for the sale belonged to everyone in the Madison organization. Furthermore, much of their business was "handed to

them on a silver platter" and was not a direct consequence of their individual initiative.

The sales manager disagreed. He maintained that straight salary gave sales reps no incentive to develop new business or to increase business with current customers, and that these objectives were the real focus of their efforts. He added that both these activities were critical to the success of the company's strategic shift in product and customer emphasis. Furthermore, he maintained that salary adjustments would be determined by the same subjective evaluations that made Madison executives uncomfortable in determining bonuses under the current system.

Continuation of Current Plan

The major argument for continuing the present plan was based upon the marketing vice president's idea that "the devil you know is better than the devil you don't." He maintained that the current system had the advantages of familiarity and control over unexpected events. He recognized, however, that the current plan was favored neither by the sales reps, who had been complaining about the subjectivity of the bonus determination, nor by the sales manager, who was particularly uncomfortable when explaining to the sales reps the basis for these subjective judgments.

Straight Commission

Straight commission was the plan favored by the sales reps. The commission rate under discussion was 0.6% of sales, paid monthly. The sales reps argued that they would be inclined to work harder if they were treated "as if they were in business for themselves," and that their efforts to maximize their own incomes would maximize the achievement of company objectives. The controller pointed out to the sales manager and the marketing vice president that straight commission meant that, as the firm grew and increased its efficiency, it could never improve its ratio of sales to cost of selling. The marketing vice president expressed the opinion that he did not want the sales reps "in business for themselves," he wanted them "working for Madison." The sales manager sympathized with both of these reservations, but he thought that straight commission might make his managing job easier because he would have to do less "booting them in the tail."

Salary Plus Annual Bonus Based on Product-Line Sales

The sales manager proposed an annual bonus based on product-line sales "over quota." He favored establishing quotas for each sales rep for each major product line-carpet fiber, yarn, and industrial fabric. At 100% of quota for each product, sales reps would receive no bonuses; for each 3% in excess of quota for each product line, a sales rep would receive a bonus of 1% of salary. Thus, if a sales rep exeeded his or her personal quota for each of the three product lines by 9%, the annual bonus would be 3% + 3% + 3% or 9% of salary. The maximum bonus would be 50% of salary. The annual bonus would be supplemented by a one-time award given for each new account, to equal one-tenth of one percent of the new account's first-year sales, with a maximum-payment of $500 per account. This payment would be made as soon as possible after the anniversary date of the new account's first order.

The controller was less than enthusiastic about this plan, maintaining that the quotas might be set too low, resulting in overpayment to the sales reps. He also wondered about the effects of windfall sales. The marketing vice president wanted to know how the sales managers planned to make the quotas fair, because sales in the past had sometimes been limited by plant capacity.

Salary Plus Quarterly Bonus Based on "Capitalized Sales Expense"

One of the product managers had passed along to the marketing vice president an article describing the "capitalized sales expense" approach to compensation. This method required that managers first determine the sales expenses that they were willing to incur. This expense was expressed as a percentage of sales. The salary and controllable expenses incurred by a sales rep were then divided by this percentage. The resulting amount, called a "bogey," was to be used as a dollar sales quota. The sales rep would receive a bonus for sales in excess of the "bogey." The bonus would be set at a fixed percentage of these excess dollar sales, at a rate below the figure for the desired sales expenses,

expressed as a percentage of sales. No bonus could exceed 50% of a sales rep's salary.

The marketing vice president was intrigued enough by this idea to calculate some percentages illustrating it. He set desired sales expenses at 1% of sales and set the bonus at 0.5% of sales in excess of bogey. He then figured the quarterly bonus for a sales rep who earned a salary of $15,000 for the three-month period, made $2,300,000 in sales, and incurred $5,000 in expenses during the same period.

$$\frac{\text{3 months' salary} + \text{3 months' controllable territory expenses}}{0.01} = \text{bogey}$$

$$(\text{3 months' sales} - \text{Bogey}) \times 0.005 = \text{bonus}$$

$$\frac{\$15,000 + \$5,000}{0.01} = \$2,000,000 = \text{bogey}$$

$$\$2,300,000 - \$2,000,000 = \$300,000$$
(sales in excess of bogey)

$$\$300,000 \times 0.005 = \$1,500$$
(bonus for the quarter)

The marketing vice president felt that this system would appear too complicated to the sales force, although he recognized that the bogey derived from capitalizing sales expense seemed less arbitrary than a quota "plucked out of the air." The controller felt that the system would be too complicated to administer, although he realized that the cost of sales would decline as the sales reps exceed their bogey. The sales manager noted that this plan neither emphasized sales by product line, nor motivated sales reps to open new accounts. But he acknowledged that the system would encourage sales reps to keep their expenses down, because spending less than budget would lower their bogey.

CASE 14-2 POWER & MOTION INDUSTRIAL SUPPLY, INC.

*I*t was 7:00 on Sunday evening when Hal Maybee returned to his office. He had spent the afternoon golfing with one of his customers, and he now had to decide what he was going to tell the head office on Monday morning with regard to new salaries for the sales staff at his branch.

Hal had just been appointed Atlantic Region District Manager for one of Canada's largest industrial distributors. His appointment was made only two weeks before, following the sudden death of Fergie McDonald, who at 48 years old, had been in charge of the company's most profitable branch. About 70 percent of the sales in Atlantic Canada, including the four most profitable product lines, were for manufacturers that the company did not represent on a national basis. There were many manufacturers in Ontario and Quebec that served central Canada with their own sales forces, and used distributors for the east and west coasts due to the distances from their head offices and the geographical dispersion of customers in those regions. Although Power Motion had sales agreements with over 400 North American manufacturers, only about 100 manufacturers were involved in 80 percent of the sales.

It was a complete surprise to Hal when he was promoted, and he knew there were people at the branch who thought they deserved it more. Exhibit 1 shows the performance evaluations that Fergie had completed on the six salespeople just before he died. Head office had intended to send only five forms to Hal, but one of the secretaries mistakenly included Fergie's evaluation of Hal as well.

Nearly three weeks previously, Fergie and Hal were making some joint calls on some pump mills in northern New Brunswick, the territory that Fergie kept for himself, even though head office wanted him to stop selling and spend more time on sales administration. During the trip, Fergie told Hal that he was given 6 percent of the total sales staff salary to be divided among them for the coming year. This was the customary way of giving salary increases at the branches, as it gave the head office the discretion to decide the total increase in the salary expense, but it gave the district managers responsibility for allocating salary increases. Fergie was told that nationally, sales increases would average about 3 percent, but his branch was among the lowest paid in the company and had been the best-performing branch for several years.

Hal did not want to express his opinions, as he knew he and Fergie would disagree. However, he did allow Fergie to express his own thoughts on the staff. There were two salespeople that Fergie had a real problem with. He viewed Jim Stanley as his biggest problem. Jim actually had seniority at the branch. He had been hired, as shipper, order desk salesperson, and secretary when the branch was only large enough to support one person other than Bob Laird, the first salesperson the company had in Atlantic Canada. Bob and Jim operated the branch for almost two years when Bob decided to hire Fergie as a salesperson to help develop the territory. When Bob retired, Jim thought he would get the position as District Manager, as he had seniority, and he had experience with all aspects of the business including managing the office and warehouse, which had grown to include seven people. He was very disappointed when the head office gave the position to Fergie, as he had no experience other than sales.

Within a year, Jim decided he wanted to get into sales. He was finally resigned to the fact that office management was a dead-end job, and the only possibility for advancement was through sales. Now, after five years, Jim was not performing as well as he should. In fact, he hated selling and spent an increasing amount of time drinking while away from home. He hinted that he wanted to get back into the office. However, when these rumors started to spread, the staff let it be known that they did not want to work under Jim again if there were any alternatives.

Fergie was thinking about giving Jim a good salary increase. First, it might make him appreciate his job more, and maybe he would put more effort into selling.

This case was prepared by H. F. MacKenzie of Memorial University of Newfoundland, Canada. The case was prepared as a basis for class discussion and is not intended to illustrate effective or ineffective handling of a management situation. All names in the case have been disguised. Copyright © 1994 by H. F. MacKenzie, Memorial University of Newfoundland, Faculty of Business Administration, St. John's, Newfoundland A1B 3X5. Reproduced by permission.

EXHIBIT 1   Evaluation of Salespeople

Salesperson	Evaluation Criteria	Far Worse Than Average			About Average		Far Better Than Average	
Dave Edison	Attitude	1	2	3	4	(5)	6	7
	Appearance and manner	1	2	3	4	5	(6)	7
	Selling skills	1	2	3	4	5	(6)	7
	Product knowledge	1	2	3	(4)	5	6	7
	Time management	1	2	3	(4)	5	6	7
	Customer goodwill	1	2	3	(4)	5	6	7
	Expense/budget	1	2	3	(4)	5	6	7
	New accounts opened	1	2	3	(4)	5	6	7
	Sales calls/quota	1	2	3	(4)	5	6	7
	Sales/quota	1	2	3	4	(5)	6	7
	Sales volume	1	2	3	(4)	5	6	7
	Sales growth	1	2	3	4	(5)	6	7
	Contribution margin	1	2	3	4	5	(6)	7
	Total score: 61							

Comments: Current salary $52,000. Territory is Cape Breton Island and the city of Moncton, N.B. Needs more product knowledge but has learned a lot since hired. A bit aggressive, but he has developed some excellent new accounts through attention to detail and follow-up support.

Salesperson	Evaluation Criteria	Far Worse Than Average			About Average		Far Better Than Average	
Arne Olsen	Attitude	1	2	(3)	4	5	6	7
	Appearance and manner	1	2	(3)	4	5	6	7
	Selling skills	1	2	(3)	4	5	6	7
	Product knowledge	1	2	3	(4)	5	6	7
	Time management	1	2	(3)	4	5	6	7
	Customer goodwill	1	2	(3)	4	5	6	7
	Expense/budget	1	2	3	4	(5)	6	7
	New accounts opened	1	2	(3)	4	5	6	7
	Sales calls/quota	1	2	3	4	5	(6)	7
	Sales/quota	1	2	(3)	4	5	6	7
	Sales volume	1	2	3	(4)	5	6	7
	Sales growth	1	2	(3)	4	5	6	7
	Contribution margin	1	2	(3)	4	5	6	7
	Total score: 46							

Comments: Current salary $44,500. Has been calling regularly on his existing accounts in southern New Brunswick (except Moncton). Although he has increased the number of sales calls, as agreed at our last review, sales have not gone up accordingly. Some concern with product knowledge. Arne knows all of our major product lines very well, but has not shown much effort to learn about many of the new lines we have added that may become our best product lines in the future. Further concern with his contribution margin. This is the fourth year in a row that it has dropped, although it is almost the same as last year.

Salesperson	Evaluation Criteria	Far Worse Than Average			About Average		Far Better Than Average	
Hal Maybee	Attitude	1	2	3	4	(5)	6	7
	Appearance and manner	1	2	3	(4)	5	6	7
	Selling skills	1	2	3	(4)	5	6	7
	Product knowledge	1	2	3	4	(5)	6	7
	Time management	1	2	3	4	5	(6)	7
	Customer goodwill	1	2	3	4	5	(6)	7
	Expense/budget	1	2	3	(4)	5	6	7
	New accounts opened	1	(2)	3	4	5	6	7
	Sales calls/quota	1	2	3	(4)	5	6	7
	Sales/quota	1	2	3	4	(5)	6	7
	Sales volume	1	(2)	3	4	5	6	7
	Sales growth	1	2	(3)	4	5	6	7
	Contribution margin	1	(2)	3	4	5	6	7
	Total score: 52							

EXHIBIT 1 **(Continued)**

Salesperson	Evaluation Criteria	Far Worse Than Average			About Average			Far Better Than Average
					Rating			

Comments: Current salary $38,500. Although still the Office Manager, Hal has taken over Newfoundland as a territory and travels there four times a year. Hal also travels to northern New Brunswick with me occasionally due to his expert product knowledge on electric and pneumatic products, which we sell to the mines and pulp mills in the two areas. Hal is very focused and successful with the big sales but needs to develop knowledge of and interest in some of the lower sales volume, less technical products, as they are generally higher-margin items. Hal has a lot of respect in the office and our efficiency has improved greatly, as has the general work atmosphere within the office.

Salesperson	Evaluation Criteria	1	2	3	4	5	6	7
Tanya Burt	Attitude	1	2	3	④	5	6	7
	Appearance and manner	1	2	3	④	5	6	7
	Selling skills	1	2	3	4	⑤	6	7
	Product knowledge	1	2	③	4	5	6	7
	Time management	1	2	3	4	⑤	6	7
	Customer goodwill	1	2	3	4	⑤	6	7
	Expense/budget	1	2	3	④	5	6	7
	New accounts opened	1	2	3	4	⑤	6	7
	Sales calls/quota	1	2	3	4	⑤	6	7
	Sales/quota	1	2	3	4	⑤	6	7
	Sales volume	1	2	3	④	5	6	7
	Sales growth	1	2	3	4	⑤	6	7
	Contribution margin	1	2	3	4	⑤	6	7
	Total score: 59							

Comments: Current salary $36,000. Very impressed with her performance. Has good knowledge of product pricing and sourcing but needs to learn more about product applications. Tanya sells mainly maintenance and operating supplies, but she has a number of accounts that buy large annual volumes, as her territory is the Halifax-Dartmouth area surrounding our warehouse. Tanya is dedicated and dependable. She has opened many new accounts for us, and I predict good success for her as she continues to develop her knowledge and selling skills.

Salesperson	Evaluation Criteria	1	2	3	4	5	6	7
Jim Stanley	Attitude	1	2	③	4	5	6	7
	Appearance and manner	1	2	③	4	5	6	7
	Selling skills	1	2	③	4	5	6	7
	Product knowledge	1	2	3	④	5	6	7
	Time management	1	②	3	4	5	6	7
	Customer goodwill	1	2	③	4	5	6	7
	Expense/budget	1	2	③	4	5	6	7
	New accounts opened	1	②	3	4	5	6	7
	Sales calls/quota	1	2	3	④	5	6	7
	Sales/quota	1	2	3	4	⑤	6	7
	Sales volume	1	2	3	④	5	6	7
	Sales growth	1	2	3	4	⑤	6	7
	Contribution margin	1	2	3	4	⑤	6	7
	Total score: 46							

Comments: Current salary $42,000. Jim seems to be performing quite well, but there is concern with his behavior. I hope that a salary increase and some direction from me will improve his performance next year. He has been making some suggestions that he might like to move back to office management because everyone thinks I will be promoting Hal to full-time sales and letting him take over my territory as well as Newfoundland. I really do not want Jim back in the office, and I think he should be a good salesperson. His sales and contribution margin are good, but part of his sales increase this year came from a new customer that has a manufacturing plant in his region but actually buys from an office located in Tanya's territory. Tanya and Jim have agreed to split the credit for the sales, as Tanya must do the selling but Jim has to service the account.

Salesperson	Evaluation Criteria	1	2	3	4	5	6	7
Buck Thompson	Attitude	1	2	3	④	5	6	7
	Appearance and manner	1	2	3	④	5	6	7
	Selling skills	1	2	3	4	⑤	6	7
	Product knowledge	1	2	3	4	5	⑥	7
	Time management	1	2	3	④	5	6	7
	Customer goodwill	1	2	3	④	5	6	7

EXHIBIT 1   (Continued)

Salesperson	Evaluation Criteria	Far Worse Than Average			About Average		Far Better Than Average	
	Expense/budget	1	2	③	4	5	6	7
	New accounts opened	1	②	3	4	5	6	7
	Sales calls/quota	1	2	③	4	5	6	7
	Sales/quota	1	2	3	④	5	6	7
	Sales volume	1	2	3	④	5	6	7
	Sales growth	1	2	3	④	5	6	7
	Contribution margin	1	2	3	④	5	6	7
	Total score: 51							

Comments: Current salary $49,000. Sells in Pictou Country, N.S., where we have a very established customer base and a variety of industries. Buck knows all of his customers very well, as he has lived in the area all of his life. He has very good selling skills and product knowledge and has been the main reason we have done so well in his territory.

Second, it would make the position more attractive than a possible return to the office, as he would not want to take a tremendous salary cut.

The other problem was Arne Olsen, the other senior salesperson. As the territory developed quickly, the branch hired a secretary just after Fergie was hired. A month later, a warehouseman was hired and Jim was promoted to Office Manager. Jim immediately hired Hal Maybee as an order desk salesperson. Within a year, another salesperson, Arne, was hired, along with a second secretary. The branch growth slowed but was steady from that point on. Arne was always an average salesperson. He never really had much motivation to perform, but he always did whatever he had to do, so that he was never in any serious trouble as far as his job was concerned. Lately, he was starting to slip a bit, and rumor had it that he was having at least one affair. He also recently bought a Mazda Miata that he drove on weekends, as he was not allowed to drive anything but the company car through the work week.

Dave Edison was with the company for just under one year. If he had had a few more years with the company, Hal knew he would have probably been the new District Manager. He came to the company from the life insurance industry, and rumor had it that he was slated for a national sales manager position within the next year, as the company was rumored to be taking on a new line of capital equipment from Europe that would be sold nationally, but would have one person at head office responsible for national sales.

Tanya Burt was also in sales for only a year. She had been hired as a secretary, but it soon became apparent that she had exceptional telephone skills. She was promoted to order desk salesperson within a year, and three years later, she requested and was given an outside sales territory. There was some concern with her product knowledge but no concern with her attitude or sales ability. Tanya was the first and only woman to be promoted to one of the company's 80 outside sales positions.

Buck Thompson had a very solid, established territory. He needed little direction, as he was doing most things very well. Fergie was a bit concerned that he was not making enough sales calls, but he certainly was performing well.

As Hal reviewed the performance evaluations, he agreed that Fergie had been very thorough and accurate in his assessment of each of the individuals. Hal wondered about the amount of salary increase he should give to each person. While he had to make this decision immediately, Hal realized there were other important decisions he would have to make soon. He recognized some of the problems Fergie had trying to decide salary increases, and these were more important for Hal, as he had to get the support of the sales staff before he could hope to overcome some of these problems. He also had to start thinking about hiring another salesperson to cover Newfoundland and northern New Brunswick, as the head office was determined that he give up responsibility for all accounts in the region. He would, however, be allowed and encouraged to call on customers with the sales staff.

TABLE 15-1   Output Measures Used in Sales Force Evaluation

Performance Measure	Percent Using	Performance Measure	Percent Using
Sales		**Profit**	
Sales volume dollars	79%	Net profit	69%
Sales volume previous year's sales	76	Gross margin percentage	34
Sales to quota	65	Return on investment	33
Sales growth	55	Net profit as a percentage of sales	32
Sales volume by product	48	Margin by product category	28
Sales volume by customer	44	Gross margin dollars	25
New account sales	42		
Sales volume in units	35	**Orders**	
Sales volume to potential	27	Number of orders	47
Accounts		Average size of order	22
Number of new accounts	69		
Number of accounts lost	33		
Number of accounts buying full line	27		

are difficult to measure and often lead to biased evaluations.[3] This same study revealed a decline in the use of input performance measures. One recent explanation is that larger sales organizations rely less on input performance measures when there are more people to evaluate. As a result, managers are putting less emphasis on such factors as number of sales calls, demonstrations, and letters/phone calls to prospects and more emphasis on profit, margin, and expense factors.

THE BIG PICTURE

A logical first step in a sales analysis is to look at aggregate sales figures for a company or division. Some sample sales figures for the Bear Computer Company are provided in Table 15-3. Bear seems to be doing well; sales have increased from $17 million to $26 million in only four years, or 18 percent annually. However, the rate of growth is declining. For some reason, Bear has been unable to maintain the sales increases that it achieved in earlier years. One excuse for such a situation is that slow growth simply reflects general economic conditions. However, industry sales have been expanding rapidly at the same time that Bear's sales gains have fallen off. The resulting impact on market share is shown in column 4. Bear's market position has fallen from 13.6 percent in 1996 to only 8.6 percent in 1999. Thus, although Bear's sales have increased 53 percent, its market share has taken a disastrous plunge. A sales increase, like the tip of the iceberg, tells only part of the story. The *iceberg principle* encourages managers to search through their data to find out what is really going on.

There could be many reasons for the 37 percent drop in market share at Bear Computer. Competitors may simply be more aggressive and may have attracted the new business from

TABLE 15-2   Input or Behavior Bases Used in Sales Force Evaluation

Base	Percent Using	Base	Percent Using
Selling expenses to budget	55%	Number of calls per day	42%
Total expenses	53	Number of reports turned in	38
Selling expenses as a % of sales	49	Number of days worked	33
Number of calls	48	Selling time vs. nonselling time	27

TABLE 15-3   Sales Data for Bear Computer Company

Year	*1* *Company* *Volume* *($ millions)*	*2* *Percentage* *Change from* *Previous Year*	*3* *Industry* *Volume* *($ millions)*	*4* *Company* *Market Share* *(percent)*
1999	26	+ 8.3	300	8.6
1998	24	+14.3	219	10.9
1997	21	+23.5	165	12.7
1996	17	—	125	13.6

Bear. Another possibility is that the product itself may be deficient in terms of performance or reliability. Because personal selling is the primary way of selling business networking computer solutions, it is a potential problem area. Bear may not have enough salespeople or sales offices, or the sales force may not be calling on the right prospects.

Dollar versus Unit Sales

Sales can also be broken out in terms of number of units sold (Table 15-4). Unit sales can be useful when inflation and other price changes distort dollar sales figures. For example, dollar sales of Bear computers went from $16.8 million in 1998 to $18.2 million in 1999. However, unit sales actually declined from 560 to 520 over the same period, meaning that the average price of a Bear computer went from $30,000 in 1998 to $35,000 in 1999. Although some of the 17 percent increase in computer prices was due to inflation, some other factor is contributing to this change. The data suggest that the sales force is trading customers up to the most expensive computers in the line. Another breakdown of sales by individual models of Bear computers would tell you what items are being ignored.

A decline in unit sales is a serious problem in an expanding market, so adjustments should be made in the wage and quota systems to achieve more balanced growth in computer sales. Unit sales growth is desirable because it keeps production lines and employees busy.

A somewhat different situation exists with Bear's line of accessory equipment (Table 15-4). Note that both dollar and unit sales increased between 1998 and 1999. However, unit sales grew much more rapidly than dollar sales, and the average unit price dropped from $1,200 in 1998 to $1,100 in 1999. These results suggest that the sales force may be cutting prices to boost unit volume. This push for market share is to be applauded as long as profit margins are not completely destroyed. Bear's software product line also experienced growth in dollar and unit sales. In this case, the sales force was able to sell more units at higher average prices. These efforts are commendable, but Bear's software sales are still far below the levels suggested by industry and company potential figures.

TABLE 15-4   Comparing Dollar and Unit Sales at the Bear Computer Company

Products	*1998 Sales*			*1999 Sales*		
	Thousands of *Dollars*	*Units*	*Avg, Price* *Per Unit*	*Thousands of* *Dollars*	*Units*	*Avg, Price* *Per Unit*
Computers	$16,800	560	$30,000	$18,200	520	$35,000
Accessories	4,800	4,000	1,200	5,200	4,727	1,100
Software	2,400	1,200	2,000	2,600	1,280	2,031
TOTAL	$24,000	5,760		$26,000	6,527	

Sales by Customer Type

Another useful approach is to break down sales by individual customers. These reviews often show that you obtain a high percentage of sales from a small number of customers. When 80 percent of your sales come from only 20 percent of your buyers, you are probably losing money serving small accounts. Some sales managers use the 80–20 principle to shift low-volume accounts to mail-order, telephone reorder systems, or the Internet. Other firms give small accounts to independent distributors so that the regular sales force can concentrate their efforts on a reduced number of large accounts. Frequently, a policy of providing extra service to large accounts leads to greater total sales for the firm.

EXPENSE ANALYSIS

Although a sales analysis provides useful data on the operation of a field sales force, it does not tell the whole story. Sales figures show trends, but they do not reveal the effects of price-cutting or the differences in selling expenses, potential, and saturation that exist across products or territories. A more complete picture of sales force efficiency can be obtained by reviewing expense data to show the effects of changes in selling tactics on the profitability of the firm.

What Expenses Are Relevant?

We believe that controllable expenses such as wages and travel are the figures that are relevant to field sales managers. Thus national advertising and production costs, which are not directly controlled by sales managers, should not be used to judge the efficiency of the sales organization. Of course, cost-of-goods-sold figures are necessary to help measure price-cutting by salespeople. Table 15-2 shows that the most popular expense measures relate selling expenses to budget figures or to sales.

Product Expenses

A logical first step in an expense analysis is to look at the differences associated with each product line. Table 15-5 shows such an analysis for the Bear Computer Company. Note that the cost of goods sold plus commissions is considerably higher for computers (70 percent) than it is for accessories (60 percent) and software (20 percent). These results can be explained in several ways. One possibility is that Bear is paying too much for parts, with the result that its manufacturing costs are simply higher than those of competitors. Another explanation is that competition has driven down selling prices in the market and raised Bear's cost-of-goods sold as a percentage of sales. A more disturbing possibility is that salespeople are cutting prices on computers to close sales so that they can raise their commission income. If this is the case, then the sales manager may need to place limits on the

TABLE 15-5 Expense Analysis by Product Line, Bear Computer Company, 1999

Products	1999 Sales (000)	CGS and Commission $	CGS as a Percentage of Sales	Contribution Margin	Contribution Margin Percentage
Computers	$18,200	$12,740	70	$5,460	30
Accessories	5,200	3,120	60	2,080	40
Software	2,600	520	20	2,080	80
Total	$26,000	$16,380	63%	$9,620	37%

sales force's authority to negotiate prices. The sales manager could also shift to a gross margin commission system so that there would be less incentive to cut computer prices. A third approach is to revise the commission structure so that salespeople can earn more by pushing the higher-margin accessories and software lines. This discussion shows that a review of the contribution margins produced by different product lines can be very helpful for sales managers.

EVALUATING SALESPEOPLE

One of the most difficult tasks you will face as a sales manager is evaluating the performance of salespeople under your control. Although appraisals are opportunities to motivate salespeople to higher levels of achievement, they also provide evidence for disciplinary action. Thus performance reviews demand that sales managers play the role of coach and judge. One consultant has said, "I'm not aware of a single company happy with the performance appraisal process."[4]

Why Are Performance Reviews Needed?

Performance reviews are usually conducted on an annual basis, although many firms conduct evaluations semiannually or quarterly.[5] While these reviews are difficult to administer, they do provide valuable information for staffing decisions and serve as a basis to improve salesperson performance. The results of performance reviews can be used to answer a number of important questions such as:

- Who should receive raises, bonuses, and prizes?
- Who should be promoted?
- What criteria should be used in hiring?
- Who needs retraining?
- What subjects should be emphasized in training classes?
- Have the company's strategic selling objectives been met?
- How should sales territories be adjusted?
- Who should be terminated?

Each of these decisions requires you to look at a slightly different set of evaluative criteria. For example, performance evaluations used for determining raises, bonuses, and prizes should emphasize activities and results related to the salesperson's current job and situation. Performance evaluations used for the purpose of promoting a salesperson into a sales management position should focus on criteria related to successful sales managers and not just current salesperson performance. Adding to the complexity of the evaluation process is the wide variety of procedures to measure how well salespeople are performing on each dimension.

Behavior versus Output Performance Measures

Although behavior control systems are more widely used than output measures, there is considerable debate as to which approach is better. A model highlighting the differences between input- and output-based systems is shown in Figure 15-2. An example of salespeople who are evaluated on input measures of performance are those who receive the majority of their compensation in salary, such as pharmaceutical, cigarette, and alcohol salespeople. For these people, number of calls, demonstrations, and displays erected are key success factors. On the other hand, managers who direct stockbrokers, insurance, and real estate agents who are paid on commission tend to emphasize output measures. Despite these preferences,

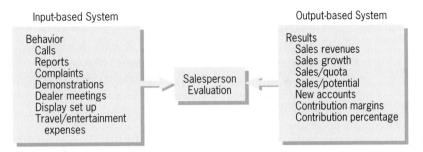

FIGURE 15-2 A Model of Salesperson Evaluation

neither group relies exclusively on input or output measures of performance. Sales jobs are multidimensional and comprehensive evaluation systems must include multiple criteria. Thus, your dilemma is how to select and balance a set of input and output factors that will achieve the best results for your organization. Our discussion of this issue begins with a review of input, or what we call behavioral measures of performance.

BEHAVIOR-BASED EVALUATION

Behavioral systems are concerned with keeping track of what happens at each stage of the sales operation. This means that management must closely monitor sales force activities and direct and intervene to improve customer relations. For example, Swissôtel reviewed the activities of their 10 U.S. salespeople to see how they were allocating their time and how many calls they were making per week.[6] The hotel company found that salespeople were spending too much time in the office preparing proposals and expense accounts instead of talking to customers. Swissôtel set a new goal of six calls per day and expected their people to spend 80 percent of their time in direct customer contact. To help make salespeople more efficient, they equipped them with cellular phones and laptop computers to provide up-to-the-minute inventory of hotel rooms. This provided salespeople with the information needed to close calls on the spot.

Behavior-based systems usually require managers to make some subjective evaluations about individual salespeople. The most common qualitative factors used in these performance evaluations are given in Table 15-6. Note that factors such as communication skills, attitude, initiative, and appearance can only be judged using subjective interpretations and rating scales. This may introduce problems of bias, halo effects, and credibility into the

TABLE 15-6 Qualitative Bases Used in Sales Force Evaluation

Base	Percent Using	Base	Percent Using
Communication skills	88%	Time management	63%
Product knowledge	85	Cooperation	62
Attitude	82	Judgment	62
Selling skills	79	Motivation	61
Initiative and aggressiveness	76	Ethical/Moral behavior	59
Appearance and manner	75	Planning ability	58
Knowledge of competition	71	Pricing knowledge	55
Team player	67	Report preparation and submission	54
Enthusiasm	66	Creativity	54

evaluation process. Despite these limitations, behavioral systems are thought to produce a number of desirable benefits.

Behavior-based evaluation procedures can lead to knowledgeable and expert salespeople who are more committed to the organization. Also, salespeople tend to be self-motivated and react favorably to peer recognition. With behavior systems, salespeople can be expected to spend more time planning their calls and on sales support activities. Finally, behavioral measures encourage salespeople to achieve company goals and better serve the needs of customers.

Support for behavior reviews is shown by a survey of 144 sales executives from a cross section of industries.[7] The managers were asked a variety of questions on behavioral and outcome-based systems. The most interesting finding was a positive relation (+0.17) between the proportion of salary in the compensation system and the achievement of sales objectives. This suggests that a high proportion of wages usually associated with behavior systems produces better results than the high commissions associated with outcome-based plans. These results must be tempered with the knowledge that they reflect the opinions of sales managers rather than the preferences of field salespeople. When 249 salespeople were surveyed, 93 percent said they preferred pay raises over the recognition awards commonly used with behavioral systems.[8]

Another study supporting the value of behavior measures compared activities of top-quartile insurance agents with bottom-quartile agents.[9] The most successful agents were more likely to be able to leverage their time by having customers deal with other agency personnel, were more willing to spend money beyond the office expense allowance, adopted a numbers approach to setting goals, and were more likely to have employees who could back them up when they were out of the office.

It's not surprising that the evaluation process is going through radical transformations in order to meet the challenges of today's economy. AT&T, for example, has recently revamped its evaluation process to help meet the strategic challenges it faces. Managers are evaluating the sales force not just on the increase in sales, but also on a number of other dimensions such as competitor product knowledge, customer knowledge, and the attainment of personal goals. To learn more about how AT&T changed its sales force evaluation process, see the Strategic Action Competency box.

Using Behavior-Based Systems

Successful implementation of behavioral evaluations requires periodic analysis of data on sales force activities. One widely used way to gather this information is through the completion of daily, weekly, or monthly *call reports* by salespeople. These reports detail who was called on, at what stage the prospect is within the sales cycle, and what follow-up activities are needed in the future. Some managers use the 10-3-1 rule, meaning that for every 10 qualified prospects, 3 will entertain a proposal and 1 will become a customer. By monitoring three key databases, a lead log, a proposal log, and an order log, managers can see how reps are moving leads through the sales cycle.

Firms that do not monitor sales force activities can create serious evaluation problems. One company gave its salesperson-of-the-year award to a rep who did not close any new accounts and lost 40 percent of his old customers. Although this person produced high sales revenues by closing a few existing customers, he was not positioned for the future because he had no new prospects to move into the proposal stage. To avoid similar situations, companies are relying on technology-based programs to help keep track of salesperson activities. For example, BellSouth uses ACT!, an activity management software developed by Symantec.[10]

A recent innovation is to have salespeople record call data directly on notebook-sized computer screens. Call report forms are presented on the screen, and salespeople make their

---

STRATEGIC AWARENESS COMPETENCY
Reaching Out Beyond Sales Quotas

AT&T, the New York-based telecommunications company, recently changed the evaluation program it uses to measure the performance of its business-to-business sales force. Instead of measuring—and compensating—its account executives, sales managers, and branch managers on sales quotas alone, the company instituted a behavior-based component to the evaluation process. Now sales professionals are measured based on three specific areas of knowledge in addition to their sales quotas.

The areas are: the business (where sales professionals are measured on their in-depth knowledge of the product line being sold, in addition to their competition's); satisfying the customer (where they are judged on their inability to demonstrate knowledge of a customer's business and be able to develop plans that would assist the customer); and people value-added (where they are judged on either how well they develop their own personal strengths, or how well they developed their own salespeople). Members of the sales staff set their own annual objectives, and are periodically appraised on their progress by a superior.

Victoria Knudson, district manager, business network sales, human resources and employee development, at the company's Basking Ridge, New Jersey, divisional office, feels the program is important because "judging salespeople on sales quotas alone isn't always the best solution. In many sales forces, less-than-average sales are not necessarily the problem, but more, a symptom of a greater problem. It's our responsibility to train the sales force so that all-around excellence can be achieved." See *www.att.com* for more about AT&T.

---

entries with a pen or keyboard. Pharmaceutical salespeople, for example, have doctors sign their names directly on the screens to request product samples. At the end of the day, reps call in with a modem and information is forwarded to central computers for processing. This speeds the collection of field data and simplifies filling of customer requests for samples, brochures, and merchandise. A side benefit of using notebook computers for call reports is that the machines have built-in clocks that allow managers to monitor field activities to ensure that reps actually make the calls they are reporting. The Internet also presents great potential for handling the details of each prospect and customer account, which can translate into a useful tool for manager evaluation and control of salespeople. An interesting Internet application for managing the sales process can be found in the Technology Competency box.

Management by Objectives   A common behavioral system is management by objectives (MBO)—also called development and performance management. With this method, salespeople and sales managers jointly set personal development goals for the subordinate that can be completed within a specific time period. Salespeople then develop an action plan to reach each goal. Written performance appraisals are presented to salespeople during review sessions with sales managers. Reps react favorably to MBO systems because they can see where they stand and know that progress toward their goals will be rewarded.

Although MBO systems work well for some firms, they are not without problems. One issue is that some sales force goals do not lend themselves to expression in quantitative terms. This problem is particularly serious with technical reps when the job often involves problem solving. Also, MBO goals can sometimes become ceilings that salespeople refuse to exceed. Perhaps the biggest weakness of MBO systems is that they require a lot of the sales manager's time and heavy paperwork. Because implementing an MBO control system

TECHNOLOGY COMPETENCY
Internet Shifts in Monitoring Salesperson Activities

Private Business, Inc., a $60-million small-business financing company, recently installed an Internet-based program to help sales managers track the sales process of its 200 salespeople. Unlike the past, where reps used to set up their own presentations and handle every detail of their customers' and prospects' accounts, they now simply access a central Internet site from the field for real-time updates on the time and location of their next appointment—information provided by marketers from home base. The information includes everything from the latest market intelligence on the business to buyer profiles. It even has directions to the buyer's office. Prior to this new system, sales reps would self-report leads and deals in any way that was convenient. "They could have been writing them on cocktail napkins and slipping them underneath the sales manager's door," jokes John Dodd, Private Business vice president. Now, with the new Internet-based system, every sales call is managed in a central data repository, and sales managers can create reports showing the number of deals pending or closed, number of sales calls made as well as the revenue generated by a particular salesperson.

One big adjustment for the sales force is the reduced amount of control over their activities. "With the new technology, some decisions get taken away from you," says Dodd. However, once the sales force adjusted to the new system, productivity increased much more than the other traditional sales force automation software Dodd tried. "There was certainly some irritation and complaining about the new system at first," says Dodd of his sales reps, "But once they saw how much their close rates and commissions shot up, they stopped grumbling."

Private Business, Inc.'s home Web page can be found at *www.privatebusiness.com.*

takes a few days per subordinate per year, a manager supervising 12 salespeople would spend more than a month every year on this activity alone!

Behavioral Observation Scales   An improvement on MBO is an approach called behavioral observation scales (BOS), which focuses on identifying a list of critical incidents that lead to job success. Salespeople, their superiors, and customers can provide inputs for this task. The key job behaviors that are identified can then be grouped together to form job dimensions. Next, five-point scales are attached to each activity. The resulting behavioral scales can be used by regional or district sales managers to measure the frequency with which subordinates engage in critical behaviors.

Scores on scale items are totaled, and categories for adequate, good, excellent, and superior performance are set by management. Use of BOS allows regional managers to measure the personal interaction skills of their district sales managers. Good people skills are often the difference between success and failure among field sales employees. Research has shown that 95 percent of failed managers are weak in this area,[11] and BOS is a good way to identify these problems.

The use of BOS is less time-consuming for sales managers than MBO systems. However, the main problem with BOS is the expense entailed in preparing reliable and valid rating scales. Also, separate job dimensions and critical incidents must be developed for each level and type of sales job.

RESULTS-BASED EVALUATIONS

In results-based evaluations, managers set performance standards for each salesperson and evaluate the results against the preset standards. Results-based evaluations have been shown to increase salesperson job attitudes when the salesperson understands what is expected and is able to modify his or her work strategy to meet the expected goals.[12] An example of a sales results system employed by Bear Computer Company is shown in Table 15-7. The figures are broken out by territory so that the manager can evaluate the performance of individual salespeople. Columns 1 and 2 show year-to-date sales volumes for 1998 and 1999. Note that Brown and West had the highest sales, with Brown also producing the largest dollar increase. When these changes are converted into percentages, we see that Smith had the best sales growth, followed by Jones (column 4). Up to this point, the figures suggest that Brown ranked number one on revenues, and Smith showed the best sales improvement.

Differences in Potential

One problem with the results-based sales figures given in columns 1 through 4 (Table 15-7) is that they do not adequately measure conditions faced by salespeople in the field. Thus the sales outputs we have observed may simply reflect differences in the size of the territories. This suggests that sales results need to be compared with the potential available in each territory.

Bear's sales potential for the four areas can be estimated from published industry figures, from the *Survey of Industrial Purchasing Power,* or from *Census of Business* data. A detailed discussion of ways to estimate potential was covered in Chapter 7. Once reliable measures of potential are available, the next step is to convert these numbers into sales quotas. For example, Jones has 26 percent of the sales potential in the area (column 5, Table 15-7). Because Bear expected district sales to increase 12 percent to $3,623,000 ($3,235,000 × 1.12 = $3,623,000), the sales quota for Jones would be 0.26 × $3,623,000, or $941,980. Similar calculations can provide sales quotas for each territory that can be compared with actual sales results.

Sales to Quota

Dividing actual territory 1 sales of $825,000 by the quota of $942,812 shows that Jones was only producing 87 percent of company expectations (column 7, Table 15-7). Also, Brown has not achieved his quota even though he has the largest potential of all (32 percent). West, who had the lowest dollar increase, was still able to sell 102 percent of his quota. Thus, two territories with large dollar increases in computer sales actually were the two weakest territories when sales were related to potential. The best performance was achieved by Smith, who had the smallest potential in the division and was third in terms of dollar sales growth. These results suggest that you should consider rewarding Smith with some of the accounts from Brown. This change may increase total sales of the division, because Brown is apparently not covering this large market adequately.

TABLE 15-7 Measuring Sales Force Output for Bear Computer Company

	1	2	3	4	5	6	7	8
Territory	Sales '98 Jan–Sept (000)	Sales '99 Jan–Sept (000)	Dollar Change	Sales Growth	Market Potential Index (percent)	Sales Quota (000)	Percentage of Quota Achieved	Sales Variance (000)
Jones	$ 750	$ 825	+ $75	10.0%	26%	$ 943	87%	– $118
Smith	500	570	+ 70	14.0	15	543	105	+ 27
Brown	1025	1110	+ 85	8.3	32	1160	96	– 50
West	960	1000	+ 40	4.2	27	977	102	+ 23
	$3235	$3505	+$270	8.3%	100.0%	$3623		

The figures in Table 15-7 also indicate that Jones needs further review. Jones achieved a 10 percent sales increase, which is better than the average for the division. However, computer sales are still $118,000 below potential (column 8). One possible explanation is Jones is new to the territory and has not had time to develop the area properly. Perhaps the area has a history of poor sales because of competitive pressure, or Jones is poorly trained and needs additional coaching from you. These examples suggest that a careful analysis of territorial sales data can help in addressing problems that affect performance results.

Contribution-Based Evaluations

Measuring salespeople on the basis of the *profit contribution* that results from their activities is often a useful exercise for sales managers. An example of a contribution profit review for Bear Computer Company is shown in Table 15-8. The analysis begins with net sales for each territory, from which the cost of goods sold and sales commissions are subtracted. This gives a *dollar contribution margin.* Note that Brown had the highest dollar margin. However, when the dollar contributions are divided by sales to give a *contribution margin percentage,* West had a 34 percent margin, compared with only 32 percent for Brown. Brown is apparently pushing a mix of items with low markups or is possibly cutting prices to gain sales volume.

Trading Profits for Revenues   The disadvantages of trading profits for volume can be clearly seen by comparing the performances of Jones and Smith. Jones appears to be selling high-profit products at list prices to generate an impressive 40 percent margin. On the other hand, Smith is cutting prices, leaving only a 25 percent contribution margin. These results help explain the sales figures reported in Table 15-7. This earlier analysis showed that Smith achieved a 14 percent sales growth and produced 105 percent of quota. The information in Table 15-8 suggests that the results were related to Smith's selling strategy—offering low prices and pushing low-markup items. Conversely, the high prices charged by Jones resulted in slower sales growth, and Jones attained only 87 percent of the planned sales quota.

An analysis of the direct selling expenses in the four computer sales territories provides another view of the results of individual efforts (Table 15-8). Even though West had the second-highest contribution margin percentage, he was tied with Brown on net profit contribution as a percentage of sales (26 percent). The reason is that Brown kept direct selling expenses to 6 percent of sales, while these expenses ran to 8 percent of sales in West's territory. Part of the problem was that West was paid more than anyone else. In addition, West's expenses for travel, food, and entertainment were relatively high. If these could be reduced to the level achieved by Brown without hurting sales, West's profits would improve substantially.

Buying Customers   Another profitability issue is raised by the activities of Jones, who produced a contribution margin that was 6 percent higher than that produced by any other territory (Table 15-8). However, the profit contribution of 28 percent was only 2 percent more than that generated by Brown and West. The explanation for the failure to push this advantage through to the bottom line lies in the various expense categories. Although Jones's salary ($55,000) seems reasonable, the amounts spent on travel, food, lodging, and entertainment appear to be excessive. While salespeople in the other three territories averaged $11,500 for these expenses, Jones spent $43,900. The typical response of a sales manager to expenditures of this size would be to pressure the salesperson to cut back so that the profit contribution would increase. However, the issue of how much control managers should place on sales expenses is a very delicate one. Salespeople need to spend enough to get the sale, but not so much that profits are reduced. Sometimes it pays to entertain customers. For example, a study revealed that the most successful insurance agents were those who

TABLE 15-8 **Measuring Territory Profit Output for Bear Computer Company**

	Territory Performance (thousands)[a]			
	Jones	*Smith*	*Brown*	*West*
Net Sales	$825	$570	$1100	$1000
Less CGS and Commissions	495	428	744	660
Contribution margin	330	142	356	340
CM as a percentage of sales	40%	25%	32%	34%
Less direct selling costs				
Sales force salaries	55.0	35.0	55.0	65.0
Travel	15.5	4.1	3.5	5.0
Food and lodging	12.5	4.0	3.2	4.5
Entertainment	11.4	0.3	0.5	1.0
Home sales office expense	4.5	2.3	2.0	4.5
Profit contribution	$231.1	$96.3	$291.8	$260.0
PC as a percentage of sales	28%	17%	26%	26%

[a]Sales figures are from Table 15-7.

exceeded their office expense budgets.[13] Thus Jones's success may be due to his ability to wine and dine clients. On the other hand, it is possible that Jones is using his expense account to offer customers under-the-table discounts on the computers. If these travel, food, and entertainment expenditures are legitimate, the manager might consider asking the other salespeople to spend more on these items.

USING MODELS FOR EVALUATION

As mentioned earlier, most sales managers use both behavioral and outcome-based factors. This combination approach allows them to appraise more effectively the multidimensional nature of the field sales job. Several evaluation models allow you to review different aspects of selling at the same time.

Four-Factor Model

Perhaps the simplest sales force evaluation model includes just four measures of performance. Individual input is gauged by the number of days worked and the total number of calls made. The output of the salesperson is measured by the number and average size of orders. These factors are combined to give the following equation:

$$\$\text{ Sales} = \text{Days worked} \times \frac{\text{Calls}}{\text{Days worked}} \times \frac{\text{Orders}}{\text{Calls}} \times \frac{\text{Sales \$}}{\text{Orders}}$$

The four-factor model indicates that sales can be increased by working more days, making more calls per day, closing more sales with customers, and increasing the sales per order. If a salesperson is not generating sufficient volume, then the problem must be a deficiency in one or more of these areas. The model must be used with caution because of the interactions among the factors. Calls, for example, have a positive correlation with sales but often have a negative relationship with sales per order. This means that even though sales increase as you make more calls, at some point the size of the order begins to decline, because there is less time to spend with each customer. Thus there appears to be an optimum number of sales calls for each salesperson that will maximize profits.

TABLE 15-9   Evaluating Performance Using Behavior and Outcome Data

Performance Factors	Pete Jones	Ann Smith
Sales (annual)	$1,400,000	$1,100,000
Days worked	210	225
Calls	1,200	1,500
Orders	480	750
Expenses	$19,000	$14,900
Calls per day	5.7	6.7
Batting average (orders per calls)	40%	50%
Sales per order	$2,916	$1,466
Expenses per call	$15.83	$9.93
Expenses per order	$39.58	$19.86
Expenses as % of sales	1.35%	1.35%

An example of the four-factor model is presented in Table 15-9. The data show that Pete's sales were about average for a salesperson in 1999 ($1,394,260), whereas Ann's were a little low.[14] However, Ann worked more days, made more calls, had lower expenses, and landed more orders. As a result, she made one more call per day and had a 50 percent *batting average* (orders per calls). Although Jones closed the sale on only 40 percent of his calls, he had a high *average order size.* Thus, despite lower values for days worked, calls per day, and batting average, Jones obtained larger orders and a higher total sales volume.

In this case, a sales manager might be tempted to encourage Ann Smith to increase the size of her average order. Suggestions of using different selling strategies to account for differences within and across territories are sometimes warranted. A first step to get Ann to focus on larger accounts, for example, could be to direct her smaller, less profitable, accounts to the Internet for reordering. Care must be taken, however, to approach only those customers who would feel comfortable with this new ordering procedure. Although larger orders should increase total sales, Ann would be making fewer and longer sales calls and possibly a reduction in her batting average. Fewer calls per day produced larger orders in Jones's territory, but it is not clear that this strategy would work as well for Smith. It is possible that Ann's average order size is lower than Pete's because her *account opportunity* is lower. For example, Ann's territory may have fewer numbers of large firms. If this is the case, then Ann's overall evaluation would be higher than Pete's. Also, Pete's expenses are $3,000 above industry averages in 1999 and Ann's are below average.[15] Jones's expenses are also sharply higher than Smith's when expressed on a per-call or order basis. It is important to point out, however, that *expenses as a percentage of sales* were the same for both representatives.

Ranking Procedures

A second way to combine sales force evaluations is to use ranking procedures. Rankings can be added up to give an overall measure of efficiency. For example, Table 15-10 shows how five salespeople ranked on 10 different input/output factors. The first factor used to evaluate performance is sales per person. Although this variable is a good overall measure, it can be deceiving. Note that Ford, for example, had the highest total sales but was last on sales to potential, suggesting that this high volume was due to a large territory. Gold, on the other hand, had low volume and high sales to potential, indicating good coverage of a limited market.

Sales to quota shows a salesperson's ability to increase revenue, and Mann was best on this factor. Sales per order is important to some firms because they have found that small orders are unprofitable. Ford, for example, achieved a high sales volume by making a large number of calls and selling small amounts to each customer. Gold had the best batting average, ranking first on the ratio of orders to calls. The gross margin percentage achieved by the salespeople shows how well they control prices and sell the right mix of products. The data suggest that Ford's low margins were the result of price-cutting to increase the *number of accounts* and boost sales. Ford was also weak on the behavioral factors measuring the number of reports turned in and expense control.

The performance of the five salespeople varied widely across the 10 factors in Table 15-10, and each person ranked first on two criteria and last on at least one factor. When the rankings are added to give an overall measure of performance, Bell, Shaw, and Mann had total scores close to 30, the expected value. However, Ford's score of 36 and Gold's score of 25 suggest that these two representatives require special attention. Although Ford had the best sales volume, he had the lowest scores on four other factors and the weakest overall record. Gold, on the other hand, was doing a good job despite low total sales. The most obvious change suggested is to shift some of Ford's territory to Gold, giving Gold more to do and providing better coverage for some of Ford's customers. Also, Ford should be encouraged to work for larger orders and told to stop cutting prices.

Summing the ranks of the factors in Table 15-10 provides a rough indication of the salespeople's performance levels, but it has some disadvantages. Perhaps the biggest weakness is that it assumes that all 10 criteria are equally important. This is rarely the case, because firms may be looking for sales growth at one point in the business cycle and profits at another.

Performance Matrix

Deficiencies of the four-factor model and ranking procedures have led to the development of a new performance matrix[16] shown in Figure 15-3. The diagram was constructed by dividing sales force sales and contribution margin percentages into high and low categories. Then averages were calculated for age, calls, and contribution dollars for salespeople falling into each cell. The four cells of the matrix have been given descriptive names to highlight comparisons among different groups. The stars in the upper-right quadrant produced the highest sales and highest gross margin percentages. Slowpokes in the lower-right cell produced good percentage margins but lower sales. Salespeople who fell into the lower-left quadrant were low on both sales and percentage margins. The compromisers in the upper-left cell had high sales and lower contribution margin percentages.

A performance matrix allows you to review and compare the accomplishments of your sales force along several input/output dimensions at the same time. Note that Figure 15-3 includes data on two input measures (calls and age as a proxy for experience) and three out-

TABLE 15-10 **Ranking Salespeople on 10 Input/Output Factors**

Ranking Factors	Ford	Bell	Shaw	Mann	Gold
Dollar sales	①	2	3	4	5
Sales to potential	5	3	4	2	①
Sales to quota	5	4	2	①	3
Sales per order	5	①	4	3	2
Number of calls	2	5	①	3	4
Orders per call	4	2	5	3	①
Gross margin percent	5	①	3	4	2
Direct selling costs	4	3	5	①	2
New accounts	①	4	2	5	3
Number of reports turned in	4	3	①	5	2
Total of ranks	36	28	30	31	25

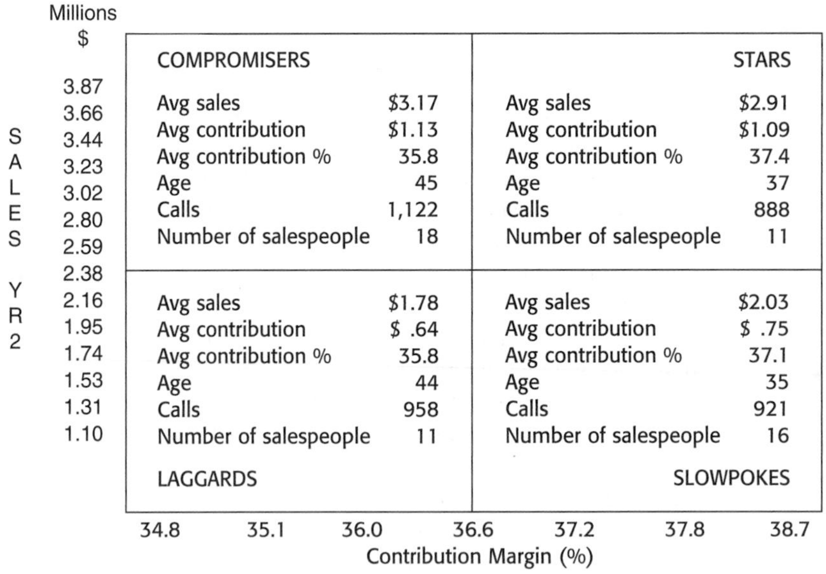

FIGURE 15-3   Performance Matrix for 56 Building Products Salespeople

put measures (sales, contribution dollars, and contribution margin percentage). In this case, the matrix shows that the youngest salespeople are either slowpokes or stars and that the oldest are laggards or compromisers. These data suggest that many reps start their careers by selling a high-margin mix of products and end it by sacrificing margins for revenue.

Data from the performance matrix shown in Figure 15-3 can be used to make a number of managerial recommendations. The 11 laggards represent a plateau problem and therefore are ripe for retraining, redeployment, or dismissal. Also, if these salespeople made more calls, they might be able to move up to the compromiser category. A crucial issue for the sales manager is deciding whether to encourage reps to become stars or compromisers. This is a tough choice because although the stars had the highest contribution percentage, the compromisers produced more sales and more contribution dollars. Thus managers looking for dollars would reward the compromisers and those seeking a higher net profit percentage would reward the stars. After reviewing the data in Figure 15-3, management of the firm changed the compensation plan from straight commission to a salary plus commission plus bonus program to tie sales efforts more closely to the profitability of the different product lines.

This example shows that a performance matrix can provide a useful way to review behavior and the results achieved by salespeople. The matrix is easy to construct and it neatly summarizes a variety of sales activities in a readable format. With this procedure, the manager's key task is to select appropriate performance measures for the review process.

Relative Performance Efficiency

Another procedure called the relative performance efficiency index uses both inputs and outputs to compare performance to a peer group. This approach employs data envelopment analysis and simulation techniques to prepare a single index of efficiency.[17] Table 15-11 shows a relative performance index of 85 percent calculated for a salesperson selling advertising space to businesses. In this case rep 22 is compared with three other salespeople who had scores of 100 percent operating in similar conditions. The analysis is based on a comparison of output measured by three variables relative to the size of four input variables. If

TABLE 15-11   Relative Performance Efficiency for Sales Rep 22

Variable Type	Variable Name	Value Measured	Value if 100% Efficient	Slack
Output	Percent Quota Attained (%)	100	120	20
Output	Supervisor Evaluation	5	5	0
Output	Sales Volume ($)	45,000	50,500	5,500
Input	Sales Training	5	5	0
Input	Salary ($)	20,000	18,000	2,000
Input	Management Ratio	3	2	1
Input	Territory Potential ($)	60,500	50,000	10,500

Reference Set			Efficiency = 0.85
	Influence		Iterations = 10
Salesperson 7	0.49		
Salesperson 20	0.43		
Salesperson 45	0.08		

salesperson 22 had been as efficient as his peers, he would have exceeded his quota by 20 percent, sold $5,500 more advertising, received $2,000 less salary, had 1 less management support person, and had operated in a smaller territory. The results of the analysis can be used by sales managers to allocate resources and make decisions on retraining. Organizations that pay their salespeople straight commissions to maximize output are rarely concerned with input factors, and relative performance indexes would not be an appropriate evaluation technique. However, some companies are experimenting with relative performance systems to reduce manager time in setting, managing, and adjudicating complaints about quotas. See the Coaching Competency box for an example of how Knoll Pharmaceutical, based in Mount Olive, New Jersey, switched from a territory-based commission plan to a relative performance pay system.

TQM AND SALES FORCE EFFICIENCY

TQM uses a strong customer orientation, a team-oriented culture, and statistical methods to analyze and improve business processes, including sales management. A typical TQM approach groups salespeople into teams to analyze current problems and suggest ways to improve sales procedures. This method includes salespeople in the quality improvement perspective and helps to develop a team orientation. For example, a sales team in Kodak's Chemical Division identified 17 behavioral activities in quality sales calls that were important determinants of territory sales.[18] Sales managers now concentrate sales force evaluation and control activities on the implementation of these behavioral elements. The idea is that continuous improvements in call quality should lead to improved territory sales. Although the use of TQM can improve sales procedures and customer satisfaction, the procedure is not easy to implement in the typical sales organization. The main problem is that TQM focuses on teamwork, whereas most sales force compensation plans reward individual salespeople with commissions based on achieving sales and volume quotas. W. Edwards Deming, one of the founders of the TQM movement, attacks quotas and commissions because they do not focus attention on improving quality or customer satisfaction. One way to solve this problem is to offer salespeople bonuses based on the achievement of quality-related activities. Recommended activities include the following:

- Team participation
- Sales process improvements

COACHING COMPETENCY
Squashing the Quota System

Knoll Pharmaceuticals recently dumped its quota evaluation system for all 600 field salespeople. The problem was that its star salespeople were not bringing home substantially more money than its lowest performers. But even those slower sellers, who were favored by the previous quota system, were unhappy. "No one thought their quota was fair," says Dave Kerr, director of strategic planning. "We spent too much time setting, managing, and adjudicating complaints about the quotas—it was just a massive, unproductive effort every four months." So Knoll adapted a relative performance evaluation plan. Knoll's managers evaluate reps' performance in terms of how reps perform against other reps with similar sales potential. Here's how it works: Incentive money is put into a company-wide pool that grows or shrinks with the company's earnings. Reps can earn a larger or smaller share of a company-wide pool of money depending on the relative performance of absolute volume growth and the percentage of volume growth for individual products. According to Kerr, the new plan is perceived to be more fair than the previous quota plan because reps are only measured against those with similar sales potential. Knoll's sales managers have also benefited. With specific product data, the new plan also allows Knoll's managers to provide coaching programs for the lower selling product lines during the evaluation period. Given that reps are selling on relative performance, and not on a fixed monthly quota, Kerr believes that sales manager coaching ideas are more likely to be implemented.

To learn more about Knoll Pharmaceutical, see their home page at *www.basf.com/businesses/consumer/knoll/index.html.*

- Suggestions implemented
- Customer satisfaction improvements
- Sales opportunities identified[19]

Points could be assigned for achievements in each category, and bonus dollars would then be paid to reward individual or group performance.

SUMMARY

Sales force evaluation is a process that compares goals with accomplishments. Our discussion has shown that the evaluation of salespeople is an essential but tricky task. You want to be able to motivate reps to higher levels of achievement while at the same time judging them on their accomplishments. This chapter has introduced you to a number of topics and issues dealing with the sales force evaluation process. You should now be able to:

1. **Conduct a sales force performance review.** The first step is to decide what you want the sales force to accomplish. Once decided, the second step is to prepare a sales plan. The third step is to set performance standards for individual products for different levels in the organization. Finally, reasons for above- and below-standard performance are analyzed, and modifications are made in future plans.

2. **Describe the criteria used to evaluate salespeople.** The most common criteria used are sales by territories, products, units sold, and customers. However, sales figures do not tell the whole story; you must also evaluate selling expenses and margins. An effective expense analysis could show whether salespeople are wasting company travel funds or cutting prices to boost their commission income.

3. **Distinguish between input and output measures of sales performance.** Input criteria measure important factors that are generally thought to be closely associated with sales, such as number of calls, days worked, and expenses. Output measures, on the other hand, look at those criteria that are direct measurements of salesperson performance, such as sales volume, number of new accounts, margins, and the number of orders. Although selecting a set of sales performance measures for a firm is difficult, one rule of thumb is to use those performance measures that are consistent with the organization's goals and objectives. Most sales managers use both input and output criteria to assess the multidimensional character of sales jobs. Ranking procedures, performance indexes, and performance matrices can be used to combine control factors to show overall effects and interactions more clearly.

4. **Discuss the importance of cost controls.** A review of expense data can show important trends for the sales manager. Controllable expenses such as wages and travel are relevant for evaluating the efficiency of the sales organization. Cost-of-goods-sold figures can also help measure the effects of price-cutting or other changes in selling tactics that may affect profits.

5. **Discuss the value of behavioral control procedures for salespeople.** Behavioral systems produce a number of desirable benefits. First, behavior-based evaluation procedures can lead to knowledgeable and expert salespeople who are more committed to the organization. Second, salespeople tend to be self-motivated and react favorably to peer recognition. With behavior systems, salespeople can be expected to spend more time planning their calls and providing sales support activities to their customers. Third, behavioral measures encourage salespeople to achieve company goals and better serve the needs of customers.

6. **Explain MBO and its advantages and disadvantages.** MBO is where a salesperson and a sales manager jointly set personal development goals for the salesperson and an action plan to reach each goal. A major advantage is that reps prefer MBO systems because they can see where they stand and know that progress toward their goals will be rewarded. One problem, however, is that some sales force goals cannot be quantified. Also, MBO goals can sometimes become ceilings that salespeople refuse to exceed. Perhaps the greatest weakness of MBO systems is that they require a lot of sales manager time.

KEY TERMS

Average order size	Evaluation	Performance matrix
Batting average	Expenses as a percentage of sales	Profit contribution
Behavioral observation scales (BOS)	Four-factor model	Ranking procedures
Behavioral systems	Iceberg principle	Relative performance efficiency index
Call reports	Input factors	Sales growth
Calls per day	Management by objectives (MBO)	Sales per order
Contribution margin percentage	New accounts	Sales to potential
Dollar contribution margin	Number of accounts	Sales to quota
80–20 principle	Output measures	

DEVELOPING YOUR COMPETENCIES

1. **Technology.** In order to use salesperson performance information, a sales manager must first correctly interpret problems and causes influencing salesperson performance. Interpretation is often assisted by better understanding the personal values and motives that are primary determinants of the individual salesperson's behavior and performance. One of the more highly accepted personal assessment instruments used for this purpose is the VALS2 survey developed by SRI.

   A version of VALS2 has recently been added to SRI's extensive set of sites on the World Wide Web and can be accessed through the URL: *<http://future.sri.com:80/vals/survey.html>*. Access this Web page and complete the VALS2 survey as provided. Immediate feedback is provided to the user regarding their personal values and motivation profile. Additional informational pages such as *<http://future.sri.com/vals/diamonds.html>* linked to this site are designed to give the user more information and discussion of their profile, what it means regarding behaviors, and how it compares with the rest of the population.

   What is your VALS typology? Consider a salesperson with this same typology. What are its implications for evaluating and motivating that individual salesperson's (a) performance and (b) job satisfaction? Why?

2. **Global Perspective.** Richard Smith is the vice president of sales and marketing for Triton Manufacturers, Inc., which manufactures electric motors. For the past seven years, the company has been doing business in Germany and Switzerland. The first three months of the company's fiscal year have ended, and Richard is preparing for the European quarterly sales review meeting.

   The managing director for the German and Switzerland operations is Helmut Schmidt. Sales in Switzerland are currently above projected targets, but sales in Germany are not keeping pace with the rate of industry or competitor growth. What factors would you need to examine to guide your evaluation and feedback to Helmut?

3. **Strategic Action.** The most successful companies reward their salespeople by growing the value of each customer. One metric used to measure customer value is the "share-of-customer." It is calculated using the ratio of business the customer gives to your firm divided by the amount of business the customer is doing with the competition. What are the strategic implications for the share-of-customer metric in the evaluation process? How would you know that a rep was on the right track when his or her relationship with the customer is strong, but the share-of-customer is low?

4. **Team Building.** Merck & Company, one of the largest pharmaceutical companies in the United States, uses a forced distribution of a bell curve to reward its employees. This means that the high-performing reps are paid considerably more than average or below-average reps. The strong emphasis on individual quantitative performance measures has met some resistance from those who believe in promoting group cooperation. Merck has responded to these concerns by offering a 100-share stock option grant to all employees. Staff turnover is running at a low 5 percent per year. Do you think this was successful in promoting a stronger team atmosphere at Merck? What else could you do to enhance a stronger team culture?

5. **Coaching.** The CEO of Vanstar Corporation found that one of his top sales reps came to the office early every morning and called customers' voice mail and left messages with her opening ideas for them for the day. When she called later, the customers always took her calls personally to respond to the ideas she had left on their machines. Should the

CEO coach everyone on using this technique? Should the CEO incorporate this activity in the company's sales performance evaluation system? How would you measure performance on this activity? To learn more about Vanstar and the recent merger with Inacom, visit their Web site at *www.inacom.com*.

6. **Self-Management.** When you focus management's attention on the activities of individual salespeople, you open a Pandora's box of possible ethical violations. Salespeople are under a great deal of pressure to meet their quotas, and some are not above offering bribes, kickbacks, and lavish entertainment to get what they want. They may even resort to lying about competitive products and sabotaging in-store promotional materials. As a field sales manager, you are expected to know when salespeople engage in these activities and how to control them.

Assume that you just started your dream job as a branch sales manager in charge of 15 salespeople. You quickly discover that a perennial problem with your field reps is expense account cheating. The previous manager allowed a certain amount of expense account cheating and now it has almost become an acceptable part of the sales culture. One of your directives from your new boss is to correct this problem. How would you deal with this issue?

IN-CLASS EXERCISES

15.1: "Missed Quota"

Justin March missed his quota—again. Since being hired six months ago he has sold 60 or 70 percent of quota every month, but he can't seem to get any higher. His manager, Tom Dooley, knows March possesses the skills to be a star performer (he hired March with high expectations), so he's been patient.

When March, a two-year sales veteran, joined Carlton Media he was given the accounts of the rep he replaced. Those accounts are performing well. Dooley has made sales calls to these customers with March, and observed that he's a natural at developing relationships and partnering. The problem is, he's slow to approach new accounts. He procrastinates on following up leads and doesn't follow through aggressively enough on contacts he does make. Dooley's doing his best to coach March through this—giving him advice on how to handle specific accounts, training him on basic sales skills—but March is slow to improve.

After looking over this month's numbers, Carlton's vice president of sales, Sarah Watts, told Dooley to give March three months to make his numbers; if he can't, fire him. To Watts, performing under 75 percent of quota for six months is cause for termination. Dooley is sure March will improve; after all, he's a natural once the account is established.

Questions:

1. How should Dooley handle this situation?
   - Should Dooley keep investing his time in helping March to improve?
   - Should he let March try to prove himself on his own?
   - Or is there a better approach?

2. What behavioral-based evaluation activities could Dooley use to help improve March's performance?

PROBLEMS*

1. You are a branch sales manager for a start-up Web fulfillment company and manage four salespeople. The company has been in business for two years and sales have been growing more than 40 percent during that time. Ninety percent of the company's sales are generated by the sales force. One reason you took the job was because you knew that the ultimate success of this business is dependent on the success of the sales staff. You also know that the long-term viability of your company will rely on the new Web fulfillment product (Product C), which was launched last year. It is a more advanced technology and is considered potentially revolutionary by the experts. In addition, the competitive advantage of this product over the others in the marketplace provides the company with a healthy 30 percent contribution margin. Products A and B, on the other hand, are similar to the competition's product offerings and have lower contribution margin (Product A = 10 percent; Product B = 15 percent). Last year your sales quotas for each product line were: $10,000/month for Product A, $16,000/month for Product B, and $10,000/month for Product C.

The year-end evaluation of your four salespeople is due to your immediate boss, the marketing director, next week. She wants to review your written evaluation of each salesperson and your recommendations and ideas for performance improvement of your sales staff.

Below are the net sales revenues for last year. An Excel spreadsheet has been developed to help you in your evaluation. When using the spreadsheet, insert the net sales and the number of sales calls shown below into the appropriate cells. The spreadsheet has the formula necessary to complete the ratios needed to complete this assignment.

Net Sales	Mayhew	Shaft	Peters	Rody
Product A	$122,000	$125,000	$130,000	$140,000
Product B	195,000	200,000	210,000	180,000
Product C	113,000	109,500	108,000	93,000
Total Sales	$420,000	$434,500	$448,000	$413,000
Number of Sales Calls	85	92	82	79

2. It is January, 2001 and you are district sales manager for the Southeast region. Annual evaluations are done and $40,000 in bonus money and $6,000 in salary increase money needs to be distributed to your six person sales force.

The company's goal is profits. Salesforce pay is salary plus commission. If the firm does very well (like in 2000), bonus money is allocated on the basis of merit.

Salespeople are prohibited from making more than 75% of their immediate supervisor's salary. Total salesperson pay is not prevented from being more than their supervisors's total pay. Your salary as district manager was $44,000 in 2000 ($41,000 in 1999 - you also have a bonus system for meeting district goals that is not discussed here). You

* Contributed by Avery Abernathy, Auburn University. Excel spreadsheets for working on these problems are available at www.wiley.com/college/dalrymple. Go to "Student Resources."

got the second biggest percent salary raise last year; it would have been number 1 except for a failure to turn in paperwork on time, largely due to Ann being chronically late with her call reports.

Salespeople have quotas for sales, new accounts, expenses and average calls per day. They are also expected to turn in paperwork in correctly done and on time.

For 1999 there were $5,000 in district salary increases and 0 merit bonuses.

District managers are responsible for setting quotas, allocating raise/merit money, and hiring/firing salespeople. As district manager you are evaluated by your superior on the following criteria:

- District total sales
- District sales to quota
- District profit (sales minus expenses)
- Following company policy (e.g., paper work done, don't violate company rules or Federal/State Laws)

On the next page is a copy of a performance printout that gives the previous year's evaluation of your six salespeople (1999 and 2000). Inflation in 2000 was 3.2%.

Questions:

1. Allocate the salary and bonus money for 2001.
2. Give a written allocation of your funds.
3. Give a written performance review to each person.
4. Each performance evaluation must be signed and dated February 1, 2001.

Note: Contribution margin, attitude, selling skills, product knowledge, and paperwork are all measured on a 1–10 scale with 1 = unacceptable and 10 = excellent; 5 is average.

In May 2000, Mr. Tull's wife was diagnosed with cancer. She has been through extensive, painful treatments.

There is an Excel spreadsheet (provided by your instructor) that has additional computations you should use to help decide 1–3 above. Hint, use the "2000 - 1999/1999" table and the "Individual Compared to 2000 Total" table to help you make your evaluation assessments.

1999 Annual Evaluation

	Joey Ramone	Justine Frischmann	Simon LeBon	Jethro Tull	Ann Wilson
Sales	$222,000.00	$191,000.00	$351,000.00	$422,500.00	$895,000.00
Sales/Quota	1.01	1.12	0.95	1.67	2.45
New Accounts	6	9	19	8	26
New Accounts/Quota	1	1.11	1.8	0.75	3
Expense/Quota	0.98	0.96	1.04	1.1	1.01
Avg. Calls/Day	4.5	3.7	4	4.9	4.2
Cont. Margin	8	7	6	5	6
Attitude	5	5	5	7	3
Selling Skills	5	7	4	8	9
Product Knowledge	7	3	5	9	7
Paperwork	7	7	7	9	1
Years with Firm	2	1	5	31	13
1999 Salary	$19,500.00	$19,000.00	$27,800.00	$30,500.00	$29,750.00
1999 Commission	$6,660.00	$5,730.00	$10,530.00	$12,675.00	$26,850.00
Salary Increase (1/1/00)	$400.00	$1,200.00	$400.00	$1,700.00	$1,300.00

2000 Annual Evaluation

	Joey Ramone	Justine Frischmann	Simon LeBon	Jethro Tull	Ann Wilson
Sales	$240,000.00	$250,000.00	$350,000.00	$300,500.00	$960,000.00
Sales/Quota	1.03	1.49	0.94	1.13	2.51
New Accounts	6	15	9	6	20
New Accounts/Quota	1	1.6	0.9	0.65	2.7
Expense/Quota	0.97	0.99	1.06	0.98	1.01
Avg. Calls/Day	4.5	4.3	3.9	4.1	4.2
Cont. Margin	7	6	4	5	6
Attitude	5	7	4	9	4
Selling Skills	6	7	4	8	9
Product Knowledge	6	5	4	9	7
Paperwork	8	8	5	6	4
Years with Firm	3	2	6	32	14
2000 Salary	$19,900.00	$20,200.00	$28,200.00	$32,200.00	$31,050.00
2000 Commission	$7,200.00	$7,500.00	$10,500.00	$9,015.00	$28,800.00
2001 Salary Increase (2/1/01)					

CASE 15-1 YORK ELECTRONICS

York is a medium-sized electronics company that specializes in the manufacture of circuit boards, customized computer chips, and test equipment. The electronic components are sold by company salespeople directly to original equipment manufacturers (OEMs), and test equipment is handled by a second group of independent reps. Bill Hicks was recently appointed national sales manager at York to supervise the company's salespeople and the independent reps.

Company sales for the Electronic and Test Equipment divisions amounted to $135 million in 1998. Test equipment sold for relatively high prices and made up the major portion of sales revenue. Independent reps were paid straight 6 percent commissions on all York equipment sales in their territories. The volume of test equipment shipments had increased 15 percent the previous year, and Bill was satisfied with the performance of the reps. Also, the reps' compensation plan made it difficult for York managers to direct their day-to-day

activities. About all Bill could do with the independent reps was to replace them if they failed to push York's equipment. York's testing products were only one of several lines of equipment carried by these reps.

Bill Hicks was convinced, on the other hand, that a review of the Electronics Division's sales force would be quite useful. York currently covered the U.S. electronics market with 18 company salespeople. The assignments of individuals and descriptions of their territories are given in Exhibit 1. Electronics salespeople acted as consultants to OEMs and helped them solve product design problems using York boards and customized chips. They were paid a base salary plus a commission and an annual discretionary bonus. Since electronics salespeople did a great deal of developmental work, their base wage amounted to about 60 percent of their total compensation. Commission rates varied from 0.3 to 1.0 percent of sales, depending on the products sold. The highest commissions were paid

EXHIBIT 1   Descriptions of Sales Territories

Territory Number	Salesperson Assigned	Area Included
1	Mary Holmes	Vermont, New Hampshire, Rhode Island, Massachusetts, Maine
2	James Potter	Connecticut, upstate New York (Rochester and east; includes Westchester County)
3	Harvey Stewart	Long Island (Nassau and Suffolk counties), western Pennsylvania (Altoona and west)
4	Jane Thomas	New York City (New York, Kings, Queens, Richmond, and Bronx counties), north Jersey, western New York from Buffalo to Rochester
5	Chad Hunter	Eastern Pennsylvania to Altoona, south Jersey, Maryland, Delaware
6	Harvey Phillips	Ohio, West Virginia, Kentucky
7	Greg Lewis	Indiana, Michigan
8	Anne Forbes	Missouri, Nebraska, Kansas, Iowa
9	Bill Fredericks	Illinois, Wisconsin, Minnesota, North and South Dakota
10	Sally Smith	California north of Santa Barbara, Oregon, Washington, Idaho
11	Fred Reilly	Los Angeles north to Santa Barbara (includes Santa Barbara, Ventura, and the western part of Los Angeles County)
12	Marilyn Reed	California south of Los Angeles (includes Orange, Riverside, San Diego, and Imperial counties)
13	George Pardo	Los Angeles (most of Los Angeles County and part of San Bernardino County)
14	Henry Dodds	Colorado, Arizona, New Mexico, Utah, Wyoming, Montana
15	Todd Young	Texas, Oklahoma, Arkansas, Louisiana
16	David Wood	Mississippi, Alabama, Tennessee
17	Tammy Cook	Virginia, North Carolina, South Carolina
18	Brad Wolf	Georgia, Florida

This case was prepared by Douglas J. Dalrymple of Indiana University.

on items with the largest gross margins. In the past, bonuses had been based on sales increases, with some attention to profitability. Each salesperson was also given a company car and an expense account to cover travel and entertainment costs.

York's sales of electronic components increased in 1998, but profits were relatively flat. Price competition was intense, and Hicks had been brought in to improve sales force productivity and profits. Bill began his analysis by collecting some performance data on his electronics sales force (Exhibit 2). After reviewing these numbers, he thought it might be useful to calculate some additional control factors such as sales per call, expenses to sales, sales growth, dollars of gross margin, and sales to potential. York measured potential by the number of manufacturers who used electronic components in each sales territory and the value of their finished product shipments. These numbers were derived from U.S. Census of Business data using SIC codes and territory boundaries. Bill decided to calculate penetration by dividing territory sales by the total value of electronics shipments in each area.

To help with his analysis, Hicks called up the new spreadsheet software that he had recently installed on his computer. He then retrieved the York file. The next step in Hicks' sales force analysis was to calculate simple correlation coefficients among his control factors. The correlations that came up on the screen varied from 0.0 to ±1.0, and they showed the direction and intensity of associations among the performance variables. For example, a strong positive correlation observed between sales and dollars of gross margin (+0.806) was expected because gross margin dollars is simply sales minus the cost of goods sold (Exhibit 3).

Once his sales analysis was complete, Hicks had a number of decisions to make. The annual sales meeting was scheduled in two weeks, and he needed to identify the best salespeople in each district and nationwide so that "Salesperson of the Year" awards could be made. He wondered whether these choices should be made on the basis of sales alone or whether he should use some combination of performance variables. He also had to identify salespeople for retraining and for possible termination. If the data showed evidence of plateauing among his middle-aged salespeople, then changes would be needed to correct this problem. Hicks would have to specify the topics needed to be covered for those picked for retraining. In addition, Bill had $55,000 in annual bonus money that he had to allocate among the electronics salespeople. He was also concerned about whether changes were needed in basic wage levels and commission rates. Another strategic question was whether York had enough electronics salespeople. If extra salespeople were hired, Bill had to decide how old they should be when hired and how much experience was necessary. In addition, he had to decide if the present sales territories needed to be redesigned. A reallocation of the territories would have to consider where to place any new salespeople. The more Bill thought about these problems, the more he was convinced that he needed one of those new computerized territory design programs he had seen advertised. Without a computer program, he would have to draw some maps to analyze the existing territories and plan for possible added salespeople.

Beyond these decisions, Hicks had to make decisions concerning the factors he wanted to emphasize to motivate his electronics salespeople to reach corporate objectives. Bill knew that his goals were unlikely to be reached if he asked his salespeople to improve on 10 different control factors all at the same time. Besides, improving some of the factors conflicted with the achievement of others. What he needed was a short list of prioritized factors to highlight at the upcoming sales meeting.

EXHIBIT 2 Sales Force Performance Data[a]

Territory Number	Sales, 1997 (millions)	Sales, 1998 (millions)	Gross Margin (%)	Calls, 1998	Years of Service	Age	Territory Size in Miles² (000)	Potential Total Number of Firms	Potential Total Value of Shipments (millions)	Salary, 1998	Commissions, 1998	Expenses, 1998	District
1	$1.839	$2.214	40%	770	2	32	58.4	1965	$9959	$34,100	$16,500	$ 4269	1
2	2.398	2.411	38	660	6	40	44.2	1461	10190	40,150	17,710	7096	1
3	2.497	2.640	33	1250	25	50	16.7	1023	4719	35,860	21,450	9510	1
4	1.509	1.739	36	900	7	34	8.7	2601	10360	37,950	11,440	15628	1
5	2.167	2.686	31	678	20	49	46.7	2264	16287	33,330	22,330	13027	1
6	1.183	1.190	44	610	3	40	104.8	2286	21195	33,000	10,450	9785	2
7	2.232	2.431	37	870	12	38	92.9	2465	23010	33,000	16,610	11797	2
8	1.561	1.632	45	580	16	46	283.3	1601	14240	33,000	11,660	22425	2
9	2.147	2.032	42	630	14	48	334.9	3306	25600	31,900	18,370	12014	2
10	2.012	2.621	40	492	3	32	356.3	3329	17980	39,600	17,380	12523	3
11	.831	.885	52	600	2	26	4.6	136	540	27,500	8,470	4741	3
12	1.658	2.251	28	1030	6	39	16.4	994	4047	33,000	12,100	4938	3
13	1.377	1.146	39	540	5	38	4.0	2127	10590	46,200	6,600	3477	3
14	1.058	1.081	49	480	2	26	662.9	1407	6407	33,000	10,560	14165	3
15	1.898	3.083	37	460	2	29	427.3	3130	26280	33,000	12,100	19431	4
16	1.856	2.578	25	820	5	36	139.1	1603	12303	33,000	14,520	18747	4
17	2.090	2.317	23	820	20	50	118.7	2167	18840	38,500	16,280	9602	4
18	1.224	1.565	39	830	5	28	112.2	2479	13232	28,050	10,340	25394	4

[a] Data are in file yorkdat.sav.

533

EXHIBIT 3   Correlations Among Sales Force Control Factors

	1998 Sales	1998 Calls	Sales/ Calls	Expenses	Exp/ Sales	Exp/ Calls	Years Service	Age	GM (%)	GM ($)	Terr. Size	No. of Firms	Value Ship.	Penetration	Sales Growth	Commissions
Sales	1.000	.285[a]	.718	.140	-.435	.115	.346	.332	-.666	.806	.000	.353	.389	.279	.637	.738
Calls	.285	1.000	-.430	-.112	-.221	-.492	.499	.371	-.562	-.047	-.583	-.318	-.343	.725	.071	.358
Sales/call	.718	-.430	1.000	.254	-.204	.517	-.079	-.035	-.174	.810	.447	.576	.587	-.203	.611	.355
Expenses	.140	-.112	.254	1.000	.807	.875	.061	-.124	-.021	.174	.428	.369	.359	-.337	.436	-.060
Exp/sales	-.435	-.221	-.204	.807	1.000	.714	-.121	-.302	.379	-.282	.445	.082	.048	-.386	.026	-.412
Exp/call	.115	-.492	.517	.875	.714	1.000	-.120	-.241	.207	.301	.718	.425	.450	-.452	.440	-.147
Years of service	.346	.499	-.079	.061	-.121	-.120	1.000	.874	-.429	.120	-.216	-.030	.117	.249	-.211	.640
Age	.332	.371	-.035	-.124	-.302	-.241	.874	1.000	-.478	.098	-.284	.057	.244	.180	-.297	.599
GM(%)	-.666	-.562	-.174	-.021	.379	.207	-.429	-.478	1.000	-.117	.356	-.111	-.125	-.354	-.420	-.430
GM ($)	.806	-.047	.810	.174	-.282	.301	.120	.098	-.117	1.000	.248	.486	.472	.064	.478	.631
Territory size	.000	-.583	.447	.428	.445	.718	-.216	-.284	.356	.248	1.000	.333	.331	-.326	.174	-.075
No. of mfg.	.353	-.318	.576	.369	.082	.425	-.030	.057	-.111	.486	.333	1.000	.846	-.570	.238	.192
Value ship.	.389	-.343	.587	.359	.048	.450	.117	.244	-.125	.472	.331	.846	1.000	-.630	.203	.236
Penetration	.279	.725	-.203	-.337	-.386	-.452	.249	.180	-.354	.064	-.326	-.570	-.630	1.000	.116	.271
Sales growth	.637	.071	.611	.436	.026	.440	-.211	-.297	-.420	.478	.174	.238	.203	.116	1.000	.131
Commissions	.738	.358	.355	-.060	-.412	-.147	.640	.599	-.430	.631	-.075	.192	.236	.271	.131	1.000

[a] Correlations of .320 and larger are significant, with a probability of error of <.10.

CASE *15-2*   ABBOTT, INC.

*O*ne snowy Saturday in January 2000, Mary Reid was reviewing the performance of her field sales force. Mary was the national sales manager for Abbott, Inc. Abbott produced vinyl siding and plastic plumbing supplies for the construction industry. Their products were sold to 120 distributors in the United States, who made them available to lumberyards, hardware stores, and contractors. The company employed 56 salespeople who worked with the distributors and made calls on contractors, retailers, and architects. Abbott had organized its sales force into five geographic districts headed by sales managers. The five sales managers reported directly to Mary Reid (Exhibit 1). Siding and plumbing fixtures were shipped by truck from company warehouses to distributors and directly to large buyers.

Salespeople were assigned fixed territories and were responsible for increasing sales in their areas. They were given quotas based on potential and past company sales in their areas. Territory performance was also measured by the penetration ratio. This ratio compared company sales with published industry data showing the volume of building contracts awarded in each territory. Salespeople who exceeded their quotas were eligible for recognition awards, larger territories, and promotions.

Field reps were paid a straight commission that ranged from 1 to 3 percent of sales. The size of the commission varied according to the experience of the salesperson. In addition, salespeople received an expense allowance that averaged $8500 per year. The five district sales managers were paid a salary and a bonus based on the volume produced in their districts.

Consolidated sales of Abbott, including the overseas division, totaled $355,670,000 in 1999. Although sales were up in 1999, net profits had declined. These results were partially due to increased competition and price cutting. Reid wanted to learn more about her sales force because she was under considerable pressure to improve profits in the new year.

Reid decided to start her analysis by calling up some basic sales force performance data on her desktop computer. These figures are shown in Exhibit 2. The territory sales quota, penetration, and contribution margin are given for 12 months, even though a few salespeople worked for less than a year. As a result, Reid adjusted calls and commissions to make it easier to compare salespeople with one another.

Next, Reid transferred her data files to the new Spreadsheet analysis program that she had acquired. This program allowed her to create new variables and perform a variety of evaluations on her field salespeople. Reid decided to calculate some simple correlation coefficients among her control variables (Exhibit 3). Age appeared to be related to sales, and there were

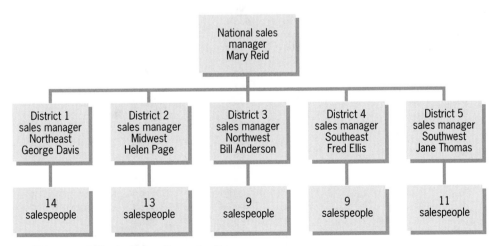

EXHIBIT 1   Abbott Sales Organization

This case was prepared by Douglas J. Dalrymple of Indiana University.

EXHIBIT 2 Sales Force Performance Data for Abbott, Inc.

Name	Age	Sales 1999 (000)	Sales 1998 (000)	Quota 1999 (000)	Penetra-tion 1999	Calls 1999	Commis-sion per Month 1999	Contri-bution Margin 1999 (000)	Sales District	Months of Work 1999
Field	54	$3.710	$2.943	$3.548	702	917	$6928	$1318.0	1	12
White	29	2.971	2.070	2.300	419	467	4990	1149.7	2	8
Evans	35	2.927	2.364	2.749	1948	1219	4075	1041.8	1	12
Long	37	2.428	1.773	2.107	315	880	4125	903.8	2	12
Hunt	30	2.298	1.753	1.899	710	1213	4905	854.9	3	12
Reed	32	2.741	2.421	2.879	2820	935	4967	977.0	1	12
Knight	33	2.577	1.948	2.228	527	1096	4198	920.4	5	12
Quinn	36	2.565	2.432	2.847	297	807	4752	961.9	2	12
Reilly	34	2.278	1.684	1.899	957	939	4305	833.8	3	12
Adams	33	1.872	1.308	3.016	338	889	3851	699.4	2	12
Zimmer	37	2.982	2.399	2.649	644	1165	5618	1105.4	3	12
Smith	27	1.669	1.751	2.098	225	780	3250	635.9	4	12
Miller	37	3.589	3.272	3.698	368	1091	6030	1329.2	2	12
Hall	51	3.755	3.322	3.739	306	1181	7107	1366.6	4	12
Vance	29	1.928	2.054	2.391	580	866	3684	698.3	3	12
Martin	27	1.292	.914	1.777	343	1178	3659	465.1	5	10
Sharp	48	3.884	3.301	3.798	1490	1354	6726	1375.9	1	12
Jones	43	3.500	2.836	3.150	1960	1180	6565	1219.1	3	12
Baker	26	2.944	2.256	2.738	571	402	4251	1120.9	2	12
Queen	37	1.945	1.886	2.248	506	492	3402	704.6	2	8
Kelly	35	2.068	1.932	2.141	342	825	4883	759.0	2	12
Lewis	60	1.501	1.295	1.339	448	1199	4466	535.1	5	12
Young	57	2.693	2.067	2.421	1123	806	6070	979.0	1	12
Isom	27	1.551	1.612	1.878	246	832	3137	584.7	2	12
Urban	38	1.099	.716	.962	231	353	3706	387.4	2	12
Green	40	1.262	1.071	1.309	453	1313	3876	468.4	5	12
Scott	67	2.243	2.042	2.767	550	968	5535	793.6	2	12
Norris	33	2.448	2.225	2.558	453	1060	4129	905.5	4	12
Ward	34	2.713	1.567	1.998	267	958	4960	996.7	4	12
Wood	45	2.541	2.670	2.811	873	1260	4918	899.3	1	12
Upchurch	49	2.759	2.583	3.086	365	969	6056	1008.8	4	12
York	65	2.606	2.400	2.697	497	1147	5352	986.7	4	12
Grant	33	2.786	2.400	2.197	441	1461	4279	1009.6	5	4
Taylor	38	2.965	2.174	2.448	1151	1373	5473	1075.8	5	12
Carter	63	3.716	2.704	3.128	1332	1047	6920	1347.0	1	12
Wolf	64	2.384	1.990	2.281	3000	614	6202	835.8	1	12
Olsen	43	2.126	2.050	2.200	455	1173	4240	785.2	5	12
Edwards	47	2.203	1.930	2.600	141	882	5870	818.8	5	8
Summers	32	4.078	2.762	3.183	602	767	6725	1472.1	1	12
Black	53	2.742	2.434	2.682	931	945	5976	998.6	3	12
Allen	38	2.617	2.475	2.898	300	938	3353	968.1	4	8
Owens	32	3.595	3.323	3.848	1861	1135	5339	1346.2	1	12
Day	63	3.358	2.801	3.282	1133	1604	8265	1205.7	1	12
Parsons	38	1.790	1.842	2.105	203	941	4029	655.9	4	12
Dunn	49	2.596	2.372	2.796	310	1162	5089	927.9	5	12
Thomas	39	1.678	1.571	1.812	907	1281	3136	608.5	3	12
Voss	30	2.192	1.875	2.469	166	673	5824	829.3	4	7
Stone	48	1.879	1.711	2.032	990	1182	5124	679.4	5	12
Zorn	30	2.011	1.739	2.281	243	568	3657	742.2	2	11
Jackson	33	1.903	1.894	2.161	450	840	3790	701.3	3	4
Nichols	36	1.609	1.690	1.898	381	1307	2527	583.3	5	12
Irwin	30	2.631	2.170	2.560	199	697	3803	987.9	2	10
Page	47	3.047	2.939	3.298	806	1200	5846	1099.6	1	12
Cook	37	2.328	2.054	2.398	664	933	4665	859.6	1	12
Walker	39	2.055	2.043	2.399	519	1099	3594	735.9	3	12
Fox	28	3.411	2.689	3.248	3322	706	5335	1187.5	1	12

EXHIBIT 3 **Correlations Among Sales Force Performance Factors, 1999**

	Age	Sales	Sales Growth 1993/1992	Sales to Quota	Pene-tration	Calls	Commis-sion per Month	Contri-bution Margin Percent	Sales per Call	Contri-bution per Call
Age	1.00	.21	−.09	.04	.16	.30	.59	−.39	−.15	−.17
Sales	.21	1.00	.22	.45	.39	.17	.76	−.15	.52	.51
Sales growth	−.09	.22	1.00	.64	.08	−.19	.22	−.05	.35	.35
Sales quota	.04	.45	.64	1.00	.19	.03	.34	−.09	.36	.35
Penetration	.16	.39	.08	.19	1.00	.08	.34	−.53	.19	.17
Calls	.30	.17	−.19	.03	.08	1.00	.22	−.28	−.68	−.67
Commission/month	.59	.76	.22	.34	.34	.22	1.00	−.27	.29	.25
Contribution percent	−.39	−.15	−.05	−.09	−.53	−.28	−.27	1.00	.18	.23
Sales/call	−.15	.52	.35	.36	.19	−.68	.29	.18	1.00	.99
Contribution/call	−.17	.51	.35	.35	.17	−.67	.23	.23	.99	1.00

some interesting correlations with other variables. Reid decided to focus on the most significant associations to see what effects they might have on sales force supervision. Based on a review of the numbers in Exhibit 3, she decided to plot some of the variables to give a performance matrix for evaluation.

Abbott's marketing manager had been asking for some recommendations on sales managers and salespeople who could be honored at the national sales meeting scheduled for February. Although it would be very easy to rank them on sales achievements, Reid wondered if she should prepare some sort of composite index that would evaluate the sales force on a variety of factors.

Reid had recently come across an article in a marketing journal suggesting that salespeople follow a career path that resembles the product life cycle. According to the article, salespeople start off exploring the sales field, go into a development phase, mature, and then experience declining performance measures as they approach retirement. The suggested relationship is shown in Exhibit 4. Note that sales are lowest in the exploration phase, grow rapidly in the development stage, level off in the mature phase, and drop off in the decline stage. Mary wondered whether the career life cycle concept described in Exhibit 4 applied to Abbott salespeople. Abbott employed a variety of sales reps ranging in age from 26 to 67; the median age was 37. Reid thought it would be useful to calculate an age distribution of the sales force to see if there was anything meaningful to be learned.

To help find out whether the career life cycle applied to Abbott, Mary decided it might be instructive to calculate the means of various performance factors for groups of salespeople divided according to the career categories described in Exhibit 4. Mary was sure that there was something to be learned about

the sales force from the performance data if she just kept her computer humming. The data in Exhibit 2 also gave an indication of the turnover rate in the sales force in 1999, and Reid wondered if some adjustments were needed in the compensation program. Reid was concerned that the results of her performance matrix and career life cycle analyses would require some changes in terms of hiring, firing, training, and motivation.

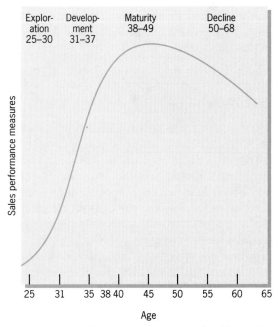

EXHIBIT 4 **Sales Force Career Path Life Cycle**

APPENDIX A

In-Class Exercises

INTRODUCTION

Twenty-eight in-class exercises have been developed for this text. Each in-class exercise presents a realistic sales management dilemma that you are asked to solve. The exercises have been written as an opportunity to address real-life complexities. There is no one right answer, but some solutions are better than others.

Each of these in-class exercises could also serve as the basis for students to develop role plays dramatizing the problem, evaluating alternative solutions, and proposing a preferred solution. Role playing is used extensively in sales and sale management training to give people a realistic preview of what they can expect on the job and to develop skills in handling critical issues. Should you enter sales as a career, you are almost sure to encounter the use of role plays. Experience in developing and participating in role plays should help you in conducting role plays in the future.

The purposes of the exercises are to give you a better overall understanding of sales management, to give you a chance to develop your own ideas regarding sales management issues, and to serve as a basis for class discussion. As with all practical exercises, it is important that all students be familiar with the exercises and develop their own approaches to resolving the main issues of the role play. The purpose of this appendix is to provide help in approaching the in-class exercises in this text.

PREPARATION

The first step in preparing your solution is to read the in-class exercise and identify the main issue or issues in the situation. Some issues are of immediate concern, while others are more long-term in nature, especially the possibility of establishing a precedent for undesirable behaviors or attitudes. The chapter preceding the role play will often provide additional insight into the general issue under consideration.

The next step is to identify alternative ways of realistically addressing the situation. Several solutions will likely occur to you, some fairly quickly. Be careful to evaluate fully the consequences of each solution in terms of potential negative short- and long-term consequences and consider whether the alternative fully addresses the problem in the role play. Be prepared to defend your chosen solution, especially in regard to its realism and the extent to which it fully addresses the core issues of the role play.

If you are asked to videotape a role play of the situation, then it would be helpful to keep the following points in mind:

- Prepare a carefully worded script to guide you through the role play, but do not read from the script during the videotaping of the role play.
- Keep in mind your surroundings for the role play and attempt to integrate appropriate props, such as products and office machines.
- Be sure to check the quality of the sound on the tape before proceeding very far into the role play itself.
- Inject your personality and humor into the exercise.

APPENDIX B

Getting a Job in Sales

Personal selling is often the first job for business students on the pathway to an executive position. All manufacturers and service organizations need qualified sales talent, and they are constantly looking for replacements. You will find sales openings listed daily in almost every newspaper in every region of the country. Although an abundant number of sales jobs are available, your task is to get an offer from a firm that meets your expectations in terms of location, compensation, travel, and opportunities for personal growth.

The easiest way to contact firms that are looking for salespeople is to sign up for interviews with companies through your campus placement office. This allows you to talk with a variety of firms about their sales opportunities in a convenient and inexpensive manner. However, you should realize that for every 30 students interviewed on campus, only three or four will be invited to headquarters for a final round of testing and secondary interviews. Also, the chances are that only one out of four final candidates will be offered a job. Thus, although campus interviews are easy to arrange, competition for jobs is often fierce.

NETWORKING

Statistics prove networking and informational interviewing to be among the top conduits for effectively locating a job in today's workplace. Off-campus networking has become increasingly important as new job opportunities have moved more to small and medium-size companies that may not interview on campus. Well-informed students and graduates are learning each day the values of networking with other sales professionals, executives, senior executives, faculty members, and others whose daily routines immerse them in the business community.

One thing to keep in mind when networking is that studies indicate that one is most likely to find a job at the third level of networking. The first level of networking consists mostly of people you know right now, while the second level are people that have been referred by the first-level people, and the third level are people to whom you have been referred by the second-level network people. This suggests that you should build a network of contacts by asking people with whom you speak for the names of additional people. It also suggests that you put some time and effort into building your network and not expect to find a job on the first round of interviews.

DIRECT MAIL CAMPAIGN

To increase the odds of getting the job you want, you may also wish to supplement the on-campus interviews and off-campus networking with a direct mail campaign. The first step in this campaign is to develop a mailing list of firms that you want to approach. Your campus placement office is a good place to look for prospects, as the office will probably have directories, as well as lists of firms that are looking for sale candidates. Also, you may want to target desirable companies whose representatives visited the campus but did not have any openings on their interview schedules. Other names of organizations can be obtained from family and friends who know people in particular firms or work with an organization. Numerous references to specific companies are made in this text and are summarized in the company index at the back of the book. If you have geographical preferences, you should pick firms that are located in the area where you want to live. Once you have a mailing list, you need to prepare your advertising message.

COVER LETTER DESIGN

Cover letters introduce you to potential employers. Good letters motivate employers to read your resume and subsequently invite you to an interview. Your cover letter expands on your resume and adds a personal touch to your approach. Effective letters present you as a warm, pleasant person who wants to be a salesperson.

Your cover letter should be directed to a decision maker rather than to the nebulous "Dear Sir" or "Dear Madam." There is no reason for a firm to respond to a letter addressed to "Sir" or "Madam." Note that the sample cover letters in Exhibits 1 and 2 are directed to Jane R. Briggs, director of college relations, and C. B. Johnson in the personnel department. When individuals receive letters, there is more of an obligation to respond.

Remember that your cover letters must be customized for each potential employer, individually typed, and personally signed by you. Mass-produced form letters usually get filed in the wastebasket. Cover letters also should be concise, yet have enough bullet points to catch the interest of the reader. The four-paragraph cover letters shown in Exhibits 1 and 2 are close to the maximum acceptable length.

The objective of the opening paragraph in a cover letter is to capture the reader's attention. One sentence describes the position for which you wish to be considered and how you learned of the opportunity. Another states your job interests and career aspirations. When appropriate, you can mention the mutual acquaintance who suggested that you write to the potential employer.

The middle paragraphs of a cover letter sell your credentials to the employer. The idea is to show how your background matches the needs of the job. For example, in Exhibit 1, Edward Bell points to his leadership activities, his readership of computer magazines, and his work in a computer store as reasons he should be hired by Hewlett-Packard to sell financial software.

All sales presentations need a strong and effective close. The last paragraph of your cover letter should ask for the interview. You need to make a positive response easy by presenting alternative interview dates and telling how you plan to follow up. Notice how Ed Bell (Exhibit 1) asks to be put in contact with a local sales rep and says when he will call.

PREPARING YOUR RÉSUMÉ

Employers often receive hundreds of résumés each day, and they spend only a few minutes reviewing each one. This means that your résumé has to be carefully designed if you expect to penetrate the clutter of competitive applicants. Job-focused résumés are more likely to get through the initial 60-second glance than

Key Points
- **Graduating**
- **Commercial sales**
- **Financial orientation**
- **Industry knowledge**
- **Leadership**
- **Transcript skills**
- **Relevant hobby**
- **Local contact**

125 S. High Street
Columbus, OH 43210
333-337-3337
April 1, 1997

Ms. Jane R. Briggs
Director of College Relations
Hewlett-Packard
Palo Alto, CA 94444

Dear Ms. Briggs:

In May I will be graduating from Ohio State with a degree in marketing supported by a strong set of courses in finance and computer applications. I am seeking a position in commercial sales which draws equally from my marketing and finance strengths. Your opportunity in calling on corporate financial managers for the purpose of selling financial software and hardware solutions excites me.

Hewlett-Packard and other hardware vendors in the computer industry offer a unique opportunity to use many of my skills. My elected leadership activities and involvement in intramural team sports give you some clues to my personality and spirit. My unofficial transcript illustrates the depth and breadth of my skills and interests in your opportunity.

I read several popular computer magazines regularly and have stayed attuned to recent developments in microcomputers and related equipment throughout college. I work part-time at a local computer retailer dealing with everyone from hackers to local business owners.

The enclosed résumé provides detail about my credentials and interests, but I need an opportunity to personally talk to you to best express how I can contribute to Hewlett-Packard. If you could put me in contact with a local representative as a shadow for a day, my talents would be clearer. I will call you on Wednesday to see when we might be able to get together.

Sincerely,

Edward R. Bell

Enclosures: Résumé
               Unofficial Transcript

EXHIBIT 1   Sample Cover Letter for Financial Sales

Source: Reproduced with permission from C. Randall Powell, *Career Planning Today,* 2nd ed. (Dubuque, Iowa: Kendall/Hunt).

Apartment 22
Stone Hill Estates
Arcola, FL 2611
407-222-2222
February 27, 1997

Mr. C. B. Johnson
Personnel Department
Professional Pharmaceuticals
Atlanta, GA 30332

Dear Mr. Johnson:

Key Points
- **Question opening**
- **Targeted field**
- **Personal qualities**
- **Industry interest**
- **Maturity**
- **Regional interview**
- **Will call**

Do you have an opening for a sales representative? With a B.S. degree in marketing and 10 hours of chemistry courses at the University of Florida, I think that my academic qualifications and personality are well suited for a career in pharmaceutical marketing.

Two summers and many part-time jobs in sales-related positions have convinced me that sales is the best entry-level position for me to begin my career as a future marketing executive. I value the freedom and independence that you offer an individual after your training program which I read about in the College Placement Office. Each of my previous employers will tell you that I work hard and thrive under pressure and challenge. Although I have not been active in campus life as a leader because I have had to work to get through school, every work supervisor has expressed pleasure at my enthusiasm to serve customers. In my last experience at Super Drugs, I worked for a pharmacist and talked with several salespeople who called on us. They all commented on the individual rewards of working in the booming health-related industry. The attached résumé only brushes the surface of my qualifications, so I hope I have the opportunity to elaborate on my credentials in person.

I am willing to work hard, study, learn, and take responsibility. May I have the privilege of an interview? Since we are several hundred miles apart, would it be possible for me to schedule an initial interview with any of your salespeople in this region? I plan to call you within the week to see if something might possibly be arranged. I need a chance to start as a sales representative because I know I can advance on my own merits with Professional Pharmaceuticals. Please call me if you need more information.

Very truly yours,

Mary T. Stuart

Enclosure

EXHIBIT 2   Sample Cover Letter for Pharmaceutical Sales

Source: Reproduced with permission from C. Randall Powell, *Career Planning Today,* 2nd ed. (Dubuque, Iowa: Kendall/Hunt).

more broadly based résumés. An outstanding example of a position-focused sales brochure résumé is presented in Exhibit 3. This creative résumé features the position description on the cover and shows a picture of Sandra Marinconz making a sales presentation to a doctor.

On page 2 of her résumé, Sandra describes her career goals, education, and activities (Exhibit 3). Observe that Sandra has placed her grades in her major ahead of her overall grade point average. The third page of Sandra's résumé highlights her work experience and her philosophy of success. Notice how well the work data are organized to emphasize Sandra's ties to sales and the pharmaceutical industry.

You should realize that there is no one standard format for résumés. Indeed, most students prepare short résumés for on-campus interviews and develop more creative résumés (Exhibit 3) for off-campus direct mail campaigns. Effective résumés employ large type and plenty of white space to make them easy to read. Heavy-textured buff paper is preferable to white copy machine paper. Often your printer will have some suggestions on what color and weight of paper are appropriate for a power résumé.

RÉSUMÉS THAT SELL

We included Sandra Marinconz's résumé in this section because it was very well received by business recruiters. Sandra actually sent this résumé out and was deluged with requests for interviews. One sales vice president called her immediately after he received the résumé and invited her to St. Louis for a visit to headquarters. Sandra's creative résumé generated a total of six job offers.

What features made Sandra's résumé so effective? First, it was job focused, well organized, and creative (pictures), and it emphasized the match between Sandra's background and pharmaceutical sales. A close reading of Sandra's résumé reveals that her overall grade point average was only 3.1 out of a possible 4.0. Sandra was not hired because of her grades, but because she had the skills and interests to get the job done. Does this mean that you should copy Sandra's design when you prepare your own résumé? The answer is clearly no, but you should realize that creativity in résumé design can reap big rewards. We believe that each résumé should be unique so that it highlights the personality, background, and career interests of its creator. Remember that the best résumés are positive, emphasize skills, use action words, stress accomplishments, incorporate buzz words from your field, and use examples to illustrate personality traits. Best of luck with your job search.

Résumé
of
Sandra A. Marinconz

<table>
<tr><td>Present Address</td><td>Permanent Address</td></tr>
<tr><td>501 D Terry Lane</td><td>8802 Branton Avenue</td></tr>
<tr><td>Bloomington, Indiana 47401</td><td>Highland, Indiana 46322</td></tr>
<tr><td>(812) 333-5741</td><td>(219) 923-6378</td></tr>
</table>

Position Description
Pharmaceutical Sales Representative

Desire to begin my career in the Health Care Industry marketing a pharmaceutical product line to physicians, pharmacies, and hospitals. Prefer a highly structured training program which combines classroom and field training to fully prepare me to begin a successful career. Would like to eventually participate in the development and achievement of corporate plans and goals. Ambition is to complete advanced sales training programs and advance into a specialty position.

EXHIBIT 3   Creative Résumé for Pharmaceutical Sales

Career Goals

SHORT-TERM GOALS (1–12 months):
- To continue learning and developing professional behaviors
- To successfully enter my sales career with a desirable and challenging position

INTERMEDIATE GOALS (1–5 years):
- To generate the maximum amount of sales and new business within my territory
- To advance either within my sales career or move into a sales management position

LONG-TERM GOALS (5 years on):
- To continue learning, developing, and sharpening my sales skills to keep up with the changing field
- To become an expert at solving problems

Education

College: INDIANA UNIVERSITY SCHOOL OF BUSINESS, Bloomington, Indiana.
Degree: BACHELOR'S DEGREE in Marketing, May 1994.
Grade Index: 3.6/4.0 in major
               3.1/4.0 overall
Coursework includes the completion of 26 hours of Marketing Electives

Activities

ACTIVE MEMBER:
- Indiana University Marketing Club (Promotions Committee)
- Indiana University Student Athletic Board (Revenues Committee)

DEAN'S HONOR LIST CANDIDATE:
- Fall Semester 1992–93

PROFESSIONAL PRACTICE LECTURES:
- Presented the benefits of an internship to Orientation students

VICE PRECINCT COMMITTEE PERSON:
- Registered precinct members to vote
- Helped coordinate community activities
- Attended county conventions

EXHIBIT 3   Continued

Work Experience

DATES	COMPANY	POSITION/ACCOMPLISHMENTS	SKILLS ACQUIRED
May-August 1993	HALLMARK MARKETING CORPORATION Indianapolis, IN	SALES INTERNSHIP: Detailing, selling and servicing all assigned retail outlets. Assisted with seasonal orders, sales objectives, and current sales programs and promotions.	• Communications • Selling • Analytical • Flexibility • Commitment
May-August 1992	ECKERD DRUGS Dallas, TX	SALES CLERK/CASHIER: Provided quality customer service. Trained new sales clerks. Supervised employees in store manager's absence. Increased the sales of Eckerd brand products.	• Learning Quickly • Managerial Skills • Team Work • Problem Solving
June-August 1990	PEPSI-COLA COMPANY Munster, IN	PRODUCT SAMPLE DISTRIBUTOR: Promoted Pepsi-Cola products in grocery outlets. Distributed samples and communicated sale information to the consumers. Also managed unsupervised working hours.	• Verbal Skills • Creativity • Persistence • Honesty • Self-Discipline

Philosophy of Success

SUCCESS IS...

- Never giving up/persistence
- Learning from mistakes and successes
- Assuming responsibility for your own behavior (NO EXCUSES!!!)
- Performing acts without the expectation of immediate rewards
- Putting forth your best effort at *all times*
- Never putting things off

References Listed on Back*

* Sandra listed 4 references on the last page of her résumé. She included: names, titles, addresses, and telephone numbers.

EXHIBIT 3   Continued

REFERENCES

Chapter 1: Introduction to Selling and Sales Management

1. David Whitford, "Another Good Day for a Dell Sales Whiz," *Fortune* (July 20, 1998), pp. 146–148.

2. This section is based on some excellent discussions of current market and sales force changes including the following: Rolph Anderson, "Personal Selling and Sales Management in the New Millennium," *Journal of Personal Selling Sales Management,* 16 (Fall, 1996), pp. 17–32; Gerald Bauer, Mark Baunchalk, Thomas Ingram, and Raymond LaForge, *Emerging Trends in Sales Thought and Practice* (Westport, CT: Quorum Books, 1998); David Cravens, "The Changing Role of the Sales Force," *Marketing Management,* Vol. 4 (Fall 1995), pp. 49–57; and Neil Rackham, *Rethinking the Sales Force* (New York: McGraw-Hill, 1999).

3. Adam Fein, "Consolidation in Wholesale Distribution: What Are the Triggers?" *I.D.A. Management Journal* (September/October 1997).

4. Kenneth R. Evans, David Good, and Theodore Hellman, "Relationship Selling: New Challenges for Today's Sales Manager," *Emerging Trends in Sales Thought and Practice,* Gerald Bauer, Mark Baunchalk, Thomas Ingram, and Raymond LaForge (eds.) (Westport, CT: Quorum Books, 1998), p. 36.

5. John DeVincentis and Lauri Kien Kotcher, "Packaged Goods Salesforces—Beyond Efficiency," *The McKinsey Quarterly,* No. 1, 1995, pp. 72–85.

6. Andy Cohen, "Designing the Process, Starting Over," *Sales & Marketing Management* (September 1995), pp. 40–44.

7. DeVincentis and Kotcher, 1995, p. 78.

8. Mark W. Johnston, Joseph F. Hair, Jr., and James Boles, "Why Do Salespeople Fail?" *Journal of Personal Selling and Sales Management,* Vol. 9, No. 3 (Fall 1989), p. 61.

9. Linda Hill, *Becoming a Manager* (Boston, MA: Harvard Business School, 1992), p. 88.

10. William Keenan, "Bravo: 10 Managers Show What It Takes to Lead and Succeed," *Sales & Marketing Management* (August 1995), p. 39.

11. Geoffrey Brewer, "Celebrate Good Times," *Sales & Marketing Management* (October 1995), pp. 53–54.

12. Charles Butler, "Why the Bad Rap?" *Sales & Marketing Management* (June 1996), pp. 62–63.

13. Our definition of sales management competencies is adapted from the definition for managerial competencies provided in Don Hellriegel, Susan Jackson, and John Slocum, *Management,* 8th edition (Cincinnati, OH: South-Western College Publishing, 1999), p. 4.

14. David Cravens, 1995, p. 51.

15. Hill, *Becoming a Manager,* 1992, p. 89.

16. The discussion in this section and the dimensions of coaching are based on Gregroy Rich, "The Constructs of Sales Coaching: Supervisory Feedback, Role Modeling and Trust," *Journal of Personal Selling & Sales Management,* 18 (Winter, 1998), pp. 53–63.

17. Frank Pacetta, *Don't Fire Them, Fire Them Up:* A Maverick's Guide to Motivating Yourself and Your Team (New York: Simon & Schuster, 1994), p. 22.

18. Gregory Rich, "The Sales Manager as a Role Model: Effects on Trust, Job Satisfaction, and Performance of Salespeople," *Journal of the Academy of Marketing Science,* 25 (Fall 1997), pp. 319–328.

19. *The Hay Report: Compensation and Benefits Strategies for 1997 and Beyond* (Philadelphia: The Hay Group, 1996).

20. Hill, *Becoming A Manager,* p. 181.

21. Hill, *Becoming A Manager,* p. 171.

22. Andy Cohen, "Small World, Big Challenge," *Sales & Marketing Management* (June 1996), pp. 69–73.

23. Bonnie Guy and W. E. Patton, "Managing the Effects of Culture Shock and Sojourner Adjustment on the Expatriate Industrial Sales Force," *Industrial Marketing Management,* 25 (1996), pp. 385–393.

24. "It's a Wired World, Are You Ready to Compete?" *Sales & Marketing Management* (March 1999), p. 33.

25. Robert W. Armstrong, Anthony Pecotich, and Brad Mills, "Does the Sales Manager Make a Difference? The Impact of Sales Management Succession Upon Departmental Performance," *Journal of Personal Selling & Sales Management* (Fall 1993), p. 22.

26. Robert W. Armstrong, Anthony Pecotich, and Brad Mills, "Does the Sales Manager Make a Difference? The Impact of Sales Management Succession Upon Departmental Performance," *Journal of Personal Selling & Sales Management* (Fall 1993), p. 22.

27. "Rob Prazmark Goes for the Gold," *Sales & Marketing Management* (December 1990), pp. 24–25.

Chapter 2: Strategic Planning and Budgeting

1. Geoffrey Brewer, "The Tough Get Going," *Sales & Marketing Management* (September 1993), p. 61.

2. This organization is based on Eric Berkowitz, Roger Kerin, Stephen Hartley, and Bill Rudelius, *Marketing* (Burr Ridge, IL: R. D. Irwin, 1994), pp. 33–56.

3. William Keenan, Jr., "The Tough Get Going," *Sales and Marketing Management* (September 1993), p. 62.

4. Michael Porter, *Competitive Strategy* (New York: Free Press, 1980).

5. George Anders, "Managed Health Car Jeopardizes Outlook for Drug 'Detailers,'" *Wall Street Journal* (September 1, 1993), p. A1.

6. Presentation by Manual Diaz, "Sales Force Conversion: From Volume to Value" (September 28, 1993).

7. Thomas Wotruba and Linda Rochford, "The Impact of New Product Introductions on Sales Management Strategy," *Journal of Personal Selling & Sales Management* (Winter 1995), pp. 35–51.

8. "Kotler Foresees Integrated Future," *Business Marketing* (September 1993), p. 85.

9. Much of the discussion in this section is adapted from Neil Rackham and John DeVincentis, *Rethinking the Sales Force* (New York: McGraw-Hill), 1999.

10. Rowland Moriarty and Ursula Moran, "Managing Hybrid Marketing Systems" *Harvard Business Review* 68 (November–December 1990), p. 146.

11. Tim Clark, "Marketing Alliances Starting to Pay Off," *Business Marketing* (May 1993), p. 46.

12. "Distributor Networks," *Sales Manager's Bulletin,* 1307 (June 30, 1993), pp. 1–2.

13. *Economic Impact: U.S. Direct Marketing Today* (New York: The Direct Marketing Educational Foundation, Inc. 1995).

14. Kathy Haley, "Telemarketing Boosts Sales Effectiveness," *Business Marketing* (August 1995), pp. B2–B5.

15. Moriarty and Moran, "Managing Hybrid Marketing Systems," p. 153.

16. Robert Conti and William Cron, "Selling in the Future: Synthesis and Suggestions," in *Emerging Trends in Sales Thought and Practice,* eds. Gerald Bauer, Mark Baunchalk, Thomas Ingram and Raymond LaForge (Wesport, CT: Quorum Books), 1998.

17. Richard Hudson, "AT&Ts Computer Business Is Planning to Build Sales Partnerships in Europe," *Wall Street Journal* (May 11, 1990), p. B5.

18. Bradley Stertz, "Chrysler's Search for Broader Alliances Intensifies Amid Strong Internal Debate," *Wall Street Journal* (June 19, 1990), p. A4.

19. John Sterlicchi and Charlotte Klopp, "Europe Faces Invasion by U.S. Cereal Makers," *Marketing News* (June 1, 1990), p. 2.

20. "IBM to Shift Business to Resellers," *Sales & Marketing Management* (March 1995), p. 36.

21. This section is based on the discussion in Frederick Webster, "The Changing Role of Marketing in the Corporation," *Journal of Marketing,* 56 (October 1992), pp. 1–17, and Roger Brooksbank, "The New Model of Personal Selling: Micromarketing," *Journal of Personal Selling & Sales Management,* 15 (Spring 1995), pp. 61–66.

22. For more information on the customer's choice of supplier relationships, see Michael Dorsch, Scott Swanson, and Scott Kelley, "The Role of Relationship Quality in the Stratification of Vendors as Perceived by Customers," *Journal of the Academy of Marketing Science,* 26 (Spring 1998), pp. 128–142.

23. For more on how partnering relationships differ, see Dan Dunn and Claude Thomas, "Partnering with Customers," *Journal of Business & Industrial Marketing,* 9 (1994), pp. 34–40.

24. Edward Doherty, "How to Steal a Satisfied Customer," *Sales & Marketing Management* (March 1990), p. 45.

25. Marvin Jolson, "Broadening the Scope of Relationship Selling," *Journal of Personal Selling & Sales Management,* 17 (Fall 1997), pp. 75–88.

26. Rackam and DeVincentis, 1999, p. 146.

27. Reported in Lisa Napolitano, "Customer-Supplier Partnering: A Strategy Whose Time Has Come," *Journal of Personal Selling & Sales Management,* 17 (Fall 1997), pp. 1–8.

28. Jeffrey Dyer, "How Chrysler Created an American Keiretsu," *Harvard Business Review* (July–August 1996), pp. 42–56.

29. John Maggs, "U.S. Paper, Car Parts Makers Decry Japan Business Tactic," *Journal of Commerce and Commercial* (October 17, 1991), p. 3.

30. Urban Lehner and Alan Murray, "Selling of America," *Wall Street Journal* (June 19, 1990), pp. A1, A12.

31. See Thomas Tice, "Managing Compensation Caps in Key Accounts," *Journal of Personal Selling & Sales Management,* 17 (Fall 1997), pp. 41–47, for more on compensation issues in enterprise relationships.

32. See Barton Weitz and Kevin Bradford, "Personal Selling and Sales Management: A Relationship Marketing Perspective," *Journal of the Academy of Marketing Science* 27 (Spring 1999), pp. 241–254, for more on conflict management.

33. William Strahle, Rosann Spiro, and Frank Acito, "Marketing and Sales: Strategic Alignment and Functional Implementation," *Journal of Personal Selling & Sales Management* (Winter 1996), pp. 1–20.

Chapter 3: Personal Selling

1. Gail Edmondson, "One Electronic SOS Clinched the Deal," *Business Week* (February 26, 1996), p. 83.

2. Robert Peterson, Michael Cannito, and Steven Brown, "An Exploratory Investigation of Voice Characteristics and Selling Effectiveness," *Journal of Personal Selling & Sales Management* (Winter 1995), pp. 1–15.

3. Greg Marshall, William Moncrief, and Felicia Lassk, "The Current State of Sales Force Activities," *Industrial Marketing Management,* 28 (1999), pp. 87–98.

4. Andy Cohen, "IBM Wants to Automate Your Sales Force," *Sales & Marketing Management,* (October 1998), p. 14.

5. Thomas Stafford, "Conscious and Unconscious Processing of Priming Cues in Selling Encounters," *Journal of Personal Selling & Sales Management* (Spring 1996), pp. 37–44.

6. Joan Giuducci, "The First 7 Seconds of a Cold Call," *American Salesman,* 43 (August 1998), p. 14.

7. Marvin Jolson, "Broadening the Scope of Relationship Selling," *Journal of Personal Selling & Sales Management,* 17 (Fall 1997), 75–88.

8. Theresa Flaherty, Robert Dahlstrom, and Steven Skinner, "Organizational Values and Role Stress as Determinants of Customer-Oriented Selling Performance," *Journal of Personal Selling & Sales Management,* 19 (Sprint 1999), pp. 1–18.

9. This discussion is based on material from the Wilson Learning Corporation, *The Counselor Salesperson* (1996).

10. Roger Brooksbank, "The New Model of Personal Selling: Micromarketing," *Journal of Personal Selling & Sales Management* (Spring 1995), 15, 61–66.

11. Arun Sharma and Rajnandini Pillai, "Customers' Decision-Making Styles and their Preferences for Sales Strategies: Conceptual Examination and an Empirical Study," *Journal of Personal Selling & Sales Management,* 16 (Winter 1996), pp. 21–34.

12. Lucette Comer and Tanya Drollinger, "Active Empathetic Listening and Selling Success: A Conceptual Framework," *Journal of Personal Selling & Sales Management,* 19 (Winter 1999), pp. 15–29.

13. We don't mean to leave the impression that logical deduction is all that is involved. For more on presentation influencing techniques see: Tommy Whittler, "Eliciting Consumer Choice Heuristics: Sales Representatives," *Journal of Personal Selling & Sales Management,* 14 (Fall 1994), pp. 41–54.

14. Karl Boedecker, Fred Morgan and Jeffrey Stoltman, "Legal Dimensions of Salespersons' Statements: A Review and Managerial Suggestions," *Journal of Marketing,* 55 (January 1991), pp. 70–80.

15. Neil Rackham, *SPIN Selling* (New York: McGraw-Hill, 1988), p. 115.

16. Based on Robert Kantin, *Strategic Proposals: Closing the Big Deal* (New York: Vantage Press, 1999).

17. David Mercer, *High-Level Selling* (Houston, TX.: Golf Publishing, 1990), p. 130.

18. Rosemary Ramsey and Ravipreet Sohi, "Listening to Your Customers: The Impact of Perceived Salesperson Listening Behavior on Relationship Outcomes," *Journal of the Academy of Marketing Science,* 25 (Spring 1997), pp. 127–137.

19. For more on handling customer concerns, see Kenneth Hunt and Edward Bashaw, "A New Classification of Sales Resistance," *Industrial Marketing Management,* 28 (1999), 109–118.

20. Kerry Rottenberger-Murtha, "What Common Mistakes Do Your Salespeople Make?" *Sales & Marketing Management* (May 1993), p. 28.

21. David Strutton and James Lumpkin, "Problem-and Emotion-Focused Coping Dimensions and Sales Presentation Effectiveness," *Journal of the Academy of Marketing Science,* 22 (Winter 1994), pp. 28–37.

22. Rottenberger-Murtha, "Common Mistakes," p. 28.

23. Sarah Lorge, "How to Close the Deal," *Sales & Marketing Management,* 150 (April 1998), p. 84.

24. *Exchange,* p. 3.

25. See, for example, John Fento, *Close! Close! Close!* (Amsterdam: Pfeiffer and Company, 1993).

26. Jon Hawes, James Strong and Bernard Winick, "Do Closing Techniques Diminish Prospect Trust?" *Industrial Marketing Management,* 25 (1996), pp. 349–360.

27. Rottenberger-Murtha, "Common Mistakes," p. 28.

Chapter 4: Account Relationship Managements

1. "Ultimate Edge," *Sales Manager's Bulletin* (September 15, 1993), pp. 1–2.

2. Marvin Jolson, "Broadening the Scope of Relationship Selling," *Journal of Personal Selling & Sales Management* (Fall 1997), pp. 75–88.

3. Allison Lucas, "Leading Edge," *Sales & Sales Management* (June 1995), p. 13.

4. William Weeks and Lynn Kahle, "Salespeople's Time Use and Performance," *Journal of Personal Selling & Sales Management* (Winter 1990), pp. 29–37.

5. For further development of the purchasing process, see Michele Bunn, "Taxonomy of Buying Decision Approaches," *Journal of Marketing* (January 1993), pp. 38–56.

6. Daniel Smith and Jan Owens, "Knowledge of Customers' Customers as a Basis of Sales Force Differentiation," *Journal of Personal Selling & Sales Management,* 15 (Summer 1995), pp. 1–16.

7. Jan Heide and Allen Weiss, "Vendor Consideration and Switching Behavior for Buyers in High Technology Markets," *Journal of Marketing* (July 1995), pp. 30–43.

8. Charles O'Neal and Kate Bertrand, *Developing a Winning JIT Marketing Strategy* (Englewood Cliffs, NJ: Prentice-Hall, 1991).

9. "Chrysler's Neon," *Business Week* (May 3, 1993), p. 119.

10. For more on developing proposals, see Robert Kantin, *Strategic Proposals* (New York: Vantage Press, 1999).

11. James Anderson and James Narus, *Business Market Management* (Upper Saddle River, NJ: Prentice-Hall, 1999), pp. 172–173

12. Barton Weitz and Kevin Bradford, "Personal Selling and Sales management: A Relationship Marketing Perspective," *Journal of the Academy of Marketing Science,* 27, 2 (1999), pp. 241–254.

13. Louis Stern, Adel El-Ansary, and Anne Coughlan, *Marketing Channels* (Upper Saddle River, NJ: Prentice-Hall, 1996).

14. Thomas Noorewier, George John, and John Nevin, "Performance Outcomes of Purchasing Arrangements in Industrial Buyer-Vendor Relationships," *Journal of Marketing* (October 1990), pp. 80–93.

15. For more on understanding buyer decision making, see Arun Sharma and Rajnandini Pillai, "Customers' Decision-Making Styles and the Preferences for Sales Strategies: Conceptual Examination and Empirical Study," *Journal of Personal Selling & Sales Management,* 16 (Winter 1996), pp. 21–34.

16. This discussion is based on concepts presented in Robert Miller, Stephen Heiman, and Tad Tuleja, *Strategic Selling* (New York: Morrow, 1985), pp. 83–87.

17. B. G. Hovovich, "Marketing After the Break-Up," *Business Marketing* (November 1991), pp. 14–16.

18. B. G. Hovovich, "Revolutionary Marketing," *Business Marketing* (March 1993), pp. 36–38.

19. Robert Krapfel, Jr., "An Advocacy Behavior Model of Organizational Buyers' Vendor Choice," *Journal of Marketing,* 49 (Fall 1985), pp. 51–59.

20. Robert Blattberg and John Deighton, "Managing Marketing by the Customer Equity Test," *Harvard Business Review* (July–August 1996), pp. 136–144.

21. For more on relationship development see James C. Anderson, "Relationships in Business Markets: Exchange Episodes, Value Creation, and Their Empirical Assessment," *Journal of the Academy of Marketing Science,* 23 (1996), pp. 346–350.

22. Gerrard Macintosh, Kenneth Anglin, David Szymanski, and James Gentry, "Relationship Development in Selling: A Cognitive Analysis," *Journal of Personal Selling & Sales Management,* 4 (Fall 1992), pp. 23–34.

23. Jan Heide and George John, "Alliances in Industrial Purchasing: The Determinants of Joint Action in Buyer-Supplier Relationships," *Journal of Marketing Research,* 27 (February 1990), p. 25.

24. For more on how teams operate, see Dawn Deeter-Schmelz and Rosemary Ramsey, "A Conceptualization of

the Functions and Roles of Formalized Selling and Buying Teams," *Journal of Personal Selling & Sales Management,* 15 (Spring 1995), pp. 47–60.

25. Jeffrey Dyer, Dong Cho and Wujin Chu, "Strategic Supplier Segmentation," *California Management Review,* 40 (Winter 1998), pp. 57–77.

26. For more on the influencers of a customer's long-term orientation, see Shankar Ganesan, "Determinants of Long-Term Orientation in Buyer-Seller Relationships," *Journal of Marketing,* 58 (April 1994), pp. 1–19.

27. Erin Anderson and Thomas Robertson, "Inducing Multi-Line Salespeople to Adopt House Brands," *Journal of Marketing* 59 (April 1995), pp. 16–31.

28. Miller et al., *Strategic Selling,* pp. 101–105.

29. For more on additional relationship binders, see David T. Wilson, "An Integrated Model of Buyer-Seller Relationships," *Journal of the Academy of Marketing Science,* 23 (1996), pp. 225–245.

30. Don Pepper and Martha Rogers, "In One-to-One Marketing Customer Interaction Vital," *Business Marketing* (February 1994), p. 9.

31. Douglas Lambert, Howard Marmorstein, and Arun Sharma, "The Accuracy of Salespersons' Perceptions of Their Customers: Conceptual Examination and an Empirical Study," *Journal of Personal Selling & Sales Management* (Winter 1990), pp. 1–9.

32. Michael Dorsch, Scott Swanson and Scott Kelley, "The Role of Relationship Quality in the Stratification of Vendors as Perceived by Customers," *Journal of the Academy of Marketing Science,* 26, 2 (1998), pp. 128–142.

33. For more on building trust see Patricia Doney and Joseph Cannon, "An Examination of the Nature of Trust in Buyer-Seller Relationships," *Journal of Marketing,* 61 (April 1997), pp. 35–51, and Robert Morgan and Shelby Hunt, "The Commitment-Trust Theory of Relationship Marketing," *Journal of Marketing,* 58 (July 1994), pp. 20–38.

34. See the work of Lucette Comer and Tanya Drollinger, "Active Empathetic Listening and Selling Success: A Conceptual Framework," *Journal of Personal Selling & Sales Management,* 19 (Winter 1999), pp. 15–29, and Rosemary Ramsey and Ravipreet Sohi, "Listening to Your Customers: The Impact of Perceived Salesperson Listening Behavior on Relationship Outcomes," *Journal of the Academy of Marketing Science,* 25, 2 (1997), pp. 127–137.

Chapter 5: Territory Management

1. David Mercer, *High-Level Selling* (Houston, TX.: Gulf Publishing, 1990), pp. 21–22.

2. "What Does a Sales Call Cost?" *Sales & Marketing Management* (September 1999) p. 56.

3. David S. Kemp, "Pray for Us All," *Sales & Marketing Management* (March 1993), p. 8.

4. For additional discussion of how companies are efficiently identifying qualified prospects, see Nancy Arnott, "Selling Is Dying" *Sales & Marketing Management* (August 1994), pp. 82–86.

5. Marvin Jolson and Thomas Wotruba, "Prospecting: A New Look at This Old Challenge," *Journal of Personal Selling & Sales Management,* 4 (Fall 1992), p. 65.

6. Michele Marchetti, "Is Cold Calling Worth It?" *Sales & Marketing Management* (August 1997), p. 103.

7. For more information on trade shows, call or write to Trade Show Bureau, 1660 Lincoln Street, Suite 2080, Denver, Colorado 80264-2001 or call 303-860-7626.

8. Jolson and Wotruba, "Prospecting," p. 61.

9. Jolson and Wotruba, "Prospecting," p. 61.

10. David Szymanski and Gilbert Churchill, "Client Evaluation Cues: A Comparison of Successful and Unsuccessful Salespeople," *Journal of Marketing Research,* 27 (May 1990), pp. 163–174.

11. "1993 Sales Manager's Budget Planner," *Sales & Marketing Management* (1993), p. 62.

12. Michele Marchetti, "1999 Sales Manager's Budget Planner" (September 1999), p. 56–57.

13. Raymond LaForge, David Cravens, and Clifford Young, "Improving Salesforce Productivity," *Business Horizons* (September–October 1982), pp. 50–59.

14. For more on response functions, decision calculus, and decision models, see Bernd Skiera and Sonke Albers, "COSTA: contribution optimizing sales territory alignment," *Marketing Science* (Summer 1998), 17, p. 196.

15. Raymond LaForge, David Cravens, and Clifford Young, "Using Contingency Analysis to Select Selling Effort Allocation Methods," *Journal of Personal Selling & Sales Management* (August 1986), p. 23.

16. For an alternative selling process model see Michael Bosworth, *Solutions Selling* (New York: McGraw-Hill, 1995).

17. This discussion is based on Stephen Heiman, Diane Sanchez, Tad Tuleja, and Robert Miller, *The New Strategic Selling* (New York: Morrow, 1998), pp. 234–269.

18. Heiman et al., *The New Strategic Selling,* p. 249.

19. Economist Intelligence Unit and Andersen Consulting, as reported in *Velocity* (Summer 1999), p. 3.

20. Rackham, *Rethinking the Sales Force,* pp. 14–16.

21. Mark Van Clieaf, "Identifying Your Most Profitable Customers," *Business Quarterly* (Winter 1996), pp. 55–60.

22. Joseph Vaccaro and Derek Coward, "Managerial and Legal Implications of Price Haggling: A Sales Manager's Dilemma," *Journal of Personal & Selling & Sales Management,* 13 (Summer 1993), pp. 79–85.

23. "1993 Sales Manager's Budget Planner," p. 75.

24. Ginger Conlon, "Plug and Play," *Sales & Marketing Management* (December 1998), p. 65.

25. For further information on the traveling salesperson problem, see Wayne Winston, *Operations Research: Applications and Algorithms* (Belmont, CA: Duxbury Press, 1994) and G. D. Eppon, F. J. Gould, C.P. Schmidt, and Rick Hesse, *Introductory Management Science* (Englewood Cliffs, NJ: Prentice-Hall, 1993).

26. For more time management in selling, see Marge Figel, "Get the Most Out of Your Time," *American Salesman* (September 1997), vol. 42, p. 3.

27. Stephen Covey, *Principle-Centered Leadership* (New York: Simon & Schuster, 1992).

28. For more information see Bernard Jaworski, Vlasis Stathkopoulos, and Shanker Krishnan, "Control Combinations in Marketing: Conceptual Framework and Empirical Evidence," *Journal of Marketing,* 57 (January 1993), p. 57–69.

Chapter 6: Sales Ethics

1. Bridget O'Brian, "Prudential Fined $20 Million by NASD Over Its Sales of Variable Life Insurance," *Wall Street Journal* (July 9, 1999), pp. C1, C11.

2. Frances A. McMorris, "Bid Rigging, Kickbacks Inflated Costs for Many Companies, Prosecutors Find," *Wall Street Journal* (February 1, 1999), p. B9.

3. Geoffrey Brewer, "On the Road Again," *Sales & Marketing Management* (January 1996), p. 50.

4. John R. Sparks and Shelby Hunt, "Marketing Researcher Ethical Sensitivity: Conceptualism, Measurement, and Exploratory Investigation," *Journal of Marketing,* 62 (April 1998), p. 105.

5. Michael Siconolfi, "Brokers May Sue Former Employers Over Firing Notices," *Wall Street Journal* (May 2, 1996), p. B7.

6. John R. Wilke, "New York Will Bar Data General Sales to State Agencies Amid Bribery Inquiry," *Wall Street Journal* (October 8, 1992), p. A5.

7. Ken Bass, Tim Barnett, and Gene Brown, "The Moral Philosophy of Sales Managers and Its Influence on Ethical Decision Making," *Journal of Personal Selling & Sales Management,* 18 (Spring 1998), pp. 1–17.

8. Niccolo Machiavelli, *The Prince* (New York: Mentor Classics), 1952.

9. Anusorn Singhapakdi and Scott J. Vitell, "Analyzing the Ethical Decision Making of Sales Professionals," *Journal of Personal Selling & Sales Management* (Fall 1991), p. 9.

10. Dawn Blalock, "For Many Executives, Ethics Appear to Be a Write-Off," *Wall Street Journal* (March 26, 1996), p. C1.

11. Milo Geyelin and Stephanie Simon, "Court Rules Employers Can Fire Older Executives to Trim Costs," *Wall Street Journal* (July 16, 1991), p. B5.

12. Ken Bass, Tim Barnett, and Gene Brown, "The Moral Philosophy of Sales Managers and Its Influence on Ethical Decision Making," *Journal of Personal Selling & Sales Management,* 18 (Spring 1998), p. 9.

13. "Most Doctors Get Gift Offers from Drug Firms, Survey Says," *Herald Times* (April 3, 1992), p. A5.

14. James P. Miller, "Mid-American Waste System CEO Quits After Indictment on Bribery Charges," *Wall Street Journal* (April 17, 1996), p. B5a.

15. "Former Sales Executive at National Medical Admits Kickback Role," *Wall Street Journal* (December 4, 1998), p. A15.

16. *Wall Street Journal* (June 20, 1989), p. B1.

17. Rob Zeiger, "Sex, Sales & Stereotypes," *Sales & Marketing Management* (July 1995), pp. 46–56.

18. Mark Maremont, "Abuse of Power," *Business Week* (May 13, 1996), pp. 86–98.

19. Leslie M. Fine, C. David Shepard, and Susan L. Josephs, "Insights into Sexual Harassment of Salespeople by Customers: The Role of Gender and Customer Power," *Journal of Personal Selling & Sales Management,* 19, No. 2 (Spring 1999), p. 29.

20. Charles Gasparino and John Connor, "Big Payday for a Whistleblower," *Wall Street Journal* (April 9, 1999), pp. C1, C22.

21. Scott Kilman, "Ex-Officials of ADM Given 2 Years in Jail," *Wall Street Journal* (July 12, 1999), pp. A3, A12.

22. Alan J. Dubinsky, Marvin A. Jolson, Ronald E. Michaels, Masaaki Kotabe, and Chae Un Lim, "Ethical Perceptions of Field Sales Personnel: An Empirical Assessment," *Journal of Sales & Marketing Management* (Fall 1992), p. 18.

23. *Wall Street Journal* (May 14, 1996), p. A1.

24. Gabriella Stern and Joann S. Lublin, "New GM Rules Curb Wining and Dining," *Wall Street Journal* (May 5, 1996), p. B1.

25. Rolph Anderson, Rajiv Mehta, and James Strong, "An Empirical Investigation of Sales Management Training Programs for Sales Managers," *Journal of Personal Selling & Sales Management,* 17 (Summer 1997), p. 61.

26. Rosemary R. Lagace, Robert Dahlstrom, and Jule B. Gassenheimer, "The Relevance of Ethical Salesperson Behavior on Relationship Quality: The Pharmaceutical Industry," *Journal of Personal Selling & Sales Management* (Fall 1991), p. 44.

27. Ken Bass, Tim Barnett, and Gene Brown, "The Moral Philosophy of Sales Managers and Its Influence on Ethical Decision Making," *Journal of Personal Selling & Sales Management,* 18 (Spring 1998), p. 11.

28. Joann S. Lublin, "Companies Try a Variety of Approaches to Halt Sexual Harassment on the Job," *Wall Street Journal* (October 11, 1991), p. B1.

Chapter 7: Estimating Potentials and Forecasting Sales

1. Rolph Anderson, Rajiv Mehta, and James Strong, "An Empirical Investigation of Sales Management and Training Programs for Sales Managers," *Journal of Personal Selling & Sales Management,* 17, No. 3 (Summer 1997), p. 61.

2. G. Pascal Zachary, "Hewlett to Post About Flat Net for 3rd Period," *Wall Street Journal* (August 15, 1989), p. 10.

3. William Keenan, "Numbers Racket," *Sales & Marketing Management* (May 1995), p. 66.

4. The seasonal indexes derived in Table 7-4 are easy to explain, but most computer programs use a more sophisticated procedure known as the ratio to moving average method.

5. Kenneth B. Kahn, "Benchmarking Sales Forecasting Performance Measures," *Journal of Business Forecasting Methods & Systems,* 17, No. 4 (Winter 1998/1999), p. 20.

6. Kenneth B. Kahn, "Revisiting Top-down Versus Bottom-up Forecasting," *Journal of Business Forecasting Methods & Systems,* 17, No. 2 (Summer 1998), p. 3.

7. John T. Mentzer, "State of Sales Forecasting Systems in Corporate America," *Journal of Business Forecasting Methods & Systems,* 16, No. 1 (Spring 1997), pp. 6–13.

8. Spyros, Makridakis, A. Anderson, R. Carbone, R. Fildes, M. Hibon, R. Lewandowski, J. Newton, E. Parzen, and R. Winkler, "The Accuracy of Extrapolation (Times Series) Methods: Results of a Forecasting Competition," *Journal of Forecasting,* 1 (April–June 1982), pp. 111–153, and Stephan P. Schnaars, "Situational Factors Affecting Forecasting Accuracy," *Journal of Marketing Research,* 21 (August 1984), pp. 290–297.

Chapter 8: Organization

1. Daniel Levine, "Justice Served," Sales & *Marketing Management* (May 1995), pp. 53–61.

2. Christien Heide, *Sales Force Compensation Survey* (Chicago: The Dartnell Corporation 1996), p. 175.

3. "Technology Raises Bar for Sales Jobs," *Wall Street Journal* (January 21, 1997), p. B1.

4. Heide, p. 175.

5. Paul Dishman and Dregg Aytes, "Exploring Group Support Systems in Sales Management Applications," *Journal of Personal Selling & Sales Management* (Winter 1996), pp. 65–77.

6. Economist Intelligence Unit and Andersen Consulting, "A Survey of More than 200 Leading Executives in North America, Europe and Asia, in *Velocity* (Summer 1999), p. 3.

7. Jerome Colletti and Gary Tubridy, *Reinventing the Sales Organization* (Scottsdale, AZ: The Alexander Group, Inc. 1993), p. 2.

8. Robert Ruekert, Orville Walker, and Kenneth Roering, "The Organization of Marketing Activities: A Contingency Theory of Structure and Performance," *Journal of Marketing,* 49 (Winter 1985), pp. 17–21.

9. Martin Everett, "Send in the Specialists," *Sales & Marketing Management* (April 1991), pp. 46–47.

10. Ravipeet Sohi, Daniel Smith, and Neil Ford, "How Does Sharing a Sales Force Between Multiple Divisions Affect Salespeople?" *Journal of the Academy of Marketing Science* (Summer 1996), pp. 195–207.

11. Alston Gardner and Stephen Bistritz, *Managing Strategic Accounts: A White Paper,* Target Marketing Systems, Inc., 1997.

12. Thomas Wotruba and Stephen Castleberry, "National Account Marketers: Who They Are and What They Do," NAMA *Journal,* 27 (Winter 1992), p. 9.

13. Adam Fein, "Understanding Evolutionary Processes in Non-Manufacturing Industries: Empirical Insights from the Shakeout in Pharmaceutical Wholesaling," *Journal of Evolutionary Economics* (July 1998), pp. 1–39.

14. Kathleen Schmidt, "Unisys Cuts Clear Path to International Recovery," *Marketing News* (September 1999), p. 4.

15. Kathy Haley, "Telemarketing Boosts Sales Effectiveness," *Business Marketing* (August 1995), pp. B2–B5.

16. Peggy Moretti, "Telemarketers Serve Clients," *Business Marketing* (April 1994), pp. 29, 31.

17. Moretti, "Telemarketers," p. 31.

18. John Tschohl, *Achieving Excellence Through Customer Service* (Englewood Cliffs, NJ: Prentice-Hall, 1991).

19. Michele Marchetti, "Looks Who's Calling," *Sales & Marketing Management* (May 1998), p. 43.

20. For a good discussion on how to address these problems, see Judith Marshall and Harrie Vredenburg, "An Empirical Study of Factors Influencing Innovation Implementation in Industrial Sales Organizations," *Journal of the Academy of Marketing Science,* 20 (Summer 1992), pp. 205–215.

21. American Telemarketing Association, 1993 *Salary Survey of Members.*

22. Dana Milbank, "Telephone Sales Reps Do Unrewarding Jobs that Few Can Abide," *Wall Street Journal* (September 9, 1993), p. A1.

23. Marilyn Stephens, Donald Weinrauch, and Karl Mann, "Leading Manufacturers Representatives Voice Their Perceptions and Recommendations for the Future: A Challenge to Marketing Educators," *National Conference for Sales Management* (1993), p. 95.

24. For more on nonfinancial means of motivating sales reps, see Paul Dishman, "Exploring Strategies for Companies that Use Manufacturers' Representatives as Their Sales Force," *Industrial Marketing Management* (Fall, 1996). pp. 453–465.

25. Steve Zunier, "Finally, Reps Get Some Respect," *Industrial Distribution,* 80 (June 1991), pp. 27–30.

26. U.S. Department of Commerce, *Census of Wholesale Trade* for 1972, 1977, 1982, 1987, Vol. 1.

27. Allen Weiss and Erin Anderson, "Converting from Independent to Employee Salesforces: The Role of Perceived Switching Costs," *Journal of Marketing Research,* 24 (February 1992), pp. 101–115.

28. John Hill and Richard Still, "Organizing the Overseas Sales Force: How Multinationals Do It," *Journal of Personal Selling & Sales Management,* 10 (Spring 1990), pp. 57–66.

29. "Sales Management in the Age of Cross-Functional Organizations," *Sales Manager's Bulletin* (August 30, 1995), p. 10.

30. Joseph Conlin, "Teaming Up," *Sales & Marketing Management* (October 1993), pp. 98–104.

Chapter 9: Territory Design

1. Tom Eisenhart, "Drawing a Map to Better Sales," *Business Marketing* (January 1990), pp. 59–61.

2. TERRALIGN, Metron, Inc., 1481 Chain Bridge Road, McLean, VA 22101.

3. "Software Directory," *Sales & Marketing Management* (December 1993), p. 102.

4. Tom Dellecave, "Lost in New York, Onboard Navigation Keeps Reps on the Right Road," *Sales & Marketing Management* (May 1996), pp. 98–103.

Chapter 10: Recruiting and Selections Personnel

1. Jim Harris and Joan Brannick, *Finding and Keeping Great Employees* (New York: American Management Association 1999), p. 135.

2. Geoffrey Brewer, "Shrink Rap," *Performance* (September 1995), p. 30.

3. Herbert M. Greenberg and Jeanne Greenberg, "Job Matching for Better Performance," *Harvard Business Review,* 58 (September–October 1980), p. 128.

4. William Keenan, "Time Is Everything," *Sales & Marketing Management* (August 1993), p. 60.

5. Erika Rasmusson, "Protecting Your Turf, Are You Reviewing Sales Territories as Often as You Should?" *Sales & Marketing Management* (April 1998), p. 90.

6. For more information on the success of first-year insurance agents, see Jacqueline Landau and James Werbel, "Sales Productivity of Insurance Agents During the First Six Months of Employment: Differences Between Older and Younger New Hires," *Journal of Personal Selling & Sales Management,* 15 (Fall 1995), pp. 33–43.

7. For more information on the causes of turnover and how to manage turnover, see Eli Jones, Donna Massey Kantak, Charles Futrell, and Mark Johnston, "Leader Behavior, Work-Attitudes, and Turnover of Salespeople: An Integrative Study," *Journal of Personal Selling & Sales Management,* 16 (Spring 1996), pp. 13–23; Pradeep Tyagi and Thomas Wotruba, "An Exploratory Study of Reverse Causality Relationships Among Sales Force Turnover Variables," *Journal of the Academy of Marketing Science,* 21 (Spring 1993), pp. 143–153; and

Jeff Sager, "A Longitudinal Assessment of Change in Sales Force Turnover," *Journal of the Academy of Marketing Science,* 19 (Winter 1991), pp. 25–36.

8. Harris and Brannick, *Finding and Keeping Great Employees,* pp. 18–19.

9. H. R. Chally Group, *How to Select a Sales Force that Sells* (1998).

10. H. R. Chally Group, *The Customer-Selected World Class Sales Excellence Research Report* (1997).

11. Charles Butler, "What Does it Take to Sell for Invacare?" *Sales & Marketing Management* (July 1995), p. 70.

12. Michele Marchetti and Chad Kaydo, "Give Us Two Weeks and We'll Give You a New Sales Force," *Sales & Marketing Management* (December 1998), p. 31.

13. Review reported in Gilbert Churchill, Neil Ford, Steve Hartley, and Orvill Walker, "The Determinants of Salesperson Performance: A Meta-Analysis," *Journal of Marketing Research* (May 1986), pp. 103–118; and Neil Ford, Gilbert Churchill, Steve Hartley, and Orvill Walker, "Selecting Successful Salespeople: A Meta-Analysis of Biographical and Psychological Selection Criteria," *Review of Marketing,* ed. Michael Houston (Chicago: American Marketing Association, 1988), pp. 90–131.

14. For more on the importance of person-job fit, see James Werbel, Jacqueline Landau, and Thomas DeCarlo, "The Relationship of Pre-entry Variables to Early Employment Organizational Commitment," *Journal of Personal Selling & Sales Management,* 16 (Spring 1996), pp. 25–36.

15. For more on the biases involved in hiring salespeople, see Greg W. Marshall, Miriam B. Stamps, and Jesse N. Moore, "Preinterview Biases: The Impact of Race, Physical Attractiveness, and Sales Job Type on Preinteriew Impressions of Sales Job Applicants," *Journal of Personal Selling & Sales Management* (Fall 1998), pp. 21–38.

16. George Freehery, "The Role of Empathy in Personal Selling," *National Conference of Sales Management* (1992), pp. 130–135.

17. H. R. Chally Group, *The Customer-Selected World Class Sales Excellence Research Report* (1997), p. 17.

18. Rosann Sprio and Barton Weitz, "Adaptive Selling: Conceptualization, Measurement, and Nomological Validity," *Journal of Marketing Research,* 27 (February 1990), pp. 61–69.

19. "Eli Lilly Lauded for Its Bedside Manner," *Sales & Marketing Management* (February 1992), p. 68.

20. Susan Meisinger, "The Americans with Disabilities Act of 1990: A New Challenge for Human Resource Managers," *Legal Report, Society for Human Resource Management* (Winter 1990), pp. 1–16.

21. Ilan Mochari, "How to Hire," *Inc.,* 19 (October 1998), p. 36.

22. Tricia Campbell, "Finding Hidden Sales Talent," *Sales & Marketing Management* (March 1999), p. 84.

23. Tricia Campbell (1999), p. 85.

24. Thomas Wotruba and Stephen Castleberry, "Job Analysis and Hiring Practices for National Account Marketing Positions," *Journal of Personal Selling & Sales Management,* 13 (Summer 1993), pp. 49–65.

25. Ilan Mochair (1998), p. 38

26. William Keenan (1993), p. 60.

27. Conversation with Stephanie N. Crisara, Manager of Professional Employment, Armstrong Cork Company, Lancaster, Pennsylvania.

28. Gary McWilliams, "Reveille for DEC's Sleepy Sales Force," *Business Week* (August 30, 1993), p. 74.

29. For more information on how to recruit college students, see Dan Weilbaker and Nancy Merritt, "Attracting Graduates to Sales Positions: The Role of Recruiter Knowledge," *Journal of Personal Selling & Sales Management,* 12 (Fall 1992), pp. 49–58.

30. Dick Schaaf, "Lessons From the 100 Best," *Training,* 27 (February 1990), p. S19.

31. Keenan, "Time Is Everything," p. 62.

32. Rene Darmon, "Where Do the Best Sales Force Profit Producers Come From?" *Journal of Personal Selling & Sales Management,* 13 (Summer 1993), p. 27.

33. Myron Gable, Charles Hollon, and Frank Dangello, "Increasing the Utility of the Application Blank: Relationship Between Job Application Information and Subsequent Performance and Turnover of Salespeople," *Journal of Personal Selling & Sales Management,* 12 (Summer 1992), pp. 51–58.

34. Timothy S. Bland and Sue S. Stalcup, "Build a Legal Employment Application," *HR Magazine,* 44 (March 1999), p. 129.

35. Keenan, "Time Is Everything," p. 61.

36. Martin Everett and Betsy Siesendanger, "What Does Body Language Really Say?" *Sales & Marketing Management* (April 1992), p. 40.

37. Jim Harris and Joan Brannick, *Finding and Keeping Great Employees,* p. 72.

38. Liz Murphy, "Did Your Salesman Lie to Get His Job?" *Sales & Marketing Management* (November 1987), p. 54.

39. Thomas Wotruba and Edwin Simpson, *Sales Management: Text and Cases* (Boston: PWS-Kent, 1992), p. 380.

40. H. R. Chally Group, *How to Select a Sales Force that Sells* (1998), p. 16.

41. Meisinger, "Americans with Disabilities Act," pp. 4–7.

42. Cathy Owens Swift, Rober Wayland, and Jane Wayland, "The ADA: Implications for Sales Managers," *National Conference for Sales Management* (1993), pp. 146–148.

43. Roy Cook and Joel Herche, "Assessment Centers: An Untapped Resource for Global Salesforce Management," *Journal of Personal Selling & Sales Management,* 12 (Summer 1992), pp. 31–39.

44. "Internship Program Attracts Quality Recruits," *Sales Manager's Bulletin* (July 15, 1993), p. 5.

45. The discussion in this section is based on The Chally Group, "The 9 Most Common Hiring Mistakes and How to Avoid Them" (1998).

46. The discussion in this section is based on John Fernandez, *Managing a Diverse Work Force: Regaining the Competitive Edge* (Lexington, MA: Lexington Books, 1991).

47. Lucette B. Comer, J.A.F. Nicholls, and Leslie J. Vermillion, "Diversity in the Sales Force: Problems and Challenges," *Journal of Personal Selling & Sales Management,* 18 (Fall 1998), 1–20.

Chapter 11: Sales Training

1. Sarah Lorge, "Getting Into Their Heads," *Sales & Marketing Management* (February 1998), pp. 59–67.

2. Neil Ford, Orville Walker, Gilbert Churchill, and Steven Hartley, "Selecting Successful Salespeople: A Meta-Analysis of Biographical and Psychological Selection Criteria," in *Review of Marketing,* ed. Michael Houston (Chicago: American Marketing Association, 1988), pp. 90–131, and Kay Keck, Thomas Leigh, and James Lollar, "Critical Success Factors in Captive Multi-Line Insurance Agency Sales," *Journal of Personal Selling & Sales Management,* 15 (Winter 1995).

3. Sarah Lorge, "Teach Your Managers Well," *Sales & Marketing Management* (June 1999), p. 40.

4. Dick Schaaf, "Lessons from the 100 Best," *Training,* 27 (February 1990), p. S19.

5. Robert Klein, "Nabisco Sales Soar After Sales Training," *Marketing News* (January 6, 1997), p. 23.

6. William Moncrief, Ronald Hoverstad, and George Lucas, "Survival Analysis: A New Approach to Analyzing Sales Force Retention," *Journal of Personal Selling & Sales Management,* 9 (Summer 1989), p. 26.

7. Frederick A. Russ, Kevin M. McNeilly, James M. Comer, and Theodore B. Light, "Exploring the Impact of Critical Sales Events," *Journal of Personal Selling & Sales Management,* 18 (Spring 1998), p. 26.

8. *Sales & Marketing Management* (September 1993), p. 61.

9. Based on conversations with William J. Bartholomew, Director of Sales, Tellabs, Inc.

10. Thayer C. Taylor, "Take Your Time," *Sales & Marketing Management* (July 1994), pp. 45–46.

11. Thayer C. Taylor, "Does This Compute?" *Sales & Marketing Management* (September 1994), pp. 115–119.

12. Robert Erffmeyer, Randall Russ, and Joseph Hair, "Needs Assessment and Evaluation in Sales Training Programs," *Journal of Personal Selling & Sales Management,* 11 (Winter 1991), pp. 17–30.

13. Saul Gellerman, "The Tests of a Good Salesperson," *Harvard Business Review,* 90 (May–June 1990), pp. 64–72.

14. John Marohl, "More on Training," *Sales & Marketing Management* (July 1993), p. 7.

15. Adel Eln-Ansary, "Sales Force Effectiveness Research Reveals New Insights and Reward-Penalty Patterns in Sales Force Training," *Journal of Personal Selling & Sales Management,* 13 (Spring 1993), p. 86.

16. William Keenan, "Are You Overspending on Training?" *Sales & Marketing Management* (January 1990), pp. 56–60.

17. Kerry Rottenberger-Mutha, "Owens-Corning Fiberglas, Corp." *Sales & Marketing Management* (September 1993), p. 56.

18. Erin Anderson and Thomas Robertson, "Inducing Multiline Salespeople to Adopt House Brands," *Journal of Marketing,* 59 (April 1995), pp. 16–31.

19. For more information on salespeople's cognitive scripts and knowledge structures, see Thomas Leigh and Patrick McGraw, "Mapping the Procedural Knowledge of Industrial Sales Personnel: A Script-Theoretic Investigation," *Journal of Marketing,* 53 (January 1989), pp. 16–34; and Thomas Ainscough, Thomas E. DeCarlo, and Thomas W. Leigh, "Building Expert Systems for Novice Salespeople from the Selling Scripts of Multiple Experts," *Journal of Services Marketing,* 10 (1996), pp. 23–40.

20. William Keenan, "What's Sales Got to Do with It?" *Sales & Marketing Management* (March 1994), pp. 66–70.

21. Michele Marchetti, "Sales Training Even a Rep Could Love," *Sales & Marketing Management* (June 1998), p. 70.

22. "Dow Makes It Big by Thinking Small," *Sales & Marketing Management* (September 1991), p. 44.

23. "Vital Statistics: 1995 Industry Report," *Training* (October 1995), p. 62.

24. The H. R. Chally Group, *The Customer Selected World Class Sales Excellence Research Report* (1998), p. 52.

25. For more on mentoring, see Ellen Pullins, Leslie Fine, and Wendy Warren, "Identifying Peer Mentors in the Sales Force: An Exploratory Investigation of Willingness and Ability," *Journal of the Academy of Marketing Science,* 24 (Spring 1996), pp. 125–136.

26. William Keenan, "Merck Co.," *Sales & Marketing Management* (September 1993), p. 62.

27. For more on role-playing in a classroom setting, see Joseph Chapman, "Building Block Method for in-Class Role-Playing," *National Conference for Sales Management* (1992), pp. 27–30; Lynn Metcalf, "Role-Playing in the Classroom: Enriching the Sales Management Course in a Resource-Limited Environment," *National Conference for Sales Management* (1992), pp. 8–12; Richard Rexelsen, "Developing Role Play as an Interactive Learning Resource," *National Conference for Sales Management* (1992), pp. 13–18.

28. "To Reinforce and Motivate Your Sales Team, Use TV-Style Quiz Shows," *Personal Selling Power* (July–August 1990), pp. 44–46.

29. Jack Falvey "The Most Neglected Training Tool," *Sales & Marketing Management* (June 1990), pp. 51–59.

30. Melanie Berger, "On-the-Job Training: Online Classes Keep Reps Up-to-Date and in the Field," *Sales & Marketing Management* (February 1998), pp. 122–125.

31. Robert M. Kahn, "21st Century training," *Sales & Marketing Management* (June 1997), p. 82.

32. Tricia Campbell, "Training the Video Game Generation," *Sales & Marketing Management* (June 1999), p. 15.

33. William Keenan, "Hewlett-Packard Strives to Connect with Its Customers," *Sales & Marketing Management* (September 1991), p. 48.

34. Erika Rasmusson, "Getting Schooled in Outsourcing," *Sales & Marketing Management* (January 1999), p. 49.

35. Keenan, "Are You Overspending on Training?" p. 59.

36. Lawrence Chonko, John Tanner, and William Weeks, "Sales Training: Status and Needs," *Journal of Personal Selling & Sales Management,* 13 (Fall 1993), pp. 81–86.

37. For more on evaluating sales training effectiveness, see Rick Mendosa, "Training: Is There a Payoff?" *Sales & Marketing Management* (June 1995), pp. 64–71.

Chapter 12: Leadership

1. "Top Reasons for Voluntary Turnover," *Sales & Marketing Management* (June 1999), p. 14.

2. See Alan J. Dubinsky, Frances J. Yammarino, Marvin A. Jolson, and William D. Spangler, "Transformational Leadership: An Initial Investigation in Sales Management," *Journal of Personal Selling & Sales Management,* 15, No. 2 (Spring 1995), p. 27; and Jeffrey K. Sager, Junsub Yi, and Charles M. Futrell, "A Model Depicting Salespeople's Perceptions," *Journal of Personal Selling & Sales Management,* 18, No. 3 (Summer 1998), pp. 1–22.

3. Interview with Joe Clayton, Executive Vice President of Marketing and Sales—Americas, Thomson Consumer Electronics (1993).

4. James Cortada, *TQM for Sales and Marketing Management* (New York: McGraw-Hill, 1993), pp. 40–41.

5. Based on John French, Jr. and Bertrm Raven, "The Bases of Social Power," in *Studies in Social Power,* ed. D. Carwright (Ann Arbor, MI: The University of Michigan Press, 1959).

6. Jennifer J. Laabs, "Change," *Personnel Journal,* 53 (July 1996), pp. 54–63.

7. Price Prichett, "Overcome Resistance," *Executive Excellence,* 14 (1997), pp. 13–14.

8. Kevin M. McNeilly and Marian B. Lawson, "Navigating Through Rough Waters," *Industrial Marketing Management,* 28 (January 1999), pp. 37–49.

9. This section is based on Jerome A. Colletti and Lawrence B. Chonko, "Change Management Initiatives: Moving Sales Organizations from Obsolescence to High Performance," *Journal of Personal Selling & Sales Management,* 17, No. 2 (Spring 1997), pp. 1–30; and Geral Bauer, Mark Baunchalk, Thomas Ingram, and Raymond LaForge, *Emerging Trends in Sales Thought and Practice* (Westport, CT: Quorum Books, 1998).

10. Frederick A. Russ, Kevin M. McNeilly, and James M. Comer, "Leadership, Decision Making and Performance of Sales Managers: A Multi-Level Approach," *Journal of Personal Selling & Sales Management,* 16, No. 3 (Summer 1996), pp. 11–12.

11. Frank Cespedes, Stephen Doyle, and Robert Freedman, "Teamwork for Today's Selling," *Harvard Business Review* (March–April 1989), p. 44.

12. "Why Teams Don't Work," *Sales & Marketing Management* (April 1993), p. 12.

13. This section is based largely on Don Hellriegel and John Slocum, *Management, 6th ed.* (Reading, MA: Addison-Wesley, 1991), pp. 544–554.

14. D. C. Feldman, "The Development and Enforcement of Group Norms," *Academy of Management Review,* 9 (1989), pp. 47–53.

15. Kevin J. Corcoran, Laura K. Petersen, Daniel B. Baitch, and Mark Barrett, *High-Performance Sales Organizations: Achieving Competitive Advantage in the Global Marketplace* (Chicago: Irwin Professional Publications, 1995).

16. Bernard Jaworski and Ajay Kohli, "Supervisory Feedback: Alternative Types and Their Impact on Salespeople's Performance and Satisfaction," *Journal of Marketing Research,* 28 (May 1991), pp. 190–201.

17. Gregory A. Rich, "The Constructs of Sales Coaching: Supervisory Feedback, Role Modeling and Trust," *Journal of Personal Selling & Sales Management,* 18, No. 1 (Winter 1998), pp. 53–63.

18. Ibid.

19. Gregory A. Rich, "The Sales Manager as a Role Model: Effects on Trust Job Satisfaction, and Performance of Salespeople," *Journal of the Academy of Marketing Science,* 25 (October 1997), pp. 319–328.

20. John Ueland, "Meetings," *Sales & Marketing Management* (August 1998), p. 49.

21. "1997 MANA Sales Meeting Survey," *Agency Sales Magazine* (August 1997), p. 36.

22. *Sales & Marketing Management* (June 22, 1992), p. 42.

23. Elaine Evans, "How to Create Sales Meeting Magic," *Personal Selling Power* (September 1990), pp. 34–35.

24. "Weary Travelers," *Sales & Marketing Management* (March 1996), p. 68.

25. Robert Cary, "Meetings," *Sales & Marketing Management* (August 1998), pp. 60–61.

26. William Keenan, Jr., "The Nagging Problem of the Plateaued Salesperson," *Sales & Marketing Management* (March 1989), pp. 36–40.

27. John Slocum, William Cron, Richard Hansen, and Sally Rawlings, "Business Strategy and the Management of Plateaued Employees," *Academy of Management Journal,* 28 (1985), pp. 133–154.

28. John Slocum, William Cron, and Linda Yows, "Whose Career Is Likely to Plateau?" *Business Horizons,* 30 (1987), pp. 31–38.

29. Minda Zetlin, "Is It Worth Keeping Older Salespeople?" *Sales & Marketing Management* (April 1995), p. 148.

30. Milan Moravee, Marshall Collins, and Clinton Tropodi, "Don't Want to Manage? Here's Another Path," *Sales & Marketing Management* (April 1990), p. 70.

31. Robin Peterson, "Beyond the Plateau," *Sales & Marketing Management* (July 1993), pp. 78–80.

32. Patrick Schul and Brent Wren, "The Emerging Role of Women in Industrial Selling: A Decade of Change," *Journal of Marketing,* 56 (July 1992), pp. 38–54.

33. Leslie M. Fine, C. David Shepherd, and Susan L. Josephs, "Insights into Sexual Harassment of Salespeople by Customers: The Role of Gender and Customer Power," *Journal of Personal Selling & Sales Management,* 19 (Spring 1999), pp. 19–34.

34. Patricia M. Buhler, "The Manager's Role in Preventing Sexual Harassment," *Supervision,* 60 (April 1999), pp. 16–19.

35. Based on Linda Lynton, "The Dilemma of Sexual Harassment," *Sales & Marketing Management* (October 1989), pp. 67–71.

36. Julia Lawlor, "Stepping Over the Line," *Sales & Marketing Management* (October 1995), p. 94.

37. Raymond Corey, "Marketing Managers: Caught in the Middle," in *Ethics in Marketing,* ed. Craig Smith and John Quelch (Homewood, IL.: Irwin, 1993), p. 41.

Chapter 13: Motivating Salespeople

1. Leslie Brennan, "Sales Secrets of the Incentive Stars," *Sales & Marketing Management* (April 1990), pp. 88–100.

2. Frederick Herzberg, "One More Time: How Do You Motivate Employees?" *Harvard Business Review,* 46 (January–February 1968), pp. 53–62.

3. Geoffrey Brewer, "What Makes Great Salespeople?" *Sales & Marketing Management* (May 1994), pp. 82–92.

4. Marvin Jolson, "The Salesman's Career Cycle," *Journal of Marketing,* 38 (July 1974), pp. 39–46.

5. The discussion in this section is based on the following articles: William L. Cron, "Industrial Salesperson Development: A Career Stages Perspective," *Journal of Marketing* (Fall 1984), pp. 41–52; William L. Cron and John W. Slocum, "The Influence of Career Stages on Salespeople's Job Attitudes, Work Perceptions and Performance," *Journal of Marketing Research* (May 1986), pp. 119–129; and Douglas Hall, "Managing Yourself: Building a Career," in A. R. Cohen, ed., *The Portable MBA in Management* (New York: Wiley, 1993), pp. 190–206.

6. For further discussion of expectancy theory, see Wesley J. Johnston and Keysuk Kim, "Performance Attribution and Expectancy Linkages in Personal Selling," *Journal of Marketing,* 58 (October 1994), pp. 68–81; and Thomas E. DeCarlo, R. Kenneth Teas, and James C. McElroy, "Salesperson Performance Attribution Processes and the Formation of Expectancy Estimates," *Journal of Personal Selling and Sales Management,* 27 (Summer 1997), pp. 1–17.

7. For a detailed discussion of role perceptions, see Jeffrey Sager, "A Structural Model Depicting Salespeople's Job Stress," *Journal of the Academy of Marketing Science,* 22 (January 1994), pp. 74–84.

8. See Gordon Badovick, "Emotional Reactions and Salesperson Motivation: An Attributional Approach Following Inadequate Sales Performance," *Journal of the Academy of Marketing* Science, 18 (Spring 1990), pp. 123–130; and Thomas E. DeCarlo, R. Kenneth Teas, and James C. McElroy, "Salesperson Performance Attribution Processes and the Formation of Expectancy Estimates," *Journal of Personal Selling and Sales Management,* 27 (Summer 1997), pp. 1–17.

9. Alan Dubinsky, Masaaki Kotabe, Chae Un Lim, and Ronald Michaels, "Differences in Motivational Perceptions among U.S., Japanese, and Korean Sales Personnel," *Journal of Business Research,* 30 (1994), pp. 175–185.

10. Linda Hill, *Becoming a Manager* (Boston: Harvard Business School Press, 1992).

11. For more on this subject, see Steven Brown and Robert Peterson, "The Effect of Effort on Sales Performance and Job Satisfaction," *Journal of Marketing,* 58 (April 1994), pp. 70–80.

12. Nancy Arnott, "Step Right Up!" *Sales & Marketing Management* (October 1994), p. 117.

13. Richard Oliver and Erin Anderson, "An Empirical Test of the Consequences of Behavior- and Outcome-Based Sales Control Systems," *Journal of Marketing,* 58 (October 1994), pp. 53–67.

14. Thomas Wotruba, "The Effect of Goal-Setting on the Performance of Independent Sales Agents in Direct Selling," *Journal of Personal Selling & Sales Management,* 9 (Fall 1989), pp. 22–29.

15. See William Ross, "Performance Against Quota and the Call Selection Decision," *Journal of Marketing Research,* 28 (August 1991), pp. 296–306, for more information on how quota difficulty may influence salespeople's strategies for achieving the quota.

16. Rene Y. Darmon, "Selecting Appropriate Sales Quota Plan Structures and Quota Setting Procedures," *Journal of Personal Selling and Sales Management* (Winter 1997), pp. 1–16.

17. For more information on the importance and use of feedback, see Bernard Jaworski and Ajay Kohli, "Supervisory Feedback: Alternative Types and Their Impact on Salespeople's Performance and Satisfaction," *Journal of Marketing Research,* 28 (May 1991), pp. 190–201; and Ajay Kohli and Bernard Jaworski, "The Influence of Coworker Feedback on Salespeople," *Journal of Marketing,* 58 (October 1994), pp. 82–94.

18. Thomas R. Wotruba and Michael L. Thurlow, "Sales Force Participation in Quota Setting and Sales Forecasting," *Journal of Marketing,* 40 (April 1976), p. 16.

19. Steven P. Brown, William L. Cron, and John W. Slocum Jr. "Effects of Trait Competitiveness and Perceived Intraorganizational Competition on Salesperson Goal Setting and Performance," *Journal of Marketing,* 62 (October 1998), pp. 88–98.

20. Marilyn E. Gist and Terence R. Mitchell, "Self-Efficacy: A Theoretical Analysis of Its Determinants and Malleability," *Academy of Management Review,* 17 (1992), pp. 183–211.

21. The Buying Power Index is reported by cities, counties, and states each July by *Sales & Marketing Management* magazine.

22. Regina Eisman, "Justifying Your Incentive Program," *Sales & Marketing Management* (April 1993), p. 43.

23. Vincent Alonzo, "Sharing the Wealth," *Sales & Marketing Management* (May 1998), pp. 30–32.

24. "What Employees Want," *Sales & Marketing Management* (June 1995), p. 41.

25. William Murphy and Ravipreet Sohi, "Sales Persons' Perceptions About Sales Contests," *European Journal of Marketing,* 29 (1996) pp. 42–66.

26. "Multiple Recognition," *Sales Manager's Bulletin,* 1295 (December 30, 1992), p. 8.

27. Steven Brown, William Cron, and Thomas Leigh, "Do Feelings of Success Mediate Sales Performance-Work Attitude Relationships?" *Journal of the Academy of Marketing Science,* 21 (Spring 1993), pp. 91–100.

28. Frank Cespedes, Stephen Doyle, and Robert Freedman, "Teamwork for Today's Selling," *Harvard Business Review* (March–April 1989), p. 8.

Chapter 14: Compensating Salespeople

1. *Sales Force Compensation Survey* (Chicago: Dartnell Corporation, 1999), p. 117.

2. *Wall Street Journal* (March 6, 1990), p. B1.

3. Robert G. Head, "Restoring Balance to Sales Compensation," *Sales & Marketing Management* (August 1992), p. 52.

4. Michele Marchetti, "Compensation Is Kid Stuff," *Sales & Marketing Management* (April 1999), pp. 53–59.

5. *Sales Force Compensation Survey* (Chicago: Dartnell Corporation, 1999), p. 38.

6. *Sales Force Compensation Survey* (Chicago: Dartnell Corporation, 1999), p. 50.

7. Bridget O'Brian, "Merrill Lynch Considers Paying Salaries to New Brokers to Cut Interest Conflicts," *Wall Street Journal* (November 20, 1995), p. A2.

8. George John and Barton Weitz, "Salesforce Compensation: An Empirical Investigation of Factors Related to Use of Salary Versus Incentive Compensation," *Journal of Marketing Research,* 26 (February 1989), p. 9.

9. *Sales Force Compensation Survey* (Chicago: Dartnell Corporation, 1999), p. 49.

10. Kissan Joseph and Manohar U. Kalwani, "The Role of Bonus Pay in Salesforce Compensation Plans," *Industrial Marketing Management,* 27 (March 1998), pp. 147–159.

11. Michele Marchetti, "Not So Easy to Digest," *Sales & Marketing Management* (February 1997), pp. 54–60.

12. Joseph and Kalwani (March 1998).

13. Ginger Trumfio, "Keeping the Lid on Turnover," *Sales & Marketing Management* (November 1995), pp. 41–42.

14. Tim Clark, "Digital Displays Signs of Recovery," *Business Marketing* (August 1993), p. 13.

15. *Sales & Marketing Management* (February 1995), p. 32.

16. Ron Donoho, "Pay Plans Get Low Marks," *Sales & Marketing Management* (December 1994), pp. 11–12.

17. Michele Marchetti, "Global Gamble," *Sales & Marketing Management* (July 1996), pp. 64–69.

18. Bridget O'Brian, "Merrill Lynch Planners Say They Face Too Much Sales Pressure," *Wall Street Journal* (May 3, 1996), p. B1.

19. Andy Cohen, "Right on Target," *Sales & Marketing Management* (December 1994), pp. 59–63.

20. *Sales Compensation in the 1990s* (Bureau of Business Practice, SMB Special Report, 1991), p. 13.

21. "Rewarding Team Players," *Sales & Marketing Management* (April 1996), pp. 35–36.

22. *Sales Force Compensation Survey* (Chicago: Dartnell Corporation, 1999), p. 163.

23. Rene Y. Darmon, "Salesmen's Responses to Financial Incentives," *Journal of Marketing Research* (July 1974), pp. 39–46.

24. Chad Kaydo, "Compensation in the Call Center," *Sales & Marketing Management* (August 1999), p. 75.

25. *Sales & Marketing Management's 1998 Productivity Study.*

26. *Sales Force Compensation Survey* (Chicago: Dartnell Corporation, 1999), p. 119.

27. *Sales Force Compensation Survey* (Chicago: Dartnell Corporation, 1999), pp. 121.

28. Peter Drucker, "Permanent Cost Cutting," *Wall Street Journal* (January 11, 1991), p. A15.

29. Lawrence B. Chonko, John F. Tanner, and William A. Weeks, "Selling and Sales Management in Action: Reward Preferences of Salespeople," *Journal of Personal Selling & Sales Management* (Summer 1992), p. 69.

30. *Sales Force Compensation Survey* (Chicago: Dartnell Corporation, 1999), p. 119.

31. Tom Dellecave, Jr., "Getting the Most from Your Web Site," *Sales & Marketing Management* (March 1997), pp. 2–4.

Chapter 15: Evaluating Performance

1. Donald W. Jackson, John L. Schlacter, and William G. Wolfe, "Examining the Bases Utilized for Evaluating Salespeoples' Performance," *Journal of Personal Selling & Sales Management,* Vol. 15, No. 4 (Fall 1995), p. 65.

2. Vlasis Stathakopoulos, "Sales Force Control: A Synthesis of Three Theories," *Journal of Personal Selling & Sales Management,* Vol. 16, No. 2 (Spring 1996), p. 1.

3. Donald W. Jackson, John L. Schlacter, and William G. Wolfe, "Examining the Bases Utilized for Evaluating Salespeoples' Performance," *Journal of Personal Selling & Sales Management,* Vol. 15, No. 4 (Fall 1995), p. 64.

4. *Wall Street Journal* (October 16, 1990), p. 1.

5. Michael H. Morris, Duane L. Davis, Jeffrey W. Allen, Ramon A. Avila, and Joseph Chapman, "Assessing the Relationships Among Performance Measures, Managerial Practices, and Satisfaction When Evaluating the Salesforce," *Journal of Personal Selling & Sales Management* (Summer 1991), p. 32.

6. Andy Cohen, "Movin' Out," *Sales & Marketing Management* (January 1996), pp. 24–25.

7. David W. Cravens, Thomas N. Ingram, Raymond W. LaForge, and Clifford E. Young, "Behavior-Based and Outcome-Based Salesforce Control Systems," *Journal of Marketing* (October 1993), p. 54.

8. Lawrence B. Chonko, John F. Tanner, and William Weeks, "Selling and Sales Management in Action: Reward Preferences of Salespeople," *Journal of Personal Selling & Sales Management* (Summer 1992), p. 69.

9. Kay L. Keck, Thomas W. Leigh, and James G. Lollar, "Critical Success Factors in Captive, Multi-Line Insurance Agency Sales," *Journal of Personal Selling & Sales Management,* Vol. 14, No. 1 (Winter 1995), pp. 17–33.

10. Michele Marchetti, "Board Games," *Sales & Marketing Management* (January 1996), p. 44.

11. Robert Troutwine, "Prepare Now and Succeed Later," College Edition of the National Business Employment Weekly, *Wall Street Journal* (Fall 1990), p. 10.

12. Sanjeev Agarwal, "Impact of Job Formalization and Administrative Controls on Attitude of Industrial Salespersons," *Industrial Marketing Management,* 28 (1999), pp. 359–368.

13. Kay L. Keck, Thomas W. Leigh, and James G. Lollar, "Critical Success Factors in Captive, Multi-Line Insurance Agency Sales," *Journal of Personal Selling & Sales Management,* Vol. 14, No. 1 (Winter 1995), pp. 17–33.

14. *Salesforce Compensation Survey* (Chicago: Dartnell, 1999), p. 20.

15. Ibid.,

16. Douglas J. Dalrymple and William M. Strahle, "Career Path Charting: Frameworks for Sales Force Evaluation," *Journal of Personal Selling & Sales Management,* Vol. 10, No. 203 (Summer 1990), pp. 59–68.

17. James S. Boles, Naveen Donthu, and Ritu Lohtia, "Salesperson Evaluation Using Relative Performance Efficiency: The Application of Data Envelopment Analysis," *Journal of Personal Selling & Sales Management,* Vol. 15, No. 3 (Summer 1995), pp. 31–49; To compute relative efficiency by adjusting for territory considerations, see Bruce K. Pilling, Naveen Donthu, and Steve Henson, "Accounting for the Impact of Territory Characteristics on Sales Performance: Relative Efficiency as a Measure of Salesperson Performance," *Journal of Personal Selling & Sales Management* (Spring 1999), pp. 35–45.

18. David W. Cravens, Raymond W. LaForge, Gregory M. Pickett, and Clifford E. Young, "Incorporating a Quality Improvement Perspective into Measures of Salesperson Performance," *Journal of Personal Selling & Sales Management* (Winter 1993), p. 11.

19. James W. Cortada, *TQM for Sales and Marketing Management* (New York: McGraw-Hill, 1993), p. 83.

CREDITS

Chapter 1

Figure 1-2: Ginger Canton, Lisa Napolitano, and Mike Pusateri, *Unlocking Profits: The Strategic Advantage of Key Account Management* (Chicago, IL: National Account Management Association, 1997), p. 44.

Figure 1-3: Thomas Muccio, "Procter & Gamble: Allocating Resources," in *Unlocking Profits: The Strategic Advantage of Key Account Management,* Ginger Canton, Lisa Napolitano, and Mike Pusateri (eds.), (Chicago, IL: National Account Management Association, 1997), p. 66.

Table 1-1: Adapted from data presented in William O'Connell and William Keenan, Jr., "The Shape of Things to Come," *Sales & Marketing Management* (January 1990), p. 39.

Chapter 2

Figure 2-3: Adapted from William Cron and Michael Levy, "Sales Management Performance Evaluation: A Residual Income Perspective," *Journal of Personal Selling & Sales Management* (August 1987), p. 58.

Strategic Action Competency: W. Chan Kim and Renee Mauborgne, "Creating New Market Space," *Harvard Business Review,* 77 (January–February 1999), pp. 88–89.

Figure 2-5: Adapted from Cron and Levy, 1987, p. 58.

Figure 2-6: Adapted from Rackam and DeVincentis, 1999, p. 27.

Figure 2-7: Adapted from Jeffrey Dyer, "How Chrysler Created an American Keiretsu, *Harvard Business Review* (July–August 1996), p. 50.

Table 2-2: Adapted from "Data Watch", *Velocity* (Spring 1999), p. 3.

Technology Competency: Tom Dellecave, "The Net Effect," *Sales & Marketing Management* (March 1996), pp. 17–21.

Global Awareness Competency: Rackham and DeVincentis, 1999, pp. 194–196.

Team-Building Competency: The HR Chally Group, *The Customer Selected World Class Sales Excellence Research Report* (1998), pp. 93–101.

Table 2-1: Source: William Strahle, *An Exploratory Study of the Relationship Between Marketing and Sales Strategy* (Bloomington: School of Business, Indiana University, unpublished doctoral dissertation, 1989), p. 153.

Table 2-2: Lisa Napolitano, "Customer-Supplier Partnering: A Strategy Whose Time Has Come," *Journal of Personal Selling & Sales Management* (Fall 1997), p. 8.

Table 2-3: Sales Force Compensation Survey (Chicago: Dartnell Corp., 1999), p. 9.

Chapter 3

Self-Management Competency: Kerry Rottenberger-Murtha, "What Common Mistakes Do Your Salespeople Make?" *Sales & Marketing Management* (May 1993), pp. 28–29.

Strategic Action Competency: Sarah Lorge, "Enron," *Sales & Marketing Management* (July 1999), pp. 48–52.

Technology Competency: Thayer Taylor, "The Automated Wake-Up Call," *Sales Marketing Management* (August, 1993), pp. 64–67.

Global Perspective Competency: George Leslie, "U.S. Reps Should Learn to Sell 'Japanese Style,'" *Marketing News,* 24 (October 29, 1990), p. 6.

Chapter 4

Figure 4-2: Adapted from Rackam and DeVincentis, 1999, p. 67.

Coaching Competency: John Caslione, "Strategic Sales Planning," presented in *Leading the High-Performance Sales Organization,* October 7, 1993.

Global Perspective Competency: Sudhir Kale, "The Cultural Domain of Cross-National Buyer-Seller Interactions," presented at the *American Marketing Association's Summer Educator Conference,* August 1993.

Strategic Action Competency: David Kirkpatrick, "IBM: From Big Blue Dinosaur to E-Business Animal," *Fortune* (April 26, 1999), pp. 116–125.

Chapter 5

Strategic Action Competency: Based on information in Dell Online, Harvard Business School Publishing, 1998.

Global Perspective Competency: Steven Prokesch, "Xerox Drives for Pole Position in Race for Eastern Europe Markets," *The Dallas Morning News* (December 31, 1990), p. 1D.

Figure 5-1: Source: Sarah Lorge, "Get More Customers Now," *Sales & Marketing Management* (November 1998), p. 50.

Figure 5-2: Adapted from Raymond LaForge, David Cravens, and Clifford Young, "Improving Salesforce Productivity," *Business Horizons* (September–October 1985), p. 54.

Figure 5-5: Sales Force Compensation Survey (Chicago: Dartnell Corp, 1999), p. 176.

Chapter 6

Figure 6-1: Thomas R. Wotruba, "A Comprehensive Framework for the Analysis of Ethical Behavior, with a Focus on Sales Organizations," *Journal of Personal Selling & Sales Management,* Vol. 10 (Spring 1990), p. 31.

Self-Management Competency: Joseph B. Cahill, "Sears is Sued Again on Auto-Center Work," *Wall Street Journal* (June 17, 1999), pp. A3, A10.

Global Perspective Competency: Glenn R. Simpson, "Foreign Deals Rely on Bribes, U.S. Contends," *Wall Street Journal* (February 23, 1999), pp. A3, A13. Glenn R. Simpson, "Mobil Defends Payments Made to Panamanians," *Wall Street Journal* (April 5, 1999), p. A24.

Strategic Action Competency: Thomas M. Burton, "Methods of Marketing Infant Formula Land Abbot in Hot Water." *Wall Street Journal* (May 25, 1993), p. A1.

Chapter 7

Table 7-1: "1999 Survey of Buying Power," *Sales & Marketing Management* (September 1999), pp. 12, 18, 21, 32.

The production employee data in Table 7-2 are from the 1992 Census of Manufacturers, Geographical Area Series, North Carolina, p. NC 11. The codes in the table are the old SIC codes that were used in the 1992 Census of Manufacturers. More recent data from the 1997 Census of Manufacturers using the new NAIC codes will be available sometime in the spring of 2000.

Table 7-2: From 1992 Census of Manufacturers, Geographical Area Series, North Carolina, p. NC 11.

Table 7-3: Douglas J. Dalrymple, "Sales Forecasting Practices: Results from a United States Survey," *International Journal of Forecasting,* 3 (1987), p. 382.

Table 7-5: *Sales & Marketing Management* (December 1994), p. 66.

Table 7-6: Steven C. Wheelwright and Spyros Makridakis, *Forecasting Methods for Management,* 4th ed. (New York: Wiley, 1985), pp. 181–182.

Strategic Action Competency: Rich Gordon, "A Role for the Forecasting Function," *Journal of Business Forecasting Methods & Systems,* Vol. 16, No. 4 (Winter 1997), pp. 3–7.

Global Perspective Competency: Mainiero Antonio, "Forecasting at Procter & Gamble in Italy," *Journal of Business Forecasting & Systems,* Vol. 16, No. 2 (Summer 1997), pp. 19–20.

Technology Competency: Shri Amrute, "Forecasting New Products with Limited History: Nabisco's Experience," *Journal of Business Forecasting Methods & Systems,* Vol. 17, No. 3 (Fall 1998), pp. 7–11.

Chapter 8

Figure 8-2: Source: Economist Intelligence Unit and Andersen Consulting: A survey of more than 200 leading executives in North America, Europe and Asia, as reported in *Velocity* (Summer 1999), p. 3.

Strategic Action Competency: "Benchmarking Tools: Strategic Account Management Innovation Study," sponsored by the Strategic Account Management Association, October 7, 1999.

Table 8-2: Peggy Moretti, "Telemarketers Serve Clients," *Business Marketing* (April 1994), pp. 29, 31.

Global Awareness Competency: "Benchmarking," October 7, 1999.

Teamwork Competency: Patricia Sellers, "How to Remake Your Sales Force," *Fortune* (May 4, 1992), pp. 100–102.

Self-Management Competency: *Sales Competencies for the 21st Century,* MOHR Inc., 1997, p. 6.

Chapter 9

Strategic Action Competency: Richard Lewis, "Putting Sales on the Map," *Sales & Marketing Management* (August 1993), pp. 78–80.

Coaching Competency: Melissa Campaneli, "A New Focus," *Sales & Marketing Management* (September 1995), pp. 56–58.

Technology Competency: Tom Eisenhart, "Drawing a Map to Better Sales," *Business Marketing* (January 1990), pp. 59–61.

Chapter 10

Table 10-1: "The Best Sales Reps Will Take on Their Bosses for You," *Purchasing* (November 7, 1996), p. 81.

Table 10-2: John Hunte and Ronda Hunte, "Validity and Utility of Alternative Predictors of Job Performance," *Psychological Bulletin,* 96 (July 1984), p. 90.

Technology Competency: Sarah Lorge, "A Real-Life SFA Success Story," *Sales & Marketing Management* (January 1999), p. 67.

Strategic Action Competency: Patricia Nakache, "Cisco's Recruiting Edge," *Fortune* (September 29, 1997), pp. 275–276.

Self-Management Competency: David Strutton and James Lumpkin, "The Relationship Between Optimism and Coping Styles of Salespeople," *Journal of Personal Selling & Sales Management,"* 13 (Spring 1993), pp. 71–82; Fiona Patterson and Jo Silvester, "Counter Measures," *People Management* (April 1998), p. 46.

Global Perspective Competency: John Hill and Meg Birdeye, "Salesperson Selection in Multinational Corporations: An Empirical Study," *Journal of Personal Selling & Sales Management,* 9 (Summer 1989), p. 45.

Chapter 11

Strategic Awareness Competency: Willima Keenan, "Getting Customers into the A.C.T.," *Sales & Marketing Management* (February 1995), pp. 58–63.

Table 11-2: Source: *Sales Force Compensation Survey* (Chicago: Dartnell Corporation, 1999), p. 143.

Table 11-3: Source: *Sales Force Compensation Survey* (Chicago: Dartnell Corporation, 1999), p. 145.

Self-Management Competency: Rekha Balu, "Whirlpool Gets Real with Customers," *Fast Company* (December 1999), pp. 74–76.

Technology Competency: Robert M. Kahn, "21st Century Training," *Sales & Marketing Management* (June 1997), p. 82.

Team-Building Competency: Sarah Lorge, "Getting Into Their Heads," *Sales & Marketing Management* (February 1998), pp. 66–67.

Chapter 12

Self-Management Competency: Rolph Anderson, Rajiv Mehta, and James Strong, "Sales Training and Education: An Empirical Investigation of Sales Management Training Programs for Sales Managers," *Journal of Personal Selling & Sales Management* (Summer 1997), pp. 53–66.

Strategic Action Competency: Adapted from R. B. Leiber, "Why Employees Love These Companies," *Fortune* (January 12, 1998), pp. 72–74; *Mary Kay Ash, Mary Kay You Can Have It All: Lifetime Wisdom from America's Foremost Woman Entrepreneur* (Prima, 1995) and the company home page for Mary Kay Cosmetics, Inc. at *www.marykay.com.*

Team Building Competency: David Stumm, *The New Sales Manager's Survival Guide* (New York: Amacom, 1985), p. 119.

Table 12-1: Source: William Keenan, "The Nagging Problem of the Plateaued Salesperson," *Sales & Marketing Management* (March 1989), p. 38.

Table 12-2: *Sales Force Compensation Survey* (Chicago: Dartnell Corporation, 1999), p. 171.

Chapter 13

Global Perspective Competency: Adapted from E. Nevis, "Using an American Perspective in Understanding Another Culture; Toward a Hierarchy of Needs for the People's Republic of China, *Journal of Applied Behavior Science,* 19 (1983), pp. 249–264.

Table 13-2: *Sales and Marketing Management* (February 1990), p. 2.

Figure 13-2: "What Makes Great Salespeople," *Sales & Marketing Management* (May 1994), pp. 82–92.

Figure 13-3: William L. Cron, "Industrial Salesperson Development: A Career Stages Perspective, *"Journal of Marketing,* 48 (Fall 1984), pp. 41–52.

Figure 13-5: Daniel A. Sauers, James B. Hunt, and Ken Bass, "Behavioral Self-Management as a Supplement for External Sales Force Control," *Journal of Personal Selling & Sales Management* (Summer 1990), p. 22.

Figure 13-6: Developed from the information in Alan J. Dubrosky and Thomas E. Barry, "A Survey of Sales Management Practices," *Industrial Marketing Management,* 11 (April 1982), pp. 133–141.

Team-Building Competency: Vincent Alonzo, "Sharing the Wealth," *Sales & Marketing Management* (May 1998), pp. 30–32.

Coaching Competency: Alfie Kohn, "Why Incentives Plans Cannot Work," *Harvard Business Review* (September–October 1993), pp. 54–63.

Chapter 14

Team-Building Competency: Don Peppers and Martha Rogers, Ph.D., "The Price of Customer Service," *Sales & Marketing Management* (April 1999), p. 20.

Technology Competency: Paula Jacobs, "Amdahl's Sales Compensation System," *CIO,* 10 (April 1, 1979), pp. 102.

Strategic Action Competency: Based on Peter Burrows, "Beyond Rock Bottom," *Business Week* (March 14, 1994), pp. 80–82; and *The Nineteenth Annual AMA Faculty Consortium On Professional Selling and Sales Management* (July 1999), Orlando, FL.

Coaching Competency: Sarah Lorge, "Warning: Pay Change on the Way," *Sales & Marketing Management* (February 1999), p. 70.

Table 14-1: *Sales Force Compensation Survey* (Chicago: Dartnell Corporation, 1999), p. 43.

Figure 14-3: *Sales Force Compensation Survey* (Chicago: Dartnell Corporation, 1999), p. 28.

Table 14-4: "Sales & Marketing Management's 1998 Productivity Study," *Sales & Marketing Management* (December 1998).

Table 14-5: *Sales Force Compensation Survey* (Chicago: Dartnell Corporation, 1999), p. 121.

Chapter 15

Table 15-1: Donald W. Jackson, John L. Schlacter, and William G. Wolfe, "Examining the Bases Utilized for Evaluating Salespeoples' Performance," *Journal of Personal Selling & Sales Management,* Vol. 15, No. 4 (Fall 1995), p. 61.

Table 15-2: Donald W. Jackson, John L. Schlacter, and William G. Wolfe, "Examining the Bases Utilized for Evaluating Salespeoples' Performance," *Journal of Personal Selling & Sales Management,* Vol. 15, No. 4 (Fall 1995), p. 62.

Table 15-6: Donald W. Jackson, John L. Schlacter, and William G. Wolfe, "Examining the Bases Utilized for Evaluating Salespeoples' Performance," *Journal of Personal Selling & Sales Management,* Vol. 15, No. 4 (Fall 1995), p. 63.

Table 15-11: James S. Boles, Naveen Donthu, and Ritu Lohtia, "Salesperson Evaluation Using Relative Performance Efficiency: The Application of Data Envelopment Analysis," *Journal of Personal Selling & Sales Management,* Vol. 15, No. 3 (Summer 1995), p. 44.

Strategic Action Competency: Based on Melissa Campanelli, "Rising to the Top: These Innovative Incentive Programs Reward Salespeople for Acting Strategically and Strengthening Customer Relations Beyond Rock Bottom," *Sales & Marketing Management* (April 1994), pp. 83–86.

Technology Competency: Dana James, "Hit the Bricks: Internet Shifts in B-to-B Sales World Mean 'Get Up and Go' or Risk Losing Jobs," *Marketing News* (September, 13, 1999), p. 1.

Coaching Competency: Sarah Lorge, "Strategies and Tools to Increase Sales," *Sales & Marketing Management* (July 1999), p. 89.

Team-Building Competency: William Keenan, Jr., "Teaming Up on a Problem," *Sales & Marketing Management* (July 1993), pp. 36–37.

KEY TERM AND SUBJECT INDEX

AUTHOR INDEX

COMPANY INDEX

CASE INDEX

Campus Library

...ust return this item on or before the date on
...ceipt.

...n this item late you will be charged a fir...
...this item by using the
...61)... the Li...ar

Leeds Metropolitan University

17 0367612 2